The Writings of Baal HaSulam

Volume One

LAITMAN
KABBALAH
PUBLISHERS

Yehuda Leib HaLevi Ashlag

The Writings of Baal HaSulam
Volume One

Copyright © 2019 by Michael Laitman

All rights reserved

Published by Laitman Kabbalah Publishers

Contact Information

E-mail: info@kabbalah.info

Website: www.kabbalah.info

Toll free in USA and Canada: 1-866-LAITMAN

1057 Steeles Avenue West, Suite 532, Toronto,
ON, M2R 3X1, Canada
Tel. 1-416-274-7287

2009 85th Street #51, Brooklyn, New York, 11214, USA
Tel. 1-800-540-3234

No part of this book may be used or reproduced in any manner without written permission of the publisher, except in the case of brief quotations embodied in critical articles or reviews.

ISBN: 978-1-77228-145-3

Library of Congress Control Number: 2019939696

Translation: Chaim Ratz

Translation Assistance: Mickey Cohen, Moshe Eisenberg

Content Review: Noga Bar Noye

Editing and Proofreading: Mary Pennock, Mary Miesem, Joseph Donnelly, Michael Kellogg, Debbie Wood

Internal Design: Chaim Ratz

Cover Design: Baruch Khovov/Inna Smirnova

Executive Editor: Chaim Ratz

Printing and Post Production: Uri Laitman

FIRST EDITION: May 2019

Second printing

Table of Contents

About the Book	5
Time to Act	7
Disclosing a Portion, Covering Two	9
The Essence of the Wisdom of Kabbalah	13
The Teaching of the Kabbalah and Its Essence	21
The Acting Mind	38
Matan Torah [The Giving of the Torah]	40
The Arvut [Mutual Guarantee]	48
The Essence of Religion and Its Purpose	57
The Peace	64
The Freedom	78
Introduction to The Book of Zohar	101
A Handmaid Who Is Heir to Her Mistress	135
The Shofar of the Messiah	139
Peace in the World	142
Exile and Redemption	156
A Speech for the Completion of The Zohar	159
One Commandment	171
The Love of God and the Love of Man	175
The Wisdom of Kabbalah and Philosophy	182
The Quality of the Wisdom of the Hidden in General	190
The Wisdom of Israel Compared to External Wisdoms	197
Body and Soul	200
Not the Time for the Livestock to Be Gathered	205
The Meaning of Conception and Birth	208
From My Flesh I Shall See God	220
You Have Made Me in Behind and Before	227
Remembering	235
The Meaning of the Chaf in Anochi	245
Four Worlds	250
This Is for Judah	254
The History of the Wisdom of Kabbalah	257
Inheritance of the Land	258
600,000 Souls	260
Concealment and Disclosure of the Face of the Creator - A	264
Concealment and Disclosure of the Face of the Creator - B	267
Introduction to A Sage's Fruit, Vol. 4 (Three Partners)	268
Introduction to the Book From the Mouth of a Sage"	271

Anyone Who Is Sorry for the Public 272
Man's Actions and Tactics 273
Righteous and Wicked 274
Rewarded—I Will Hasten It; Not Rewarded—in Its Time 276
Introduction to The Study of the Ten Sefirot 278
Introduction to "From the Mouth of a Sage" 332
The Prophecy of Baal HaSulam 340
The Nation 343
The Study of the Ten Sefirot, Part One, Inner Observation 368
Foreword to The Book of Zohar 391
Matter and Form in the Wisdom of Kabbalah 411
General Preface 412
Introduction to the Book Panim Meirot uMasbirot 439
Introduction to the Preface to the Wisdom of Kabbalah 473
Preface to the Wisdom of Kabbalah 479
Preface to the Sulam Commentary 548
HaIlan (The Tree) 583
Poems of Baal HaSulam 601

About the Book

For the first time, we are seeing the publication of the essential writings of the greatest Kabbalist of the 20th century, Rav Yehuda Leib HaLevi Ashlag (1885-1954), also known as Baal HaSulam [author of the *Sulam* (Ladder commentary on *The Zohar*)].

The Writings of Baal HaSulam contains all the texts required for any person interested in learning the wisdom of Kabbalah, from Baal HaSulam's first composition, *Introduction to the Book, Panim Meirot uMasibrot*, published in 1927, through *The Writings of the Last Generation*, which was written in the 1950s and describes the structure of the future society.

The book contains:

- All the introductions and forewords written by Baal HaSulam as preparation to learn his three key compositions: *Panim Meirot uMasibrot* (a commentary on the ARI's *Tree of Life*), the *Sulam* [ladder] commentary on *The Book of Zohar*, and *The Study of the Ten Sefirot*.
- All the essays that Baal HaSulam wrote so as to spread the wisdom of Kabbalah among the general public.
- All the letters that Baal HaSulam sent to his disciples and which contain guidance for those marching on the spiritual path.
- All the articles contained in the book *Shamati* [*I Heard*], which detail one's inner work, as written by Baal HaSulam's firstborn son and successor, Rav Baruch Shalom HaLevi Ashlag (better known as RABASH), who put on paper what he had heard from his father.
- *Histaklut Pnimit* [Inner Reflection]—commentaries and elaborations on the topics presented in Part 1 of the book *The Study of the Ten Sefirot*.
- The book *Beit Shaar HaKavanot* [*Gatehouse of Intentions*]: *Commentaries on the writings of the ARI*.
- *The Writings of the Last Generation*, a collection of notes from the 1950s in which Baal HaSulam analyzes political regimes and presents a model for the construction of the future society.

In addition to the learning material, we included in the final part, poems that Baal HaSulam wrote.

Explanations and translations into English are marked in square brackets [example].

We are certain that delving into the authentic writings of Baal HaSulam will help those who do so on their spiritual advancement and search for life's meaning, and will help advance all of humanity to a new and better world.

"Only through the expansion of the wisdom of Kabbalah in the masses will we obtain complete redemption. For this reason, we must establish seminaries and compose books to hasten the dissemination of the wisdom throughout the nation."

Baal HaSulam, *Introduction to the Book, Panim Meirot UMasibrot*

The editors

Time to Act

For a long time now, my conscience has burdened me with a demand to come out and create a fundamental composition regarding the essence of Judaism, religion, and the knowledge of the authentic wisdom of Kabbalah, and spread it among the nation, so people will come to know and properly understand these exalted matters in their true meaning.

Previously in Israel, prior to the development of the printing industry, there were no fallacious books among us relating to the essence of Judaism, as there were hardly any writers among us who could stand behind their words for the simple reason that in most cases, an unreliable person has no renown.

Therefore, if, by chance, one dared to write such a composition, it was not worthwhile for any scribe to copy it, as he would not be paid for his labor, which, for the most part, was a considerable sum. Thus, such a composition was doomed from the start.

In those days, knowledgeable people, too, had no interest in writing such books, since the general public did not need that knowledge. Quite the contrary, they had an interest in hiding the matter in secret chambers because "It is the glory of God to conceal a thing." We were commanded to conceal the essence of the Torah and the work from those who did not need it, or were unworthy of it, and to not degrade it and display it in shop windows for the lusting eyes of the boastful, because thus the glory of God demands of us.

But ever since the printing of books has become popular, and writers no longer need scribes, the price of books has been reduced. This has paved the way for unreliable writers to publish whatever books they please, for money or for glory. But they do not take their own actions into account and do not examine the consequences of their work.

From that time on, publications of the aforementioned kind have significantly increased, without any learning or reception mouth-to-mouth from a qualified rav [teacher/great one/sage] or even knowledge of earlier books that dealt with this topic. Such writers fabricate theories of their own empty shells, and relate their words to the most exalted matters, to thus portray the essence of the nation and its fabulous treasure. As fools, they know not how to be scrupulous, or have a way by which to learn it. They instill faulty views to generations, and in return for their petty lusts, they sin and make the nations sin for generations to come.

Recently, their stench has soared ever upward because they have plunged their nails into the wisdom of Kabbalah, not minding that this wisdom has been closed and locked behind a thousand doors to this day, to the point that no person may understand the true meaning of even a single word of it, much less the connection between one word and the next.

This is because in all the genuine books that have been written to this day, there are but clues that barely suffice for a knowing disciple to understand their meaning from the mouth of a wise and qualified Kabbalist sage. And there, too, "the owl nests and lays [its eggs], and hatch, and brooded in its shade." These days, such conspirators multiply and make such delights that disgust those who behold them.

Some of them even go as far as to assume the place of the leaders of the generation, pretending to know how to sort through the books of the first [sages] and tell which of them is worthy of studying and which is not, since it is filled with fallacies, and they arouse contempt and wrath. Until today, the work of such scrutiny had been limited to one in ten leaders of a generation; and now the ignorant abuse it.

Therefore, the public's perception of these matters has been greatly corrupted. In addition, there is an atmosphere of frivolity, and people think that a glance at one's leisure is sufficient for the study of such exalted matters. They skim over the ocean of wisdom and the essence of Judaism in a single glance like that angel, and draw conclusions based on their own states of mind.

These are the reasons that have prompted me to go out of my way and decide that it is time to "do for the Lord" and salvage what can still be salvaged. Thus, I have taken upon myself to reveal a certain portion of the true essence, which relates to the above matter, and spread it in the nation.

Disclosing a Portion, Covering Two

There is an idiom among great sages when they come to disclose a profound matter: They begin their words with "I am disclosing a portion and covering two portions." Our sages took great care not to utter words needlessly, as they instructed, "A word is a Sela [ancient coin]; silence is two" (*Megillah* 18a, "Introduction of The Book of Zohar," Item 18).

This means that if you have a priceless word whose worth is one rock, know that not saying it is worth two rocks. This refers to those who utter needless words without pertinent content or use except to decorate the style in the eyes of the reader. This was strictly forbidden in the eyes of our sages, as is known to those who examine their words, and as I will prove in the following essays. Hence, we must be attentive to understand this common idiom of theirs.

Three Kinds of Concealment of the Wisdom

There are three parts in the secrets of the Torah. Each part has its own reason for being concealed. They are called by the following names:

1. Unnecessary,

1. Impossible,

1. The counsel of the Lord is to those who fear Him.

There is not a single fraction of this wisdom where scrutinies of these three parts do not apply, and I will clarify them one at a time.

1. Unnecessary

This means that no one will benefit from their disclosure. Of course, this is not such a great loss because there is only the issue of the cleanness of the mind here, to warn of those actions defined as "so what," meaning "So what if I did this, there is no harm in it."

But you should know that in the eyes of the sages, "so what" is considered the worst corruptor, since all the destructors in the world, those that have been and those that will be, are the "so what" kind of people. This means that they engage in needless matters and occupy others in needless matters. Hence, no student would be accepted before it was certain that he would be cautious in his ways, so as not to reveal what was not necessary.

2. Impossible

This means that the language does not compel them to say anything of their quality, due to their great sublimity and spirituality. Hence, any attempt to clothe them in words may only mislead the examiners and deflect them to a false path, which is considered the worst of all iniquities. Therefore, to reveal anything in these matters requires permission from above. This is the second part of the concealment of the wisdom. Yet, this permission, too, requires explanation.

Permission from Above

This matter is explained in the book *The Gate to Rashbi's Words* by the ARI (in the portion, *Mishpatim*, *The Zohar*, 4:100, beginning with words, "Yochai's son knew how to hide"): "Know that some of the souls of the righteous are from the phase of the surrounding light, and some are from the phase of the inner light. (You will find their meaning in my book *Panim Meirot*, Gate *Makifin*, Branch 48.) Those who are of the surrounding light kind have the power to speak of the secrets and concealments of the Torah by way of great covering and concealment so that only those worthy of it will understand them.

Rabbi Shimon Bar-Yochai's soul was of the surrounding light kind. Hence, he had the power to clothe the words and teach them in a way that even if he taught them to many, only the worthy of understanding would understand. This is why he was given "permission" to write *The Book of Zohar*.

The permission was not "granted" to write a book in this wisdom to his teachers or to the first ones who preceded them in writing in this wisdom, even though they were certainly more knowledgeable in this wisdom than he. But the reason is that they did not have the power to dress the matters as did he. This is the meaning of what is written, "Yochai's son knew how to guard his ways." Now you can understand the great concealment in *The Book of Zohar* that Rashbi wrote, that not every mind can grasp his words.

The essence of his words: Explaining matters in the wisdom of truth is not dependent whatsoever on the greatness or smallness of the Kabbalist sage. Rather, it is about the illumination of a soul dedicated to this matter. The illumination of this soul is considered "giving permission" from above to disclose the upper wisdom. We therefore learn that one who has not been rewarded with this permission must not make clarifications in this wisdom, as he cannot clothe those subtle matters in their proper words in a way that will not fail the students.

For this reason, we did not find a single book in the wisdom of truth that precedes Rashbi's *The Book of Zohar*, since all the books in the wisdom prior to his are not categorized as clarifications of the wisdom, but are mere intimations, without an order of cause and consequence, as is known to the knowledgeable ones.

I should add, as I had received from books and from authors, that since the time of Rashbi and his disciples, the authors of *The Zohar*, until the time of the ARI there was not a single writer who understood the words of *The Zohar* and the *Tikkunim* [corrections] like the ARI. All the compositions before his time are mere intimations in this wisdom, including the books of the sage RAMAK.

And the same words that were said about the Rashbi should be said about the ARI himself—that his predecessors were not given permission from above to disclose the interpretations of the wisdom, and the ARI was given this permission. This does not distinguish any greatness or smallness at all, since it is possible that the merit of the ARI's predecessors was much greater than his, but they were not given permission for it. For this reason, they refrained from writing commentaries that relate to the essence of the wisdom, but settled for brief intimations that were not in any way linked to one another.

Therefore, since the books of the ARI appeared in the world, all who study the wisdom of Kabbalah have left their hands from all the books of the RAMAK, and all the first and the great ones who preceded the ARI, as it is known among those who engage in this wisdom. They have attached their spiritual lives solely to the writings of the ARI in a way that the essential books, considered proper interpretations in this wisdom, are only *The Book of Zohar*, the *Tikkunim*, and following them, the books of the ARI.

3. The Counsel of the Lord Is to Those Who Fear Him

This means that the secrets of the Torah are revealed only to those who fear His name, who keep His glory with their hearts and souls, so as never to commit any manner of blasphemy. This is the third part of the concealment of the wisdom.

This part is the strictest in regard to the concealment, as this kind of disclosure has failed many. From the midst of those stem all the charmers, whisperers, and "practical" Kabbalists, who hunt souls with their cunningness, and the mystics who use withered wisdom that came from under the hands of unworthy students, to produce bodily benefit for themselves or for others. The world has suffered much from this and is suffering still.

Know that the root of the concealment was only this part. From here the sages took excessive strictness in testing the disciples, as our sages said (*Hagigah* 13a), "A summary is given only to a chief justice, and to one whose heart is worried," and "*Maase Beresheet* is not to be studied in twos, nor is *Merkava* to be explored alone." There are many others like that, and this whole fear is for the above reason.

For this reason, few are the chosen who have been rewarded with this wisdom, and even those who passed all their tests and examinations are sworn by the most serious oaths not to reveal anything of those three parts. (In this regard, see in the introduction to *The Book of Creation* by Rabbi Moshe Burtril.)

Do not misunderstand my words, in that I have divided the concealment of the wisdom into three parts. I do not mean that the wisdom of truth itself is divided into these three parts. Rather, I mean that these three parts branch out from every single detail of this wisdom, since they are the only three manners of scrutiny that are always applied to this wisdom.

However, here we should ask, If it is true that the strictness of the concealment of the wisdom is so severe, from where were all the thousands of compositions in this wisdom taken? The answer is that there is a difference between the first two parts and the last part. The primary burden lies only in the above third part, for the reason explained above.

But the first two parts are not under a permanent prohibition, since sometimes an issue in the "unnecessary" is reversed, stops being unnecessary for some reason, and becomes necessary. Also, the part "impossible" sometimes becomes possible. This is so for two reasons: either because of the development of the generation or by being given permission from above, as it happened to Rashbi and to the ARI, and to smaller extents to their formers. All the genuine books written in the wisdom emerge from these discernments.

This is what they mean by their idiom, "I disclosed a portion and I will cover two portions." They mean that it happened that they revealed something new that their predecessors did not envision. This is why they imply that they are revealing only one portion, meaning he is revealing the first part of the three parts of concealment, and leaves two parts concealed.

This indicates that something happened which is the reason for that disclosure: Either the "unnecessary" received the form of "necessary," or he was given "permission from above," as I have explained above. This is the meaning of the idiom, "I am disclosing a portion."

The readers of these essays, which I intend to print during the year, should know that they are all innovations, which are not introduced purely as such, in their precise content, in any book preceding me. I received them mouth to mouth from my teacher, who was authorized for it, meaning that he, too, received from his teachers mouth to mouth.

And although I had received them under all the conditions of covering and watchfulness, by the necessity introduced in my essay "Time to Act," the "unnecessary" part has been inverted for me and became "necessary." Hence, I have revealed this portion with complete permission, as I have explained above. Yet I will keep the other two portions as I am commanded.

The Essence of the Wisdom of Kabbalah

Before I go about elucidating the history of the wisdom of Kabbalah, conversed about by many, I find it necessary to begin with a thorough clarification of the essence of this wisdom, which I believe so few know. Naturally, it is impossible to speak of the history of something before we know the thing itself.

Although this knowledge is wider and deeper than the sea, I will exert with all the strength and knowledge I have acquired in this field to clarify and illuminate it from all sides, enough for any person to draw the right conclusions, as they truly are, leaving no room for error, as is often the case in such matters.

What the Wisdom Is About

This question comes to the mind of every right-minded person. To properly address it, I will provide a reliable and lasting definition: This wisdom is no more and no less than a sequence of roots that cascade by way of cause and consequence, following fixed, determined laws that interweave into a single, exalted goal described as "the revelation of His Godliness to His creatures in this world."

And here there is a conduct of general and particular:

General—the whole of humanity, obligated to eventually come to this immense development, as it is written, "For the earth shall be full of the knowledge of the Lord, as water covers the sea" (Isaiah 11, 9). "And they shall teach no more every man his neighbor, and every man his brother, saying, know the Lord, for they shall all know Me, from the least of them to the greatest of them" (Jeremiah 31, 33), and he says, "Your Teacher will no longer hide Himself, and your eyes will behold your Teacher" (Isaiah 30).

Particular—that even before the perfection of the whole of humanity, this rule is implemented in a chosen few individuals in every generation. These are the ones who are endowed, in each generation, with certain degrees of revelation of His Godliness. These are the prophets and the men of God, and as our sages said, "There is no generation without such that are as Abraham, Isaac, and Jacob" (*Midrash Rabbah*, *Beresheet*, Portion 74). Thus, you see that the revelation of His Godliness is implemented in each generation, as our sages, whom we find trustworthy, proclaim.

The Abundance of *Partzufim*, *Sefirot*, and Worlds

According to the above, a question arises: Since this wisdom has but one, special, and clear role, why is there an abundance of *Partzufim*, *Sefirot*, and interchangeable connections, which are so prevalent in the books of Kabbalah?

Indeed, if you take the body of a small animal, whose only task is to nourish itself so it may exist in this world long enough to procreate and carry on its species, you will find in it a complex structure of millions of fibers and tendons, as physiologists and anatomists have found, and there is much there that humans have yet to find. From the above, you can conclude the vast variety of issues and channels that need to connect in order to fashion and reveal that sublime goal.

Two Conducts—from Above Downward and from Below Upward

This wisdom is generally divided into two parallel, equal, and identical orders, like two drops in a pond. The only difference between them is that the first order extends from above downward, to this world, and the second order begins in this world and traverses from below upward precisely by the same routes and make-ups imprinted at their root when they appeared from above downward.

The first order is called "the order of descent of the worlds, *Partzufim*, and *Sefirot*," in all their occurrences, whether lasting or transient. The second order is called "attainments or degrees of prophecy and Holy spirit." A person rewarded with it must follow the same trails and inlets, and gradually attain each detail and each degree, precisely by the same rules that were imprinted in them upon their emanation from above downward.

This is so because the matter of revelation of Godliness does not appear at once, as with the revelation of corporeal things, but gradually, over a period of time, depending on the cleansing of the one who attains, until one discovers all the degrees that are prearranged from above downward. Because they come in an order of attainment one after the other and one above the other, as do rungs of a ladder, they are called "degrees" [steps].

Abstract Names

Many believe that all the words and the names in the wisdom of Kabbalah are a kind of abstract names, since it deals with Godliness and spirituality, which are above time and space, where even our imagination has no hold. For this reason, they have decided that all that is said about such matters is only abstract names, or even more sublime and exalted than abstract names, as they are completely and from the outset devoid of imaginary elements.

But this is not the case. On the contrary, Kabbalah uses only names and appellations that are concrete and real. It is an unbending law for all Kabbalists that "Anything we do not attain, we do not define by a name and a word."

Here you must know that the word "attainment" [Heb: *Hasagah*] means the ultimate degree of understanding. It derives from the phrase, *Ki Tasig Yadcha* ["Your hand shall attain"]. That means that before something becomes utterly lucid, as though gripped in one's hand, Kabbalists do not consider it attained, but by other names such as understanding, comprehension, and so on.

The Actuality in the Wisdom of Kabbalah

Actual things are found even in the corporeal reality set before our eyes, although we have neither perception nor an image of their essence. Such are the electricity and the magnet, which are called "fluidum."

Nevertheless, who can say that these names are not real, when we have completely satisfactory awareness of their actions, and we are utterly careless about the fact that we have no perception of the essence of the subject itself, namely electricity in itself.

This name is as tangible and as close to us as though it were entirely perceived by our senses. Even little children are familiar with the word "electricity," as well as they are familiar with words such as "bread," "sugar," and so on.

Moreover, if you wish to exercise your tools of scrutiny, I shall tell you that as a whole, as there is no perception of the Creator whatsoever, so is it impossible to attain the essence of any of His creatures, even the tangible objects that we feel with our hands.

Thus, all we know about our friends and relatives in the world of action before us are nothing more than "acquaintance with actions." These are prompted and born by the association of their encounter with our senses, which render us complete satisfaction although we have no perception whatsoever in the essence of the subject.

Furthermore, you have no perception or attainment whatsoever even in your own essence. Everything you know about your own essence is nothing more than a series of actions extending from your essence.

Now you can easily conclude that all the names and appellations that appear in books of Kabbalah are indeed real and factual, although we have no attainment in the subject matter whatsoever. This is so because those who engage in them have the complete satisfaction of inclusive perception in its ultimate wholeness, meaning also, merely perception of actions that are prompted and born from the association of the upper light and its perceivers.

However, it is quite sufficient, for this is the rule: "All that is measured and extends from His guidance so as to become a reality, the nature of creation, is completely satisfactory." This is just as one will not wish for a sixth finger in his palm because the five fingers are quite sufficient.

The Corporeal Terms and the Physical Names in Books of Kabbalah

Any reasonable person will understand that when dealing with spiritual matters, much less with Godliness, we have no words or letters with which to contemplate. This is because our whole vocabulary is but combinations of the letters of our senses and imagination, and how can they assist where there are neither imagination nor senses?

Even if we take the subtlest word that can be used in such matters, meaning the word "upper light," or even "simple light," it is still imaginary and borrowed from the sunlight or a candlelight, or a light of contentment one feels upon resolving some doubt. How can we use them in spiritual matters and Godly ways? They offer the examiner nothing more than falsehood and deceit.

It is particularly so where one needs to find some rationale in these words to help one in the negotiations customary in the research of the wisdom. Here the sage must use rigorously accurate definitions for the eyes of the readers.

Should the sage fail with but a single unsuccessful word, he will confuse and mislead the readers. They will not understand at all what he says before and after it, and everything connected to that word, as is known to anyone who examines books of wisdom.

Thus, one should wonder how it is possible for Kabbalists to use false words to explain the interconnections in this wisdom. Also, it is known that there is no definition through a false name, for the lie has no legs and no stance.

Indeed, here you must first know the "law of root and branch" by which the worlds relate to one another.

The Law of Root and Branch by Which the Worlds Are Related

Kabbalists have found that the form of the four worlds named *Atzilut*, *Beria*, *Yetzira*, and *Assiya*, beginning with the first, highest world, called *Atzilut*, down to this corporeal, tangible world, called *Assiya*, is exactly the same in every item and event. This means that everything that eventuates and occurs in the first world is found unchanged in the next world, below it, too. It is likewise in all the worlds that follow it, down to this tangible world.

There is no difference between them, but only a difference of degree perceived in the substance of the elements of reality in each and every world. The substance of the elements of reality in the first, uppermost world, is finer than in all the ones below it. And the substance of the elements of reality in the second world is thicker than in the first world, but finer than all that is of a lower degree.

This continues similarly down to this world before us, whose substance of the elements of its reality is coarser and darker than in all the worlds preceding it. However, the shapes and elements of reality and all their occurrences come unchanged and equal in every world, both in quantity and quality.

They compared it to the conduct of a seal and its imprint: All the shapes in the seal are perfectly transferred in every detail and intricacy to its imprinted object. So it is with the worlds: Each lower world is an imprint of the world above it. Hence, all the forms in the higher world are meticulously copied, in both quantity and quality, to the lower world.

Thus, there is not an element of reality or an occurrence of reality in a lower world that you will not find its likeness in the world above it, as identical as two drops in a pond. And they are called "root and branch." That means that the item in the lower world is deemed a branch of its pattern found in the higher world, which is the root of the lower element, as this is where that item in the lower world has been imprinted and made to be.

That was the intention of our sages when they said, "You have not a blade of grass below that has not a fortune and a guard above that strike it and tell it, 'Grow'!" (Omissions of *The Zohar*, p 251a [source in Hebrew], *Beresheet Rabbah*, Chapter 10). It follows that the root, called "fortune," compels it to grow and assume its attribute in quantity and quality, as with the seal and its imprint. This is the law of root and branch that applies to every detail and occurrence in reality, in every single world, in relation to the world above it.

The Language of the Kabbalists Is a Language of Branches

This means that the branches indicate their roots, being their molds that necessarily exist in the upper world. This is because there is nothing in the reality of the lower world that does not stem from its superior world. As with the seal and the imprint, the root in the upper world compels its branch in the lower one to reveal its entire form and attribute, as our sages said, that the fortune in the world above, related to the grass in the world below, strikes that grass and forces it to complete its growth. Because of this, each and every branch in this world well defines its mold situated in the higher world.

Thus, Kabbalists have found a set and annotated vocabulary sufficient to create an excellent spoken language. It enables them to converse with one another of the dealings in the spiritual roots in the upper worlds by merely mentioning the lower, tangible branch in this world, which is well defined to our corporeal senses.

The listeners understand the upper root to which this corporeal branch points because it is related to it, being its imprint. Thus, all the beings of the tangible creation and all their instances have become to them like well-defined words and names, indicating the high spiritual roots. Although there cannot be a verbal expression in their spiritual place, as it is above any imagination, they have earned the right to be expressed by utterance through their branches, arranged before our senses here in the tangible world.

This is the nature of the spoken language among Kabbalists by which they convey their spiritual attainments from person to person and from generation to generation by word of mouth and in writing. They fully understand one another, with all the required accuracy needed for negotiating in a research of wisdom, with precise definitions one cannot fail in. This is so because each branch has its own natural, unique definition, and this absolute definition indicates its root in the higher world.

Bear in mind that this language of branches of the wisdom of Kabbalah is better suited to explain the terms of the wisdom than all our ordinary languages. It is known from the theory of nominalism that the languages have been disrupted by the masses, meaning that due to excessive use of the words, they are being emptied of their accurate content, resulting in great difficulties to convey precise deductions from one to another by word of mouth or in writing.

This is not the case with the Kabbalah's language of branches: It is derived from the names of the creations and their occurrences, set before our eyes, and defined by the unchangeable laws of nature. The readers and the listeners will never be misled into a misunderstanding of the words being offered to them, since the natural definitions are absolute and cannot be breached.

Conveyance from a Wise Kabbalist to an Understanding Receiver

Thus wrote Nachmanides in his introduction to his commentary on the Torah, and Rav Chaim Vital also wrote similarly in the essay *Pesi'ot*: "The readers should know that they will not understand a single word of all that is written in these essays, unless when they are conveyed from a wise Kabbalist to the ear of a wise receiver who understands with his own mind." Also, in the words of our sages (*Hagigah* 11b): "One does not study the *Merkava* [structure/epithet to the wisdom of Kabbalah] on one's own, unless he is wise and understands with his own mind."

Their words are thoroughly understood when they say that one must receive from a wise Kabbalist. But why the necessity for the disciple to first be wise and understanding with his own mind? Moreover, if he is not so, then he must not be taught, be he the most righteous person in the world. Additionally, if one is already wise and understands with his own mind, what need has he to learn from others?

From the aforesaid, their words are understood with utter simplicity: We have seen that all the words and utterances our lips pronounce cannot help us clarify even a single word from the spiritual, Godly matters above the imaginary time and space. Instead, there is a special language for these matters, the language of the branches, according to their relation to their upper roots.

However, this language, though very suitable for its task of delving into the studies of this wisdom, more than other languages, is only so if the listener is wise in his own right, meaning that he knows and understands the way the branches relate to their roots. It is so because these relations are not at all clear when looking from the lower to the upper. In other words, it is impossible to make any deduction or semblance concerning the upper roots by observing the lower branches.

Quite the contrary, the lower is studied from the higher. Thus, one must first attain the upper roots the way they are in spirituality, above any imagination and with pure attainment, as was explained in the essay, "The Essence of the Wisdom of Kabbalah," Item 4, "The Actuality in the Wisdom of Kabbalah." And once he has thoroughly attained the upper roots with his own mind, he may examine the tangible branches in this world and know how each branch relates to its root in the upper world, in all its orders, in quantity and quality.

When one knows and thoroughly comprehends all this, he has a common language with his teacher, namely the language of the branches. Using it, the Kabbalist sage may convey all the studies in the wisdom conducted in the upper, spiritual worlds, both what he had received from his teachers and the expansions in the wisdom he had discovered by himself. This is because now they have a common language and they understand each other.

However, when a disciple is not wise and comprehends that language on his own, meaning how the branches indicate their roots, naturally, the teacher cannot convey even a single word of this spiritual wisdom, much less negotiate with him in the scrutiny of the wisdom. Since they have no common language they can use, they become as mute. Thus, it is necessary that *Maase Merkava*, which is the wisdom of Kabbalah, will not be taught unless he is wise and understands with his own mind.

We must ask further: How then, has the disciple grown so wise as to know the relations of branch and root through tracing the upper roots? The answer is that here man's efforts are in vain; it is the Creator's help that we need! He fills those whom He favors with wisdom, understanding, and knowledge to acquire sublime attainments. Here it is impossible to be assisted by any flesh and blood!

Indeed, once He has grown fond of a person and has endowed him with the sublime attainment, one is then ready to come and receive the vastness of the wisdom of Kabbalah from a wise Kabbalist, for only now do they have a common language.

Appellations Alien to the Human Spirit

With all that is said above, you will understand why we sometimes find appellations and terms that are very alien to the human spirit in books of Kabbalah. They are abundant in the fundamental books of Kabbalah, which are *The Book of Zohar*, the *Tikkunim*, and the books of the ARI. It is indeed bewildering why these sages used such lowly appellations to express such exalted, holy notions.

Yet, you will fully understand it once you have acquired the above conceptions. This is because it is now clear that no language in the world can be used to explain this wisdom except for one that is intended for just that end, namely the language of the branches according to the relations to the upper roots.

Thus, obviously, no branch or occurrence of a branch should be neglected because of its inferior degree, or not use it to express the desired concept in the interconnections in the wisdom, as there is no other branch in our world to take its place.

As no two hairs nurse from the same foramen, we do not have two branches that relate to a single root. Hence, by leaving an incident unused, we lose the spiritual concept corresponding to it in the upper world, as we have not a single word to utter in its place and indicate that root. In addition, such an incident would impair the entire wisdom in all its vastness, since now there is a missing link in the chain of the wisdom connected to that concept.

This mutilates the entire wisdom, for there is no other wisdom in the world where matters are so fused and intertwined by way of cause and effect, primary and consequential, as is the wisdom of Kabbalah, connected from top to bottom just like a long chain. Therefore, upon the temporary loss of but a small cognizance, the entire wisdom darkens before our eyes, for all its matters are tightly connected to one another, literally fusing into one.

Now you will not wonder at the occasional use of alien appellations. They have no freedom of choice with appellations, to replace the bad with the good or the good with the bad. They must always use the branch or the incident, which precisely points to its upper root in all its necessary measure. Moreover, the matters must be expanded so as to provide an accurate definition for the eyes of their fellow readers.

The Teaching of the Kabbalah and Its Essence

What is the wisdom of Kabbalah? As a whole, the wisdom of Kabbalah concerns the revelation of Godliness, arranged on its paths in all its aspects—those that have been revealed in the worlds and those that are destined to be revealed, and in all the manners that can ever be revealed in the worlds, to the end of time.

The Purpose of Creation

Since there is no act without some purpose, it is certain that the Creator had a purpose in the creation set before us. The most important thing in this whole diverse reality is the sensation given to the animals—that each of them feels its own existence. And the most important sensation is the noetic sensation, given to man alone, by which one also feels what is in the other—others' pains and comforts. Hence, it is certain that if the Creator has a purpose in this creation, its subject is man. It is said about this, "All of the Lord's works are for him."

But we must still understand what was the purpose for which the Creator created this lot. Indeed, it is to elevate him to a higher and more important degree, to feel his Creator like the human sensation, which is already given to him. And as one knows and feels one's friend's wishes, so he will learn the ways of the Creator, as it is written about Moses, "And the Lord spoke to Moses face to face, as a man speaks to his friend."

Any person can be as Moses. Undoubtedly, anyone who examines the evolution of Creation before us will see and understand the great pleasure of the Operator, whose operation evolves until he acquires that wondrous sensation of being able to converse and deal with one's Creator as one speaks to one's friend.

From Above Downward

It is known that the end of the act is in the preliminary thought. Before one begins to think about how to build a house, one contemplates the apartment in the house, which is the purpose. Subsequently, one examines the blueprint to make it suitable for this task.

So it is with our matter. Once we have learned about the purpose, it is also clear to us that all the aspects of creation, in its every corner, inlet, and outlet, are completely prearranged for the purpose of nurturing the human species from within it, to improve its qualities until it can feel the Creator as one feels one's friend.

These ascents are like rungs of a ladder, set and arranged degree by degree until it is completed and achieves its goal. And you should know that the quality and quantity of these rungs is set in two realities: 1) the existence of material substances, 2) the existence of spiritual concepts.

In the language of Kabbalah, they are called "from above downward" and "from below upward." This means that the corporeal substances are a sequence of disclosure of His light from above downward—from the first source, when a measure of light was cut off from His essence and was restricted *Tzimtzum* by *Tzimtzum* [restriction by restriction] until the corporeal world was formed out of it with corporeal creatures at its very bottom.

From Below Upward

Afterward begins an order from below upward. These are all the rungs of the ladder by which the human race develops and climbs until it reaches the purpose of creation. These two realities are explained in their every detail in the wisdom of Kabbalah.

The Necessity to Study Kabbalah

An opposer might say, "Therefore, this wisdom is for those who have already been rewarded with a measure of revelation of Godliness, but what necessity can the majority of the people have for knowing this sublime wisdom?"

Indeed, there is a common opinion that the prime goal of religion and the Torah is only the cleansing of actions, that all that is desired concerns observing the physical *Mitzvot* [commandments] without any additions or anything that should result from it. Had that been so, those who say that studying the revealed is sufficient are right in matters that concern the practice.

Yet, this is not the case. Our sages already said, "Why should the Creator mind if one slaughters at the throat or at the back of the neck? After all, the *Mitzvot* were only given to cleanse people." Thus, there is a purpose beyond the observance of practices, for the practices are merely preparations for this purpose. Hence, clearly, if the actions are not arranged for the desired goal, it is as if nothing exists. And it is also written in *The Zohar*: "A *Mitzva* [commandment] without an aim is like a body without a soul." Hence, the aim, too, should accompany the act.

Also, it is clear that the aim should be a true aim, worthy of the act, as our sages said about the verse, "'And I will set you apart from the peoples, that you should be Mine,' so your separation will be for My Name. Let not one say about pork, 'It is impossible.' Rather, let one say, 'It is possible, but what can I do that my Father in heaven has sentenced me?'"

Thus, if one avoids pork because of abomination or because of some bodily harm, this aim does not help at all for it to be considered a *Mitzva*, unless one has the unique and proper intention that the Torah forbade. So it is with every *Mitzva*, and only then is one's body gradually cleansed by observing the *Mitzvot*, which is the desired purpose.

Hence, the study of physical conducts is not enough; we need to study those things that produce the desirable intention: to observe everything with faith in the Torah and in the Giver of the Torah, that there is a judgment and there is a Judge.

Who is so foolish as to not understand that faith in the Torah and in reward and punishment, which have the *Segula* [power/merit/quality] to yield this great thing, require much study in the proper books? Thus, even before the act, a study that qualifies the body is required, to grow accustomed to faith in the Creator, His law, and His Providence. Our sages said about this, "I have created the evil inclination; I have created for it the Torah as a spice." They did not say, "I have created for it the *Mitzvot* as a spice," since "Your guarantor needs a bondsman himself," as the evil inclination desires licentiousness and will not let him observe the *Mitzvot*.

The Torah as a Spice

The Torah is the only spice to annul and subdue the evil inclination, as our sages said, "The light in it reformed them."

The Majority of the Words of the Torah Are for Study

This reconciles why the Torah speaks at length about parts that do not concern the practical part but only the study, meaning the introduction with the work of creation, the whole of the book of *Beresheet* [Genesis], the book of *Shemot* [Exodus], most of *Devarim* [Deuteronomy], and needless to say, legends and commentaries. Yet, since they are what the light is stored in, his body will be cleansed, the evil inclination will be subdued, and he will come to faith in the Torah and in reward and punishment. This is the first degree in the observance of the work.

A Candle Is a *Mitzva* and the Torah Is Light

It is written, "A candle is a *Mitzva* and the Torah is light." As one who has candles but no light to light them sits in the dark, one who has *Mitzvot* but no Torah sits in the dark. This is because the Torah is light by which the darkness in the body is illuminated and lit up.

Not All Portions of the Torah Are of Equal Light

According to the *Segula* [power/merit] mentioned in the Torah, that is, considering the measure of light in it, it is certain that the Torah should be divided into degrees according to the measure of light that one can receive from studying it. Clearly, when one ponders and contemplates words of Torah that pertain to the revelation of the Creator to our fathers, they bring the examiner more light than when examining practical matters.

Although they are more important with respect to the practices, with respect to the light, the revelation of the Creator to our fathers is certainly more important.

Anyone with an honest heart who tried to ask to receive the light of the Torah will admit to this.

Necessity and Unfolding of the Expansion of the Wisdom

Since the whole of the wisdom of Kabbalah speaks of the revelation of the Creator, naturally, there is none more successful teaching for its task. This is what the Kabbalists aimed for—to arrange it so it is suitable for studying.

And so they studied in it until the time of concealment (it was agreed to conceal it for a certain reason). However, this was only for a certain time, and not forever, as it is written in *The Zohar*, "This wisdom is destined to be revealed at the end of days, and even to children."

It follows that the above-mentioned wisdom is not at all limited to the language of Kabbalah, as its essence is a spiritual light that emerges from His essence, as it is written, "Can you send forth lightning, that they may go and say to you, 'Here we are,'" referring to the two above-mentioned ways: from above downward and from below upward.

These matters and degrees expand according to a language suitable for them, and they are truly all the beings in this world and their conducts in this world, which are their branches. This is so because "You have not a blade of grass below that does not have an angel above, which strikes it and tells it, 'Grow!'" Thus, the worlds emerge and are imprinted from one another like a seal and imprint, and all that is in one is in the other down to the corporeal world, which is their last branch, but contains the world above it like an imprint of a seal.

Thus, it is easy to know that we can speak of the upper worlds only by their corporeal, lower branches, which extend from them, or of their conducts, which are the language of the Bible, or by secular teachings or by people, which is the language of Kabbalists, or according to agreed-upon names. This was the conduct in the Kabbalah of the *Ge'onim* since the concealment of *The Zohar*.

Thus, it has been made clear that the revelation of the Creator is not a one-time revelation but an ongoing matter that is revealed over a period of time, sufficient for the disclosure of all the great degrees that are revealed from above downward and from below upward. On top of them, and at the end of them, appears the Creator.

It is like a person proficient in all the countries and people in the world. He cannot say that the whole world has been revealed to him before he has completed his examination of the last person and the last country. Until one has achieved this, he has not attained the whole world.

Similarly, the attainment of the Creator unfolds in preordained ways. The seeker must attain all those ways in both the upper and the lower. Clearly, the upper worlds are the important ones here, but they are attained together because there is no difference in their shapes, only in their substance. The substance of a higher world is finer, but the shapes are imprinted from one another, and what exists in the higher world necessarily exists in all the worlds below it, since the lower one is imprinted by it. Know that these realities and their conducts, which the seeker of the Creator attains, are called "degrees," since their attainment is arranged one atop the other, like rungs of a ladder.

Spiritual Expressions

The spiritual has no image; hence, it has no letters with which to contemplate. Even if we declare in general that it is simple light, descending and extending to the seeker until one clothes and attains it in the amount sufficient for His revelation, this, too, is a borrowed expression. This is so because everything that is called "light" in the spiritual world is not like sunlight or candlelight.

What we refer to as light in the spiritual world is borrowed from the human mind whose nature is such that when a doubt is resolved in a person, one discovers a kind of abundance of light and pleasure throughout the body. This is why we sometimes say "the light of the mind," although this is not so. The light that shines in those parts of the substance of the body that are unsuitable for receiving resolved scrutinies is certainly something inferior to the mind. Hence, those lower, inferior organs can receive it and attain it, too.

Yet, to be able to name the mind by some name, we call it "the light of the mind." Similarly, we call the elements of the reality of the upper worlds "lights," as they bring those who attain them abundance of light and pleasure throughout the body, from head to toe. For this reason, we may call one who attains, "clothing," for he has clothed that light.

We might ask, Would it not be more correct to call them by names used in scrutiny, such as "observation" or "attainment," or express ourselves with expressions that emphasize the phenomena of the contemplating mind? The thing is that this is nothing like the conducts of the intellectual phenomena, since the mind is a particular branch among all the elements of reality. Hence, it has its own ways of manifestation.

This is not so with degrees, as they are a complete whole, which contains all the elements that exist in a world. Each element has its own particular ways. For the most part, the perception of matters in degrees is similar to the perception of animate bodies: When one attains some essence, one attains the whole of it, from head to toe.

If we judge by the laws of the contemplating mind, we can say that he has attained everything he could attain in that essence, and even if he contemplated it for another thousand years, he would not add to it even an iota. Yet, in the beginning it is very similar to... meaning he sees everything but understands none of what he sees. Yet, by the passing of time he will have to attain additional matters, similar to *Ibur* [conception/impregnation], *Yenika* [nursing], *Mochin* [adulthood], and *Ibur Bet* [second *Ibur*], and then he begins to feel and use his attainments in every way he wishes.

However, in truth, he did not add a thing to the attainments he had achieved in the beginning. It is rather like ripening: Previously it was unripe, so he could not understand it, and now its ripening has been completed.

Thus, you see the big difference from the conducts of the phenomena of the mind. For this reason, the definitions we are accustomed to use will not suffice for us with phenomena of the mind. We are compelled to use only the conducts that apply to corporeal matters, since their shapes are completely similar, although their substance is utterly remote.

Four Languages Are Used in the Wisdom of Truth

Four languages are used in the wisdom of truth:

1. The language of the Bible, its names, and appellations.
2. The language of laws. This language is very close to the language of the Bible.
3. The language of legends, which is very far from the Bible, since it has no consideration of reality. Strange names and appellations are attributed to this language, and it also does not relate to concepts by way of root and its branch.
4. The language of *Sefirot* and *Partzufim*. In general, sages had a strong tendency to conceal it from the ignorant, since they believed that wisdom and ethics go hand in hand. Hence, the first sages hid the wisdom in writing, using lines, dots, tops, and bottoms. This is how the [Hebrew] alphabet was formed with the twenty-two letters before us.

The Language of the Bible

The language of the Bible is the primary, rudimentary language, perfectly suited for its task, as for the most part, it contains a relation of root and branch and is the easiest language to understand. This language is also the oldest; it is the Holy Tongue, attributed to *Adam ha Rishon*.

This language has two advantages and one disadvantage. Its first advantage is that it is easy to understand, and even beginners in attainments immediately understand all that they need. The second advantage is that it clarifies matters extensively and deeply than all other languages.

Its disadvantage is that it cannot be used for discussing particular issues or connections of cause and consequence because every matter must be clarified in its fullest measure, as it is not self-evident to which element it is referring, unless by presenting the matter in its entirety. Hence, to emphasize the smallest detail, a complete story must be presented. This is why it is unsuitable for small details or for connections of cause and consequence.

Also, the language of prayers and blessings is taken from the language of the Bible.

The Language of Laws

The language of laws is not of reality, but only of the existence of reality. This language is taken entirely from the language of the Bible according to the roots of the laws presented there. It has one advantage over the Bible: It greatly elaborates on every matter and hence points to the upper roots more accurately.

However, its great disadvantage compared to the language of the Bible is that it is very difficult to understand and is the most difficult of all the languages. Only a complete sage, called "entering and exiting without harm," will attain it. Of course, it also contains the first disadvantage, as it is taken from the Bible.

The Language of Legends

The language of legends is easy to understand through the allegories that perfectly fit the desired meaning. In superficial examination, it is even easier to understand than the language of the Bible. Yet, for complete understanding, it is a very difficult language as it does not confine itself to speaking in sequences of root and branch, but only in allegories and marvelous wit. However, it is very rich in resolving abstruse and odd concepts that concern the essence of the degree in its state, for itself, which cannot be explained in the languages of the Bible and laws.

The Language of Kabbalists

The language of the Kabbalists is a language in the full sense of the word: very precise, both in terms of root and branch and concerning cause and consequence. It has the unique merit of being able to express subtle details in this language without any limits. Also, through it, it is possible to approach the desired matter directly, without the need to connect it with what precedes it or follows it.

However, despite all the sublime merits that you find in it, there is a great drawback in it, that it is difficult to attain. It is almost impossible to attain it except from a Kabbalist sage and from a sage one who understands with his own mind. This means that even one who understands the rest of the degrees from below upward and from above downward with his own mind will still not understand anything in this language until he receives it from a sage who has already received the language from his teacher face to face.

The Language of Kabbalah Is Contained in All of Them

The names, appellations, and *Gematrias* belong entirely to the wisdom of Kabbalah. The reason they are found in the rest of the languages, too, is that all the languages are included in the wisdom of Kabbalah, since they are all particular cases that the other languages must be assisted with.

But one should not think that these four languages, which serve to explain the wisdom of the revelation of Godliness, evolved one at a time, over time. The truth is that all four appeared before the sages of truth simultaneously.

In truth, each consists of all the others. The language of Kabbalah exists in the Bible, such as the standing on the *Tzur* [rock], the thirteen attributes of mercy in the Torah and in *Micah*. To an extent, it is sensed in each and every verse. There are also the *Merkavot* [chariots/structures] in Isaiah and Ezekiel, and atop them all *The Song of Songs*, which is purely the language of Kabbalah in its entirety. It is similar in laws and in legends, and all the more so with the matter of the unerasable holy names, which bear the same meaning in all the languages.

The Order of the Evolution of the Languages

There is a gradual development in everything, and the easiest language to use is one whose development is completed before the others. Hence, the first products were in the language of the Bible, as it is the most convenient language and was very prevalent at the time.

Following it came the language of laws, since it is completely immersed in the language of the Bible, as well as because it was needed in order to show the people how to implement the laws.

The third was the language of legends. Although it is found in many places in the Bible, too, it is only as an auxiliary language because its wit rushes the perception of matters. However, it cannot be used as a basic language, as it lacks the precision of root and its branch. Thus, it was rarely used and hence did not develop.

Even though legends were used extensively during the time of the Tannaim and the Amoraim, it was only in conjunction with the language of the Bible, to open the words of our sages—Rabbi... started, etc., (and other suffixes). In truth, expansive use of this language by our sages began after the concealment of the language of Kabbalah during the days of Rabbi Yochanan Ben Zakai and shortly before his time, meaning seventy years prior to the ruin of the Temple.

The last to evolve was the language of Kabbalah. This was so because of the difficulties in understanding it: In addition to attainment, one needs to understand the meaning of its words. Hence, even those who understood it could not use it since, for the most part, they were alone in their generation and had no one with whom to study. Our sages called that language *Maase Merkavah* [structure/chariot] since it is a special language by which one can discuss the details of the *Harkavot* [structures/compositions] of the degrees in one another, and not at all with any other.

The Language of Kabbalah Is Like Any Spoken Language, and Its Advantage Is in the Meaning Contained within a Single Word

At first glance, the language of Kabbalah seems like a mixture of the three above-mentioned languages. However, one who understands how to use it will find that it is a unique language in and of itself from beginning to end. This does not pertain to the words, but to their instructions. This is the whole difference between them.

In the first three languages, there is almost no instruction to a single word, allowing the examiner to understand what the word implies. Only by joining several words, and sometimes also portions, can their content and instruction be understood. The advantage in the language of Kabbalah is that each and every word in it discloses its content and instruction to the examiner in utter precision, no less than in any other human tongue: Each word carries its own precise definition that cannot be replaced with another.

Forgetting the Wisdom

Since the concealment of *The Zohar*, this important language has gradually been forgotten, as its users became fewer. Also, there was a cessation of one generation where the receiving sage did not convey it to an understanding receiver. Since then, there has been an immeasurable deficit.

You can evidently see that Kabbalist Rabbi Moshe de Leon, who was the last to possess it and by whom it was revealed to the world, did not understand one word of it, since in those books where he introduces pieces from *The Book of Zohar*, it is evident that he did not understand the words at all, as he interpreted it according to the language of the Bible. He completely confused the understanding, although he himself had a wonderful attainment, as his compositions demonstrate.

So it was for generations: All the Kabbalists dedicated their entire lives to understanding the language of *The Zohar* but could not find their hands or legs, since they forced the language of the Bible on it. Hence, this book was sealed before them as it was to Rabbi Moshe de Leon himself.

The Kabbalah of the ARI

This was so until the arrival of the unique Kabbalist, the ARI. His attainment was above and beyond any boundary, and he opened the language of *The Zohar* for us and paved our way in it. Had he not passed away so young, it is hard to imagine the amount of light that would be drawn out of *The Zohar*. The little we have been granted with has paved a way and inlet, and true hope that over the generations our understanding would grow to fully grasp it.

Yet, you must understand the reason why all the great sages who followed the ARI abandoned all the books that they compiled in this wisdom and in the commentaries on *The Zohar*, and nearly prohibited themselves even from seeing them, and dedicated their lives to the words of the ARI. This was not because they did not believe in the sanctity of the sages preceding the ARI; God forbid that we should think so. Anyone with eyes in the wisdom could see that the attainment of those great sages in the wisdom of truth was immeasurable. Only an ignorant fool could doubt them. However, their logic in the wisdom followed the first three languages.

Although each language is true and fitting in its place, it is not completely fitting, and quite misleading to understand the wisdom of Kabbalah contained in *The Zohar* using these orders, since this is a completely different language, since it was forgotten. For this reason, we do not use their explanations, either the explanations of Rabbi Moshe de Leon himself or those of his successors, as their words in interpreting *The Zohar* are not true, and to this day we have but one commentator—the ARI.

In light of the above-said, it follows that the internality of the wisdom of Kabbalah is no different from the internality of the Bible, the Talmud, and the legends. The only difference between them is in their explanations.

This is similar to a wisdom that has been translated into four languages. Naturally, the essence of the wisdom has not changed at all by the change of language. All we need to think of is which translation is the most convenient for conveying the wisdom to the reader.

So is the matter before us: The wisdom of truth, meaning the wisdom of the revelation of Godliness in His ways to the created beings, like secular teachings, must be passed on from generation to generation. Each generation adds a link to its predecessors, and thus the wisdom evolves. Moreover, it becomes more suitable for expansion in the public.

Hence, each sage must pass on to his students and to the following generations everything he has inherited in the wisdom from earlier generations, as well as the additions with which he himself has been rewarded. Clearly, the spiritual attainment—as it is attained by the attaining—cannot be passed on to another, and all the more so be written in a book, since spiritual objects cannot come in letters of the imagination whatsoever (even though it is written, "...and by the ministry of the prophets have I used similitudes," it is not literally so).

The Order of Conveying the Wisdom

Thus, how can one who attains convey one's attainments to the generations and to students? Know that there is only one way for this: the way of root and branch. All the worlds and everything that fills them, in their every detail, emerged from the Creator in one, unique, and unified thought. And that thought alone hung down and created all the many worlds, creations, and their conducts, as explained in *The Tree of Life* and in *Tikkuney Zohar*.

Hence, they are all equal to one another, like seal and imprint, where the first seal is imprinted in all of them. As a result, we call the closer worlds to the thought about the purpose, "roots," and we call the farther worlds from the purpose, "branches." This is so because the end of the act is in the preliminary thought.

Now we can understand the common idiom in the legends of our sages: "and watches it from the end of the world to its end." Should they not have said, "...from the beginning of the world to its end"? Yet, there are two ends: an end according to the distance from the purpose, meaning the last branches in this world, and 2) an end called "the final purpose," since the purpose is revealed at the end of the matter.

But as we have explained, "The end of the act is in the preliminary thought." Hence, we find the purpose at the beginning of the worlds. This is what we refer to as "the first world," or "the first seal." All other worlds stem from it, and this is why all creations—still, vegetative, animate, and speaking—in all their incidents exist in their fullest form right at the first world. And what does not exist there cannot appear in the world, since one does not give what one does not have.

Root and Branch in the Worlds

Now it is easy to understand the matter of root and branch in the worlds. Each of the manifold still, vegetative, animate, and speaking in this world has its corresponding part in the world above it, without any difference in its form but only in its substance. Thus, an animal or a rock in this world is a corporeal matter, and its corresponding animal or rock in the higher world is a spiritual matter, occupying no space or time. However, their quality is completely the same.

And here we should certainly add the matter of relation between matter and form, which is naturally conditioned on the quality of form, too. Similarly, with the majority of the still, vegetative, animate, and speaking in the upper world, you will find their similitude and likeness in the world above the upper. This continues through the first world where all the elements are completed, as it is written, "And God saw everything that He had made, and behold, it was very good."

This is why the Kabbalists wrote that the world is at the center of everything, indicating the above, that the end of the act is the first world, meaning the goal. Also, the remoteness from the goal is called "the descent of the worlds from their Emanator" down to this corporeal world, the farthest from the purpose.

However, the end of everything corporeal is to gradually develop and achieve the goal that the Creator had designed for it, meaning the first world. Compared to this world, which we are in, it is the last world, meaning the end of the matter. This is why it seems that the world of the purpose is the last world, and we, people of this world, are in between them.

The Essence of the Wisdom of Truth

Now it is clear that as the emergence of the living species in this world and the conduct of their existence are a wondrous wisdom, the appearance of the Godly abundance in the world, the degrees and the conduct of their actions, unite to create a wondrous wisdom far more than the science of physics. This is so because the science of physics is merely knowledge of the arrangements of a particular kind existing in a particular world. It is unique to its subject, and no other science is included in it.

This is not so with the wisdom of truth. Because it is knowledge of the whole of the still, vegetative, animate, and speaking in all the worlds, in all their instances and conducts, as they were included in the thought of the Creator, that is, in the purposeful subjects, for this reason, all the teachings in the world, from the least of them to the greatest of them, are wondrously included in it, as it equalizes all the various teachings, the most different and the most remote from one another, as the east from the west. It makes them all equal, meaning until the orders of each teaching are compelled to come by its ways.

For example, the science of physics is arranged precisely by the order of the worlds and the *Sefirot*. Similarly, the science of astronomy is arranged by that same order, and so is the science of music, etc. Thus, we find that all the teachings are arranged in it and follow a single connection and a single relation, and they are all like the relation of the child to its progenitor. Hence, they are contingent upon one another; that is, the wisdom of truth is contingent upon all the teachings, and all the teachings are contingent upon it. This is why we do not find a single genuine Kabbalist without comprehensive knowledge in all the teachings of the world, since they acquire them from the wisdom of truth itself, as they are included in it.

The Meaning of Unity

The greatest wonder about this wisdom is the incorporation in it: All the elements of the vast reality are incorporated in it until they come into a single thing—the Almighty, who contains them together.

In the beginning, you find that all the teachings in the world are reflected in it. They are arranged within it precisely by its orders. Subsequently, we find that all the worlds and the orders in the wisdom of truth itself, which are immeasurable, unite under only ten realities, called "Ten *Sefirot*."

Afterward, these ten *Sefirot* arrange in four manners, which are the four-letter Name. Then, these four manners are included in the tip of the *Yod*, which implies the *Ein Sof* [Infinity/no end].

In this way, one who begins in the wisdom must begin with the tip of the *Yod*, and from there to the ten *Sefirot* in the first world, called "the world of *Adam Kadmon*." From there one sees how the numerous details in the world of *Adam Kadmon* necessarily extend by way of cause and consequence by the same laws we find in astronomy and physics, meaning constant, unbreakable laws that necessarily stem from one another, hanging down from one another, from the tip of the *Yod* down to all the elements in the world of *Adam Kadmon*. From there they are imprinted by one another from the four worlds by way of seal and imprint until we arrive at all the elements in this world. Afterward, they are reintegrated in one another until they all come to the world of *Adam Kadmon*, then to the ten *Sefirot*, then to the four-letter Name [*HaVaYaH*], up to the tip of the *Yod*.

We could ask, "If the material is unknown, how can we scrutinize it rationally"? Indeed, such as that you will find in all the sciences. For example, when studying anatomy—the various organs and how they impact one another—these organs have no similarity to the general subject, which is the whole, living human being. However, over time, when you thoroughly know the wisdom, you can establish a general relation of all the details upon which the body is conditioned.

So it is here: The general subject is the revelation of Godliness to His creations, by way of the purpose, as it is written, "...for the earth shall be full of the knowledge of the Lord." However, a beginner certainly has no knowledge of this general subject, which is conditioned by all of them. For this reason, one must acquire all the details and how they impact one another, as well as their causes by way of cause and consequence, until one completes the whole wisdom. When one thoroughly knows everything, if he has a refined soul, it is certain that he will ultimately be rewarded with the general subject.

Even if he is not rewarded, it is still a great reward to acquire any perception of this great wisdom whose advantage over all other teachings is as the value of their subjects. As the advantage of the Creator over His creations is valued, so this wisdom, whose subject is Him, is far more valuable than the wisdom whose subject is His creatures.

It is not because it is imperceptible that the world refrains from contemplating it. After all, an astronomer has no perception of the stars or the planets but only of their movements, which they perform with wondrous wisdom that is predetermined in wondrous guidance. Similarly, the knowledge in the wisdom of truth is not more hidden than this, as even beginners thoroughly understand the moves. Rather, the whole prevention was because Kabbalists very wisely hid it from the world.

Giving Permission

I am glad that I was born in such a generation when it is permitted to disclose the wisdom of truth. And should you ask how I know that it is permitted, I will reply that it is because I have been given permission to disclose. That is, until now, the ways by which it is possible to publicly engage and to fully explain each word have not been revealed to any sage. And I, too, have sworn by my teacher not to disclose, as did all the disciples before me. However, this oath and this prohibition apply only to those manners that are given orally from generation to generation, back to the prophets and before. Had these ways been revealed to the public, they would have caused much harm, for reasons known only to us.

Yet, the way in which I engage in my books is a permitted way. Moreover, I have been instructed by my teacher to expand it as much as I can. We call it "the manner of clothing the matters." You will see in the writings of Rabbi Shimon Bar Yochai that he calls this way "giving permission," and this is what the Creator has given me to the fullest extent. We deem it as dependent not on the greatness of the sage, but on the state of the generation, as our sages said, "Little Samuel was worthy, etc., but his generation was unworthy." This is why I said that my being rewarded with the manner of disclosing the wisdom is only because of my generation.

Abstract Names

It is a grave mistake to think that the language of Kabbalah uses abstract names. On the contrary, it touches only upon the actual. Indeed, there are things in the world that are real even though we have no perception of them, such as the magnet and electricity. Yet, who would be so foolish as to say that these are abstract names? After all, we thoroughly know their actions, and we do not care at all that we do not know their essence. In the end, we refer to them as subjects of the actions related to them, and this is a real name. Even an infant who is just learning to speak can name them, if he only begins to feel their actions. This is our law: All that we do not attain, we do not define by name.

The Essence Is Not Perceived by the Corporeal Beings

Moreover, even the things that we imagine we attain by their essence, such as rocks and trees, after honest examination we are left with zero attainment in their essence, since we only attain their actions, which occur in conjunction with the encounter of our senses with them.

Soul

For example, when Kabbalah states that there are three forces, 1) body, 2) animate soul, 3) soul of *Kedusha* [holiness], this does not refer to the essence of the soul. The essence of the soul is fluid; it is what psychologists refer to as "self" and materialists as "electric."

It is a waste of time to speak of its essence, as it is not arranged for impression through the touch of our senses, as with all corporeal objects. However, by observing in the essence of this fluid three kinds of actions in the spiritual worlds, we thoroughly distinguish between them by different names, according to their actual operations in the upper worlds. Thus, there are no abstract names here, but rather tangible ones in the full sense of the word.

The Advantage of My Commentary over Previous Commentaries

We can be assisted by secular teachings in interpreting matters in the wisdom of Kabbalah since the wisdom of Kabbalah is the root of everything and they are all included in it. Some were assisted by anatomy, as it is written, "From my flesh shall I see God," and some were assisted by philosophy. Latterly, there is extensive use of the wisdom of psychology. But all these are not considered true commentaries since they do not interpret anything in the wisdom of Kabbalah itself, but only show us how the rest of the teachings are included in it. This is why the readers cannot be assisted by one place in another place. ...even though the wisdom of serving the Creator is the closest wisdom to the wisdom of Kabbalah from all the external teachings.

And needless to say, it is impossible to be assisted by interpretations according to the science of anatomy, or by philosophy. For this reason, I said that I am the first interpreter by root and branch, and cause and consequence. Hence, if one were to understand some matter through my commentary, he can be certain that wherever he finds this matter appears in *The Zohar* and in the *Tikkunim*, he can be assisted by it, as with the commentaries on the literal where you can be assisted by one place for all the other places.

The style of interpreting according to external teachings is a waste of time because it is nothing more than a testimony to the genuineness of one over the other. An external teaching needs no testimony, as Providence has prepared five senses to testify to it, and in Kabbalah one should (nevertheless) understand the argument of the litigator prior to bringing testimony to the argument.

The Style of Interpreting According to External Teachings

This is the source of the mistake of the Rav Shem Tov: He interpreted *The Guide for the Perplexed* according to the wisdom of Kabbalah, and he did not know, or pretended not to know, that the wisdom of medicine, or any other wisdom, could be interpreted according to the wisdom of Kabbalah no less than the wisdom of philosophy. This is so because all the teachings are included in it and were imprinted by its seal.

Of course, *The Guide to the Perplexed* did not refer at all to what the Rav Shem Tov interpreted, and he did not see how... in *The Book of Creation*, he interpreted the Kabbalah according to philosophy. I have already proven that such a style of commentaries is a waste of time, since external teachings need no testimony, and it is pointless to bring testimony to the truthfulness of the wisdom of Kabbalah before its words are interpreted.

It is like a prosecutor who brings witnesses to verify his words before he has explained his arguments (except for books that deal with the work of the Creator, since the wisdom of serving the Creator truly needs witnesses to its truthfulness and success, and we should be assisted by the wisdom of truth).

However, all the compositions in this style are not at all a waste. After we thoroughly understand the wisdom itself, we will be able to receive much assistance from analogies, how all the teachings are included in it, as well as the manners by which to seek them.

Attaining the Wisdom

There are three orders in the wisdom of truth:

1. The originality in the wisdom. It requires no human assistance, as it is entirely a gift of the Creator, and no stranger shall interfere with it.

2. The understanding of these sources, which one attains from above. It is like a person before whom the whole world is set, yet he must exert and study to understand this world. Although he sees everything with his own eyes, there are fools and there are wise. This understanding is called "the wisdom of truth," and *Adam ha Rishon* was the first to receive a sequence of sufficient knowledge by which to understand and to successfully utilize the maximum of everything he saw and attained with his eyes.

   The order of this knowledge is given only from mouth to mouth. And there is also an order of evolution in them, where each can add to his friend or regress (whereas in the first discernment everyone receives equally without adding or subtracting, like Adam, in understanding the reality of this world. In viewing it, all are equal, but this is not so in understanding it—some evolve from generation to generation and some regress). And the order of its conveyance is sometimes called "conveying the Explicit Name," and it is given under many conditions, but only orally and not in writing.

3. This is a written order. It is a completely new thing, since besides containing much room for the development of the wisdom, through which each inherits all the expansions of his attainments to the following generations, there is another magnificent power in it: All who engage in it, although they still do not understand what is written in it, are purified by it, and the upper lights draw closer to them. This order contains four languages, as we have explained above, and the language of Kabbalah exceeds them all.

The Order of Conveying the Wisdom

The most successful way for one who wishes to learn the wisdom is to search for a genuine Kabbalist and follow all his instructions, until one is rewarded with understanding the wisdom in one's own mind, meaning the first discernment. Afterward, one will be rewarded with its conveyance mouth to mouth, which is the second discernment, and after that, understand in writing, which is the third discernment. Then, one will have inherited all the wisdom and its instruments from his teacher with ease and will be left with all his time to develop and expand.

However, in reality there is a second way: Through one's great yearning, the sights of heaven will open before him and he will attain all the origins by himself. This is the first discernment. Yet, afterward, one must still labor and exert extensively until he finds a Kabbalist sage before whom he can bow and obey, and from whom to receive the wisdom by way of conveyance face to face, which is the second discernment.

Then comes the third discernment. Since he is not attached to a Kabbalist sage from the outset, the attainments come with great efforts and consume much time, leaving little time to develop in it. Also, sometimes the knowledge comes after the fact, as it is written, "and they shall die without wisdom." These are ninety-nine percent and what we call "entering but not exiting." They are as fools and ignorant in this world, who see the world set before them but do not understand any of it, except for the bread in their mouths.

Indeed, in the first way, too, not everyone succeeds, since after being rewarded with attainment, the majority of them become complacent and cannot subjugate themselves to their teacher sufficiently, as they are not worthy of the conveyance of the wisdom. In this case, the sage must hide the essence of the wisdom from them, and "they shall die without wisdom," "entering but not exiting."

This is so because there are harsh and strict conditions in conveying the wisdom, which stem from necessary reasons. Hence, very few are regarded highly enough by their teachers for them to find them worthy of this thing, and happy are the rewarded.

The Acting Mind

It is written that every person is obliged to attain the root of his soul. This means that the aspired-for purpose of the created being is *Dvekut* [adhesion] with His qualities, as it is written, "And to cleave unto Him." Our sages interpreted that this is the *Dvekut* with His attributes: "As He is merciful," etc. His qualities are the holy *Sefirot*, and this is the acting mind that guides His world and by which He allots them His bestowal and goodness.

We must understand why this is called "*Dvekut* with the Creator," as it seems to be mere learning. I will explain it with an allegory: In every operation in the world, the mind of its operator remains in that operation. In a table, one can attain the carpenter's mind and deftness in his craft, whether great or small. This is so because while working, he built it with his mind and the qualities of his mind. And one who observes this operation and considers the mind imprinted in it, during this act, he is attached to the mind that performed it, meaning they actually unite.

In truth, there is no distance or cessation between spirituals, even when they are in distinct bodies. But the mind in them cannot be distinguished, since what knife can cut the spiritual and leave it separated? Rather, the main difference between spirituals is in their qualities—praiseworthy or blameworthy—and the composition, since a mind that calculates astronomy will not cling to one that contemplates natural sciences.

There is great diversity even within the same teaching, for if one exceeds another in even one element, it separates the spirituals from one another. But when two sages contemplate the same teaching and have the same measure of knowledge, they are in fact united, for what separates them?

Hence, when one contemplates another's action and attains the mind of the sage who performed it, they have the same mind and power. Now they are completely united, like a man who met his beloved friend on the street, he embraces him and kisses him, and because of their great unity, it is impossible to separate them.

Hence, the rule is that in the speaking, the mind is the best-adjusted force between the Creator and His creatures. It is considered the medium, meaning He emanated a spark of that force, and through that spark, everything returns to Him.

It is written, "In wisdom You have made them all," meaning that He created the whole world with His wisdom. Hence, one who is rewarded with attaining the manners by which He created the world and its conducts is adhered to the Mind that performed them. Thus, he is adhered to the Creator.

This is the meaning of the Torah being all the names of the Creator, which belong to the created beings. And by their merit, the created being attains the Mind that does everything, since the Creator looked in the Torah when He created the world, and one achieves illumination through creation and forever adheres to that Mind; thus, he is adhered to the Creator.

Now we understand why the Creator showed us His tools of craftsmanship, for do we need to create worlds? But from the above-mentioned, we gather that the Creator has shown us His conducts so we may know how to adhere to Him, which is "cleave unto His attributes."

Matan Torah [The Giving of the Torah]

"Love your friend as yourself" (Leviticus 19:18)

Rabbi Akiva says, "This is a great *Klal* [collective/rule] in the Torah"
(*Beresheet Rabbah*, Chapter 24).

1) This statement of our sages demands explanation. The word *Klal* [collective/rule] indicates a sum of details that, when put together, form that collective. Thus, when he says about the *Mitzva* [commandment] "love your friend as yourself," that it is a great *Klal* in the Torah, we must understand that the rest of the 612 *Mitzvot* [commandments] in the Torah, with all their interpretations, are no more and no less than the sum of the details inserted and contained in that single *Mitzva*, "love your friend as yourself."

This is quite perplexing because you can say this regarding *Mitzvot* between man and man, but how can that single *Mitzva* contain all the *Mitzvot* between man and God, which are the essence and the vast majority of the laws?

2) If we can still strain to find some way to reconcile their words, there comes before us a second saying, even more conspicuous, about a convert who came to Hillel (*Shabbat* 31a) and told him, "Teach me the whole of the Torah while I am standing on one leg." And he replied, "Anything that you hate, do not do to your friend" (the translation of "love your friend as yourself"), "and the rest is its commentary; go study."

Here before us is a clear law, that in all 612 *Mitzvot* and in all the writings in the Torah there is none that is preferred to the *Mitzva*, "love your friend as yourself." This is because they only aim to interpret and allow us to observe the *Mitzva* of loving others properly, since he specifically says—"the rest is its commentary; go study." This means that the rest of the Torah is interpretations of that one *Mitzva*, that the *Mitzva* to love your friend as yourself could not be completed were it not for them.

3) Before we delve into the heart of the matter, we must observe that *Mitzva*, since we were commanded: "Love your friend as yourself." The word "yourself" tells us, "love your friend to the same extent you love yourself, not one bit less." In other words, you must constantly and vigilantly satisfy the needs of every person at least in the Israeli nation, no less than you are always vigilant to satisfy your own needs.

This is utterly impossible, for not many can satisfy their own needs during their daily work, so how can you tell them to work to satisfy the wishes of the entire nation? And we couldn't possibly think that the Torah exaggerates, for it warns us to not add or subtract, indicating that these words and laws were given with utter precision.

4) And if this is still not enough for you, I will tell you that the simple explanation of that *Mitzva* of loving your fellow person is even harsher, for we must put the needs of our friends before our own. It is written in the Tosfot in the name of the Jerusalem

[Talmud] (*Kidushin* 20a) regarding the verse "Because he is happy with you," said about a Hebrew slave: "When sometimes he has but one pillow, if he lies on it himself and does not give it to his slave, he does not observe 'Because he is happy with you,' for he is lying on a pillow and the slave, on the ground. If he does not lie on it and does not give it to the slave, as well, it is Sodomite rule. It turns out that, against his will, he must give it to his slave while the master himself lies on the ground."

We also find the same rule in the verse about the measure of loving others, for here, too, the text compares the satisfaction of the friend's needs to the satisfaction of one's own needs, as with the example of "Because he is happy with you" regarding the Hebrew slave. Thus, here too, if he has but one chair and his friend does not, the law is that if he sits on it and does not give it to his friend, he breaks the *Mitzva*, "Love your friend as yourself," since he is not fulfilling the needs of his friend as he fulfills his own.

If he does not sit on it and also does not give it to his friend, it is as evil as Sodomite rule. Therefore, he must let his friend sit on it while he himself will sit on the ground or stand. Clearly, this is the law regarding all the needs that one has, and one's friend lacks. Now go and see if this *Mitzva* is in any way feasible.

5) We must first understand why the Torah was given specifically to the Israeli nation and not to all the people in the world equally. Is there, God forbid, nationalism involved here? Of course, only an insane person would think so. In fact, our sages have already examined this question, and this is what they meant by their words (*Avoda Zarah* 2b): "The Creator gave it to every nation and tongue, and they did not accept it."

But what they find bewildering is why, then, were we called "the chosen people," as it is written, "The Lord has chosen you," since no other nation wanted it? Moreover, there is a fundamental question in the matter: Can it be that the Creator came with His law in His hands to negotiate with those savage peoples, or through his prophets? Such a thing has never been heard of and is completely unacceptable.

6) But when we fully understand the essence of the Torah and *Mitzvot* that were given to us, and their desired purpose, to the extent our sages instructed us, which is the purpose of the great creation that is set before our eyes, we will understand everything. The first concept is that there is no act without a purpose. There is no exception from this rule except for the lowest of the human species or infants. Therefore, it is certain that the Creator, whose exaltedness is inconceivable, would not act—be it a great or a small act—without some purpose.

Our sages tell us about that, that the world was created only for the purpose of observing Torah and *Mitzvot*, meaning, as our sages explained, that the aim of the Creator from the time He created His creation is to reveal His Godliness to others, since the revelation of His Godliness reaches the creature as pleasant bounty that is ever growing until it reaches the desired measure.

By this, the lowly rise with true recognition and become a *Merkava* [chariot/structure] to Him, and to cling unto Him until they reach their final completion: "The eye has not seen a God besides you." And because of the greatness and glory of that perfection, the Torah and the prophecy, too, refrain from uttering even a single word of exaggeration here, as our sages implied about this (*Berachot* 34b), "All the prophets made their prophecies only for the days of the Messiah, but for the next world, 'The eye has not seen a God besides you,'" as is known to the knowledgeable ones.

This perfection is expressed in the words of the Torah and the prophecy and in the words of our sages in the simple word, *Dvekut* [adhesion]. Because of the widespread use of this word by the masses, it has lost almost all its content, but if you reflect on that word for even an instant, you will be overwhelmed by its wondrous stature, for if you picture the exaltedness of the Creator and the lowliness of the creature, you will be able to perceive the value of *Dvekut* of one with the other. Then you will understand why we ascribe that word the purpose of the whole creation.

It turns out that the purpose of the whole of creation is for the lowly creatures to be able, by observing Torah and *Mitzvot*, to rise ever upward, ever developing until they are rewarded with *Dvekut* with their Creator.

7) But here came the sages of *The Zohar* and asked why we were not created in this high stature of *Dvekut* with Him to begin with. What reason did He have to burden us with this labor and burden of creation and the Torah and *Mitzvot*? They replied, "He who eats that which is not his is afraid to look at his face." This means that one who eats and enjoys the labor of one's friend is afraid to look at his face because by doing so he becomes increasingly humiliated until he loses his human form. Because that which extends from His wholeness cannot be deficient, He gave us room to earn our exaltedness by ourselves, through our work in Torah and *Mitzvot*.

These words are most profound and I have already explained them in my book, *Panim Masbirot on The Tree of Life*, Branch One [and in the book, *The Study of the Ten Sefirot, Histaklut Pnimit*, Part One]. Here I will explain them briefly to make them understandable for all.

8) This matter is like a rich man who took a man from the market and fed him and gave him gold and silver and every desirable thing each day. Each day, he showered him with more gifts than the day before. Finally, the rich man asked, "Tell me, have all your wishes been fulfilled?" And he replied, "Not all of my wishes have been fulfilled, for how good and how pleasant it would be if all those possessions and precious things came to me through my own work, as they have come to you, and I would not be receiving the charity of your hand." Then the rich man told him, "In this case, there has never been born a person who could fulfill your wishes."

It is a natural thing, since on one hand he experiences greater and greater pleasure, the more he showers presents upon him. But on the other hand, it is hard for him to tolerate the shame of the excessive goodness with which the rich showers him.

This is because there is a natural law that a receiver feels shame and impatience upon receiving gifts from a giver out of compassion and pity.

From here extends a second law, that never will anyone be able to satisfy the needs of his friend to the fullest, because ultimately, he will not be able to give him the nature and form of self-possession, as only with it is the desired perfection attained.

But this relates only to the creatures, whereas regarding the Creator, it is completely impossible and unacceptable. This is the reason He has prepared for us the toil and the labor of Torah and *Mitzvot*, to produce our exaltedness by ourselves, because then the delight and pleasure that comes to us from Him, meaning everything that is included in the *Dvekut* with Him, will all be our own possession that has come to us through our own efforts. Then we will feel ourselves as the owners, without which there cannot be a sensation of wholeness.

9) Indeed, we need to examine the heart and the source of this natural law, and who it was that fathered the flaw of shame and impatience that we feel upon receiving charity from another. It is understood from a law that is known to scientists, that each branch bears the same nature as its root, 1) and that the branch also desires, seeks, and craves, and benefits from all the conducts of the root. 2) Conversely, all the conducts that are not in the root, its branch removes itself from them, cannot tolerate them, and is harmed by them. This law exists between each root and its branch and cannot be breached.

This opens before us a door to understand the source of all the pleasures and pains in our world. Since the Creator is the root of His creations, we feel all that exists in Him, and which extends to us directly from Him, as pleasant and delightful, for our nature is close to our root. And everything that is not in Him and does not extend to us directly from Him, but contradicts creation itself, will be against our nature and difficult for us to tolerate. Thus, we love to rest and hate to move so much that we do not make a single movement if not for the attainment of rest. This is so because our root is not in motion but at rest, and no motion exists in Him whatsoever. Therefore, it is against our nature and loathsome to us, as well.

By the same token, we love wisdom, strength, and wealth, etc., because all those exist in Him Who is our Root. And hence, we hate their opposites, such as foolishness, weakness, and poverty, since they do not exist in our Root at all. This makes us feel hateful and loathsome, and pains us immeasurably.

10) This is what gives us the foul taste of shame and impatience when we receive from others by way of charity, because in the Creator there is no such thing as reception of favors, as from whom would He receive? Because this element does not exist in our Root, we feel it as repulsive and loathsome. On the other hand, we feel delight and pleasure every time we bestow upon others since that conduct exists in our Root, which gives to all.

11) Now we have found a way to examine the purpose of creation, which is to cling unto Him, in its true appearance. This exaltedness and *Dvekut*, which is guaranteed to come to us through our work in Torah and *Mitzvot*, is no more and no less than the equivalence of the branches with their Root. All the gentleness and pleasure and sublimity become a natural extension here, as we have said above, 1) that pleasure is only the equivalence of form with the Maker. When we equalize in every conduct with our Root, we sense delight. 2) Everything we encounter that is not in our Root becomes intolerable, disgusting, or considerably painful to us, as is necessitated by that concept. And we naturally find that our very hope depends on the extent of our equivalence of form with our Root.

12) These were the words of our sages (*Beresheet Rabbah* 44) when they asked, "Why should the Creator mind whether one slaughters at the throat or at the back of the neck? After all, the *Mitzvot* were given only to cleanse people." That cleansing means the cleansing of the turbid body, which is the purpose that emerges from the observation of all the Torah and *Mitzvot*, for "A wild ass will be turned into man," since when one emerges out of the bosom of creation, one is in utter filth and lowliness, meaning a multitude of self-love that is imprinted in him, and his every movement revolves solely around himself without a shred of bestowal upon others.

Thus, then one is at the farthest distance from the Root, on the other end, 1) since the root is all bestowal without a hint of reception, 2) whereas the newborn is in a state of complete self-reception without a hint of bestowal. Therefore, his situation is regarded as being at the lowest point of lowliness and filth in our human world.

The more he grows, the more he receives from his environment portions of "bestowal upon others," depending on the values and development in that environment. And then one is initiated into observing Torah and *Mitzvot* for the purpose of self-love, for reward in this world and in the next world, called *Lo Lishma* [not for Her sake], since one cannot be accustomed any other way.

As one grows, he is told how to observe *Mitzvot Lishma* [for Her sake], which is with an aim solely to bring contentment to his Maker. As Maimonides said (*Hilchot Teshuva*, Chapter 10), "Women and children should not be told of observing Torah and *Mitzvot Lishma* since they will not be able to bear it. But when they grow and acquire knowledge and wisdom, they are taught to work *Lishma*." It is as our sages said, "From *Lo Lishma*, one comes to *Lishma*," defined by the aim to bring contentment to one's Maker and not for any self-love, under any circumstances.

Through the natural remedy of engagement in Torah and *Mitzvot Lishma*, which the Giver of the Torah knows, as our sages said (*Kidushin* 30b), "The Creator says, 'I have created the evil inclination; I have created for it the Torah as a spice.'" Thus, that creature develops and marches upward in degrees of the above-said exaltedness until he loses all remnants of self-love and all the *Mitzvot* in his body rise, and he performs all his actions only to bestow, so even the necessity that he receives flows in the direction of bestowal, meaning so he can bestow. This is why our sages said, "The *Mitzvot* were given only to cleanse people."

13) If indeed there are two parts in the Torah: 1) *Mitzvot* between man and the Creator, 2) *Mitzvot* between man and man, both aim for the same thing—to bring the creature to the final purpose of *Dvekut* with Him. Furthermore, even the practical side in both of them is really one and the same, for when one performs an act *Lishma*, without any mixture of self-love, meaning without drawing any benefit for himself, then one does not feel any difference whether one is working to love one's friend or to love the Creator.

This is so because it is a natural law for any being that anything outside one's own body is regarded as unreal and empty. And any movement that a person makes to love another is performed with a reflected light and some reward that will eventually return to him and serve him for his own benefit. Thus, such an act cannot be considered "love of others" because it is judged by its end. It is like rent that pays off only in the end. However, the act of renting is not considered love of another.

But making any movement only as a result of love for others, without any spark of reflected light or hope for any kind of reward in return is completely impossible by nature. It is written in *The Zohar* about this with regard to the nations of the world: "Every *Hesed* [mercy/grace] that they do, they do for themselves."

This means that all the good that they do, either toward their friends or toward their God, is not for their love for others but for self-love, since this matter is completely unnatural.

Therefore, only those who observe Torah and *Mitzvot* are capable of this since by accustoming themselves to observe Torah and the *Mitzvot* in order to bring contentment to their Maker, they gradually depart from the bosom of the natural creation and acquire a second nature, being the above-mentioned love of others.

This is what brought the sages of *The Zohar* to exclude the nations of the world from love of others, when they said, "Every *Hesed* that they do, they do for themselves," for they are not involved in observing Torah and *Mitzvot Lishma*, and the only reason they serve their gods is for reward and salvation in this world and in the next. Thus, their worship of their gods is because of self-love, too, and they will never perform an act that is outside the boundaries of their own bodies, for which they will be able to lift themselves even as a hairsbreadth above their basic nature.

14) Thus we can clearly see that toward those who observe Torah and *Mitzvot Lishma*, there is no difference between the two parts of the Torah, even on the practical side. This is because before one accomplishes it, one is compelled to feel any act of bestowal—either toward another person or toward the Creator—as emptiness beyond conception. But through great effort, one slowly rises and attains a second nature, and then one attains the final goal, which is *Dvekut* with Him.

Since this is so, it is reasonable to think that the part of the Torah that deals with man's relationship with his friend is better capable of bringing one to the desired goal since the work in *Mitzvot* between man and God is regular and specific, and is not demanding, and one becomes easily accustomed to it, and everything that is done out of habit is no longer useful. But the *Mitzvot* between man and man are changing and irregular, and demands surround him wherever he turns. Hence, their cure is much more certain and their aim is closer.

15) Now we can understand the words of Hillel HaNasi to the proselyte, that the essence of the Torah is "Love your friend as yourself," and the remaining six hundred and twelve *Mitzvot* are but an interpretation and preparation for it (see Item 2). And even the *Mitzvot* between man and the Creator are regarded as a preparation for that *Mitzva*, which is the final aim emerging from the Torah and *Mitzvot*, as our sages said, "The Torah and *Mitzvot* were given only so as to cleanse Israel" (Item 12), which is the cleansing of the body until one acquires a second nature defined as "love for others," meaning the one *Mitzva*: "Love your friend as yourself," which is the final aim of the Torah, after which one immediately obtains *Dvekut* with Him.

But one must not wonder why it was not defined in the words: "And you will love the Lord your God with all your heart and with all your soul and with all your might." He did this for the above reason that indeed, with respect to a person who is still within the nature of creation, there is no difference between the love of the Creator and the love of his fellow person, for anything that is from another is unreal to him.

And because that proselyte asked of Hillel HaNasi to explain to him the desired outcome of the Torah, so his goal would be near and he would not have to walk a long way, as he said, "Teach me the whole Torah while I am standing on one leg," he defined it for him as love of his friend since its aim is nearer and is revealed faster (Item 14), since it is mistake-proof and is demanding.

16) In the above words, we find a way to understand our concept from above (Items 3 and 4) about the contents of that *Mitzva*, "Love your friend as yourself," how the Torah compels us to do something that cannot be done.

Indeed, know that for this reason, the Torah was not given to our holy fathers—Abraham, Isaac and Jacob—but was held until the exodus from Egypt, when they came out and became a complete nation of six hundred thousand men of twenty years of age or more. For then, each member of the nation was asked if he agreed to that exalted work. And once each and every one in the nation agreed to it with heart and soul, and said "We will do and we will hear," it became possible to observe the whole of the Torah, and that which was previously impossible became possible.

This is because it is certain that if six hundred thousand men abandon their work for the satisfaction of their own needs and worry about nothing but standing guard so their friends will not lack a thing, and moreover, they will engage in this with great love, with their very heart and soul, in the full meaning of the *Mitzva*, "Love your friend as yourself," it is then beyond doubt that no one in the nation will need to worry about his own well-being.

Because of this, one becomes completely free of securing his own survival and can easily observe the *Mitzva*, "Love your friend as yourself," obeying all the conditions given in Items 3 and 4. After all, why would he worry about his own survival when six hundred thousand loyal lovers stand by, ready with great care to make sure he lacks nothing of his needs?

Therefore, once all the members of the nation agreed, they were immediately given the Torah, for now they were capable of observing it. But before they grew into a complete nation, and certainly during the time of the fathers, who were unique in the land, they were not truly qualified to observe the Torah in its desirable form, since with a small number of people it is impossible to even begin with engagement in *Mitzvot* between man and man to the extent of "Love your friend as yourself," as explained in Items 3 and 4. This is why they were not given the Torah.

17) From all the above, we can understand one of the most perplexing phrases of our sages: "All of Israel are responsible for one another." This seems to be completely unjust, for is it possible that if someone sins or commits a sin that upsets his Maker, and I have no acquaintance with him, the Creator will collect his debt from me? It is written, "Fathers will not be put to death for children," etc., and "Each man will be put to death for his own sin," so how can they say that I am responsible for the sins of even a complete stranger, of whom I know neither him nor his whereabouts?

And if that is not enough for you, see *Masechet Kidushin*, 40b: "Rabbi Elazar, the son of Rabbi Shimon, says: 'Since the world is judged by its majority and the individual is judged by its majority, if he performed one *Mitzva*, happy is he, for he has sentenced the world to the side of merit. And if he commits one sin, woe unto him, for he has sentenced himself and the world to the side of sin, as it is said, 'one sinner destroys much good.'"

Thus, Rabbi Elazar, son of Rabbi Shimon, has made me responsible for the whole world, since he thinks all the people in the world are responsible for one another, and each person brings merit or sin to the whole world by his deeds. This is twice as perplexing.

But according to the above said, we can understand their words very simply; we have shown that each of the 613 *Mitzvot* in the Torah revolves around that single *Mitzva*: "Love your friend as yourself." And we find that such a state can only exist in a complete nation whose every member agrees to it.

The Arvut [Mutual Guarantee]

(Continued from "Matan Torah")

"All of Israel are responsible for one another" (*Sanhedrin* 27b, *Shavuot* 39a).

This is to speak of the *Arvut* [mutual guarantee], when all of Israel became responsible for one another. Because the Torah was not given to them before each and every one from Israel was asked if he agreed to take upon himself the *Mitzva* [commandment] of loving others in the full measure expressed in the words "Love your friend as yourself," as explained in the article "Matan Torah," Items 2 and 3, examine it thoroughly there. This means that each and every one in Israel would take upon himself to care and work for each member of the nation, to satisfy all their needs, no less than the measure imprinted in him to care for his own needs.

Once the whole nation unanimously agreed and said, "We will do and we will hear," each member of Israel became responsible that no member of the nation will lack anything. Only then did they become worthy of receiving the Torah, and not before.

With this collective responsibility, each member of the nation was liberated from worrying about the needs of his own body and could observe the *Mitzva*, "Love your friend as yourself" in the fullest measure and give all that he had to any needy person since he no longer cared for the existence of his own body, as he knew for certain that he was surrounded by six hundred thousand loyal lovers standing ready to provide for him, as explained in the article, "Matan Torah," Item 16.

For this reason, they were not ready to receive the Torah at the time of Abraham, Isaac, and Jacob, but only when they came out of Egypt and became a complete nation. Only then was there a possibility to guarantee everyone's needs without any care or concern.

However, while they were still mingled with the Egyptians, a portion of their needs was necessarily given into the hands of these savages, permeated with self-love. Thus, the portion that is given into the hands of foreigners will not be secured for any person from Israel because his friends will not be able to provide for those needs, as they will not be in possession of them. Consequently, as long as the individual is troubled with concerns for himself, he is unfit to even begin to observe the *Mitzva*, "Love your friend as yourself."

Thus, you evidently find that the giving of the Torah had to be delayed until they came out of Egypt and became a nation on their own, meaning when all their needs were provided for by themselves, independently of others. This qualified them to receive the above *Arvut*, and then they were given the Torah. It turns out that even after the reception of the Torah, if a handful from Israel betray and return to the filth of self-love, without consideration of others, that same amount of need that is put in the hands of those few would burden each one in Israel with the need to provide for it themselves because those few will not pity them at all.

Hence, the fulfillment of the *Mitzva* of loving one's friend will be prevented from the whole of Israel. Thus, these rebels cause those who observe the Torah to remain in their filth of self-love, for they will not be able to engage in the *Mitzva*, "Love your friend as yourself," and complete their love of others without their help.

You therefore see that all of Israel are responsible for one another, both on the positive side and on the negative side. On the positive side, if they keep the *Arvut* to the point that each one cares and satisfies the needs of his friends, they can fully observe the Torah and *Mitzvot* [commandments], meaning to bring contentment to their Maker, as mentioned in "Matan Torah," Item 13. On the negative side, if a part of the nation does not want to keep the *Arvut*, but to wallow in self-love, they cause the rest of the nation to remain immersed in their filth and lowliness without finding a way out of their filth.

18) Therefore, the Tana described the *Arvut* as two people who were on a boat, and one of them began to drill a hole in the boat. His friend said, "Why are you drilling?" He replied, "Why should you mind? I am drilling under me, not under you." So he replied, "Fool! We will both drown together in the boat!"

Meaning, as we said, since those rebels wallow in self-love, by their actions, they build an iron wall that prevents the observers of the Torah from even beginning to fully observe the Torah and *Mitzvot* in the measure of words "Love your friend as yourself," which is the ladder for achieving *Dvekut* [adhesion] with Him. Indeed, how right were the words of the proverb that said, "Fool, we will both drown together in the boat!"

19) Rabbi Elazar, son of Rashbi, clarifies the matter of *Arvut* even further. It is not enough for him that all of Israel be responsible for one another, but the whole world is included in the *Arvut*. Indeed, there is no dispute here, for everyone admits that initially, it is enough to begin with one nation for the observance of the Torah, meaning for the beginning of the correction of the world, as it was impossible to begin with all the nations at once. It is as they said, that the Creator went with the Torah to every nation and tongue and they would not receive it. In other words, they were immersed in the filth of self-love up to their necks, some in adultery, some in robbery and murder and so on, until it was impossible to even conceive, in those days, to even ask if they agreed to retire from self-love.

Therefore, the Creator did not find a nation or a tongue qualified to receive the Torah, except for the children of Abraham, Isaac, and Jacob, whose ancestral merit reflected upon them, as our sages said, "The fathers observed the whole Torah even before it was given." This means that because of the exaltedness of their souls, they could attain all the ways of the Creator with respect to the spirituality of the Torah, which stems from their *Dvekut* with Him without first needing the ladder of the practical part of the Torah, which they had no possibility of observing at all, as written in "Matan Torah," Item 16.

Undoubtedly, both the physical refinement and the mental exaltedness of our holy fathers greatly influenced their sons and their sons' sons, and their righteousness reflected upon that generation, whose members all assumed that sublime work, and each and every one stated clearly, "We will do and we will hear." Because of this, we were chosen, out of necessity, to be a chosen people from among all nations. Hence, only the members of the Israeli nation were admitted into the required *Arvut*, and not the nations of the world at all, since they did not participate in it. This is the plain reality, so how could Rabbi Elazar dispute it?

20) But the end of the correction of the world will only be by bringing all the people in the world under His work, as it is written, "And the Lord will be King over all the earth; in that day, the Lord will be one and His name one." The text specifies, "on that day," and not before. And there are several more verses, "For the earth will be full of the knowledge of the Lord..." "...and all the nations will flow unto him."

But the role of Israel toward the rest of the world resembles the role of our holy fathers toward the Israeli nation: As the righteousness of our fathers helped us develop and refine ourselves until we became worthy of receiving the Torah, for were it not for our fathers, who observed the whole of the Torah before it was given, we would certainly not be any better than the rest of the nations, as mentioned in Item 19, so it is upon the Israeli nation—through engagement in Torah and *Mitzvot Lishma* [for Her sake]—to qualify itself and all the people of the world to develop until they take upon themselves that sublime work of the love of others. This is the ladder to the purpose of creation, which is *Dvekut* with Him.

Thus, each and every *Mitzva* that each person from Israel performs in order to bring contentment to one's Maker, and not for any reward and self-love, helps, to some extent, with the development of all the people of the world. This is because it is not done at once, but by a slow, gradual development, until it increases to such a degree that they can shift all the people in the world to the desired refinement. And this is what our sages call "shifting the balance to merit," meaning that the desired weight of purity has been achieved. They compared it to weighing on a scale, where the shifting of the balance is the achievement of the desired weight.

21) These are the words of Rabbi Elazar, son of Rabbi Shimon, who said that the world is judged by its majority. He was referring to the role of the Israeli nation to qualify the world for a certain measure of refinement, until they are worthy of taking upon themselves His work, no less than Israel were worthy at the time they received the Torah. In the words of our sages, it is considered that they had attained enough virtues to overcome the side of sin, which is the filthy self-love.

Clearly, if the side of merit, which is the sublime attainment of the benefit of loving others, transcends the filthy side of sin, they become qualified for the decision and the agreement to say, "We will do and we will hear," as Israel said. But before they obtain sufficient merits, self-love will certainly prevail and they will refuse to assume His burden.

Our sages said, "He who performs one *Mitzva* is happy, for he has sentenced himself and the whole world to the side of merit." This means that an individual from Israel finally adds his own part to the final decision, as one who weighs sesame seeds and adds them one by one to the scale until the balance shifts. Certainly, each one takes part in this shifting, for without him, the sentencing would never be completed. Similarly, it is said about the acts of an individual from Israel that he sentences the whole world to the side of merit. This is because when the matter ends and the whole world has been sentenced to the side of merit, each and every one will have a share in this shifting, for were it not for his actions, the shifting would have been deficient.

Thus you find that Rabbi Elazar, son of Rabbi Shimon, does not dispute the words of our sages that all of Israel is responsible for one another. Rather, Rabbi Elazar, the son of Rabbi Shimon, speaks of the correction of the whole world in the future, whereas our sages speak of the present, when only Israel have taken upon themselves the Torah.

22) And this is what Rabbi Elazar, son of Rabbi Shimon, quotes from the writings: "One sinner destroys much good." It has already been explained in Item 20 that the impression that comes to a person when engaging in *Mitzvot* between man and the Creator is completely the same as the impression he gets when engaging in *Mitzvot* between man and man, since one is obliged to perform all the *Mitzvot Lishma* [for Her sake], without any hope for self-love, meaning that no light or hope returns to him through his trouble in the form of reward or honor, etc. Here, at this exalted point, the love of the Creator and the love of his friend unite and actually become one, as said in the article, "Matan Torah," Item 15.

In this manner one affects a certain measure of advancement on the ladder of love for others in all the people of the world in general, since that degree, which that individual caused by his actions, whether large or small, ultimately joins the future in shifting the world to the side of merit, since his share has been added and joins the shift.

As written in Item 20 in the allegory about the sesame seeds, one who commits one sin, meaning he cannot overcome and conquer his filthy self-love, and therefore steals or does something of the sort, sentences himself and the whole world to the side of sin. This is because with the disclosure of the filth of self-love, the lowly nature of creation is reinforced. Thus, he takes away a certain amount from the sentencing to the final side of merit, like a person removing from the scale that single sesame seed his friend had put there.

Thus, to that extent, he slightly elevates the side of sin. It turns out that he regresses the world, as they said, "One sinner destroys much good." Because he could not overcome his petty lust, he pushed the spirituality of the whole world backward.

23) With these words, we clearly understand what we said above in Item 5 about the Torah being given specifically to the Israeli nation, because it is certain and unequivocal that the purpose of creation lies on the shoulders of the whole of the human race, black, or white, or yellow, without any essential difference.

But because of the descent of human nature to the lowest degree, which is the self-love that rules over all of humanity without restraint, there was no way to negotiate with them and persuade them to agree to take upon themselves, even as a mere promise, to exit their narrow frame into the wide world of love of others. The exception was the Israeli nation because they were enslaved in the savage kingdom of Egypt four hundred years in horrible torments.

Our sages said, "As salt sweetens meat, suffering scours man's sins." This means that they bring to the body great refinement. In addition, the refinement of their holy fathers assisted them, as said in Item 16, which is the most important, as some of the verses of the Torah testify.

Because of these two prefaces, they were qualified for it. This is why the text refers to them in singular form, as it is written, "And Israel camped there before the mountain," which our sages interpret as "as one man with one heart."

This is because each and every person from the nation completely detached himself from self-love, and wanted only to benefit his friend, as we have shown above in Item 16 regarding the meaning of the *Mitzva*, "Love your friend as yourself." It turns out that all the individuals in the nation had come together and became one heart and one man, for only then were they qualified to receive the Torah.

24) Thus, because of the above necessity, the Torah was given specifically to the Israeli nation, solely to the descendants of Abraham, Isaac, and Jacob, for it was inconceivable that any stranger would take part in it. Yet, because of this, the Israeli nation had been constructed as a sort of passageway by which sparks of refinement would flow onto the entire human race throughout the world.

And these sparks of refinement multiply daily, like one who gives to the treasurer until they are filled sufficiently, meaning until they develop to such an extent that they can understand the pleasantness and tranquility that are found in the kernel of love of others, for then they will know how to shift the balance to the side of merit, and will place themselves under His burden, and the side of sin will be eradicated from the earth.

25) Now there remains for us to complete what we have said in the previous article, "Matan Torah," Item 16, about the reason that the Torah was not given to the fathers, since the *Mitzva*, "Love your friend as yourself," the axis of the whole Torah and around which all the *Mitzvot* revolve, so as to clarify and interpret it, cannot be observed by an individual, but only through the prior consent of an entire nation.

This is why it took until they came out of Egypt, when they became become worthy of observing it. Then they were first asked if each and every one in the nation agreed to take that *Mitzva* upon himself. And once they agreed to it, they were given the Torah. However, there still remains to clarify where we find in the Torah that the children of Israel were asked that question, and that they agreed to it prior to receiving the Torah.

26) Bear in mind that these matters are evident to every educated person in the invitation that the Creator had sent to Israel through Moses prior to the reception of the Torah. It is as it is written (Exodus 19:5), "'Now, if you surely listen to My voice and keep My covenant, then you will be a *Segula* [virtue/power/cure] unto Me from among all peoples, for all the earth is Mine; and you will be unto Me a kingdom of priests and a holy nation. These are the words that you will say to the children of Israel.' And Moses came and called for the elders of the people and set before them all these words which the Lord had commanded him. And all the people answered together and said, 'All that the Lord has said, we will do.' And Moses reported the words of the people unto the Lord."

These words do not seem to fit their role, since common sense dictates that if one offers one's friend to do some work and wants him to agree, he should give him an example of the nature of that work and its reward. Only then can the receiver examine it, whether to decline or to accept.

But here, in these two verses, we seem to find neither an example of the work nor its reward, because he says, "If you surely listen to My voice and keep My covenant," and he does not interpret the voice or the covenant and to what they apply. And then He says, "Then you will be a *Segula* unto Me from among all peoples, for all the earth is Mine." It is not clear whether He commands us to labor to be a *Segula* from among all peoples, or whether this is a promise of benefit for us.

We must also understand the connection to the words, "for all the earth is Mine." All three translations—Unkelos, Yonatan Ben Uziel, and the Jerusalem Talmud—find it difficult to interpret these words, as is the case with all the interpreters—RASHI, Nachmanides, etc. Even Ezra says, in the name of Rabbi Marinos, that the word "for" means "although." He interprets, "Then you will be a *Segula* unto Me from among all peoples although all the earth is Mine." Even Ezra himself tends to agree with it, but that interpretation does not coincide with our sages, who said that "for" serves for four meanings: "either," "lest," "but," and "that."

And he even adds a fifth interpretation: "although." And then the writing ends, "and you will be unto Me a kingdom of priests and a holy nation." Here, too, it is not self-evident if this is a *Mitzva*, and one must exert in this, or a promise of benefit. Also, the words "a kingdom of priests" are not repeated or explained anywhere in the Bible.

The important thing here is to determine the difference between "a kingdom of priests" and "a holy nation," for by the ordinary meaning of priesthood, it is one with holiness, and it is therefore obvious that a kingdom where all are priests is a holy nation, so the words "holy nation" seem redundant.

27) However, by all that we have explained from the beginning of the essay until now, we learn the true meanings of the words as their roles should be—to resemble a negotiation of offer and consent. This means that with these words, He really does offer them the whole form and content of the work in Torah and Mitzvot, and its worthwhile reward.

The work in Torah and Mitzvot is expressed in the words, "And you will be unto Me a kingdom of priests." A kingdom of priests means that all of you, from the youngest to the oldest, will be as priests. Just as the priests have no land or any corporeal possessions since the Creator is their lot, so will the entire nation be organized so that the land and all that is in it will be dedicated to the Creator. And no person should have any other engagement in it but to observe the Mitzvot of the Creator and satisfy the needs of his fellow person so his friend will lack none of his wishes, so that no person will need to have any worry about himself.

In this way, even secular works such as harvesting, sowing, etc., are considered to be precisely like the work with the sacrifices that the priests performed in the Temple. How is it different if I observe the Mitzva of making sacrifices to the Creator, which is a Mitzva to do, or if I observe the Mitzva to do, "Love your friend as yourself"? It follows that he who harvests his field in order to feed his fellow person is the same as one who sacrifices to the Creator. Moreover, it makes sense that the Mitzva, "Love your friend as yourself," is more important than one who makes the sacrifice, as we have shown above in Items 14, 15.

Indeed, this is not the end of the matter, for the whole of the Torah and the Mitzvot were given for the sole purpose of cleansing Israel, which is the cleansing of the body, as written in Item 12, after which he will be granted the true reward of Dvekut with Him, which is the purpose of creation, as written in Item 15. That reward is expressed in the words "a holy nation," as through the Dvekut with Him we have become holy, as it is written, "You will be holy to the Lord your God, for I the Lord your God, who sanctifies you, am holy."

And you see that the words "a kingdom of priests" express the complete form of the work on the axis of "Love your friend as yourself," meaning a kingdom that is all priests, that the Creator is their possession, and they have no self-possession of all the mundane possessions. We must admit that this is the only definition through which we can understand the words, "a kingdom of priests," for you cannot interpret it with regard to the sacrifices on the altar since this cannot be said about the whole nation, for who would be making the sacrifices?

Also, with regard to taking the gifts of the priesthood, who would be the givers? And also, to interpret the holiness of the priests, it has already been said "a holy nation." Therefore, this must certainly mean that it is only that the Creator is their domain, that they lack any material possession for themselves, meaning the full measure of the words "Love your friend as yourself," which encompasses the whole of the Torah. And the words "a holy nation" express the full form of the reward, which is the *Dvekut*.

28) Now we fully understand the previous words, for he says, "Now, if you surely listen to My voice and keep My covenant," meaning make a covenant on what I am telling you here: to be My *Segula* from among all peoples. This means that you will be My *Segula*, and sparks of refinement and cleansing of the body will pass through you onto all the peoples and the nations of the world, for the nations of the world are not yet ready for this, and at any rate, I need one nation to start with now, so it will be as a remedy for all the nations. For this reason, He ends, "for all the earth is Mine," meaning all the peoples of the earth belong to Me, as do you, and are destined to adhere to Me, as written in Item 20.

But now, while they are still incapable of performing that role, I need a virtuous people. If you agree to be the remedy for all the nations, I command you to "be unto Me a kingdom of priests," which is the love of others in its final form of "Love your friend as yourself," the axis of all the Torah and *Mitzvot*. And "a holy nation" is the reward in its final form of *Dvekut* with Him, which includes all the rewards that can even be conceived.

These are the words of our sages in clarifying the ending, "These are the words which you will say to the children of Israel." They made the precision, "These are the words," no more and no less. This is perplexing: How can you say that Moses would add or take away from the words of the Creator to the point that the Creator had to warn him about it? We find no such example in the whole of the Torah. On the contrary, the Torah says about him: "for he is the trusted one in all My house."

29) Now we can fully understand that concerning the form of work in its last manner, as explained in the words "a kingdom of priests," which is the final definition of "Love your friend as yourself," it was indeed conceivable for Moses to restrain himself and refrain from disclosing the full manner of the work all at once, for fear that Israel would not want to detach themselves from all material possessions and give all their fortune and assets to the Creator, as instructed by the words, "a kingdom of priests."

It is much like Maimonides wrote, that women and children must not be told the manner of the clean work, which must be in order not to be rewarded, and wait until they grow, become wise, and have the courage to execute it. Therefore, the Creator gave him the above warning, "no less," to offer them the true nature of the work, in all its sublimity, expressed in the words, "a kingdom of priests."

Regarding the reward that is defined in the words "a holy nation," it was possible for Moses to contemplate interpreting and elaborating further about the pleasantness and the sublime subtleness that come with *Dvekut* with Him, to persuade them to accept this extreme, to completely detach themselves from any worldly possessions, as do priests. Hence, he was warned, "no more," but be vague and do not explain the whole reward included in the words, "a holy nation."

The reason for this is that had he told them about the wondrous things in the essence of the reward, they would necessarily use and assume His work in order to obtain that wonderful reward for themselves. This would be considered working for themselves, for self-love. That, in turn, would falsify the whole purpose, as written in Item 13.

Thus we see that regarding the form of the work expressed in the words "a kingdom of priests," he was told, "no less." And about the unclear measure of the reward, expressed in the words "a holy nation," he was told, "no more."

The Essence of Religion and Its Purpose

In this article, I would like to resolve three issues:

1. What is the essence of religion?
2. Is its purpose intended for this world or for the next world?
3. Is its purpose to benefit the Creator or the created beings?

At first glance, the reader might be surprised by my words and will not understand these three questions that I have set before me as the topic of this essay. 1) For who is it who does not know what is religion, 2) and especially its reward and punishment, which we hope to obtain primarily in the next world? And needless to say, regarding the third question, that everyone knows that it is to benefit the created beings, to guide them to delight and happiness, and what else need we add to this?

Indeed, I have nothing more to add. But because they are so familiar with these three concepts from infancy, they do not add or further examine them for the rest of their lives, and this shows their lack of knowledge about these exalted matters, which are necessarily the very foundation upon which the whole structure of religion lies.

Therefore, you tell me, how is it possible that a child of twelve or thirteen years of age can already thoroughly grasp these three subtle notions, and so sufficiently that he will not need to add any further learning for the rest of his life?

Indeed, here lies the problem! For this rash conjecture brought with it all the recklessness and wild conclusions that have come into our world in our generation and has brought us to a state where the second generation has almost completely slipped from under our hands.

The Absolute Good

To avoid tiring the readers with long discussions, I have relied on all that I wrote in the previous essay ["The Arvut"], and especially on all that is explained in the essay, "Matan Torah," which are all like a preface to the exalted matter ahead. Here I will speak briefly and simply, to make it clear to everyone.

First, we must understand the Creator—He is the absolute good. This means that it is utterly impossible that He would ever cause any sorrow to anyone. And this we take to be the first concept, for common sense clearly shows that the basis for any evil-doing in the world stems only from the will to receive.

This means that the eagerness to benefit ourselves makes us harm others due to our will to satisfy ourselves. Thus, if no being would find contentment in favoring itself, no being would ever harm another. And if we sometimes find some being that harms another without any will to receive for its own pleasure, it does this only because of an old habit that originated in the will to receive, a habit that now rids it of the need to find a new reason.

Because it is clear to us that the Creator is complete in and of Himself and needs no one to help Him to completion since He precedes everything, it is therefore clear that He does not have any will to receive. Because He has no will to receive, He is fundamentally devoid of a desire to harm anyone; it is as simple as that.

Furthermore, it makes perfect sense to us, as the first concept, that He possesses a desire to bestow goodness upon others, meaning to His creatures. This is evidently shown by the great creation that He has created and set before us, for in this world there are beings that necessarily experience either a good feeling or a bad one, and that feeling necessarily comes to them from the Creator. Once it becomes absolutely clear that there is no aim to harm in the nature of the Creator, it necessitates that the creatures receive only benefits from Him, for He has created them only to bestow upon them.

Thus, we learn that He has only a desire to bestow goodness, and it is utterly impossible that any harmfulness might be in His domain, which could emit from Him. Hence we have defined Him as "the absolute good." Once we have learned this, let us look at the actual reality that is guided by Him, and how He bestows only goodness upon them.

His Guidance Is Purposeful Guidance

By observing nature's systems, we understand that any being of the four types—still, vegetative, animate, and speaking—however small, as a whole and in particular, is under a purposeful guidance, meaning a slow and gradual growth by way of cause and effect, as a fruit on a tree, which is guided well toward its final outcome of becoming a sweet and fine-looking fruit.

Go and ask a botanist how many phases the fruit undergoes from the time it becomes visible until it is completely ripe. Not only do its preceding phases show no evidence of its sweet and fine-looking end, but as if to anger, they show the opposite of the final outcome. That is, the sweeter the fruit is at its end, the more bitter and unsightly it is in the earlier phases of its development.

And so it is with the animate and speaking types: The beast, whose mind is little at its end, is not so flawed while it grows, whereas man, whose mind is great at his end, is very flawed while developing. "A day-old calf is called an ox," meaning it has the strength to stand on its own legs and walk, and the intelligence to avoid hazards on its way. But a day-old human being lies seemingly senseless. Should one who is not accustomed to the conducts of this world examine these two newborns, he would certainly conclude that the human infant will amount to nothing and the calf will become a new Napoleon, meaning if he were to judge by the wisdom of the calf compared to the senseless and mindless child.

Thus, it is evident that His guidance over the reality that He has created is in the form of purposeful guidance, without taking into consideration the order of the phases of development, for they deceive us and prevent us from understanding their purpose, being always opposite to their final shape.

It is about such matters that we say, "There is none so wise as the experienced." Only one who is experienced has the opportunity to see the created being in all its phases of development, all the way through its completion, and can calm things down so as to not to fear those spoiled images that the created being undergoes in the phases of its development, but believe in its fine and pure end. The reason for this gradual order that is mandatory for every created being is thoroughly explained in the wisdom of Kabbalah, and there is nothing more to add here.

Thus, we have thoroughly shown the conducts of His guidance in our world, which is only a purposeful guidance. The attribute of goodness is not at all apparent before creation arrives at its completion, its final ripeness. On the contrary, it rather always wears a cloak of corruption in the eyes of the beholders. Thus you see that the Creator bestows upon His creatures only goodness, but that goodness comes by way of purposeful guidance.

Two Paths: A Path of Pain and a Path of Torah

We have shown that the Creator is the absolute good. He watches us in complete benevolence without a hint of evil and in a purposeful guidance. This means that His guidance compels us to undergo a series of phases, by way of cause and effect, preceding and resulting, until we are qualified to receive the desired benefit. At that time, we will arrive at our purpose as a ripe and fine-looking fruit. By this we understand that this purpose is guaranteed for us all, or else you doubt His guidance, saying it is insufficient for its purpose.

Our sages said, "*Shechina* [Divinity] in the lower ones—a high need." That is, since His guidance is purposeful and aims to eventually bring us to *Dvekut* [adhesion] with Him, so He would reside within us, this is regarded as a high need, meaning if we do not come to that, we will find ourselves regarding His guidance as flawed.

This is similar to a great king who had a son at an old age, and he was very fond of him. Hence, since the day he was born, he thought of only good things for him. He collected the finest, wisest, and most precious books in the kingdom and built for him a school. He sent after the finest builders and built palaces of pleasure. He gathered all the musicians and singers and built for him concert halls, and called the finest bakers and chefs to provide him with all the delicacies in the world.

But alas, the son grew up to be a fool, with no desire for knowledge. And he was blind and could not see or feel the beauty of the buildings. He was also deaf, unable to hear the singers. And he was diabetic, permitted to eat only coarse flour bread, arising contempt and wrath.

However, such a thing may happen to a flesh and blood king, but cannot be said about the Creator, where there cannot be any deceit. Therefore, He has prepared for us two paths of development:

1. The first is a path of suffering, which is the conduct of development of creation from within itself. By its own nature, it is compelled to follow a way of cause and effect in varying, consecutive states, which slowly develop us until we come to a resolution to choose the good and reject the bad, and to be qualified for the purpose as He desires. But that path is indeed a long and painful one.

2. Therefore, He has prepared for us a pleasant and good way, which is the path of Torah and *Mitzvot*, which can qualify us for our purpose painlessly and quickly.

It turns out that our final aim is to be qualified for *Dvekut* with Him—for Him to reside within us. That aim is a certainty and there is no way to deviate from it, since His guidance supervises us in both paths, which are the path of suffering and the path of Torah. But looking at the actual reality, we find that His guidance comes simultaneously in both paths, which our sages refer to as "the way of the earth" and "the way of Torah."

The Essence of Religion Is to Develop in Us the Sense of Recognition of Evil

Our sages say, "Why should the Creator mind whether one slays at the throat or at the back of the neck? After all, the *Mitzvot* were only given to cleanse people" (*Beresheet Rabbah* 44a). That cleansing has been thoroughly clarified in the article "Matan Torah," Item 12, but here I would like to clear up the essence of that development, which is attained through engagement in Torah and *Mitzvot*.

Bear in mind that it is the recognition of the evil within us that engagement in *Mitzvot* can slowly and gradually purify those who delve in them. And the scale by which we measure the degrees of cleansing is the measure of the recognition of the evil within us.

Man is naturally ready to repel and root out any evil from within him. In this, all people are the same. But the difference between one person and the next is only in the recognition of evil. 1) A more developed person recognizes in himself a greater measure of evil, and hence repels and separates the evil from within to a greater extent. 2) The undeveloped senses in himself only a small amount of evil, and will therefore repel only a small amount of evil. As a result, he leaves all his filth within, for he does not recognize it as filth.

To avoid tiring the reader, we will clarify the general meaning of good and bad, as it has been explained in the article, "Matan Torah," Item 12. Evil, in general, is nothing more than self-love, called "egoism," since it is opposite in form from the Creator, who has no will to receive for Himself, but only to bestow.

We have explained in "Matan Torah," Items 9 and 11, that 1) pleasure and sublimity are measured by the extent of equivalence of form with the Maker. 2) Suffering and intolerance are measured by the extent of disparity of form from the Maker. Thus, egoism is loathsome to us and very painful, as its form is opposite from the Maker.

But this loathing is not divided equally among us. Rather, it is given in varying measures. The crass, undeveloped person does not recognize egoism as bad at all. Therefore, he uses it openly, without any shame or restraint, stealing and murdering in broad daylight wherever he can. The somewhat more developed sense some measure of their egoism as bad and are at least ashamed to use it in public, stealing and killing openly. But in secret, they still commit their crimes, but are careful that no one will see them.

The even more developed sense egoism as so loathsome that they cannot tolerate it in them and reject it completely, as much as they detect of it, until they cannot, and do not want to enjoy the labor of others. Then begin to emerge in them sparks of love of others, called "altruism," which is the general attribute of goodness.

But that, too, evolves gradually. First develops love and desire to bestow upon one's family and kin, as in the verse, "Do not ignore your own flesh." When one develops further, one's attribute of bestowal expands to all the people around him, being one's townspeople or one's nation. And so one adds until he finally develops love for the whole of humanity.

Conscious Development and Unconscious Development

Bear in mind that two forces serve to push us up the rungs of the aforementioned ladder, until we reach its head in the sky, which is the purposeful point of equivalence of form with our Maker. The difference between these two forces is that the first pushes us involuntarily, meaning not of our own choice. This force pushes us from behind, and it is called "from behind." We defined it as "the path of suffering" or "the way of the earth."

And from it stems the philosophy of morality called "ethics," which is based on empirical knowledge, through examination of the practical reason. The essence of that teaching is but a summary of the evident damages that result from the nucleons of egoism.

These experiences come to us by chance, not as a result of our conscious choice, but they are certain to lead us to their goal, for the image of evil grows ever clearer to our senses. And to the extent that we recognize its damages, to that extent we remove ourselves from it and climb to a higher rung on the ladder.

The second force pushes us voluntarily, meaning of our own choice. That force pulls us from before and is called "from before." This is what we defined as "the path of Torah and *Mitzvot*," for engaging in *Mitzvot* and the work to bring contentment to our Maker rapidly develops in us that sense of recognition of evil, as we have shown in "Matan Torah," Item 13.

Here we benefit twice:

1) We do not have to wait for life's ordeals to push us from behind, whose measure of pushing is measured only by the amount of agony and destruction inflicted upon us by finding the evil within us. Rather, as we work for the Creator, that recognition develops in us without any prior suffering or ruin. On the contrary, through the subtle pleasantness we feel when working solely for Him, to bring Him contentment, there develops within us a relative recognition of the lowliness of these sparks of self-love—that they are obstacles on our way to receiving that subtle taste of bestowal upon the Creator. Thus, the gradual sense of recognition of evil evolves in us through times of delight and great tranquility, through reception of the good while serving the Creator out of our sensation of the pleasantness and gentleness that reach us due to the equivalence of form with our Maker.

2) We save time, for it operates according to "our own volition," thus enabling us to increase our work and hasten time as we please.

Religion Is Not for the Sake of the People, but for the Sake of the Worker

Many are mistaken and compare our holy Torah to ethics. But this has come to them because they have never tasted religion in their lives. I call upon them: "Taste and see that the Lord is good." It is true that ethics and religion both aim at the same thing—to raise man above the filth of the narrow self-love and bring him to the apex of love of others.

But still, they are as far one from the other as the distance between the thought of the Creator and the thought of people. For religion extends from the thoughts of the Creator, and ethics comes from thoughts of flesh and blood and from their life's experiences. Hence, there is an evident difference between them, both in practical aspects and in the final aim. 1) For the recognition of the bad and the good that develops in us through ethics, as we use it, is relative to the success of the society. 2) With religion, however, the recognition of good and evil that develops in us as we use it is relative to the Creator alone, meaning from the disparity of form from the Maker to equivalence of form with Him, which is called *Dvekut* [adhesion], as clarified in "Matan Torah," Items 9-11.

They are also completely removed from one another regarding the goal: 1) The goal of ethics is the well-being of society from the perspective of practical reason, derived from life's experiences. But in the end, that goal does not promise one who practices it any elevation above the boundaries of nature. Hence, this goal is still subject to criticism, for who can prove to an individual the extent of his benefit in such a conclusive manner that he will be compelled to even slightly diminish his own self for the sake of the well-being of society? 2) The religious goal, however, guarantees the well-being of the individual who follows it, as we have already shown that when one comes to love others, he is in direct *Dvekut*, which is equivalence of form with his Maker, and along with it man passes from his narrow world, filled with pain and impediments, to an eternal and broad world of bestowal upon the Creator and upon people.

You will also find a significant difference regarding the support because 1) engaging in ethics is supported by gaining people's favor, which is like a rent that finally pays off. When one becomes accustomed to this work, he will not be able to ascend on the degrees of ethics for he will now be used to such work that is well rewarded by society, which pays for his good deeds. 2) Yet, by observing Torah and *Mitzvot* in order to bring contentment to his Maker without any reward, he climbs the rungs of ethics precisely to the extent of his engagement, since there is no payment on his path, and each penny is added to a great amount. Finally, he acquires a second nature, which is bestowal upon others without any self-reception except for one's bare sustenance.

Now he has really been liberated from the incarcerations of creation, for when one detests any self-reception and his soul loathes the petite physical pleasures and respect, he finds himself roaming free in the Creator's world, and he is guaranteed that no damage or misfortune will ever come upon him, since all the damages come to a man only through the self-reception imprinted in him.

Thus, we have thoroughly shown that the purpose of religion is only for the individual who engages in it, and not at all for the use or benefit of common people, although all his actions revolve around the benefit of people and are measured by these acts. Yet, this is but a passage to the sublime goal, which is equivalence with the Maker. Now we can understand that the purpose of religion is collected while living in this world, and examine closely in "Matan Torah," Item 6, regarding the purpose of the general public and of the individual.

But regarding the reward in the next world, this is a different matter which I will explain in a separate essay.

The Peace

(An empirical, scientific research about the necessity
of the work of the Creator)

"The wolf shall dwell with the lamb and the leopard shall lay down with
the kid, and the calf and the young lion and the fatling together,
and a little child shall lead them."

"And it shall come to pass on that day, that the Lord shall set His hand again,
a second time, to recover the remnant of His people, who shall be left from
Ashur and from Egypt, from Patros and from Kush, and from Elam and from
Shin'ar, and from Hamat, and from the islands of the sea" (Isaiah 11).

"Rabbi Shimon Ben Halafta said, 'The Lord did not find a vessel to hold the
blessing for Israel but peace, as was said. 'The Lord will give strength to His
people; the Lord will bless His people with peace'" (end of *Masechet Okatzin*).

After having demonstrated in previous articles the general form of His work, whose essence is nothing more and nothing less than the love of others, practically determined as "bestowal upon others," meaning that the actual manifestation of love of others is bestowal of goodness upon others, love of others should therefore be determined as bestowal upon others, which is best suited for its content, aiming to ensure that we do not forget the intention.

Now that we know for certain the conduct of His work, there still remains to inquire whether we accept this work on faith alone, without any scientific, empirical basis, or do we also have an empirical basis for this. This is what I want to prove in the essay before us. But first I must thoroughly prove the subject itself, meaning who it is who accepts our work.

But I am not an enthusiast of formative philosophy, since I dislike theoretically based studies, and it is well known that most of my contemporaries agree with me, for we are too familiar with such foundations, which are rickety foundations, and when the foundation fluctuates, the whole building tumbles.

Therefore, I have come here to speak only through critique of empirical reason, beginning from the simple recognition no one disagrees with, through proving analytically [separating the various elements in an issue], until we come to determine the uppermost topic. And it will be tested synthetically [the connection and unity between matters, such as inference and the "all the more so"], how His work is confirmed and reaffirmed by simple recognition from the practical aspect.

Contradictions in Providence

Every reasonable person who examines the reality before us finds two complete opposites in it. When examining creation, its reality and conducts, there is an apparent and affirmed leadership of great wisdom and skill, 1) both regarding the formation of reality and 2) the securing of its existence in general.

Let us take the making of a human being as an example: The love and pleasure of the progenitors is its first reason, guaranteed to perform its duty. When the essential drop is extracted from the father's brain, Providence has very wisely secured a safe place for it, which qualifies it to receive life. Providence also gives it its daily bread in the exact amount. Providence has also prepared a wonderful foundation for it in the mother's womb so that no stranger might harm it.

It tends to its every need like a trained nanny who will not forget it for a moment until it has acquired the strength to emerge into our world. At that time, Providence briefly lends it just enough strength to break the walls that surround it, and like a trained, armed warrior, it breaks an opening and emerges into the world.

Then, too, Providence does not abandon it. Like a loving mother, it brings it to such loving, loyal people it can trust, called "Mother" and "Father," to assist it through its days of weakness until it grows and can sustain itself. As man, so are all the animals, plants, and inanimate; all are wisely and mercifully cared for to ensure their own existence and the continuation of their species.

But those who examine that reality from the perspective of provision and persistence of existence can clearly see great disorder and confusion, as though there were no leader and no guidance. Everyone does that which is right in his own eyes, building himself on the ruin of others, the evil thrive and the righteous are trampled mercilessly.

Bear in mind that this oppositeness, set before the eyes of every sensible, educated person, has preoccupied humanity even in ancient times. And there are many methods to explain these two apparent opposites in Providence, which occupy the same world.

First Method: Nature

This method is an ancient one. Since they did not find a way and an outlet to bring these two evident opposites closer, they came to assume that the Creator, Who created all these, Who watches mightily over His reality lest any of it be canceled, is mindless and senseless.

Hence, although He watches over the existence of reality with wondrous wisdom, He Himself is mindless and does all that senselessly. If there had been any reason and feeling in Him, He would certainly not leave such malfunctions in the provision of reality without pity or compassion for the tormented. For this reason, they named

Him "Nature," meaning a mindless, heartless Supervisor. For this reason, they believe that there is no one to be angry at, pray to, or justify before Him.

Second Method: Two Authorities

Others were more sophisticated. They found it difficult to accept the premise of nature's supervision, since they saw that the supervision over reality, to secure its existence, is a far deeper wisdom than any human culmination. They could not agree that the overseer over all these is Himself mindless, for how can one give that which one does not possess? Can one teach one's friend while he himself is a fool?

How can you say about He who performs before us such astute and wise deeds that He does not know what He is doing, that He does it by chance, which it is evident that chance cannot arrange any orderly deed, devised in wisdom, much less secure its eternal existence? Hence, they came to a second assumption that there are two supervisors here: one creates and sustains the good, and the other creates and sustains the bad. And they have greatly elaborated that method with evidence and proofs along their way.

Third Method: Multiple Gods

This method was born out of the bosom of the method of two authorities. This is because they had divided and separated each of the general actions for itself, meaning strength, wealth, domination, beauty, famine, death, disorder, and so on. They appointed each its own supervisor, and expanded the matter as they wished.

Fifth Method: Left His Operation

Recently, when knowledge increased and they saw the tight linkage among all parts of creation, they recognized the concept of multiple gods to be completely impossible. Thus, the question of the oppositeness sensed in creation reawakened.

This led them to a new assumption—that the Supervisor of reality is indeed wise and feeling, but because of His exaltedness, which is beyond conception, our world is deemed a grain of sand, nothing in His eyes. It is not worthwhile for Him to bother with our petty matters, which is why our livelihood is so disordered and every man does that which is right in his own eyes.

Alongside these methods, there existed religious methods of Godly unity. But this is not the place to examine them, as I only wanted to examine the origins from which the foul methods and puzzling assumptions that vastly dominated and expanded at different times and places were taken.

We find that the basis on which all the above methods were born and emerged is the contradiction between the two types of Providence detectable in our world, and all these methods came about only to mend that great rift.

Yet, nothing is new under the sun, and not only is that great rift not been mended, it grows and expands before us into a terrible chasm without seeing or hoping for a way out of it. When I look at all those attempts that humanity has been making for several thousand years to no avail, I wonder if we should not seek the mending of this great rift from the Supervisor's point of view at all, but rather accept that this great correction is in our own hands.

Necessity to Practice Caution with the Laws of Nature

We can all plainly see that the human species must lead a social life, meaning we cannot exist and sustain ourselves without the help of society. Therefore, imagine an event where one retires from society to a desolate location and lives there a life of misery and great pain due to his inability to provide for his needs. That person would have no right to complain about Providence or his fate. And if that person were to do that, meaning complain and curse his bitter fate, he would only be displaying his stupidity, for while Providence has prepared for him a comfortable, desirable place in society, he has no justification to retire from it to a desolate place. Such a person must not be pitied, since he goes against the nature of creation. Since he has the option to live as Providence has ordered him, he should not be pitied. That sentence is agreed upon by all of humanity without dispute.

And I can add and establish it on a religious basis and give it such a form: Since Providence extends from the Creator, who undoubtedly has a purpose in His actions, since no one acts without a purpose, we find that anyone who breaks a law from the laws of nature that He has imprinted in us, corrupts the purposeful aim.

Because the purpose is undoubtedly built over all the laws of nature, none excluded, just as the clever worker would not add or subtract even a hairsbreadth of the necessary actions to attain the goal, he who spoils even a single law harms and damages the purposeful aim that the Creator has set and will therefore be punished by nature. Hence, we, too, creatures of the Creator, must not pity him because he desecrates the laws of nature and defiles the purpose of the Creator. That, I believe, is the form of the sentence.

And I believe that it is not a good idea for anyone to contradict this form that I have given to the sentence, since the words of the sentence are one. For what is the difference if we say that the supervisor is called "nature," meaning mindless and purposeless, or saying that the supervisor is wondrously wise, knowing, feeling, and has a purpose in his actions?

In the end, we all admit and agree that we are obliged to observe the commandments of Providence, meaning the laws of nature. And we all admit that one who breaks the commandments of Providence, meaning the laws of nature, should be punished by nature, and must not be pitied by anyone. Thus, the nature of the sentence is the same, and the only difference is in the motive: They maintain that the motive is necessary, and I maintain that it is purposeful.

To avoid having to use both tongues from now on, 1) nature, 2) a supervisor, between which, as I have shown, there is no difference regarding the following of the laws, it is best for us to agree and accept the words of the Kabbalists that *HaTeva* [the nature] has the same numerical value [in Hebrew] as *Elokim* [God]—eighty-six. Then, I will be able to call the laws of God "nature's *Mitzvot* [commandments]," or vice-versa (the *Mitzvot* of *Elokim* by the name "nature's laws"), for they are one and the same, and we need not discuss it further.

Now it is vitally important for us to examine nature's *Mitzvot*, to know what it demands of us, lest it would mercilessly punish us. We have said that nature obligates humankind to lead a social life, and this is simple. But we need to examine the *Mitzvot* that nature obliges us to observe in that respect, meaning with respect to the social life.

In general examination, we find that there are only two *Mitzvot* to follow in society. These can be called 1) "reception" and 2) "bestowal." This means that each member must, by nature, receive his needs from society and must benefit society through his work for its well-being. And if one breaks one of these two *Mitzvot*, he will be mercilessly punished.

We need not excessively examine the *Mitzva* [singular for *Mitzvot*] of reception, since the punishment is carried out immediately, which prevents any neglect. But in the other *Mitzva*, that of bestowal upon society, not only is the punishment not immediate, but it is given indirectly. Therefore, this *Mitzva* is not properly observed.

Thus, humanity is being fried in a heinous turmoil, and strife and famine and their consequences have not ceased thus far. The wonder about it is that nature, like a skillful judge, punishes us according to our development. For we can see that to the extent that humankind develops, the pains and torments obtaining our sustenance and existence also multiply.

Thus you have a scientific, empirical basis that His Providence has commanded us to observe with all our might the *Mitzva* of bestowal upon others in utter precision, in such a way that no member from among us would work any less than the measure required to secure the happiness of society and its success. As long as we are idle performing it to the fullest, nature will not stop punishing us and take its revenge.

And besides the blows we suffer today, we must also consider the drawn sword for the future. The right conclusion must be drawn—that nature will ultimately defeat us and we will all be compelled to join hands in following its *Mitzvot* with all the measure required of us.

Proof of His Work by Experience

But he who wishes to criticize my words might still ask, "Although I have thus far proven that one must work to benefit people, where is the proof that it has to be done for the sake of the Creator?"

Indeed, history itself has troubled in our favor and has prepared for us an established fact, sufficient for a full appreciation and unequivocal conclusion: Everyone can see how a large society such as that of Russia, with hundreds of millions in population, more land than the whole of Europe, second to none in wealth and raw materials, and which has already agreed to lead communal life and practically abolished private property altogether, where each worries only about the well-being of society, has seemingly acquired the full measure of the virtue of bestowal upon others in its full meaning, as far as the human mind can grasp.

And yet, go and see what has become of them: Instead of rising and exceeding the achievements of the capitalist countries, they have sunk ever lower. Now, they not only fail to benefit the lives of the workers a little more than in the capitalist countries, they cannot even secure their daily bread and clothes on their flesh. Indeed, this fact puzzles us, since judging by the wealth of that country and its plentiful population, it seems unreasonable that it would have to come to this.

But this nation has sinned one sin which the Creator will not forgive: All this precious and exalted work, namely bestowal upon others, which they have begun to perform, must be for the sake of the Creator and not for the sake of humanity. Because they do their work not for His sake, from nature's point of view, they have no right to exist.

Try to imagine if every person in that society were anxious to observe the *Mitzvot* of the Creator to the extent of the verse: "And you will love the Lord your God with all your heart, and with all your soul, and with all your might," and to that extent would rush to satisfy the needs and wishes of one's friend in the full measure imprinted in man to satisfy his own wishes, as it is written, "Love your neighbor as yourself." If the Creator Himself were the goal of every worker while working for the well-being of society, meaning that the worker would expect this work for the sake of society to reward him with *Dvekut* [adhesion] with Him, the source of all goodness and truth and every pleasantness and softness, there is no doubt that within a few years they would rise in wealth over all the countries of the world combined. That is because then they would be able to utilize the raw materials in their lush soil, would truly be an example for all the countries, and would be considered blessed by the Creator.

But when all the work of bestowal upon others is based solely on the benefit of society, it is a rickety foundation, for who or what would obligate the individual to toil for society? From a dry, lifeless principle, one can never hope to derive motive power for movement even in developed individuals [motive power: a purposeful force that moves every body and allots it strength to exert, like fuel in a machine], much less for undeveloped people. Thus, the question is where would the worker or the farmer find sufficient motive power to work, for his daily bread will not increase or decrease by his efforts, and there are no goals or rewards before him. It is well known to researchers of nature that one cannot perform even the slightest movement without motive power, without somehow benefiting oneself.

When, for example, one moves one's hand from the chair to the table, it is because he thinks that by putting his hand on the table he will enjoy it more. If he did not think so, he would leave his hand on the chair for the rest of his life without moving it at all. It is all the more so with greater efforts.

And if you say that there is a solution—to place them under supervision so that anyone who is idle at his work will be punished by denial of salary, I will ask, "Do tell me where the supervisors themselves would take the motive power for their work?" Because standing at one place and watching over people to motivate them to work is a great effort, too, perhaps more so than the work itself. Therefore, it is as though one wishes to switch on a machine without fueling it.

Hence, they are doomed by nature, since nature's laws will punish them because they do not adapt themselves to obeying its commands—performing these acts of bestowal upon others in the form of work for the sake of the Creator, to achieve through it the purpose of creation, which is *Dvekut* with Him. It was explained in the article, "Matan Torah," Item 6, that this *Dvekut* comes to the worker in the measure of His pleasant and pleasurable bounty, which increases up to the desired measure for rising to know His genuineness, ever developing until he is rewarded with the excessiveness implied in the words, "The eye has not seen a God besides you."

And imagine that the farmer and the worker were to sense this goal before them while working for the well-being of society, they would certainly not need any supervisors, since they would already have sufficient motive power for a great effort, enough to raise society to the ultimate happiness.

Indeed, understanding that matter in such a way requires great care and proven conducts. But everyone can see that without it they have no right to exist from the perspective of the obstinate, uncompromising nature, and this is what I wanted to prove here.

Thus, I have evidently proven from the perspective of empirical reason—out of the practical history unfolding before our very eyes—that there is no other cure for humanity but to assume the commandment of Providence to bestow upon others in order to bring contentment to the Creator in the measure of the two verses.

The first is "love your friend as yourself," which is the attribute of the work itself. This means that the measure of work to bestow upon others for the happiness of society should be no less than the measure imprinted in man to care for his own needs. Moreover, he should put his fellow person's needs before his own, as it is written in the article, "Matan Torah," Item 4.

The other verse is, "And you will love the Lord your God with all your heart, with all your soul, and with all your might." This is the goal that must be before everyone's eyes when laboring for one's friend's needs. This means that he labors and toils only to be liked by the Creator, as He said, "and they do His will."

"And if you wish to listen, you will feed on the fruit of the land," for poverty and torment and exploitation will be no more in the land, and the happiness of each and every one will rise ever higher, beyond measure. But as long as you refuse to assume the covenant of the work for the sake of the Creator in the fullest measure, nature and its laws will stand ready to take revenge on you. And as we have shown, it will not let go until it defeats us and we accept its authority in whatever it commands.

Now I have given you a practical, scientific research according to the critique of empirical reason regarding the absolute necessity of all people to assume the work of the Creator with all their hearts, and souls, and might.

Clarification of the Excerpt from the Mishnah: "Everything Is in Deposit, and a Net Is Spread Over All of Life"

Now that we have learned all the above, we can understand an unclear excerpt in *Masechet Avot*, Chapter 3, Item 16. It reads as follows: "He (Rabbi Akiva) would say, 'All is in deposit, and a net is spread over all of life. The store is open and the shopkeeper sells by deferred payment; the book is open and the hand writes. And anyone who wishes to borrow may come and borrow, and the collectors return regularly, day-by-day, and collect from a person knowingly and unknowingly. And they have what to rely on, and the judgment is true, and all is ready for the feast.'"

That excerpt did not remain an abstruse allegory without reason, without even a hint as to its meaning. It tells us that here there is great depth to delve into. Indeed, the knowledge we have thus far acquired clarifies it very well indeed.

The Wheel of Transformation of the Form

First, let me present the view of our sages concerning the unfolding of the generations of the world: Although we see the bodies changing from generation to generation, this is only the case with the bodies. But the souls, which are the essence of the body's self, do not vanish, to be replaced, but move from body to body, from generation to generation. The same souls that were at the time of the flood came also during the time of Babylon, and in the exile in Egypt, and in the exodus from Egypt, etc., until this generation and until the end of correction.

Thus, in our world, there are no new souls the way bodies are renewed, but only a certain amount of souls that incarnate on the wheel of transformation of the form, for each time they clothe a new body and a new generation.

Therefore, with regard to the souls, all generations since the beginning of creation to the end of correction are as one generation that has extended its life over several thousand years until it developed and became corrected as it should be. And the fact that in the meantime, each has changed his body several thousand times is completely irrelevant because the essence of the body's self, called "the soul," did not suffer at all by these changes.

And there is much evidence pointing to that, and a great wisdom called "the secret of the incarnation of the souls." And while this is not the place to explain it, because of the great importance of the matter, it is worthwhile to point out to the uneducated that reincarnation occurs in all the objects of the tangible reality, and each object, in its own way, lives an eternal life.

Although our senses tell us that everything is transient, it is only how we see it. In fact, there are only incarnations here, and each item is not still and does not rest for a moment, but incarnates on the wheel of transformation of the form, losing nothing of its essence along its way, as physicists have shown.

And now we come to clarify the excerpt: "All is in deposit." It has been compared to someone who lends money to his friend for a business in order to make him a partner in the profit. To make sure that he does not lose his money, he gives it to him as collateral, and thus he is free from any uncertainty. The same applies to the creation of the world and its existence, which the Creator has prepared for humans to engage in and to eventually attain by it the exalted goal of *Dvekut* [adhesion] with Him, as is explained in "Matan Torah," Item 6. Thus, one must wonder, who would compel humanity to engage in His work until they finally come to this exalted end?

Rabbi Akiva tells us about this, "All is in deposit." This means that everything that the Creator had placed in creation and given to people, He did not give to them recklessly, but secured Himself with collateral. And should you wonder what collateral He was given, he responds to this by saying, "and a net is spread over all of life." This means that the Creator has cleverly devised a wonderful net and spread it over all of humanity, so that no one will escape. All the living beings must be caught there in that net and necessarily accept His work until they attain their sublime goal. This is the collateral by which the Creator secured Himself that no harm would come to the work of creation.

Afterward, he interprets it in detail and says, "The store is open." This means that this world seems to us like an open shop, without an owner, and anyone who passes through may receive abundantly, as much as one wishes, free of any charge. However, Rabbi Akiva warns us that the shopkeeper is selling by deferred payment. In other words, although you cannot see any shopkeeper here, know that there is a shopkeeper, and the reason that he is not demanding payment is because he sells it to you by deferred payment.

And should you say, "How does he know my debt?" To this he replies, "The book is open and the hand writes," meaning there is a general book in which each act is written without losing even one. And the aim surrounds the law of development that the Creator has imprinted in humanity, which prompts us ever forward.

This means that the corrupt conducts in the states of humanity are the very ones that generate the good states. And each good state is nothing but the fruit of the work in the bad state that preceded it. Indeed, these values of good and bad do not refer to the value of the state itself, but to the general purpose: Each state that brings humanity closer to the goal is considered good, and one that deflects them from the goal is considered bad.

By this standard alone is the "law of development" built—the corruption and the wickedness that appear in a state are considered the cause and the generator of the good state, so that each state lasts just long enough to grow the evil in it to such an extent that the public can no longer bear it. At that time, the public must unite against it, destroy it, and reorganize in a better state for the correction of that generation.

And the new state, too, lasts just as long as the sparks of evil in it ripen and reach such a level that they can no longer be tolerated, at which time it must be destroyed and a more comfortable state is built in its stead. And so the states clear up one by one and degree by degree until they come to such a corrected state that there will be good without any sparks of evil.

You find that all the seeds from which the good states grow are only the corrupted deeds themselves, meaning that all the exposed evils that come from under the hands of the wicked in the generation join and accumulate to a great sum until they weigh so heavily that the public can no longer bear them. Then they rise up and ruin it and create a more desirable state. Thus you see that each wickedness becomes a condition for the driving force by which the good state is developed.

These are the words of Rabbi Akiva: "The book is open and the hand writes." Any state that the generation is in is like a book, and all the evildoers are as writing hands because each evil is carved and written in the book until they accumulate to an amount that the public can no longer bear. At that time, they destroy that bad state and rearrange themselves in a more desirable state. Thus, each and every act is calculated and written in the ledger, meaning in the state.

He says, "All who wish to borrow may come and borrow." This means that one who believes that this world is not like an open store without an owner, but that there is an owner present, a shopkeeper who stands in his store and demands of each customer the right price for the merchandise he is taking from the store, meaning toil in His work while he is nourished by that store, in a manner that is certain to bring him to the purpose of creation, as He pleases, such a person is regarded as one who wishes to borrow. Thus, even before he stretches his hand to take something from this world, which is the store, he takes it as a loan, in order to pay its listed price. That is, he takes it upon himself to work to achieve His goal during the time he lives off the store, in a way that he promises to pay his debt by achieving the desired goal. Therefore, he is regarded as one who wishes to borrow, meaning that he pledges to return the debt.

Rabbi Akiva describes for us two kinds of people: The first are the "open store" kind, who regard this world as an open store without a shopkeeper. He says about them, "The book is open and the hand writes." That is, although they do not see that there is an account, all their actions are nonetheless written in the book, as explained above. This is done by the law of development imprinted in creation against humanity's will, where the deeds of the wicked themselves necessarily engender the good deeds, as we have shown above.

The second kind of people is called "those who want to borrow." They take the shopkeeper into consideration, and when they take something from the store, they only take it as a loan. They promise to pay the shopkeeper the listed price, meaning attain the goal by it. He says about them, "All who wish to borrow may come and borrow."

And if you say, "What is the difference between the first kind, whose goal comes to them from the law of development, and the second kind, whose goal comes to them by self-enslavement to His work? Are they not equal in attaining the goal?"

In that regard, he continues, "The collectors return regularly, day-by-day, and collect from a person knowingly and unknowingly." Thus, in truth, both pay their daily portion of the debt. And just as the forces that emerge by engaging in His work are deemed the loyal collectors who collect their debt in portions every day, until it is completely paid, the mighty forces imprinted in the law of development are also deemed as loyal collectors who collect their daily portions of the debt until it is paid in full. This is the meaning of "and the collectors return regularly, day by day, and collect from a person."

However, there is a great difference and a great distance between them, meaning "knowingly and unknowingly." The first kind, whose debt is collected by the collectors of development, pay their debt unknowingly. Rather, stormy waves come upon them through the strong wind of development and push them from behind, forcing them to step forward.

Thus, their debt is collected against their will and with great pains by manifestations of the forces of evil, which push them from behind. But the second kind pay their debt, which is attainment of the goal knowingly, of their own accord, by repeating the actions that hasten the development of the sense of recognition of evil, as explained in the article, "The Essence of Religion and Its Purpose."

Through this work their gain is twofold: The first gain is that these forces, which appear out of His work, are set before them as a pulling, magnetic force (from before). They chase it of their own free will with the spirit of love. Needless to say, they are free from any kind of sorrow and suffering like the first kind.

The second gain is that they hasten the desired goal, for they are the righteous and the prophets who attain the goal in each generation, as is explained in the essay, "The Essence of the Wisdom of Kabbalah," in the section, "What Does the Wisdom Revolve Around?"

Thus you see that there is a great distance between those who pay knowingly and those who pay unknowingly, as the advantage of the light of delight and pleasure over the darkness of pain and agony. He says further: "They have what to rely on, and the judgment is true." In other words, he promises all those who pay knowingly and willingly that "they have what to rely on," that there is great strength in His work to bring them to the sublime goal, and it is worthwhile for them to harness themselves under His burden.

And of those who pay unknowingly, he says, "and the judgment is true." Seemingly, one must wonder why Providence permits those corruptions and agonies to appear in the world, in which humanity is being fried mercilessly.

He says about this that this "judgment is true," since "all is ready for the feast," for the true goal. And the sublime delight that is destined to emerge with the revelation of His purpose in creation, when all the trouble and toil and anguish that befall us over times and generations will seem like a host who greatly troubles himself to prepare a great feast for the invited guests. And he likens the anticipated goal that must finally be revealed to a feast whose guests attend with great delight. This is why he says, "and the judgment is true, and all is ready for the feast."

Such as that you will also find in *Beresheet Rabbah*, Chapter 8, regarding the creation of man: The angels asked the Creator, "What is a man, that you are mindful of him, and the son of man, that you visit him? Why do you need this trouble?"

The Creator told them, "So why were Tzona and Alafim created?" What is this like? There is an allegory about a king who had a tower filled abundantly but no guests. What pleasure does a king have in his full tower? They promptly said to Him, "Lord of the world, the Lord our Master, how great is Your name in all the land. Do that which pleases You."

Interpretation: The angels that saw all the pain and agony that was to befall humanity wondered "Why do you need this trouble?" The Creator replied to them that indeed He had a tower filled abundantly, but only this humanity was invited to it. And of course, the angels weighed the pleasures in that tower, awaiting its guests, against the agony and trouble that awaited humanity. And once they saw that it was worthwhile for humanity to suffer for the good that awaited us, they agreed to man's creation, just as Rabbi Akiva said, "The judgment is true, and all is ready for the feast." From the beginning of creation, all people have reservations, and the thought of the Creator necessitates them to come to the feast, knowingly or unknowingly.

And now all will see the truth in the words of the prophet (Isaiah 11) in the prophecy of peace: "The wolf shall dwell with the lamb, and the leopard shall lay down with the kid." And he reasoned that "The earth will be full of the knowledge of the Lord, as the waters cover the sea."

Thus, the prophet conditions peace in the whole world with the filling of the whole world with the knowledge of the Creator, just as we have said above, that the tough, egoistic resistance among people, along which international relationships deteriorate, all these will not cease from the world by any human counsel or tactic, whatever it may be.

Our eyes can see how the poor, sick person is turning over in dreadful, intolerable pains, and humanity has already thrown itself to the extreme right, as with Germany, or to the extreme left, as with Russia. But not only did they not ease the situation for themselves, they have worsened the malady and agony, and the voices rise up to heaven, as we all know.

Thus, they have no other choice but to come to accept His burden in knowledge of the Creator, meaning to aim their actions to the will of the Creator and to His purpose, as He had planned for them prior to creation. When they do this, it is plain to see that with serving Him, all envy and hatred will be abolished from humanity, as I have shown above, since then all members of humanity will unite into one body and one heart, full of the knowledge of the Lord. Thus, world peace and the knowledge of the Creator are one and the same.

Immediately following, the prophet says, "And it will come to pass in that day, that the Lord will set His hand again a second time to recover the remnant of His people...and gather together the dispersed of Judah from the four corners of the earth." Thus we learn that world peace comes before the gathering of the Diaspora.

Now you can understand the words of our sages at the end of *Masechet Okatzin*: "The Creator did not find a vessel to hold the blessing for Israel but peace," as it says: "The Lord will give strength to His people, the Lord will bless His people with peace." Seemingly, one should wonder at the allegory, "a vessel to hold the blessing for Israel." And also, how does one conclude that from these words?

But these words become clear to them like the prophecy of Isaiah that world peace precedes the gathering of the Diaspora. This is why the verse says, "The Lord will give strength to His people," meaning that in the future, when the Creator gives His people strength, meaning eternal resurrection, "the Lord will bless His people with peace." This means that He will first bless His people, Israel, with peace in the whole world, and subsequently, He will "set his hand again the second time to recover the remnant of his people."

Our sages said about the reason for the words: Therefore, the blessing of peace in the whole world precedes the strength, meaning the redemption, because "God did not find a vessel to hold the blessing for Israel but peace." Thus, as long as self-love and egoism exist among the nations, Israel, too, will not be able to serve the Creator in purity, in bestowal upon others, as it is written in the explanation of the words, "And you will be to me a kingdom of priests," in the essay, "The Arvut." We see this from experience, for the coming to the land and the building of the Temple could not persist and receive the blessings that the Creator had sworn to our fathers.

This is why they said, "God did not find a vessel to hold the blessing," meaning that thus far, Israel did not have a vessel to hold the blessing of the fathers. Therefore, the oath that we can inherit the land for eternity has not been fulfilled, since world peace is the only vessel that enables us to receive the blessing of the fathers, as in the prophecy of Isaiah.

Meaning of Foreign Words [non-Hebrew words used in the text]

- Altruism: love of others.
- Analysis: separating the various elements in a matter.
- Synthesis: the connection and unity between matters, such as inference and the "all the more so."
- Motive power: a purposeful force, the strength to exert, which acts like fuel in a machine.
- From behind: a force that pushes something from behind.
- From before: a force that pulls something from before.

The Freedom

"'*Harut* [engraved] on the tablets'; do not pronounce it *Harut*, but rather *Herut* [freedom], to show that they were liberated from the angel of death."

[*Shemot Rabbah* 41]

These words need to be clarified, for how is the matter of acceptance of the Torah related to one's liberation from death? Furthermore, once they have attained an eternal body that cannot die through the acceptance of the Torah, how did they lose it again? Can the eternal become absent?

Freedom of Will

To understand the sublime concept, "freedom from the angel of death," we must first understand the concept of freedom as it is normally understood by all of humanity.

It is a general view that freedom is deemed a natural law, which applies to all of life. Thus, we see that animals that fall into captivity die when we rob them of their freedom. This is a true testimony that Providence does not accept the enslavement of any creature. It is with good reason that humanity has been struggling for the past several hundred years to obtain a certain measure of freedom of the individual.

Yet, this concept, expressed in that word, "freedom," remains unclear, and if we delve into the meaning of that word, there will be almost nothing left, for before you seek the freedom of the individual, you must assume that any individual, in and of himself, has that quality called "freedom," meaning that one can act according to one's choice of one's own free will.

Pleasure and Pain

However, when we examine the acts of an individual, we will find them compulsory. He is compelled to do them and has no freedom of choice. In a sense, he is like a stew cooking on a stove; it has no choice but to cook, since Providence has harnessed life with two chains: pleasure and pain.

The living creatures have no freedom of choice—to choose pain or reject pleasure. And man's advantage over animals is that man can aim at a remote goal, meaning agree to a certain amount of current pain, out of choice of future benefit or pleasure to be attained after some time.

But in fact, there is no more than a seemingly commercial calculation here, where the future benefit or pleasure seems preferable and advantageous to the agony they are suffering from the pain they have agreed to assume presently. There is only a matter of deduction here—where they deduct the pain and suffering from the anticipated pleasure, and there remains some surplus.

Thus, only the pleasure is extended. And so it sometimes happens that we are tormented because the pleasure we received is not the surplus we had hoped for compared to the agony we suffered. Hence, we are in deficit, just as are merchants.

And when all is said and done, there is no difference here between man and animal. And if this is the case, there is no free choice whatsoever, but a pulling force drawing them toward any passing pleasure and rejecting them from painful circumstances. And Providence leads them to every place it chooses by means of these two forces without asking their opinion in the matter.

Moreover, even determining the type of pleasure and benefit are entirely out of one's own free choice, but follows the will of others, as they want, and not he. For example: I sit, I dress, I speak, and I eat. I do all these not because I want to sit that way, or talk that way, or dress that way, or eat that way, but because others want me to sit, dress, talk, and eat that way. It all follows the desire and fancy of society, and not my own free will.

Furthermore, in most cases, I do all these against my will. For I would be more comfortable behaving simply, without any burden. But I am chained with iron shackles, in all my movements, to the fancies and manners of others, which make up the society.

So tell me, where is my freedom of will? On the other hand, if we assume that the will has no freedom, and we are all like machines operating and creating through external forces, which force them to act this way, it means that we are all incarcerated in the prison of Providence, which, using these two chains, pleasure and pain, pushes and pulls us to its will, to where it sees fit.

It turns out that there is no such thing as selfishness in the world, since no one here is free or stands in his own right. I am not the owner of the act and I am not the doer because I want to do. Rather, it is because I am worked upon against my will and without my awareness. Thus, reward and punishment become extinct.

And it is quite odd not only for the religious, who believe in His Providence and can rely on Him and trust that He aims only for the best in this conduct. It is even stranger for those who believe in nature, since according to the above-said, we are all incarcerated by the chains of blind nature, with no awareness or accountability. And we, the chosen species, with reason and knowledge, have become a toy in the hands of the blind nature, which leads us astray, and who knows where?

The Law of Causality

It is worthwhile taking some time to grasp such an important thing, meaning how we exist in the world as beings with a "self," where each of us regards himself as a unique entity, acting on its own, independent of external, alien, and unknown forces, and in what this being—the self—becomes revealed to us.

It is true that there is a general connection among all the elements of reality before us, which abides by the law of causality, by way of cause and effect, moving forward. And as the whole, so is each item for itself, meaning that each and every creature in the world from the four types—still, vegetative, animate, and speaking—abides by the law of causality by way of cause and effect.

Moreover, each particular form of a particular conduct, which a creature follows while in this world, is pushed by ancient causes, compelling it to accept that change in that conduct and not another whatsoever. This is apparent to all who examine the ways of nature from a pure scientific point of view and without a mixture of bias. Indeed, we must analyze this matter to allow ourselves to examine it from all sides.

Four Factors

Bear in mind that every emergence occurring in the beings of the world must be perceived not as extending existence from absence, but as existence from existence, through an actual entity that has shed its previous form and has robed its current one.

Therefore, we must understand that in every emergence in the world there are four factors where from the four of them together arises that emergence. They are called by the names:

1. The source.

2. The unchanging conduct of cause and effect related to the source's own attribute.

3. Its internal conducts of cause and effect which change by contact with alien forces.

4. The conducts of cause and effect of alien things which affect it from the outside.

I will clarify them one at a time.

The First Reason: the Source, the First Matter

A) The "source" is the first matter, related to that being. For "there is nothing new under the sun," and anything that happens in our world is not existence from absence, but existence from existence. It is an entity that has stripped off its former shape and taken on another form, different from the first. And that entity, which shed its previous form, is defined as "the source." In it lies the potential destined to be revealed and determined at the end of the formation of that emergence. Therefore, it is clearly considered its primary cause.

The Second Reason: Cause and Effect that Stem from Itself

B) This is a conduct of cause and effect related to the source's own attribute, and which is unchanging. Take, for example, a stalk of wheat that has rotted in the ground and arrived at a state of sowing many stalks of wheat. Thus, that rotten state is deemed the "source," meaning that the essence of the wheat has stripped off its former shape, the shape of wheat, and has taken on a new quality, that of rotten wheat, which is the seed called "the source," which has no shape at all. Now, after rotting in the ground, it has become suitable for robing another form, the form of many stalks of wheat, intended to emerge from that source, which is the seed.

It is known to all that this source is destined to become neither grain nor oats, but only equalize with its former shape, which has left it, being the single stalk of wheat. Although it changes to a certain degree in quality and quantity, for in the former shape it was a single stalk, and now there are ten stalks, and in taste and appearance, too, the essence of the shape of the wheat remains unchanged.

Thus, there is a conduct of cause and effect here, ascribed to the source's own attribute, which never changes. Thus, grain will never emerge from wheat, as we have said, and this is called "the second reason."

The Third Reason: Internal Cause and Effect

C) This is the conduct of the internal cause and effect of the source, which changes upon encountering the alien forces in its environment. Thus, we find that from one stalk of wheat, which rots in the ground, many stalks emerge, sometimes larger and better wheat than prior to sowing.

Therefore, there must be additional factors involved here, collaborating and connecting with the force concealed in the environment, meaning the "source." And because of this, the additions in quality and quantity, which were absent in the previous form of wheat, have now appeared. Those are the minerals and the materials in the ground, the rain, and the sun. All these operate on it by administering from their forces and joining the force within the source itself. And through the conduct of cause and effect, they have produced the multiplicity in quantity and quality in that emergence.

We must understand that this third factor joins the internality of the source, since the force hidden in the source controls them. In the end, all these changes belong to the wheat and to no other plant. Hence, we define them as internal factors. However, they differ from the second factor, which is utterly unchanging, whereas the third factor changes in both quality and quantity.

The Fourth Reason: Cause and Effect through Alien Things

D) This is a conduct of cause and effect of alien things that act upon it from the outside. In other words, they have no direct relation to the wheat, like minerals, rain, or sun, but are alien to it, such as nearby things or external events, such as hail, wind, etc.

And you find that four factors combine to the wheat throughout its growth. Each particular state that the wheat is subject to during that time becomes conditioned on the four of them, and the quality and quantity of each state is determined by them.

As we have portrayed in the wheat, so is the rule in every emergence in the world, even in thoughts and ideas. If, for example, we picture some conceptual state in a certain individual, such as a state of a person being religious or non-religious, or an extreme orthodox or not so extreme, or midway, we will understand that that state was established in that person by the four above factors.

Hereditary Possessions

The cause of the first reason is the source, which is its first substance. Man is created existence-from-existence, meaning from the minds of its progenitors. Thus, to a certain extent, he is like a replication from book to book. This means that almost all the matters that were accepted and attained in the fathers and forefathers are replicated here, as well.

But the difference is that they are in an abstract form, like the sowed wheat that is not fit for sowing until it has rotted and shed its former shape. So is the case with the drop of sperm from which man is born: There is nothing in it of its forefathers' shapes, only abstract force.

For the same ideas that were concepts in his forefathers have turned into mere tendencies in him, called "instincts" or "habits," without even knowing why one does what he does. Indeed, they are hidden forces he had inherited from his ancestors in a way that not only do the material possessions come to us by inheritance from our ancestors, but the spiritual possessions and all the concepts that our fathers engaged in also come to us by inheritance from generation to generation.

From here come the manifold tendencies that we find in people, such as a tendency to believe or to criticize, a tendency to settle for material life or desiring only spiritual, moral wholeness, despising a worthless life, stingy, yielding, insolent, or shy.

All these pictures that appear in people are not their own property, which they have acquired, but mere inheritance that had been given to them by their ancestors. It is known that there is a special place in the human brain where these hereditaments reside. It is called "the elongated brain," or "subconscious," and all the tendencies appear there.

But because the concepts of our ancestors, acquired through their experiences, have become mere tendencies in us, they are considered the same as the sowed wheat, which has taken off its former shape and has remained bare, having only potential forces fit of receiving new forms. In our matter, these tendencies will robe the forms of concepts. This is considered the first matter, and this is the primary factor, called "source." In it reside all the forces of the unique tendencies he had inherited from his progenitors, which are defined as "ancestral heritage."

Bear in mind that some of these tendencies come in a negative form, meaning the opposite of the ones that were in the ancestors. This is why they said, "All that is concealed in the father's heart emerges openly in the son."

The reason for this is that the source takes off its former shape in order to take on a new form. Hence, it is close to losing the shapes of the concepts of the ancestors, like the wheat that rots in the ground loses the shape that existed in the wheat. However, it still depends on the other three factors, as I have written above.

Influence of the Environment

The second reason is an unchanging, direct conduct of cause and effect, related to the source's own attribute. Meaning, as we have clarified with the wheat that rots in the ground, the environment in which the source rests, such as soil, minerals, and rain, air, and the sun affect the sowing by a long chain of cause and effect in a long and gradual process, state by state, until it ripens.

And that source retakes its former shape, the shape of wheat, but differing in quality and quantity. In their general aspect, they remain completely unchanged; hence, no grain or oats will grow from it. But in their particular aspect, they change in quantity, as from one stalk emerge a dozen or two dozen stalks, and in quality, as they are better or worse than the former shape of the wheat.

It is the same here: Man, as a "source," is placed in an environment, meaning in the society. He is necessarily affected by it, as the wheat from its environment, for the source is but a raw form. Thus, through the constant contact with the environment and the society, he is gradually impressed by them through a chain of consecutive states, one by one, as cause and effect.

At that time, the tendencies included in his source change and take on the form of concepts. For example, if one inherits from his ancestors a tendency to stinginess, as he grows he builds for himself concepts and ideas that conclude decisively that it is good for a person to be stingy. Thus, although his father was generous, he might inherit from him the negative tendency—to be stingy—for the absence is just as much inheritance as the presence.

Or, if one inherits from one's ancestors a tendency to be open-minded, he builds for himself concepts and draws from them conclusions that it is good for a person to be open-minded. But where does one find those sentences and reasoning? He takes all this from the environment unconsciously, for they impart upon him their views and likings in the form of gradual cause and effect.

Hence, man regards them as his own possession, which he acquired through his free thought. But here, too, as with the wheat, there is one unchanging part of the source, which is that in the end, the tendencies he had inherited remain as they were in his forefathers. This is called "the second factor."

Habit Becomes a Second Nature

The third reason is a conduct of direct cause and effect, which affect the source and change it. Because the inherited tendencies in man have become concepts due to the environment, they operate in the same directions that these concepts define. For example, a man of frugal nature, in whom the tendency to stinginess has been turned into a concept, through the environment, perceives frugality through some reasonable definition.

Let us assume that by this conduct he protects himself from needing other people. Thus, he has acquired a scale for frugality, and when that fear is absent, he can waive it. It follows that he has changed substantially for the better from the tendency he had inherited from his forefathers. And sometimes one manages to completely uproot a bad tendency. This is done by habit, which has the ability to become a second nature.

In that, the strength of man is greater than that of a plant, for wheat can change only in its own part, whereas man can change through the cause and effect of the environment, even in the general parts, meaning to completely uproot a tendency and invert it to its opposite.

External Factors

The fourth reason is a conduct of cause and effect that affects the source by things that are completely alien to it and operates on it from the outside. This means that these things are not at all related to the source's growth conduct to affect it directly. Rather, they operate indirectly. For example, finances, burdens, or the winds, etc., have their own complete, slow, and gradual order of states by way of "cause and effect" that change man's concepts for better or for worse.

Thus, I have set up the four natural factors that each thought and idea that appears in us is but their fruits. Even if one were to sit and contemplate something all day long, he will not be able to add or to alter what those four factors give him. Any addition he can add is in the quantity: whether a great intellect or a small one. But in the quality, he cannot add one bit. This is because they are the ones that compellingly determine the nature and shape of the idea and the conclusion against our will, without asking our opinion. Thus, we are at the hands of these four factors, as clay in the hands of a potter.

Free Choice

However, when we examine these four factors, we find that although our strength is not enough to face the first factor, the source, we still have the ability and free choice to protect ourselves against the other three factors by which the source changes in its individual parts, and sometimes in its general part, as well, through habit, which endows it with a second nature, as explained above.

The Environment as a Factor

This protection means that we can always add in the matter of choosing our environment, which are the friends, books, teachers, and so on. It is like a person who inherited a few stalks of wheat from his father. From this small amount, he can grow many dozens of stalks through his choice of the environment for his source, which is fertile soil that contains all the necessary minerals and raw materials that nourish the wheat abundantly.

There is also the matter of the work of improving the environmental conditions to fit the needs of the plant and the growth, for the wise will do well to choose the best conditions and will succeed. And the fool will take from whatever comes before him and thus turn the sowing to a curse rather than a blessing.

Thus, all his praise and his gain depend on the choice of the environment in which to sow the wheat. But once it has been sown in the selected location, the wheat's absolute shape is determined according to the measure that the environment is capable of providing.

So is the case with our topic, for it is true that the desire has no freedom. Rather, it is operated by the above four factors. And one is compelled to think and examine as they suggest, denied of any strength to criticize or change, as the wheat that has been sown in its environment.

However, there is freedom for the will to initially choose such an environment, such books, and such guides that impart upon him good concepts. If one does not do this but is willing to enter any environment that appears before him and read any book that falls into his hands, he is bound to fall into a bad environment or waste his time on worthless books, which are abundant and more accessible. In consequence, he will be forced into foul concepts that make him sin and condemn. He will certainly be punished, not because of his evil thoughts or deeds, in which he has no choice, but because he did not choose to be in a good environment, for in this there is definitely a choice.

Therefore, he who strives to continually choose a better environment is worthy of praise and reward. But here, too, it is not because of his good thoughts or deeds, which come to him without his choice, but because of his effort to acquire a good environment, which brings him these good thoughts and actions. It is as Rabbi Yehoshua Ben Perachya said, "Make for yourself a rav and buy for yourself a friend."

The Necessity to Choose a Good Environment

Now you can understand the words of Rabbi Yosi Ben Kisma (Avot, Chapter 6), who replied to a person who offered him to live in his town, and he would give him millions of gold coins for it: "Even if you give me all the gold and silver and jewels in the world, I will live only in a place of Torah." These words seem inconceivable to our simple mind, for how could he relinquish millions of gold coins for such a small thing as living in a place where there are no disciples of Torah, while he himself was a great sage who needed to learn from no one? Indeed, a mystery.

But as we have seen, it is a simple thing and should be observed by each and every one of us. Although each one has his own source, the forces are revealed openly only through the environment one is in. This is similar to the wheat sown in the ground, whose forces become apparent only through its environment, which is the soil, rain, and sunlight.

Thus, Rabbi Yosi Ben Kisma correctly assumed that if he were to leave the good environment he had chosen and fall into a harmful environment in a city where there is no Torah, not only would his former concepts be compromised, but all the other forces hidden in his source, which he had not yet revealed in action, would remain concealed. This is because they would not be subject to the right environment that would be able to activate them.

And as we have clarified above, only in the matter of the choice of environment is man's reign over himself measured, and for this he should receive reward or punishment. Therefore, one must not wonder that a sage such as Rabbi Yosi Ben Kisma chose the good and declined the bad, and was not tempted by material or corporeal things, as he deduces there: "When one dies, one does not take with him silver, gold, or jewels, but only Torah and good deeds."

And so our sages warned, "Make for yourself a rav and buy for yourself a friend." And there is also the choice of books, as we have mentioned, for only in this is one rebuked or praised—in his choice of the environment. But once he has chosen an environment, he is at its hands as clay in the hands of the potter.

The Mind's Control over the Body

Some external contemporary sages, after contemplating the above matter and seeing how man's mind is but a fruit that grows out of the events of life, concluded that the mind has no control whatsoever over the body. Rather, only life's events, imprinted in the physical tendons of the brain, control and activate man. Man's mind is like a mirror, reflecting the shapes before it. Although the mirror is the carrier of these shapes, it cannot activate or move the shapes reflected in it.

So is the mind. Although life's events, in all their manners of cause and effect, are seen and recognized by the mind, the mind is nonetheless utterly incapable of controlling the body, to bring it into motion, meaning to bring it closer to the good or push it away from the bad. This is because the spiritual and the physical are completely remote from one another, and there is no intermediary tool between them to enable the spiritual mind to activate and operate the corporeal body, as has been discussed at length.

But where they are smart, there they disrupt. Man's imagination uses the mind just as the microscope serves the eyes: Without the microscope, we would not see anything harmful, due to its smallness. But once we see the harmful being through the microscope, we distance ourselves from the noxious element.

Thus, it is the microscope that brings man to distance himself from the harm, and not the sense, for the sense did not detect the harm-doer. And to that extent, the mind fully controls man's body, to push it away from bad and pull it toward the good. Thus, in all the places where the attribute of the body fails to recognize the beneficial or the detrimental, it needs only the mind's knowledge.

Furthermore, since man knows his mind, which is a true conclusion from life's experiences, he can therefore receive knowledge and understanding from a trusted person and take it as law, although his life's events have not yet revealed these concepts to him. It is like a person who asks the advice of a doctor and obeys him even though he understands nothing with his own mind. Thus, one uses the mind of others no less than one uses one's own.

As we have clarified above, there are two ways for Providence to make certain that man achieves the good, final goal: The path of suffering and the path of Torah. All the clarity in the path of Torah stems from this. For these clear conceptions that were revealed and recognized after a long chain of events in the lives of the prophets and the men of God, there comes a man who fully utilizes them and benefits from them, as though these concepts were events of his own life. Thus, you see that one is exempted from all the ordeals one must experience before he can develop that clear mind by himself. Thus, one saves both time and pain.

It can be compared to a sick man who does not wish to obey the doctor's orders before he understands by himself how that advice would cure him, and therefore begins to study medicine by himself. He could die of his illness before he learns medicine.

So is the path of suffering compared to the path of Torah. One who does not believe the concepts that the Torah and prophecy advise him to accept without self-understanding must come to these concepts by himself by following the chain of cause and effect from life's events. These are experiences that greatly rush and can develop the sense of recognition of evil in them, as we have seen, without one's choice, but because of one's efforts to acquire a good environment, which leads to these thoughts and actions.

The Freedom of the Individual

Now we have come to a thorough and accurate understanding of the freedom of the individual. However, this relates only to the first factor, the source, which is the first substance of every person, meaning all the characteristics we inherit from our fathers and our forefathers and by which we differ from each other.

This is because even when thousands of people share the same environment in such a way that the other three factors affect all of them equally, you will still not find two people who share even one attribute. This is because each of them has his or her own unique source. This is like the source of the wheat: Although it changes a great deal by the three latter factors, it still retains the preliminary shape of wheat and will never take on the form of another species.

The General Shape of the Progenitor Is Never Lost

So it is that each "source" that had taken off the preliminary shape of the progenitor and had taken on a new shape as a result of the three factors that were added to it, and which change it significantly, the general shape of the progenitor still remains, and will never assume the shape of another person who resembles him, just as oat will never resemble wheat.

This is so because each and every source has its own long sequence of generations comprised of several hundred generations, and the source includes the conceptions of them all. However, they are not revealed in it in the same ways they appeared in the ancestors, that is, in the form of ideas, but only as abstract forms. Therefore, they exist in him in the form of abstract forces called "tendencies," "nature," and "instincts," without knowing their reason or why he does what he does. Thus, there can never be two people with the same attribute.

The Necessity to Preserve the Freedom of the Individual

Know, that this is the one true possession of the individual that must not be harmed or altered. This is because the end of all these tendencies, which are included in the source, is to materialize and assume the form of concepts when that individual grows and becomes knowledgeable, as a result of the law of evolution, which controls that chain and prompts it ever forward, as explained in the article, "The Peace." Also, we learn that each and every tendency is bound to turn into a sublime and immeasurably important concept.

Thus, anyone who eradicates a tendency from an individual and uproots it from him causes the loss of that sublime and wondrous concept, intended to emerge at the end of the chain, for that tendency will never again emerge in any other body. Accordingly, we must understand that when a particular tendency takes the form of a concept, it can no longer be distinguished as good or bad, as such distinctions are recognized only when they are still tendencies or immature concepts, and in no way are any of them recognized when they assume the shape of real concepts, as will be thoroughly explained in the following essays.

From the above-said, we learn what a terrible wrong inflict those nations that force their reign on minorities, depriving them of freedom without allowing them to lead their lives according to the tendencies they have inherited from their ancestors. They are regarded as no less than murderers.

Even those who do not believe in religion or in purposeful guidance can understand the necessity to preserve the freedom of the individual by watching nature's systems, for we can see how all the nations that ever fell, throughout the generations, came to it only due to their oppression of minorities and individuals, which had therefore rebelled against them and ruined them. Hence, it is clear to all that peace cannot exist in the world unless we take into consideration the freedom of the individual. Without it, peace will not be sustainable and ruin will prevail.

Thus, we have clearly defined the essence of the individual with utmost accuracy, after the deduction of all that he takes from the public. But now we face a question: "Where, in the end, is the individual himself?" All we have said thus far concerning the individual is perceived as only the property of the individual, inherited from his ancestors. But where is the individual himself, the heir and the carrier of that property, who demands that we guard his property?

From all that has been said thus far, we have yet to find the point of "self" in man, which stands before us as an independent unit. And why do I need the first factor, which is a long chain of thousands of people, one after the other, from generation to generation, with which we set the image of the individual as an heir? And why do I need the other three factors, which are the thousands of people standing side by side in the same generation? In the end, each individual is but a public machine, ever ready to serve the public as it sees fit.

In other words, he has become subordinate to two types of public: From the perspective of the first factor, he has become subordinate to a large public from past generations, standing one after the other. From the perspective of the three other factors, he has become subordinate to his contemporary public.

This is indeed a universal question. For this reason, many oppose the above, natural method. Although they thoroughly know its validity, they choose instead metaphysical methods, dualism, or transcendentalism to depict for themselves some spiritual object and how it sits within the body, as man's soul. That soul is what teaches and operates the body, and it is man's essence and his "self."

Perhaps these interpretations could ease the mind, but the problem is that they have no scientific solution as to how a spiritual object can have any contact with physical atoms in the body, to bring it into any kind of motion. All their wisdom and delving did not help them find a sufficient bridge to cross that wide and deep crevice between the spiritual entity and the corporeal atom. Hence, science has gained nothing from all these metaphysical methods.

The Will to Receive—Existence from Absence

To move a step forward in a scientific manner here, all we need is the wisdom of Kabbalah. This is because all the teachings in the world are included in the wisdom of Kabbalah. Concerning spiritual lights and vessels (in the commentary on *Tree* of Life, Branch 1), we learn that the primary innovation, from the perspective of creation, which He has created existence from absence, applies to one and only aspect, defined as the "will to receive." All other matters in the whole of creation are not innovations at all; they are not existence from absence but existence from existence. This means that they extend directly from His essence, as the light extends from the sun. There, too, there is nothing new, since what is found in the core of the sun extends outwards.

However, the will to receive is complete novelty. Prior to creation such a thing did not exist in reality since He has no quality of will to receive at all, as He precedes everything... so from whom would He receive?

For this reason, this will to receive, which He extracted as existence from absence, is complete novelty. But everything else is not considered an innovation that could be called "creation." Hence, all the vessels and the bodies, from spiritual worlds and from physical worlds, are deemed spiritual or corporeal substance whose nature is to want to receive.

Two Forces in the Will to Receive: An Attracting Force and a Rejecting Force

You need to discern further that we distinguish two forces in that force called "will to receive":

1. The attracting force.
2. The rejecting force.

The reason is that each body, or vessel, defined as the will to receive, is indeed limited, meaning how much it will receive and the quality it will receive. Therefore, all the quantity and quality that are outside one's boundaries appear to be against one's nature; hence, he rejects them. Thus, that "will to receive," although it is deemed an attracting force, it is compelled to become a rejecting force, as well.

One Law for All the Worlds

Although the wisdom of Kabbalah mentions nothing of our corporeal world, there is still only one law for all the worlds (as written in the article, "The Essence of the Wisdom of Kabbalah," section "The Law of Root and Branch"). Thus, all the corporeal entities in our world, that is, everything within that space, be it still, vegetative, animate, a spiritual object or a corporeal object, if we want to distinguish the unique self of each of them, how they differ from one another, even in the smallest particle, it amounts to no more than that "desire to receive." This is its entire particular form, from the perspective of the generated creation, limiting it in quantity and quality. As a result, there is an attracting force and a rejecting force in it.

Yet, anything that exists in it besides these two forces is regarded as the bounty from His essence. That bounty is equal for all creatures and presents no innovation with respect to creation as it extends existence from existence.

Also, it cannot be ascribed to any particular unit, but only to things that are common to all parts of creation, small or large. Each of them receives from that bounty according to the limit of its will to receive, and this limit defines each individual and unit.

Thus, I have evidently—from a purely scientific perspective—proven the self (ego) of every individual in a scientific, completely criticism-proof method, even according to the system of the fanatic, automatic materialists. From now on, we have no need for those lame methods dipped in metaphysics.

And of course, it makes no difference whether this force of the will to receive is a result and a fruit of the material that had produced it through chemistry, or the material is a result and a fruit of that force. This is because we know that the main thing is that only this force, imprinted in every being and atom of the "will to receive," within its boundaries, is the unit by which it is separated and distinguished from its environment. This applies to both a single atom or a group of atoms, called a "body."

All other discernments in which there is more than that force are not related in any way to that particle or group of particles, with respect to itself, but only with respect to the whole, which is the bounty extended to them from the Creator, which is common to all parts of creation together, without distinction of specific created bodies.

Now we will understand the matter of the freedom of the individual, according to the definition of the first factor, which we called the "source," where all previous generations, which are the fathers and forefathers of that individual, have imprinted their nature. As we have clarified, the meaning of the word "individual" is but the boundaries of the will to receive, imprinted in its group of molecules.

Thus you see that all the tendencies he has inherited from his ancestors are indeed no more than boundaries of his will to receive, either related to the attracting force in him, or to the rejecting force in him, which appear before us as tendencies to stinginess or generosity, a tendency to mingle with people or to be a hermit, and so on.

Because of this, they really are his self (ego), fighting for its existence. Thus, if we eradicate even a single tendency from that individual, we are regarded as cutting off an actual organ from his essence. It is also considered a genuine loss for all creation, since there is no other like it, nor will there ever be someone like him in the whole world.

After we have thoroughly clarified the just right of the individual according to the natural laws, let us turn and see just how practical it is, without compromising the theory of ethics and statesmanship. And most important: how this right is applied by our holy Torah.

Taking after the Collective

Our scriptures say: "Take after the collective." This means that wherever there is a dispute between the collective and the individual, we are obliged to rule according to the will of the collective. Thus, you see that the collective has a right to expropriate the freedom of the individual.

But we are faced with a different question here, even more serious than the first. It seems as though this law regresses humanity instead of promoting it. This is because while most of humanity is undeveloped, and the developed ones are always a small minority, if you always determine according to the will of the majority, which are the undeveloped and the reckless, the views and desires of the wise and developed in society, which are always the minority, will never be heard and be taken into consideration. Thus, you seal off humanity's fate to regression, for it will not be able to make even a single step forward.

However, as is explained in the article "The Peace," section "Necessity to Practice Caution with the Laws of Nature," since we are ordered by Providence to lead a social life, we have become obligated to observe all the laws pertaining to the sustenance of society. And if we are somewhat negligent, nature will take its revenge in us, regardless of whether or not we understand the reasons for the laws.

And we can see that there is no other arrangement by which to live in society except following the law of "Taking after the collective," which sets every dispute and tribulation in society in order. Thus, this law is the only instrument that gives society sustainability. For this reason, it is considered one of the natural *Mitzvot* [commandments] of Providence, and we must accept it and guard it meticulously, regardless of our understanding.

This is similar to the rest of the *Mitzvot* in the Torah: All of them are nature's laws and His Providence which come to us from above downward. I have already described ("The Essence of the Wisdom of Kabbalah," "The Law of Root and Branch") how the whole of reality seen in the nature of this world is only because they are extended and taken from laws and conducts of upper, spiritual worlds.

Now you can understand that the *Mitzvot* in the Torah are but laws and conducts set in higher worlds, which are the roots of all of nature's conducts in this world of ours. Hence, the laws of the Torah always match the laws of nature in this world as two drops of water. Thus, we have proven that the law, "Taking after the collective," is the law of Providence and nature.

A Path of Torah and a Path of Suffering

Yet, our question about the regression, which had emerged from this law, is still not settled by these words. Indeed, this is our concern—to find ways to mend this. But Providence, for itself, does not lose because of this, for it has enveloped humankind in two ways—the "path of Torah," and the "path of suffering"—in a way that guarantees humanity's continuous development and progress toward the goal without any reservations ("The Peace," "Everything Is in Deposit"). Indeed, obeying this law is a natural, necessary commitment.

The Collective's Right to Expropriate the Freedom of the Individual

We must ask further: Things are justified when matters revolve around issues between people. Then we can accept the law of "Taking after the collective," through the obligation of Providence, which instructs us to always look after the well-being and happiness of the members. But the Torah obliges us to follow the law of "Taking after the collective" in disputes between man and the Creator, as well, although these matters seem completely unrelated to the existence of society.

Therefore, the question still stands: How can we justify that law, which obligates us to accept the views of the majority, which is, as we have said, undeveloped, and reject and annul the views of the developed, who are always a small minority?

As we have shown in the second tractate ("The Essence of Religion and Its Purpose," "Conscious Development and Unconscious Development"), the Torah and the Mitzvot were given only to purify Israel, to develop in us the sense of recognition of evil imprinted in us at birth, which is generally defined as our self-love, and to come to the pure good defined as "love of others," which is the one and only passage to the love of the Creator.

Accordingly, the Mitzvot between man and the Creator are considered tools that detach man from self-love, which is harmful for society. It is thus obvious that the topics of dispute regarding Mitzvot between man and the Creator relate to the problem of society's sustainability. Thus, they, too, fall into the framework of "Taking after the collective."

Now we can understand the conduct of discriminating between Halachah [Jewish law] and Agadah [legends]. This is because only in Halachot [plural for Halachah] does the law, "individual and collective, Halachah [law] as the collective" apply. It is not so in the Agadah, since matters of Agadah stand above matters that concern the existence of society, for they speak precisely of the matter of people's conducts in matters concerning man and the Creator, in that part where the existence and physical happiness of society has no consequence.

Thus, there is no justification for the collective to annul the view of the individual and "every man will do that which was right in his own eyes." But regarding Halachot that deal with observing the Mitzvot of the Torah, they all fall under the supervision of society since there cannot be any order except through the law, "Take after the collective."

For Social Life, the Law, Take after the Collective

Now we have come to a clear understanding of the sentence concerning the freedom of the individual. Indeed, there is a question: Where did the collective take the right to expropriate the freedom of the individual and deny him of the most precious thing in life, freedom? Seemingly, there is no more than brute force here.

But as we have clearly explained above, it is a natural law and the decree of Providence. And because Providence compels each of us to lead a social life, it naturally follows that each person is obligated to secure the existence and well-being of society. And this cannot happen but through imposing the conduct of "taking after the collective," ignoring the opinion of the individual.

Thus, you evidently see that this is the origin of every right and justification that the collective has to expropriate the freedom of the individual against his will, and to place him under its authority. Therefore, it is understood that with regard to all those matters that do not concern the existence of the material life of the society, there is no justification for the collective to rob and abuse the freedom of the individual in any way. If they do so, they are deemed robbers and thieves who prefer brute force to any right or justice in the world, since here the obligation of the individual to obey the will of the collective does not apply.

In Spiritual Life, Take after the Individual

It turns out that as far as spiritual life is concerned, there is no natural obligation on the individual to abide by society in any way. On the contrary, here applies a natural law over the collective, to subjugate itself to the individual. And it is clarified in the article, "The Peace," that there are two ways by which Providence has enveloped and surrounded us, to bring us to the end: a path of suffering, which develops us in this manner unconsciously, and a path of Torah and wisdom, which consciously develops us in this manner without any agony or coercion.

Since the more developed in the generation is certainly the individual, it follows that when the public wants to relieve themselves of the terrible agony and assume conscious and voluntary development, which is the path of Torah, they have no choice but to subjugate themselves and their physical freedom to the discipline of the individual, and obey the orders and remedies that he will offer them.

Thus you see that in spiritual matters, the authority of the collective is overturned and the law of taking after the individual is applied, that is, the developed individual. For it is plain to see that the developed and the educated in every society are always a very small minority. It follows that the success and spiritual well-being of society is bottled and sealed in the hands of the minority.

Therefore, the collective is obliged to meticulously guard all the views of the few, so they will not perish from the world. This is because they must know for certain, in complete confidence, that the truer and more developed views are never in the hands of the collective in authority, but in the hands of the weakest, that is, in the hands of the indistinguishable minority. This is because every wisdom and everything precious comes into the world in small quantities. Therefore, we are cautioned to preserve the views of all the individuals due to the collective's inability to sort them out.

Criticism Brings Success; Lack of Criticism Causes Decadence

We must further add that reality presents to our eyes extreme oppositeness between physical matters and concepts and ideas regarding the above topic, for the matter of social unity, which can be the source of every joy and success, applies particularly to bodies and bodily matters in people, and the separation between them is the source of every calamity and misfortune.

But with concepts and ideas, it is the complete opposite: Unity and lack of criticism are deemed the source of every failure and hindrance to all the progress and intellectual fertilization. This is because drawing the right conclusions depends particularly on increasing disagreements and separation between views. The more contradictions there are between views and the more criticism there is, the more the knowledge and wisdom increase, and matters become more suitable for examination and clarification.

The degeneration and failure of intelligence stem only from the lack of criticism and disagreement. Thus, evidently, the whole basis of physical success is the measure of unity of the society, and the basis for the success of intelligence and knowledge is the separation and disagreement among them.

It turns out that when humankind achieves its goal, with respect to the success of the bodies, by bringing them to the degree of complete love of others, all the bodies in the world will unite into a single body and a single heart, as written in the article, "The Peace." Only then will all the happiness intended for humanity become revealed in all its glory. But against that, we must be watchful not to bring the views of people so close that disagreement and criticism among the wise and scholarly might be terminated, for the love of the body naturally brings with it proximity of views. And should criticism and disagreement vanish, all progress in concepts and ideas will cease, as well, and the source of knowledge in the world will dry out.

This is the proof of the obligation to caution with the freedom of the individual regarding concepts and ideas. For the whole development of the wisdom and knowledge is based on that freedom of the individual. Thus, we are cautioned to preserve it very carefully, in a manner that each and every form within us, which we call "individual," that is, the particular force of a single person, generally named the "will to receive."

Ancestral Heritage

All the details of the pictures that this will to receive includes, which we have defined as the source, or the first reason, whose meaning includes all the tendencies and customs inherited from his ancestors, which we picture as a long chain of thousands of people who were alive once, and stand one atop of the other, each of them is an essential drop of his progenitors, and that drop brings each person all the spiritual possessions of his progenitors into his elongated brain, called "subconscious." Thus, the individual before us has, in his subconscious, all the thousands of spiritual legacies from all the individuals represented in that chain, which are his progenitors and ancestors.

Thus, just as the face of each and every person differs, so their views differ. There are no two people on earth whose opinions are identical, because each person has a great and sublime possession bequeathed to him from his ancestors, and which others have no shred of them.

Therefore, all those possessions are considered the individual's property, and society is cautioned to preserve its flavor and spirit so it does not become blurred by its environment. Rather, each individual should maintain the integrity of his inheritance. Then, the contradiction and oppositeness between them will remain forever, to forever secure the criticism and progress of the wisdom, which is all of humanity's advantage and its true eternal desire.

After we have come to a certain measure of recognition of man's selfishness, which we have determined as a force and a desire to receive, being the essential point of the bare being, it has also become thoroughly clear to us, from all sides, the original possession of each body, which we have defined as "ancestral heritage." This pertains to all the potential tendencies and qualities that have come into his source by inheritance, which is the first substance of every person, meaning the initial seed of his forefathers.

Now we have found the door to resolving the intention of our sages in their words that by receiving the Torah, they were liberated from the angel of death. However, we still need further understanding regarding selfishness and the above-mentioned ancestral heritage.

Two Discernments: A) Potential, B) Actual

First, we must understand that although this selfishness, which we have defined as the force of will to receive, is the very essence of man, it cannot exist in reality even for a second. (For it is known that there is a discernment and a discernment in the "potential," and the thing we call "potential" is in the thought, before it emerges from potential to actual, and is established only in the thought.) For what we call "potential," before it emerges from potential to actual, exists only in our thought, meaning that we can determine it only in the thought.

But in fact, there cannot be any real force in the world that is dormant and inactive. This is because the force exists in reality only while it is revealed in action. By the same token, you cannot say about an infant that it is very strong when it cannot lift even the lightest weight. Instead, you can say that you see in that infant that when it grows, it will manifest great strength.

However, we do say that that strength we find in man when he is grown was present in his organs and his body even when he was an infant, but that strength had been concealed and was not evident. It is true that in our minds we could determine (the powers destined to manifest), since the mind asserts it. However, in the infant's actual body there is certainly no strength at all, since no strength manifests in the infant's actions, since no force was revealed in the infant's actions.

So it is with appetite. This force will not appear in a man's body in the actual reality when the organs cannot eat, meaning when he is full. But even when one is full, the force of appetite exists, but it is concealed within one's body. After some time, when the food has been digested, it reappears and manifests from potential to actual.

However, such a sentence (of determining a force that has not yet been revealed in actual fact) belongs to the conducts by which the thought perceives. However, it does not exist in reality, since when satiated, we feel very clearly that the force of appetite is gone, and if you search for it, you will not find it.

It turns out that we cannot display a potential as a subject that exists in and of itself, but only as a predicate. Thus, when an action occurs in reality, at that time the force manifests in the action.

Yet, we necessarily find two things here in the perceiving process: a subject and a predicate, that is, potential and actual, such as the force of appetite, which is the subject, and the image of the food, which is the predicate and the action. In reality, however, they come as one. It will never occur that the force of appetite will appear in a person without picturing the food he wishes to eat. Thus, these are two halves of the same thing. The force of appetite must dress in the image of the thing being eaten, since there is revealing only through clothing in an image. You therefore see that the subject and the predicate are presented here as two halves of the same thing, whose appearance and disappearance are simultaneous.

Now we understand that the will to receive, which we presented as selfishness, does not mean that it exists so in a person as a craving force that wishes to receive in the form of a passive predicate. Rather, this pertains to the subject, meaning that it dresses in an image of things he deems worthy of receiving. It is like the force of appetite, which dresses in the image of a thing worthy of being eaten, and whose action appears in the form of the thing being eaten and in which it clothes. We call this action, "desire," meaning the force of appetite revealed in the action of the imagination.

So it is with our topic—the general will to receive, which is the very essence of man. It appears and exists only through dressing in shapes of objects that are likely to be received, for then it exists as the subject, and in no other way. We call this action, "life," meaning man's vitality, which means that the force of the will to receive dresses and acts within the desired objects. And the measure of revelation of this action is the measure of his vitality, as we have explained in the act we call "desire."

Two Creations: A) Man, B) A Living Soul

From the above, we can clearly understand the verse: "And the Lord God formed man of the dust of the ground, and breathed into his nostrils the breath of life; and man became a living [Haya] soul [Nefesh]." Here we find two creations:

1. Man himself,

2. The living soul itself.

The verse says that in the beginning, man was created as dust from the ground, a collection of molecules in which resides the essence of man, meaning his will to receive. That force, the will to receive, is present in every element of reality, as we have explained above. Also, all four types emerged from them: 1) still, 2) vegetative, 3) animate, 4) speaking.

In that respect, man has no advantage over any part of creation. This is the meaning of the verse in the words, "dust from the ground."

However, we have already seen that this force, called "will to receive," cannot exist without dressing and acting in a desired object, and this action is called "life." And accordingly, we find that before man has arrived at the human forms of reception of pleasure, which differ from those of other created beings, he is still considered a lifeless, dead person, since his will to receive has no place in which to dress and manifest its actions, which are the manifestations of life.

This is the meaning of the verse, "and breathed into his nostrils the breath of life," which is the general form of reception suitable for humans. The word *Nishmat* [breath of] comes from the word *Samin* [placing] the ground for him, which is like "value." (And the origin of the word "breath" is understood from the verse (Job 33:4): "The spirit of God has made me, and the breath of the Almighty has given me life," and see the commentary of the MALBIM there.) The word "soul" [*Neshama*] has the same syntax structure as the words, "missing" [*Nifkad*], "accused" [*Ne'esham*], and "accused" [*Ne'eshama*—female term of *Ne'esham*].

And the meaning of the words, "and breathed into his nostrils" is that He instills a soul [*Neshama*] in his internality and an appreciation of life, which is the sum of the forms that are worthy of reception into his will to receive. Then, that force, the will to receive, enclosed in his molecules, has found a place in which to dress and act, meaning in those forms of reception that he had obtained from the Creator. And this action is called "life," as we have explained above.

And the verse ends, "and man became a living soul." This means that since the will to receive has begun to act by the measures of those forms of reception, life instantly manifested in it and it "became a living soul." However, prior to the attainment of those forms of reception, although the force of the will to receive had been imprinted in him, it is still considered a lifeless body, since it has no place in which to appear and to manifest in action.

As we have seen above, although man's essence is only the will to receive, it is still taken as half of a whole, as it must clothe in a reality that comes its way. For this reason, it and the image of possession it depicts are literally one, for otherwise it would not be able to exist for even a moment.

Therefore, when the machine of the body is at its peak, meaning until his middle-age, his ego stands upright in all the height imprinted in him at birth. Because of this, he feels within him a large and powerful measure of the will to receive. In other words, he craves great wealth and honor, and anything that comes his way. This is so because of the perfection of man's ego, which attracts shapes of structures and concepts that it dresses in and sustains itself through them.

But when half his life is through, begin the days of the decline. By their content, these are his dying days. A person does not die in an instant, just as he did not receive his life in an instant. Rather, his candle, being his ego, withers and dies bit by bit, and along with it die the images of the possessions he wishes to receive.

He begins to relinquish many possessions he had dreamed of in his youth, and he gradually relinquishes great possessions according to his decline over the years. Finally, in his truly old days, when the shadow of death hovers over all his being, a person finds himself in "times of no appeal," since his will to receive, his ego, has withered away. Only a tiny spark of it remains, hidden from the eye, from clothing in some possession. Therefore, there is no appeal or hope in those days for any image of reception.

Thus, we have proven that the will to receive, along with the image of the object expected to be received, are one and the same. Their manifestation is equal, their stature is equal, and so is the length of their lives.

However, there is a significant distinction here in the form of the yielding at the time of the decline of life. That yielding is not a result of satiation, like a person who relinquishes food when he is full, but a result of despair. That is, when the ego begins to die during the days of decline, it senses its own weakness and approaching death. Therefore, a person lets go and gives up the dreams and hopes of his youth.

Observe carefully the difference between that and the yielding due to satiation, which causes no grief and cannot be called "partial death," but is like a worker who completed his work. Indeed, relinquishment out of despair is full of pain and sorrow, and can therefore be called "partial death."

Freedom from the Angel of Death

Now, after all that we have learned, we find a way to truly understand the words of our sages when they said, "'*Harut* [carved] on the stones,' do not pronounce it *Harut*, but rather *Herut* [freedom], for they have been liberated from the angel of death."

It has been explained in the articles, "Matan Torah" and "The Arvut," that prior to the giving of the Torah, they had assumed the relinquishment of any private property to the extent expressed in the words, "a kingdom of priests," and the purpose of the whole of creation—to adhere to Him in equivalence of form with Him: As He bestows and does not receive, they, too, will bestow and not receive. This is the last degree of *Dvekut* [adhesion], expressed in the words, "a holy nation," as it is written at the end of the article, "The Arvut."

I have already brought you to realize that man's essence, meaning his selfishness, defined as the will to receive, is only half a thing, and can only exist when clothed in some image of a possession or hope for possession. Only then is our matter complete and can be called "man's essence."

Thus, when the children of Israel were rewarded with complete *Dvekut* on that holy occasion, their vessels of reception were completely emptied of any worldly possession and they were adhered to Him in equivalence of form. This means that they had no desire for any self-possession, but only to the extent that they could bestow contentment, so their Maker would delight in them.

And since their will to receive had clothed in an image of that object, it had clothed in it and bonded with it into complete oneness. Therefore, they were certainly liberated from the angel of death, for death is necessarily an absence and negation of the existence of something. But only while there is a spark that wishes to exist for its own pleasure is it possible to say about it that that spark does not exist because it has become absent and died.

However, if there is no such spark in man, but all the sparks of his selfness clothe in bestowal of contentment upon their Maker, then he neither becomes absent nor dies. For even when the body is annulled, it is only annulled with respect to self-reception, in which the will to receive is dressed and can only exist in it.

However, when he achieves the aim of creation and the Creator receives pleasure from him, since His will is done, man's essence, which clothes in His contentment, is granted complete eternity, like Him. Thus, he has been rewarded with freedom from the angel of death. This is the meaning of the words of the Midrash (*Midrash Rabbah, Shemot*, 41): "Freedom from the angel of death." And in the Mishna (*Avot*, Chapter 6): "*Harut* [carved] on the stones; do not pronounce it *Harut*, but rather *Herut* [freedom], for none are free, unless they engage in the study of Torah."

Introduction to The Book of Zohar

1) In this introduction, I would like to clarify matters that are seemingly simple, matters that everyone fumbles with and for which much ink has been spilled attempting to clarify. Yet we have not reached a concrete and sufficient knowledge of them.

Question No. 1: What is our essence?

Question No. 2: What is our role in the long chain of reality, of which we are but small links?

Question No. 3: When we examine ourselves, we find that we are so corrupted and low, and there is nothing more contemptible than us. And when we examine the Operator who has made us, we are compelled to be at the highest degree, for there is none so praiseworthy as Him, for it is necessary that only perfect operations will stem from a perfect operator.

4. Our mind asserts that He is The Good Who Does Good, and there is nothing higher than Him. How, then, did He create so many created beings that suffer and agonize all through their lives? Is it not the way of the good to do good, or at least not to do so much harm?

5. How is it possible that the infinite, who has neither beginning nor end, will produce finite, mortal, and flawed created beings?

2) In order to fully clarify all this, we need to make some preliminary inquiries, and not, God forbid, where it is forbidden, in the Creator's self, of which we have no thought or perception whatsoever, and thus have no thought or utterance of Him, but where we are commanded to inquire, meaning the inquiry of His deeds. It is as the Torah commands us: "Know the God of your father and serve Him," and as it says in the poem of unification, "By Your actions we know You."

Thus, inquiry No. 1 is, How can we picture a new creation, something new that is not included in Him before He creates it, when it is obvious to any observer that there is nothing that is not included in Him? Common sense also dictates it, for how can one give what one does not have?

Inquiry No. 2: If you say that from the aspect of His almightiness, of course He can create existence from absence, something new that is not in Him, there arises the question—what is this reality which can be determined as having no place in Him at all, but is completely new?

Inquiry No. 3: Kabbalists have said that man's soul is a part of God above, so there is no difference between Him and the soul, except He is the "whole" and the soul is a "part." They compared it to a rock carved from a mountain. There is no difference between the rock and the mountain, except that one is the "whole" and the other is a "part." Thus, we must ask: It is one thing that a stone carved from the mountain is separated from it by an ax made for that purpose, causing the separation of the "part" from the "whole." But how can you picture this about Him, that He will separate a part of His self until it departs His self and becomes separated from Him, meaning a soul, to the point that it can be understood only as part of His self?

3) Inquiry No. 4: Since the chariot of the Sitra Achra [other side] and the shells is so far from His holiness, from one end to other, until such remoteness is inconceivable, how can it be extended and made from holiness, much less that His holiness will sustain it?

Inquiry No. 5: The matter of the revival of the dead: Since the body is so contemptible that immediately at birth it is doomed to death and burial, and moreover, *The Zohar* said that before the body rots entirely, the soul cannot ascend to its place in the Garden of Eden, while there are still remnants of it. Therefore, why must it return and rise at the revival of the dead? Could the Creator not delight the souls without it?

Even more bewildering is what our sages said, that the dead are destined to rise with their flaws, so they will not be mistaken for another, and after that He will cure their flaws. We must understand why the Creator should mind that they would not be mistaken for another, to the point that for this He would recreate their flaws and then would have to cure it.

Inquiry No. 6: Regarding what our sages said, that man is the center of reality, that the upper worlds, this corporeal world, and everything in them, were created only for him (*The Zohar, Tazria*, 40), and obligated man to believe that the world had been created for him (*Sanhedrin* 37). It is seemingly hard to grasp that for this trifling human—whose value is no more than a wisp compared to the reality of this world, much less compared to all the upper worlds, whose height and sublimity is immeasurable—the Creator had troubled Himself to create all these for him. And also, why does man need all this?

4) To understand these questions and inquiries, the only tactic is to examine the end of the act, that is, the purpose of creation, for nothing can be understood in the middle of the process, but only at its end. And it is clear that there is no act without a purpose, for only the insane can act purposelessly.

I know that there are those who cast over their backs the burden of Torah and Mitzvot [pl. of Mitzva], saying the Creator has created the whole of reality, then left it alone, that because of the worthlessness of the created beings, it is not fitting for the exalted Creator to watch over their mean little ways. Indeed, without knowledge they have spoken, for it is impossible to decide on our lowliness and nothingness before we decide that we have created ourselves with all our corrupted and loathsome natures.

But while we decide that the Creator, who is utterly perfect, is the one who created and designed our bodies, with all their good and indecent inclinations, surely, there can never emerge an imperfect act under the hand of the perfect operator, as each act testifies to its performer. What fault is it of a bad garment if some no-good tailor made it?

Such as this we find in (*Masechet Taanit* 20): A tale about Rabbi Elazar, son of Rabbi Shimon, who came across a very ugly man. He said to him, "How ugly is that man." The man replied, "Go and tell the craftsman who made me, 'How ugly is this instrument that you have made.'" Thus, those who claim that because of our lowliness and nothingness, it is beneath Him to watch over us, and so He has left us, do nothing but display their ignorance.

Try to imagine if you were to meet a person who would create created beings precisely so they would suffer and agonize their whole lives as we do, and not only that, but cast them behind his back without even looking after them to help them a little. How contemptible and low you would regard him! Can such a thing be thought of Him?

5) Therefore, common sense dictates that we grasp the opposite of what appears to be on the surface, and decide that we are truly noble and worthy created beings, of immeasurable importance, meaning truly worthy of the worker who had made us. For any fault you wish to perceive in our bodies, behind all the excuses that you give to yourself, falls only on the Creator, who created us and the nature within us, for it is clear that He created us and not we.

He also knows all the ways that stem from the evil nature and attributes He has installed in us. It is as we have said, that we must contemplate the end of the act, and then we will be able to understand everything. It is as the saying goes, "Do not show a fool a job half done."

6) Our sages have already said (*Tree of Life, Shaar HaKlalim*, beginning of Chapter 1) that the Creator created the world for no other reason but to delight His created beings. And here is where we must place our minds and all our thoughts, for it is the ultimate aim of the act of the creation of the world.

We must bear in mind that since the thought of creation was to bestow upon His created beings, He had to create in the souls a great measure of desire to receive what He had thought to give them. For the measure of each pleasure and delight depends on the measure of the will to receive it. The greater the will to receive, the greater the pleasure; and the lesser the will to receive, to that extent, the pleasure from reception decreases. Thus, the thought of creation itself necessarily dictates the creation of an excessive will to receive in the souls, to fit the immense pleasure that His almightiness thought to bestow upon the souls, for the great delight and the great desire to receive go hand in hand.

7) Once we have learned this, we come to a full understanding of the second inquiry in complete clarity. We have learned what is the reality that can be clearly determined, which is not a part of His essence, to the extent that we can say that it is a new creation, existence from absence. Now that we know for certain that the thought of creation, to delight His created beings, necessarily created a quality of a desire to receive from Him all the goodness and pleasantness that He had planned for them, that will to receive was clearly not included in His essence before He created it in the souls, as from whom could He receive? It follows that He created something new that is not in Him.

And yet, we understand that according to the thought of creation, there was no need to create anything more than that will to receive since this new creation is sufficient for Him to fulfill the entire thought of creation, which He had thought to bestow upon us. But all the filling in the thought of creation, all the benefits He had planned to render us, stem directly from His self, and He has no reason to recreate them since they are already extended existence from existence to the great will to receive in the souls. Thus, we evidently see that all the substance in the innovated creation, from beginning to end, is only the will to receive.

8) Now we have come to understand the words of the Kabbalists in the third inquiry. We wondered how it was possible to say about the souls that they were a part of God above, like a stone that is carved from a mountain, that there is no difference between them except that one is a "part" and the other is the "whole." And we wondered: It is one thing to say that the stone that is carved from the mountain becomes separated by an ax made for that purpose, but how can you say this about His essence? And also, what was it that separated the souls from His essence and excluded them from the Creator to become created beings?

From the above, we clearly understand that as the ax cuts and splits a physical object in two, the disparity of form divides the spiritual into two. For example, when two people love one another, you say that they are attached to one another as one body. And when they hate one another, you say that they are as far from one another as the east from the west. But there is no issue of nearness or remoteness of location here. Rather, it implies equivalence of form: When they are equal in form, and one loves what the other loves and hates what the other hates, they love one another and are attached to one another.

And if there is some disparity of form between them, and one of them likes something that the other hates, to the extent that they differ in form, they become hateful and distant from one another. And if, for example, they are opposite in form, where everything that one likes, the other hates, and everything the other hates is liked by the first, they are regarded as remote as the east from the west, meaning from one end to the other.

9) You therefore find that in spirituality, the disparity of form acts like the ax that separates corporeal objects, and the measure of the distance is according to the measure of oppositeness of form. From this we learn that since the will to receive His delight has been imprinted in the souls, and we have shown that this form is absent in the Creator, as from whom would He receive, that disparity of form that the souls acquired separates them from His essence like the ax that carves a stone from the mountain. Because of that disparity of form, the souls were separated from the Creator and became created beings. However, everything the souls acquire of His light extends from His essence, existence from existence.

It follows that with respect to His light, which they receive in their vessel, which is the will to receive, there is no difference whatsoever between them and His essence, since they receive it existence from existence, directly from His essence. The only difference between the souls and His essence is that the souls are a part of His essence, meaning that the measure of light that they received in their vessel, being the will to receive, is already a separate part from the Creator, as it is predicated in the disparity of form of the will to receive. This disparity of form made it a part by which they were separated from the "whole" and became a "part." Thus, the only difference between them is that one is the "whole" and the other is a "part," as a stone that is carved from a mountain. Scrutinize this carefully, for it is impossible to elaborate further in such an exalted place.

10) Now we can begin to understand the fourth inquiry: How is it possible that the chariot of impurity and the shells would emerge from His holiness, since it is at the other end of His holiness? Also, how can it be that He supports and sustains it? Indeed, first we must understand the meaning of the existence of the impurity and the shells.

Know that this great will to receive, which we determined was the very essence of the souls by creation—for which they are fit to receive the entire filling in the thought of creation—does not remain in this form within the souls. Had it remained in them, they would have to remain eternally separated from Him since the disparity of form in them would separate them from Him.

In order to correct this separation, which lies on the vessel of the souls, He created all the worlds and separated them into two systems, as in the verse "God has made them one opposite the other." These are the four worlds ABYA of Kedusha [holiness], and opposite them the four worlds ABYA of impurity. And He imprinted the desire to bestow in the system of ABYA of Kedusha, and removed from them the will to receive for themselves, and placed it in the system of the worlds ABYA of impurity. Because of this, they have become separated from the Creator and from all the worlds of Kedusha.

For this reason, the shells are called "dead," as in the verse "sacrifices of the dead," and so are the wicked who follow them, as our sages said, "The wicked, in their lives, are called 'dead,'" since the will to receive imprinted in them in oppositeness of form to His holiness separates them from the Life of Lives, and they are far from Him from one end to the other. It is so because He has no interest in reception, only in bestowal, whereas the shells have no interest in bestowing, but only to receive for themselves, for their own delight, and there is no greater oppositeness than this. You already know that spiritual remoteness begins with some disparity of form and ends in oppositeness of form, which is the farthest possible distance in the last degree.

11) The worlds cascaded onto the reality of this corporeal world to a place where there is a body and a soul, and a time of corruption and a time of correction. For the body, which is the will to receive for oneself, extends from its root in the thought of creation through the system of the worlds of impurity, as it is written, "Man is born a wild ass's colt." He remains enslaved under the authority of that system for the first thirteen years, and this is the time of corruption.

By engaging in Mitzvot from thirteen years of age onward, in order to bestow contentment upon his Maker, he begins to purify the will to receive for himself, imprinted in him, and slowly turns it to the aim to bestow. By this he extends a holy soul from its root in the thought of creation. It passes through the system of the worlds of Kedusha and dresses in the body. This is the time of correction.

So he accumulates degrees of holiness from the thought of creation in Ein Sof [Infinity], until they aid him in turning the will to receive for himself in him, to be entirely in the form of reception in order to bestow contentment upon his Maker, and not at all for his own benefit. By this, one acquires equivalence of form with his Maker, for reception in order to bestow is regarded as pure bestowal.

It is written in *Masechet Kidushin*, p 7, that with an important man, she gives and he says—by this you are sanctified. Because when his reception is in order to delight the one who gives him, it is deemed absolute bestowal and giving. Thus, one acquires complete adhesion with Him, for spiritual adhesion is but equivalence of form, as our sages said, "How is it possible to adhere unto Him? Rather, adhere on to His qualities." By this, one becomes worthy of receiving all the delight, pleasure, and gentleness in the thought of creation.

12) Thus we have clearly explained the correction of the will to receive, imprinted in the souls by the thought of creation. For the Creator has prepared for them two systems, one opposite the other, through which the souls pass and become divided into two discernments, body and soul, which dress in one another.

Through Torah and Mitzvot, they finally turn the form of the will to receive to be as the form of the desire to bestow, and then they can receive all the goodness in the thought of creation. And along with it, they are rewarded with a strong adhesion with Him, because through the work in Torah and Mitzvot, they have been rewarded with equivalence of form with their Maker. This is regarded as the end of correction.

Then, since there will no longer be any need for the foul Sitra Achra [other side], it will be eliminated from the earth and death will be swallowed up forever. And all the work in Torah and Mitzvot that was given to the world in general during the six thousand years of the existence of the world, and to each person during one's seventy years of life, is only to bring them to the end of correction—the above-mentioned equivalence of form.

The issue of the formation and extension of the system of shells and impurity from His holiness has also been thoroughly clarified now: It was necessary in order to extend by it the creation of the bodies, which would then be corrected through Torah and Mitzvot. If our bodies, with their corrupted will to receive, were not extended through the system of impurity, we would never be able to correct it, for one does not correct that which is not in him.

13) Indeed, we still need to understand how the will to receive for oneself, which is so flawed and corrupted, could extend from, and be in the thought of creation in Ein Sof, whose unity is beyond words and beyond description. The thing is that by the very thought to create the souls, His thought completed everything, for He does not need an act, as do we. Instantaneously, all the souls and worlds that were destined to be created emerged filled with all the delight and pleasure and the gentleness that He had planned for them, in the final perfection that the souls were destined to receive at the end of correction, after the will to receive in the souls has been fully corrected and has turned into pure bestowal, in complete equivalence of form with the Emanator.

This is so because in His eternalness, past, present, and future are as one. The future is as the present, and there is no such thing as time in Him (*The Zohar*, *Mishpatim*, Item 51, *New Zohar*, *Beresheet*, Item 243). Hence, there was never an issue of a corrupted will to receive in its separated state in Ein Sof.

On the contrary, that equivalence of form, destined to be revealed at the end of correction, appeared instantly in His eternalness. Our sages said about this (*Pirkei de Rabbi Eliezer*): "Before the world was created, there were He is one and His name One," for the separated form in the will to receive had not been revealed in the reality of the souls that emerged in the thought of creation. Rather, they were adhered to Him in equivalence of form by way of "He is one and His name One."

14) Thus you necessarily find that on the whole, there are three states to the soul:

The First State is their existence in Ein Sof, in the thought of creation, where they already have the future form of the end of correction.

The Second State is their existence during the six thousand years, which were divided by the above two systems into a body and a soul. They were given the work in Torah and Mitzvot in order to invert their will to receive and turn it into a desire to bestow contentment upon their Maker, and not at all for themselves.

During the time of that state, no correction will come to the bodies, only to the souls. This means that they must eliminate from within them any form of self-reception, which is considered the body, and remain with but a desire to bestow, which is the form of the desire in the souls. Even the souls of the righteous will not be able to rejoice in the Garden of Eden after their demise, but only after their bodies have completely rotted in the dust.

The Third State is the end of the correction of the souls after the revival of the dead. At that time, the complete correction will come to the bodies, too, for then they will turn reception for themselves, which is the form of the body, to take on the form of pure bestowal, and they will become worthy of receiving for themselves all the delight, pleasure, and pleasantness in the thought of creation.

And with all that, they will attain strong adhesion by the force of their equivalence of form with their Maker, since they will not receive all this because of their desire to receive, but because of their desire to bestow contentment upon their Maker, since He derives pleasure when they receive from Him. For purposes of brevity, from now on I will use the names of these three states, namely "first state," "second state," and "third state," and you will remember all that is explained here in every state.

15) When you examine the above three states, you will find that one completely necessitates the other, in a way that if one were to be canceled, the others would be canceled, too.

For example, if the third state—the inversion of the form of reception to the form of bestowal—had not been revealed, it is certain that the first state in Ein Sof would never have been able to emerge, since the wholeness emerged there only because the future third state was already there, as though it is the present. All the wholeness that was depicted there in that state is like a reflection from the future into the present. But if the future could be canceled, there would not be any present. Thus, the third state necessitates the existence of the first state.

It is all the more so when something is canceled in the second state, where there is all the work that is destined to be completed in the third state, the work in corruptions and corrections and the extensions of the degrees of the souls. Thus, how will the third state come to be? Hence, the second state necessitates the third state.

And so it is with the existence of the first state in Ein Sof, where the wholeness of the third state already exists. It necessitates that it will be adapted, meaning that the second and third states will be revealed in the complete wholeness that is there, no less and no more in any way.

Thus, the first state itself necessitates the expansion of two corresponding systems in the second state, to allow for the existence of a body in the corrupted will to receive, through the system of impurity, and then we can correct it. Had there not been the system of the worlds of impurity, we would not have that will to receive and we would not be able to correct it and achieve the third state, for one cannot correct that which is not in him. Thus, we need not ask how the system of impurity came to be from the first state, for it is the first state that necessitates its existence in the form of the second state.

16) Therefore, one might wonder if perhaps choice had been taken from us, since we must be completed and come to the third state, since it is already present in the first. The thing is that the Creator has prepared for us two ways in the second state in order to bring us to the third state:

The first is the path of observing Torah and Mitzvot [commandments], as has been explained above.

The second is the path of suffering, since the suffering itself purifies the body and will eventually compel us to invert our will to receive into the form of a desire to bestow, and cling to Him. It is as our sages said (*Sanhedrin* 97b), "If you repent, good; and if not, I will place over you a king such as Haman who will force you to repent." Our sages said about the verse "will hasten it in its time": "If they are rewarded, I will hasten it; and if not, in its time."

This means that if we are rewarded through the first path, by observing Torah and Mitzvot, we thus hasten our correction, and we do not need the harsh and bitter agony and the long time needed to experience them, so they will compel us to reform. And if not, "in its time," meaning only when the suffering completes our correction and the time of correction is forced upon us. And the punishments of the souls in Hell are also included in the path of suffering.

But one way or the other, the end of correction, namely the third state, is mandatory because of the first state. Our choice is only between the path of suffering and the path of Torah and Mitzvot. Thus we have thoroughly clarified how the three states of the souls are interconnected and necessitate one another.

17) From all the above, we thoroughly understand the third inquiry we asked, that when we examine ourselves, we find ourselves to be as corrupted and as contemptible as can be. But when we examine the Operator who created us, we must be at the highest level, of which there is none more praiseworthy as He, as becoming of the Operator who created us, because the nature of the perfect Operator is to perform perfect operations.

Now we can understand that our body, with all its trifle incidents and possessions, is not at all our real body. Our real, eternal, and complete body already exists in Ein Sof, in the first state, where it receives its complete form from the future third state, that is, receiving in the form of bestowal, in equivalence of form with Ein Sof.

And if our first state necessitates that we receive the shell of our body in the second state, in its corrupted and loathsome form, which is the will to receive for oneself alone, which is the force that separates us from Ein Sof, so as to correct it and allow us to receive our eternal body in actual fact, in the third state, we need not resent it. Our work can only be done in this transitory and wasteful body, for "one does not correct that which is not in him."

Thus, we are already in that measure of wholeness worthy and fitting of the perfect Operator who has made us, even in our current, second state. This body does not blemish us in any way since it is destined to expire and die, and had been prepared for us only for the duration required in order to cancel it and acquire our eternal form.

18) This settles our fifth inquiry: How could it be that transitory, momentary, and worthless actions would extend from the eternal? According to the above, we see that, indeed, we have already been extended as is fitting for His eternalness—eternal and perfect beings. Our eternalness requires that the shell of the body, which was given to us only for work, be transitory and wasteful. If it remained in eternity, we would remain forever separated from the Life of Lives.

We have said before, in Item 13, that this form of our body, which is the will to receive for ourselves alone, is not at all present in the eternal thought of creation, for there we are in the form of the third state. Yet, it is mandatory in the second state, in order to allow us to correct it.

We must not ponder the state of the rest of the beings in the world besides man, since man is the center of creation, as will be written below in Item 39. All other created beings do not have any value in themselves, but to the extent that they help man achieve his wholeness. Hence, they rise and fall with him without any consideration of themselves.

19) With this we settle our fourth inquiry: Since the nature of the good is to do good, how did He create beings that would be tormented and agonized throughout their lives? As we have said, all this agony is necessitated from our first state, where our complete eternity, which comes from the future third state, compels us to go either by the path of Torah or by the path of suffering, and reach our eternal state in the third state (as said in Item 15).

And all this agony is felt only by the shell of our body, created only to be perished and buried. This teaches us that the will to receive for oneself in us was created only to be eradicated, abolished from the world, and be turned into a desire to bestow. The pains we suffer are but revelations of its nothingness and the harm in it. Indeed, when all human beings agree to abolish and eradicate their will to receive for themselves and have no other desire but to bestow upon their friends, all worries and harm-doers in the world would cease to exist. We would all be assured of a healthy and complete life, since each of us would have a whole world caring for us, and satisfying all our needs.

Yet, while each of us has only a desire to receive for oneself, this is the source of all the worries, suffering, wars, and slaughter we cannot escape. They weaken our bodies with all sorts of sores and maladies, and you find that all the agonies in our world are but manifestations offered to our eyes, to prompt us to revoke the evil shell of the body and assume the complete form of the desire to bestow. It is as we have said, that the path of suffering itself can bring us to the desired form. Bear in mind that the Mitzvot between man and man come before the Mitzvot between man and the Creator since bestowing upon one's friend brings one to bestow upon the Creator.

20) After all that we have said, we come to the resolution of our first inquiry: What is our essence? Our essence is as the essence of all the details in reality, which is no more and no less than the will to receive, as written in Item 7. But it is not as it is now, in the second state, which is the will to receive only for oneself, but as it stands in the first state, in Ein Sof, in its eternal form, which is reception in order to bestow contentment upon his Maker, as written in Item 13.

Although we have not yet reached the third state in actual fact, and we still need time, it does not blemish our essence whatsoever, since our third state is necessitated from the first. Thus, "all that is bound to be collected is deemed collected." And the need for time is regarded a deficiency only where there is doubt whether one will complete what needs to be completed in time.

But since we have no doubt about it, it is as though we have already reached the third state. And that body, too, given to us in its present, corrupted form, does not blemish our essence, since it and all its possessions are to be completely eradicated along with the whole system of impurity, which is their source, and all that is bound to be burned is deemed burned, regarded as though it never existed.

But the soul that is dressed in that body, whose essence is also purely a desire—but a desire to bestow, which is extended to us from the system of the four worlds of ABYA of Kedusha—exists forever, as written in Item 11. This is because this form of a desire to bestow is in equivalence of form with the Life of Lives and is not in any way exchangeable. This matter will be completed below, from Item 32 onward.

21) Do not be led astray by the philosophers who say that the very essence of the soul is an intellectual substance, and that it only exists through the concepts it learns, that it grows through them and that they are its very essence. And the question of the persistence of the soul after the departure of the body depends entirely on the extent of concepts it has acquired, until in the absence of the concepts, there remains nothing to continue. This is not the view of Torah. It is also unacceptable, and anyone who ever tried to acquire knowledge knows and feels that the mind is a possession and not the actual possessor.

But as we have said, the whole substance of the innovated creation, both the substance of the spiritual objects and the substance of the corporeal objects, is no more and no less than a desire to receive. Although we said that the soul is entirely a desire to bestow, it is only through corrections of clothing of reflected light that it receives from the upper worlds, from which it comes to us. The meaning of this clothing is thoroughly explained in "Preface to the Wisdom of Kabbalah," Items 14, 15, 16, and 19.

Yet, the very essence of the soul is a will to receive, as well. And the only difference we can tell between one object and another is only by its desire, for the desire in any essence creates needs, and the needs create thoughts and concepts so as to obtain those needs, which the will to receive demands.

As human desires differ from one another, so do their needs, thoughts, and ideas. For instance, those whose will to receive is limited to beastly desires, their needs, thoughts, and ideas are dedicated to satisfying that will to receive in its entire beastliness. Although they use the mind and reason as humans do, it is, however, enough for the slave to be as his master. And it is like the beastly mind, since the mind is enslaved and serves the beastly desire.

And those whose will to receive is strong mainly in human desires—such as respect and control over others—which are absent in the beast, the majority of their needs, thoughts, and ideas revolve solely around satisfying that desire as much as they can. And those whose will to receive is intensified mainly for acquisition of knowledge, the majority of their needs, thoughts, and ideas are to satisfy that desire as much as they can.

22) These three desires are present in most every person; however, they are merged in different quantities in each one, hence the difference from one person to another. And from the corporeal attributes we can deduce about the attributes of spiritual objects according to their spiritual value.

23) Thus, spiritual human souls—through the clothing of reflected light that they receive from the upper worlds from which they come—have only a desire to bestow contentment upon their Maker. That desire is their essence and the core of the soul. It turns out that once dressed in a human body, it generates needs and thoughts and ideas to satisfy its desire to bestow to the fullest, meaning to bestow contentment upon its Maker, according to the measure of its desire.

24) The core and the essence of the body is but a desire to receive for itself, and all its incidents and possessions are fulfillments of that corrupted will to receive, which had initially been created only to be eradicated from the world in order to achieve the complete third state at the end of correction. For this reason, it is mortal, transitory, and contemptible, along with all its possessions, like a fleeting shadow that leaves nothing in its wake.

Since the core and the essence of the soul is but a desire to bestow, and all its incidents and possessions are fulfillments of that desire to bestow, which already exists in the eternal first state, as well as in the future third state, it is immortal and irreplaceable. Rather, it and all its possessions are eternal and exist forever. Absence does not apply to them at all when the body dies. On the contrary, the absence of the form of the corrupted body greatly strengthens it and enables it to rise to the Garden of Eden.

Thus we have clearly shown that the persistence of the soul in no way depends upon the concepts it has acquired, as philosophers claim. Rather, its eternity is in its very essence, in its desire to bestow, which is its essence. And the concepts it acquires are its reward, not its essence.

25) From here stems the full resolution of the fifth inquiry: Since the body is so corrupted that the soul is not in all its purity before the body rots in the ground, why does it return at the revival of the dead? And also, the question about the words of our sages: "The dead are destined to be revived with their flaws, so it will not be said, 'It is another'" (*The Zohar*, Emor, 17).

And you will clearly understand this matter from the thought of creation itself, from the first state. We have said that since the thought was to delight His creations, He had to create an overwhelmingly excessive will to receive all that bounty, which is in the thought of creation, for "the great delight and the great will to receive go hand in hand," as said in Items 6-7. We stated there that this excessive will to receive is all the new substance He had created, for He needs nothing more than that in order to carry out the thought of creation. And it is the nature of the perfect Operator not to perform redundant operations, as written in the Poem of Unification: "Of all Your work, not a thing did You forget, omit, or add."

We also said there that this excessive will to receive has been completely removed from the system of Kedusha and was given entirely to the system of the worlds of impurity, from which come the bodies, their sustenance, and all their possessions in this world. When one reaches thirteen years of age, he begins to attain a holy soul through engaging in the Torah. At that time, he is nourished by the system of the worlds of Kedusha according to the measure of the soul of Kedusha he has attained.

We also said above that during the six thousand years that are given to us for work in Torah and Mitzvot, no corrections come from this to the body, meaning to the excessive will to receive in it. All the corrections that come through our work relate only to the soul, which climbs through them on the degrees of Kedusha and purity, meaning only to increase the desire to bestow that is extended with the soul.

For this reason, the body will ultimately die, be buried, and rot since it did not undergo any correction. Yet, it cannot remain that way, for if the excessive will to receive perished from the world, the thought of creation would not be realized—meaning the reception of all the great pleasures that He intended to bestow upon His created beings, for "the great will to receive and the great pleasure go hand in hand." And to the extent that the desire to receive it is diminished, to that extent the delight and pleasure from reception are diminished.

26) We have already stated that the first state necessitates the third state, to emerge to the full extent that is in the thought of creation in the first state, not omitting anything of it, as said in Item 15. Therefore, the first state necessitates the revival of the dead bodies. That means that their excessive will to receive, which had already been eradicated and rotted in the second state, must now be revived in all its excessive measure, without any restraints, meaning with all its past flaws.

Then begins the work anew, to invert that excessive will to receive to work only to bestow. And then we will have doubled our gain:

1. We would have a place to receive all the delight and pleasure and gentleness in the thought of creation, since we would already have a body with its greatly excessive will to receive, which goes hand in hand with these pleasures.

2. Since our reception in that manner would be only in order to bestow contentment upon our Maker, that reception would be regarded as complete bestowal, as said in Item 11. That would bring us to equivalence of form, which is adhesion, which is our form in the third state. Thus, the first state absolutely necessitates the revival of the dead.

27) Indeed, there cannot be revival for the dead, but only near the end of correction, toward the end of the second state. For once we have been rewarded with denying our excessive will to receive, and have been granted the will to only bestow, and once we have been endowed with all the wonderful degrees of the soul, called Nefesh, Ruach, Neshama, Haya, Yechida, through our work at negating this will to receive, we have come to the greatest perfection, until the body could be revived with all its excessive will to receive, and we are no longer harmed by it by being separated from our adhesion.

On the contrary, we overcome it and give it the form of bestowal. Indeed, this is done with every corrupt quality that we wish to remove from ourselves. 1) We must completely remove it until there is nothing left of it. 2) Next, we can receive it again and conduct it in the middle way. But as long as we have not fully removed it from ourselves, it is impossible to conduct it in the desired, medium way.

28) Our sages said, "The dead are destined to be revived with their flaws, and then be healed." This means that in the beginning, the same body is revived, which is the excessive will to receive, without any restraints, just as it grew under the Merkava [structure] of the worlds of impurity, before the Torah and Mitzvot have purified it in any way. This is the meaning of "with all their flaws."

Next, we embark on a new kind of labor—to insert all that excessive will to receive in the form of bestowal. Then it is healed, because now it obtained equivalence of form. And they said that the reason is "so it will not be said, 'It is another,'" meaning so it will not be said about it that it is in a different form than the one it had in the thought of creation. This is so because that excessive will to receive stands there, aiming to receive all the bounty in the thought of creation.

It is only that in the meantime it has been given to the shells for purification. But in the end, it must not be a different body, for if it were diminished in any way, it would be deemed entirely different, and thus unworthy of receiving all the bounty in the thought of creation, as it receives there in the manner of the first state.

29) Now we can resolve the above second inquiry: What is our role in the long chain of reality, of which we are but tiny links, during the short span of our days? Know that our work during the seventy years of our days is divided into four divisions.

The first division is to obtain the excessive will to receive without restraints in its full, corrupted measure from under the hands of the four impure worlds ABYA. If we do not have that corrupted will to receive, we will not be able to correct it, for "one cannot correct that which is not in him."

Thus, the will to receive imprinted in the body at birth is insufficient. Rather, it must also be a chariot for the impure shells for no less than thirteen years. This means that the shells must control it and give it from their lights, for their lights increase its will to receive. That is because the fulfillments that the shells grant the will to receive only expand the demands of the will to receive.

For example, at birth, he has a desire for only a hundred, and not more. But when the Sitra Achra provides the one hundred, the will to receive immediately grows and wants two hundred. Then, when the Sitra Achra provides fulfillment for the two hundred, the desire immediately expands and wants four hundred. If one does not overcome it through Torah and Mitzvot, and purifies the will to receive to turn it into bestowal, one's will to receive expands throughout one's life until eventually he dies without obtaining half his wishes. This is regarded as being under the authority of the Sitra Achra and the shells, whose role is to expand and enhance his will to receive and make it exaggerated and completely unrestrained, to provide one with all the material he needs to work with and correct.

30) The second division is from thirteen years and on. At that time, the point in his heart, which is the posterior of the soul of Kedusha, is given strength. Although it is dressed in his will to receive at birth, it only begins to awaken after thirteen years, for the above-said reason, and then one begins to enter the authority of the system of the worlds of Kedusha to the extent that one engages in Torah and Mitzvot.

The primary purpose of that time is to obtain and intensify the spiritual will to receive, since at birth, one has only a will to receive for corporeality. Therefore, although one has obtained the excessive will to receive before he turned thirteen, it is still not the completion of the growth of the will to receive, for the primary intensification of the will to receive is only to spirituality.

This is because, for example, prior to turning thirteen, one's will to receive wishes to devour all the wealth and respect in this corporeal world. This is evidently not an eternal world, and for all of us it is but a fleeting shadow. But when one obtains the excessive spiritual will to receive, one wishes to devour, for one's own delight, all the wealth and delights in the next, eternal world, which is an eternal possession for him. Thus, the majority of the excessive will to receive is completed only with the desire to receive spirituality.

31) It is written (in *New Tikkunim* 97b) about the verse (Proverbs 30), "The leech has two daughters: 'Give, give.'": "A leech means Hell. And the wicked ones who are caught in that Hell cry as dogs '*Hav! Hav!* [give, give],'" meaning "give us the wealth of this world, give us the wealth of the next world."

Yet it is a much more important degree than the first, since aside from obtaining the full measure of the will to receive, giving one all the material one needs for one's work, this is the degree that brings one to Lishma [for Her sake]. It is as our sages said (*Pesachim* 50b): "One should always engage in Torah and Mitzvot Lo Lishma [not for Her sake], as from Lo Lishma, one comes to Lishma."

Hence, this degree, which comes past the thirteen years, is deemed Kedusha. This is considered the holy maid that serves her mistress, which is the holy Shechina [Divinity], since the maid brings one to Lishma and he is rewarded with the instilling of the Shechina. Yet, one should take every measure suited to come to Lishma, for if one does not strain for this and does not achieve Lishma, he will fall into the trap of the impure maid, which is the opposite of the holy maid, whose role is to confuse a person, so the Lo Lishma will not bring him to Lishma. It is said about her: "A handmaid that is heir to her mistress" (Proverbs 30), for she will not let one near the mistress, who is the Holy Shechina.

And the final degree in this division is that he will fall passionately in love with the Creator, as one becomes infatuated in a corporeal love, until the passion remains before one's eyes all day and all night, as the poet says, "When I remember Him, He does not let me sleep." Then it is said of him: "A desire fulfilled is a tree of life" (Proverbs 13). This is because the five degrees of the soul are the Tree of Life, which stretches over five hundred years. Each degree lasts a hundred years, meaning it will bring him to receive all five discernments NRNHY [Nefesh, Ruach, Neshama, Haya, Yechida] explained in the third division.

32) The third division is the work in Torah and Mitzvot Lishma, in order to bestow and not receive reward. This work cleanses the will to receive for oneself in him and inverts it into a desire to bestow. To the extent that one purifies the will to receive, he becomes suitable and able to receive the five parts of the soul called NRNHY (below Item 42). This is because they stand in the desire to bestow (see Item 23) and cannot clothe one's body as long as the will to receive—which is opposite, or even different in form from the soul—controls it.

That is because the matter of clothing and equivalence of form go hand in hand, as said in Item 11. When one is rewarded with being entirely in the desire to bestow and not at all for oneself, he will be rewarded with obtaining equivalence of form with his upper NRNHY, which extend from their origin in Ein Sof in the first state, through the ABYA of Kedusha, and will immediately extend to him and clothe him in a gradual manner.

The fourth division is the work conducted after the revival of the dead. This means that the will to receive, which had already been completely absent through death and burial, is now revived in its excessive, worst will to receive, as our sages said, "The dead will be revived with their flaws," as written in Item 28. At that time, it is turned into reception in the form of bestowal. However, there are a chosen few who were given this work while still alive in this world.

33) Now remains the clarification of the sixth inquiry, which is the words of our sages who said that all the worlds, upper and lower, were created only for man. It seems very peculiar that for man, whose worth is but a wisp compared to the reality before us in this world, much less compared to the upper, spiritual worlds, the Creator would go to all the trouble of creating all these for him. And even more peculiar is what would man need all these vast spiritual worlds for?

You should know that any contentment of our Maker from bestowing upon His creations depends on the extent that the created beings feel Him—that He is the giver, and He is the one who delights them. Then He takes great pleasure in them, as a father playing with his beloved son, to the extent that the son feels and recognizes the greatness and exaltedness of his father, and his father shows him all the treasures he had prepared for him, as it is written (Jeremiah 31): "Ephraim, my darling son, is he a child of joy? For whenever I speak of him, I do remember him still. Hence, My heart yearns for him, I will surely have mercy on him, says the Lord."

Observe these words carefully and you can come to know the great delights of the Lord with those whole ones who have been granted feeling Him and recognizing His greatness in all those manners He has prepared for them, until they are like a father with his darling son, like a father with his child of joy. We need not continue about this, for it is enough for us to know that for this contentment and delight with those whole ones, it was worth His while to create all the worlds, higher and lower alike.

34) To prepare His creations to attain the aforementioned exalted degree, the Creator wanted to do it by an order of four degrees that evolve from one another, called "still," "vegetative," "animate," and "speaking." These are, in fact, the four phases of the will to receive, by which the upper worlds are divided. For although the majority of the desire is in phase four of the will to receive, it is impossible for phase four to appear at once, but by its preceding three phases, in which, and through which, it gradually develops and becomes revealed until it is fully completed in the form of phase four, as explained in *The Study of the Ten Sefirot*, Part 1, Item 50.

35) In phase one of the will to receive, called "still," which is the initial manifestation of the will to receive in this corporeal world, there is but a collective force of movement for the whole of the still category. But no motion is apparent in its particular items. This is because the will to receive generates needs, and the needs

generate sufficient movements to satisfy the need. Since there is only a small will to receive, it dominates only the whole of the category at once, but its power over the particular items is indistinguishable.

36) The vegetative is added to it, which is phase two of the will to receive. Its measure is greater than in the still, and its will to receive dominates each and every one of its items, since each item has its own movement, expanding to the length and to the width, and moving toward the sun. Also, the matter of eating, drinking, and secretion of waste is also apparent in each item. However, the sensation of freedom and individuality is still absent in them.

37) Atop that comes the animate category, which is phase three of the will to receive. Its measure is already completed to a great extent, for this will to receive already generates in each item a sensation of freedom and individuality, which is the life that is unique to each unit separately. Yet, they still lack the sensation of others, meaning they have no preparation to share others' pains or joys.

38) Above all comes the human species, which is phase four of the will to receive. It is the complete and final measure, and its will to receive includes the sensation of others, as well. And if you wish to know the precise difference between phase three of the will to receive, which is in the animate, and the fourth phase of the will to receive in man, I will tell you that it is as the value of a single created being compared to the whole of reality.

This is because the will to receive in the animate, which lacks the sensation of others, can only generate needs and desires to the extent that they are imprinted in that creature alone. But man, who can feel others, too, becomes needy of everything that others have, too, and is thus filled with envy to acquire everything that others have. If he has a hundred, he wants two hundred, and so his deficiencies and needs forever grow until he wishes to devour all that there is in the whole world.

39) Now we have shown that the Creator's desired goal for the creation He had created is to bestow upon His creations, so they would know His truthfulness and greatness, and receive all the delight and pleasure He had prepared for them, in the measure described in the verse "Ephraim my darling son, is he a child of joy?" Thus, you clearly find that this purpose does not apply to the still and the great spheres, such as the earth, the moon, or the sun, however luminous and vast they may be, and not to the vegetative or the animate, for they lack the sensation of others, even from among their own species. Therefore, how can the sensation of the Godly and His bestowal apply to them?

Humankind alone, having been prepared with the sensation of others of the same species, who are similar to them, after working in Torah and Mitzvot, when they invert their will to receive to a desire to bestow and achieve equivalence of form with their Maker, they receive all the degrees that have been prepared for them in the upper worlds, called NRNHY. By this they become qualified to receive the purpose of the thought of creation. Thus, the purpose of the creation of all the worlds was for man alone.

40) And I know that it is completely unacceptable in the eyes of some philosophers. They cannot agree that man, whom they regard as ignoble and worthless, is the center of the great and sublime creation. But they are like a worm that was born inside a radish. It lives there and thinks that the world of the Creator is as bitter, dark, and small as the radish in which it was born. But as soon as it breaks the peel of the radish and peeps out, it says in bewilderment: "I thought the whole world was like the radish I was born in, and now I see a grand, enlightened, beautiful, and wondrous world before me!"

So, too, are those who are immersed in the shell of the will to receive they were born with, and did not try to take the unique spice, which are the practical Torah and Mitzvot, which can break this hard shell and turn it into a desire to bestow contentment upon the Maker. It is certain that they must determine according to their worthlessness and emptiness, as they truly are. They cannot comprehend that this vast reality had been created only for them.

Indeed, had they engaged in Torah and Mitzvot to bestow contentment upon their Maker, with all the required purity, and would try to break the shell of the will to receive in which they were born, and would assume the desire to bestow, their eyes would promptly open to see and attain for themselves all the degrees of wisdom, intelligence, and clear mind that have been prepared for them in the spiritual worlds. Then they would say for themselves what our sages said, "What does a good guest say? 'Everything the host has done, he has done only for me.'"

41) But there still remains to clarify why man needs all the upper worlds the Creator had created for him? What use has he of them? Bear in mind that the reality of all the worlds is generally divided into five worlds, called a) Adam Kadmon, b) Atzilut, c) Beria, d) Yetzira, and e) Assiya. In each of them are innumerable details, which are the five Sefirot KHBTM [Keter, Hochma, Bina, Tifferet, and Malchut]. The world of AK [Adam Kadmon] is Keter, the world of Atzilut is Hochma, the world of Beria is Bina, the world of Yetzira is Tifferet, and the world Assiya is Malchut.

The lights clothed in those five worlds are called YHNRN. The light of Yechida shines in the world of Adam Kadmon, the light of Haya in the world of Atzilut, the light of Neshama in the world of Beria, the light of Ruach in the world of Yetzira, and the light of Nefesh in the world of Assiya.

All these worlds and everything in them are included in the holy name, Yod-Hey-Vav-Hey, and the tip of the Yod. We have no perception in the first world, AK. Hence, it is only implied in the tip of the Yod of the name. This is why we do not speak of it and always mention only the four worlds ABYA. Yod is the world of Atzilut, Hey–the world of Beria, Vav–the world of Yetzira, and the bottom Hey is the world of Assiya.

42) We have now explained the five worlds that include the entire spiritual reality that extends from Ein Sof to this world. However, they are incorporated in one another, and in each of the worlds there are the five worlds, the five Sefirot KHBTM, in which the five lights NRNHY are dressed, corresponding to the five worlds.

And besides the five Sefirot KHBTM in each world, there are the four spiritual phases: still, vegetative, animate, and speaking—where 1. man's soul is regarded as the speaking, 2. the animate is regarded as the angels in that world, 3. the vegetative category is called "dresses," 4. and the still category is called "halls." Also, they all robe one another: The speaking category, which is the souls of people, clothes the five Sefirot KHBTM, which is the Godliness in that world (the matter of the ten Sefirot, which are Godliness, will be explained in the "Preface to The Book of Zohar"). The animate category, which is the angels, clothes over the souls; the vegetative, which is the dresses, clothe the angels; and the still, which is halls, surround them all.

This clothing means that they serve one another and evolve from one another, as we have explained concerning the corporeal still, vegetative, animate, and speaking in this world (Items 35-38). As we said there, the three phases—still, vegetative, and animate—did not emerge for themselves, but only so the fourth phase, which is man, might develop and rise by them. Therefore, their role is only to serve man and be useful to him.

So it is in all the spiritual worlds. The three phases—still, vegetative, and animate—appeared there only to serve and be useful to the speaking phases there, which is man's soul. Therefore, it is considered that they all clothe man's soul, meaning to serve him.

43) When man is born, he immediately has Nefesh of Kedusha [holiness]. Yet, not actually Nefesh, but the posterior phase of Nefesh, meaning its last phase, which, due to its smallness, is called a "dot." It clothes man's heart in one's will to receive, which is found primarily in man's heart.

Know this rule, that all that applies to the whole of reality applies to each world, even in the smallest particle that can be found in that world. Thus, as there are five worlds in the whole of reality, which are the five Sefirot KHBTM, so there are five Sefirot KHBTM in each and every world, and five Sefirot in every little element in that world.

We have said that this world is divided into still, vegetative, animate, and speaking, corresponding to the four Sefirot HBTM: 1) still corresponds to Malchut, 2) vegetative corresponds to Tifferet, 3) animate to Bina, and 4) speaking to Hochma. 5) And the root of them all corresponds to Keter. But as we have said, even in a single element from each and every category in the still, vegetative, animate, and speaking contains the four categories of still, vegetative, animate, and speaking. Hence, even in a single element of the speaking category, meaning even in one person, there are also still, vegetative, animate, and speaking, which are the four parts of his will to receive, where the dot from the Nefesh of Kedusha is clothed.

44) Prior to the thirteen years, there cannot be any revelation of the point in one's heart. But after thirteen years, when he begins to engage in Torah and Mitzvot, even without any intention, meaning without love and fear, as is fitting when serving the King, even in Lo Lishma, the point in one's heart begins to grow and show its action.

This is so because Mitzvot do not need an intention. Even actions without intentions can purify one's will to receive, but only in the first degree, called "still." To the extent that he purifies the still part of the will to receive, he builds the 613 organs of the point in the heart, which is the still of the Nefesh of Kedusha.

And when one completes all 613 Mitzvot in action, it completes the 613 organs in the point in the heart, which is the still of the Nefesh of Kedusha, whose 248 spiritual organs are built by observing the 248 Mitzvot to do, and its 365 spiritual tendons are built through observing the 365 Mitzvot not to do, until it becomes a complete Partzuf of Nefesh of Kedusha. Then the Nefesh rises and clothes the Sefira [sing. of Sefirot] of Malchut in the spiritual world of Assiya.

And all the spiritual elements of still, vegetative, and animate in that world, which correspond to that Sefira of Malchut of Assiya, serve and aid that Partzuf of Nefesh of one who has risen there, to the extent that the soul perceives them. Those concepts become its spiritual nourishment, giving it strength to grow and multiply until it can extend the light of the Sefira of Malchut of Assiya in all the desired completeness to shine in man's body. And that complete light helps one add exertion in Torah and Mitzvot and receive the remaining degrees.

And we have stated that immediately at the birth of man's body, a point of the light of Nefesh is born and dresses in him. So it is here: When his Partzuf of Nefesh of Kedusha is born, a point from its adjacent higher degree is born with it, meaning the last degree of the light of Ruach of Assiya, and dresses inside the Partzuf of Nefesh.

So it is in all the degrees. With each degree that is born, the last phase in the degree above it instantaneously appears within it. This is because this is the whole connection between the upper one and the lower one up to the highest degree. Thus, through this point, which exists in it from the upper one, it becomes able to rise to the next higher degree.

45) And that light of Nefesh is called "the light of the still of Kedusha in the world Assiya," since it corresponds to the purity of the still part of the will to receive in man's body. It shines in spirituality like the still category in corporeality. It has been explained above, in Item 35, that its particles have no individual motion, but only a collective motion, common to all the elements equally. So it is with the light of Partzuf Nefesh of Assiya: Although there are 613 organs in it, which are 613 different

forms in the manners of receiving the abundance, these differences are not apparent in it, but only a general light, whose action enfolds all of them equally, without distinction of the particular elements in it.

46) Bear in mind that although the Sefirot are Godliness, and there is no difference in them from the top of Keter in the world of AK to the bottom of the Sefira of Malchut in the world of Assiya, there is still a great difference with respect to the receivers, since the Sefirot are considered lights and vessels, and the light in the Sefirot is pure Godliness. But the vessels, called KHBTM in each of the lower worlds—Beria, Yetzira, Assiya—are not considered Godliness. Rather, they are covers that conceal the light of Ein Sof within them and ration a certain amount of its light to the receivers, so each of them will receive only according to the level of its purity.

In this respect, although the light itself is one, we name the lights in the Sefirot NRNHY because the light is divided according to the qualities of the vessels. Malchut is the coarsest cover, hiding the light of Ein Sof. The light it passes from Him to the receivers is only a small portion, related to the purification of the still body of man. This is why it is called Nefesh.

The vessel of Tifferet is more refined than the vessel of Malchut. The light it transfers from Ein Sof relates to the purification of the vegetative part of man's body, since it acts in it more than the light of Nefesh. This is called "the light of Ruach."

The vessel of Bina is more refined still than Tifferet, and the light it transfers from Ein Sof relates to the purification of the animate part of man's body, and it is called "the light of Neshama."

The most refined of all is the vessel of Hochma. The light it transfers from Ein Sof relates to the purification of the speaking part of man's body. It is called "the light of Haya," and its action is beyond measurement.

47) In Partzuf Nefesh, which one attains through engaging in Torah and Mitzvot without the intention, there is already a point from the light of Ruach clothed in there. And when one strengthens and engages in Torah and Mitzvot with the desired intention, he purifies the vegetative part of his will to receive in him, and to that extent builds the dot of Ruach into a Partzuf. And by performing the 248 Mitzvot "to do" with intention, the dot expands through its 248 spiritual organs. And by observing the 365 Mitzvot not to do, the dot expands through its 365 tendons.

When it is completed with all 613 organs, it rises and clothes the Sefira of Tifferet in the spiritual world of Assiya, which extends to him a greater light from Ein Sof, called "the light of Ruach," which corresponds to the purification of the vegetative part in man's body. And all the elements of the still, vegetative, and animate in the world of Assiya, related to the level of Tifferet, aid one's Partzuf of Ruach to receive the lights from the Sefira Tifferet in all its entirety, as was explained above concerning the light of Nefesh. Because of this, it is called "vegetative of Kedusha."

The nature of its illumination is like the corporeal vegetative: There are distinct differences in motion in each of its elements. Likewise, the spiritual light of vegetative already has enough strength to shine in unique ways for each and every organ of the 613 organs in Partzuf Ruach. Each of them manifests the power of action related to that organ. Also, with the emergence of Partzuf Ruach, the dot of the degree above it emerged from it, a dot of the light of Neshama, which dresses in its internality.

48) And by engaging in the secrets of Torah and the flavors of the Mitzvot, he purifies the animate part of his will to receive, and to that extent builds the point of the soul, dressed in him in its 248 organs and 365 tendons. When its construction is completed and it becomes a Partzuf, it rises and dresses the Sefira Bina in the spiritual world of Assiya. This vessel is much more refined than the first vessels, TM [Tifferet and Malchut]. Hence, it transfers to it a great light from Ein Sof, called "light of Neshama."

All the items of still, vegetative, and animate in the world of Assiya, related to the level of Bina, serve and aid one's Partzuf of Neshama to receive all its lights from the Sefira Bina, as has been explained about the light of Nefesh. It is also called "animate of Kedusha" because it corresponds to the purification of the animate part of man's body. So is the nature of its light, as has been explained about the corporeal animate, Item 37, which gives a sensation of individuality to each of the 613 organs of the Partzuf, so each of them feels alive and free, without any dependency on the rest of the Partzuf.

At last, it is discerned that its 613 organs are 613 Partzufim [pl. of Partzuf], unique in their light, each in its own way. The advantage of this light over the light of Ruach, in spirituality, is as the difference between the animate, the still, and vegetative in corporeality. Also, a dot is extended from the light of Haya of Kedusha, which is the light of the Sefira of Hochma, with the emergence of Partzuf Neshama, and dresses in its internality.

49) Once he has been rewarded with the great light called "the light of Neshama," each of the 613 organs in that Partzuf fully shine in their own unique way, each as an independent Partzuf. Then there opens before him the possibility to engage in each Mitzva according to its true intention, for each organ in Partzuf Neshama illuminates for him the paths of each Mitzva related to that organ.

Through the great power of those lights, he purifies the speaking part of his will to receive and inverts it into a desire to bestow. And to that extent, the point of the light of Haya, dressed within him, is built in its spiritual 248 organs and 365 tendons.

When it is completed into a complete Partzuf, it rises and dresses the Sefira of Hochma in the spiritual world of Assiya, which is an immeasurably refined vessel. Therefore, it extends a tremendous light to him from Ein Sof, called "the light of Haya" or Neshama to Neshama, and all the elements in the world of Assiya, which are the still, vegetative, and animate related to the Sefira of Hochma, aid him in receiving the light of the Sefira of Hochma to the fullest.

It is also called "speaking of Kedusha" since it corresponds to the purification of the speaking part in man's body. The value of that light in Godliness is as the value of the speaking in the corporeal still, vegetative, animate, and speaking. This means that one obtains the sensation of others in a way that the measure of that light relative to the measure of the spiritual still, vegetative, and animate is as the measure of the corporeal speaking relative to the corporeal still, vegetative, and animate. And the light of Ein Sof, dressed in this Partzuf, is called "the light of Yechida."

50) Indeed, you should know that these five lights, NRNHY, received from the world of Assiya, are but NRNHY of the light of Nefesh and have nothing of the light of Ruach. This is because the light of Ruach is only in the world of Yetzira, the light of Neshama is only in the world of Beria, the light of Haya is only in the world of Atzilut, and the light of Yechida, only in the world of AK.

But as we said above, everything that exists in the whole appears in all the items, too, down to the smallest possible item. Thus, all five qualities, NRNHY, exist in the world of Assiya, as well, although they are only NRNHY of Nefesh. Similarly, all five qualities, NRNHY, exist in the world of Yetzira, which are the five parts of Ruach. Also, there are all five qualities, NRNHY, in the world of Beria, which are the five parts of Neshama. So it is in the world of Atzilut, which are the five parts of the light of Haya; and so it is in the world of AK, which are the five parts of the light of Yechida. The difference between the worlds is as we have explained in the distinctions between each of the NRNHY of Assiya.

51) Know that repentance and purification are not accepted unless they are totally permanent, so he will not return to folly, as it is written, "When is there Teshuva [repentance]? When He who knows the mysteries will testify that he will not return to folly." Thus, as we have said, if one purifies the still part of his will to receive, he is rewarded with a Partzuf of Nefesh of Assiya and ascends and clothes the Sefira of Malchut of Assiya.

This means that he will certainly be granted the permanent purification of the still part, in a way that he will not return to folly. Then he will be able to rise to the spiritual world of Assiya, for he will have definite purity and equivalence of form with that world.

But as for the rest of the degrees, which we have said are Ruach, Neshama, Haya, and Yechida of Assiya, corresponding to them, one should purify the vegetative, animate, and speaking parts of one's will to receive, so they will clothe and receive those lights. Yet, the purity does not need to be permanent, "until He who knows the mysteries will testify that he will not return to folly."

That is so because the whole of the world of Assiya, with all its five Sefirot KHBTM, are actually only Malchut, which relates only to the purification of the still. And the five Sefirot are but the five parts of Malchut.

Therefore, since he has already been rewarded with purifying the still part of the will to receive, he already has equivalence of form with the whole of the world of Assiya. However, each Sefira in the world of Assiya receives from its corresponding phase in the worlds above it. For example, the Sefira Tifferet of Assiya receives from the world of Yetzira, which is all Tifferet and the light of Ruach; the Sefira Bina of Assiya receives from the world of Beria, which is all Neshama; and the Sefira Hochma of Assiya receives from the world of Atzilut, which is all Hochma and the light of Haya.

For this reason, although he has permanently purified only the still part, if he has purified the remaining three parts of his will to receive, even if not permanently, he can receive Ruach, Neshama, and Haya from Tifferet, Bina, and Hochma of Assiya, though not permanently, since when one of the three parts of his will to receive awakens, he immediately loses these lights.

52) After he permanently purifies the vegetative part of his will to receive, he permanently rises to the world of Yetzira, where he attains there up to the degree of Ruach permanently. There he can also attain the lights of Neshama and Haya from the Sefirot Bina and Hochma that are there, which are considered Neshama of Ruach and Haya of Ruach, even before he has been granted with purifying the animate and speaking parts permanently, as we have seen regarding the world of Assiya. Yet, this is not permanent, for after he has permanently purified the vegetative part of his will to receive, he is already in equivalence of form with the whole of the world of Yetzira, to its highest degree, as written about the world of Assiya.

53) After he purifies the animate part of his will to receive, and turns it into a desire to bestow, "until He who knows all mysteries will testify that he will not return to folly," he is already in equivalence of form with the world of Beria. He rises there and permanently receives up to the light of Neshama. And through the purification of the speaking part of his body, he can rise up to the Sefira Hochma and receive the light of Haya that is there, although he has not purified it permanently, as with Yetzira and Assiya. But the light, too, does not shine for him permanently.

54) When one is rewarded with permanent purification of the speaking part in his will to receive, he is granted equivalence of form with the world of Atzilut, and he rises there and permanently receives the light of Haya. When he is rewarded further, he receives the light of Ein Sof, and the light of Yechida dresses in the light of Haya, and there is nothing more to add here.

55) Thus, we have clarified what we asked in Item 41, "Why does man need all the upper worlds, which the Creator created for him? What need has man of them?" Now you will see that one cannot bring contentment to one's Maker if not with the

help of all these worlds. This is because he attains the lights and degrees of his soul, called NRNHY, according to the measure of the purity of his will to receive. And with each degree he attains, the lights of that degree assist him in his purification.

Thus, he rises in degrees until he achieves the amusements of the final aim in the thought of creation, see Item 33. It is written in *The Zohar*, *Noah*, Item 63, about the verse, "He who comes to purify is aided." It asks, "With what is he aided?" And it replies that he is aided with a holy soul, for it is impossible to achieve the desired purification, the thought of creation, except through the assistance of all the NRNHY degrees of the soul.

56) You should know that all the NRNHY we have spoken of thus far are the five parts by which the whole of reality is divided. Indeed, all that is in the whole exists even in the smallest element in reality. For example, even in the still phase of the spiritual Assiya alone, there are five phases of NRNHY to attain, which are related to the five general phases of NRNHY.

Thus, it is impossible to attain even the light of still of Assiya except through the four parts of the work. Therefore, there is not a person from Israel who can excuse himself from engaging in all of them according to his stature. 1) One should engage in Torah and Mitzvot with intention, in order to receive the phase of Ruach according to his stature. 2) He should engage in the secrets of the Torah according to his stature, in order to receive the phase of Neshama according to his stature. 3) And the same applies to the Taamim [flavors] of the Mitzvot, for it is impossible to complete even the smallest light in Kedusha without them.

57) Now you can understand the aridity and the darkness that have befallen us in this generation, such as we have never seen in all the generations preceding us. It is so because even the servants of the Creator have abandoned the engagement in the secrets of the Torah.

Maimonides has already given a true allegory about that. He said that if a line of a thousand blind people walks along the way and there is at least one leader among them who can see and lead them, they are guaranteed to walk on the right path and not fall into pits and traps since they follow the sighted one who leads them. But if that person is missing, they are certain to stumble over every hurdle on the way and will all fall into the pit.

So is the matter before us. If the servants of the Creator had, at least, engaged in the internality of the Torah and extended a complete light from Ein Sof, the whole generation would have followed them, and everyone would be certain of their way, that they would not fall. But if even the servants of the Creator have distanced themselves from this wisdom, it is no wonder the whole generation is failing because of them. And because of my great sorrow, I cannot elaborate on that!

58) However, I do know the reason: It is mainly because 1) faith has diminished in general, 2) faith in the holy ones, the sages of the generations in particular, and 3)

the books of Kabbalah and *The Zohar* are full of corporeal parables. Hence, people are afraid lest they will lose more than they will gain since they could easily fail with materializing. This is what prompted me to compose a sufficient interpretation on the writings of the ARI, and now on *The Zohar*. And I have completely removed that concern, for I have evidently explained and proven the spiritual meaning of every thing, that it is stripped and devoid of any corporeal image, above space and above time, as the readers will see, to allow the whole of Israel to study *The Book of Zohar* and be warmed by its sacred light.

I have named that commentary *The Sulam* (Ladder) to show that the purpose of my commentary is as the role of any ladder: If you have an attic filled abundantly, all you need is a ladder to climb. And then, all the bounty in the world is in your hands. But the ladder is not a purpose in and of itself, for if you pause on the rungs of the ladder and do not enter the attic, your goal will not be achieved.

So it is with my commentary on *The Zohar*, for the way to fully clarify these most profound of words has not yet been created. Nonetheless, with my commentary, I have constructed a path and an entrance for any person by which to rise and delve and scrutinize *The Book of Zohar* itself, for only then will my aim with this commentary be completed.

59) All those who know the ins and outs of *The Book of Zohar*, meaning understand what is written in it, unanimously agree that *The Zohar* was written by the Godly Tanna [a sage from the time of the Mishnah] Rabbi Shimon Bar Yochai. Only some of those who are far from this wisdom doubt this pedigree and tend to say, relying on fabricated tales of opposers of this wisdom, that its author is the Kabbalist Rabbi Moshe De Leon, or others of his time.

60) As for me, since the day I have been endowed, by the light of the Creator, with a glance into this holy book, it has not crossed my mind to question its origin, for the simple reason that the content of the book brings to my heart the merit of the Tanna Rashbi [Rabbi Shimon Bar Yochai] far more than all other Tannaim [pl. of Tanna]. And if I were to clearly see that its author is some other name, such as Rabbi Moshe De Leon, then I would praise the merit of Rabbi Moshe De Leon more than all the Tannaim, including Rashbi.

Indeed, judging by the depth of the wisdom in the book, if I were to clearly find that its composer is one of the forty-eight prophets, I would consider it much more acceptable than to relate it to one of the Tannaim. Moreover, if I were to find that Moses himself received it from the Creator Himself on Mount Sinai, then my mind would really be at peace, for such a composition is worthy of him. Hence, since I have been blessed with compiling a sufficient commentary that enables every examiner to acquire some understanding of what is written in the book, I think I am completely excused from further toil in this examination, for any person who is knowledgeable in *The Zohar* will now settle for no less than the Tanna Rashbi as its composer.

61) Accordingly, the question arises, "Why was *The Zohar* not revealed to the early generations, whose merit was undoubtedly greater than the latter ones and who were more worthy of it?" We must also ask, "Why was the commentary on *The Book of Zohar* not revealed before the time of the ARI, and not to the Kabbalists that preceded him?" And the most perplexing question, "Why were the commentaries on the words of the ARI and on the words of *The Zohar* not revealed since the days of the ARI through our generation?" (See my introduction to the book *Panim uMasbirot* on *Tree of Life*, Item 8).

The question is, Is the generation worthy? The answer is that during the six thousand years of its existence, the world is like one Partzuf divided into three thirds: Rosh [head], Toch [interior], Sof [end], meaning HBD [Hochma, Bina, Daat], HGT [Hesed, Gevura, Tifferet], NHY [Netzah, Hod, Yesod]. This is what our sages wrote, "Two millennia of Tohu [chaos], two millennia of Torah, and two millennia of the days of the Messiah" (*Sanhedrin* 97a).

In the first two millennia, considered Rosh and HBD, the lights were very small. They were regarded as Rosh without a Guf [body], having only lights of Nefesh. This is because there is an inverse relation between lights and vessels: In the vessels, the rule is that the first vessels grow first in each Partzuf, and in the lights it is the opposite: The smaller lights dress in the Partzuf first.

Thus, as long as only the upper parts are in the vessels, the vessels of HBD, only lights of Nefesh descend to dress there, which are the smallest lights. This is why it is written about the first two millennia that they are regarded as Tohu. And in the second two millennia of the world, which are vessels of HGT, the light of Ruach descends and clothes in the world, which is considered the Torah. This is why it is said about the two middle millennia that they are Torah. And the last two millennia are vessels of NHYM [Netzah, Hod, Yesod, Malchut]. Therefore, at that time the light of Neshama dresses in the world, which is the greater light; hence, they are the days of the Messiah.

This is also the conduct in each particular Partzuf. In its vessels of HBD, HGT through its Chazeh [chest], the lights are covered and do not begin to shine, disclosed Hassadim, meaning the revelation of the illumination of the upper Hochma occurs only from the Chazeh down, in its NHYM. This is the reason that before the vessels of NHYM began to show in the Partzuf of the world, which are the last two millennia, the wisdom of *The Zohar* in general, and the wisdom of Kabbalah in particular, were hidden from the world.

But during the time of the ARI, when the time of the completion of the vessels below the Chazeh had drawn closer, the light of the upper Hochma was revealed in the world through the soul of the Godly Rabbi Isaac Luria [the ARI], who was ready to receive that great light. Hence, he revealed the essentials in *The Book of Zohar* and in the wisdom of Kabbalah until he overshadowed all his predecessors.

Yet, since these vessels were not yet completed, since he passed away in 1572, the world was not yet worthy of discovering his words, and his words were known only to a chosen few who were not permitted to reveal them to the world.

Now, in our generation, since we are nearing the end of the last two millennia, we were given permission to reveal his words and the words of *The Zohar* in the world to a great extent. Thus, from our generation onward, the words of *The Zohar* will become increasingly revealed in the world until the full measure is revealed, by the will of the Creator.

[Item 62 is missing in the original manuscript]

63) Now you can understand that there really is no end to the merit of the first generations over the last, as this is the rule in all the Partzufim [pl. of Partzuf] of the worlds and of the souls, the more refined one is the first to be selected into the Partzuf. Therefore, the vessels HBD were sorted first in the world and in the souls.

Thus, the souls in the first two millennia were infinitely higher. Yet, they could not receive the full measure of the light due to the absence of the lower parts in the world and in themselves, namely the HGT NHYM.

Likewise, afterward, in the two middle millennia, when the vessels HGT were selected into the world and in the souls, the souls were indeed very refined, in and of themselves, since the merit of the vessels of HGT is close to that of HBD, as it is written in the "Introduction of The Book of Zohar," p 6. Yet, the lights were still concealed in the world due to the absence of the vessels from the Chazeh down in the world and in the souls.

Thus, in our generation, although the essence of the souls is the worst in reality, which is why they could not be selected for Kedusha until today, they are the ones that complete the Partzuf of the world and the Partzuf of the souls with respect to the vessels, and the work is completed only through them. Now, when the vessels of NHY are being completed, and all the vessels—Rosh, Toch, Sof—are in the Partzuf, full measures of light are being drawn, in Rosh, Toch, and Sof, to all who are worthy of them, meaning complete NRN, as said above. Hence, only after the completion of these lowly souls can the highest lights manifest, and not before.

64) Indeed, even our sages asked this question, in *Masechet Berachot*, p 20: "Rav Papa said to Abaye: 'How were the first different, that a miracle happened to them, and how are we different, that a miracle is not happening to us?' Is it because of the study? During the years of Rav Yehuda, the whole study was in [Masechet] *Nezikin*, whereas we are learning the six volumes [of the Mishnah]. And when Rav Yehuda delved in *Okatzin*, he said, 'I saw Rav and Shmuel here, whereas we are learning thirteen *Yeshivot* in *Okatzin*. And when Rav Yehuda took off one shoe, the rain came, whereas we torment our souls and cry out, and no one notices us.' He replied, 'The first gave their souls to the sanctity of the Lord.'"

Thus, although it was obvious, both to the one who asked and to the one who answered, that the first were more important than they were, with respect to the Torah and the wisdom, Rav Papa and Abaye were more important than the first. Thus, although the first generations were more important than the latter generations in the essence of their souls, because the more refined is sorted out to come to the world first, nevertheless, with respect to the wisdom of the Torah, it is increasingly revealed in the latter generations. This is so for the reason we have mentioned, that the overall level is completed specifically by the latter ones. This is why more complete lights are drawn to them although their own essence is far worse.

65) Hence, we could ask, Why, then, is it forbidden to disagree with the first in the revealed Torah? It is because, as far as the practical part of the Mitzvot is concerned, it is to the contrary, the first were more complete in them than the last, since the act is extended from the holy vessels of the Sefirot, and the secrets of the Torah and the Taamim [flavors] of the Mitzva are extended from the lights in the Sefirot.

You already know that there is an inverse relation between lights and vessels: In the vessels, the higher ones grow first, see Item 62, which is why the earlier ones were more complete in the practical part than the latter ones. But with the lights, the lower ones enter first, so the last are more complete than the first.

66) Bear in mind that in everything there is internality and externality. In the world in general, Israel, the descendants of Abraham, Isaac, and Jacob, are regarded as the internality of the world, and the seventy nations are regarded as the externality of the world. Also, there is internality within Israel themselves, which are the complete servants of the Creator, and there is externality—those who do not devote themselves to the work of the Creator. Among the nations of the world, there is internality, as well, which are the righteous of the nations of the world, and there is externality, which are the crass and the harmful among them.

Additionally, among the servants of the Creator among the children of Israel, there is internality, being those rewarded with comprehension of the soul of the internality of the Torah and its secrets, and externality, who merely observe the practical part of the Torah.

Also, there is internality in every person from Israel—the Israel within him—which is the point in the heart, and externality—which is the nations of the world within him, which is the body itself. But even the nations of the world within him are regarded as proselytes, since by adhering to the internality, they become like proselytes from among the nations of the world who came and adhered to the whole of Israel.

67) When a person from Israel enhances and dignifies his internality, which is the Israel in him, over the externality, which are the nations of the world in him, that is, he dedicates the majority of his efforts to enhance and exalt his internality, to benefit his soul, and gives little efforts, the mere necessity, to sustain the nations of the world in him, meaning the bodily needs, as it is written (*Avot* 1), "Make your

Torah permanent and your work temporary," by so doing, he makes the children of Israel soar upward in their wholeness in the internality and externality of the world, as well, and the nations of the world, which are the externality, to recognize and acknowledge the value of the children of Israel.

And if, God forbid, it is to the contrary, and an individual from Israel enhances and appreciates his externality, which is the nations of the world in him, more than the quality of Israel in him, as it is written (Deuteronomy 28), "The stranger that is in the midst of you," meaning the externality in him "shall rise higher and higher above you," and you, yourself, the internality, the Israel in you, "shall come down lower and lower." With these actions, he causes the externality of the world in general—the nations of the world—to soar ever higher, overcome Israel, degrade them to the ground, and the children of Israel—the internality in the world—will plunge deep down.

68) Do not be surprised that one person's actions bring elevation or decline to the whole world, for it is an unbreakable law that the general and the particular are equal, like two drops of water. Hence, all that applies to the general applies also to the particular. Moreover, the parts make what is found in the whole, for the general can appear only after the appearance of the parts in it, and according to the quantity and quality of the parts. Evidently, the value of an act of an individual elevates or lowers the entire collective.

That will clarify to you what is written in *The Zohar*, that by engaging in *The Book of Zohar* and the wisdom of truth they will be rewarded with emerging from exile to complete redemption to complete redemption from exile (*Tikkunim*, end of *Tikkun* No. 6). We might ask, What has the study of *The Zohar* to do with the redemption of Israel from among the nations?

69) From the above said we can thoroughly understand that the Torah, too, contains internality and externality, as does the entire world. Therefore, one who engages in the Torah has these two degrees, as well. When one increases one's toil in the internality of the Torah and its secrets, to that extent, one makes the virtue of the internality of the world—which are Israel—soar high above the externality of the world, which are the nations of the world. And all the nations will acknowledge and recognize Israel's merit over them, until the realization of the words, "And the peoples will take them and bring them to their place, and the house of Israel will possess them in the land of the Lord" (Isaiah 14), and also "Thus says the Lord God, Behold, I will lift up my hand to the nations, and set up my standard to the peoples, and they will bring your sons in their arms, and your daughters will be carried on their shoulders" (Isaiah 49).

But if, God forbid, it is to the contrary, and a person from Israel degrades the merit of the internality of the Torah and its secrets, which deals with the conducts of our souls and their degrees, and the intellectual part and the flavors of the Mitzvot with regard to the merit of the externality of the Torah, which deals only with the practical part, and even if one does occasionally engage in the internality of the Torah, and dedicates a little of one's time to it, when it is neither day nor night, as though it were redundant, by this one disgraces and degrades the internality of the world, which are the children of Israel, and raises the externality of the world over them, meaning the nations of the world. They will humiliate and disgrace the children of Israel, and will regard Israel as redundant, as though the world has no need for them.

Furthermore, by this they make even the externality in the nations of the world overpower their own internality, for the worst among the nations of the world, the harmful and the destructors of the world, rise above their internality, who are the righteous of the nations of the world. Then they make all the ruin and the heinous slaughter that our generation had witnessed, may the Creator protect us from here on.

Thus you see that the redemption of Israel and the whole of Israel's merit depend on the study of *The Zohar* and the internality of the Torah. And vice-versa, all the destructions and the decline of the children of Israel are because they have abandoned the internality of the Torah, degraded its merit, and made it seemingly redundant.

70) This is what is written in the *Tikkunim* [corrections] of *The Zohar* (Tikkun 30, "Second Path"): "Awaken and rise for the Shechina, for you have an empty heart, without the understanding to know and to attain it, although it is within you." The meaning of the matter is as it is written (Isaiah 40), a voice says, "Call!" as in "Call! Is there anyone who answers you? To which of the holy ones will you turn?" And she says, "What can I call, all that is flesh is hay; they are all as beasts that eat hay, and all their mercies are as the flower of the field; every mercy that they do, they do for themselves."

The meaning of this is as it is written (Isaiah 40): "A voice says, 'Call!'" that a voice pounds in the heart of each and every one from Israel, to cry and to pray for the raising of the Shechina, which is the collection of all the souls of Israel. He brings evidence from the text, "Call! Is there anyone who answers you?" for calling means praying.

But the Shechina says, "What can I call?" That is, I have no strength to raise myself from the dust, for "All that is flesh is hay," they are all like beasts, eating grass and hay. This means that they observe the commandments mindlessly, like beasts. "Every mercy that they do, they do for themselves," meaning that in the commandments they perform, they have no intention to do them in order to bring contentment to their Maker. Rather, they observe the commandments only for their own benefit.

"And even all those who exert in Torah, every mercy that they do, they do for themselves." Even the best among them, who dedicate all their time to engagement in the Torah, do it only to benefit their own bodies, without the desirable aim: to bring contentment to their Maker.

"At that time, the spirit leaves and will not return to the world." It is said about the generation of that time: "A spirit leaves and will not return to the world." This is the spirit of the Messiah, meaning the spirit of the Messiah, who must deliver Israel from all their troubles until the complete redemption, to fulfill the words, "The earth will be full of the knowledge of the Lord." That spirit has left and does not shine in the world.

"Woe unto them who cause him to leave the world and not return to the world, for they are the ones who make the Torah dry, and do not want to engage in the wisdom of Kabbalah." Woe unto those people who make the spirit of Messiah leave and depart from the world, and not be able to return to the world. They are the ones who make the Torah dry, without any moisture of sense and reason, for they confine themselves only to the practical part of the Torah and do not want to try to understand the wisdom of Kabbalah, to know and to learn the secrets of the Torah and the flavors of Mitzva [commandment].

"Woe unto them, for they cause poverty and ruin, looting and killing, and destruction in the world." Woe unto them, for with these actions they bring about the existence of poverty, ruin, and robbery, looting, killing, and destructions in the world.

71) The reason for their words is as we have explained, that when all those who engage in the Torah degrade their own internality and the internality of the Torah, leaving it as though it were redundant in the world, and engage in it only at a time that is neither day nor night, and they are in it like blind people searching the wall, by this they intensify their own externality, the benefit of their own bodies. Also, they regard the externality of the Torah as higher than the internality of the Torah. By these actions, they make all the forms of externality in the world overpower all the parts of internality in the world, each according to its essence.

This is so because 1) the externality in the whole of Israel, meaning the nations of the world in them, overpowers and revokes the internality in the whole of Israel, who are those who are great in the Torah. 2) Also, the externality in the nations of the world—the destructors among them—overpower and revoke the internality among them, who are the righteous of the nations of the world. 3) Additionally, the externality of the whole world, being the nations of the world, overpower and revoke the children of Israel, who are the internality of the world.

In such a generation, all the destructors among the nations of the world raise their heads and wish primarily to destroy and to kill the children of Israel, as it is written (*Yevamot* 63), "No calamity comes to the world but for Israel." This means, as it is written in the above *Tikkunim*, that they cause poverty, ruin, robbery, killing, and destructions in the whole world.

After, through our many faults, we have witnessed all that is said in the abovementioned *Tikkunim*, and moreover, the judgment struck the very best of us, as our sages said (*Baba Kama* 60), "And it begins with the righteous first," and of all the glory Israel had had in the countries of Poland and Lithuania, etc., there remains but the relics in our holy land, now it is upon us, relics, to correct that dreadful wrong. Each of us remainders should take upon himself, heart and soul, to henceforth intensify the internality of the Torah and give it its rightful place according to its merit over the externality of the Torah.

Then, each and every one of us will be rewarded with intensifying his own internality, meaning the Israel within him, which is the needs of the soul over his own externality, which is the nations of the world within him, being the needs of the body. And that force will come to the whole of Israel, as well, until the nations of the world within us recognize and acknowledge the merit of the great sages of Israel over them, and they will listen to them and obey them.

Additionally, the internality of the nations of the world, the righteous of the nations of the world, will overpower and submit their externality, who are the destructors. The internality of the world, too, who are Israel, will rise in all their merit and virtue over the externality of the world, who are the nations.

Then, all the nations of the world will recognize and acknowledge Israel's merit over them, and will fulfill the words (Isaiah 14), "And the peoples will take them and bring them to their place, and the house of Israel will possess them in the land of the Lord." And also (Isaiah 49), "And they will bring your sons in their arms, and your daughters will be carried on their shoulders." This is the meaning of what is written in *The Zohar* (*Nasso*, p 124b), "Through your composition," which is *The Book of Zohar*, "they will be redeemed from exile with mercy." Amen, would that be so.

A Handmaid Who Is Heir to Her Mistress

This requires a thorough explanation. To make it clear to all, I will choose to interpret the matter by what is revealed to us for this reason and extends to us here in the conduct of this world.

Internality and Externality

The thing is that the upper roots extend their power by cascading until their branches appear in this world, as it is written in the explanation of branch and root. As a whole, the worlds are regarded as internality and externality, like a heavy load that none can lift or move from place to place. Hence, the advice is to divide the load into small parts and subsequently transfer them one at a time.

It is similar in our matter: Since the purpose of creation is invaluable, for a tiny spark such as man's soul can rise in its attainment higher than the ministering angels, as our sages said about the verse, "Now it will be said to Jacob and to Israel: 'What has God wrought!'" They interpreted that the high angels will ask Israel, "What has God wrought?"

The Evolution of Israel (Internality)—One at a Time

This abundance will come to us only by developing one at a time. As in the above allegory, even the heaviest load can be lifted if we split it into pieces and raise them one at a time. Not only the general purpose comes to us in this manner, but even the physical purpose, which is but a preparation for the general purpose, comes to us through gradual and slow development.

Hence, the worlds have been divided into internality and externality, where each world contains illuminations suitable to operate in a slow development, and they are called "the internality of the world."

Evolution of the Nations of the World (Externality)—at Once

Opposite them are illuminations that can act only at once; hence, when they appear here in their worldly branches and are given control, not only do they not correct, they even ruin.

Our sages call it "unripe," as it is written concerning the Tree of Knowledge and *Adam HaRishon*, that they ate unripe fruit. This means that it is truly a dainty delight, immeasurably pleasant, and is destined to delight man, but in the future, not at present, as it is still growing and developing. This is why they compared it to an unripe fruit, since the fig, too, which is the sweetest, most pleasant fruit, when eaten prematurely, will upset one's stomach and he will die.

Indeed, we should ask, "Who is the one who brings such an act into the world?" After all, it is known that there is no action in our world that comes without a strike in the upper root. Know that this is what we call "the control of the externality," as in the verse, "God has made one opposite the other." It contains a force that pushes and rushes toward the revelation of the internal guidance, as our sages said, "I place upon them a king such as Haman, and against their will they will repent."

The Internality Are the People of Israel

Once we have clarified the upper roots, we will clarify the branches in this world. Know that a branch that extends from the internality are the people of Israel, who have been chosen as the operators of the correction and the general purpose. They contain the preparation required for growing and developing until they come to move the nations to achieve the general goal.

The Externality Are the Nations of the World

The branch that extends from the externality is the rest of the nations. They have not been imparted the qualities that make them worthy of receiving the conducts of development of the purpose one at a time. Rather, they are fit to receive the correction at once and to the fullest, according to their upper root. Hence, when they receive dominion from their root, they destroy the virtues in the children of Israel and cause suffering in the world.

A Slave and a Handmaid

The upper roots, called "Externality," as we have explained above, are generally called a "handmaid" and a "slave." This aims to show that they do not intend to harm at all, as it may seem in superficial observation. Instead, they serve the internality like a slave and a handmaid serve their master.

The Externality Rule When Israel Do Not Demand Depth in Their Work

The above-mentioned control of the externality is called "the exile of Israel among the nations of the world." Through it, they inflict many forms of suffering, degradation, and ruin upon the Israeli nation. However, to be brief, we will explain only what is revealed through a general observation, which is the general purpose. This concerns the idol-worship and superstition, as it is written, "They mingled with the nations and learned from their actions." This is the most terrible and dangerous poison, which destroys the souls of Israel, as it brings their vanities closer to the human reason. In other words, they do not require great depth to understand them, and thus plant the foundations of their work in the hearts of the children of Israel.

Although an Israeli man is quite unfit to accept their vanities, in the end they do induce idolatry and filth, down to blatant heresy, until he says, "all faces are equal."

The Reason for the Concealment of Kabbalah

Now you can understand the matter of the concealment of the wisdom of the hidden from the eyes of the external ones, as well as what the sages said, "A gentile must not be taught Torah." There seems to be a contradiction between this and the Tanna [great sage in the early CE years] Devei Eliyahu, who said, "Even a gentile, even a slave, and even a handmaid who sit and learn Torah, the *Shechina* [Divinity] is with them." Thus, why did the sages prohibit teaching the Torah to gentiles?

Teaching the Torah to Gentiles

Indeed, the Tanna Devei Eliyahu relates to a converted gentile, or at least to one who retired from idol-worship, from superstition. Our sages, conversely, referred to one who did not retire from idol-worship and wanted to know Israel's law and wisdom in order to strengthen and fortify their idolatry. You might say, "Why should we care if this gentile has become more pious in his idol-worship because of our Torah? If it does not help, what harm will it do?"

Rashbi's Weeping

Indeed, this is what Rashbi cried about before he explained an important secret in the wisdom of the hidden, as it is written, "Rabbi Shimon wept, 'Woe if I tell, and woe if I do not tell. If I tell, the sinners will know how to serve their idols; and if I do not tell, the friends will lose that matter.'"

He was afraid that this secret would come by the hands of idol-worshippers, and they would perform their idolatry with the force of this holy mind. This is what prolongs our exile and brings upon us all the afflictions and the ruins, as we now see before us, since the sages of the nations studied all the books of the children of Israel and turned them into delicacies to strengthen their faith, meaning their wisdom, called "theology."

Two Harms from Revealing Israel's Wisdom to the Nations of the World

They have done two harms:

1. Besides clothing in our cloak, saying that all of that wisdom is by attainment of their own holy spirit, these mimics gained their reputation at our expense. By this, they strengthen their false teaching and obtain the strength to deny our holy Torah.

2. An even greater harm came upon us: One who observes their theology discovers in it concepts and wisdom concerning the work of God that seem truer and more genuine than our wisdom. This is so for two reasons: The first is that they

are a large society, and among them are great and proficient philologists who know their work: to make matters acceptable to uneducated people. Philology comes from external teachings, and certainly a society of eight billion people can produce many more and much greater philologists than our society of fifteen million can. Hence, one who observes their books falls into doubting that they might be right, or even worse, of course. The second, and the most important reason is that the sages of Israel conceal the wisdom of religion from the masses behind closed doors. However they can, the sages of each generation offer simple explanations to the masses and reject them with all kinds of tricks from the desire to even approach and touch the wisdom of the hidden.

Woe if I Tell

They do this for fear that the matters will fall into the hands of idol-worshippers, as Rashbi wrote, "If I tell, the sinners will know how to serve their masters." After all, we suffer plenty even for the tiny things they stole from our vessels, which have seeped to them past all the vigil guarding.

The Reason for the Concealment of Kabbalah

This clarifies what would happen to us if our sages revealed the wisdom of the hidden to all. And since we conceal, as long as our ordinary person is unfit to be given the secrets of Torah, he has no knowledge whatsoever in the wisdom of religion. Hence, such a person is obviously inspired and elated when he finds the trifling wisdom and explanations in their theology, whose essence is but a collection of stolen concepts from our hidden, with added literary dainties. Once one sees this, he says and denies our practical law and ends in complete heresy.

A Handmaid Who Is Heir to Her Mistress

This is called "a handmaid who is heir to her mistress," since the very power of the mistress—the control of the internality—is by the force of our wisdom and knowledge, as it is written, "we are distinguished, I and Your people, from all the people that are upon the face of the earth." Now, the handmaid has stepped forth and prides herself in public that she is the heir of this wisdom. Know that this power of theirs is the chain by which they tie the legs of the children of Israel in the exile under their dominion.

Chains of Exile

Thus, the essence of the chains of exile and its power come from the wisdom of Torah and its secrets, which they have managed to steal and place in their vessels passed all the watchful guarding we have put up. With it, they mislead the masses, saying they have inherited the work of the Creator, and cast doubt and heresy, too, in the souls of Israel.

The Shofar* of the Messiah

Redemption Only through Kabbalah

Know that this is what it means that the children of Israel are redeemed only after the wisdom of the hidden is revealed to a great extent, as it is written in *The Zohar*, "With this composition, the children of Israel emerge from exile." This is because at that time, there was hope for redemption, as the writing of *The Zohar*, which began in the days of Rashbi, was during the days of Bar-Kokhva. Rabbi Akiva, Rashbi's teacher, said about him: "There will step forth a star out of Jacob." Also, after the ruin of Beitar, there was great hope.

Writing *The Zohar* and Concealing It

Because of this, Rashbi permitted himself and disclosed the wisdom of the hidden in his books, *The Zohar* and the *Tikkunim*. However, it was with great care, since he permitted only Rabbi Aba to write, for he could disclose with intimation, so only the sages of the children of Israel would understand, and the sages of the nations would not understand, for fear that the wicked would know how to serve their masters. For this reason, as soon as they saw that the time was too soon for Israel's redemption, they hid it. That was at the time of the sages, the Savoraim, since we find much that our sages, the Savoraim, wrote their matters inside *The Zohar*.

Disclosing the Kabbalah Is the Creator's Will

Indeed, it was the Creator's will that it would appear. This is why it wandered onto the widow of Rabbi Moshe de Leon. She inherited the manuscript from her husband, and he probably told her nothing of the prohibition to disclose, and she, by chance, put it up for sale.

Israel's Troubles Are because of the Disclosure of Kabbalah

Indeed, to this day, this matter caused many ruins in the house of Israel for the above reasons.

The Benefit from Disclosing the Kabbalah

However, there is no bad without good. Therefore, this control that the nations have obtained by stealing the secrets of Torah gave a big thrust to the development of holiness. In my assessment, we are in a generation that is standing at the very

---

* A *Shofar* is a ram's horn. When blown like a trumpet during prayer on some Jewish holidays, it symbolizes a call for awakening.

threshold of redemption, if we only know how to spread the wisdom of the hidden to the masses.

First Benefit

Apart for the simple reason of "He has swallowed down riches, and he will vomit them up," for this will reveal to all what is between my son and my father-in-law, and the difference between the core of the nucleus and the upper *Klipa* [shell], from which all the sages of the nations in the world peeled. This is because all the camps of Israel that have denied the Torah are sure to return to the Creator and to His work.

Second Benefit

There is another reason for it: We have proof that there is a precondition for redemption—for all the nations of the world to acknowledge Israel's law, as it is written, "And the land will be full of knowledge," as in the example of the exodus from Egypt, where there was a precondition that Pharaoh, too, would acknowledge the true God and His laws, and would allow them to leave.

Redemption through Disclosing Kabbalah to the Nations of the World

This is why it is written that each one from the nations will hold a Jewish man and lead him to the holy Land. It was not enough that they could leave by themselves. You must understand from where the nations of the world came by such a will and idea. Know that this is through the dissemination of the true wisdom, so they will evidently see the true God and the true law.

Dissemination of the Wisdom of Kabbalah the World Over

The dissemination of the wisdom in the masses is called a "*Shofar*." Like the *Shofar*, whose voice travels a great distance, the echo of the wisdom will spread the world over, so even the nations will hear and acknowledge that there is Godly wisdom in Israel.

The Revelation of Kabbalah to All the Nations Is the Revelation of Eliyahu (Elijah)

This task was said about Eliyahu the prophet, since the disclosure of the secrets of Torah is always referred to as "the disclosure of Eliyahu." It is as they have said, "Let it rest until Elijah comes," and also, "The Tishbi will answer the questions and problems." This is why they said that three days (a known intimation) prior to the coming of the Messiah, Elijah would walk on the hilltops and blow a great horn, etc.

Disclosing the Kabbalah to All the Nations Is a Precondition for the Complete Redemption

You must understand these intimations: This issue of the *Shofar* is only the disclosure of the wisdom of the hidden in great masses; it is a necessary precondition that must be met prior to the complete redemption.

And the books that have already been revealed through me in this wisdom will testify to it, that matters of the greatest importance have been spread out like a gown for all to see. This is a true testimony that we are already at the threshold of redemption, and the voice of the great *Shofar* has already been heard, though in the distance, for it still sounds very softly.

Indeed, every greatness requires prior smallness, and there is no great voice if it is not preceded by a soft sound. And this is the way of the *Shofar*: Its voice grows progressively. And who better than I knows that I am not at all worthy of being even a messenger and a scribe for disclosing such secrets, much less to understand them down to their roots. So why has the Creator done so to me? It is only because the generation is worthy of it, as it is the last generation, which stands at the threshold of complete redemption. For this reason, it is worthy of beginning to hear the voice of the *Shofar* of the Messiah, which is the revealing of the secrets, as has been explained.

Peace in the World

Scrutinies and inquiries concerning matters that cause absence of peace, suggestions of world reformers and testing them against reality, observing the "good" that is founded on "mercy and truth, justice and peace," as implied in the book of Psalms.

"Mercy and truth met; justice and peace kissed. Truth will spring forth from the earth, and justice was reflected from heaven. The Lord, too, will give the good, and our land will yield its crop" (Psalms 85).

Everything Is Evaluated Not by Its Appearance at a Given Moment, but According to Its Level of Development.

Everything in reality, good or bad, and even the most harmful in the world, has a right to exist and must not be destroyed and eradicated from the world. We must only mend and reform it because any observation of the work of creation is enough to teach us about the greatness and perfection of its Operator and Creator. Therefore, we must understand and be very careful when casting a flaw on any item of creation, saying it is redundant and superfluous, as that would be slander about its Operator.

It is common knowledge that the Creator did not complete creation when He created it. And we can see in every corner of reality, in the general and in the particular, that it abides by laws of gradual development, from absence to completion of growth. For this reason, when the fruit tastes bitter in the beginning of its growth, we do not consider it a flaw in the fruit since we all know the reason: The fruit has not completed its development.

So it is in every element of reality: When an element seems to us as bad and harmful, it is but a self-testimony of that element, that it is still in a transition phase in the process of its development. Hence, we must not decide that it is bad, and it is not wise for us to cast a flaw in it.

The Weakness of "World Reformers"

This is the key to understand the weakness of world reformers throughout the generations. They regarded man as a machine that is not operating properly and needs mending, meaning to remove its broken parts and replace them with working ones.

This is the tendency of all world reformers—to eradicate any harmful and bad in the human species... and it is true that had the Creator not stood against them, they would certainly have by now cleansed man entirely, leaving in him only what is good and useful.

But because the Creator meticulously watches over all the elements in His creation, not letting anyone destroy a single thing in His domain, but only reform it and make it useful and good, all the reformers of the above-mentioned kind will vanish from the earth, and bad qualities will not vanish. They exist and count the degrees of development that they must still traverse until they complete their ripening.

At that time, the bad attributes themselves will turn to good and useful ones, as the Creator had initially planned for them. It is like a fruit on the tree that sits and waits and counts the days and months it must still wait before the completion of its ripeness, at which time its taste and sweetness will become evident to every person.

Rewarded—I Will Hasten It, Not Rewarded—In Its Time

We must know that the above-mentioned law of development, which is spread over the whole of reality, is certain to reform all evil to good and useful, and acts through the power of the government of heaven above, meaning without asking permission from the people, dwellers of the earth. However, the Creator placed knowledge and authority in the hands of man and permitted him to accept the above-mentioned law of development under his own authority and government, and handed him the ability to hasten the process of development as he wishes, freely and completely independent of the boundaries of time.

It turns out that there are two authorities here acting in the above-mentioned conduct of development: One is the authority of heaven, which is sure to turn anything harmful and evil to good and useful, but it will come in its time, in its own way, heavily, and after a long time. Then there is the authority of the earth. When the "evolving object" is a living, feeling being, it suffers horrendous torments and pains while under the "steamroller of development" which carves its way ruthlessly.

The "authority of the earth," however, consists of people who have taken this above-mentioned law of development under their own government and can free themselves entirely from the chains of time, and who greatly accelerate time, namely the completion of the ripeness and correction of the object, which is the end of its development.

Such are the words that our sages said (*Sanhedrin* 98) about the complete redemption and complete correction of Israel, and thus they clarified the verse "I the Lord will hasten it in its time": Rewarded—I will hasten it, not rewarded—in its time.

They wish to say that if Israel are rewarded and take the law of development that their bad attributes must go through in order to invert them into good ones, they will bring it under their own government. In other words, they will set their minds and hearts to correct all the bad attributes in them and turn them into good ones by themselves. Then, "I will hasten it," meaning they will be completely freed from the chains of time. And from now on, this end depends on their own will, meaning only by the greatness of the deed and the mindfulness. Thus, they hasten the end.

But if they are not rewarded with developing their bad attributes under their own authority, but leave it under the authority of heaven, they, too, are certain to attain the end of their redemption and the end of their correction. This is because there is complete certainty in the government of heaven, which operates by the law of gradual development, degree by degree, until it turns any evil and harmful to good and beneficial as the fruit on a tree. The end is guaranteed, but in its time, meaning it is completely connected and dependent on time.

According to the above-mentioned law of gradual development, one must go through many degrees, which tend to come heavily and very slowly and lengthily, and stretch over a very long time before one reaches the end. Because the objects we are discussing are evolving, sensing, living beings, they, too, must suffer great agony and pains in those states of development, since the compelling force that exists in those degrees in order to raise man from a lower degree to a higher one is but a pushing force of pain and torments that has accumulated in the lower degree and that can no longer be tolerated. Because of this, they must leave that degree and rise to a higher one. It is as our sages said, "The Creator places over them a king whose decrees are as harsh as Haman's, Israel repent, and He reforms them."

Therefore, the end is certain to come to Israel by the above-mentioned law of gradual development, and it is called "in its time," meaning tied to the chains of time. And Israel's guaranteed end, by taking the development of their qualities under their own authority is called "I will hasten it," meaning completely independent of time.

Good and Bad Are Evaluated by the Actions of the Individual toward Society

Before we examine the correction of evil in the human race, we must first determine the value of those abstract terms, "good" and "bad." When we define an act or an attribute as good or bad, we should clarify with regard to whom that attribute or act is good or bad.

To understand this, we must thoroughly know the proportional value between the individual and the collective, between the individual and the collective that the individual lives in and nourishes from, in both matter and in spirit.

Reality shows us that an individual cannot exist in isolation without a sufficient number of people around him to serve him and help him provide for his needs. Hence, man is inherently born to lead a social life. Each and every individual in society is like a wheel that is linked to several other wheels placed in a machine. This single wheel has no freedom of movement in and of itself but continues with the motion of the rest of the wheels in a certain direction to qualify the machine to perform its general function.

And if there is some malfunction in the wheel, the malfunction is not evaluated relating to the wheel itself, but according to its service and role with respect to the whole machine.

And in our subject, the benefit of each and every person within his collective is evaluated not according to his own benefit, but according to his service to the public. And vice-versa, we appreciate the measure of evil of each and every individual only according to the harm one inflicts upon the public in general, and not by one's own individual value.

These matters are crystal clear both from the perspective of the truth in them, and from the perspective of the good in them. This is because what is found in the collective is only what is found in the individual, and the benefit of the collective is the benefit of each and every individual. He who harms the collective takes his share in the harm, and he who benefits the collective takes his share in the benefit, since individuals are parts of the whole, and the whole is not worth in any way more than the sum of its individuals.

It thus turns out that the collective and the individual are one and the same, and the individual is not harmed because of his enslavement to the collective, since the freedom of the collective and the freedom of the individual are one and the same, too, and as they share the good, they also share the freedom. Thus, good attributes and bad attributes, good deeds and bad deeds are evaluated only with respect to the benefit of the public.

Of course, the above words apply if all the individuals perform their role toward the public to the fullest and receive no more than they deserve, nor take from their friend's share. But if a part of the collective does not behave accordingly, as a result, they not only harm the collective, but they, too, are harmed.

We should not discuss further something that is known to all, and the aforesaid is only to show the drawback, the place that needs correction, namely that each and every individual will understand that his own benefit and the benefit of the collective are one and the same, and by this, the world will come to its full correction.

The Four Attributes, Mercy, Truth, Justice, and Peace, in the Individual and in the Collective

Once we know full well the desired attribute of goodness, we should examine the things and the means at our disposal in order to hasten that delight and happiness.

Four attributes are provided for that purpose: mercy, truth, justice, and peace. These attributes have been used by all world reformers thus far. It is more correct to say that it is with these four attributes that human development has advanced thus far through the government of heaven, in a gradual path, until it brought humankind to its current state.

It has already been written that it would be better for us to take the law of development under our own hands and government, for then we will rid ourselves of any torment that the developmental history has in store for us henceforth. Thus, we should scrutinize and examine those four properties in order to thoroughly understand what we have been given thus far, and by them know what aid we should hope to get from them in the future.

Practical Difficulties in Determining the Truth

When we discuss good attributes in theory, there is certainly no better attribute than the attribute of truth. This is because all the good that we have defined above in the relationship between the individual and the collective is when the individual gives and fully plays his part toward the collective, and also takes his share from the collective justly and honestly. All this is but the truth, but the drawback is that in fact, the collective does not accept this attribute at all. Thus, the practical difficulty in the above-mentioned truth is proven from itself: There is some drawback and a cause here that makes it unacceptable to the collective. We must examine what is that drawback.

When you closely examine the above-mentioned truth from the perspective of its practical feasibility, you will necessarily find it vague and complicated, and it is impossible for the human eye to scrutinize it, since the truth requires that we equalize all the individuals in the collective, so they receive their share according to their labor, no more and no less. This is the one true basis which cannot be doubted, for it is certain that anyone who wishes to enjoy the labor of his friend, his acts are against the above-mentioned reason and clear truth.

But how do we think that we can scrutinize that truth in a way that is acceptable to the collective? For example, if we evaluate something according to the apparent labor, meaning according to the number of hours, and compel each one to work an equal number of hours, we will still not discover the attribute of truth at all. Moreover, there is an evident lie here for two reasons: The first is the physical side, and the second is the mental side of the worker.

That is because by nature, the power to work is not equal in each and every person. One person in the society labors in one hour of work, due to his weakness, much more than another who works two hours or more.

And there is also a psychological matter here, since he who is very lazy by nature exhausts himself in one hour more than his friend in two hours or more. According to the perspective of the evident truth, we should not compel one part of society to labor more than the other part for the satisfaction of the needs of their lives. But in truth, the naturally strong and nimble in society benefit from the labor of others and exploit them maliciously against the attribute of truth, for they labor very little compared to the weak and lazy in society.

And if we also consider the natural law, "Taking after the majority," then such a truth that takes the number of hours of apparent work as a basis is completely infeasible, since the weak and the lazy are always the vast majority in society, and they will not allow the nimble and strong minority to exploit their strength and labor. Thus, you see that the above-mentioned basis, which is the labor of the individual on the condition of the evident truth, and with it the majority in the society, is completely impractical, since it cannot be examined and evaluated in any way.

Thus, you find that the attribute of truth has no practical ability to organize the path of the individual and the path of the collective in an absolute and satisfactory manner. Also, it is completely insufficient for organizing life at the end of the correction of the world.

Furthermore, there are even greater difficulties here because there is no clearer truth than nature itself. And it is natural that each and every individual feels himself in the world of the Creator, as a sole ruler, that all the others were created only to ease and improve his life, without feeling any obligation whatsoever to give anything in return.

In simple words, we will say that the nature of each and every person is to exploit the lives of all other people in the world for his own benefit, and all that he gives to another is only out of necessity. Even then, there is exploitation of others in it, but it is done cunningly, so his friend will not notice it and concede willingly.

The reason for this is that the nature of every branch is close to its root. Because man's soul extends from the Creator, who is one and unique, and everything is His, likewise, man, who extends from Him, feels that all the people in the world should be under his own governance and for his own private benefit. This is an unbreakable law. The only difference is in people's choices: One chooses to exploit people by obtaining lowly lusts, and one by obtaining governance, while the third by obtaining respect. Furthermore, if one could do it without much effort, he would agree to exploit the world with all three together—wealth, governance, and respect. However, he is forced to choose according to his possibilities and capabilities.

This law can be called "the law of singularity in man's heart." No person escapes it (rather each and every one takes his share in that law), the great according to his size, and the small according to his size.

Thus, the above law of singularity in the nature of every person is neither condemned nor praised, as it is a natural reality and has a right to exist like all parts of reality. And there is no hope to eradicate it from the world or even slightly blur its form, just as there is no hope to eradicate the entire human race from Earth. Therefore, we will not be lying at all if we said about this law that it is the absolute truth.

Since it is undoubtedly so, how can we even try to ease one's mind by promising him equality with all the people in the collective? Nothing is further from human nature than this, while one's sole inclination is to soar higher, above the whole collective.

Thus we have thoroughly clarified that there is no real possibility to bring good and joyful conducts to the life of the individual and the life of the collective by following the attribute of truth in a way that it will ease the mind of each and every individual, so he may completely agree to it, as it should be at the end of correction.

In the Absence of the Ability to Establish the Attribute of Truth, They Tried to Establish the Basic Attributes

Now let us turn to the remaining three attributes: mercy, justice, and peace. It seems that to begin with, they were created only to be used as support for the attribute of truth, which is very weak in our world. From here, developmental history began to climb its slow and straggler degrees in its progress toward organizing the lives of the collective.

In theory, the whole society willingly agreed and took it upon themselves not to deviate in any way from the truth. But in fact, they conducted themselves completely opposite from the truth, as was agreed. Since then, it has been the fate of truth to always be in the hands of the most deceitful and never in the hands of the weak and righteous, so they could even be somewhat assisted by the attribute of truth.

When they could not establish the attribute of truth in the life of the collective, the exploited and the weak increased within society, and from here emerged the attributes of mercy and justice to do their actions in the conduct of society, since the existence of the whole society compelled the successful ones among them to support the straggling, so as to not harm the society in general. Therefore, they behaved with them indulgently, meaning with mercy and charity.

But it is only natural that under such conditions, the straggling and exploited proliferate, until there are enough of them to protest against the successful and start quarrels and fights. From here emerged the attribute of "peace" in the world. Thus, all those attributes—mercy, charity, and peace—emerged and were born out of the weakness of truth.

This is what caused society to divide into sects. Some adopted the attributes of mercy and charity, giving of their own possessions to others, and some adopted the attribute of truth, meaning "What's mine is mine and what's yours is yours."

In simpler words, we can divide the two sects into "constructors" and "destructors." Constructors are those who want construction, the benefit of the collective, for which they are often willing to give of their own possessions to others. But those who are naturally prone to destruction and recklessness were more comfortable clinging to the attribute of truth, meaning "What's mine is mine and what's yours is yours," for their own benefit, and would never want to give up anything of their own to others without taking into consideration the risk to the well-being of the collective, for they are destructors by nature.

Hopes for Peace

Once those conditions brought society a great deal of strife and risked the well-being of society, the "peacemakers" appeared in society. They have assumed control and power and renewed the social life based on new conditions, which they considered true, to suffice for the peaceful existence of society.

Yet, the majority of those peacemakers, which spring up after every dispute, naturally come from among the destructors, meaning from the seekers of truth, by way of "What's mine is mine and what's yours is yours." This is because they are the powerful and courageous ones in society, called "heroes" and "courageous," for they are always willing to renounce their own lives and the lives of the whole collective, if the collective disagrees with their views.

But the constructors in society, who are the men of mercy and charity, who care for their own lives and for the life of the collective, refuse to risk themselves or the public in order to impose their opinion on the collective. Hence, they are always on the weak side in society, called "the faint-hearted" and "the coward."

It is therefore obvious that the hand of the reckless brave will always be on top, and it is natural that all the peacemakers come from among the destructors and not from the constructors. By this, we see how the hope for peace, which our generation so yearns for, is futile both from the perspective of the subject and from the perspective of the predicate.

For the subjects, who are the peacemakers of our time and in any generation, meaning those who have the power to make peace in the world, are forever made of the human substance we call "destructors," for they are seekers of truth, meaning to establish the world on the attribute of "What's mine is mine and what's yours is yours."

It is natural that those people defend their opinions firmly, to the point of risking their own lives and the life of the entire collective. And this is what gives them the power to always prevail over the human substance called "constructors," the seekers of mercy and charity, who are willing to give up of their own for the sake of others in order to save the world, since they are the faint-hearted and the coward.

It turns out that seeking truth and the destruction of the world are one and the same, and the seeking mercy and the construction of the world are one and the same, too. Therefore, we should not hope from the destructors to establish the peace.

And it is hopeless to hope for peace from the predicate, meaning from the conditions of peace itself, since the proper conditions for the well-being of the individual and the well-being of the collective, according to the criterion of truth that these peacemakers so desire, have not been established. And it is a must that there will always be a large minority in society who are dissatisfied with the conditions offered to them, as we have shown above regarding the weakness of the truth. They will always remain a ready and willing fuel for the new quarrelsome people and for new peacemakers who will always follow.

The Well-Being of a Certain Collective and the Well-Being of the Whole World

Do not be surprised if I mix together the well-being of a particular collective with the well-being of the whole world, because indeed we have already come to such a degree where the whole world is considered one collective and one society. That is, because each person in the world draws his life's marrow and his livelihood from all the people in the world, he thereby becomes enslaved, to serve and care for the well-being of the entire world.

We have proven above that the total subordination of the individual to the collective is like a small wheel in a machine. He draws his life and his happiness from that collective, and therefore the well-being of the collective and his own well-being are one and the same, and vice-versa. Therefore, to the extent that a person is enslaved to himself, he necessarily becomes enslaved to the collective, as we have spoken at length above.

And what is the extent of that collective? This is determined by the perimeter of the drawing of the individual from them. For example, in historic times, that perimeter was only the perimeter of one family, meaning the individual needed aid only from his own family members. At that time, he had to be subordinate only to his own family.

In later times, families gathered into towns and counties, and the individual became enslaved to his town. Later, when the towns and counties joined into states, the individual was supported by all his countrymen for the happiness of his life. Thus, he became enslaved to all the people in the country. Therefore, in our generation, when each person is aided for his happiness by all the countries in the world, it is necessary that to that extent, the individual becomes enslaved to the whole world, like a wheel in a machine.

Therefore, the possibility of making good, happy, and peaceful conducts in one country is inconceivable when it is not so in all the countries in the world, and vice versa. In our time, the countries are all linked in the satisfaction of their needs of life, as individuals were in their families in earlier times. Therefore, we can no longer speak or deal with just conducts that guarantee the well-being of one country or one nation, but only with the well-being of the whole world, for the benefit or harm of each and every person in the world depends and is measured by the benefit of all the individuals the world over.

Although this is, in fact, known and felt, still the people in the world have not yet grasped it properly. Why? Because such is the conduct of development in nature: The act comes before the understanding, and only actions will prove and push humanity forward.

In Practical Life, the Four Attributes Contradict One Another

If the above practical difficulties, which disturb us helpless people on our way, are not enough, we have in addition a further mix-up and great battle regarding the psychological predispositions. That is, the attributes themselves, within each and every one of us individually, are unique and contradictory to one another, for the four above attributes, mercy, truth, justice, and peace, which were divided in the nature of people, whether by development or by rearing, are in and of themselves contradictory to one another. If we take, for example, the attribute of mercy in its abstract form, we find that its government contradicts all other attributes, meaning that by the laws of the rule of mercy, there is no place for the appearance of the other attributes in our world.

What is the attribute of mercy? Our sages defined it (Avot 5), "What's mine is yours and what's yours is yours"—*Hasid* [having the quality of *Hesed* (mercy)]. And if all the people in the world were to behave by this quality, it would cancel all the glory of the attribute of truth and judgment, for if each and every one were naturally willing to give everything he had to others, and take nothing from another, then the whole interest in lying to one another would disappear. Also, it would be irrelevant to discuss the quality of truth, since truth and falsehood are relative to one another. If there were no falsehood in the world, there would be no concept of truth. Needless to say, all the other attributes, which came only to strengthen the attribute of truth because of its weakness, would be canceled.

Truth is defined by the words "What's mine is mine, and what's yours is yours." This contradicts the attribute of mercy and cannot altogether tolerate it, since in truth, it is unjust to labor and strain for another, since besides failing his friend and accustoming him to exploit others, truth dictates that every person should treasure his own assets for a time of need, so he will not have to be a burden on his fellow man.

Moreover, there is not a person without relatives and heirs that, in truth, should come before others, for so nature dictates, and one who gives his property to others lies to his relatives and heirs by not leaving them anything.

Also, peace contradicts justice because to make peace in the public, there must be conditions that by content promise the nimble and the smart, which invest their energy and wisdom, to become rich, and the negligent and naïve to be poor. Hence, he who is more energetic takes his share and the share of his negligent friend and enjoys such a good life that there is not enough left for the negligent and naive to merely provide for their necessary livelihood. Hence, they remain completely bare and destitute in many ways.

It is certainly unjust to punish the negligent and the naive so harshly for no evil, for what is their sin and what is the crime of those wretched people if Providence did not grant them agility and acumen that they should be punished with torments harsher than death?

Thus, there is no justice whatsoever in the conditions of peace. Thus, peace contradicts justice and justice contradicts peace, for if we order the division of property justly, meaning give to the negligent and naive a substantial portion of the part that the nimble and the energetic have, then these powerful and initiating people will certainly not rest until they overthrow the government that enslaves the great and energetic ones, and exploits them in favor of the weak. Therefore, there is no hope for the peace of the collective. Thus, justice contradicts peace.

The Attribute of Singularity in the Egoism Effects Ruin and Destruction

You see how our attributes collide and fight one another. Not only among sects, but within each person, the four attributes dominate him at once or one at a time, and fight within him until it is impossible for common sense to organize them and bring them to complete consent.

The truth is that the root of this whole disorder within us is no more than the above-mentioned attribute of singularity, which exists in each of us, whether less or more.

Although we have clarified that it comes from a sublime reason, that this attribute extends to us directly from the Creator, who is singular in the world and the Root of all creations, still, since the sensation of singularity has settled in our narrow egoism, it affects ruin and destruction until it became the source of all the ruins that were and will be in the world.

Indeed, there is not a single person in the world who is free from it, and all the differences are only in the ways it is used—for the desires of the heart, for governance, or for honor—and this is what distinguishes people from one another.

But the equal side in all the people of the world is that each of us stands ready to exploit all the people for his own private benefit with every means at one's disposal without taking into any consideration that he is going to build himself on the ruin of his friend. It is completely inconsequential what allowance each of us gives himself, according to his chosen direction, since the desire is the root of the intellect and not the intellect the root of the desire. In truth, the greater and more outstanding one is, precisely to that extent, his attribute of singularity is greater and outstanding.

Using the Nature of Singularity as a Subject of Evolution in the Collective and in the Individual

Now we will penetrate into the understanding of the direct conditions that will finally be accepted by humanity at the time of the appearance of world peace, and to know how these conditions are good to bring a life of happiness to the individual and to the public, and the willingness in humanity to want to finally burden themselves with these special conditions.

Let us return to the matter of singularity in the heart of every person, which is poised to swallow the whole world for his own pleasure. Its root extends directly from the Unique One to the people, who are His branches. Here there is a question that demands an answer: How can it be that such a corrupted form will appear in us so as to become the father of all harm and ruin in the world, and how from the Source of every construction extends the source of every destruction? We cannot leave such a question unanswered.

Indeed, there are two sides to the coin of the above-mentioned singularity. If we examine it from its upper side, from the perspective of its equivalence with the Unique One, it works only in the form of bestowal upon others, for the Creator only bestows and has nothing of the form of reception. He lacks nothing nor needs to receive anything from the created beings He has created. Therefore, the singularity that extends to us from Him must also act only in forms of bestowal upon others, and not at all to receive for ourselves.

On the other side of that coin, meaning in terms of how it actually works within us, we find that it operates in the complete opposite direction, since it operates only in forms of reception for oneself, such as the desire to be the single most wealthy person in the world. Thus, the above two sides are as far apart from one another as the east from the west.

This gives us the solution to our question: "How is it possible that within that singularity which stems and comes to us from He who is unique in the world, Who is the source of every construction, serves in us as the source of every destruction?" This has come to us because we use that precious tool in the opposite direction, which is self-reception.

I am not saying that the singularity in us will never act in us in a form of bestowal, for you cannot deny that amongst us are people whose singularity operates in them in the form of bestowal upon others, too, such as those who spend their money for the common good, or those who dedicate all their efforts to the common good, etc.

Yet, those two sides of the coin that I have described speak only of the two points in the development of creation that bring everything to completion, starting in absence, and gradually climbing the rungs of development, from one degree to the degree above it, and from there to the higher still, until it comes to its final height, which is its preordained measure of completeness, where it will remain forever.

The order of development of the two points is, A) the starting point, the lowest degree, which is close to complete absence. It is described as the second side of the coin. B) The point of final height, where it rests and exists forever. This is described in the first side of the coin.

But this era that we are in has already developed to a great extent and has already risen many degrees. It has already risen above its lowest phase, which is the above-mentioned second side, and has come significantly closer to the first side.

For this reason, there are already people among us who use their singularity in forms of bestowal upon others. Yet, they are still few, as we are still in the midst of the path of development. When we achieve the highest point of the degrees, we will all be using our singularity only in a form of bestowal upon others, and there will never be any case of any person using it in a manner of self-reception.

According to these words, we have found an opportunity to examine the conditions of life in the last generation—the time of world peace, when the whole of humanity achieves the level of the first side and will use their singularity only in a manner of bestowal upon others, and not at all in a manner of reception for oneself. And it is good to copy here the above-mentioned form of life so it will serve us as a lesson and a role model to settle our minds under the flood of the waves of our lives; perhaps it is worthwhile and possible in our generation, too, to experiment in resembling this above form of life.

The Condition of Life in the Last Generation

First, everyone must thoroughly understand and explain to his surroundings that the well-being of society, which is the well-being of the state and the well-being of the world, are completely interdependent. As long as the laws of society are not satisfactory to each and every individual in the state, and leave a minority that is dissatisfied with the government of the state, that minority conspires under the government of the state and seeks to overthrow it.

If its power is not sufficient to fight the government of the state face to face, it will seek to overthrow it indirectly, such as by inciting countries against each other and bringing them to war, for it is natural that at wartime there will be many more dissatisfied people with whom they will have hope to achieve the critical mass to overthrow the government of the state and establish a new leadership that is convenient for them. Thus, the well-being of the individual is a direct cause for the well-being of the state.

Furthermore, if we take into consideration that always-existing part in the state for whom war is their craft and their every hope of success—such as professional soldiers and suppliers of ammunition—who are always a very prominent minority in terms of social quality, and if we add to them the dissatisfied minority from the current laws, then at any given moment, you have a vast amount of people craving war and bloodshed.

Thus, peace in the world and peace in the country are interdependent. Hence, we necessarily find that even that part of the state which is currently satisfied with life, who are the nimble and the clever, they still have a lot to be concerned about for the safety of their lives due to the tensions with those who strive to overthrow them. If they understood the value of peace, they would be happy to adopt the conduct of life in the last generation, for "all that a man has will he give for his life."

Pain vs. Pleasure in Self-Reception

Thus, when we examine and thoroughly grasp the above plan, we will see that the whole difficulty lies in changing our nature from a desire to receive for ourselves to a desire to bestow upon others, as those two things deny one another. At first glance, the plan seems imaginary, as something that is above human nature. But when we delve into the matter, we will find that the whole contradiction from reception for oneself to bestowal upon others is nothing but psychological, for in fact, we do bestow upon others without benefiting ourselves. This is so because although self-reception manifests itself in us in various ways, such as property, possessions that the heart, eye, and palate covet, etc., all those are defined by one name: "pleasure." Thus, the very essence of reception for oneself that a person desires is nothing but the desire for pleasure.

Now, imagine that if we were to collect all the pleasures one feels during his seventy years of life and put it on one side, and collect all the sorrow and suffering one feels on the other side, if we could see the balance, we would prefer not to be born at all. If this is so, then what does one receive during one's life? If we assume that one obtains twenty percent of pleasure in his life compared to eighty percent of suffering, then if we put them one opposite the other, there would remain sixty percent of suffering unrewarded.

But this is all a private calculation, as when one works for oneself. But in a global calculation, the individual produces more than he receives for his own pleasure and sustenance. Thus, if the direction were to change from self-reception to bestowal, the individual would enjoy the entire produce he produces without much pain.

Exile and Redemption

Harmony between Religion and the Law of Development or Blind Fate

"And among those nations you will have no repose and there will be no resting place for your feet" (Deuteronomy 28:65). "And that which comes to your mind will not be at all, in that you say, 'We will be as the nations, as the families of the lands'" (Ezekiel 20:32).

The Creator will evidently show us that Israel cannot exist in exile, and will find no rest as the rest of the nations that mingled among the nations and found rest, and assimilated in them until no trace was left of them. Not so is the house of Israel. This nation will find no rest among the nations until it realizes the verse, "And from there you will seek the Lord your God, and you will find Him for you will demand Him with all your heart and all your soul."

This can be examined by studying Providence and the verse that states about us, "The Torah is true and all its words are true, and woe to us as long as we doubt its truthfulness." And we say about all the rebuke that is happening to us that it is chance and blind fate. This has but one cure—to bring the troubles back on us to such an extent that we will see that they are not coincidental but steadfast Providence, intended for us in the holy Torah.

We should clarify this matter by the law of development itself: The nature of the steadfast guidance that we have attained through the holy Torah, as in the path of Torah in Providence (see the article "The Freedom"), a far more rapid development than the other nations has come to us. And because the members of the nation developed so, there was always the necessity to go forward and be extremely meticulous with all the *Mitzvot* [commandments] of the Torah. Because they would not do so, but wished to include their narrow selfishness, meaning the *Lo Lishma* [not for Her sake], this developed the ruin of the First Temple, since they wished to extol wealth and power above justice, as do other nations.

But because the Torah prohibits this, they denied the Torah and the prophecy and adopted the manners of the neighbors so they could enjoy life as much as the selfishness demanded of them. Because they did so, the powers of the nation disintegrated: Some followed the selfish kings and officers, and some followed the prophets, and that separation continued until the ruin.

In the Second Temple, it was even more noticeable, since the beginning of the separation was publicly displayed there by unvirtuous disciples, headed by Tzadok and Bytos. Their mutiny against our sages revolved primarily around the obligation of *Lishma* [for Her sake], as our sages said, "Wise men, be careful with your words." Because they did not want to retire from selfishness, they created communities of this deplorable kind and became a great sect called "Tzdokim," who were the rich and the officers, pursuing selfish desires, unlike the path of Torah. They fought against the Prushim, and they are the ones who brought the Roman kingdom's rule over Israel. They are the ones who would not make peace with the imperious, as our sages advised according to the Torah, until the house was ruined and the glory of Israel was exiled.

The Difference between a Secular Ideal and a Religious Ideal

A secular ideal stems from humanity and hence cannot raise itself above humanness. Conversely, a religious ideal, which stems from the Creator, can raise itself above humanity. This is because the basis for a secular ideal is equalization and the price of glorifying man, and he acts in order to boast in the eyes of people. And although he is sometimes disgraced in the eyes of his contemporaries, he still relies on other generations and it is still a precious thing for him, like a gem that greatly satisfies its owner although no one knows of it or cherishes it.

A religious ideal, however, is based on glory in the eyes of the Creator. Hence, he who follows a religious ideal can raise himself above humanity.

So it is among the nations of our exile. As long as we followed the path of Torah, we were safe, for it is known to all the nations that we are a highly developed nation and they wanted our cooperation. They exploit us, each according to their own selfish desires, but we still had great power among the nations, so after all the exploitation, there still remained a handsome portion left for us, greater than for the civilians of the land.

But because people rebelled against the Torah in their aspiration to execute their selfish ploys, they lost life's purpose, meaning the work of the Creator, and replaced the sublime goal for selfish goals of life's pleasures. Thus, anyone who attained fortune raised his goal with glory and beauty. In consequence, where the religious man scattered his monetary surplus on charity, good deeds, building seminaries, and other such collective needs, the selfish ones scattered their surplus on the joys of life: food and drink, clothing and jewels, and equalized themselves with the prominent in that nation.

By these words, I only mean to show that the Torah and the natural law of development go hand in hand in wondrous unity even with blind fate. Thus, the bad incidents in the exile, which we have much to tell of from the days of our exile, were all because we embezzled the Torah. Had we kept the commandments of the Torah, no harm would have come to us.

Congruity and Unity between Torah and Blind Fate, and the Development of Human Calculation

Hence, I hereby propose to the House of Israel to say to our troubles, "Enough!" and at the very least make a human calculation regarding those adventures that they have inflicted on us time and time again. And here, too, in our own country, where we want to reestablish our statehood, we have no hope of holding on to the ground as a nation as long as we do not accept our holy Torah without any allowances, to the last condition of the work Lishma, and not for one's own sake, with any residue of selfishness, as I have proven in the article "Matan Torah."

If we do not establish ourselves accordingly, then there are classes among us, and we will undoubtedly be pushed, once to the right and once to the left, like all the nations. And much more so, since the nature of the developed is that they cannot be restrained, for any important view that comes from a developed, opinionated person, will not bow its head before anything and knows no compromise. This is why our sages said, "Israel is the fiercest among the nations," as one whose mind is broader is most obstinate.

This is a psychological law, and if you do not understand me, go and study this lesson among the contemporary members of the nation: While we have only begun to build, time has already disclosed our fierceness and assertiveness of the mind, and that which one builds, the other ruins.

...This is known to all, but there is only one innovation in my words: They believe that in the end, the other side will understand the danger and will bow his head and accept their view. But I know that even if we tie them up together, one will not surrender to the other even a little, and no danger will interrupt anyone from carrying out his ambition.

In a word: As long as we do not raise our goal above the corporeal life, we will have no corporeal resurrection, for the spiritual and the corporeal in us cannot dwell together. We are the children of the idea, and even if we are immersed in forty-nine gates of materialism, we will still not give up the idea. Hence, it is the holy purpose of for His sake that we need.

A Speech for the Completion of The Zohar

(Given to celebrate the completion of the publication of the
Sulam [ladder] commentary on *The Book of Zohar*)

It is known that the desired purpose from the work in Torah and *Mitzvot* [commandments] is to adhere to the Creator, as it is written, "and to adhere to Him." We should understand what *Dvekut* [adhesion] with the Creator means, since the thought has no perception of Him whatsoever.

Indeed, our sages have discussed this question before me, asking about the verse, "and to adhere to Him": "How can one adhere to Him? After all, He is a consuming fire." And they replied, "Adhere unto His qualities: As He is merciful, so you are merciful; as he is compassionate, so you are compassionate."

This is perplexing; how did our sages drift from the literal text? After all, it is explicitly written, "and to adhere to Him." Had the meaning been to adhere to His qualities, it would have to be written, "adhere to His ways," so why does it say, "and to adhere to Him"?

The thing is that in corporeality, which takes up space, we understand *Dvekut* as proximity of place, and we understand separation as remoteness of place. But in spirituality, which does not occupy any space, *Dvekut* and separation do not mean proximity or remoteness of place, since they do not occupy any space. Rather, we understand *Dvekut* as equivalence of form between two spirituals, and we understand separation as disparity of form between two spirituals.

As the axe cuts and separates a corporeal object into two, by removing the parts from one another, disparity of form distinguishes the spiritual and divides it in two. If the disparity of form between them is small, we say that they are a little far from one another. If the disparity of form is great, we say that they are very far from one another. If they are of opposite forms, we say that they are as far from each other as two extremes.

For example, when two people hate each other, it is said about them that they are as separated from one another as the east from the west. And if they love each other, it is said about them that they are as attached to one another as a single body.

This does not concern nearness or remoteness of location. Rather, it is about equivalence of form or disparity of form. This is so because when people love each other, it is because there is equivalence of form between them. Because one loves everything that one's friend loves, and hates all that one's friend hates, they are attached to one another and love one another.

However, if there is any disparity of form between them, and one loves something even though one's friend hates that thing, they are hateful of each other and remote from one another to the extent of their disparity of form. And if they are opposite so that everything that one loves, one's friend hates, it is said about them that they are as remote and as separate as the east from the west.

You find that disparity of form in spirituality acts like the axe that separates in corporeality. Similarly, the measure of remoteness of location and the measure of the separation in them depends on the measure of disparity of form between them. Also, the measure of *Dvekut* between them depends on the measure of equivalence of form between them.

Now we understand how right our sages were when they interpreted the verse, "and to adhere to Him," as *Dvekut* with His qualities—"As He is merciful, so you are merciful; as He is compassionate, so you are compassionate." They did not deflect the text from the literal meaning. Quite the contrary, they interpreted the text precisely according to its literal meaning, since spiritual *Dvekut* can only be depicted as equivalence of form. Hence, by equalizing our form with the form of His qualities, we become attached to Him.

This is why they said, "as He is merciful." In other words, all His actions are to bestow and benefit others, and not at all for His own benefit, since He has no deficiencies that require complementing. And also, He has no one from whom to receive. Similarly, all your actions will be to bestow and to benefit others. Thus, you will equalize your form with the form of the qualities of the Creator, and this is spiritual *Dvekut*.

There is a discernment of "mind" and a discernment of "heart" in the above-mentioned equivalence of form. The engagement in Torah and *Mitzvot* in order to bestow contentment upon one's Maker is equivalence of form in the mind. This is because the Creator does not think of Himself—whether He exists or whether He watches over His creations, and other such doubts. Similarly, one who wishes to achieve equivalence of form must not think of these things, as well, when it is clear to him that the Creator does not think of them, since there is no greater disparity of form than that. Hence, anyone who thinks of such matters is certainly separated from Him and will never achieve equivalence of form.

This is what our sages said, "Let all your actions be for the sake of the Creator," that is, *Dvekut* with the Creator. Do not do anything that does not yield this goal of *Dvekut*. This means that all your actions will be to bestow and to benefit your fellow person. At that time, you will achieve equivalence of form with the Creator—as all His actions are to bestow and to benefit others, so you, all your actions will be only to bestow and to benefit others. This is the complete *Dvekut*.

We could ask about it, "How can one's every action be to benefit others? After all, one must work to sustain oneself and one's family." The answer is that those deeds that one does out of necessity, to receive one's bare necessities for sustenance, that necessity is neither praised nor condemned. This is not considered doing something for oneself whatsoever.

Anyone who delves into the heart of things will certainly be surprised at how one can achieve complete equivalence of form, so all one's actions will be to give to others, while man's very essence is only to receive for oneself. By nature, we are unable to do even the smallest thing to benefit others. Instead, when we give to others, we are compelled to expect that in the end, we will receive a worthwhile reward. If one as much as doubts the reward, one will refrain from acting. Thus, how can one's every action be only to bestow upon others and not at all for oneself?

Indeed, I admit that this is a very difficult thing. One cannot change the nature of one's own creation, which is only to receive for oneself, much less invert one's nature from one extreme to the other, meaning not to receive anything for oneself, but rather act only to bestow.

Yet, this is why the Creator gave us Torah and *Mitzvot*, which we were commanded to do only in order to bestow contentment upon the Creator. Had it not been for the engagement in Torah and *Mitzvot Lishma* [for Her sake], to bring contentment to the Creator with them, and not to benefit ourselves, there would have been no tactic in the world that could help us invert our nature.

Now you can understand the rigorousness of engaging in Torah and *Mitzvot Lishma*. If one's intention in the Torah and *Mitzvot* is not to benefit the Creator, but to benefit oneself, not only will the nature of the will to receive in him not be inverted, but rather, the will to receive in him will be much more than what he was given by the nature of his creation, as I explained in the introduction to the *Sulam* commentary in the first volume, see there Items 30-31.

But what are the virtues of one who has been rewarded with *Dvekut* with the Creator? They are not specified anywhere, except in subtle intimations. Yet, to clarify the matters in my essay, I must disclose a little, as much as necessary.

I will explain the matters through an allegory. The body with its organs are one. The whole of the body exchanges thoughts and sensations with each of its organs. For example, if the whole body thinks that a certain organ should serve it and please it, this organ immediately knows that thought and provides the contemplated pleasure. Also, if an organ thinks and feels that the place it is in is narrow, the rest of the body immediately knows that thought and sensation and moves it to a comfortable place.

However, should an organ be cut off from the body, they become two separate entities; the rest of the body no longer knows the needs of the separated organ, and the organ no longer knows the thoughts of the body, to serve it and to benefit it. But if a physician came and reconnected the organ to the body as before, the organ would once again know the thoughts and needs of the rest of the body, and the rest of the body would once again know the needs of the organ.

According to this allegory, we can understand the merit of one who has been rewarded with *Dvekut* with the Creator. I have already demonstrated (in the "Introduction to the Book of Zohar," Item 9, and in my commentary on the *Idra*

Zuta) that the soul is an illumination that extends from His self. This illumination has been separated from the Creator by the Creator's clothing it with a will to receive. This is so because the thought of creation, to do good to His creations, created in each soul a desire to receive pleasure. Thus, this disparity of form of the will to receive separated that illumination from His self and turned it into a separate part from Him. See there in the source, since this is not the place to elaborate on this.

It follows that each soul was included in His self prior to its creation. But with creation, meaning along with the nature of the desire to receive pleasure that has been instilled in it, it acquired disparity of form and was separated from the Creator, whose only wish is to bestow. This is so because, as we have explained above, disparity of form separates in spirituality as the axe does in corporeality.

Thus, now the soul is completely similar to the allegory about the organ that was cut off and separated from the body. Even though prior to the separation, they—the organ and the whole body—were one and exchanged thoughts and sensations with one another, after the organ has been cut off from the body they have become two entities. Now one does not know the other's thoughts or needs. It is even more so after the soul is dressed in a body of this world: All the connections it had prior to the separation from His self have stopped, and they are like two separate entities.

Now we can easily understand the merit of one who has been rewarded with adhering to Him once more, meaning rewarded with equivalence of form with the Creator by inverting the will to receive imprinted in him through the power in Torah and *Mitzvot*. This was the very thing that separated him from His self. He turned it into a desire to bestow, and all of one's actions are only to bestow and to benefit others, as he has equalized his form with the Maker. It follows that he is just like the organ that was once cut off from the body and has reconnected to the body: It knows the thoughts of the rest of the body once again, just as it did prior to the separation from the body.

So is the soul: After it has acquired equivalence with Him, it knows His thoughts once more, as it knew prior to the separation from Him due to the will to receive's disparity of form. Then the verse, "Know the God of your father," comes true in him, as then he is rewarded with complete knowledge, which is Godly knowledge, and he is rewarded with all the secrets of the Torah, as His thoughts are the secrets of the Torah.

This is the meaning of what Rabbi Meir said: "Anyone who learns Torah *Lishma* is granted many things. The secrets and flavors of Torah are revealed to him, and he becomes like an ever-flowing spring." As we have said, through engagement in Torah *Lishma*, meaning by aiming to bring contentment to his Maker through his engagement in the Torah, and not at all for his own benefit, he is guaranteed to cling to the Creator. This means that he will achieve equivalence of form, and all his actions will be to benefit others and not himself at all, just like the Creator, whose every action is only to bestow and to benefit others.

By this, one returns to *Dvekut* with the Creator as was the soul prior to its creation. Hence, he is granted many things and is rewarded with the secrets and the flavors of the Torah. Because he has reconnected with the Creator, he knows once more the thoughts of the Creator like the allegory about the organ that has been reattached to the body. The thoughts of the Creator are called "secrets and flavors of the Torah." Thus, one who learns Torah *Lishma* is rewarded with the secrets and flavors of Torah being revealed to him, and he becomes like an ever-flowing spring due to the removal of the partitions that separated him from the Creator, so he has become one with Him again, as before one was created.

Indeed, the whole Torah, revealed and concealed, is the thoughts of the Creator, without any difference. Yet, it is like a person drowning in the river, whose friend throws him a rope to save him. If the drowning person catches the rope in its near part, his friend can save him and pull him out of the river.

So is the Torah: Being entirely the thoughts of the Creator, it is like a rope that the Creator throws to people to save them and pull them out of the *Klipot* [shells]. The end of the rope, which is near to all the people, is the revealed Torah, which requires no intention or thought. Moreover, even when there is a faulty thought in the *Mitzvot*, the Creator still accepts it, as it is written, "One must always engage in Torah and *Mitzvot Lo Lishma* [not for Her sake], since from *Lo Lishma* he will come to *Lishma* [for Her sake]."

Hence, the Torah and *Mitzvot* are the end of the rope, and there is not a person in the world who cannot grip it. If one tightly grips it, meaning is rewarded with engaging in Torah and *Mitzvot Lishma*, to bring contentment to one's Maker and not to oneself, the Torah and *Mitzvot* lead one to equivalence of form with the Creator. This is the meaning of "and to adhere to Him."

At that time, one will be rewarded with attaining all the thoughts of the Creator, called "secrets of the Torah" and "flavors of the Torah," which are the rest of the rope. However, one is awarded it only after one has achieved complete *Dvekut*.

The reason we compare the Creator's thoughts, meaning the secrets of the Torah and the flavors of the Torah, to a rope is that there are many degrees in the equivalence of form with the Creator. Hence, there are many degrees in the rope in attaining the secrets of the Torah. One's measure of attainment of the secrets of the Torah, of knowing His thoughts, is as the measure of equivalence of form with the Creator.

Overall, there are five degrees: *Nefesh, Ruach, Neshama, Haya, Yechida*, each of which consists of all of them. Also, each contains five degrees, and each of those contains at least twenty-five degrees.

They are also called "worlds," as our sages said, "The Creator is destined to grant each righteous 310 worlds." The reason why the degrees of attaining Him are called "worlds" is that the name *Olam* [world] has two meanings:

All those who come into that world have the same sensation, and everything that one sees, hears, and feels, all those who come into that world see, hear, and feel, as well.

All those who come into that "hidden" world cannot know or attain anything in another world.

These two degrees are also found in attainment:

Anyone who has been rewarded with a certain degree knows and attains in it everything that those who came to that degree attained in all the generations that were and that will be. He has common attainment with them as though they are in the same world.

All who come to that degree will not be able to know or attain what exists in another degree. It is like this world: They cannot know anything of what exists in the world of truth. This is why the degrees are called "worlds."

For this reason, those with attainment can compose books and put their attainments in writing in intimations and allegories. They will be understood by all who have been rewarded with the degrees that the books describe, and they have common attainment with them. But those who have not been rewarded with the full measure of the degree as the authors will not be able to understand their intimations. It is even more so with those who have not been rewarded with any attainment; they will not understand a thing about them since they have no common attainments.

We have already said that the complete *Dvekut* and complete attainment is divided into 125 degrees overall. Accordingly, prior to the days of the Messiah, it is impossible to be granted all 125 degrees. And there are two differences between the generation of the Messiah and all other generations:

1. Only in the generation of the Messiah is it possible to attain all 125 degrees, and in no other generation.

2. Throughout the generations, those who ascended and were rewarded with *Dvekut* were few, as our sages wrote about the verse, "I have found one person in a thousand, where a thousand enter the room, and one comes out to the light," meaning to *Dvekut* and attainment. But in the generation of the Messiah, each and every one can be rewarded with *Dvekut* and attainment, as it was said, "For the earth will be full of the knowledge of the Lord," "And they will teach no more every man his neighbor and every man his brother, saying, 'Know the Lord,' for they will all know Me, from the least of them to the greatest of them."

An exception is Rashbi and his generation, the authors of *The Zohar*, who were granted all 125 degrees in completeness, even though it was prior to the days of the Messiah. It was said about him and his disciples: "A sage is preferable to a prophet." Hence, we often find in *The Zohar* that there will be none like the generation of Rashbi until the generation of the Messiah King. This is why his composition made such a great impression in the world, since the secrets of the Torah in it occupy the level of all 125 degrees.

This is why it is said in *The Zohar* that *The Book of Zohar* will be revealed only at the End of Days, the days of the Messiah. This is so because we have already said that if the degrees of the examiners are not at the full measure of the degree of the author, they will not understand his intimations since they do not have a common attainment.

Since the degree of the authors of *The Zohar* is at the full level of the 125 degrees, they cannot be attained prior to the days of the Messiah. It follows that there will be no common attainment with the authors of *The Zohar* in the generations preceding the days of the Messiah. Hence, *The Zohar* could not be revealed in the generations before the generation of the Messiah.

This is a clear proof that our generation has come to the days of the Messiah. We can see that all the interpretations of *The Book of Zohar* before ours did not clarify as much as ten percent of the difficult places in *The Zohar*. Even in the little they did clarify, their words are almost as abstruse as the words of *The Zohar* itself.

But in our generation, we have been rewarded with the *Sulam* [Ladder] commentary, which is a complete interpretation of all the words of *The Zohar*. Moreover, not only does it not leave an unclear matter in the whole of *The Zohar* without interpreting it, the clarifications are based on a straightforward analysis, which any intermediate examiner can understand. And since *The Zohar* appeared in our generation, it is a clear proof that we are already in the days of the Messiah, at the outset of that generation of which it was said, "for the earth will be full of the knowledge of the Lord."

We should know that spiritual matters are not like corporeal matters, where giving and receiving come as one. In spirituality, the time of giving and the time of receiving are separate. This is because first it was given from the Creator to the receiver, and in this giving, He only gives him a chance to receive. However, he has not received anything until he is properly sanctified and purified, and then one is rewarded with receiving it. Thus, it may take a long time between the time of giving and the time of receiving.

Accordingly, saying that this generation has already come to the verse, "for the earth will be full of the knowledge of the Lord," refers only to the giving. Yet, we have not yet come to a state of reception. When we are purified, sanctified, studied, and exerted in the desired amount, the time of reception will arrive and the verse, "for the earth will be full of the knowledge of the Lord," will come true in us.

Also, it is known that redemption and the complete attainment are intertwined. The proof is that anyone who is drawn to the secrets of the Torah is also drawn to the land of Israel. This is why we were promised, "for the earth will be full of the knowledge of the Lord," only at the End of Days, during the time of redemption.

Thus, as we have not yet been rewarded with a time of reception in the complete attainment, but only with a time of giving, by which we have been given a chance to achieve complete attainment, so it is with redemption. We have been rewarded with it only in the form of giving. The fact of the matter is that the Creator delivered our holy land from the foreigners and has given it back to us, yet we have not received the land into our own authority, since the time of reception has not yet come, as we explained concerning the complete attainment.

Thus, He has given but we have not received, since we have no economic independence, and there is no political independence without economic independence. Moreover, there is no redemption of the body without redemption of the soul. As long as the majority of the people are captive in the foreign cultures of the nations and are incapable of Israel's religion and culture, the bodies, too, will be captive under the alien forces. In this respect, the land is still in the hands of foreigners.

The proof is that no one is excited about the redemption, as it should have been with redemption after two millennia. Not only are those in the Diaspora not inclined to come to us and delight in the redemption, but a large portion of those that have been redeemed and are already dwelling among us are anxiously waiting to get rid of this redemption and return to the countries from which they came.

Thus, even though the Creator has delivered the land from the hands of the nations and has given it to us, we have not received it and we are not enjoying it. But with this giving, the Creator has given us an opportunity for redemption, to be purified and sanctified and assume the work of the Creator in Torah and *Mitzvot Lishma*. At that time, the Temple will be built and we will receive the land into our own authority. Then we will experience and feel the joy of redemption.

But as long as we have not come to this, nothing will change. There is no difference between the current manners of the land and the way it was while still under the hands of foreigners, in law, in economy, and in the work of the Creator. Thus, all we have is an opportunity for redemption.

It follows that our generation is the generation of the days of the Messiah. This is why we have been granted the redemption of our holy land from the hands of the foreigners. We have also been rewarded with the revelation of *The Book of Zohar*, which is the beginning of the realization of the verse, "For the earth will be full of the knowledge of the Lord." "And they will teach no more… for they will all know Me, from the least of them unto the greatest of them."

Yet, with those two, we have only been rewarded with giving from the Creator, but we have not received anything into our own hands. Instead, we have been given a chance to begin with the work of the Creator, to engage in Torah and *Mitzvot Lishma*. Then we will be granted the great success that is promised to the generation of the Messiah, which all the generations before us did not know. And then we will be rewarded with the time of reception of both the complete attainment and the complete redemption.

Thus, we have thoroughly explained our sages' reply to the question, "How is it possible to adhere to Him? which they said means 'adhere to His qualities.'" This is true for two reasons: 1) Spiritual *Dvekut* is not in proximity of place, but in equivalence of form. 2) Since the soul was separated from His self only because of the will to receive, which the Creator had imprinted in it, once He separated the will to receive from it, it naturally returned to the previous *Dvekut* with His self.

However, all this is in theory. In fact, they have not answered anything with the explanation of adhering to His qualities, which means to separate the will to receive, imprinted in the nature of creation, and arriving at the desire to bestow—the opposite of its nature.

What we explained, that one who is drowning in the river should grip the rope firmly, and before he engages in Torah and *Mitzvot Lishma* in a way that he will not return to folly, it is not considered gripping the rope firmly, the question returns: Where will one find motivation to wholeheartedly exert solely to bring contentment to one's Maker? After all, one cannot make a single movement without any benefit for himself, like a machine cannot work without fuel. If there is no self-benefit, but only contentment to his Maker, he will have no fuel for work.

The answer is that anyone who sufficiently attains His greatness, the bestowal he bestows upon Him is inverted into reception, as it is written in *Masechet Kidushin* (p 7a): With an important person, when the woman gives him money, it is regarded for her as reception, and she is sanctified.

So it is with the Creator: If one achieves His greatness, there is no greater reception than contentment to one's Maker. This is sufficient fuel to toil and wholeheartedly exert to bring contentment to Him. But clearly, as long as one has not sufficiently attained His greatness, he will not regard giving contentment to the Creator as reception enough for him to give one's heart and soul to the Creator.

Therefore, each time he truly aims only to bring contentment to his Maker and not to himself, he will immediately lose the strength to work, as he will be like a machine without fuel, since one cannot move a limb without drawing some benefit to oneself. It is even more so with such great labor as giving one's heart and soul, as dictated in the Torah. Undoubtedly, he will not be able to do so without drawing some reception of pleasure for himself.

Indeed, obtaining His greatness in a measure that bestowal becomes reception, as mentioned concerning an important person, is not at all difficult. Everyone knows the greatness of the Creator, who created everything and consumes everything, without a beginning and without an end, and whose sublimity is endless.

Yet, the difficulty in that is that the measure of the greatness does not depend on the individual, but on the environment. For example, even if one is filled with virtues but the environment does not appreciate him as such, he will always be low-spirited and will not be able to take pride in his virtues, although he has no doubt that they are true. And conversely, a person with no merit at all, but the environment respects him as though he is virtuous, that person will be filled with pride, since the measure of importance and greatness is given entirely to the environment.

When a person sees that the environment slights His work and does not properly appreciate His greatness, he cannot overcome the environment. Thus, he cannot obtain His greatness, and becomes negligent during his work, like them.

Since he does not have the basis for obtaining His greatness, he will obviously not be able to work in order to bring contentment to his Maker and not to himself, for he will have no motivation to exert, and "if you did not labor and find, do not believe." The only advice for this is either to work for oneself or not to work at all, since bestowing contentment upon his Maker will not be for him tantamount to reception.

Now you can understand the verse, "In the multitude of people is the king's glory," since the measure of the greatness comes from the environment under two conditions:

The extent of the appreciation of the environment.

The size of the environment. Thus, "In the multitude of people is the king's glory."

Because of the great difficulty in the matter, our sages advised us: "Make for yourself a rav [teacher/great person] and buy yourself a friend." This means that one should choose for oneself an important and renowned person to be his rav, and from him he will be able to come to engaging in Torah and *Mitzvot* in order to bring contentment to his Maker. This is so because there are two extenuations concerning one's rav:

1. Since he is an important person, the student can bestow contentment upon him, based on the sublimity of his rav, since bestowal becomes as reception for him. This is a natural fuel, so one can always increase his acts of bestowal. Once a person grows accustomed to engaging in bestowal upon the rav, he can transfer it to engaging in Torah and *Mitzvot Lishma* toward the Creator, too, since habit becomes a second nature.

2. Equivalence of form with the Creator does not help if it is not forever, "Until He who knows the mysteries will testify that he will not return to folly." This is not so with equivalence of form with his rav. Since the rav is in this world, within time, equivalence of form with him helps even if it is only temporary and he later turns sour again.

Thus, every time one equalizes one's form with one's rav, he adheres to him for a time. As a result, he obtains the knowledge and thoughts of the rav, according to his measure of *Dvekut*, as we explained in the allegory about the organ that has been cut off from the body and was reunited with it.

For this reason, the student can use his rav's attainment of the Creator's greatness, which inverts bestowal into reception and sufficient fuel to give one's heart and soul. At that time, the student, too, will be able to engage in Torah and *Mitzvot Lishma* with his very heart and soul, which is the remedy that yields eternal *Dvekut* with the Creator.

Now you can understand what our sages said (*Berachot* 7b): "Serving in the Torah is greater than learning it, as it is said, 'Elisha the son of Shaphat is here, who poured water on Elijah's hands.' It did not say 'learned,' but 'poured.'" This is perplexing; how can simple acts be greater than studying the wisdom and the knowledge?

But according to the above, we thoroughly understand that serving the rav with one's body and soul in order to bring contentment to his rav brings him to *Dvekut* with his rav, meaning to equivalence of form. By this he receives the thoughts and knowledge of the rav by way of "mouth-to-mouth," which is *Dvekut* of spirit with spirit. In this way, he is rewarded with obtaining His greatness sufficiently to turn bestowal into reception, to become sufficient fuel for devotion, until he is rewarded with *Dvekut* with the Creator.

This is not so concerning learning Torah with his rav, as this must be for his own benefit and does not yield *Dvekut*. It is considered "from mouth to ear." Thus, serving brings the student the rav's thoughts, and the learning—only the rav's words. Thus, the merit of serving is greater than the merit of learning as the importance of the rav's thoughts compared to the rav's words, and as the importance of "mouth-to-mouth" compared to "from mouth to ear."

However, all this is true if the service is in order to bestow contentment upon his rav. Yet, if the service is to benefit himself, such service cannot bring him to *Dvekut* with his rav, so learning with the rav is certainly more important than serving him.

Yet, as we have said concerning obtaining His greatness, an environment that does not properly appreciate Him weakens the individual and prevents him from obtaining His greatness. This is certainly true concerning one's rav, as well. An environment that does not properly appreciate the rav prevents the student from being able to properly obtain the greatness of his rav.

For this reason, our sages said, "Make for yourself a rav and buy yourself a friend." This means that one can make a new environment for oneself. This environment will help him obtain the greatness of his rav through love of friends who appreciate his rav. Through the friends' discussing the greatness of the rav, each of them receives the sensation of his greatness. Thus, bestowal upon his rav becomes reception and sufficient motivation to an extent that will bring one to engage in Torah and *Mitzvot Lishma*.

It was said about this, "The Torah is acquired by forty-eight virtues, by serving of sages, and by meticulousness of friends." This is so because besides serving the rav, one needs the meticulousness of friends, as well, meaning the friends' influence, so they will influence him so he obtains the greatness of his rav. This is so because obtaining the greatness depends entirely on the environment, and a single person cannot do a thing about it whatsoever.

Yet, there are two conditions to obtaining the greatness:

Always listen and accept the appreciation of the environment to the extent of their greatness.

The environment should be great, as it is written, "In the multitude of people is the king's glory."

To receive the first condition, each student must feel that he is the smallest among all the friends. In that state, he will be able to receive the appreciation of the greatness from everyone, since the great cannot receive from a smaller one, much less be impressed by his words. Rather, only the small is impressed by the appreciation of the great.

For the second condition, each student must extol the virtues of each friend and cherish him as though he were the greatest in the generation. Then the environment will influence him as though it were a great environment, as it should be, since quality is more important than quantity.

One Commandment

> "If he performs one *Mitzva* [commandment], he is happy, for he has sentenced himself and the whole world to the side of merit."

There is no serving the Creator and observing the *Mitzvot* [commandments] except *Lishma* [for Her sake]—meaning to bring contentment to one's Maker. Yet, our sages have already instructed to engage in Torah and *Mitzvot* even *Lo Lishma* [not for Her sake], since "from *Lo Lishma* he will come to *Lishma*"... I say that the first and only *Mitzva* that guarantees the achievement of the aspiration to attain *Lishma* is to resolve not to work for oneself, apart for the necessary works—merely to provide for one's sustenance. In the rest of the time, he will work for the public: to save the oppressed, and every being in the world that needs salvation and benefit.

Serving People According to the Commandment of the Creator

There are two advantages to this *Mitzva*: 1) Each one will understand that he is working because this work is approved and agreeable to all the people in the world. 2) This *Mitzva* may better qualify him to observe Torah and *Mitzvot Lishma*, since the preparation is part of the goal. This is so because by accustoming oneself to serving people, one benefits others and not oneself. Thus, one gradually becomes fit to observe the *Mitzvot* of the Creator under the required condition—to benefit the Creator and not himself. Naturally, the intention should be to observe the *Mitzvot* of the Creator.

The Part of the Torah Concerning Relations between Man and Man

There are two parts to the Torah: one concerns man and the Creator, and the other concerns man and man. And I call upon you, at any rate, to engage and assume that which concerns man and man, for by this you will also learn the part that concerns man and the Creator.

Speech, Thought, and Action

Work, of any kind, should include thought, speech, and action.

We have already explained the "practical" part of the one *Mitzva*: One should agree to dedicate all of one's free time to benefit the people in the world. The aspect of "thought" is more imperative in this *Mitzva* than in *Mitzvot* relating to man and the Creator since in *Mitzvot* between man and the Creator, the "act" in itself testifies that the intention is to benefit one's Maker, as there is no other room for such an action but Him.

Yet, with what concerns man and man, they are justified in and of themselves, since human conscience necessitates them. However, if one performs them from this perspective, he has not done a thing. In others words, these actions will not bring him closer to the Creator and to actual work *Lishma*.

Thus, each person should think that he is doing all this only to bring contentment to his Maker and to resemble His ways: As He is merciful, so I am merciful, and as He always imparts good, so do I. This image, coupled with good deeds, will bring him closer to the Creator in a way that will equalize his form with spirituality and with *Kedusha* [holiness], and he will become like a seal, fit to receive the true Higher Abundance.

The "speech" refers to the prayer in the mouth—during the work and in fixed times—for the Creator to turn one's heart from reception to bestowal. Also, it is contemplating the Torah and matters that promote achieving it.

Bringing Contentment to One's Maker Inadvertently

It is hopeless to wait for a time when a solution is found that enables one to begin the work of the Creator in *Lishma*. As in the past, so is now, and so will it be: Every servant of the Creator must begin the work in *Lo Lishma*, and from that achieve *Lishma*.

The way to achieve this degree is not limited by time, but by his qualifiers, and by the measure of one's control over one's heart. Hence, many have fallen and will fall in the field of working *Lo Lishma*, and will die without wisdom. Yet, their reward is nevertheless great, since one's mind cannot appreciate the true merit and value of bringing contentment to one's Maker. Even if one works not under this condition, since one is not worthy of another way, one still brings contentment to one's Maker. This is called "unintentionally."

Prophetic Truth in Physical Measurement

Since it is an absolute certainty, the prophetic abundance must be received in those combinations of letters completely suitable for the spirit of beginners, that is, to benefit them and to be open to the self-interest of that generation. Only then is it guaranteed that the word of the Creator is accepted by the generation in the form of *Lo Lishma*, for the Creator did not prepare them in any other way.

Hence, this is the sign of a true prophet: His prophecy is best suited for the physical success of his contemporaries, as it is written, "And what great nation has statutes and ordinances so righteous as all this law which I set before you today?" It is so because the nearness of the physical success will confirm their truthfulness, that in the end, this is indeed the entry point.

The Necessity to Observe the 613 Commandments

The 613 *Mitzvot*, considered the holy Names, are private Providence for all who approach the reception of the Godly abundance. One must experience all these orders without a single exception. Hence, the complete ones crave them with their hearts and souls, to keep them down to their corporeal branches, as it is written, "In every place where I mention My name, I will come to you and bless you."

The Wisdom of Truth

Earlier sages chose a private way for themselves, and I have chosen a general way, since in my view, it better suits the Godly matter to be clothed in eternal letter combinations that will never change. I wish to say that with physical success, they will not change at any place or at any time. For this reason, my words are limited.

Because of the above reason, I was compelled to express spirituality in a general manner. Yet, instead, I chose to explain all the details and spiritual combinations down to very small details, which have no other source or origin other than this collective, meaning the purity of Kabbalah. And since I clarify the spiritual details without clothing in corporeal combinations, it will do much good to the development of attainment. This wisdom is called "the wisdom of truth."

Prophecy

There cannot be mistakes or lies in prophecy, as how can there be a mistake in the light of truth that stems from the Creator? Rather, it is as certain as the rain and snow that fall from the sky on the ground and do not return there until their mission is successfully accomplished. Yet, there is a difference in the receiver, in the ground: Soil that has been prepared by stone removal and by plowing is better suited to receive than unprepared soil. Everything depends on the preparation.

Also, there are certainly differences in the receiving prophets. One is not at the same degree as the other. This greatness or smallness is measured by the preparation in that prophet: One in a lower degree due to absence of superb preparation will necessarily miss some inclination in the course of the light that pours upon him, of which it could be said that the light of prophecy does not suffer any mistakes. Yet, one's smallness causes him multiplication in letter combinations, which is multiplication of conduits and vessels until he attains prophecy.

Prophetic Success Is Speed

Although the truth in the prophecy ultimately appears in the desirable success, a prophet of a smaller degree still compels a longer way upon the people to whom he was sent. Conversely, one of a great degree, whose preparation is more complete, will suffer no deflection upon receiving one's prophecy from the Creator. Hence, he will not multiply the vessels and conduits, for which his prophecy will be clear, concise, and easily accepted by those to whom he was sent.

The Small May Succeed More than the Great

Besides the above words, it is possible for the smallest of prophets to succeed in his prophecy even more than the greatest prophet—concerning the above-mentioned speed—since he relies on revelations of prior prophets who paved his way for him. Obviously, it also depends on the development of his listeners, since clear and concise words require a more developed generation, so they can understand him. If these two additions are added to one of small degree, he can succeed far more than a great one.

Prophecy through the Generations

Although Moses received the Torah and the laws for all the generations, to such an extent that the prophet is not entitled to make any innovations, his prophecy was only given for a time. This is supported by the verse, "A prophet from the midst of you, from your brothers, like Me, will the Lord your God raise up for you, and to him you will listen." If Moses' prophecy were enough for all eternity, why would the Creator raise other prophets like him? Clearly, his prophecy was effective only for its time. When that time is through, the Creator sends another prophet to continue and complete His will.

Yet, the prophet is not permitted to renew or take away anything, for this would mean that there was a deficiency in the prior prophet. Rather, the words of the Creator are always complete, as it is written, "I am the first, and I am the last." Rather, his only task is to extend that same prophecy to those generations that are no longer worthy of receiving from the first.

And the last prophet is the Messiah, who completes them all. He, too, is certainly not permitted to add or take away, but his success will be greater, since the whole generation will be fit to accept his words and be completed through him. This is so for two above reasons: either because of their greatness, or because of his contemporaries, or because of both.

The Essence of Prophetic Success

The essence of prophetic success is to extend the upper light to the dwellers below. The one who brings it the lowest is the most successful. Above and below are measured in spirit and in physical benefit, since the physicality obtained by prophecy is the point that gives people footing, and it is known that the focal point in the work of the Creator is the first footing.

A General Force and a Particular Force

Their uniqueness is the unity of the Creator and the *Shechina* [Divinity]. A particular force is the prohibition on reception down to the lowest degree. The general force is increase of bestowal to the point of "with all his heart and soul."

The Love of God and the Love of Man

> "'Love your friend as yourself,' Rabbi Akiva says this is a great rule in the Torah" (*Beresheet Rabbah* 24).

Collective and Individual

The above statement—although it is one of the most famous and cited sayings—is still unexplained to everyone with all its vastness. This is because the word *Klal* [rule/or collective] indicates a sum of details that relates to the above collective, where each and every detail carries a part within it in a way that the gathering of all the details together creates that collective.

If we say "a great *Klal* in the Torah," it means that all the texts and the 612 *Mitzvot* [commandments] are the sum total of the details that relate to the verse, "Love your friend as yourself." It is difficult to understand how such a statement can contain the sum-total of all the *Mitzvot* in the Torah. At most, it can be a *Klal* for the part of the Torah and sentences that relate to the *Mitzvot* between man and man. But how can you include the greater part of the Torah, which concerns work between man and the Creator in the verse, "Love your friend as yourself"?

That which You Hate, Do Not Do to Your Friend

If we can somehow reconcile the above words, there come the words of Old Hillel to that foreigner who came to him and asked him to convert him, as it says in the Gemara, "Convert me so that you will teach me the whole Torah while I am standing on one leg." He told him, "That which you hate, do not do to your friend. This is the whole Torah, and the rest is its commentary, go study." We see that he told him that the whole Torah is the interpretation of the verse, "Love your friend as yourself."

Now, according to the words of Hillel—the teacher of all the Tannaim [sages during the early CE centuries], and by whom laws are interpreted—it is perfectly clear to us that the primary purpose of our holy Torah is to bring us to that sublime degree where we can observe this verse, "Love your friend as yourself," for he says explicitly, "The rest is its commentary, go study." That is, they interpret for us how to come to that rule.

It is surprising that such a statement can be correct in most issues of the Torah, which concern sentences between man and the Creator, when every beginner evidently knows that this is the heart of the Torah and not the interpretation explaining the verse, "Love your friend as yourself."

Love Your Friend as Yourself

We should also examine and understand the meaning of the verse itself when he says, "Love your friend as yourself." The literal meaning of it is to love your friend to the same extent that you love yourself. However, we see that the public cannot be like that at all. If it had said, "Love your friend as much as your friend loves you," there would still not be many who could fully observe it, yet it would be acceptable.

But to love my friend as much as I love myself seems impossible. Even if there were but one person in the world besides me, it would still be impossible, much less when the world is full of people. Moreover, if one loved everyone as much as one loves oneself, he would have no time for himself, for it is certain that one satisfies one's own needs without neglect, and with great passion, for one loves oneself.

It is not so concerning the needs of the collective: He has no strong reason to stimulate his desire to work for them. Even if he had a desire, could he still keep this statement literally? Would his strength endure? If not, how can the Torah obligate us to do something that is not in any way achievable?

We should not imagine that this verse was said as an exaggeration, for we are warned and insist on "You will neither add nor take away from it." All the interpreters agreed to interpret the text literally. Moreover, they said that one must satisfy the needs of one's friend even in a place where one is himself deficient. Even then he must satisfy the needs of his friend and leave himself deficient.

The Tosfot interpret *Kidushin* 20, "One who buys a Hebrew slave, it is as though he buys a master for himself." The *Tosfot* interpret there in the name of the Jerusalem [Talmud] that "Sometimes he has but one pillow. If he lies on it himself, he does not observe, 'For he is happy with you.' If he does not lie on it and does not give it to his slave, it is sodomite rule. It turns out that against his will he must give it to his servant. Thus, he has bought himself a master."

One Mitzva [Commandment]

This raises several questions: According to the aforesaid, we all sin against the Torah. Moreover, we do not observe even the primary part of the Torah, since we observe the details but not the actual rule. It is written: "When you observe the will of the Creator, the poor are in others and not in you," for how can there be poor when everyone does what the Creator wants and loves their friends as themselves?

The issue of the Hebrew slave that the Jerusalem [Talmud] presents needs further study: The meaning of the text is that even if the foreigner is not Hebrew, he must love him like himself. And how could one explain that the rule for the foreigner is the same as that of the Hebrew, since "One law and one ordinance should be both for you and for the stranger who dwells with you." The word *Ger* [proselyte/foreigner] also means a "residing proselyte," meaning one who does not accept the

Torah, except for retiring from idolatry. It is written about such a person: "You may give it to the stranger who is within your gates."

This is the meaning of one Mitzva that the Tanna speaks of when he says, "If he performs one Mitzva, he shifts himself and the entire world to the side of merit." It is very difficult to understand what the entire world has to do with this. We should not force an explanation that it is when one is half unworthy and half worthy, and the whole world is half unworthy and half worthy, for if we say so, we are missing the whole point.

Moreover, the whole world is full of gentiles and tyrants, so how can he see that they are half unworthy and half worthy? He can see about himself that he is half unworthy and half worthy, but not that the entire world is such. Furthermore, the text should have at least stated "The whole of Israel." Why did the Tanna add the entire world here? Are we guarantors for the nations of the world, to add them to our account of good deeds?

We must understand that our sages spoke only of the practical part of the Torah, which leads to the desired purpose from the world and from the Torah. Therefore, when they say one Mitzva, they certainly mean a practical Mitzva. This is certainly as Hillel says, meaning "Love your friend as yourself." It is by this Mitzva alone that one attains the real goal, which is *Dvekut* [adhesion] with the Creator. Thus, you find that with this one Mitzva, one observes the entire goal and purpose.

Now there is no question about the Mitzvot between man and the Creator because the practical ones among them have the same purpose of cleansing the body, the last point of which is to love your friend as yourself, whose immediate subsequent stage is *Dvekut*.

There is a general and a particular in this. We come from the particular to the general, for the general leads to the ultimate goal. Thus, it certainly makes no difference from which side to begin, from the particular or from the general, for the most important thing is that we begin and not quit in the middle until we reach our goal.

And to Adhere to Him

There still remains room to ask, "If the whole purpose of the Torah and all of creation is but to raise the base humanity to become worthy of that wonderful sublimity, and to adhere to Him, He should have created us with that sublimity to begin with instead of troubling us with the labor of creation, and the Torah and Mitzvot.

We could explain this with the words of our sages: "One who eats that which is not his is afraid to look at his face." This means that anyone who feeds on the labor of others is afraid (ashamed) to look at his own form, for his form is inhuman.

Because no deficiency comes from His wholeness, He has prepared for us this work, so we may enjoy the labor of our own hands. This is why He created creation in this base form. The work in Torah and Mitzvot lifts us from the baseness of creation, and through it we achieve our sublimity by ourselves. Then we do not feel the delight and pleasure that comes to us from his generous hand as a gift, but as the owners of that pleasure.

However, we must still understand the source of the baseness that we feel upon receiving a gift. Nature scientists know that the nature of every branch is close to its root. The branch loves all the conducts in the root, wants them, covets them, and derives benefit from them. Conversely, the branch stays away from everything that is not in the root; it cannot tolerate them and is harmed by them.

Because our root is the Creator, Who does not receive but bestows, we feel sorrow and degradation upon every reception from another.

Now we understand the purpose of adhering to Him. The sublimity of *Dvekut* [adhesion] is only the equivalence of the branch with its root. On the other hand, the whole matter of baseness is only the remoteness from the root. In other words, each being whose ways are corrected to bestow upon others rises and becomes capable of adhering to Him, and every being whose way is reception and self-love is degraded and removed far from the Creator.

As a remedy, the Torah and *Mitzvot* have been prepared for us. In the beginning, we are to observe it *Lo Lishma* [not for Her sake], meaning to receive reward. This is the case during the period of *Katnut* [smallness], as education. When one grows, one is taught to observe Torah and *Mitzvot Lishma* [for Her sake], meaning to bring contentment to one's Maker, and not for self-love.

Now we can understand the words of our sages who asked, "Why should the Creator mind whether one slaughters at the throat, or slaughters at the back of the neck? After all, the *Mitzvot* [commandments] were given only so as to cleanse people through them."

But we still do not know what that cleansing means. With the aforesaid, we understand that "Man is born a wild ass's colt," completely immersed in the filth and baseness of self-reception and self-love, without any spark of love for one's fellow person and bestowal. In that state, one is at the farthest point from the Root.

When one grows and is educated in Torah and *Mitzvot* defined only by the aim to bring contentment to one's Maker and not at all for self-love, one comes to the degree of bestowal upon one's fellow person through the natural remedy in the study of Torah and *Mitzvot Lishma*, that the Giver of the Torah knows, as our sages said, "I have created the evil inclination; I have created for it the Torah as a spice."

By this the creature develops in the degrees of the above-said sublimity until one loses any form of self-love and self-reception, and one's every attribute is to bestow or to receive in order to bestow. Our sages said about this, "The *Mitzvot* were given only in order to cleanse people by them," and then one adheres to one's Root to the extent of the words, "and to adhere to Him."

Two Parts to the Torah:
Between Man and the Creator and Between Man and Man

Even if we see that there are two parts to the Torah—the first, *Mitzvot* between man and the Creator, and the second, *Mitzvot* between man and man—they are both one and the same thing. This means that the practice of them and the desired goal from them are one: *Lishma*.

It makes no difference if one works for one's friend or for the Creator, since it is engraved in the created being at birth that anything that comes from another appears empty and unreal.

Because of this, we are compelled to begin in *Lo Lishma*, as Maimonides says, "Our sages said: 'One should always engage in Torah, even if *Lo Lishma*, since from *Lo Lishma* he comes to *Lishma*.' Therefore, when teaching the young, the women, and the uneducated, they are taught to work out of fear and to receive reward. Until they accumulate knowledge and gain wisdom, they are told that secret bit by bit, and are accustomed to that matter with ease until they attain Him and know Him and serve Him out of love."

...Thus, when one completes one's work in love of others and bestowal upon others through the final point, one also completes one's love for the Creator and bestowal upon the Creator. And there is no difference between the two, for anything that is outside one's body, meaning outside one's self-interest, is judged equally—whether it is to bestow upon one's friend or to bestow contentment upon one's Maker.

This is what Hillel Hanasi assumed, that "Love your friend as yourself" is the ultimate goal in the practice, as it is the clearest nature and form to man.

We should not be mistaken about actions, since they are set before his eyes. He knows that if he puts the needs of his friend before his own needs, then he is in the quality of bestowal. For this reason, he does not define the goal as "And you will love the Lord your God with all your heart and with all your soul and with all your might," for indeed they are one and the same, since he should also love his friend with all his heart and with all his soul and with all his might, as this is the meaning of the words "as yourself." He certainly loves himself with all his heart and soul and might, and with the Creator, he may deceive oneself, but with his friend it is always spread out before his eyes.

Why Was the Torah Not Given to the Patriarchs?

By this we have clarified the first three questions. But there still remains the question how it is possible to observe it, for it is seemingly impossible. You should know that this is why the Torah was not given to the patriarchs but to their children's children, a complete nation of 600,000 men from 20 years of age and on. They were asked if each and every one were willing to take upon himself these sublime work and goal, and after each and every one said "We will do and we will hear," the matter became possible, for it is clear beyond doubt that if 600,000 men have no other engagement in life but to stand guard and see that no need is left unsatisfied in their friends, and they even do it with true love, with all their soul and might, there is absolutely no doubt that there will not be a need in any person in the nation to worry about his own sustenance, for he will have 600,000 loving and loyal people watching over him so not a single need is left unsatisfied.

This answers why the Torah was not given to the patriarchs, for in a small number of people, the Torah cannot be observed. It is impossible to begin the work of *Lishma* as is described above, which is why the Torah was not given to them.

All of Israel Are Responsible for One Another

In light of the above, we can understand a perplexing saying by our sages who said, "All of Israel are responsible for one another." Furthermore, Rabbi Elazar, son of Rabbi Shimon, adds, "The world is judged by its majority."

It follows, that we are also responsible for all the nations of the world. I wonder; this seems inconceivable, for how can one be responsible for the sins of a person whom he does not know? It is said specifically, "The fathers will not be put to death for the children, and the children will not be put to death for the fathers; every man will be put to death for his own sin."

Now we can understand the meaning of the words in utter simplicity, for it has been explained that it is utterly impossible to observe Torah and *Mitzvot* unless the entire nation participates.

It follows that each one becomes responsible for his friend. This means that the reckless make the observers of the Torah remain in their filth, for they cannot be completed in bestowal upon others and love of others without their help. Thus, if some in the nation sin, they make the rest of the nation suffer because of them.

This is the meaning of what is written in the Midrash, "Israel, one of them sins and all of them feel." Rabbi Shimon said about this: "It is like people who were seated in a boat. One of them took a drill and began to drill under him. His friends told him, 'What are you doing?' He replied, 'Why do you care? Am I not drilling under me?' They replied, 'The water is rising and flooding the boat.'" As we have said above, because the reckless are immersed in self-love, their actions create an iron fence that prevents the observers of Torah from even beginning to observe the Torah and *Mitzvot* properly.

Now we will clarify the words of Rabbi Elazar, son of Rabbi Shimon, who says, "Since the world is judged by its majority, and the individual is judged by its majority, if one performs one *Mitzva*, happy is he, for he has sentenced himself and the entire world to the side of merit. If he commits one sin, woe unto him for he has sentenced himself and the entire world to the side of sin, as it is said, 'And one sinner destroys much good.'"

We see that Rabbi Elazar, son of Rabbi Shimon, takes the matter of the *Arvut* [mutual responsibility] even further, for he says, "The world is judged by its majority." This is because in his opinion, it is not enough for one nation to receive the Torah and *Mitzvot*. He came to this opinion either by observing the reality before us, for we see that the end has not yet come, or he received it from his teachers.

The text also supports him, as it promises us that at the time of redemption, "The earth will be full of the knowledge of the Lord," and also, "All the nations will flow onto Him," and many more verses. This is the reason he conditioned the *Arvut* on the entire world, to tell you that an individual, too, cannot come to the desired goal by observing Torah and *Mitzvot*, if not through the assistance of all the people in the world.

Thus, each and every *Mitzva* that an individual performs affects the whole world. It is like a person who weighs beans on a scale, and each and every bean he puts on the scale induces the desired final decision. Likewise, each *Mitzva* that the individual performs before the whole earth is full of knowledge develops the world so it will come to this.

It is said, "And one sinner destroys much good," since through the sin he commits, he reduces the weight on the scale, as though that person took back the bean he had put on the scale. By this, he turns the world backwards.

Why Was the Torah Given to Israel?

Now we can answer the question why the Torah was given to the Israeli nation without the participation of all the nations of the world. The truth is that the purpose of creation applies to the entire human race, none excluded. However, because of the lowliness of the nature of creation and its power over people, it was impossible for people to be able to understand, determine, and agree to rise above it. They did not demonstrate the desire to relinquish self-love and come to equivalence of form, which is *Dvekut* with His attributes, as our sages said, "As he is merciful, so you are merciful."

Thus, because of their ancestral merit, Israel succeeded, and over 400 years they developed and became qualified, and sentenced themselves to the side of merit. Each and every member of the nation agreed to love his fellow man.

Being a small and single nation among seventy great nations, when there are a hundred gentiles or more for every one of Israel, when they had taken upon themselves to love their fellow person, the Torah was then given specifically to qualify the Israeli nation, to qualify itself.

However, by this the Israeli nation was to be a "passage." This means that to the extent that Israel cleanse themselves by observing the Torah, so they pass their power on to the rest of the nations. And when the rest of the nations also sentence themselves to the side of merit, the Messiah will be revealed, whose role is not only to qualify Israel to the ultimate goal of *Dvekut* with Him, but to teach the ways of the Creator to all the nations, as it is written, "And all nations will flow unto Him."

The Wisdom of Kabbalah and Philosophy

What Is Spirituality?

Philosophy has gone through a great deal of trouble to prove that corporeality is the offspring of spirituality and that the soul begets the body. Still, their words are utterly unacceptable to the heart. Their primary mistake is their erroneous perception of spirituality: They determined that spirituality fathered corporeality, which is certainly a fib.

Every father must have some resemblance to his offspring. This relation is the path and the route through which his offspring is extended. In addition, every operator must have some relation to its operation by which to contact it. Since you say that spirituality is denied of any corporeal incidents, then such a path does not exist, or a relation by which the spiritual can contact and set it into any kind of motion.

However, understanding the meaning of the word "spirituality" has nothing to do with philosophy. This is because how can they discuss something that they have never seen or felt? What do their rudiments stand on?

If there is any definition that can tell spiritual from corporeal, it belongs only to those who have attained a spiritual thing and felt it. These are the genuine Kabbalists; thus, it is the wisdom of Kabbalah that we need.

Philosophy with Regard to His Essence

Philosophy loves to concern itself with His essence and prove the rules of negation that apply to Him. However, Kabbalah has no dealings whatsoever with it, for how can something be defined in what is unattainable and imperceptible? Indeed, a definition by negation is just as valid as a definition by confirmation. If you see an object from afar and recognize its negatives, meaning all that it is not, that, too, is considered seeing and some extent of recognition. If an object is truly out of sight, even its negative characteristics are not apparent.

If, for example, we see a black image from a distance, but can still determine that it is neither a person nor a bird, it is regarded as seeing. If it had been even farther still, we would have been unable to determine that it is not a person.

This is the origin of their confusion and invalidity. Philosophy loves to pride itself on understanding all the negation about His essence. Conversely, the sages of Kabbalah put their hand to their mouth in this place and do not give Him even a simple name, for anything that we do not attain, we cannot define by name or word, for a word designates some degree of attainment. However, Kabbalists do speak a great deal about His illumination in reality, meaning all those illuminations they have actually attained, as validly as tangible attainment.

The Spiritual Is a Force without a Body

This is what Kabbalists define as "spirituality," and that is what they talk about. It has no image or space or time or any corporeal value (and in my opinion, philosophy has generally worn a mantle that is not its own, for it has pilfered definitions from the wisdom of Kabbalah and made delicacies with human understanding. Had it not been for that, they would never have thought of fabricating such acumen). However, it is only a potential force, meaning not a force that is clothed in an ordinary, worldly body, but a force without a body.

A Spiritual Kli [Vessel] Is Called "A Force"

This is the place to point out that the force that spirituality speaks of does not refer to the spiritual light itself. That spiritual light extends directly from His essence and is therefore the same as His essence. This means that we have no perception or attainment in the spiritual light, too, that we may define by name. Even the name "light" is borrowed and is not real. Thus, we must know that the name "force," without a body, refers specifically to the spiritual Kli.

Lights and Kelim [Vessels]

Therefore, we must not inquire how the sages of Kabbalah, which fill the entire wisdom with their insights, differentiate between the various lights. However, these observations do not refer to the lights themselves, but to the impression of the Kli, which is the above-mentioned force, affected by its encounter with the light.

Kelim and Lights (in the meaning of the words)

Here is where the line between the gift and the love that it creates must be drawn. The lights, meaning the impression on the Kli, which is attainable, is called "form and matter together." The impression is the form, and the above-mentioned force is the matter.

However, the love that is created is regarded as "form without matter." This means that if we separate the love from the gift itself, as though it was never clothed in any tangible gift, but only in the abstract name "the love of the Creator," it is regarded as a "form." In that event, the practice of it is regarded as "Formative Kabbalah." However, it would still be regarded as real, without any similarity to formative philosophy since the spirit of this love remains in the attainment, completely separated from the gift, meaning the light itself.

Matter and Form in Kabbalah

The reason is that although this love is merely a consequence of the gift, it is still far more important than the gift itself. It is like a great king who gives a small object to a person. Although the gift itself hasn't any value, the king's love and attention make it priceless and precious. Thus, it is completely separated from the matter, being the light and the gift, in a way that the work and the distinction remain carved in the attainment with only the love itself, while the gift is seemingly forgotten from the heart. Therefore, this aspect of the wisdom is called the "Formative Wisdom of Kabbalah," which is the most important part in the wisdom.

ABYA

This love consists of four parts that are much like human love: When we first receive the present, we still do not refer to the giver of the gift as one who loves us, all the more so if the giver of the present is important and the receiver is not equal to him.

However, the repetitive giving and the perseverance will make even the most important person seem like a true, equal lover. This is because the law of love does not apply between great and small, as two real lovers must feel equal.

Thus, you can measure four degrees of love here. The incident is called *Assiya*, the repetition of the giving of gifts is called *Yetzira*, and the appearance of the love itself is called *Beria*.

It is here that the study of the Formative Wisdom of Kabbalah begins, for it is in this degree that love is separated from the gifts. This is the meaning of "and creates darkness," meaning the light is removed from *Yetzira* and the love remains without light, without its gifts.

Then comes *Atzilut*. After it has tasted and entirely separated the form from the matter, as in, "and creates darkness," it became worthy of ascending to the degree of *Atzilut* where the form clothes the substance once more, meaning light and love together.

The Origin of the Soul

Everything spiritual is perceived as a separated force from the body because it has no corporeal image. However, because of that, it remains isolated and completely separated from the corporeal. In such a state, how can it set anything corporeal in motion, much less beget anything physical, when it has no relation by which to come in contact with the physical?

The Element of Oxygen

However, the truth is that the force itself is also considered a genuine matter, just as any corporeal matter in the concrete world, and the fact that it has no image that the human senses can perceive does not reduce the value of the substance, which is the "force."

Take a molecule of oxygen as an example: It is a constituent of most materials in the world. Yet, if you take a bottle with pure oxygen when it is not mixed with any other substance, you will find that it seems as though the bottle is completely empty. You will not be able to notice anything about it; it will be completely like air, intangible and invisible to the eye.

If we remove the lid and smell it, we will find no scent; if we taste it, we will find no flavor, and if we put it on scales, it will not weigh more than the empty bottle. The same applies to hydrogen, which is also tasteless, odorless, and weightless.

However, when putting these two elements together, they will immediately become a liquid—drinking water that possesses both taste and weight. If we put the water inside active lime, it will immediately mix with it and become as solid as the lime itself.

Thus, the elements oxygen and hydrogen, in which there is no tangible perception whatsoever, become a solid body. Therefore, how can we determine about natural forces that they are not a corporeal substance just because they are not arranged in such a way that our senses can perceive them? Moreover, we can evidently see that most of the tangible materials in reality consist preliminarily of the element of oxygen, which human senses cannot perceive or feel!

Moreover, even in the tangible reality, the solid and the liquid we can vividly perceive in our tangible world might turn to air and fumes at a certain temperature. Likewise, vapors may solidify when the temperature drops.

In that event, we should wonder how one gives that which one does not possess. We clearly see that all the tangible images come from elements that are in and of themselves intangible and do not exist as materials in and of themselves. Likewise, all the fixed pictures that we know and use to define materials are inconstant and do not exist in their own right. Rather, they only dress and undress forms under the influence of conditions such as heat or cold.

The primary part of the corporeal substance is the "force" in it, though we are not yet able to tell these forces apart, as with chemical elements. Perhaps in the future they will be discovered in their pure form, as we have only recently discovered the chemical elements.

Equal Force in the Spiritual and the Physical

In a word: All the names that we attribute to materials are completely fabricated, meaning stem from our concrete perception in our five senses. They do not exist in and of themselves. On the other hand, any definition we ascribe to the force, which separates it from the material, is also fabricated. Even when science reaches its ultimate development, we will still have to regard only the actual reality, meaning that within any material operation we see and feel, we must perceive its operator, who is also a substance, like the operation itself. There is a correlation between them, or they would not have come to it.

We must know that this erring of separating the operating force from the operation comes from the formative philosophy, which insisted on proving that the spiritual act influences the corporeal operation. That resulted in erroneous assumptions such as the above, which Kabbalah does not need.

Body and Soul in the Upper Ones

The opinion of Kabbalah in this matter is crystal clear, excluding any mixture of philosophy. This is because in the minds of Kabbalists, even the spiritual, separated, conceptual entities, which philosophy denies having any corporeality and displays them as purely conceptual, bear substance, in the view of Kabbalists, although they attained the spirituality, more sublime and abstract, they still consist of body and soul, like the physical human.

Therefore, you need not wonder how two can win the prize, saying that they are complex. Furthermore, philosophy believes that anything complex will eventually disintegrate and decompose, meaning die. Thus, how can one declare that they are complex and eternal?

Lights and *Kelim*

Indeed, their thoughts are not our thoughts, for the way of the sages of the Kabbalah is one of finding actual proof of attainment, making its revocation through intellectual pondering impossible. But let me clarify these matters so that everyone can understand them.

First, we must know that the difference between lights and *Kelim* [vessels] is created immediately in the first emanated being from *Ein Sof* [Infinity/no end]. Naturally, the first emanation is also the most complete and purer than everything that follows it. It is certain that it receives this pleasantness and completeness from His essence, Who wishes to grant it every pleasantness and pleasure.

It is known that the measurement of the pleasure is the will to receive it. That is because what we most want to receive feels as the most pleasurable. Because of this, we should discern two observations in this first emanation: the "will to receive" that receives the essence, and the received essence itself.

We should also know that the will to receive is what we perceive as the "body" of the emanated being, meaning its primary essence, being the *Kli* [vessel] to receive His goodness. The second is the essence of the good that is received, which is His light, which is eternally extended to that emanation.

It follows that we necessarily distinguish two discernments that clothe one another even in the most sublime spiritual that the heart can conceive. It is the opposite of the opinion of philosophy, which fabricated that the separated entities are not complex materials. It is necessary that that "will to receive," which necessarily exists in the emanated (for without it there would be no pleasure but coercion, and no feeling of pleasure), is absent in His essence. This is the reason for the name "emanated," since it is no longer His essence, for from whom would He receive?

However, the bounty that it receives is necessarily a part of His essence, for here there need not be any innovation. Thus, we see the great difference between the generated body and the received abundance, which is deemed His essence.

How Can a Spiritual Beget a Corporeal?

It is seemingly difficult to understand how the spiritual can beget and extend anything corporeal. This question is an ancient philosophical query that much ink has been spilled attempting to resolve it.

The truth is that this question is difficult only if one follows their doctrine, for they determined the form of spirituality without any connection to anything corporeal. This produces a difficult question: How can the spiritual lead to or father anything corporeal?

But it is the view of the sages of Kabbalah that this is not difficult at all, for their terms are the complete opposite from those of philosophers. They maintain that any spiritual quality equalizes with the corporeal quality like two drops in a pond. Thus, the relationships are of the utmost affinity, and there is no separation between them except in the substance: The spiritual consists of a spiritual substance and the corporeal consists of a corporeal substance.

However, all the qualities in spiritual materials apply also to corporeal materials, as has been explained in the article, "The Essence of the Wisdom of Kabbalah."

The old philosophy presents three opinions as obstacles before my explanation: The first is their decision that the power of the human intellect is the eternal soul, man's essence. The second is their conjecture that the body is an extension and a consequence of the soul. The third is their saying that spiritual entities are simple objects and not complex.

Materialistic Psychology

Not only is it the wrong place to argue with them about their fabricated conjectures, but also the time of supporters of such views has already passed and their authority revoked. Also, we should thank the experts of materialistic psychology for that, which built its plinth on the ruin of the former, winning the public's favor. Now everyone admits to the nullity of philosophy, for it is not built on concrete foundations.

This old doctrine became a stumbling rock and a deadly thorn to the sages of Kabbalah because where they should have subdued before the sages of Kabbalah, and assumed abstinence and prudence, sanctity, and purity before the sages disclosed before them even the smallest thing in spirituality, they easily received what they wanted from the formative philosophy. Without payment or price, they watered them from their fountain of wisdom to satiation and refrained from laboring in the wisdom of Kabbalah until the wisdom has almost been forgotten from Israel. Hence, we are grateful to materialistic psychology for handing it a deadly blow.

I Am Solomon

The above matter is much like a fable that our sages tell: Asmodeus [the devil] drove King Solomon four hundred parasangs [a distance unit] from Jerusalem and left him with no money or means of sustenance. Then he sat in King Solomon's throne while the king was begging at the doors. Every place he went, he said: "I am Ecclesiastes!" but none believed him. So he went from town to town declaring, "I am Solomon!" But when he came to the Sanhedrin, they said: "A fool does not utter the same folly all the time, saying, 'I was once a king.'"

It seems as though the name is not the essence of a person, but rather the owner of the name is. Therefore, how can a wise man such as Solomon not be recognized if he is indeed the owner of the name? Moreover, it is the person who dignifies his name and he should display his wisdom!

Three Preventions

There are three reasons that prevent us from knowing the owner of a name:

1. Because of its truthfulness, the wisdom becomes clear only when all its details appear together. Therefore, before one knows the whole wisdom, it is impossible to see even a fraction of it. Thus, it is the publicity of its truthfulness that we need, so as to have enough prior faith in it to make a great effort.

2. Just as Asmodeus the demon wore the clothes of King Solomon and inherited his throne, philosophy sat on the throne of Kabbalah with easier concepts to grasp, for the lie is quickly accepted. Therefore, there is a twofold trouble here: First, the wisdom of truth is profound and laborious, whereas the false philosophy is easily grasped. The second is that it is superfluous because philosophy is quite satisfying.

3. As the demon claims that King Solomon is mad, philosophy mocks and dismisses Kabbalah.

However, as long as wisdom is sublime, it is elevated above the people and separated from it. Because he was the wisest man, he was also higher than every man. Thus, the finest scholars could not understand him, except those friends, meaning the Sanhedrin, whom he taught his wisdom every day for days and years. They are the ones who understood him and publicized his name in the entire world.

The reason for it is that a small idea is explained in five minutes and is thus attainable by anyone and can be easily publicized. Conversely, a big idea will not be understood in less than several hours. It may even take days or years, depending on the intelligence. Accordingly, the greatest scholars will be understood only by a select few in the generation, since profound concepts are founded on much prior knowledge.

It is therefore not surprising that the wisest of all men, who was exiled to a place where he was not known, could not demonstrate his wisdom or even show a hint of his wisdom before they believed that he was the owner of the name.

It is the same with the wisdom of Kabbalah in our time: The troubles and the exile that have come upon us brought us to forget it (and if there are people who do practice it, it is not in its favor, but rather harms it, for they did not receive it from a Kabbalist sage). Hence, in this generation, it is as King Solomon in exile, declaring, "I am the wisdom, and all the flavors of religion and Torah are in me," yet none believe it.

But this is perplexing, for if it is a genuine wisdom, can it not display itself like all other wisdoms? It cannot. As King Solomon could not display his wisdom to the scholars at the place of his exile and had to come to Jerusalem, the place of the Sanhedrin, who learned and knew King Solomon, and testified to the depth of his wisdom, so it is with the wisdom of Kabbalah: It requires great sages who examine their hearts and study it for twenty or thirty years. Only then will they be able to testify to it.

And as King Solomon could not prevent Asmodeus from sitting on his throne, pretending to be him until he arrived in Jerusalem, sages of Kabbalah observe philosophic theology and complain that they have stolen the upper shell from their wisdom, which Plato and his Greek predecessors had acquired while studying with the disciples of the prophets in Israel. They have stolen basic elements from the wisdom of Israel and wore a cloak that is not their own. To this day, philosophic theology sits on the throne of Kabbalah, being heir under her mistress.

And who would believe the sages of Kabbalah while others sit on their throne? It is as they did not believe King Solomon in exile, for they knew him to be sitting on his throne, meaning the demon, Asmodeus. As King Solomon had no hope of revealing the truth, for the wisdom is deep and cannot be revealed by testimony or by experimentation except to those believers who dedicate themselves to it with heart and soul.

Just as the Sanhedrin did not recognize King Solomon as long as the falsehood of Asmodeus did not appear, Kabbalah cannot prove its nature and truthfulness, and no revelations will suffice for the world to know it before the futility and falsehood of theological philosophy that has taken its throne becomes apparent.

Therefore, there was no such salvation for Israel as when materialistic psychology appeared and struck theological philosophy on its head a lethal blow. Now, any person who seeks the Creator must bring Kabbalah back to its throne and restore its past glory.

The Quality of the Wisdom of the Hidden in General

There are two parts in any understanding (recognition of reason). The first is in material elements, meaning the nature of the objects in the reality before us. The second is in the figurative elements devoid of those objects, meaning forms of mind and reason itself.

We shall call the first "material learning," which is empirical, and is called "physics" ... and we shall call the second one "figurative learning," which is theoretical, and is called "logic."

Material Learning Is Also Divided into Two, which Are Four

Sometimes we can minimize it into speaking of what is above nature. This is called "the wisdom of what is beyond nature," meaning according to specific subjects of the superior mind.

There are four parts here:

1. Material learning from the part called "Nature's Law" which is empirical;
2. Material learning from the part called "Nature's Law" which is the wisdom of what is beyond nature;
3. Material learning from the part called *Atik* [ancient], which is empirical and practical;
4. Material learning from the part called *Atik*, which is only the wisdom of what is beyond nature.

Figurative Learning

Figurative learning is one whose predicate is the upper one. In material learning, the predicates are the degrees called "worlds" and *Partzufim*.

And yet, it is empirical and practical. Clearly, the superior principle in the wisdom of the hidden does not become any clearer now because it requires complete study in and of itself, and I have already shown that it is the revelation of His Godliness to His creatures, as explained in the essay "The Essence of the Wisdom of Kabbalah," as I have elaborated there. Once you understand this, you will understand my explanation of the quality of the wisdom in general.

This Superior Principle Is Defined in One, Unique, and Unified

One: It is obvious that the upper one is one. He comprises the whole of reality and all the times—past, present, and future—for one cannot give that which one does not have. Had the whole of reality and the existence of reality not been included in Him, they would not have emerged from Him, as is evident to any scrutinizer, and without minding that we find corruptions in the manners of the existence of reality.

Indeed, know that this is the study that the sages of the hidden call "one." The first to study it was Abraham the Patriarch. (This is explained in the *Book of Creation* and is therefore attributed to Abraham the Patriarch.) This means that there aren't two authorities here—good and bad—but only good.

Unique: This indicates that He is still united and does not change because we feel the bad, not even in the relation between Him and His creations. For example, when a sick person comes to a physician to pull out a thorn, the physician who pulls it out hurts the patient. This is not considered that he has now changed and is doing harm. Rather, the physician and the patient, who loved one another before, are still loving even during the painful cutting. This is called "unique."

Unified: This indicates that His attitude toward creation, as a Creator, is only to disclose His uniqueness, for all the pleasantness, all the wisdom, and all the *Dvekut* [adhesion] are expressed in this unification.

Material and Empirical Learning

Material learning is to know the approach of the whole of reality of people, and their manners of existence, and manners of their development, from the first cause through their arrival in this world, both from above downward and from below upward. The main thing to know about them is the cause and consequence that applies to them, for this is the picture of every wisdom, like nature's law and the law of life.

Practical Learning

It is the nature of those degrees that one who attains finds in them tremendous pleasure and delight when he attains them. This extends from one's coming into the will of the upper one, since the ways of His guidance over the existence of the world are by no more than two equal forces where one who desires their work draws them by enjoying during the work. That pleasure compels them to it, and one who does not want them to work repels them through suffering, when the creature suffers during the work and therefore leaves it.

This law is observed in full by animals and humans, as it serves the purpose. For this reason, its guidance becomes complicated and must change every single moment. Sometimes, the law is denied through the law of habit that becomes second nature for it.

The Nature of the Degrees

The nature of the degrees to the attaining is as the nature of animals. That is, the law of reward and punishment is observed strictly and inexorably, and even habit will not change it.

Two Parts to Material Studies

There are two parts to material studies: 1) reality, 2) their existence—the quantity and quality of their sustenance and how they are obtained: by whom and by what. For this reason, there is a very bitter taste in the spaces between each two degrees, and those who attain them loathe them vehemently. It is made and drawn upon them so they will not remain there in the middle, as is the case with simple animals. However, sometimes the attaining turn back when they remember the great delight that is there.

Klipa [Shell/Peel]: No Turning Back in Spirituality

When they return, it is already a different degree, and it is called *Klipa* in relation to the initial degree.

Two Parts to Practical Learning

There are two parts to practical learning: The first is *Kedusha* [holiness]; the second is *Klipa*. Sometimes, for some reason, sages, too, return to the place where there is the taste of a great delight in order to do something. However, they promptly leave there and resume their place. For this reason, the return is also called *Kedusha*.

And yet, for the most part, only the frightened and those of weak desire return there, wishing to avoid passing through the path between the degrees, which they find bitter, so they remain stuck there because they cannot rise to their aspired height.

The Manner of Work in the Names

The manner of work in the names is extension of much pleasantness. At that time one can draw that spirit also in one's friend, who is very inspired. By this he can heal him or command him and force him to do his will.

2. Practical Kabbalah

The Loss in Every Proliferation

We have explained above, concerning practical learning, that the Creator compels the creature through the light of pleasure in the work that dresses in it. What the Creator does not want, He prevents through the light of suffering that dresses in it. This is the meaning of the loss in every proliferation. "The more possessions, the more worry," etc., since there is a limit to every will of the Creator, as He desires many actions up the ladder of development. Were there no limit to every pleasure, the creature would become immersed in one activity his whole life and would not climb the degrees. Hence, Providence limits him by pains that result from any excessive pleasure.

Beastly Payment and Human Payment

There is immediate pleasure in which there is no issue of hope, but is rather repaid immediately. Then, there is a remote, anticipated pleasure, whose payment is aspired for at a later date. The first is called "sensual payment," and the second is the "intellectual" one. The first applies to all living beings, and its conduct is certain and undisrupted. The latter is suitable only for the scrutinizing human, and the ways are disrupted. It is so because since its payment is delayed, he becomes suitable for disruptions and preventions that confuse him in his work.

The Power of Payment, a Causal Power

Conscious payment, sensual payment: These are human payment and beastly payment, which are the two forces of Providence, by which animals do the tasks they are assigned by His Providence.

The Standard for the Sages

Indeed, there are many degrees in the human species itself, for it is measured by the sense of development of each one, and by the measure of one's retreat from the beastly world and into the human world. When one is insufficiently developed, one cannot wait for the payment very long, and chooses jobs with instantaneous reward, even if for a lower price. A more developed person might wait and choose works that pay better, even if the payment comes after a very long time. Know that this is the standard for the sages, for it depends on the material development of each one, and anyone who can prolong the payment can get a bigger reward.

What Is Development?

Therefore, you will see that the majority of the learned ones, as soon as they have completed their learning and can enjoy the fruits of their work, abandon the study and go out to trade with the people and be rewarded. But the minority restrain themselves and continue to learn, each according to one's own talents. It is so because they want to receive a greater reward, such as to be among the greatest in the generation or be innovators. Naturally, after some time their peers become very jealous of them.

The Power of the Goal

Know that this is the standard for the development of the generations, meaning the power to restrain and prolong the time of payment, and choose the higher sum. For this reason, in those generations great inventors proliferated because in our generation there are more with this kind of talent. Their exertion is immeasurable because their sense of restraining is highly developed both for prolonging the time and for exerting.

Returning Power or "Causal Power"

There is no movement among all the animals that is not repaid. It is called the "Power of the Goal," and the degrees are evaluated only according to the sensation of the reward, meaning by development. The more one is developed, the more one senses. Hence, the power of the goal acts in such a person to a greater extent and can significantly increase and enhance one's effort.

The second one is the above-stated, meaning the "power of anticipation for the time of payment." That causal power is evaluated by two: The first is the sense of the price. That sensation is the sum of the price, where one who is more sensitive is also more expensive and the causal power is increased.

The second is the power to wait for a later time, for even a higher price requires having a more developed body that can sense the remoteness. Also, any development that unfolds in the human species is only those two above-mentioned sensations: the sensation of price, and the sensation of remoteness, and the measure of wisdom rises through them to its apex.

Practical Kabbalah

Know that the governance of the above-mentioned sensations are sensed primarily in those who attain, since the pleasantness of each degree is so great, and its reward is always near, so one has no reason to be in pain and climb to a higher degree.

The Spirit of Pleasure and Intellectual Pleasure

Moreover, there are spirit and wisdom here, and they are one. But in regard to the receiver, who consists of body and mind, they are sensed as two forces: The body has a calm spirit, and the mind has great intellect. For this reason, the body must lose of its spirit when it rises to receive knowledge and reason.

3. The Essence of Mystery and Its Departments

Below, I wish to give the reader a clear understanding of the prohibition to use practical Kabbalah, as well as witchcraft and various forms of prevalent esotericism, in order to provide a sound basis from which to extend scientific research.

In our time, many scholars have delved over this issue, exerting to lay a scientific, empirical basis under this matter. Indeed, they have given it much thought. To the best of my knowledge, they have not found any scientific basis that is worth consideration due to their lack of knowledge concerning the origin of this esotericism, which the human mind cannot reach.

What has brought me to touch upon this topic is that I saw the ignorance of the masses as far as discerning such matters, causing them to mix together various forms of esotericism. Therefore, I have now come to show the origin and foundation of this type of esotericism.

I have already explained in part one [here] that there are three parts in the wisdom of the hidden, being material, figurative, and practical learning. In the third part, called "practical learning," I explained how practical Kabbalists work not according to nature, since they have retreated to the initial degrees where there are plentiful pleasantness and sweetness. For this reason, their vital spirit significantly increases, such as you see among ordinary people whose strong will power activates the ones whose desire is weaker, forcing them to act as they wish, and without any thinking or understanding or any benefit for themselves, they follow and obey their every wish.

Similarly, when one who has attained exerts to attain those degrees that yield great vitality and spirit, they can activate it in their friends to a certain extent, as well. It is so because the nature of the spiritual is as the nature of the fish at sea where the big swallows the small when it thinks of it. And here, only thought acts, and the rest is indeed not thought but desire and spirit, since a thought does not move even the thinker himself, so how will it move another? Instead, the desire receives and is depicted according to the image of that thought of the one with the bigger desire and acts in the smaller one. Psychologists define it as "power of thought," but it is a mistake because it is a desire and not a thought.

Also, know that this active power is so mighty that it can induce imaginations in one's friend to the exact same extent that every person has the power to imagine in one's own mind. And with regard to dominion, it is much more powerful than the one who imagines in one's own mind. It is so because one who depicts by himself has the power of intellectual critique opposite the imagination. If it denies that imagination, that imagination is weakened and cannot work at all.

This is not so when one is activated by another. At that time, one is in a state of anarchy, without any work of one's machine, called "the brain." For this reason, there will never be any criticism, but the imagination he has obtained from the other works in him as though he had long ago agreed to it wholeheartedly, and above any criticism, as though it is a type of prejudice.

Moreover, one can clothe and suck the spirit of one's friend inside until he feels his feelings—to an extent—and even his memories, and can contemplate them and determine which of them is desirable and notify him. This is why it is written that they "deny the household of above," for although only the foul ones have come to them, they remain and use them permanently, and intensify their vital spirit more than genuine sages.

Three Thirds in the Concealment of the Wisdom

There are three thirds in the concealment of the wisdom of truth. The first is the unnecessary, the second is the impossible, and the third is "The glory of God is to conceal a matter." I will clarify them one at a time.

The First Third: The Unnecessary

This part has no loss in it at all, of course, except for the matter of cleanness of the mind, since we find that triviality is the most harmful saboteur. All the destructors in the world are "triviality" people, meaning contemplate trivial matters and announce trivial announcements. This is why we do not accept a disciple before he has sworn to remove himself from these saboteurs.

Second Third: The Impossible

This part, of course, requires no oath. However, because it is possible to disclose it with erroneous words and take pride in it in the eyes of the masses, it is included in the oath, as well.

Third Third: The Glory of God Is to Conceal a Matter

This part is the gravest in the concealment, for it has caused many casualties. Know that all the sorcerers and cunning ones that ever were come only from such disclosures where immature disciples erred in the matters and went out to teach anyone they came across, without considering if they were fit for it. They went out and used the wisdom for human purposes—for lust and honor—and they have taken the sanctities of the Creator to secularism and to the street. This is what is called "practical Kabbalah."

The Wisdom of Israel Compared to External Wisdoms

The Standard by which to Evaluate a Wisdom

The value of any wisdom in the world is according to the purpose that it yields. This is the goal to which all the scrutinies aim. Therefore, a wisdom without some purpose is inconceivable except for infants playing games, since to pass the time they come and this is their purpose, according to their value. For this reason, a wisdom is not evaluated by keenness and proficiency, but according to the merit of the purpose that it yields.

You therefore find that any external wisdom is only for the purpose of corporeality, which is sure to be gone today or tomorrow. In that case, it is sufficient for the subject to be as the predicate.

Although the wisdom has many advantages over these subjects, for wherever it is, it is nonetheless a spiritual object, but we have already said that it is evaluated by the purpose, which is its persistence for eternity. If the purpose is transitory and fleeting, it is lost along with it.

Now we have a standard by which to gauge the significance of the wisdom of Israel compared to an external wisdom. It concerns only the understanding of the ways of the Creator over His creations and adhering to Him. It follows that the very essence of this wisdom relies on the Creator. And because the importance of the Creator compared to His creations, which He has created, is inconceivable, the merit of the wisdom of Israel compared over external wisdoms is also inconceivable.

Because the very essence of our wisdom is ever valid and eternal, our entire wisdom will also remain eternal. And because it concerns being favored and approaching the Creator, which is the finest goal that can be perceived, one who engages in it, and certainly one who is rewarded with it, is the finest among the speaking species.

Fools Have No Desire

But fools have no desire. Therefore, the house of Israel are few, as our sages have written, "A thousand people commence with the Bible [Torah], a hundred with the Mishnah, ten with the Talmud, and one of them comes out (to teach)."

"I saw the children of the ascent, and they are few." There are many reasons for it, but the main one is that all who begin with it wish to taste it in full, and the smallest of the measures of those fools is to at least know the righteousness of His guidance.

There is a sort of a duty to know, and it can be made known, according to the spirit of the fool. But "What shall we do to our sister in the day when she is spoken for"? After all, our wisdom can be interpreted in every way, except for the language of the stomach, for the subjects of this wisdom do not need the language of the stomach. This is what we wanted to clarify, and we shall clarify it in a separate essay, for it is the beginning of the confusion and its end.

You Shall Live a Sorrowful Life

Go and see, and you will find that there is one prerequisite to every wisdom, even to external wisdoms: "Live a sorrowful life." It is a well-known thing that anyone who has merited the title "sage" disparages every worldly pleasure. According to the measure of the abstention that one's soul chooses to tolerate due to the affliction of pursuing the wisdom, to that very extent does one find it.

Thus, we should ask one question regarding all the sages in the world together: Every love emerges from one's own flesh and self, and returns to one's own self and flesh. Thus, how do all the sages fail in loving wisdom, whose beginning and end is nothing but the labor of the flesh?

Indeed, any experienced person knows that the greatest of all the world's imaginable pleasures is to win people's favor. Obtaining this coveted thing is worth making every effort and worldly concession. This is the magnet to which the finest in every generation are drawn, and for which they trivialize the whole of the worldly life.

Also, each wisdom comes with its own terminology, whose progenitors had established and by which they explained their wishes. That language is a mediator—close to the wisdom itself and close to the ones engaging in it—since there is a great advantage to it in that it uses few words to explain many things.

The Carriers of the Wisdom of Truth, and the Carriers of an External Wisdom

According to the merit of the wisdom of truth, it is evident that the prerequisite that applies to any wisdom applies to it, as well: to disparage worldly life. But in addition to that is the need to disparage the collective magnet—winning people's favor.

An external sage disparages worldly life in order to be saved from wasting one's precious time on obtaining it. Such is the case with all the fools—due to their fondness of worldly life, they waste their time on it. The sage is saved from them like a fugitive due to his choice to ridicule worldly life. In return for this, he will obtain wisdom during that same time.

By this you can deduce regarding the sages of truth, that as long as they do not disparage the collective magnet—winning people's favor—they are not at all ready to obtain this wisdom. That person will waste his time on winning people's favor and will be as the fools who waste their time on worldly life. Such a person's heart is not free to achieve a pure and clean wisdom, and is unfit to win the Creator's favor, and this is simple.

Now you can understand why our wisdom was undesirable to ordinary people, and why they do not regard it even as an inferior wisdom. They are mistaken because of the different subjects, for the whole purpose of external wisdom is to win people's favor. Therefore, they exert to cloak their wisdom with a superficial garment that even the fools will accept, since they are the majority, and they are the ones who make every famous person known.

Concealing the Wisdom of Truth from the Fools

But the sages of truth had no interest in showing part of the wisdom to an extent that the fools will accept, since there is no need for these fools. I wish to say that even if the sages of the generation strove to educate them about the truth so they would accept it, still, not because of this will they commence with the Torah.

The fool has no desire unless by the revealing of his heart and matters that are close to him, namely that relate to worldly pleasures. I have already explained that the fool does not remain in folly due to his loathing of the wisdom, but due to his nearness to people's delights, for his whole life will not suffice to satisfy half his wishes. For this reason, he has no time for wisdom, even if he likes it, and even if the sages, who are famous in external wisdoms, were regarded as fools and worldly compared to this wisdom due to their nearness to winning people's favor, which in relation to this wisdom is tantamount to worldly lusts and bodily satiations.

Our Sages Did Not Disclose Development from the Wisdom of Truth

Because of it, our sages did not disclose to the fools any development from the wisdom of truth, for it is a great offense, as our sages said, "As one is commanded to say what is heard, one is also commanded not to say what is not heard." It is also written in *The Zohar* in many places: "Woe if I tell; woe if I do not tell. If I tell, the unworthy will know how to serve their master," etc. Because of the importance of the wisdom—to avoid needlessly making it empty words in the mouths of the fools, as those who are fed by the passion of their hearts will not be nourished by the brightness of the *Shechina* [Divinity] for certain, as our sages said, "All whose heart is proud," etc.

This is the reason why each time the wicked kingship spreads over the generation, our holy Torah is promptly sentenced to be burned, as has happened to us several times, even in our generation. It was so because they loathed the wisdom of His uniqueness, which is always sour in the eyes of the fools, as I have explained that they do not find any purpose in it by which to satisfy their foul lusts. On the contrary, they are robbed because of it, for they cannot enjoy, and they do not enjoy incest in public—the only thing that pacifies their hearts.

Body and Soul

Before I clarify this exalted matter, it is important for me to note that although all the readers seem to consider it impossible to clarify and bring such a matter closer to the human mind, except by relying on abstract, philosophical concepts, as is usually the case with such scrutinies, since the day I have discovered the wisdom of Kabbalah and dedicated myself to it, I have distanced myself from abstract philosophy and all its branches as the east is distant from the west. Everything that I will write henceforth will be from a purely scientific perspective, in utter precision, and by means of simple recognition of practical, useful things.

Although I will mention their words below, it will be only to indicate the difference between what the human mind can conjure up and what can be understood using the concepts of the Torah and the prophecy, which are based on practical foundations (as I have shown in "The Essence of the Wisdom of Kabbalah").

I would like to hereby thoroughly clarify the terms "body" and "soul" as they truly are, since truth and commonsense are one and the same, since the truth is available for anyone, but only according to the spirit of the Torah and by removing all the distorted concepts that have taken root among the people. These are primarily taken from abstract methods from which the spirit of our Torah is utterly removed.

Three Methods in the Concepts of Body and Soul

In general, we find that the methods that abound in the world concerning the concepts of body and soul are gathered into three methods:

1) The Method of Faith

The method of faith argues that all that exists is the spirit or the soul. They believe that there are spiritual objects separated from one another by quality. They are called "souls of people," and they exist independently, prior to dressing in a human body. Afterward, when the body dies, the death does not apply to it, since a spiritual object is a simple object. In their view, death is but separation of the elements comprising the object.

This is possible with physical objects, comprised of several elements which death disintegrates. But the spiritual soul, which is an utterly simple object, lacking any multiplicity, cannot be separated in any way, as this separation would annul its existence. Hence, the soul is eternal and exists forever.

The body, as they understand it, is like clothing over this spiritual object. The spiritual soul clothes in it and uses it to manifest its forces: the good qualities and all kinds of concepts. Also, it provides the body with life and motion and guards it from harm. Thus, the body itself is lifeless, motionless, and contains nothing but dead matter, as we see once the soul departs it—when it dies—and all the signs of life we see in human bodies are but manifestations of the powers of the soul.

2) The Method of Believers in Duality

Those who believe in duality think of the body as a complete creation, standing, living, and nourishing, and safekeeping its existence in all that is required. It does not need any assistance from any spiritual object.

Yet, the body is not considered man's essence. Man's primary essence is the perceiving soul, which is a spiritual object, as in the view of the supporters of the first method.

The difference between these two methods is only in the concept of the body. Following the extensive developments in physiology and psychology, they have found that Providence has provided for all of life's needs within the machine of the body itself. This, in their view, restricts the role of the soul's functionality within the body solely to concepts and virtues of the spiritual kind. Thus, while they believe in duality, in both methods together, they say that the soul is the reason for the body, meaning that the body is a result, extending from the soul.

3) The Method of the Deniers

The method of deniers of spirituality, who acknowledge only corporeality. Supporters of this method completely deny the existence of any kind of abstract spiritual object within the body. They have evidently proven that man's mind, too, is but a product of the body, and depict the body as an electronic machine with wires that stretch from the body to the brain and are operated by encounters with external things.

Also, they send their sensations of pain or pleasure to the brain, and the brain instructs the organ what to do. Everything is operated by wires and cords built for this task. They move the organ away from sources of pain and toward sources of pleasure. Thus, they clarify all of man's conclusions from life's events.

Also, what we feel as concepts and rationalities within our minds are but images of corporeal occurrences within the body. Man's preeminence over all animals is that our minds are developed to such an extent that all the body's events are depicted in our brains as images that we experience as concepts and rationalities.

Thus, the mind and all its deductions are but products that extend from the events of the body. In addition, there are proponents of the second method who completely agree with this method but add the spiritual, eternal object to it, called "the soul that dresses within the machine of the body." This soul is man's essence, and the machine of the body is but its clothing. Thus, I have laid out in general terms all that human science has thus far contrived in the concepts of "body" and "soul."

The Scientific Meaning of Body and Soul According to Our Torah

Now I shall explain this exalted matter according to our Torah, as our sages have explained it to us. I have already written in several places that there is not a single word of our sages, not even in the prophetic wisdom of Kabbalah, that relies on a theoretical basis. It is a known fact that man is naturally doubtful, and each conclusion that the human mind deems certain, it deems uncertain after some time. Hence, one doubles the efforts of one's study and invents another conclusion and once again declares that it is certain.

But if one is a genuine student, he will walk around this axis all of one's life, since yesterday's certainty has become today's uncertainty, and today's certainty becomes tomorrow's uncertainty. Thus, it is impossible to determine any definite conclusions for more than a day.

Revealed and Concealed

Today's science has sufficiently understood that there is no absolute certainty in reality. Yet, our sages arrived at this conclusion several thousand years earlier. Hence, concerning religious matters, they guided and forbade us not only to refrain from drawing any conclusions based on theory, but even prohibited us from being assisted by such theories, even by way of negotiations.

Our sages divided the wisdom into two matters: revealed and concealed. The revealed part contains everything we know from our direct consciousness, as well as the concepts built upon practical experience, without any assistance from scrutiny, as our sages said, "A judge has only what his eyes see."

The concealed part contains all those concepts we had heard from trusted people or have acquired by ourselves through general understanding and perception of them. However, we cannot sufficiently approach it so as to criticize it with a healthy mind, with straightforward cognizance. And this is regarded as "concealed," where we were advised to accept matters with "simple faith." And with all that concerns religion, we have been strictly forbidden to even look at matters that could arouse us to scrutinize and study them.

Yet, these names, "revealed" and "concealed," are not permanent names, applying to certain kinds of knowledge, as the masses think. Rather, they apply only to the human consciousness. Thus, one refers to all those concepts one has already discovered and has come to know through actual experience as "revealed," and regards all the concepts that are yet to be recognized in this manner as "concealed."

Thus, throughout the generations, there is not a person who does not have these two divisions, where in his revealed part, he is permitted to delve and scrutinize, since it has a real basis, and in the part that is concealed from him, even a shred of scrutiny is forbidden, since he has no real basis there.

Permitted and Forbidden in Using Human Science

Hence, we who follow in the footsteps of our sages are not permitted to use the human science, except with knowledge that has been proven by actual experiences and of whose validity we have no doubt. Therefore, we cannot accept any religious principle from the above three methods, all the more so concerning concepts of body and soul, which are the fundamental concepts and the subject of religion as a whole. We can only accept concepts of life sciences taken from experiments that no one can doubt.

Clearly, such a proof cannot be found in any spiritual matter, but only in physical matters, set up for perception by the senses. Hence, we are permitted to use the third method, to an extent. It engages only in matters of the body, in all those conclusions that have been proven by experiments, and which no one doubts. Other conjectures, which combine the logic of their method and other methods, are faulty and forbidden for us. One who uses them breaches, "Do not turn to the idols."

Yet, this third method is foreign and loathsome to the human spirit. There is hardly any truly educated person who is able to accept it. This is so because according to them, man's human form has been erased and vanished. Man has been made into a machine that walks and works by other forces. In their opinion, man has no free choice whatsoever, but is rather pushed by nature's forces, and all his actions are compulsory. Hence, man has no reward or punishment, since no judgment, punishment, or reward apply to one who has no freedom of will.

Such a thing is utterly unthinkable, and not only for the religious, who believe in reward and punishment, since believing in His Providence, that all of nature's forces are guided by Him, assures them that everything has a good and desirable cause. Yet, this method is even stranger in the eyes of the nonreligious, who believe that everyone is given to the hands of the blind, mindless, and aimless nature. These intelligent ones are like toys in its hands, led astray, and who knows where? Hence, this method has become despised and unaccepted in the world.

Indeed, know that the method of those who conceive duality came only to correct this above-mentioned distortion. For this reason, they have decided that the body, which is but a machine according to the third method, is not at all the real human. Man's real essence is something altogether different—invisible and imperceptible to the senses. It is a spiritual entity, clothed and hidden within the body. This is man's "self," the "I." The body and everything within it are considered possessions of that eternal and spiritual I, as they have written.

Yet, by their own admission, this whole method is lame since they cannot explain how a spiritual entity, being the soul or the self, can move the body or decide anything concerning it. This is because following the philosophical precision itself, the spiritual has no contact whatsoever with the physical. It has absolutely no impact on it, as they themselves have written.

The Accusation against Maimonides

Yet, even without this question, their method would have been forbidden among Israel, as we have explained above. It is important that you know that the whole accusation against Maimonides by Israel's sages and the harsh judgment to burn his books were not because they had any doubt of the righteousness and piousness of Maimonides himself. Rather, it was only because he used philosophy and metaphysics, which were at their peak at the time, as assistance in his books. Maimonides wished to save them from it, yet the sages did not agree with him.

Needless to say, today our generation has already recognized that metaphysical philosophy contains no real content upon which it is worthwhile to spend one's time. Hence, it is certainly forbidden for anyone to take any spices from their words.

Not the Time for the Livestock to Be Gathered

"It is not the time for the livestock to be gathered. Water the sheep, and go, pasture them" (Genesis 29:7). It is known that all the words of the righteous turn upwards, as it was said to him, "And it was revealed by the shepherds of Haran." It is so because it was impossible to roll the stone from the mouth of the well of the revealing of Rachel before all the herds were gathered and the stone was rolled off from the well's mouth.

In my humble opinion, it can be said that before each revelation, there must be covering, as in the darkness of the morning. For this reason, since Jacob arrived at the well of Rachel's revealing to Jacob, he did not feel Rachel's love as during the entire way, as he followed her with his cane through the Jordan.

This is why he set out for the upper well, for the well was blocked by the rock, and Jacob means elevating the externality. Hence, he set out to the externality. (This is the meaning of "And he sat on the well," meaning sitting.)

He promptly stood in prayer, and a man set out to the shepherds of the flock. (Why, etc.,) "It is not the time for the livestock to be gathered. Water the sheep, and go, pasture them," as in (Song of Songs 1:7) "Where do you pasture," and "Where do you make it lie down." And the reply came to him, "We cannot, until all the flocks have gathered." That is, until Jacob achieves a coupling in externality, the whole of Israel, including the four mothers, are dependent on him alone. This is why his work was thus far alone, not in public, for he did not need any assistance from others and was the strongest in the work without ever being tired.

But at that moment, when it was his time to mate with Rachel to elicit seventy souls, he promptly felt weariness, and this is what he spoke and prayed about. (Indeed he knew) and this is the meaning of Jacob not rolling the stone from the well's mouth prior to the disclosure of Rachel. However, upon Rachel's disclosure before him, the *Zivug Eynaim* (coupling of the eyes) was completed. Therefore, at that time all of Israel were included in him. Thus, all the herds of that time had already gathered, and therefore, "[he] rolled the stone from the well's mouth."

But from then on, when the seventy souls of Jacob expanded into 600,000 souls, the matter returned to its initial state, requiring the gathering of all the herds in order to roll off the stone from the well's mouth. And when the power of one part is missing, it causes weakness in the whole level. This is the meaning of (Braita de Rabbi Ishmael) an individual that requires a collective, and anything that was in the collective and has departed the collective, does not testify to itself, but departed in order to testify to the entire collective, since (Psalms 103:15) "As for man ... as a bud of the field, so he will bud."

The whole point of the buds rises into a single flower, the collective of Jacob and the tribes, a complete bed. This places a unique boundary for each and every soul, as in receiving light from above in this world, in the work, and one is greater than the other, one is higher than the other, and no face is like another.

The depiction of those boundaries is identical to the image of the lines and dots of the flower, where the boundaries in each part and dot on the flower form the beauty of the flower. But when the dot or the part in the flower extends its boundary, whether a little or a lot, it makes the whole flower unsightly. It is impossible to take only part of the flower and examine it alone, for then that part has neither beauty nor glory.

This is the meaning of the allegory in *The Zohar* (*The Sulam* [Ladder] commentary, *Nasso*, Item 19) about two who boarded a boat, and one was drilling under him. His friend admonished him, "Why are you drilling?" And that fool replied, "Why should you care? I am drilling under me!" But indeed, the individual spoils the beauty of the entire image.

From this we understand that in the ruin of the First Temple, the craftsman and the locksmith did not save the Temple from ruin because the majority of their contemporaries spoiled the beauty, though in them there was no flaw, for prophecy is not present in a flawed place, not even in the slightest.

This is the meaning of a prayer in public, that one must not exclude oneself from the public and ask for oneself, not even to bring contentment to one's maker, but only for the entire public. It is so because one cannot extend one's boundary while the boundaries of the rest of the buds of the flower remain where they are, for as smallness blemishes the beauty, so does greatness, since the boundaries of all the lines and circles of the flower must be related.

This is the meaning of (Psalms 22:21) "Save my soul from the sword, my only one from the dog." One who departs from the public to ask specifically for one's own soul does not build. On the contrary, he inflicts ruin upon his soul, as in (*Midrash Rabbah*, Chapter 7, Item 6) "All who is proud," etc., for there cannot be one who retires from the public unless with an attire of pride. Woe unto him, for he inflicts ruin on his soul, for one who takes from the flower, not only does he condemn the beauty of the flower in general, that there is a flaw in their value, but even that specific part has no glory or beauty whatsoever, and no color in the eye will regard him.

For this reason, he ruins his soul, and also causes the giving of his *Yechida* (only one) to a dog, meaning BON, the parting of the points, while MA is the connection into a single flower, and *Yechida* is the one who receives the light of MA, and every person has a *Yechida*, meaning his own expansion.

This is what causes every boundary, meaning man's sensation of himself as a unique self, meaning an only one. Indeed, at the root, he is called *Yechida* (only one) because there, all the souls of Israel are only one, one collective, as in "counting a number and there is no number," and as in "collective and individual," as in choice.

And all that is required of one's work is to extend upon himself the light of *Yechida*, which will be completed only when all the herds have gathered.

Even during work, when one prays alone, against his will he departs from the public and ruins his soul, which is from the *Chazeh* and below, as in the revealing and particularizing of the souls. Moreover, *Yechida* passes to the dog even at the root, as in the expanding of the name *BON* into (Isaiah 56:10) "Dumb dogs cannot bark." That is, their cry will not rise to the heaven whatsoever, to the *Zivug* of MA and BON, meaning to unite, but is rather given to a dog, meaning the separation, as in *Hav! Hav!* (bark, but also "give" in Hebrew) of the daughters of Hell.

This is the meaning of (Exodus 10:23) "And all the children of Israel had light in their dwellings," meaning their dwelling on the throne, which is from the *Chazeh* and below. It is a place where *Hassadim* are revealed and expand (for in NHY, the internality does not disappear and there are no intestines there), and also, "a dog will not bark" (Exodus 11:7). That is, there was not even an awakening of anyone from the children of Israel to demand anything personal, as in *Hav! Hav!*, for no one needed anything because they did not feel as separate selves, and this was their power to come out of Egypt with a mighty hand.

Thus, every one must gather with all of one's strength into the whole of Israel with every plea to the Creator in the prayer and in the work, for it is insolence and great disgrace to disclose one's nakedness before, etc.

This is the meaning of (Exodus 20:23) "And you shall not go up by steps to My altar," meaning as an individual, where one is above the other. And especially that he desires to boast over the seed of holiness, and a holy nation does not need him. He marches on the heads of the holy nation and demands greatness over them. This is a disgrace we must not mention henceforth.

Instead, he should include himself in the only one, the root of all of Israel, as in (Isaiah 44:6) "I am the first and I am the last." And then his strength is just as Jacob's strength. At that time he will be able to roll the stone from over the well's mouth with a mighty hand, and will water all the herds from a well of water, for the previous boundary will be lifted from all the souls of Israel, both below him and above him.

Moreover, the depictions of the boundaries of the flower that render glory and beauty will not change at all, for they will remain in their former depiction. But the boundary of the holiness in general will be expanded greatly, causing light to all the children of Israel in their dwellings. And then, even his own personal dog will remain dumb, for the light of beauty will appear, as in his dwelling place, meaning from the *Chazeh* and below, for so is the nature of the light of the collective that is on the individual who has been annulled with regard to his own individuality, and he does not feel himself.

The Meaning of Conception and Birth

1. Rules

General and Particular

The scrutiny of the educated in creation, in the first concept, is defined as emulating the work of the Creator. The work of the Creator is called "Providence," or the "nature of creation."

They are not called "body," but rather "simple matter of flesh and blood in its still [inanimate] form," completely amorphous. It is so because anything that is called by the name "form" is regarded as a spiritual force and is not a body.

This gives us a law by which all bodies are equal. However, as Earth is a single body that cannot be divided into many—for we do not find any change of form in it from one part to another—the still cannot be divided into many elements.

Also, all the power of proliferation in the world is a wonderful, spiritual force. For this reason, anything that is general is suitable and praiseworthy, for it comes from the spiritual force, and anything that is particular is contemptible and lowly. This designates the difference between a selfish person and one who is dedicated to one's nation.

There is no doubt that the merit of the collective is defined by its power of proliferation, for if we have decided that the power of proliferation is a spiritual and important matter, then if the proliferation is greater, he is more important.

It follows that one who is dedicated to one's nation is more important than one who is dedicated to one's town, and one who is dedicated to the world is more important than one who is dedicated to one's nation. This is the first concept.

Birth in Spirituality

Therefore, as there is birth of an individual, in relation to the construction of the bodies, there is birth of the collective. This is done by renewal of the spiritual force, meaning development of the concepts is birth for the collective, for in the spiritual, disparity of form divides the worlds from one another. This birth means arriving at the world of correction.

The Exodus from Egypt Is Called Birth

If we are speaking of the proliferation in the spiritual essence, it is similar to the corporeal case of being born from the mother's womb—which is a dark and spoiled world with all kinds of filth and unpleasantness—into a world lit up by perfection, the world of correction.

By this we understand the meaning of the preparation as defined in the kingdom of the priests, who have come to it by the prophecy of Moses, and for which they were rewarded with freedom from the angel of death and the reception of the Torah. At that time, they needed a new birth into the air of the enlightened world, called in the verse, "A pleasant land, good and broad."

Stillborn

That newborn was stillborn because after the pregnancy—which is the iron melting pot and the enslavement in Egypt—came the birth. But they were still unfit to breathe the spirit of life from the enlightened world, where they were given a promise they would come, until the count began, and the war with Amalek, and the trials with the water, etc., and they arrived at the Sinai desert. Sinai (as our sages said) means *Sinaa* [hatred], for they are pronounced the same, meaning the affliction entailed in every illness.

The Birth to Father and Mother

At that time they became worthy of breathing the spirit of life, and the prophecy "And you shall be unto Me a kingdom of priests and a holy nation" came true in them—first, a kingdom of priests, to revoke their personal possessions, and subsequently, a holy nation which is to bestow contentment upon their Maker through "love your neighbor as yourself."

In corporeality, the newborn falls into loving and loyal hands, who are the father and the mother, who guarantee its sustenance and health. Likewise, once each one has been prepared with 600,000 who care for one's sustenance, they breathe the spirit of life, as it is written, "And Israel encamped there before the mount," and RASHI interpreted, "as one man with one heart."

2. Posterior and Anterior

Man's eyes are before him. This implies that he can look only to the future in a manner of growth from below upward. However, he cannot look behind him, in the manner of conception, from above downward (as it is written about Lot, "Look not behind you").

Hence, man is denied any real knowledge because he is devoid of the beginning. He is like a book whose first half is missing, so its content cannot be understood at all. The whole advantage of those who attain is that they are rewarded with attaining the conception, too, meaning the progression from above downward.

Man includes everything, and this is evidently seen when he looks and contemplates something. Everyone knows that he is not looking outside his own body and ideas whatsoever, yet he attains the whole world, knows what people think, assesses how to be liked by them, and adapts himself to their wishes.

In order to know that, he only needs to look inside himself, and he already understands the thoughts of his contemporaries because everyone is equal, and a person contains all the people within. The restriction on one's knowledge is that one does not know one's own conception or remembers anything from that time so as to be able to say anything about it.

The Fiftieth Gate

This is the meaning of the verse, "You will see My back, but My face shall not be seen." Moses attained the meaning of conception, meaning all the discernments from above downward, in full. It is called "the posterior of the spiritual worlds," and all he lacked was to look at the "face," as well, meaning to see the future through the end of the correction. This is called "fifty gates of *Bina*," since the level of *Bina* is one hundred gates, and *Bina* is named by Kabbalists, *Ima* [mother], as she is the mother of the whole world. One who is rewarded with attaining all one hundred gates in her is rewarded with the revelation of completeness.

Their fifty gates from behind are the conception, meaning the progression from above downward, and their fifty gates from before are the necessary path of development through the end of correction. At that time, "The whole earth shall be full of the knowledge of the Lord," and "They shall teach no more each man his neighbor and each man his brother saying 'Know the Lord,' for they shall all know Me, from the least of them to the greatest of them."

This is the meaning of Moses' prayer, "Show me please Your glory," meaning all fifty gates of *Bina* from before. And the Creator said to him, "You shall see My back"; it is enough that you see all fifty in My posterior, from above downward. "But My face shall not be seen," since you will not see all the fifty from before, "For man shall not see Me and live," meaning before it is due time, when the vessels have fully adapted and developed.

Prior to this, one must die by seeing this because the *Kelim* [vessels] will not be able to receive that great light and will be canceled. This is the meaning of what is written, "Fifty gates of *Bina* were created in the world, and all but one were given to Moses."

But in spirituality there is no lack. Rather, it is all or nothing, as in "A slightly broken vow is a completely broken vow." But in the end, when the measure of the *Kelim* grow and develop sufficiently, they will be fit for attaining the fiftieth gate. (You should also know that there are two kinds of attainment: prophecy and wisdom. With respect to wisdom, Moses attained what all the sages attained. But with respect to prophecy, he could not attain. It is about this that our sages said, "A sage is preferable to a prophet," and they also said that Solomon attained the fiftieth gate.)

The Soul Begets the Body: Conception and Growth

We find two progressions in sown wheat:

1. From the time it is placed in the ground, when it begins to strip itself of its form. This is regarded as begetting, until it becomes naught, meaning the substrate of negation of its progenitors' form, and the actual becomes potential. Until then, it is regarded as conception, extending from the progression from above downward.

2. When it comes to the final point, the growth begins. This is the progression from below upward until it obtains the level of its progenitor.

General and Particular Are the Same

General and particular are as identical as two drops in a pond. It is so both externally, in the state of the planet in general, and internally, for even in the smallest atom we find a complete system of sun and planets circling it, just as in the universe. Likewise, man is the internality of the world, and you find within man all the images of the upper worlds, *Atzilut*, *Beria*, *Yetzira*, and *Assiya*. It is as Kabbalists said, "*Atzilut* is the *Rosh* [head], *Beria* is up to the *Chazeh* [chest], *Yetzira* is from there to *Tabur* [navel], and *Assiya* is from the *Tabur* down."

For this reason, there is a progression from above downward in man's conception, too, meaning a slow expansion from the progenitor, the mother, until one completely detaches from her as one emerges to the world, moving from operating to operated, from the authority of the progenitor to one's own authority.

At that time begins the progression from below upward, the days of nursing, when still attached to the mother's breasts, until the form is fully completed in the final level of the progenitors.

However, *Adam HaRishon* [the first man] was a creation of the Creator. He was certainly not born from a woman, but from the dust of the earth, as were the rest of the first creations, who were formed from that dust, as it is written, "All was from the dust." And yet, that dust extends from the upper worlds that precede it.

It is so because above, too, there are light and *Kli* [sing. of *Kelim*]. The light is in the forms in the reception, and the *Kli* is the will to receive the forms that suit them. That *Kli*, which is the will to receive, is never constant, neither in terms of importance, nor in terms of an independent reality that stands on its own, but only with what it receives. Thus, it has no more merit than what is received.

For example, a poor man who wishes to acquire wealth is no more important than a poor man who is content with his lot and does not aspire for wealth. On the contrary, he is worse than him because the will to receive becomes one with the received matter, and they are only two halves of one thing. When each half is separated, it has no value in itself, which you can discuss with or negotiate.

3. What Is a Soul?

The Law of Development According to the Wisdom of Kabbalah

It is impossible to examine anything before you see it from its beginning to its end. And since one feels only what comes from within (just as ophthalmologists have found that the colors are not the same in both eyes, but there is rather an agreement here), therefore, first one must know oneself through and through, at least since the time of conception [impregnation] to the time of adulthood. And because this is not so, for one begins to know oneself only when becoming a complete human being, one is therefore devoid of the ability to self-scrutinize.

No Person Knows Himself

The second reason is that to know something, you must primarily observe its negative qualities. And one cannot see one's own faults (and to the same extent that one can borrow from what one sees in others, one looks in a mirror that does not illuminate), since anything bad that one must receive comes to one as pleasure, for otherwise he would not receive it. Also, it is a law that wherever there is pleasure, a person does not regard it as bad, except after many experiences that develop in them. However, this requires days and years, as well as memory, conclusions, and observations, of which not everyone is capable. For this reason, no person knows himself.

But Kabbalists have attainment and attain a matter in full. That is, they are rewarded with attaining all those degrees in reality that one can attain. This is considered that they have attained a matter in full, and that complete matter is called a "soul."

That Soul Is the Possession of *Adam HaRishon*

I have already explained above, in item 2, that the worlds are attained in two ways—from above downward and from below upward. First, one attains from above downward, the hanging down of the soul, and then from below upward, being the attainment itself.

The first progression is called *Ibur* [impregnation] because it is tantamount to a drop that gradually detaches from the father's brain and becomes impregnated in the mother until it emerges to the world. This is regarded as the last degree from above downward, meaning taking into consideration the cause of the newborn. After all, until then it was still connected in some part to its father and mother, meaning the cause, and as it came into the world it became independent, and this is the order from above downward.

And the reason for all this is that His thought is unique. Hence, all incidents are the same, and the general is similar to the particular.

Conception and Growth of a Body as a Soul

From the moment of one's birth, when one is at the farthest point, begins the return to attainment, from below upward. This is called the "law of development," which follows the exact same ways and inlets that descended from above downward.

Kabbalists attain it, but to corporeal eyes they seem as ordinary states—slow, gradual—until one's level grows and becomes like one's father and mother. At that time one is regarded as having attained all the degrees from below upward, meaning a complete degree.

4. From Above Downward and From Below Upward

The Growth Testifies to the Conception

And since the two progressions, from above downward and from below upward, are as similar as two drops in a pond, we can understand the progression from above downward by observing the progression from below upward, which is the second progression of the development, namely the growth.

You find that there are four states in the four worlds, ABYA, beginning with *Assiya*, such as when examining the progression of the growth of a fruit from the planting to its complete ripening.

1. Before the signs of fruition appear in it. These are all the laws of the states in the fruit. This is the world of *Assiya*.

2. From the time when you can eat it and be satiated, although it is still tasteless. This is *Yetzira*.

3. From the time when some flavor can be detected in it. This is *Beria*.

4. From the time when its full flavor and beauty appear, and this is *Atzilut*. This order is from below upward.

Every Emanated and Born Comes in Two Ways

The whole issue of from above downward and from below upward that was explained in the four worlds, ABYA, applies even to the smallest item in the worlds, meaning in every cause and consequence. A cause is the father, the root, the agent. A consequence means that it was operated and done by the cause. For this reason, it is regarded as an offspring, a branch, or an extension and cause.

The meaning of these two progressions is understood in the particular just as in the general. From above downward is a way of separating the cause from its consequence until it emerges and becomes an authority on its own. And from below upward is the law of development that awakens it to grow from below upward until it attains its cause. That is, it becomes completely equal to it.

As we have explained above, the corporeal father and offspring that comes from the father's brain to the birth is the time of the ascent from below upward. You should discern likewise in all four types: still, vegetative, animate, and speaking.

As it is in the emanation of the elements of spirituality, so it is in all the worlds. It is so because from *Ehad* [one/unique] emerges the *Yechida* [also unique], and all the ways that that *Yechida* received necessitate all the subsequent successions, both in the general and in the particular.

5. Emulating Creation

The Birth of the Happy Humanity

When looking at the seal of the work of creation, we find there the words, "Which God has created to do." This means that the work of the Creator, which is set in the creation before us, is given to us in order to do and to add to it. Otherwise, the words *to do* would have been completely redundant and meaningless, and it would have to say, "For in it He rested from all His work which God has created." So why were the words *to do* added here? It must be that this verse teaches us that the full extent of the work that the Creator has left in creation is in the exact measure, no more and no less, but the extent that enables us to perform its development and completion by ourselves.

In truth, our entire development in creation is but emulation of it. All the flavors and beauty of colors that we innovate and devise are but emulation of the tasteful colors that we find in flowers. And so is a carpenter; from where does he know about making a four-legged table, if not by emulating the work of the Creator, who has made creations that stand on four legs? Or, from where would he know about combining two pieces of wood if not by emulating the organs of the body, which are joined together, so he went and built in the wood accordingly?

People observe and study the reality set before us in perfect reason and beauty. Afterward, when they understand it, they emulate it and do likewise. Subsequently, that example becomes a basis for another example, until man has created a handsome world full of inventions.

By looking at creation, planes were built with wings like birds. A radio was built to receive sound waves like the ears. In short, all of our successes are presented before us in creation and in reality as is, and all we need is to emulate it, and do.

Reality and the Existence of Reality Deny One Another

Reality—meaning reality in general, and all its parts that are created as creations in relation to that which belongs to their existence—we find that it is well set up, with every beauty and pleasantness, without any deficiency whatsoever. Truly, an enlightened world. But when we place opposite that the existence of this reality, meaning the manners by which these creations feed and sustain themselves, they are awry, disordered, tasteless, and very unrestrained. However, we have already explained about reality and the existence of reality in general in the essay "The Meaning of Unity," and learn it from there.

Conclusion and Birth

From all this you should know that the general is always equal to the particular, that the Creator in and of Himself does not feel the proliferation, as He is always in the singular authority, and you can conclude the benefit of the collective from that of the individual.

And as the existence and birth of the individual—which the Creator has set up by the force of nature—is tested from the moment of birth and emergence to the place that the Creator has prepared, which is called "this world." It is considered that He has made certain that one will fall into the hands of loyal lovers who will tend, heal, and care for all of one's needs in complete devotion and love.

The same is true of the collective. If it wishes to be born and emerge to the world corrected for the whole collective, it is necessary to see that this general child falls into the hands of loyal parents who will love it just as devotedly as would a father and a mother, meaning through the commandment of love of others. This is similar to the preparation for the giving of the Torah.

However, here we engage only in the human species and see how much of the pleasantness and good the work of the Creator has set up concerning one's existence, to keep one until one is worthy of being called upon in the shape of a working human. And when we take the order of one's own existence, how much of the loathed and terrible is in it—wherever one turns, one condemns, and one's very existence is built on the ruin of one's neighbor.

6. The Corrected and the Needy of Man's Work

Which God Has Created to Do

Know that the Creator needed the work of creation only to the extent that man was not given the strength to work there. Similar to digestion, the Creator created everything in such a way that the digestion of the food in our stomach happens without effort on our part.

However, from the point where one can work—as this is all the flavor and contentment of the Creator who wanted to enjoy His work, meaning to fashion creations that can add, delight, and create like Him, but has no wish whatsoever to cook our food which is on the stove for us without our awareness, since we can do this by ourselves.

This is similar to a teacher and a student where the whole intention of the teacher is to give the student the strength to be like him, and to teach other students, like him. Likewise, the Creator is pleased when His creations create and innovate like Him. Yet, our whole power to innovate and develop is not real innovation. Rather, it is a type of emulation. And the more the emulation matches the work of nature, to that extent is our level of development measured.

From this we know that we have the power to correct ourselves, the existence of reality, like nature's pleasant example of reality. The proof of this is that had the Creator not worked His full Providence in that discernment, too, for "Is the Lord's hand short?" Rather, it is necessary that in this place, which is our own correction, we are able to correct ourselves.

7. Movement as a Sign of Life

Still, Vegetative, Animate - Speaking

With regard to spiritual life, people are divided into two: 1) still, vegetative, animate; 2) speaking. The still, vegetative, and animate are regarded as completely lifeless. The speaking is regarded as alive.

Life is the power of movement. It is known that the beginning of life is done by two completely contradictory actions.

When the speaking is born, it is also regarded as lifeless until it is awakened through pushes, since its *Kelim* are ready to receive life and movement while still in the mother's womb. Upon the emergence to the world, the air of the world affects it with chillness to which it is not accustomed, and this causes the awakening of the contraction.

And after the first contraction, it must spread once more to its former measure. These two things—contraction and expansion—are the first step that gives it life.

However, sometimes, due to weakness of the birth, the fetus weakens and the contraction is not awakened in it, since the reception of the chillness of the air of the world is too weak to affect its contraction. This causes it to be born dead, meaning that it still did not have a place and a reason for life—which begins with contraction—to clothe in it.

Without internal contraction, there is no expansion. It is so because it by no means expands more than its boundary, so there is no movement. And the sign of a creature that is ready for the light of life is that it at least has the power to contract for some reason. At that time comes the light of life and makes the expansion, and the first movement of life occurs. For this reason, movement will not cease from it and it becomes a living, moving being.

That first movement is called "a soul," meaning the spirit of life that breathes in his nostrils, as it is written, "and breathed into his nostrils the breath of life."

However, the still, vegetative, and animate do not possess that power to make an internal contraction, for whatever reason. Because of this, the light of life cannot clothe in them and cause expansion.

He has given an inexorable law that without contraction and expansion, the *Kli* will not be able to expand beyond its boundary. Hence, the still, vegetative, and animate are sentenced to eternal death.

But the speaking is truly fit for life. However, it is born dead, as was said above, since it requires some reason and cause that will act upon it and at least make the first contraction. This happens to it by the cold air that comes to it from Torah and good deeds.

The Quality of the Contraction

The contraction should be by the power of the creature itself. We discern two kinds of contraction: The first is contraction as a result of an external cause, such as coolness. The second is contraction that comes from the vessel itself.

1. As you see when spanking and pressing the newborn to wake it up, although each press and spank causes a contraction in the newborn's body, the expansion that returns does not return because of the light of life, but because of the structure of the *Kli* itself, which must always maintain its exact boundary and custom. Hence, when some element comes and presses it, the *Kli* has the power to return to its place by the force that causes its positive boundary.

2. If the contraction happens from within the *Kli* itself, and not due to an external cause, it cannot return to its previous boundary whatsoever because the contraction that took place in it was from its own structure. Thus, it cannot return to its original boundary.

The Creator is the exception, meaning that a new, personal light should expand in it and return it to its custom. That light is added to the original light to be in it permanently. That is, each time it contracts, the light returns and causes it to expand to its previous size. That light is called "life."

Two Contractions—Partial and General. Opposite Them, Two Expansions

The blood is the soul. It is so because the red color needs the white color to connect to it, and then it is called "blood." Before it has permanently joined it, it is not regarded as blood because at that time there are lying and rising in it. This is so because its nature is *O-Dem* [two Hebrew words that mean "or blood"], and then irregular rising is painted in it, which is only called "the color *O-Dem* [redness]," from the words, "Be still for the Lord." For this reason, the color falls from it again and it becomes white, colorless, which is irregular lying [resting].

When the two join, they become tendons of life's blood.

When the two become tendons of life's blood, making the contradictions in it, one becomes the living soul, meaning the O is cut off from the *Odem* [red], leaving *Dam* [blood] permanently. And yet, the lying and rising that were before, now they conjoin in this blood.

Hence, we discern two kinds in blood: red and white. That is, the same red and white that were operating one at a time before have now conjoined and made this blood, which is called a "living soul." Know that this is the meaning of the partial contraction and partial expansion which are called *Nefesh* [soul] and *Ruach* [spirit].

However, that light, which made the expansion—the partial of the soul—is a general, wonderful upper light. For this reason, it fills and complements every kind of contraction inscribed in that structure.

It is known that there was already white in that body, in the part that is unfit to receive the *O-Dem* color [red], since ... of the redness were robbed and fell when they join together in vain, etc. For this reason, once the light completed the first expansion of the light of the above-mentioned living soul, it refills that old contraction that was made in it initially. This is what is called "general expansion" or "tendons of the brain," extending from the red material whose form has been completely wiped away.

This is the meaning of what is written, "And breathed into his nostrils" [in Hebrew it is written, "noses"], two noses. First, a nose of red-white. Second, a nose of the white that is completely wiped away. "And the man became a living soul," first out of the red-white nose, which is the blood and the first expansion, but finally it was the soul of life because it expanded in the second nose of the wiped away white, as well, which is a soul and is regarded as GAR.

You should also know that the first expansion of tendons of blood relates to the bottom, bodily brain, called marrow. There. ...operating without one's awareness since the intermediate state, from the first nose to the second nose, is the time of nurturing of ... ... and then the light works completely without one's awareness, for he has not attained his soul.

And the second expansion in the tendons from marrows kept for it as the second oppositeness, which is called the "second nose," is the relation of the upper brain: ... ... to the three *Mochin* that operate consciously in him. This is called ...

Oppositeness between Head and Body

It has been explained that in the tendons from the marrow, the red is on the right. This is the color and the being that is formed on this paper. The white is the complete left, for the second nose is also erased from it, and even the color disappears from it so that the red is the being and the white is the absence.

The opposite of it is blood tendons, since the red is the left, meaning O that has been joined in advance, and as "river" and "maybe." Conversely, although the white is lying, this image still becomes "right" and rising. For this reason, it is an eternal soul, which no longer needs color. And the red color that remains and is inscribed in advance has now been put to the left, in *Gevura*. It is called *Dam* [blood] without the O [of *Odem* (red)] so that the white is on the right, for it is not needed, and the red color will not occur in it, and the red is regarded as left, only *Gevura*, which is called "blood."

Here you need to understand that the *Reshimo* [recollection] of the above-mentioned red in the first nose—and their tendons, which rose to the left, after the second nose, regarded as a soul—is erased and permanently passes away from this structure. For this reason, the head, the brain, is white without any red at all.

Ibur [Conception]

During pregnancy, the fetus is just like a plant. Its movements are not regarded as movements of life since the movements are done by its mother, of which the fetus is a part.

Its environment is called "abdomen," and the mother is the boundary of the environment that is cast upon it, and it eats what its mother eats, etc., and the birth begins with the head.

The Essence of Life

Knowing the living is the self-essence. Movement is defined by contraction (see above), for no creation can extend its boundary even as a hairsbreadth.

This extends from the head, for there the giving of this power is restricted to slightly less than its boundary, regarding the question.

You should know that as long as another force contracts it below its size, this does not make the inanimate animate. Rather, it must contract of its own. But how can this be while it is still inanimate? This requires a prayer to be rewarded with the upper force.

By that we can understand the concealed under the surrounding light, and the meaning of "for man shall not see Me and live," for the living can move, and if it still cannot contract then it is not alive, but still. This is the meaning of "The righteous' death is with a kiss," meaning they lose the power of contraction.

From My Flesh I Shall See God

Qualification for the Nurturing of the Soul

It is impossible to sustain one's body in the world without a certain amount of knowledge about the corporeal nature, such as knowing which drugs are lethal and what things burn or harm, as well as knowledge and assessment of what is in one's friend's heart, without which it is impossible to exist in the material world.

Just so, man's soul cannot exist in the next world until it has acquired a certain amount of the nature of the systems of the spiritual worlds, their changes, couplings, and generations.

We discern three periods in the body: The first is from the time of birth, when one has no knowledge whatsoever, and all that is required to know in order to exist comes from the father and the mother, and one is sustained by their keeping and wisdom. This state is the first *Katnut* [smallness/infancy].

The second is when a person has grown and acquired some knowledge. At that time one can keep from things that harm one's body through joint keeping—that of the parents, and that of one's own. This is the second *Katnut*.

The third is the state of *Gadlut* [greatness/adulthood] when one has acquired sufficient knowledge for life, to look after oneself enough to survive. At that time one departs the authority of one's father and mother and acquires autonomy. This is the third state, the state of *Gadlut*.

Likewise, concerning the soul, a person reincarnates until one acquires the wisdom of truth in full. Without them, the soul cannot reach its full level. But it is not that the knowledge one has acquired raises the level of the soul. Rather, it is the soul's inherent nature that it will not grow by its own effort before it has acquired the knowledge of the spiritual nature. Its growth depends on the measure of its knowledge.

The reason this is so is that if it could grow without knowing, it would be harmed, like an infant who is ignorant and cannot walk. If it could walk on its feet, it would throw itself into a fire.

However, the growth comes primarily through good deeds which depend on attaining the wisdom of truth. And both the knowledge and the good deeds depend on attaining the wisdom of truth. And for the above reason, both come together. This is the meaning of "If you know not ... go forth," "go forth and see," etc.

Therefore, each complete soul attains all the souls from *Adam HaRishon* to the end of correction, as one perceives one's acquaintances and neighbors, and according to one's knowledge guards oneself from them, or connects and lives with them. And it is not surprising that one attains all the souls, since spirituality does not depend on time or place, and there is no death there.

Body and Soul

Every body is impatient and ill-tempered, for its livelihood is through incarnations through the seven years of famine and the seven years of abundance. It is an inexorable law that the years of famine cause the years of abundance to be forgotten and the body reincarnates between them like stones that have been ground by water. And another plight awaits all around it—it imagines that one's friend is happy and content.

This comes because at its basis, the soul is ground between the good inclination and the evil inclination. It incarnates between them, at times feeling relief by the surrounding good inclination, and at times suffers an additional plight from the surrounding evil inclination.

Obtaining Knowledge in the Corporeal and in the Spiritual

The connection between the body and the soul is only that in the former, things happen to it naturally and by themselves, and in the latter they happen through work and joint relation between the spiritual and the corporeal.

The advantage of the spiritual over the corporeal is that in the corporeal there is reality even without attaining all the incidents, similar to the perception of an infant who does not know the reason for the thing, and will also not eat something that is harmful to it. But in the spiritual, no reality is attained prior to knowing the events and their outcomes. To the extent of the knowledge of the events, so is the attainment of one's own greatness and the attainment of the surrounding spiritual reality.

Revelation of the Works of the Creator—in Concealment

"Then I was by Him as a master craftsman; and I was daily a delight." Our sages interpreted it to mean that prior to the days of the Messiah, when receiving proselytes, the craftsmen come out toward them, and each craftsman plays with him. On the first day, he reveals the light, on the second, he makes the firmament, etc. These are the six workdays, and all delight in resting on the seventh day, placing in it sanctity and blessing to the worlds.

This is the meaning of what our sages said, that prior to bringing the first fruit, all the craftsmen stand before them. That is, precisely when they are called "wise." However, the craftsmen do not stand before disciples of the wise. Come and see how great is a commandment in its time.

The merit of the Shabbat [Sabbath] is that in it is the blessing and *Kedusha* [holiness] to correct all the weekdays. Although it seems as though the correction depends on the workdays and not on the days of rest, in which one does not work at all, it is not so. Rather, the blessing and *Kedusha* of the Shabbat corrects the weekdays.

Indeed, each correction seemingly requires work. But in truth, the power of the Creator appears in full only in concealment, for when the power of concealment disappears from the world, perfection promptly appears by itself. And as one who throws one's staff to the firmament, the staff flies up because the power of the thrower is in it. Therefore, the entire duration of the flight is attributed to the power of the thrower. Also, the strength of the thrower appears at that time.

Conversely, during its whole return and fall toward the earth, the power of the thrower is not attributed to the fall at all. Rather, it returns to its root by itself, without any assistance.

Similarly, the work of the Creator is apparent in all the concealments. But in the return to wholeness, no work or power are required because in the absence of the preventing force, it returns to its root and wholeness by itself.

This is the meaning of "And God rested on the seventh day ... for in it, He rested from all His work." That is, on that day the power of the work of the Creator was removed from the world, after having worked to establish it in its current form throughout the workdays. But on the seventh day, no power worked, but it was left alone, as it is written, "And I will take away My hand." Thus, naturally, the force of wholeness is imprinted specifically on that day so that the power of concealment will not work here.

Attaining the Spiritual Form

It is likewise in attaining the spiritual form. The attaining errs in its two forms: 1) that it will not be imaginary whatsoever; 2) that its attainment will be beyond any doubt, just as one does not doubt one's own existence.

The title "spiritual" indicates that it is resembled to the wind [in Hebrew *Ruach* means both "spirit" and "wind"], where although the wind has no edge, similitude, or appearance, no person doubts its existence, since one's life depends on it. If the wind is sucked out of a house, should an animal be taken there, it will die. Hence, its existence is obvious for it is one's life.

And from the corporeal we can understand the spiritual: The essence of the inner mind is similar to the interior of the body, which is called "the soul of every flesh," regarded as a being with its deficiency.

Likewise, the internality of the mind, called "the intellectual soul," is also a deficient being.

It is so because such a being that feels its existence, feels its deficiencies. This is not so in animals, which are completely devoid of that perception and are completely devoid of the intellectual soul and its internality.

Because of this, they feel its deficiency to the extent required for their physical existence. Its vitality is measured by the extent of the consistency of the sensation of lack. And if it does not feel a lack, it cannot feed itself and continue its existence, and it dies. Moreover, its size and health depend on the sensation of the lack, like the corporeal body, where the healthier also has a greater appetite, and therefore eats more, and thus grows bigger and healthier.

The Need to Attain the Emanator

We must still know the lack that the intellectual soul feels. Let me tell you that it is the need to attain its emanator, for it is engraved in its nature to crave to know its emanator and creator, since it feels its own existence. That is, it has been prepared by default to search what is above.

It cannot be said that this lack is not defined in attaining its emanator, but that it rather pursues all the secrets and wishes to know about supernatural things and incarnations, and about what is in one's friend's heart, and so forth.

This is not according to the rule that I have written above, that the internality of the matter is that which does not extend oneself. If it were, a lack for attainment would be depicted only in its Maker. But it is clear that only this attainment is an internal lack, which is not called "an offshoot." But an inquiry in the creatures is an extension toward others, for had there not been creations in the world—such as if it were the only creation—it would not have been pursuing to attain them whatsoever.

But attaining its emanator is a deficiency toward itself, and this is its being. That is, it feels itself as an emanated being. All its events aim toward it, and this is the deficiency that it feels—that it will be able to attain its emanator. And to the extent that it perceives that vision, we can accurately measure the size of its own body.

Attaining the Emanator

It is written, "For you did not see any image." This requires interpretation, for what fool would think or gather that there is any corporeal similitude in the Creator? But in truth, this is why there is attainment in the Creator in the world, for no desire awakens for that which does not exist in reality.

Rather, we can discuss this in the spiritual kind and in its ordinances, which is more spiritual than the whole of reality. This is the meaning of the mind whose form grips man's sensation in discerning truth and falsehood. This distinction is called "the mind's body," according to the perception of the corporeal ones. For this reason, this discernment was defined as a "part of God above," which is truly devoid of any similitude, but is only gripped in the senses and is called a "decision" or "reality," or "absence of reality," which is clarified in laws and ways. That verse is called "the body of the mind and its image." We can say about it that this verse is a part of God above, for which this image is included in oneself and one's perception of oneself and one's existence.

The image in this verse is a complete and constant image of its situation, which cannot be completely annulled, or slightly. It is called a "proven and necessary form without additions or subtractions."

This is the meaning of "'I, and you shall not have,' we heard them from the Mighty One." The word "I" includes "You shall not have," meaning that if the Creator had necessarily been revealed to them, no law or warning would have been depicted—"You shall not have"—but the Creator would have been revealed to them by His will, and it would not be an imperative.

It is like a person who shows his wealth to his friend and tells him, "I can show it to you, but now you do not recognize my wealth at all. So exert yourself to remember this form, and then I will want to give you part of my wealth, let alone that you will see all my wealth, as long as you keep this form in your memory. That is, I did not give you this decision by an imperative on which there is no ruler. Rather, I am the ruler, for all the earth is mine." All the seeing is with His simple will. And when I want, you will not remember even what you saw in the vision. And when I want, you will always see Me. Moreover, I will also remind you all the forgotten things. This is from the wonders of the Creator, who cannot be depicted by any intellect, meaning to grasp the matter in full while keeping that man's mind, and it is voluntary and not compulsory to remain for the governance of the upper one.

Recognizing the Attainment—Only by the Path of Torah

I wonder at the researchers of Godliness, whose entire research is a disgrace to us, for they exert to bring evidence to what is known and does not require evidence, and repel and slight what is concealed because of the denial of the corporeal boundaries.

The truth is that the first perception does not need any philosophical proof, since it is the first concept wherever one turns. It is similar to asking a person, "Who wrote this wondrous book of wisdom?" And he answered that indeed, there is no such a sage in the world, but it just happened that his little boy spilled ink on those parchments, which then spread in the form of letters, creating these combinations in connections of wondrous words of wisdom.

Indeed, all concealments are from His guidance over the creatures, and their denial is also among the corporeal boundaries. But about this they keep utterly silent, for indeed it can only be kept in the way of Torah and *Mitzvot* [commandments], and not by any scrutiny in the world.

You should also know that the confirmation of reality must extend from the sensation of Providence. This is called "complete awareness," which brings with it

His love and His pleasant abundance. It is not so with that which extends through the dry, intellectual scrutiny; this knowledge neither adds nor subtracts.

This is the meaning of what our sages said, that there is he who is present, and he who is absent. It follows that all the souls of Israel were present in Mount Sinai because from that event extend all the souls of Israel throughout the generations. It is as we said, that it concerns the bodily soul, which is a being and its deficiency is with it. Extending its vitality depends on determining the deficiency, for were the seeing not positive, the intellectual soul would not have been deficient any longer. Thus, it would not be able to eat to satiation and would therefore be canceled altogether.

But it is a wonder that the rule about seeing is that the desire promptly accompanies it without any forcing, and promptly gives nourishment to establish this desire, as it is written, "that your days may be multiplied" which is the keeping of the Torah and its statutes. In this way, the law about seeing is evident as though they have received it from Sinai today, and each day it is as new to them, for on that depends the law regarding seeing. But when they break any law in the Torah, they promptly remain in the dark, as blind people who have never seen light.

The Essence of the Intellectual Perception

You already know that the intellectual ones, with bodies, are not robbed of knowing their emanator whatsoever, just as they are not robbed of knowing their friends, who are like them. It is so because a friend, like a brother, does not recognize only their spirit and internality, without any clothing, since the mind itself is already wrapped in clothing, meaning the power of imagination.

And because one cannot imagine a spiritual form, that whole kind is invisible to him. And yet, his gaze constantly falls on the externality, meaning one's friend's body and his physical movements. And by persistence, they will thoroughly recognize all the spiritual degrees in it, for this is all he wants to know, and not his own bodily flesh, of course.

He will not feel any lack or sadness at not knowing his mind and degrees in its actual, spiritual form, for he is not obligated to know his friend more than he knows himself. And even his own internality he does not attain.

For this reason, when the creature is well versed in all the laws of nature and its corporeal ordinances, and observes them diligently, it can be said that he knows the Creator face to face. It is as one speaks to one's friend, where each of his parts is adhered to his friend in similarity, meaning a power of imagination of intellectual forms and movements.

And when we research the essence of the mind to the best of our ability, we will find that it is by the gathering of spiritual beings, and from that collection extends its "conducts." That is, all of man's advantage over the beast is that in man there is an organ that can gather within it spiritual beings.

Likewise, the advantage of one person over another is in the amount of the power of the above-mentioned extension, and in the forms of the beings themselves, for one extends important beings, and another—beings that are not so important.

The difference between a spiritual being and the governance is that a boundary of the being is an intellectual image that extends and is present in one's mind unchanged, meaning it cannot be explained through events that happen over time.

And the governance falls under the influence of time and place. It is just as one who is naturally stingy can give a big donation once in his life, due to the place or the timing.

Extensions that Gather in Man's Mind

Know that the above-mentioned preparation, called "man's mind," is like a drop from the extract of all the organs and qualities of the corporeal body. It becomes attached to the first extensions that gather and extend to one's mind.

For example, while still a child, a person watches the conducts of the world and its Creator. Some of them become attached to knowledge, some to wealth, and some to power. If he chooses the quality of knowledge, because he likes it, it follows that he drew into himself a good creation from which good conducts will extend. But if he clings to wealth, it is said that he drew into his mind an inferior spiritual being.

Later, when he grows, he sees more measures. For example: One person leaves all his corporeal possessions and dedicates himself to learning, while another chooses learning but still engages in worldly matters. If the child nurtures the merit of the first, then he has extended a good being into his mind. But if he favors the second one, then he has drawn into himself an inferior being.

Afterward come types of learning—from the Creator or from the created beings—and afterward he checks whether to receive reward or not to receive reward. All those images are created beings, and from that collection, one substance is made, called "mind."

You Have Made Me in Behind and Before

"You have made me in behind and before," meaning the revelation and concealment of the face of the Creator. This is because indeed, "His kingdom rules over all," and everything will return to its root because there is no place vacant of Him. But the difference is in the present or the future, because one who is rewarded with connecting the two worlds discovers His clothing in the present, that everything that is done is a clothing for the revelation of the *Shechina* [Divinity].

This is deemed the present, meaning that now, too, he comes out in royal attire and evidently shows to everyone that the rider is not subordinate to the horse. But although it seemingly appears that the horse leads its rider, the truth is that the horse is provoked to any movement only by the sensation of the rider's bridle and headstall. This is called "The construction of the stature of the *Shechina*," and it is also called "face-to-face."

But one who has not yet come to dedicate all his movements to the Creator alone, and the horse does not equalize its movements to the rider's bridle and headstall, but appears to do the opposite... and crowns the handmaid on the mistress, this is discerned as "behind." That is, you should not think that you are drawing away from *Kedusha* [holiness], for "that which comes into your mind shall not be at all."

Thus says the Lord: "Surely with a mighty hand," etc., "For the outcast shall not be cast out from Him," and the whole wheel turns to come to the *Kedusha*, to its root. Therefore, although it seems that the horse leads the rider by its ignoble desire, the truth is not so. It is the rider who leads the horse to his destination. However, it is not apparent in the present, but in the future. Hence, in this way there is also contact, but it is back to back, meaning not according to the will of the one who dresses or the will of the dresser.

But those who do His will, meaning reveal by themselves the royal attire in the present, are connected face to face through the good will of the one who dresses and the good will of the dresser, for precisely this is His wish.

This is the meaning of "Because you did not serve the Lord your God with gladness." You will serve Him anyhow, but the difference is that this way is "in distress and under pressure meaning unwillingly, and the other way is by reason of the abundance of all things, meaning willingly.

It is also written in the *Midrash*: "The Creator looks upon the deeds of the righteous and the deeds of the wicked, and does not know which the Creator wants, whether their deeds, etc. When he says, 'And God saw the light, that it was good; and God divided,' it means in the deeds of the righteous."

This means that the Creator examines, meaning connects with all the deeds and conducts, and everything returns to its root. Hence, the question is, Which way is more desirable? In that regard, the *Midrash* is assisted by the verse, "And God saw the light, that it was good," meaning disclosure, which is in the deeds of the righteous. This is our sages' meaning in saying, "Long and short, and short and long."

World—Concealment

This is the meaning of "You have made them all In wisdom [*Hochma*]; the earth is full of Your possessions." Everything is kept in the thirty-two paths of wisdom; hence, "the earth is full of Your possessions," and no place is vacant from Him, for everything goes to its root. Now, however, it is concealed, and is therefore called *Olam* [world], from the word *He'elem* [concealment].

And the Light that hides and clothes in the world is called "a point," considered a *Yod*. It is divided into the two *Heys*: a world of concealment and a world of revelation. And all of man's work is to reveal this point and extend it from the world to the world in the form of *Vav*, meaning the *Vav* between the two *Heys*, to reveal to all the plentiful light that extends from the surrounding light to the surrounded, meaning the two *Heys*, as in *Bina*, *Yesod*, *Malchut*.

Surrender, Separation, Sweetening

There are three discernments required of a man in the desirable path: surrender, separation, sweetening, meaning "lights in deficient writing,"* since the light of this world was created out of darkness, "As the advantage of the light from within the darkness," and "What good is a candle during the day?" its light does not shine in the daytime. This is the meaning of the *Klipa* [shell/peel] that precedes the fruit. For this reason, he who becomes a partner to the Creator in the work of creation brings out the light from the darkness, meaning considers how lowly and ignoble one is compared to the *Kedusha* [holiness] of above, and how filthy are his clothes. Through it, the light becomes surrounded.

In regard to the Creator's question, "to fear the great and terrible name," he intensifies with great strength to subdue the evil within him, so the evil servant and evil maid will surrender to the mistress, who dwells with them in the midst of their *Tuma'a* [impurity], until he feels in his soul that the awakening for externality has expired and surrendered. At that time, he will be rewarded with "separation," distinguishing between the light and the darkness, and will not replace bad for good or good for bad. And should he replace, meaning the awakening of the inclination that is necessary to him, it will be dedicated to the Creator only. This is considered "sweetening," the craving for the Creator, as in true love.

This discernment comes after he separates between good and evil, between the exaltedness of the Creator and his own ignobility. He will observe "You shall uproot

---

* Translator's Note: In Hebrew, words can be written with or without vowels. In the case of the word "Light," it means writing with or without the letter Vav.

the evil from within you," for he will be very ashamed of its doers. Then he will be rewarded with sweetening the remains of his inclination, which cannot be rooted out, and will elevate them to their real root.

Remember and Keep Were Said in One Utterance

"Remember and Keep" were said in one utterance. What the mouth cannot say and the ear cannot hear, and the heart cannot think or contemplate, etc. We must understand why this was said in this way, and what it means to us.

It is written, "Man and beast You save, O Lord." Our sages said, "These are people who are of cunning mind and pretend to be as beasts." This means that the whole path of creation that the Creator created is regarded as two opposites in one subject, and all the combinations in the world were made in this way, and this is the whole of the work of creation.

The Power of Speech

However, in the work of creation, the Creator revealed only one part of this discernment, as it is written, "By the word of the Lord were the heavens made," for He took fire and water and mixed them into a single subject. And the Creator imprinted the power of speech in man, so he would partner with Him in the work of creation, so he, too, would create worlds with his speech from this discernment, meaning two opposites in the same subject, for another innovation... in the world.

This is the way of the righteous, who cleave to the Creator: From all their utterances, the worlds were created according to the word of the Creator, as well as the operating force in the operated, since He had already imprinted in their mouths the twenty-two letters [of the Hebrew alphabet] by which He had created the world. What I wish to say is that they have this Segula [power/remedy] within them.

And the reason why the doing does not end in this world by speech alone is because of the descents of this world in materialization. For this reason, nothing appears by speech, but only by hands and legs. However, in truth, the Creator has imprinted sufficient force in speech by which to disclose all the actions, since the force of the Operator is in the operated, and we, too, express with our mouths the same twenty-two letters.

Yet, the *Klipot* [shells/peels] cover and weaken that force, and the Creator wished to cleanse Israel from the *Klipot*, so He gave them Torah and *Mitzvot* [commandments] by which they draw near to his *Kedusha* [holiness], and the *Shechina* [Divinity] speaks from their mouths in purity. At that time, they perform deeds with their speech.

The Blessing of the Righteous

This is the meaning of the blessings of the righteous, who reveal by their utterances more than an ordinary person can reveal with his hands and legs. When an ordinary person wishes to do good to his friend, give him much money in his hands and make him rich. Yet, he does not know if this will last very long.

But the whole one, who wishes to do good to his friend, gives him a blessing with his mouth—some short words of richness—and the act of enrichment instantaneously appears on his friend, etc.

How is one rewarded with this? This happens through Torah and *Mitzvot*, meaning that by doing His will, one's form becomes similar to one's Maker. In truth, however, the whole issue of Torah and *Mitzvot* that connect to a person are also of the above-mentioned kind, meaning the two opposites in the same subject. This is the main thing that is desired, since the Creator created the world with the Torah, and the force of the Operator is in the operated. This is the essence of the knowledge, which we do not know: When these two opposites unite into a single *Guf* [body] in one's mind, he becomes desirable to his Maker and is considered "a whole man."

The End of a Matter Is Better than Its Beginning

In essence, the giving of the Torah in this lowly world is an opposite thing, for the angels erred in it. This is the meaning of "The end of a matter is better than its beginning." Interpretation: "The end of a matter" is the bottom of the degree, meaning at the creation of the world for all to see, when it requires no scrutiny. This is what the books call "first concepts." That is, if one does not eat, he will starve; if he touches fire, he will burn; and if he throws himself into the water, he will drown, etc. These things are understood by animals and beasts, too, since the animate mind will tell them this. This is why it is called "the end of a matter."

"The beginning of a matter" is the mind of the Torah, which is not attained even for the speaking, meaning to all the uneducated people, except to the descendants of Jacob, the Creator's chosen ones. In the world, good and evil are mixed. To distinguish between good and evil, the writing tells us that the primary way of the good is the "end of a matter," meaning to behave in a way that the lowly discuss, through what is attained to all the people, but to connect the mind of the Torah to it. This is so because this is the purpose of the opposites in the world, and the whole man must connect and unite in his mind in real unity. And this is called "good," as it is written, "The end of a matter," if it is well connected from its start, meaning the mind of the Torah and the animate mind actually connect into one.

Two Opposites in One Subject

This is the meaning of the words of our sages, "'Man and beast You save, O Lord,' these are people of a cunning mind, who pretend to be as beasts." We have explained above that these two opposites unite in them to one. Take, for example, what is written, "Without flour, there is no Torah; without Torah, there is no flour." In the first part, it is an animate mind—a mind attained by all. In the second part, it is the mind of the Torah, since how are the provision of flour and the power of the Torah connected? But from the Torah, we understand that the Creator never removes His Providence from the world even for a moment; hence, He benefits those who heed his will and hears their prayer.

Accordingly, those who have been rewarded with their labor being in the Torah certainly do not need to work as the uneducated, since they ask of the One who truly has, and He will give them, as it is written, "Since they are followers, their Torah is preserved and their work is blessed." The Tanna tells us, "Without flour," etc., meaning that the desirable way is to connect them, meaning to pretend to be as a beast, to know that without flour there is no Torah and hence to try one's hardest with what his corporeal mind teaches him to do in order to obtain flour and food for his body.

Indeed, the law of the Torah permits, for "He delights not in the strength of the horse; He takes no pleasure in the legs of a man. The Lord wants those who fear Him, who await His mercy." Hence, why should He touch and strip a carcass in the market? To not need people, he prefers to engage in the Torah—to fear the Creator and to await His mercy, for "He does not want the legs of a man," etc.

Yet, the Tanna teaches to exert with all one's might for flour, since without it there is no Torah, and it is preferable to desecrate one Shabbat [Sabbath] in order to observe many Shabbats, etc., although you know that "Without flour, there is no Torah." This means that the labor and exertion do not bring or yield the flour, but only the observance of Torah and fear of heaven, for "He does not want the legs of a man." This is two opposites when they actually unite into one, in those who do as the beast and know that it is futile, and everything comes to him from the King's table. Such a man is called "whole."

This is the meaning of the verse, "Happy is the man who has put his trust in the Lord and did not turn to the arrogant or to those who lapse into falsehood." He unites the two things: He trusts in the Creator, strains with all his might to provide food for his home, but knows that all his deeds and all his efforts are but arrogance and falsehood, and he puts his trust in the Creator.

It is written, "For the rod of wickedness shall not rest upon the lot of the righteous." This means that although their acts are similar, etc., why? The writing interprets, "So the righteous put not forth their hands unto iniquity," for they completely accept the burden of the kingdom of heaven and know that He is the one who gives you strength.

The reason for it is to see how far the righteous' faith in the Creator reaches. Although the Creator knows the thoughts, the deeds must still be clear to the righteous himself, since the nature of matter is that it does not let the righteous believe in themselves until they evidently and actually see, and they are always afraid that they will inflict sin and fall from their degree during the act.

The Quality of Jacob the Patriarch

Now we can understand what our sages said, that Jacob returned to the small tins. It is indeed a wonder that at such a time, when he saw Esau coming to kill him and to rob all that he had, he still considered staying in the place of danger by himself, to salvage the little tins. And he did not believe in his life, as it is written, "And Jacob was very fearful," etc., "and he divided the people... into two camps."

However, this is thoroughly explained with the above-mentioned, because the above-mentioned way—man and beast—was the quality of Jacob the Patriarch, who became a *Merkava* [chariot/structure] for this quality. It is as it is written in the books: Abraham the Patriarch became a *Merkava* for the quality of love, and Isaac the Patriarch to the quality of fear.

These two qualities are opposites, for one who loves is not afraid and always trusts his loved one, and love will cover all crimes. Conversely, one who fears does not trust, for if he trusted, he would not be afraid at all. But Jacob the Patriarch, the senior from among the Patriarchs, became a *Merkava* for the quality of mercy, meaning these two opposites in one subject—love and fear together—which is the essence of this quality.

This is the meaning of the verse, "And Jacob was very fearful," etc., "and he divided the people... into two camps," to leave himself some remains. Also, he sent him gifts, perhaps he would make peace with him.

And you see that his conduct in that regard was the same as that of a completely ordinary person, for what is the difference if a person is worried of starvation and seeks all kinds of tactics all day long to provide for his livelihood, or if he is worried that his enemy might rob him of his possessions and kill him, and does all that he can in that regard?

This was RASHI's question: Why was Jacob the Patriarch afraid? After all, He promised him, "And I will keep you," etc. He explained that he feared lest he would cause the sin. We should be more meticulous and say that it should have said, "lest he caused, and not lest he would cause." This reconciles it, since indeed, Jacob the Patriarch had the complete measure of love, meaning confidence, and he had no doubt at all that the Creator would keep him and he would not lack a thing. Yet he behaved like an ordinary person and pretended to fear, as the animate mind necessitates, to find a straightforward tactic for it, that he was very fearful of the 400 men with him. By this, he was seemingly distracted from the confidence in order to truly fear. Through it, he built his guard the way those who fear an enemy do—he divided the camps and gave presents, etc.

And why did he do this if he were not really afraid, for he trusted in the Creator? It was the fear that he would cause sin, since in his humbleness, the righteous does not believe in himself, that he will not fall from his degree during the act. Therefore, he prepared every worldly means of salvation against the enemy. And after all that, he assumed in his heart that it was arrogance and falsehood, and put his trust in the Creator and prayed to the Creator.

Now we understand why he remained for the little tins, to announce that along with the fear, he had the complete measure of love, completely flawless, and he valued even little tins, for he knew full well that no enemy or foe would touch his possessions, at all.

The Difference between One who Serves the Creator and One who Does Not Serve Him

This distinguishes between one who serves the Creator and one who does not serve Him. One who is truly afraid and does not trust would not notice the little tins at a time of worry that an enemy might come and strike mothers with their children and destroy everything. But a servant of the Creator, along with the labor and effort due to the fear, knows for certain and trusts His mercy—that all is his and that no stranger will control his possessions. And even at such a time, he is able to watch over the little tins, like the righteous, who are fond of their wealth.

Hence, in the giving of the Torah, we were given the strength through "remember and keep were said in one utterance. What the mouth cannot say, and the ear hear and the heart think or contemplate." This means that it is written that "Remember" is the love and "Keep" is the fear, which are two opposites. They were said to us and given to us as one, to unite them. Although they are really opposite, and it is incomprehensible to the corporeal mind and heart how such a thing can exist in reality, it is the power of the Torah that one who adheres to it is rewarded with it—being connected and united in his heart, as in the quality of Jacob the Patriarch.

The *Klipa* [shell/peel] of Ishmael and the *Klipa* of Esau

This is what Jacob said to his sons during the years of famine: "Why do you fear?" And RASHI interprets, "Why do you fear the children Ishmael and the children of Esau as though you are satiated?" This is perplexing: The children of Esau dwelled in Seir, and the children of Ishmael in the Paran desert, and what business did they have with them? He needed to be more concerned about the Canaanite and the Hittite, his neighbors in the land.

This is reconciled by the above-mentioned: RASHI made two interpretations: 1) Why should you appear satiated? and 2) Why should you be slimmed by famine? Now we understand that this is what Jacob had said to them: "If you eat to satiation, you should fear the children of Ishmael; and if you become gaunt from starvation, you should fear the children of Esau." This means that it is written that Ishmael is the *Sigim* [dross] of silver (love) and Esau is *Sigim* of gold (fear).

This is what Jacob had taught his sons: If you grip to the quality of love, and trust in the Creator that His hand will not grow short even in the years of famine, you should fear the *Klipa* of Ishmael. And if you grip only to the quality of fear and restrict your eating, you should fear the *Klipa* of Esau, who nurses from that quality. Hence, best eat to satiation and unite a thing in that time with the quality of fear: Go down and buy for us food from Egypt, for by this you will be saved from both *Klipot*.

Remembering

Remembering and Forgetting, Keeping and Losing

During the exile, considered "the female world," the work is in keeping. One who flaws one's work might lose what he is given. And *Dvekut* [adhesion] in this world is by the force of keeping, and the adornment of the force of keeping is by the elevation of the emotion, as well as the elevation of one's wholeness and the strength of his *Dvekut*.

However, in the future, there will be no fear of loss or theft, for "Death shall be swallowed up forever," and here the work is limited to "remembering." Although accordingly, one form should have sufficed, the nature of the body is to grow tired of the same form. Hence, forms must be dressed and undressed one at a time, so the body will appear to have a different form each time to increase the desire. This is similar to blocking the horse's eyes while it is circling the grindstone, so as not to tire it.

This is most profound and grave since it is simple: His will from the servant is the most praiseworthy. Also, it is known that the closer the work is to nature, the better it is. The rule is that if one of the two lovers' love increases to a complete and utter measure, meaning "natural and complete," the whole force of love will quench in the other.

Although his reason will evidently show the lover's measure of love, his ability to love his friend in return will not grow at all. On the contrary, according to the sensation of the totality of the lover, the sense of love will gradually die out in him, for he will not fear him, as his love is absolute. For this reason, the measure of spirituality, the love in the nature of the loved subject, will be annulled and corrupted.

Indeed, His will is to proclaim His love yet allow room for "expanding the boundaries of love."

These two are opposites for when his love becomes known, it acquires a mandatory form, like perfect and natural love. Hence, there is zero room for work, to expand the love, since the complete and loyal lover is dissatisfied with the reward of the loved one in return for his love, as it is written, "If you are righteous, what will you give Him?"

On the contrary, when the loved one feels that his lover has a desire to love him in return for some reward, that place becomes deficient since when there is a desire for reward, his love changes when the reward is absent. Thus, the love is not absolute. For this reason, it is not complete and natural, but conditional. When the condition is canceled, the love is canceled, as in "a vision of peace, and there is no peace."

It is evidently known that the cursed does not adhere to the blessed, as it is written, "Will give wisdom to the wise." And the servitude in adding and expanding the wholeness does not relate at all to one who is deficient, but to the truly complete worker. And to the complete worker, it seems that he has no room for work at all.

This is the meaning of the "remembering," such as when one tells the one he loves, "Here is a bag full of gems, to show my love." In this way, the loved one strains to accurately count the sum of gems in order to reveal the love in his own heart, too. In this way, the love itself does not change at all when his work is not counted, since he already has them.

However, to return some reward to the one who loves him, he touches the gems extensively in order to be rewarded with always showing the great measure of the love. In this way, the feelings of love always reach from one to the other and multiply, while the essence is not changed.

This is the meaning of adopting different combinations. Although the essence is the same, not to lose or corrupt even a tiny spark of the potential disclosure of the hidden forces that always exists in the matter, it appears in new combinations each time which the corporeal eye has never seen. By this, the matter tastes a new flavor and harnesses itself to suffer and return always and forever. This is similar to many meals from which the matter is satisfied and wishes to duplicate that form many times, or to couplings, since new flavors are always available for it.

Now you understand the association of matter in a body and a soul. Due to the matter that is rooted in "forgetfulness," and even worse, by quenching any kind of absolute love, by this it gives the soul room for mandatory work, meaning to return in different combinations every time. Otherwise, the flaw will reach the soul, as well, because of the mask in the roots of the above-mentioned matter. Even though the love itself is perfect and complete, it is seemingly covered due to the matter. By being compelled to return and repeat, the additions increase beyond the fund, and the boundaries of love wondrously expand.

Now you understand the meaning of "the third generation may enter into the assembly of the Lord." In the first generation there was the *Klipa* [shell/peel] of the Egyptian, as though the place was too narrow. This is because although the lover and the loved one are in the desirable wholeness, they lack room in which to expand and multiply because due to the suction of the matter, the soul must disclose the love in the matter, too.

There is no solution to it except to evidently show his love, with great work and great force, since the matter has no other language but emotions. Hence, to the extent of his feeling of love, she finds herself compelled to return reward with sublime work and great force. Therefore, when the soul feels His complete and utter love, unconditioned by anything, the work of the matter falls entirely, for "One does not give money for nothing." This is a law in the corporeal nature (for making room). Hence, at that time, the substance strains with its gratitude and subjugation according to its feelings, meaning repeatedly praising and thanking.

And according to the above-mentioned, the matter grows weary of the first combination and the first flavor, which causes him diminution of sensation and hence diminution of gratitude until he stops even this tiny work. And since he remains without work, and sees the absolute love, he places the *Klipa* of the Egyptian, the upper straight [narrow].

Subsequently, in the second generation, there was the exact same *Klipa* as in the first generation, with the added *Klipa* of the Edomite, meaning not to return or repeat at all, as was the custom in the first generation, which, nonetheless, had a good reason to disclose the feeling from the gratitude.

But "the third generation that are born unto them may enter into the assembly of the Lord," for in the third generation that place is revealed. That is, in the holy *Atik*, the ark-cover was regarded as the mercy seat, and the two were sensed together. This means that making a place for work promptly reveals a great measure of the light of love, that henceforth he will know that prevention of returning a reward prevents the light of love. For this reason, he exerts until he finds the return of the reward even when he is in a state of wholeness, for he must, against his will, resolve the riddle from the whole, and there is none who is whole. Henceforth, he is a tool ready for work.

We could say that there is room for the complete worker to serve in other bodies to complement them, for this is not completeness in Nature, for Nature mandates revealing, meaning the actual returning of the reward, so he will not be dependent on the view of others, lest he will not be found. But one who finds servitude in himself is always serving God and never rests. And to that extent, the light of His love is never ending, ceaseless.

Two Points

Two points to each aspiration: one in absence, and the other from satiation onward. The difference between them is that the aspiration that stems from fear of absence—while soaring to the highest levels, to the choicest—still, when weary, he settles for the poorest of the poor, and eats to satiation, and to cover *Atik* so it will not be absent. But the aspiration that stems from the point of satiation, meaning that he will not be deficient whatsoever without it, at that time he is not content with little whatsoever and aspires only to the choicest in reality. And if it is not in that measure, but is rather ordinary, he will not want to work and toil for it at all.

For example: One who is leaning toward playing music is deficient until he acquires it. He will not rest until he has acquired a certain measure of ability to play. Even if he is told that he has no hope of becoming a renowned musician, but only a common one, he will still not give up his aspiration and will settle for less, exerting to at least acquire the little he can acquire. But one who has no inherent inclination toward playing music to begin with, and feels no hunger for this knowledge, should a musician approach him and tell him he should exert over this lore, he will reply to him even before he has completed his question, "I have no doubt that I will not achieve greatness in this teaching, and to be a common player, is the world deficient without me?"

Indeed, it is embedded by His providence over man that any aspiration that emerges after the point of satiation will not be desirable except for the choicest at that time.

By this you will understand a profound matter: Although the generations are declining in value, they are expanding in the desired deficiency and the final correction. It is so because the first generations, who were as the sons of Adam, they themselves had a great and awful deficiency in the prevention of Godly work. For this reason, their aspiration to serve Him emerged from the point of their absence. Hence, they did not expand in their aspiration, for fear of losing it entirely, and they were quiet and content with the little they had attained. This is why they had small and short movements in their work, for due to their recognition of the great value, they settled for little.

This is the meaning of the declining merit of the generations until they arrived at the final shrinkage in our generation, when authors' wisdom is foul and they who fear sin are loathed. In that state the crowd feels content and are not obliged to God's work at all, nor feel any lack in its absence. Even those who do engage in work, it is merely out of habit. They have no thirst or aspiration to finding any speck of knowledge in their work.

And should a sage tell them, "Come, let me teach you wisdom, to understand and to instruct in the word of God," they already know their reply: "I already know that I will not be as Rashbi and his friends, and let things stay as they are, and I wish I could observe the literal in full." However, it is said about them, "The fathers have eaten sour grapes, and the children's teeth grow blunt," for they engage in Torah and *Mitzvot* [commandments] that are unripe, and their children's teeth will grow utterly blunt, and they wonder why they need this work. It is for you, and not for Him, and you, too, blunt its teeth. This is the form of our generation, with which we are dealing.

But with what is written and explained above, you will understand that in this melting pot we can be very hopeful because henceforth, each learned one whose heart is yearning for the work of the Creator will not be at all among those who are content with less, since the point of his aspiration does not emerge from absence, but from the point of satiation. For this reason, all who come to cling to Torah and *Mitzvot* will not settle for anything less than being the first in the generation, meaning to actually know his Creator. He will not want to waste his energy on the work of the common folk at all, but only on the choicest—true nearness to the Creator, and to know in his mind that the Creator has chosen him.

Indeed, in our generation we do not find true workers except those chosen few who have already been endowed with a Godly soul, a part of God above. It is as the poet wrote, "My knee is pure, extending from cistern streams / the name of the one who chooses you, to walk before Him / etc., ...You are before Him as are all who stand before Him / who approach the Lord. My knee, you know the will of the likeminded / the name of knowing your objects, and paying momentarily."

But they who have not attained this honorable and exalted merit have no love or fear at all in the work. This was not so in previous generations whatsoever, since the servants of the Creator did not aspire for such a high level at all, and each one served the Creator as he understood.

By this you will understand that the correction actually began prior to the reception of the Torah, in the generation of the desert. This is why there was a great awakening in that generation, "It is our wish to see our king," as it is written in the *Midrash*. But then they sinned, meaning settled for a messenger, saying, "You will speak to us and we will listen, and let God not speak to us lest we will die."

This is the meaning of the breaking of the tablets and all the exiles. But in the generation of the Messiah, this matter will be corrected because that awakening will return, and when they attain Him, they will no longer sin because they have already suffered twofold for all their sins.

The desired goal is none other than the very choicest. This is the meaning of "And they shall teach no more every man his neighbor, and every man his brother saying, 'Know the Lord,' for they shall all know Me, from the least of them to the greatest of them." This will be the first condition for all who begin the work.

My words do not relate to those who settle for working and laboring to benefit people, and much less so for satisfying their contemptible cravings. Rather, it is for those who feel that it is not worthwhile to toil for people, but only for the Creator.

It is so because there are many factions to judgment day: 1) to satisfy material passions, 2) to benefit people, 3) to improve their own knowledge, or that of others. But all these are forces of concealment of the face, for they are all nothing compared to the merit of the Creator, of course.

Attaining a True Thing

There is a spiritual substance on which the letters of the prayer are carved. The substance is the whitest of white parchment. It is also called "white fire," meaning that it is as though that white color comes by fire and turns into fire, crushing and sitting with all its might.

The letters are sparks of fear and love. That is, the deficiency of fear and love are evident and sensed. This is the meaning of the black fire, since that color seems as though it is more deficient and sunken than the rest of the colors. For this reason, in the very beginning, that was the sight.

Initially, the white parchment was seen which is sufficiently processed with power and with whiteness. This is the meaning of the disclosure of the crown and its glow in *Assiya*. The meaning of *Assiya* is the parchment, as in "And the foreskin she shall not borrow from her neighbor" in one who "has been joined together." The disclosure of the crown is the true revealed love, up to *Duchra* [male] of *Arich Anpin*, and the shattering is the letters of the fear. Understand that this is truly the book of heaven.

Know that it is true from every angle. For this reason, a man will not truly attain something for which he has no lack, or for which he is not truly deficient. For this reason, any attainment that comes as a mere extra is not regarded as true attainment as he is not deficient without it. Hence, there is falsehood in the labor, in the exertion, for it is as though for something that he truly needs.

This is why external teachings are false wisdom. That is, the work to attain it must be under a complete condition, as though for something that he truly needs and finds. But when he has found and obtained it, he sees that he was not at all deficient without it. Hence, it is a lie and falsehood.

This is not so with the wisdom of serving the Creator. On the contrary, he does not know at all how to sense its absence in its true form. Only when he finds it does he see how deficient he was without it. This is why it is true attainment from every angle.

It is similar to one who pays for an object twice its value. He sighs because his friend had cheated him, and that purchase is false and fraudulent since the imagination was fooling him.

But regarding the intentions, it is not the doctor who should be asked, but the patient, for he needs *Kedusha* [holiness] and purity in the work of the Creator, in order to intend, and the intentions will be preparations for his soul for installment of the *Kedusha*.

Also, we need not ask if the Torah is good, or if morals are good, or if "in all your ways you shall know Him," since the doctor can ask the patient about all that. If he is not in pain then he is certain of his healing, so the patient is the one who knows. This is the meaning of what is written in *The Zohar*: "A man must not look where one shouldn't," meaning that looking does not make him feel *Kedusha* and purity.

Accepting Our Sages as Reliable Witnesses

There are two kinds of servitude—one for the light, and the other for the *Kelim* [vessels]—as it is impossible to speak or to understand degrees in the lights, much less say that one will be rewarded with some light, for there is no such thing as part in spirituality, and "a vow that has been slightly broken is completely broken."

(I wonder at the acting mind and the minister of the world together. One gives the power of birth in a seed of adultery in an adulterous, and one bestows stately buildings on false and fictitious foundations.) I am referring to Aristotle who commanded that he be glorified upon his ascent to heaven for his invention of a false foundation that sufficed as a target for the arrows of his narrow mind, and for the exhaustion of all his spirit. This came to him because he saw in the books of Israel profound wisdom built on the foundations of Kabbalists, and compared himself to them like a copycat, showing that his merit was as theirs, as he lied about himself. Had the prophecy been true, he would have been ready for it.

But our way is not his way, and a Kabbalist does not leave a false foundation, as he had left his foundations. Rather, although our sages and their teachings have given us in Kabbalah, but in that, they are as faithful witnesses, eyewitnesses, and nothing more. Instead, they teach us the way by which they were awarded being eyewitnesses. When we understand, our wisdom will be as theirs, and we will attain a true and real foundation, and upon a glorious, eternal building.

The reason for this conduct is that in all things there are a first substance and a first concept. Concerning worldly concepts, which are hidden and immersed in material descriptions, we attain them by removing the form, meaning from the first concept to the second concept, and so forth, until the desirable concept. For this reason, we come by the first concept very easily, as with a small part of the whole.

This is not so with the heavenly. On the contrary, the first concept is the hardest to attain. It is called *Nefesh* of *Assiya*, and when we acquire the form of *Nefesh* of *Assiya* through Kabbalah—for attainment is denied of the fool from the heavenly, but through Kabbalah it is possible. Through it we learn the heavenly wisdom, and then we will have the right to attain the received foundation as the nature of the thing that is attained, and it will be possible to reconcile what is received as is natural with all concepts.

But the fictitious foundation of his fictitious wisdom cannot be attained, as "It is enough to come from judgment to be as the judged." Thus, the whole building remains as a false building of eternal disgrace.

The Soul of the Proselyte

The pain that a severed organ feels is during the time of the judgment, the time of the severing. But afterward, all the pain and deficiency remain in the whole body. Similarly, an organ feels pleasure when it is reconnected to the body, but subsequently, the pleasure leaves it as though it has died and returns to the rest of the body. This explains the verse "And that soul will be cut off from its people," indicating that any pain and deficiency are only for the general public, as though it has been cut off from the people.

Likewise, the pleasure of the soul of the proselyte is only when it connects to the whole nation, the choicest of the species. But when it connects to the wholeness, the personal pleasure returns to the whole.

It is an intimation to what people say, "An old man and a child are equal," meaning that one who begins in the wisdom is equal to one who is complemented with it, except for the filling of wisdom, which serves his king and not himself. But the whole question is in the meantime, that it is work of the mind, entirely for oneself and for one's own completion.

For example: The servants of the king and the distinguished ministers of the king all serve the king. This is not so when they learn for their own completion: They work for themselves, like a house full of texts of wisdom and songs of praise. But when they fall into the hands of the licentious, they only boast with superficial matter that is revealed on paper, and they use it for their contemptible needs ... losing a precious trait from themselves and from the whole world due to the worldliness in them, arousing contempt and wrath.

The heart aches even more when sages see with their own eyes the filthy ones come into the houses of the wisdom of Israel and take their superficial matter from the words—meaning the beauty of the words—for the work of their hands: vain and phony allegories.

The orders of the wisdom are established on the foundations of true Kabbalah, attained by the knowledgeable. The form of wisdom is stripped into the work of a craftsman (and in my view, were it not for this mirror they would not have had the nerve to fabricate foundations from their hearts), building wittiness on the foundations of falsehood and desolation, as did Aristotle and his company in heaven, and as ... do in corporeality. It is even more so with those who come with disclosed filth, making them targets for his arrows of stupidity, to boast before others as stupid as himself. They cannot be forgiven.

It is an evident example; no deficiency in the world is established in corporeality at all. Rather, every deficiency and wholeness is imprinted in spirituality. That is, in the beginning of wholeness that will be depicted in the world, He will have no need to change any corporeal incident, but only to bless the spiritual. For instance, we see that a man assumes great pains and jolts along the way to gain wealth, even by taking great risks. Then, against your will, the depicting power from the hope of fortune subdues him and turns the evil into a great benefit until in every bit of his soul he places himself in jeopardy for the uncertain preparation.

Therefore, it is not far at all if the Creator draws near—meaning the reward for the labor, as much as one can. He will not feel any agony or pain in the exertion.

Three Factions

The Torah is like a whole world from which three factions enjoy in different ways. The first faction is the masses. These have not been prepared to make any form abstract unless they have no desire for any form but the first substance from all that fills the world and comes directly to the senses and to the imagination.

The second form is one who has been prepared to be able to make the material form abstract, and to take and enjoy another form, close to spirituality, which is found beneath it. This is an emotional, intellectual delight, meaning from separate concepts imprinted in these material images.

The third form, to the third faction, is one who has been prepared to acquire general forms from separate concepts imprinted in both spiritual and corporeal forms. These tie a thread to a thread, and pull by pull they descend to the deep and rise to the heaven. This form is found after abstracting the above-mentioned second form.

Similarly, three completions come from the Torah to the three above-mentioned factions. The first faction is completed with the first matter. The second faction is completed by form, and the third faction is completed by inclusion, which is abstracting a form from a form, and a thread from a thread. Certainly, one who does not favor people more than matter will certainly not be completed by the Torah more than his will and attainments. This is what Maimonides meant—that one must learn logic before the wisdom of truth.

However, from experience we know and see that there are indirect influence and power in the light in it, which can suddenly lift one above the first faction up to the degree of a man from the third faction. It follows that he works to obtain a needle and obtains a house full of silver and gold.

This World and the Next World

There is no difference between this world and the next world, except that one is temporary and one is eternal. But there is no possession in this world, or in the next world, that is not a separate spiritual matter. Of course, the measure that one has acquired from this kind in the temporary one will remain his in the eternal one. This is the view of the whole ones, and Maimonides, too, admits it.

However, this cannot be disclosed to the masses because they will not listen and will not pay attention to the work of leaving that small portion to their crass imagination.

It is like a craftsman whose hearing is not influenced by any ordinary sound in the world, but only by a great noise. But if all the musicians and singers came together they would provide for his hearing only a crass and noisy sound, and specifically unpleasant.

Likewise, it is impossible to speak to the masses about anything spiritual except through a chaotic racket. Words of reason will not help them because their souls have not been prepared to enjoy forms that ride atop materialism. Hence, they cling only to the first image of creation that is near them, being the thickness in corporeality. For this reason, words of the next world must also be expressed in the manner attached to this kind.

Therefore, it is forbidden to speak with them of the intellectual form in the substance of the eternal, for the substance would break, they would not attain that form and would be denied of both. For this reason, I will make for them a special composition, to provide a general depiction that is close to the truth regarding the form of the Garden of Eden and Hell. Afterward, I will be able to speak of the persistence of the soul with the best among them.

Succinctly speaking, know that the form of this world is a separate, spiritual one, and is not thick or crass, except in the eyes of the material ones, but not in the form of the Creator. For this reason, he finds all those forms within him.

It follows that at the end of correction, precisely the crass matter will be gone, and the separate forms from these images—both from reality and from the order of existence of reality, such as eating and drinking—will all remain in eternity since nothing is lost except the matters and their foundations.

But in the forms, there is no loss. They will not suffer at all from the ruin of their first matter which has already done its part. And if you are one of true form, it is easy to understand how to take off the forms from the filthy materials in the world, such as adultery, gluttony, and self-love, as these forms will remain in spirituality in the form of a separate mind.

They will remain in two discernments: The first discernment is every form toward personal consideration. The second discernment is every form toward a general discernment.

These forms are forever called "carcasses of the wicked," as it is written, "And they shall go forth, and look upon the carcasses of the men who have rebelled against Me." From this we can easily understand the forms of holiness. This is the reward and punishment, and it is felt by the owner in this world, too.

But after the stripping off of the above-mentioned form, there is another abstraction which is more general. It is called "the world of revival," and "Neither has the eye seen," in which even the prophets do not engage, but each one who understands receives from a Kabbalist sage.

By this you will understand the words, "A transgression does not quench a Mitzva [commandment]" since the carrier brings both forms together to the spiritual world. In one he delights, and in the other he is judged. This is the meaning of "The Creator does not deny the reward from any creation."

And what Maimonides wrote, that there is faith only after the depiction of the operated in one's soul, I wish to say that it is by virtue of the Godly gift, as He discerned regarding the attainment of the lights from one another. This does not contradict what I have written.

Here I have explained the completion that comes to the above-mentioned first and second factions. But as for what comes to the third faction, I have implied but did not explain.

*The Meaning of the Chaf in Anochi**

Malchut that is clothed in the worlds is called *Ani* [me/I]. It cascades to *Assiya*, which is the separation, where each person feels as a separate entity, sensing the "self," and by its expansion wishes to conquer the entire world for one's own will and pleasure. This is the power of the shattering in *Assiya*, "I will rule," meaning from holy sparks that were not yet sorted. This is called "the serpent's skin" which is the good and bad in the *Klipa* [shell/peel], Noga.

There are two souls in the creature in which one acquires. They clothe in two spirits: the "vital soul" and the "intellectual soul." One is from the *Klipa* Noga, and one is a part of God above. It is also called "The soul of every flesh is its blood" which is the vital soul. The intellectual soul is the point in the heart (prior its completion, as in "And my heart is awake"). Because the vital soul extends from the *Klipa* Noga, it is called "coincidental," the opposite of eternal. The holy soul is called "eternal," which is a part of God above.

The Difference between the Bodies of Idol Worshippers and the Bodies of Israel

Now we should scrutinize according to what is written, "One does not lift a finger below unless one is mentioned above." It is also written, "The nations are as a drop of a bucket and are counted as the small dust of the scales." How can both be observed, for it is obvious that Providence and the dust of the scales or the drop of a bucket do not go together, as there is no thought without an act in the Creator, or an act without a purpose even in people?

Indeed, this is why there is a difference between the bodies of idol worshippers and the bodies of Israel. The body of a servant of the Creator is judged by Him in private Providence, to the Creator's will, the desired purpose. For this reason, although the body is an inconsequential *Klipa* [shell/peel] from its onset, it still appeared in the Creator's thought as a tool for work. But the bodies of idol worshippers, which are unfit for serving the Creator, and which are not eternal, private Providence is unified in them only in general, and not in particular. It is as one who weighs meat on scales: He knows in his mind that over time some dust will remain on the scales, but that thought is not regarded as such because it is without an intention, for why would he need the dust, and he does not need the body at all!

Let me offer an allegory: A person buys a box with letters for printing, and gives them to the worker to print books with them. It follows that all the printing is done by the landlord's supervision, although he is not the operator.

But it is one thing with motionless letters, for which they are not under the landlord's monitoring, as this was never his intention, and all the thoughts regarding

---
* *Chaf* is a letter in the word *Anochi* (me).

the above kind were only about actions but not about emptiness and nothingness. Also, the merit of the landlord is not diminished by inactive letters, since he is not the operator, naturally. However, the merit of the operator does indeed diminish because he is idle and makes little use of the blessing that extends from the direct preparation that he gives to him.

The lesson is that the printing operator is the vital soul which extends from the *Klipa* Noga with two forms—good or bad—and the points are taken from the point in the heart while the body of the letters are from the spaces of the whole world.

Ani [me/I]–Anochi [also me/I]

If the printer draws near to good neighbors, who give him ways and hints of good combinations, that printer acquires a new form, called "one golden pan of ten shekels, full of incense." The form of the initial feeling of the *Ani* is swallowed in a new form of *Anochi*, and this is the reward for his good act. At that time, his merit reaches the merit of the author, like an uneducated printer who prints books. Over time, by looking in the books for his own needs, he becomes learned and writes books like his prior landlords, as well as gives his books to other printers and raises their pay.

But if the printer is in a bad environment, and he is made to print bad combinations, punctuated from the *Klipa* of the point in their hearts, the left hollow, he becomes as lost and forsaken as they are, like the dust of a bucket.

A Coincidental Form and an Eternal Form

By this you can understand that the printer and the box of letters are all coincidental and not eternal, and the author does not take them into consideration in and of themselves at all. It is just as one who hires an employee to do some work does not regard the beauty of his face or his appearance, for they are not the issue. What is important is his strength and loyalty, and on that the landlord's guidance focuses, and not on the rest of his qualities, which are merely coincidental with regard to him (although they are to be noticed for other discernments: for mating, and for being liked by friends, and this is regarded as the general). The focus of his author's thought is in direct, undistorted combinations due to work, so they are fit to disclose the wisdom concealed in those combinations, so all who sees them will acquire his form by himself and will become as wise as he. His intention to create a new creation, as spiritual as Himself, is similar to the desire of corporeal beings—man, fowl, and beast—to preserve the species.

This is the meaning of the preservation of the soul for eternity, regarded as the one *Chaf* [one of the Hebrew letters] that the printer purchased. It is the "new *Anochi*," for then it acquires a new form, as the author himself, and makes by himself good and steadfast combinations full of blessing and light. The combinations remain for eternity as *Kelim* [vessels] of *Hochma* [wisdom], and his one *Chaf*, which is his *Anochi*, is filled abundantly with pleasures of joy, gladness, and preciousness, which are his lot for eternity.

It follows that knowing and choosing come as one since the printer has no freedom of choice, for he is printing other people's books and not his own. However, when he is rewarded with taking off that form and putting on the form of *Anochi*, he becomes one of the chosen among the nation, chosen by God above, as it is written in the *Midrash*, "'Therefore, choose life,' as one who takes his son's hands, places them on a good portion, and tells him, 'Choose this for yourself,' as it is written, 'Therefore, choose life.'"

We might say that his knowledge necessitates the act, and if he knew that the *Ani* would acquire the *Anochi*, then he would be compelled to acquire it. If so, what is the reward for his actions? This is the meaning of "If you walk contrary to Me, I will walk with rage against you" to teach you that the acquired form is a new spiritual being that is made by taking off the corporeal form. Any printer who gives his coincidental form and is ready for the Creator, the Creator is ready to take off his coincidental form and replace it with a new, spiritual one, creating in him a new heart and a new spirit.

This is so with one who prints good books and focuses on benefiting from them in eternity. But with one who prints bad combinations, who focuses on enjoying them and what has already been imprinted in him at birth, he clings to the pollution [lit. nocturnal ejaculation] in an inconsequential, passing world. And therefore, "I, too, will walk against you with rage."

Thus, it is clear to you that this question has nothing to do with spirituality, for it is impossible to derive from corporeality. For example, if the Creator knows that Reuben will have a son, then Reuben must have a son even without the coupling of male and female. Such a thing is unthinkable since we should say according to the nonsense of this question that He knew everything you'd do after all the scrutinies, and that you are compelled.

And the printer who clings to the pollution necessarily falls under the rage, as well, and we should not say that he does not deserve to be punished, since he has no choice or free will, for the punishment is the form he is in, as in prior to creation and absence. It is not a punishment from the Creator, but that He did not create one who does not want to be created and take off his coincidental form and adopt a new, spiritual, eternal form.

In that regard, we could ask about the affliction of the souls in Hell. This relates to the point in the heart before it is included in its root. It must emit its pollution from the material world, which is a bitter punishment for it, and is not regarded as revenge, but rather as a great salvation. This is very deep and understand it as *Arvut* [(mutual guarantee) could also mean "pleasantness"], as general.

No Plurality in the Essence of Eternity

...Indeed, one who sows for bread is not meticulous in choosing the place, the particular place, but in the positive relation between the place and his seed. Any place where he sows and finds sufficient bread, he is content without profit and without even a little of the value of the place itself, for it is the same everywhere. This is the meaning of what one must say, "The world was created for me," since the whole world is worthwhile for him. The whole world was created only to command this for there is no plurality in the essence, discernments of eternity, and all the forms of the souls are one and unique essence, since there is no "part" in spirituality, and the whole issue of deficiency and correction is a new creation made by taking off the old form. These are the entertainments of the Creator, as in "The king is glorified in the multitude of the people."

Understand that there is no plurality of entertainment in the Creator in the general redemption of the entire world at once, more than the redemption of one soul at one time. It is so because remote people and bodies were not added without time, for one at a time is called "two couplings," of heaven and of earth. Two people at one time are called "one coupling," and the soul is jointly theirs, completely equally, without subtraction or addition, as in luck, time, cause, or age, for all who are born at the same time share the same sign (fortune).

Thus, it is clear that the main purpose of the creation of the 6,000 years is to multiply generations and times in which the couplings will change and multiply, but not to multiply bodies. Otherwise, it will be difficult, for He could have created all the bodies of the 6,000 years in one year. Moreover, it is known ... so the bodies are renewed, and the first ones themselves incarnate and come in time and in generations, meaning their "vital soul" which is the root of the speaking.

Therefore, he does not care at all which body will disclose the desire as long as the desire is disclosed, by whomever it is disclosed. It is just as it does not matter what the face of the printer looks like, as long as the book is printed. But the printers themselves, who are numerous in the world, are as the drop of a bucket and the dust of the scales, consumed and lost by their own rage. However, we do need a printer who is skilled in his work, and anyone who takes on the work takes his complete reward, and knowing does not necessitate his face in particular, but rather everyone whose heart is kind will raise a contribution to the Lord, and the more one hurries, the better it is, in and of itself.

Creation Is Primarily the Eternity in Creation

Explanation: The Creator is omnipotent, and therefore although the creatures are as beasts, still, one who is rewarded with annulling one's will before the Creator's will, He gives him and creates within him a new spirit and a new heart, and enthrones him over all His works, as in "By Me kings reign." It is similar to a viceroy, to whom all the governance of the state is given, and one who is favored by that rewarded one, He takes him from the providence attributed to the shells and places him under the Providence that is established for eternity, and He will do the will of those who fear Him. This is the meaning of "As I create worlds, so the righteous create worlds."

It is so because creation is primarily about the eternity in creation, where the eternal in the first creation of this world, meaning Adam HaRishon, the Creator's creation, is attributed to the Creator. But from Adam onward that creation is given to the righteous in each generation. They are the ones leading the worlds as they wish and desire, and "a righteous sentences and the Creator executes."

Know that for this reason, the providence of corporeality need not change at all, since spirituality is not bound by the corporeal boundary, and it is fitting for completion over all the boundaries in the corporeal reality.

This is why the world is filled with immeasurable corpses, to such an extent that even if 600,000 righteous are established, they will still be able to engage in creating new worlds. However, everything follows the internality, which is Providence, where the righteous establishes and the Creator executes. And the sense of surplus on that will be as the drop of a bucket or as the dust of the scales, and nature cannot regard what is worthless.

The vital soul is regarded as corrupted and about to be burned, without the value of being. It is called "pollution" to imply that the sensation of being of his own self is under the rage of pollution, and incidental. However, a soul that acquires a part of God above is called "being," and this is the meaning of "to give to those who love Me being [substance], and to fill their treasuries." Only of this being can we speak, and not of all the *Klipot* [shells/peels] that preceded its making, whose being is merely coincidental, present during the work, and finally destroyed. The heaven and earth will wear out like a garment, and only the acquired desire will remain for all eternity.

By that "being" is there plurality according to the generations and times as incarnations. For this reason, there is no division in the innovation of the "being" between one body and all the bodies in the world, since analysis and plurality are dependent on "times."

Four Worlds

Attainment, as a whole, comes by matter and form whose beginning is the being. Also, the attained sustains the "being" which is devoid of matter and form. This is considered "the four worlds," perceived in everything that exists (meaning, a world is giving and receiving), and all our engagements are in matter and form, in creating and doing, on which the work relies.

This is so because creation is their whole and does not quite expand in the perception of the mind. Also, the form essentially divides the doing, meaning the materials, into many details, each with its own unique form. And the mind thoroughly cleaves to it and abundantly expands through it to distinguish one thing from another, to divide and to tell one thing from another. This is the purpose of the work: to know the advantage of light over darkness in every detail that exists, as it is written, "All is clarified in the thought."

Four Forms: Dot, Line, Area, Cube

All the forms in the world are dot, line, area, and cube, which is an area multiplied from all directions. These four forms contain all the types of shapes in the world, and all that exists on land exists in the ocean of wisdom, meaning in the upper worlds, to which this world is but an imprint, cascading from the spiritual worlds above, which we are destined to attain in the next world.

However, during the work, during our existence in this world, we have no other attainments unless they are clothed in corporeal dresses, which are corporeal shapes without which we are unable to perceive or understand anything.

Hence, we attain all the *Vavs* in the name *HaVaYaH*, which contain all the shapes in the world, which are dot, line—*Yod*, *Vav*, and the two *Heys*—area and cube. The last *Hey* is the disclosure of the first *Hey* but in a more corporeal way, meaning a form that occupies space. This is not so with the three other forms, which do not take up any space.

In truth, we also attain the beginning of the dot, implied by the tip of the *Yod*, which is the reason why this name is the origin of all the names. That is, each name is discerned as giving and receiving, for there is no thought or perception in His essence whatsoever, but rather in influences that come to us from Him, as in "The earth is full of Your possessions." In this, this whole creation is His names. A worker who is attentive to the matter and unites the matter with its root devotes the name to the heaven. That is, a "name" is that thing that one observes and knows its Giver, and that thing is the receiver. This is *Shem* [name] from *Shamayim* [sky/heaven], *Yam* [sea] from *Shamayim*, and this is the meaning of "Who created these."

This is the meaning of... meaning one part of the created beings in this world is in the dark without a name for people to examine, as this thing stems from Him, since it seems to be against His will. But in general, we know that His kingdom rules over all, and when the worker comes to that thing and delves in it and examines it, this, too, is given from His abundance. Thus, it sanctifies the name of the Creator and raises the holy spark from the *Klipa* [shell/peel], which is the whisperer that separates the Champion.

And to the extent of the scrutiny and the awareness in the thought of the worker, the "Name" grows and sanctifies.

In general, all of Israel believe and unite with His Name twice, every day with love. But that unity should appear in the thought of the worker with every... and in complete recognition. This is called raising *Mayin Nukvin* [MAN] and the descent of *Mayin Duchrin* [MAD], since the labor... which is the MAD, repeatedly rises, adding to one's awareness every time until... And this worker becomes a partner of the Creator in the work of creation. As the Creator creates worlds, he, too, creates worlds.

This is considered a whole world—giving and receiving, which is called a "world," that is, heaven and earth. This is the meaning of the saying that the righteous always create new heaven and earth.

The Act of Mitzvot [commandments]

Although in truth, all is clarified in the thought, actual deeds from below must be evoked, as well. This is because everything must expand through the world of *Assiya* [action], which is the actual disclosure, when *Kedusha* [holiness] and the revelation of His kingdom spread through *Assiya*, and "everyone will recognize," etc. Hence, for the complete *Segula* [power/remedy], it is to evoke the uniqueness of the Creator in everything in practice, and this is the essence of the whole work of *Mitzvot*.

Three Covenants

Now you understand the three covenants: covenant of the eyes, covenant of the tongue, and circumcision. This means that unification and raising *Mayin Nukvin* are done primarily in one's thought. Still, this recognition is not completed there before one's internal recognition appears outwardly. The Master's face is desired and appears in three places: a) covenant of the tongue, b) eyes, and c) circumcision, each according to its own quality. Some things are completed in what cleaves to it by what one sees, and some things are completed by words or real actions.

With circumcision, less is better. And the evidence is that the work with the eyes is good, whether before oneself or before a friend. But it must not be so with circumcision; it is a great offense. About his wife, too, it was said, "as though unwillingly." The reason is that man is the last degree of all the holiness; hence, the

Klipa clothes his *NHY*. This is the meaning of warming, becoming fire, fire for the Name (the letters *Yod*, *Hey*) has risen.

Perhaps this is the meaning of "A handsome maiden with no eyes." This is because it is known that each *Partzuf* clothes the *NHY* of the upper *Partzuf* and is considered the *Peh* [mouth] of the lower one, the *Yesod* [foundation] of the upper one. Hence, we could say that the *Eynaim* [eyes] of the lower one are at the place of *Yesod* of the upper one. It turns out that the *Eynaim* of the upper one are completely missing.

It follows that we clothe the *Kedusha* only in the form of our eye and mouth. Hence, all our unifications are only in those two covenants: mouth and eye. Know that the Creator has instilled power in those two covenants—to give all the shapes of the world from one to the other—meaning from teacher to student, in text or orally. It turns out that there is power in the study to receive all the wisdom in the world through text, as well as in the mouth—to give all the abundance in the world to one's friend.

...The creation of all the worlds was only for the Torah and for... seemingly a sublime and abstruse wisdom, to bring it to Israel. For this reason, he used... the above-mentioned three covenants. This is the meaning of the Written Torah and the Oral Torah, where the writing... affects, etc., and all is one.

Otiot and Nekudot [Letters and Points]

Transfer of their influence is through *Otiot* [letters] and *Nekudot* [points]. The eye perceives only letters and points, from which the heart understands. Similarly, the mouth is affected only by letters. This is why it is called "*Lev*" [heart, as well as 32 in *Gematria*], since it receives the *Hochma* [wisdom] through the thirty-two paths of bestowal—twenty-two letters and ten dots—as this is essentially the shapes of the world and what is in it with respect to the boundaries of the wisdom and the sustenance of the world.

This is the meaning of the four-letter-name *HaVaYaH*, which contains every shape in speech and in text, since the construction of the letters is from dots and lines: each dot is a *Tzimtzum* [restriction] and each line an expansion.

Atzmut [Self/Essence] and Kelim [Vessels]

Atzmut revolves around two kinds of Lights: 1) relating to the Operator, and 2) relating to the operated. This is the meaning of male and female, line and *Reshimo*, soul and body, king and kingship, the Creator and His *Shechina* [Divinity], mercy and judgment, for the work is completed with the true union.

The *Atzmut* governs and appears on the *Kli* [sing. of *Kelim*] to the extent of the awakening of the *Kli* and its preparation. This is the meaning of the states of ZON, since the whole issue of *Nukva* is only about those who receive according to their preparation in their work.

These two discernments are distinguished in all the creatures. And the nature of the *Atzmut* is that it appears to the eye only by the *Kli* in which it is clothed. It is recognized through the *Kli*, and almost no part of the *Atzmut* is perceived, but only the *Kli* that clothes the *Atzmut*, "and from my flesh I shall see."

And since the closeness of the Creator to His creatures is recognized through the Torah, as in the gift "from Mattanah to Nahaliel"* which is discerned as the actual Creator. One can say that one knows Him even though there is neither perception nor thought in Him at all, for if you say that you know your twin brother, who was born with you, you do not know more than his *Kli*, in which his *Atzmut* is clothed.

And of course, all the words of Torah and prayer in which His guidance is evident are said to be the actual revelation of Godliness and natural recognition. This is the meaning of "The Torah, the Creator, and Israel are one."

---

* Translator's note: In Hebrew, *Mattanah* means "gift" and *Nahaliel* means "rivers of God."

This Is for Judah

(From a commentary on the Passover Haggadah [narrative])

"This is the bread of poverty that our fathers ate in the land of Egypt." The *Mitzva* [commandment] of eating *Matza* [the Passover unleavened bread] was given to the children of Israel even before they went out from Egypt after the future exodus, which was to be in haste. It follows that the *Mitzva* of eating a *Matza* was given to them while they were still enslaved, and the aim of the *Mitzva* was for the time of redemption, since then they departed in haste.

This is why we like to remember the eating of *Matzas* in Egypt even today, since we, too, are as when we were enslaved abroad. Also, with this *Mitzva*, we aim to extend the redemption that will happen soon in our days, Amen, just as our fathers ate in Egypt.

"This year–here... next year–free." It is written above that with the aim of this *Mitzva* we can evoke the guaranteed redemption, destined for us, as in the *Mitzva* of eating the *Matza* of our fathers in Egypt.

"We were slaves..." It is written in *Masechet Pesachim* (p 116a), "Begins with denunciation, and ends with praise." Concerning the denunciation, Rav and Shmuel were in dispute: Rav said to begin with "In the beginning, our fathers were idol worshipers," and Shmuel said to begin with "We were slaves." The practice follows Shmuel.

We need to understand their dispute. The reason for "beginning with denunciation and ending in praise" is as it is written, "As the advantage of the light from within the darkness." We must remember the issue of the denunciation, for through it we acquire thorough knowledge of the mercies of the Creator that He did with us.

It is known that all of our beginning is only in denunciation, since "absence precedes presence." This is why "a wild ass's colt is born a man." And in the end, he acquires the shape of a man. This applies to every element in Creation, and this was so in the rooting of the Israeli nation, too.

The reason for this is that the Creator elicited Creation existence from absence. Hence, there is not a single creation that was not previously in absence. However, this absence has a distinct form in each element in creation, because when we divide reality into four types–still, vegetative, animate, and speaking–we find that the beginning of the still is necessarily complete absence.

However, the beginning of the vegetative is not complete absence but merely from its former degree, which, compared to itself, is considered absence. And in the matter of sowing and decay, which are necessary for any seed, it is received from the shape of the still. Also, it is the same with the absence of the animate and the speaking: The vegetative form is regarded as absence with respect to the animate, and the animate form is regarded as absence with respect to the speaking.

Hence, the text teaches us that the absence that precedes man's existence is the form of the beast. This is why it is written, "a wild ass's colt is born a man," as it is necessary for every person to begin in the state of a beast. The writing says, "Man and beast You save, O Lord." As a beast is given all that it needs for its sustenance and the fulfillment of its purpose, He also provides man with all that is necessary for his substance and the fulfillment of his purpose.

Therefore, we should understand where is the advantage of man's form over the beast, from the perspective of their own preparation. Indeed, this is discerned in their wishes, since man's wishes are certainly different from those of a beast. And to that extent, God's salvation of man differs from God's salvation of a beast.

Thus, after all the inquiries and scrutinies, we find that the only need in man's wishes, which does not exist in the whole of the animate species, is the awakening toward Godly *Dvekut* [adhesion]. Only the human species is ready for it, and none other.

It follows that the whole issue of presence in the human species is in that preparation imprinted in him to crave His work, and in this he is superior to the beast. Many have already said that even the intelligence in craftsmanship and in political conducts is present, with great wisdom, in many specimens in the animal world.

Accordingly, we can also understand the matter of the absence that precedes the existence of man as the negation of the desire for God's proximity, since this is the animate degree. Now we understand the words of the *Mishnah* that said, "Begins with denunciation, and ends with praise." This means that we must remember and research the absence that precedes our existence in a positive manner, as this is the denunciation that precedes the praise, and from it we will understand the praise more profoundly, as it is written, "Begins with denunciation, and ends with praise."

This is also the meaning of our four exiles, exile after exile, which precede the four redemptions, redemption after redemption, up to the fourth redemption, which is the complete perfection that we hope for soon in our days, Amen. Exile refers to "absence that precedes the presence," which is redemption. And since this absence is what prepares for the *HaVaYaH* ascribed to it, like the sowing that prepares the reaping, all the letters of *Ge'ula* [redemption] are present in *Gola* [exile], except for the *Aleph*, since this letter indicates the "*Aluph* [Champion] of the world."

This teaches us that the form of the absence is but the negation of the presence. And we know the form of the presence—redemption—from the verse, "And they shall teach no more every man his neighbor …for they shall all know Me, from the least of them unto the greatest of them." Hence, the form of the previous absence, meaning the form of exile, is only the absence of the knowledge of the Creator. This is the absence of the *Aleph*, which is missing in the *Gola*, and present in the *Ge'ula*—the *Dvekut* with the "Champion of the world." This is precisely the redemption of our souls, no more and no less, as we have said that all the letters of *Ge'ula* are present in *Gola* but the *Aleph*, which is the "Champion of the world."

To understand this weighty issue, that the absence in itself prepares the presence ascribed to it, we should learn from the conducts of this corporeal world. We see that in the concept of freedom, which is a sublime concept, only a chosen few perceive it, and even they require appropriate preparations. The majority of the people are utterly incapable of perceiving it. Conversely, with regard to the concept of enslavement, small and great are equal, and even the least among the people will not tolerate it.

(We saw that in Poland, they lost their kingdom only because the majority of them did not properly understand the merit of freedom and did not keep it. Hence, they fell under the burden of subjugation under the Russian government for a hundred years. During that time, they all suffered under the burden of subjugation and from least to great, they desperately sought freedom. Although they did not yet assume the taste of freedom as it truly is, and each of them imagined it as they wanted, in the absence of freedom, which is subjugation, it was thoroughly engraved in their hearts to cherish and like freedom. For this reason, when they were liberated from the burden of subjugation, many of them were bewildered, not knowing what they have gained by this freedom. Some of them even regretted it and said that their government was burdening them with even more taxes than the foreign government and wished for their return. This was so because the force of absence did not sufficiently affect them.)

Now we can understand the dispute between Rav and Shmuel. Rav interprets the Mishnah as beginning with denunciation, so that through it the salvation will be thoroughly appreciated. Hence, he says to begin from the time of Terah, and does not say what Shmuel does, since in Egypt, His love and work were already planted in some in the nation. Also, the added difficulty of enslavement in Egypt is not a deficiency in itself in the life of the nation called "Adam."

And Shmuel does not interpret like Rav, since the concept of the freedom of the nation in knowing the Creator is a sublime concept that only a few understand, and this is through appropriate preparations, but the majority of the nation has not achieved this attainment.

Conversely, everyone grasps the difficulty of subjugation, as Even Ezra wrote in the beginning of the portion *Mishpatim*, "Nothing is harder for man than to be in the authority of another man like him."

He interprets the Mishnah that because absence prepares the presence, it is considered a part of His salvation, and we should be grateful also for this. Hence, we should not begin with "In the beginning, our fathers were idol worshipers," since that time is not even regarded as "absence that precedes the presence," since they are completely devoid of the human type of presence, since they were completely removed from His love.

Hence, we begin with the enslavement in Egypt when the sparks of His love were burning in their hearts, to an extent, but due to impatience and hard work, it was being quenched each day. This is considered "absence that precedes presence," which is why he says to begin with "we were slaves."

The History of the Wisdom of Kabbalah

The first book that we have in this wisdom is *The Book of Creation*, which some attribute to Abraham the Patriarch, and so it is written on its cover. However, most authors attribute it to the Tanna, Rabbi Akiva. This seems to make sense since only in his days was writing permitted in the Oral Torah. Hence, besides the books of the Bible, we hardly have any books that predate the generation of Rabbi Akiva, due to the known prohibition that you are not permitted to say written words out loud, and you are not permitted to write down words that are said out loud. But after the ruin of the Temple and the scattering of the nation from its land, they feared that the Torah would be forgotten from Israel so they permitted the writing because "It is time to do for the Lord; they have broken Your Torah [law]."

At that time, the disciples of Rabbi Akiva began to write the whole of the Oral Torah that they knew. Each of them took upon himself a special faction. Rabbi Meir redacted the *Mishnah*, Rabbi Yehuda redacted the *Tosaftot*, and Rabbi Shimon Bar Yochai redacted the wisdom of Kabbalah in which they were proficient, and composed *The Book of Zohar* and the *Tikkunim*.

Thus, as the *Mishnah* is a compilation and assembly of laws and innovations of all the generations leading to the generation of Rabbi Meir, *The Zohar* is a compilation and assembly of the wisdom of Kabbalah from all the first ones who preceded Rashbi and were only written in Rashbi's name because he redacted them. Of course, he also added his own innovations.

However, the disciples of Rabbi Akiva did not sign their books so that no additions would be added to them. On the contrary, with their books, they created a beginning so that others who followed them would add clarifications, scrutinies, and innovations to the compositions that they had begun. This was the same manner that was customary when they engaged in Oral Torah, where the latter ones clarified and scrutinized, and sometimes disputed the view of the former ones, and added to the former ones. This is why you find in the *Mishnah* innovations and sayings from other Tannaim [pl. of Tanna] who lived after the time of Rabbi Meir.

This continued until the generation of Rabbi Yehuda HaNassi, who found that the generations were declining and were no longer worthy of disputing the former ones. Also, there was the fear that unworthy disciples would contradict the words of the former ones. Hence, he arose and sealed the *Mishnah*, and since then it has not been permitted to anyone to add anything to the *Mishnah* or dispute any of the rules introduced there.

However, there was no signing on *The Zohar* because it was intended for concealment and was absent among the masses except for among the heads of the generations, who secretly kept it. For this reason, the composition remained ... and each of the heads of the generations added to it as he saw fit, and this continued until the time of our sages the Savoraim.

(The rest is missing)

Inheritance of the Land

[From a manuscript]

Israel will not return to their land until they are all in one bundle.

Our sages said, "Israel will not be redeemed until they are all in one bundle."

2) We must understand how Israel's unity pertains to redemption.

3) First we should consider the matter of "By what will I know," etc., "for your descendants will be strangers," etc., "and afterward they will come out with great substance." It is not clear how it answers Abraham's question.

4) We should understand the whole matter of this creation, in which man suffers so, what is it for? Could He not delight His creations without all this?

5) It is written in the books that the souls cannot receive the good reward for which He created the world and the souls if they do not have a *Kli* [vessel] ready to receive. And the only way one can obtain that *Kli* is through labor and toil to observe the *Mitzvot* [commandments] through the pressure and the wars that one fights with the evil inclination, and the numerous preventions and troubles. The affliction and labor in Torah and *Mitzvot* provide a *Kli* for the soul so it may be fit to receive all the delight and pleasure for which He created all creations.

6) Now we can understand the words of Ben He He in the Mishnah, *Avot*, which says, "According to the sorrow, so is the reward." This means that the reward is measured by the amount of sorrow. This is perplexing, for how is one's sorrow related to one's reward?

7) With the above said, we can thoroughly understand that all the sorrow and labor that have been prepared in the world are to provide the *Kli* to receive the good reward through labor in Torah and *Mitzvot*. Thus, naturally, the greater one's sorrow in Torah and *Mitzvot*, the greater is one's *Kli*. Naturally, he can receive a greater reward.

8) Now we can understand the Creator's answer to the question of Abraham the patriarch, "By what will I know," etc. Abraham's question was because he saw, in his spirit of holiness, the excessively great reward that Israel is destined to receive by inheriting the land, since observing the *Mitzvot* depends entirely on the land. This is why Abraham the patriarch wondered, "How will I know that I will inherit it?" That is, How will I know that the children of Israel will be able to receive such a great reward and such a great excessiveness, as from where would they have *Kelim* so big as to receive this wondrous thing? The Creator told him about this, "Your descendants will be strangers, and they will be enslaved and tormented 400 years," for then they will have great labor in Torah and *Mitzvot*. This is when he understood that in this way they will certainly obtain the great vessels of reception, and the reply was completely satisfactory.

9) It follows from our words that inheriting the land requires much preparation, since the *Segula* [merit/power/cure] of Torah and *Mitzvot* depend entirely on this, as through it one is rewarded with all the abundance and benefit that the Creator has contemplated with regard to all the souls of Israel before He created them. This is also why Abraham the patriarch was perplexed and did not understand from from where would they take such great vessels of reception so as to be rewarded with the holiness of the land. Finally, the Creator told him that laboring in Torah and *Mitzvot* in the exile in Egypt will provide them with these great vessels and they will be fit for the holy land.

10) This is perplexing: It is one thing with regard to those who engage in Torah, but what about those who engage in worldly matters, who are not at all prepared to engage in Torah? How will they be rewarded these vessels?

11) The answer is that this is why they said in the above-mentioned commentary that Israel are not redeemed before they are all in one bundle. It is so because all of Israel are indeed one body, where each and every organ has its unique role. For example, the head contemplates intellect and reason; the hands work and provide nourishments for the head, while the head itself is exempted from working and does not need to work, since the hands are quite sufficient. Likewise, the hands do not need to calculate how to work because the head is quite enough for him. Likewise, the hands do not need to think or contemplate on how to work since the head is completely enough for him.

12) If Israel become one bundle, like one body, where the workers—who are the hands of the body—provide for the head, the labor and sorrow of those who engage in Torah and work will complement for the workers... and this clarifies the commentary [Israel are not redeemed until they are all] in one bundle, and "a redeemer has come to Zion ... will walk."

600,000 Souls

It is said that there are 600,000 souls, and each soul divides into several sparks. We must understand how it is possible for the spiritual to divide, since initially, only one soul was created, the soul of *Adam HaRishon*.

In my opinion, there is indeed only one soul in the world, as it is written (Genesis 2:7), "and breathed into his nostrils the soul [also "breath" in Hebrew] of life." That same soul exists in all the children of Israel, complete in each and every one, as in *Adam HaRishon*, since the spiritual is indivisible and cannot be cut—which is rather a trait of corporeal things.

Rather, saying that there are 600,000 souls and sparks of souls appears as though it is divided by the force of the body of each person. In other words, first, the body divides and completely denies him of the radiance of the soul, and by the force of the Torah and the *Mitzva* [commandment], the body is cleansed, and to the extent of its cleansing, the common soul shines on him.

For this reason, two discernments were made in the corporeal body: In the first discernment, one feels one's soul as a unique organ and does not understand that this is the whole of Israel. This is truly a flaw; hence, it causes along with the above-mentioned.

In the second discernment, the true light of the soul of Israel does not shine on him in all its power of illumination, but only partially, by the measure he has purified himself by returning to the collective.

The sign for the body's complete correction is when one feels that one's soul exists in the whole of Israel, in each and every one of them, for which he does not feel himself as an individual, for one depends on the other. At that time, he is complete, flawless, and the soul truly shines on him in its fullest power, as it appeared in *Adam HaRishon*, as in "He who breathed, breathed from within Him."

This is the meaning of the three times of a person:

1) A spark of a soul, the act by way of sparkling, as in prohibiting and permitting.

2) A particular soul, one part out of 600,000. It is permanently completed, but its flaw is with it. This means that his body cannot receive the whole of the soul, and feels himself as being distinct, which causes him a lot of pains of love.

Subsequently, he approaches wholeness, the common soul, since the body has been cleansed and is entirely dedicated to the Creator and does not pose any measures or screens and is completely included in the whole of Israel. ... ...

We learned that "If even one man came before his Master in complete repentance, the Messiah King would come at once." It seems to mean, as they said (Song of Songs

1), "Moses is equal to 600,000." We need to understand this, since this would mean that there are twice 600,000 souls—the soul of Moses and the souls of Israel.

But the truth is that there is no more than one soul, as it is known by the measure of each and every soul that purifies and cleanses itself from its filth. Hence, when all the souls are corrected, they will draw onto them the entire upper soul of *Atzilut* to each and every soul, since the spiritual is indivisible. At that time, "And the Lord will be King over all the earth" (Zechariah, 14:9). Hence, while even a single soul is denied of complete purity, the extension of this *Kedusha* [Holiness] will be deficient in every soul from Israel.

And when a single soul from Israel is purified from all its filth, it will draw onto itself the whole of the soul of *Atzilut*, and through it, all the souls of its generation will be corrected. This is the meaning of one being dependent on the other, as it is written (*Sanhedrin* 11), "It was befitting for the *Shechina* [Divinity] to be upon him, but his generation was unworthy of it."

The content of the words is unanimously bewildering, that the same soul that was rewarded with purification immediately strives to increase the grace of the generation and asks for them until it elevates its entire generation to its merit.

This is the meaning of "Moses is equal to 600,000." Because he was their faithful shepherd, he had the same *Kedusha* that the whole generation merited.

Indeed, the whole is found within each item, since in the end, all the souls will unite into one discernment, returning to their spiritual root. Hence, all the miracles and wonders and all the journeys that the whole world has experienced during the 6,000 years should be experienced by each individual soul. The good soul draws to it from all the discernments of *Kedusha* before it and after it, and the bad soul does the opposite.

And the changing times are considered generations. However, each generation behaves according to its judge, by the mind that judges it, since it receives from the *Kedusha* of that time.

For this reason, each soul is willing to draw the souls of Moses, Aaron, Samuel, David, and Solomon within it, as times that it experiences. During the exodus from Egypt and the reception of the Torah, the soul of Moses appears on him; in the seven that they conquered, the soul of Joshua; and in the building of the Temple, the soul of King Solomon, etc.

This does not refer to the above-mentioned souls in particular, but according to the rule that we said that the spiritual is indivisible, as soon as one is rewarded with a soul, he is rewarded with the soul of the whole of Israel, but according to one's merit and place. Hence, at a time when one is rewarded with these wonders, one receives into himself the abundance of the soul in that disclosure. For this reason, the name of the owner of that disclosure is truly upon him.

They said (*Shabbat* 67; *Baba Metzia* 113), "All of Israel are sons of kings." Also, "A king who dies, all of Israel are worthy of kingship" (Jerusalem Talmud, *Masechet Horaiot* 3, 5). This is a great secret, for in all the previous generations, which were but a preparation for *Malchut*, special *Kelim* [vessels] were required for anointment of their judges, such as the souls of Moses and Samuel. But the final purpose depends on the whole of Israel, since when a tiny part of a tiny spark is missing, the end will not be able to appear. Hence, all of Israel are worthy of kingship, since everyone is equal in this true discernment.

For this reason, there is no special *Kli* [vessel] for drawing that wholeness, but anyone who cleanses and purifies his soul to be worthy of extending the revelation of *Malchut* in the world will truly be called King David. This is the meaning of "David, King of Israel, is indeed alive" (*Rosh Hashanah* 25), for he has not died at all. His *Kli* is within each and every soul from Israel. This is not so with the soul of Moses, which is found in only the wise disciples in the generation, as well as in prophets and priests.

This is the meaning of "A king who dies, all of Israel are worthy of kingship" (Jerusalem Talmud; *Masechet Horaiot* 3, 5). This is also the meaning of exempting the public.

This is the meaning of "Near the Messiah, insolence will soar" (*Sutah* 49), and "They will be insolent toward each other, the child will behave insolently against the elder, and the base against the honorable" (Isaiah 3:5). This means that even an ignoble child will dare to extend His kingship to the world as though he were one of the elders and honorable in the generation.

This is so because should the ignoble, who has a lowly and base soul at its root, aim his heart and purify his deeds to be worthy, he will be rewarded with extending the whole of the soul of a holy nation in his soul with all the wonders that the holy nation has tasted thus far. This is because they were all but preparations for this wholeness.

Hence, even that particular soul must taste everything, and he will buy his world in one hour due to the ability of that generation to extend the crown of His kingship, which contains everything: "And all need the owner of the needles, and every element in it is required" (*Berachot* 64; *Baba Batra* 145).

This is the meaning of their words: "Even if one man came before his Master in complete repentance, the Messiah King would come at once." This means that whoever it was, even if only one man in the generation were rewarded with extending that soul by himself, he will be able to reward his whole generation, since all who are committed to the matter exempt the public and can do much praying and continue until he is rewarded for the sake of his entire generation.

This is not so with other kinds of redemptions, which were but preparations and did not belong to each and every one. For example, the giving of the Torah belonged specifically to the generation of the desert and to Moses. Any other generation, even if they were more worthy, would not extend that discernment, and neither would any other person besides Moses, for they are interdependent.

However, the Messiah is ready for each and every generation. Because of this, He is also ready for each and every person to extend the discernment of the Messiah, as in "All who are committed to the matter," as mentioned above.

The reason is that anointments concern the correction of the *Kelim* and the portrayal of all the *Kelim* as equal, since any division among them is only in their *HBD*, according to their measures. Hence, from the minister who sees the King's face to the one who sits behind the grindstone, all are equal servants in restoring the old glory, and in this there are no degrees between one another.

Concealment and Disclosure of the Face of the Creator - A

First concealment

(Depiction): His Face is not revealed; that is, the Creator does not behave toward a person according to His Name—The Good Who Does Good. Rather, it is to the contrary—one is afflicted by Him or suffers from poor income and many people wish to collect their debts from him and make his life bitter. His whole day is filled with troubles and worries. Or, one suffers from poor health and disrespect from people. Every plan he begins, he fails to complete, and he is constantly dissatisfied.

In this manner, of course one does not see the Creator's Good Face, that is, if he believes that the Creator is the one who does these things to him, either as a punishment for transgressions he committed or to reward him in the end. This follows the verse, "Whom the Lord loves, He rebukes," and also, "The righteous begin with suffering, since the Creator wishes to eventually impart them great tranquility."

Yet, one does not fail in saying that all this came to him by blind fate and by nature without any reason or consideration. Rather, one strengthens in believing that the Creator, with His guidance, caused him all these. This is nonetheless considered seeing the Creator's back.

Second concealment

The second concealment, which the books refer to as "concealment within concealment," means that one cannot see even the Creator's back. Instead, one says that the Creator has left him and does not watch over him. He ascribes all the sufferings he feels to blind fate and to nature, since the ways of Providence become so complicated in his eyes as to lead him to denial.

This means (depiction) that one prays and gives charity over one's troubles but is not answered whatsoever. And precisely when he stops praying for his troubles, he is answered. Whenever he strengthens in believing in Providence and makes his deeds good, luck turns its back to him and he mercilessly falls back. And when he denies and begins to worsen his ways, he becomes very successful and is greatly relieved.

He does not find his sustenance in proper manners, but through deceit of people or desecration of Shabbat [Sabbath]. Or, all of his acquaintances who observe Torah and *Mitzvot* [commandments] suffer poverty, illness, and are despicable in the eyes of people. These observers of Mitzvot seem impolite to him, innately brainless, and so hypocritical that he cannot bear to be among them for even a minute.

Conversely, all his wicked acquaintances, who mock his faith, are very successful, well to do, and healthy. They know no sickness; they are clever, virtuous, and good-tempered. They are carefree, confident, and tranquil all day, every day.

When Providence arranges things in this manner for a person, it is called "concealment within concealment." This is because then one collapses under one's weight and cannot continue to strengthen the belief that his pains come to him from the Creator for some hidden reason. Finally, he fails, becomes heretic and says that the Creator does not watch over His creations whatsoever, and all that transpires, transpires by blind fate and nature. This is not seeing even the back.

Depiction of Disclosure of the Face

One's request to become stronger in believing in His guidance over the world during the concealment brings one to contemplate the books, the Torah, and to draw from there the illumination and understanding how to strengthen his faith in His guidance. These illuminations and observations that one receives through the Torah are called "the Torah as a spice." When they accumulate to a certain amount, the Creator has mercy on him and pours upon him the spirit from above, that is, the higher abundance.

But once he has completely discovered the spice—the light of Torah that one inhales into one's body—through strengthening in faith in the Creator, one becomes worthy of guidance with His face revealed. This means that the Creator behaves with him as is fitting to His name, "The Good Who Does Good."

His name shows us that He is good and does good to all His creations in all the forms of benefit, sufficient for every kind of receiver in the whole of Israel, for certainly, the delight and pleasure of one is not like the delight and pleasure of another. For example, one who engages in wisdom will not enjoy honor and wealth, and one who does not engage in wisdom will not enjoy great attainments and innovations in the wisdom. Thus, He gives wealth and honor to one, and wondrous attainments in the wisdom to another.

Thus (depiction), he receives abundant good and great tranquility from the Creator and is always satisfied, since he obtains his livelihood with ease and to the fullest, never knows trouble or pressure, knows no illness, is highly respected by people, easily completes any plan that comes to his mind, and succeeds wherever he turns.

And when he needs something, he prays and is immediately answered, as He always answers anything that he demands of Him, and not a single prayer is denied.

When one strengthens in good deeds, his success substantially increases, and when he is negligent, his success proportionally decreases.

All of his acquaintances are decent, well to do, healthy, highly respected in the eyes of people, and have no worries at all. They are at peace all day and every day. They are smart, truthful, and so comely that he feels blessed and delighted to be among them.

Conversely, all of his acquaintances who do not follow the path of Torah are of poor livelihood, troubled by heavy debts, and do not have even a single moment's rest. They are sick, in pain, and despised by people. They seem to him mindless, ill-mannered, wicked and cruel toward people, deceitful, and such sycophants that it is intolerable to be among them.

Concealment and Disclosure of the Face of the Creator - B

Depiction of Concealment of the Face

1) Suffering torments such as deficient income, poor health, degradations, failing to accomplish plans, and emotional dissatisfaction.

2) Praying without being answered. Declining when bettering one's ways, such as avoiding deceiving his friends, and succeeding when worsening one's ways. One's sustenance does not come in proper ways, but only by deception, stealing, or desecrating the Shabbat [Sabbath].

3) All of one's acquaintances who walk on the straight path suffer poverty, ill health, and degradations of all kinds, and one's wicked acquaintances mock him each day. They are successful, healthy, wealthy, tranquil, and carefree.

4) All of his righteous acquaintances who observe Torah and *Mitzvot* [commandments] seem to him cruel, egotistical, odd, or innately stupid and impolite, as well as hypocritical. He finds it repulsive to be with them, even in the Garden of Eden, and he cannot bear to be with them even a moment.

Depiction of Disclosure of the Face

1) Reception of abundance and tranquility, obtainment of one's livelihood with ease and to the fullest. One never feels scarcity or ill health; he is respected wherever he turns, and successfully and easily accomplishes every plan that comes to his mind.

2) When one prays, he is immediately answered. When he betters his ways, he is very successful, and when he worsens his ways, he loses his success.

3) All of one's acquaintances who walk on the straight path are wealthy, healthy, know no illness, are highly respected by people, and dwell in peace and tranquility. Conversely, acquaintances who do not follow the straight path are of poor income, filled with burdens and sorrow, ill, and contemptible in the eyes of people.

One regards all the righteous acquaintances as clever, reasonable, well-mannered with people, truthful, and so comely that it is most pleasurable to be among them.

Introduction to A Sage's Fruit, Vol. 4 (Three Partners)

The manuscripts of the books before us were before the RABASH. He proofread them as he had proofread the previous books. Once, when I brought him a part of a manuscript to proofread, he gave me the essay, "Three Partners," and said he intended to write the introduction based on that essay, as it reflects the book before us.

Regrettably, we were not blessed with his editing the introduction. On a bitter and mournful day, on the fifth of *Tishrey*, *Tav-Shin-Nun-Bet* [September 13, 1991], the RABASH passed away.

Here, I bring the complete essay as he had given it to me:

"Our sages said, 'There are three partners in man: the Creator, his father, and his mother. His father sows the white… his mother sows the red… and the Creator places within him a spirit and a soul'" (*Nidah* 31).

"Man" means the souls within him, as our sages said (*Yevamot* 61), "You are called 'Man.'" This is the Israeli soul, for in this he is distinguished and separated from the nations of the world.

Man consists of two things: matter and form. We refer to creation as "matter," and to the Creator as the "form." It follows that we necessarily have three partners: the Creator, who gives the soul and the light that sustains the *Kli* [vessel], which is called "installing of the *Shechina* [Divinity]," as He installs His *Shechina* in the *Kli*, while the *Kli* is drawn from the father and the mother—his father gives the white, and his mother, the red.

As man consists of two things, so the *Kli* consists of two things: 1) a desire to receive, 2) the force that detains. The completeness of the *Kli* cannot consist of one matter—desire to receive. Rather, it must also consist of corrections of the *Kli*, called "the force that detains," which prevents his desire from receiving.

Therefore, he receives the desire to receive from the mother, the environment, and he receives the corrections of the *Kli* from the father, his teacher, and the light, the form that clothes inside the *Kli*, is called "the Creator."

"Father" means the teacher, as our sages said (*Sanhedrin* 19): "Anyone who teaches his friend's son Torah … it is as though he begot him." "Mother" means the friends, for one acquires from one's friends "blushes," meaning *Gevurot*. As much as the teacher exerts in him and places whiteness in him, whitening the redness he had acquired from his friend, as soon as he leaves the teacher's house and enters the environment, he immediately loses all the desires, passions, and inclinations he had strenuously acquired with his teacher's help.

Yet, the loss is not so great since in the end, he ascends higher and higher until he reaches the summit, for through the sling that throws him time and again from his teacher to the environment and from the environment to his teacher, the *Kli* is formed and he becomes fit for the instilling of the *Shechina*, where the Creator is the middle line that decides and makes peace between them, as in, "For He will speak peace unto His people" (Psalms 85:9).

By these three, man is born. If he lacks one of them, he will not be able to be born, for the Creator cannot give this bad that he acquires from the society.

If we find this perplexing, since the Creator is almighty, so why can He not impart the thickness and the bad? After all, it is known that everything we see, understand, and feel does not mean that reality is as we see it, for all the forms we attribute to reality do not impress or activate it.

The rule is that the lower one cannot act upon the upper one, but only to the contrary: The upper one can act on the lower one. Yet, the Creator imprinted in us this power so we would sense some form in reality, and say about it that only this is the reality, that there is nothing above it, a higher quality, and what we feel, see, and understand is the truth.

Yet, we must know that all this is nothing less and nothing more than a true, complete degree. The degree on which we stand now compels us to feel this way, so that by this we will achieve the real goal. It is known that there are many degrees in order to achieve wholeness. This is why there are many feelings, and each feeling is true, for otherwise, if we do not perceive this way and feel this way, we will not achieve what we must achieve.

But in the end, we cannot force reality to be in the form that it appears to us, for it shows us according to what the goal compels us, according to our smallness. It is like a father who sees his son climbing a rickety ladder and shows him a cruel face so as to scare him from climbing, while his intention is to save him from death. Can we assert that the cruel form of the father is really him and say that indeed the son has a cruel and mean-hearted father because he does not give him what he wants? Rather, each time the matter depends on corrections, the corrections give the shapes, and not reality, since we cannot grasp reality.

Concerning what we asked above, if the Creator is almighty, why can He not impart the thickness and the bad, the answer is that when a person obtains only thickness and evil, he does not believe that the Creator is the doer of all these. Before one is rewarded with private Providence, he cannot grasp that He does and will do all the deeds, even the bad deeds that manifest in our world.

For this reason, he must acquire through the environment—the society. But in order not to remain inside the environment, he must have a teacher who will always pull him toward him and will not give him time to sink in the mire. This is called the "white" in him, and only in this way is the *Kli* that is fit for the light of the Creator and His Torah to be on is fashioned.

We can also say that it is impossible to attribute the bad to the Creator since he is the absolute good. Hence, as long as one feels bad states, he must say that they come from elsewhere, from the environment. But in truth, when one is rewarded with seeing only good and that there is no bad in the world, and everything is turned to good, then he is shown the truth, that the Creator did everything because He is almighty, and He alone did, does, and will do all the deeds.

Introduction to the Book *From the Mouth of a Sage"*

"Abraham was old and of many days, and the Lord blessed Abraham with everything" (Genesis 24:1). Noam Elimelech interprets (portion *Hayeh Sarah*) that when he came to the degrees of "days," regarded as *Hassadim* [mercies], "the Lord blessed him with everything," meaning with the whole of Israel, for the righteous who draws bestowal does not aim for himself at all, for he will not need them at all. Rather, his only intention is the salvation of the whole of Israel, and he will not fear for himself at all, as though he is not present in this world at all. Only the Creator watches over the righteous and blesses him with the whole of Israel, and this is "The Lord blessed Abraham with everything."

It seems that this is the meaning of "Anyone who asks for mercy for his friend and needs the same thing is answered first" (*Baba Kama* 92). In other words, a righteous who truly needs that thing, as well, but for all his sanctity does not feel it, and when he prays he aims for all of Israel to be redeemed, this is why he is answered first in person, since the Creator knows that he will not stop his sanctity due to his personal salvation, and as before, so now, he will be just as enthusiastic about praying for the comfort of Israel for he will not feel himself at all, as though he is not present in the world. Understand this well, for this is the whole of man.

Anyone Who Is Sorry for the Public

"Anyone who is sorry for the public is rewarded with seeing the comfort of the public, and anyone who is not sorry," etc. (*Taanit* 21). Interpretation: We have already said that the revelation of Godliness to His creatures as revelation is in answering those who call Him. This is why the *Shechina* [Divinity] is called "woman of valor," and this is the meaning of receiving the abundance as *Nukva* and ZA, for the complete redemption is in Isaac, for you are our father. "There is no flavor in an old man, and no counsel in the young" (*Shabbat* 89). "For Abraham does not know us and Israel does not recognize us" (Isaiah 63:16). This is the meaning of "To the extent that one appreciates, so one is allotted" (*Megillah* 12, *Sotah* 8). That is, according to the size of the hole in the *Kli* [vessel], meaning the receptacle and its insides, that lack will always be filled, not less and not more. Therefore, a servant of the Creator who is not sorry for the public but feels only his own personal lack, his receptacle for abundance is also not greater. As a result, he will not be able to receive the collective revelation of Godliness in the form of the comfort of the public, since he did not prepare a *Kli* to receive this collective discernment, but only his individual discernment.

Conversely, one who is sorry for the public and feels the troubles of the public as his own trouble is rewarded with seeing the complete revelation of the *Shechina*, meaning the comfort of the whole of Israel. Because his lack is a collective lack, the abundance of *Kedusha* [holiness] is also collective.

By this you will understand the matter of "The righteous have no rest" (end of *Berachot*, end of *Moed Katan*). Interpretation: Since the abundance is blessed according to the level of the lack and longing of the righteous, to that extent, not less and not more, they always exert to deepen and expand their receptacle, for the Giver has no measure, only the receiver. "More than the calf wants to nurse," etc., (*Pesachim* 112) so their entire intention in life is to strengthen their yearning and make for themselves a receptacle in order to bring contentment by expanding the boundaries of *Kedusha* in the blessing of the Creator.

This is the meaning of "Search for her as a hidden treasure" (Proverbs 2:4), and this is the meaning of "As a deer yearns" (Psalms 42:2). "And give Him no rest" (Isaiah 62:7), "My soul longs for Your salvation" (Psalms 119:81). However, one must always consist of both, meaning the male, too, Jacob, as in "They who fear Him shall have no lack" (Psalms 34:10), as I received the meaning of the words "And two rams" (Exodus 29:1, Leviticus 23:18), meaning male and female.

We must understand, for they said "virtue more than calamity" (*Sotah* 11, *Sanhedrin* 100), and here they said "To the extent that one appreciates" (*Megillah* 12, *Sotah* 8). Perhaps it is that here it is according to the amount, and here it is according to the level, since he is in her amount and she is in her level.

Man's Actions and Tactics

One Depiction Emerges from All the Actions

All the actions and tactics of an individual are a single procession that the Emanator has set up out of choosing Him with love. One depiction emerges from all of these actions, as bright as an object of the heaven in purity, for they are all united and integrated in one another through cause and effect, reason and result, until all the actions unite into a single act, as in "the working of the Lord, for it is fearful" (Exodus 34:10), as is known to those who know the wisdom of the hidden, a personal redemption. This is the meaning of the unity of actions from actions, meaning that many actions emerge from each created being, and in the end they will unite in one another until they literally become one action. This unification comes in every creature and its actions.

Unity of Actions

There is the unity of actions that emerges from the real Operator, who creates all those created beings that do these deeds. The value of the created beings compared to Him is as the value of the actions compared to the created beings. Hence, after all the actions of the creatures unite into an act, as in "If to the Bible (*Pesachim* 86, and a change of wording), for that particular creature, afterward, all the souls in the world must unite and merge into one soul, truly one, which emerges out of all the souls and they truly become one, as in the beginning of creation, when only one man [Adam] was created, and from his *Zivugim* [couplings], he engendered sons, and the sons follow in his ways, making *Zivugim* until this world is made, with seventy nations, and from within them, the seed of Israel. At the end of correction, they will merge in one another until all of them will become one man like *Adam HaRishon*.

Righteous and Wicked

(from manuscripts of Baal HaSulam that have never been published)

When a person becomes cleansed so as to adhere to the Creator, he is all to bestow and has nothing in him of the will to receive. Thus, how will he receive His abundance, with which He wished to delight His creatures? For this reason, the Creator has imprinted within each person that he will consist of all the people in the world. That is, the views and natures of all the people in the world will reign and unite in each person in the world, since the thoughts and views of people pass from one to the other.

Therefore, once a person has been cleansed and becomes a complete righteous, then, too, he is connected to the wicked of the whole world, who impart upon him their will to receive against his will and inadvertently. For this reason, the righteous is ready to awaken with a desire and receive His delight, which is the purpose of heaven and earth.

In this manner, this righteous truly consists of sparks of souls of wicked and righteous from the whole world, from the past and from the future. After he corrects the souls of the righteous with whom he is included, and properly adheres through them in order to bestow, the souls of the wicked included in him begin to open their mouths to receive pleasures. At that time, a person becomes a *Kli* [vessel] to receive His delight, and he achieves his purpose since he has a desire to bestow, which causes *Dvekut* [adhesion] in equivalence of form, and he has a desire to receive through the souls of the wicked included in him. This makes him a *Kli* to receive His delight and abundance.

Then the souls of the righteous envy the actions of the wicked since they see that the Creator's desire, to delight His creatures, comes mainly through the actions of the wicked, for the actions of the righteous cause only *Dvekut*, which is the desire of the lower one, but the actions of the wicked cause the purpose of the Creator's will, namely to delight His creatures.

However, in truth, the souls of the wicked are unfit to hold the abundance they received since they connected to the righteous only in order to evoke in them the desire to receive His delight, while the righteous, who have already been rewarded with *Dvekut* with Him and a desire to bestow, gain twofold now: They have *Dvekut*, and they also receive His delight in order to bestow, which is mainly what is desired. He said that the righteous have already been fully completed through the wicked, and then all the souls of the wicked are taken off from the level of the righteous since they can receive only for themselves and not in order to bestow, as do the righteous.

Private Providence and Guidance of Reward and Punishment

The path of suffering is private Providence, and the path of Torah is guidance of reward and punishment. This explains the questions about knowing and choice, since indeed, each created being must sin, as it is written, "There is not a righteous in the land who will not sin" (Ecclesiastes 7:20), and every creature must repent, as it is written, "No outcast shall be cast out from Him" (2 Samuel 14:14), and also "The earth shall be full of knowledge" (Isaiah 11:9). However, this necessity becomes clarified through nature's reins of physical pleasure and suffering that lead a person to where Providence wishes, as it is written in the essay, "The Essence of Religion and Its Purpose."

However, there is also the path of Torah, for people who are closer and more capable of development, as it is written, "He saw that the righteous are few; He stood and planted them in each and every generation" (*Yoma* 38b). Also, "There is not a generation without the likes of Abraham, Isaac, and Jacob" (according to *Midrash Rabbah, Beresheet* 56:9). They can pass on from their wisdom to the masses, who are not developed, and this passing is called "the path of Torah" [author's note: meaning Oral Torah, since the written Torah is also Oral Torah because he who tells you ABC can also say ZYX]. Because of this, the masses who have accepted the path of the righteous become fit to receive their completion in their own generation although according to the order of private Providence, they must reincarnate a hundred more generations before they accept the law of their development from nature, and all this time and suffering are considered for them a great reward if they follow the words of their teacher, or as heavy punishments if they do not follow them. This is the meaning of "Cutting off and dying are in the hands of heaven," meaning they fall once more into the hands of nature because of the offense.

This is the meaning of *Teshuva* [repentance/returning], that they become tied once more to the path of Torah (this is also the meaning of Hell and the Garden of Eden, which concern the cleansing of the soul that it undergoes in the period between one body and another incarnation. In the meantime, it acquires a certain correction until all the matters and good or bad forces that it did in the first incarnation are tied to it. This is the meaning of reception, and we will not clarify it here.).

Rewarded—I Will Hasten It; Not Rewarded—in Its Time

"If they are rewarded—I will hasten it; if they are not rewarded—in its time" (*Sanhedrin* 98, Jerusalem Talmud, *Taanit* 81:1). It is written, "No outcast shall be cast out from Him" (2 Samuel 14:14). Also, "If you sinned, what will you perform in Him?" (Job 35:6), since the power of His uniqueness has already been given in this creation for the moment when it is completed by itself, as in "Of all that You want, You have forgotten nothing and you have not omitted one thing" (Song of Unification for Friday). Also, "No work preceded Your work," since He did everything well in its time and it is set well in advance.

However, what He did leave for His servants to grow in is the matter of "If they are rewarded, I will hasten it." This is the meaning of the four hundred years that was said to Abraham the Patriarch between the divides, and they went out to 216 years, for this was the reward for their work. This is the meaning of being immersed in forty-nine gates of *Tuma'a* [impurity] and there was fear of the fiftieth gate, so the Creator pitied them and redeemed them, for there is the place of redemption for Israel. This was in return for their work, and this is the meaning of what he said, that He had them skip the end due to the hardship of enslavement.

This is what it means that in the days of the Messiah and the next world, the wicked become dust and are placed under the feet of the righteous (see *Tosafta Sanhedrin*, Chapter 13, 41). It is as in "These are for everlasting life, and these are for disgrace and everlasting contempt" (Daniel 12:2). This is also the meaning of "He takes his share and the share of his friend in the Garden of Eden" (*Hagiga* 15, *Yalkut Shimoni*, Jeremiah, Chapter 17, 299). Although in truth, "No outcast shall be cast out from Him" (2 Samuel 14:14), this is so when all of the time of the 6,000 years is completed, at the end of which there is that time of the end, whose *Segula* [power] is to reveal that light of the power of unification that corrects everything and returns it to the wholeness of unity. But by the power of the righteous and their deeds that hasten the end, meaning that that light that was to emerge by itself in its time, they extended it early through the power of their deeds. For this reason, the whole of the corrected world at that time belongs specifically to the righteous themselves. Moreover, they are rewarded with the part of their friends, who were not rewarded by their actions, and therefore have no interest in being at that time, since the world is already corrected and "sins will cease from the land" (Psalms 104:35). At that time, they exist specifically in a manner of dust and everlasting contempt.

This is the meaning of *Kof-Tzadi* [forming the word "end" in Hebrew], *Reish-Dalet-Vav*, being four hundred years [in *Gematria*], and *Kof-Tzadi* [190 in *Gematria*] years is the merit of the righteous, and this is the future redemption.

This is the meaning of "You will see your world in your life" (*Berachot* 17), since when the *Sitra Achra* [other side] sees that the soul overcomes with corrections, she pours out all her wrath on it until it is sometimes captured in its net. Then she has permission to push the soul through the 49th gate. The *Sitra Achra* wants to push her through the 50th gate, as well, but there is where she completely fails, as in "He has fallen into the hole which he made" (Psalms 7:16). "He is punished by the work of his own hands" (*Pesachim* 28), since the Creator Himself seemingly becomes revealed over her and redeems her.

Introduction to The Study of the Ten Sefirot

1) At the outset of my words, I find a great need to break an iron wall that has been separating us from the wisdom of Kabbalah, since the ruin of the Temple to this generation. It lies heavily on us and arouses fear of being forgotten from Israel.

However, when I begin to speak to anyone about engaging in this study, his first question is, "Why should I know how many angels are in the sky and what their names are? Can I not keep the whole Torah in all its details and intricacies without this knowledge?"

Second, he will ask, "The sages have already determined that one must first fill one's belly with Mishnah and Gemara, and who can deceive himself that he has already completed the whole of the revealed Torah, and lacks only the wisdom of the hidden?"

Third, he is afraid that he will turn sour because of this engagement. This is because there have already been incidents of deviation from the path of Torah because of engagement in Kabbalah. Hence, "Why do I need this trouble? Who is so foolish as to place himself in danger for no reason?"

Fourth: Even those who favor this study permit it only to holy people, servants of the Creator, and not all who wish to take the Lord may come and take.

Fifth, and most important, "There is a conduct in our midst that, when in doubt, keep this: Do as the people do," and my eyes see that all those who study Torah in my generation have one view, and refrain from studying the hidden. Moreover, they advise those who ask them that it is undoubtedly preferable to study a page of Gemara instead of this engagement.

2) Indeed, if we set our hearts to answer but one very famous question, I am certain that all these questions and doubts will vanish from the horizon, and you will look unto their place to find them gone, meaning this indignant question that the whole world asks, namely, "What is the meaning of my life?" In other words, these numbered years of our life that cost us so heavily, and the numerous pains and torments that we suffer for them, to complete them to the fullest, who is it who enjoys them? Or even more precisely, whom do I delight?

It is indeed true that historians have grown weary contemplating it, and particularly in our generation, no one even wishes to consider it. Yet the question stands as bitterly and as vehemently as ever. Sometimes it meets us uninvited, pecks at our minds and degrades us to the ground before we find the famous ploy of flowing mindlessly in the currents of life as always.

3) Indeed, it is to resolve this great riddle that the verse says, "Taste and see that the Lord is good." Those who keep the Torah and *Mitzvot* [commandments] correctly are the ones who taste the taste of life. They are the ones who see and testify that the Lord is good, as our sages say, that He created the worlds to do good to His creations, since it is the conduct of The Good to do good.

Yet, those who have not yet tasted the taste of life of keeping Torah and *Mitzvot* cannot feel or understand that the Lord is good, as our sages said, that when the Creator created us, His sole purpose was to benefit us. Hence, we have no other counsel but to keep the Torah and *Mitzvot* as they should be.

It is written in the Torah (portion *Nitzavim*): "See, I have set before you this day life and good, and death and evil." This means that prior to the giving of the Torah, we had only death and evil before us, as our sages say, "The wicked, in their lives, are called 'dead,'" since their death is better than their lives, as the pain and suffering they endure for their sustenance is many times greater than the little pleasure they feel in this life.

However, now we have been granted Torah and *Mitzvot*, and by keeping it we are rewarded with the real life, joyful and delightful to its owner, as it is written, "Taste and see that the Lord is good." Hence, the writing says, "See, I have set before you this day life and good," which you did not have in reality at all prior to the giving of the Torah.

And the writing ends, "Therefore, choose life, so you may live, you and your descendants." There is a seemingly repeated statement here: "choose life, so you may live." Yet, it is a reference to life in keeping Torah and *Mitzvot*, which is when there is real life. However, a life without Torah and *Mitzvot* is harder than death. This is the meaning of the words of our sages, "The wicked, in their lives, are called 'dead.'"

The writing says, "so you may live, you and your descendants." It means that not only is a life without Torah joyless to its owner, but one also cannot delight others. One finds no contentment even in one's progeny, since the life of his progeny is also harder than death. Hence, what gift does he bequeath them?

However, not only does one who lives in Torah and *Mitzvot* enjoy his own life, but he is even happy to bear children and bequeath them this good life. This is the meaning of "so you may live, you and your descendants," for he receives additional pleasure in the life of his progeny, of which he was the cause.

4) Now you can understand the words of our sages about the verse, "Therefore, choose life" (See RASHI's interpretation). It states, "I instruct you to choose the part of life, as one who says to his son: 'Choose for yourself a good part in my land.' He places him on the good part and tells him, 'Choose this for yourself.'" It was said about this, "Lord, the portion of my inheritance and of my cup, You support my lot. You placed my hand on the good fate, to say, 'Take this for you.'"

The words are seemingly perplexing. The verse says, "Therefore, choose life." This means that one makes the choice by himself. However, they say that He places him on the good part. Thus, is there no longer choice here? Moreover, they say that the Creator puts one's hand on the good fate. This is indeed perplexing, because if this is so, where then is man's choice?

Now you can see the true meaning of their words. It is indeed true that the Creator Himself puts one's hand on the good fate by giving him a life of pleasure and contentment within the corporeal life that is filled with torment and pain, and devoid of any content. One necessarily departs and escapes them when he sees, even if it seemingly appears amidst the cracks, a tranquil place to escape there from this life, which is harder than death. Indeed, there is no greater placement of one's hand by Him than this.

And one's choice refers only to the strengthening. This is because there is certainly a great effort and exertion here before one refines one's body to be able to keep the Torah and Mitzvot correctly, not for his own pleasure, but to bring contentment to his Maker, which is called Lishma [for Her sake]. Only in this manner is one endowed with a life of happiness and pleasantness that come with keeping the Torah.

Before one comes to that refinement, there is certainly a choice to strengthen in the good way by all sorts of means and tactics. One should do whatever his hand finds the strength to do until he completes the work of refinement and will not fall under his burden midway.

5) According to the above, you will understand the words of our sages in the Masechet Avot: "Such is the path of Torah: Eat bread with salt, drink little water, sleep on the ground, lead a sorrowful life, and labor in the Torah. If so you do, happy are you; happy in this world and happy in the next world."

We must ask about their words: How is the wisdom of Torah different from the other teachings in the world, which do not require this self-tormenting and sorrowful life, but the labor itself is enough to acquire those teachings? Even though we labor extensively in the Torah, it is still not enough to acquire the wisdom of the Torah, except through the mortification of bread with salt and a sorrowful life.

The end of the words is even more surprising, as they said, "If so you do, happy are you in this world, and happy are you in the next world." This is because it is clear that it is possible to be happy in the next world. But in this world, while I torment myself in eating and drinking and sleeping, and I lead a sorrowful life, would it be said about such a life, "happy are you in this world?" Is this the meaning of a happy life in this world?

6) However, according to what is explained above, that engagement in the Torah and observing the Mitzvot correctly—under its strict condition to bestow contentment to one's Maker and not for one's own pleasure—is impossible to achieve except through great labor and exertion in purifying the body.

The first tactic is to accustom oneself not to receive anything for one's pleasure, even the permitted and necessary things for the existence of one's body, such as eating, drinking, sleeping, and other such necessities. In this manner, one will detach oneself completely from any pleasure that comes to him, even in the necessities, in the fulfillment of one's sustenance, until he leads a sorrowful life in its literal meaning.

Then, after one becomes accustomed to it and his body possesses no desire to receive any pleasure for itself, it is now possible for him to engage in the Torah and keep the Mitzvot in that manner, too, in order to bestow contentment upon his Maker and not at all for his own pleasure.

When one acquires this, he is rewarded with tasting the happy life, filled with delight and pleasure without any blemish of sorrow, which appear in the practice of Torah and Mitzvot Lishma. It is as Rabbi Meir says (Avot 6), "Anyone who engages in the Torah Lishma is granted many things. Moreover, the whole world is worthwhile for him, the secrets of Torah are revealed to him, and he becomes as a flowing spring."

It is about him that the verse says, "Taste and see that the Lord is good." One who tastes the flavor of the practice of Torah and Mitzvot Lishma is endowed with seeing the intention of creation, which is to do only good to His creations, as it is the conduct of The Good to do good. Then he rejoices and delights in the number of years of life that the Creator has granted him, and the whole world is worthwhile for him.

7) Now you will understand the two sides of the coin of engagement in Torah and Mitzvot: The first side is the path of Torah, meaning the extensive preparation one must make to prepare the purification of his body before he is rewarded with actual keeping of Torah and Mitzvot.

In that state, he necessarily engages in Torah and Mitzvot Lo Lishma [not for Her sake], but mixed with delighting himself, since he has not yet refined and cleansed his body from the will to receive pleasure from the vanities of this world. During this time, one must lead a sorrowful life and labor in the Torah, as it is written in the Mishnah.

However, after one completes the path of Torah, has already refined his body, and is now ready to keep the Torah and the Mitzvot Lishma, to bring contentment to his Maker, he comes to the other side of the coin, which is a life of pleasure and great tranquility, to which the intention of creation—"to do good to His creations"—refers, meaning the happiest life in this world and in the next world.

8) This explains the great difference between the wisdom of the Torah and the rest of the teachings in the world: Acquiring the other teachings in the world does not improve life in this world whatsoever, since they do not even render mere gratification for the torments and suffering one experiences during one's life. Hence, one need not correct one's body, and the labor that he gives in return for them is quite sufficient, as with all other worldly possessions acquired in return for labor and toil.

However, the sole purpose of engagement in Torah and Mitzvot is to make a person worthy of receiving all the goodness in the intention of creation, "to do good to His creations." Hence, one must necessarily refine one's body to merit that Godly goodness.

9) This also thoroughly clarifies the words of the Mishnah: "If so you do, happy are you in this world." They made this precision deliberately, to indicate that a happy life in this world is available only for those who have completed the path of Torah. Thus, the mortification in eating, drinking, sleeping, and a sorrowful life that are mentioned here apply only while being on the path of Torah. This is why they meticulously stated, "Such is the path of Torah."

And when one completes this path of *Lo Lishma* in sorrowful life and mortification, the Mishnah ends, "...happy are you in this world." This is because you will be granted that happiness and goodness in the intention of creation, and the whole world will be rewarding for you, even this world, and all the more so the next world.

10) *The Zohar* (*Beresheet*, Item 348 in *The Zohar* with the *Sulam* [ladder] commentary, *Beresheet* 1) writes about the verse, "And God said, 'Let there be light,' and there was light," let there be light for this world and let there be light for the next world. This means that the works of creation were created in their full stature and form, as our sages said, meaning in their fullest glory and perfection. Accordingly, the light that was created on the first day emerged in all its perfection, which contains the life of this world, too, in utter pleasantness and gentleness, as expressed in the words, "Let there be light."

However, to prepare a place of choice and labor, He stood and concealed it for the righteous in the future, as our sages said. Hence, they said in their pure words, "Let there be light for this world." However, it did not remain so, but rather "let there be light for the next world."

In other words, they who practice Torah and *Mitzvot Lishma* are rewarded with it only in the future, meaning at the time that will come in the future, after the completion of the refinement of their body in the path of Torah. Then they are rewarded with that great light in this world, too, as our sages said, "You will see your world in your life."

11) However, we find and see in the words of the sages of the Talmud that they have made the path of Torah easier for us than the sages of the Mishnah. This is because they said, "One should always practice the Torah and *Mitzvot*, even *Lo Lishma*, and from *Lo Lishma* he will come to *Lishma*, since the light in it reforms him."

Thus, they have provided us with a new means instead of the penance presented in the above-mentioned Mishnah, *Avot*: the "light in the Torah." It bears sufficient power to reform one and bring him to practice Torah and *Mitzvot Lishma*.

They did not mention penance here, but only that engagement in Torah and *Mitzvot* alone provides one with that light that reforms, so one may engage in Torah and *Mitzvot* in order to bring contentment to his Maker and not at all for his own pleasure. And this is called *Lishma*.

12) Yet, it seems we must question their words. After all, we have found a few students whose practice in Torah did not help them to come to *Lishma* through the

light in it. Indeed, practicing Torah and Mitzvot *Lo Lishma* means that one believes in the Creator, in the Torah, and in reward and punishment, and engages in the Torah because the Creator commanded the engagement, but associates his own pleasure with bringing contentment to his Maker.

If, after all one's trouble in the practice of Torah and Mitzvot, he will learn that no pleasure or personal benefit came to him through this great exertion and strain, he will regret having made all his efforts. This is because from the very beginning, he has misled himself thinking that he, too, would enjoy his exertion. This is called *Lo Lishma* (as it is written in the *Tosfot, Rosh Hashanah*).

Nonetheless, our sages permitted the beginning of the practice in Torah and Mitzvot also *Lo Lishma*, since from *Lo Lishma* one comes to *Lishma*. However, there is no doubt that if that student has not yet been rewarded with faith in the Creator and His law, but still has doubts, it is not about him that our sages said, "From *Lo Lishma* he will come to *Lishma*." It is not about him that they said that by engaging in it, the light in it reforms them (*Midrash Rabbah, Ptichta de Eicha*, and the Jerusalem Talmud, *Hagigah*, Chapter 1, Rule 7, "From *Lo Lishma*, one comes to *Lishma*" (*Eicha Rabbah, Peticha* 2).

This is so because the light in the Torah shines only to those with faith. Moreover, the measure of that light is as the measure of the force of one's faith. Yet, to those without faith it is the opposite, as it is written, "To the left leaning in it – a potion of death" (*Shabbat* 88), for they receive darkness from the Torah and their eyes darken.

13) Sages have already presented a nice allegory about this matter regarding the verse, "Woe unto you who desire the day of the Lord! Why do you need the day of the Lord? It is darkness and not light" (Amos 5). There is an allegory about a rooster and a bat that were awaiting the light. The rooster said to the bat, "I await the light for the light is mine. But you, why do you need the light?" (*Sanhedrin* 98b).

Clearly, those students who were not endowed with coming from *Lo Lishma* to *Lishma* due to their lack of faith, and therefore did not receive any light from the Torah, will therefore walk in darkness and shall die without wisdom.

But those who were imparted complete faith are guaranteed in the words of our sages that because they engage in the Torah even *Lo Lishma*, the light in it reforms them. They will be imparted the Torah *Lishma*, which brings a happy and good life in this world and in the next world, even without the prior affliction and sorrowful life. It is about them that the verse says, "Then shall you delight in the Lord and I will make you ride upon the high places of the earth."

14) Concerning such a matter as the above, I once interpreted the saying of our sages, "He whose Torah is his trade." The measure of his faith is apparent in his practice of Torah because the letters of the word *Umanuto* [his trade] are the same [in Hebrew] as the letters of the word *Emunato* [his faith].

It is like a person who trusts his friend and lends him money. He may trust him with a pound, but if he asks him for two pounds he will refuse to lend him. He might also trust him with a hundred pounds but not more. Also, he might trust him enough to lend him half his possessions, but not all his possessions. Finally, he may trust him with all his possessions without a hint of fear. This last faith is considered "complete faith," and the previous forms are considered "incomplete faith." Rather, it is partial faith, whether more or less.

Similarly, one allots oneself only an hour a day to practice Torah and work out of the measure of his faith in the Creator. Another allots two hours, according to the measure of his faith in the Creator. The third does not neglect even a single moment of his free time without engaging in Torah and work. Thus, only the faith of the last one is complete since he trusts the Creator with all his possessions. The previous ones, however, their faith is still incomplete.

15) Thus, it has been thoroughly clarified that one should not expect that engagement in Torah and *Mitzvot Lo Lishma* will bring him to *Lishma*, except when one knows in one's soul that he has been granted faith in the Creator and in His Torah as it should be. This is because then the light in it reforms him and he will be rewarded with "the day of the Lord," which is all light, for the *Kedusha* [holiness] of faith purifies one's eyes to enjoy His light until the light in the Torah reforms him.

Yet, those without faith are as bats. They cannot look at the light of day because the daylight has been inverted for them to a more terrible darkness than the darkness of the night, as they are only fed in the darkness of the night.

Likewise, the eyes of the faithless are blinded to the light of the Creator. Hence, the light becomes darkness for them, and the potion of life is turned into a potion of death for them. It is about them that the writing says, "Woe unto you who desire the day of the Lord! Why do you need the day of the Lord? It is darkness and not light." Thus, first, one must make one's faith complete.

16) This answers yet another question in the *Tosfot* (*Taanit*, p 7), who say there, "Anyone who practices Torah *Lishma*, his Torah becomes to him a potion of life. And anyone who practices Torah *Lo Lishma*, his Torah becomes to him a potion of death." They asked, "Yet, we said, 'One should always engage in the Torah, even if *Lo Lishma*, since from *Lo Lishma* he will come to *Lishma*.'"

According to the explained above, we should divide it simply: One who engages in Torah for the *Mitzva* of learning Torah, and believes in reward and punishment, but associates self-pleasure and benefit with the intention to bring contentment to his Maker, the light in it will reform him and he will achieve *Lishma*. And one who learns Torah not for the *Mitzva* of learning Torah, since he does not believe in reward and punishment to the extent that he should labor so much for it, but exerts only for his own pleasure, it becomes a potion of death for him, since for him, the light in it is turned to darkness.

17) Hence, the student pledges, prior to the study, to strengthen himself in faith in the Creator and in His guidance in reward and punishment, as our sages said, "Your employer is liable to pay you the reward for your work." One should aim one's labor to be for the *Mitzvot* of the Torah, and in this way, he will be rewarded with enjoying the light in it, and his faith will strengthen and grow through the power in this light, as it is written, "It shall be health to your navel, and marrow to your bones" (Proverbs 3:8).

Then one can be certain that from *Lo Lishma* he will come to *Lishma*, in a way that even one who knows about himself that he has not been rewarded with faith still has hope through the practice of Torah, for if he sets his heart and mind to attain faith in the Creator through it, there is no greater *Mitzva* than this. It is as our sages said, "Habakkuk came and stressed only this: 'A righteous shall live by his faith'" (*Makkot* 24).

Moreover, there is no other counsel but this, as it is written (*Baba Batra*, p 16a), "Raba said, 'Job wished to rid the whole world of judgment. He said to Him, 'Master of the world, You have created the righteous; You have created the wicked; who holds You down?''"

And RASHI interprets there: "You have created the righteous through the good inclination; You have created the wicked through the evil inclination. Hence, none are saved from Your hand, for who holds You down? Coerced are the sinners." And what did the friends of Job reply? "Indeed, you revoke fear and impair prayer before God; the Creator created the evil inclination, He has created for it the Torah as a spice" (Job 15).

RASHI interprets there: "Created for it the Torah," which is a spice that revokes "thoughts of transgression," as it is said, "If you come across this villain, pull him to the seminary. If he is a stone, he will soften. Hence, not coerced are they, for they could save themselves" (*Kidushin*, p 30).

18) Clearly, they cannot rid themselves of the judgment. If they say that they received that spice and still have thoughts of transgression, meaning that they are still in doubt and the evil inclination has not yet melted, for the Creator, Who created it and gave the evil inclination its strength, evidently knew to create the remedy and the spice liable to wear off the power of the evil inclination and eradicate it altogether.

And if one practices Torah and fails to remove the evil inclination from himself, it is either that he has been negligent in giving the necessary labor and exertion in the practice of Torah, as it is written, "I did not labor and found, do not believe," or perhaps he did put in the necessary amount of labor, but has been negligent in the quality.

This means that while practicing Torah, they did not set their minds and hearts to draw the light in the Torah, which brings faith to one's heart. Rather, they have been absent-minded about the principal requirement demanded of the Torah, namely the light that yields faith. And although they initially aimed for it, their minds went astray during the study.

Either way, one cannot rid oneself of the judgment by arguing coercion, for our sages strictly state, "I have created the evil inclination; I have created for it the Torah as a spice." If there had been any exceptions in this, then Job's question would remain valid.

19) Through all that has been explained thus far, I have removed a great complaint about the words of Rav Chaim Vital in his introduction to *Shaar HaHakdamot* [*Gate to Introductions*] by the ARI, and the introduction to the book *Tree of Life*. He writes, "Indeed, one should not say, 'I shall go and engage in the wisdom of Kabbalah' before he engages in the Torah, Mishnah, and Talmud. This is because our sages have already said, 'One should not enter the PARDESS* unless he has filled his stomach with meat and wine.'"

This is like a soul without a body: It has no reward or act or consideration before it is connected in a body, when it is whole, corrected in the *Mitzvot* of the Torah, in 613 *Mitzvot*.

Conversely, when one is occupied with the wisdom of the Mishnah and Babylonian Talmud, and does not give a part to the secrets of Torah and its concealments, as well, it is like a body that sits in the darkness without a human soul, God's candle, which shines within it. Thus, the body is dry and does not draw from a source of life.

Thus, a wise disciple, who practices Torah *Lishma*, should first engage in the wisdom of the Bible, the Mishnah and the Talmud, as long as his mind can tolerate. Afterward, he will delve into knowing his Maker in the wisdom of truth.

It is as King David commanded his son Solomon: "Know the God of your father and serve Him." And if that person finds the study of the Talmud heavy and difficult, he is better off leaving it once he has tested his luck in this wisdom, and engage in the wisdom of truth.

It is written, "A disciple who has not seen a good sign in his learning within five years will also not see it" (*Hullin*, p 24). Thus, every person for whom learning is easy must dedicate a portion of one or two hours a day to study the *Halachah* [Jewish conducts] and explain and interpret the questions in the literal *Halachah*.

20) These words of his seem very perplexing: He says that before one succeeds in the study of the revealed, one should already engage in the wisdom of truth. This contradicts his own words from before, that the wisdom of Kabbalah without the literal Torah is as a soul without a body, having no deed, consideration, or reward.

The evidence he brings of a disciple who did not see a good sign is even more perplexing, for did our sages say that he should therefore abandon the learning of Torah? Certainly, it is to caution him to examine his ways and try with another teacher or in another portion. But he must certainly not leave the Torah, even the literal Torah.

---

* See explanation in the essay PARDESS.

21) Another perplexity is that both the words of Rav Chaim Vital and the words of the Gemara imply that one needs some specific preparation and merit to be rewarded with the wisdom of Torah. Yet, our sages said (*Midrash Rabbah*, portion "And This Is the Blessing"), "The Creator said to Israel: 'Regard, the whole wisdom and the whole Torah are easy: Anyone who fears Me and observes the words of the Torah, the whole wisdom and the whole Torah are in his heart.'"

Thus, we need no prior merit here, but only by virtue of fear of the Creator and the keeping of *Mitzvot* is one granted the whole wisdom of the Torah.

22) Indeed, if we examine his words, they will become as clear to us as the purity of the heavens themselves. What he wrote, "he is better off leaving his hand off it, once he has tested his luck in the wisdom of the revealed," does not refer to luck of wit and erudition. Rather, it is as we explained above in the interpretation of "I have created the evil inclination; I have created for it the Torah as a spice." It means that he has delved and exerted in the revealed Torah, and still the evil inclination is in power and has not melted at all. This is because he is still not saved from thoughts of transgression, as RASHI writes above in the explanation, "I have created for it the Torah as a spice."

Hence, he advises him to leave it and engage in the wisdom of truth, for it is easier to draw the light in the Torah while practicing and laboring in the wisdom of truth than in laboring in the revealed Torah. The reason is very simple: The wisdom of the revealed Torah is clothed in external, corporeal clothes, such as stealing, plundering, torts, etc. For this reason, it is difficult and heavy for any person to aim his mind and heart to the Creator while learning, so as to draw the light in the Torah.

It is even more so for a person for whom learning the Talmud itself is heavy and arduous. How can he remember the Creator during the study, since the scrutiny concerns corporeal matters, and cannot come in him simultaneously with the intention for the Creator?

Therefore, he advises him to engage in the wisdom of Kabbalah, as this wisdom is clothed entirely in the names of the Creator. Then he will certainly be able to easily aim his mind and heart to the Creator during the study, even if it is very difficult for him to study, for the study of the issues of the wisdom and the Creator are one and the same, and this is very simple.

23) Hence, he brings good evidence from the words of the Gemara: "A disciple who has not seen a good sign in his study after five years will also not see it." Why did he not see a good sign in his study? Certainly, it is only due to absence of the intention of the heart, and not for any lack of aptitude, as the wisdom of Torah requires no aptitude.

Instead, as it is written in the above *Midrash*: "The Creator said to Israel, 'Regard, the whole wisdom and the whole Torah are easy: Anyone who fears Me and observes the words of the Torah, the whole wisdom and the whole Torah are in his heart.'"

Of course, one must accustom oneself in the light of Torah and *Mitzvot*, and I do not know how much. One might remain in waiting all of his seventy years. Hence, the Braita warns us (*Hulin* 24) not to wait longer than five years.

Moreover, Rabbi Yosi says that only three years are quite sufficient to be granted the wisdom of the Torah (*Hulin* 24). If one does not see a good sign after this long, he should not fool himself with false hopes and deceit, but know that he will never see a good sign.

Hence, one must immediately find himself a good tactic by which to succeed in achieving *Lishma* and to be rewarded with the wisdom of the Torah. The Braita did not specify the tactic, but it warns not to remain in the same situation and wait longer.

This is the meaning of the Rav's words, that the surest and most successful tactic is the engagement in the wisdom of Kabbalah. One should leave one's hand entirely from engagement in the wisdom of the revealed Torah, since he has already tested his luck in it and did not succeed. And he should dedicate all his time to the wisdom of Kabbalah, where his success is certain for the above-said reasons.

24) This is very simple, for these words have no connection to the study of the revealed Torah, in anything that one must actually practice, for "It is not the ignorant who is pious, and a mistaken learning makes for evil, and one sinner destroys much good." Hence, one must necessarily repeat them as much as is necessary so as not to fail in one's practice.

Rather, here it speaks only of the study of the wisdom of the revealed Torah, to explain and scrutinize questions that arise in the interpretation of the laws, as Rav Chaim Vital himself deduces there. It refers to the part of the study of the Torah that is not performed in practice, or to the actual laws.

Indeed, here it is possible to be lenient and learn from the abbreviations and not from the origins. However, this, too, requires extensive learning, since one who knows from the origin is not as one who knows it from a brief scan of some abbreviation. In order not to err in this, Rav Chaim Vital says at the very outset of his words that the soul connects to the body only when it is complete, corrected in the *Mitzvot* of the Torah, in 613 *Mitzvot*.

25) Now you will see how all the questions we presented in the beginning of the introduction are complete folly. They are the obstacles that the evil inclination spreads in order to hunt innocent souls, to dismiss them from the world, robbed and abused.

Examine the first question, where they imagine that they can keep the whole Torah without knowing the wisdom of Kabbalah. I say to them: Indeed, if you can keep the study of Torah and the observance of the *Mitzvot* appropriately, *Lishma*, meaning only in order to bring contentment to the Maker, then indeed, you do not need to study Kabbalah. This is because then it is said about you, "One's soul shall teach him." This is because then all the secrets of the Torah will appear before you like an ever flowing spring, as in the words of Rabbi Meir in the above Mishnah (*Avot*), and you will need no assistance from the books.

However, if you are still learning *Lo Lishma*, but hope to merit *Lishma* by this, then I ask you: "How many years have you been doing so?" If you are still within the five years, as the Tana Kama says, or within the three years, as Rabbi Yosi says, then you can still wait and hope.

But if you have been practicing the Torah *Lo Lishma* for more than three years, as Rabbi Yosi says, and five years, as the Tana Kama says, then the Braita warns you that you will not see a good sign in this path you are treading! Why delude your souls with false hopes when you have such a near and sure tactic as the study of the wisdom of Kabbalah, as I have shown the reason above, that the study in the issues of the wisdom and the Creator Himself are one?

26) Let us also examine the second question, which is that one must first fill one's belly with Mishnah and Gemara. Everyone agrees that it is indeed so. Yet, this is all true if you have already been endowed with learning *Lishma*, or even *Lo Lishma*, if you are still within the three years or the five years. However, after that time, the Braita warns you that you will never see a good sign, and so you must test your success in the study of Kabbalah.

27) We must also know that there are two parts to the wisdom of truth: The first, called the "secrets of Torah," must not be exposed except by intimation, and from a Kabbalist sage to a disciple who understands in his own mind. *Maase Merkava* and *Maase Beresheet* belong to that part, as well. The sages of *The Zohar* refer to that part as "the first three *Sefirot*, *Keter*, *Hochma*, *Bina*," and it is also called "the *Rosh* [head] of the *Partzuf*."

The second part is called the "flavors of Torah." It is permitted to disclose them and indeed, a great *Mitzva* to disclose them. *The Zohar* refers to it as the "seven lower *Sefirot* of the *Partzuf*," and it is also called the *Guf* [body] of the *Partzuf*.

Every single *Partzuf* of *Kedusha* [holiness] consists of ten *Sefirot*. These are called *Keter*, *Hochma*, *Bina*, *Hesed*, *Gevura*, *Tifferet*, *Netzah*, *Hod*, *Yesod*, *Malchut*. The first three *Sefirot* are called the *Rosh* of the *Partzuf*, and the seven lower *Sefirot* are named the *Guf* of the *Partzuf*. Even the soul of the lower man contains the ten *Sefirot* in their above names, as well, and every single discernment, in the upper and in the lower.

The reason why the seven lower *Sefirot*, which are the *Guf* of the *Partzuf*, are called "flavors of Torah" is the meaning of the verse, "and the palate tastes its food." The lights that appear under the first three, namely the *Rosh*, are called *Taamim* [flavors], and *Malchut* of the *Rosh* is called *Chech* [palate].

For this reason, they are called *Taamim* of Torah. This means that they appear in the palate of the *Rosh*, which is the source of all the *Taamim*, which is *Malchut* of *Rosh*.

From there down it is not forbidden to disclose them. Quite the contrary, the reward of one who discloses them is immeasurable and boundless.

Also, these first three *Sefirot* and these seven lower *Sefirot* expand both in the general and in the most particular item that can be divided. Thus, even the first three *Sefirot* of the *Malchut* at the end of the world of *Assiya* belong to the section of the "secrets of Torah," which are forbidden to be disclosed. And the seven lower *Sefirot* in the *Keter* of the *Rosh* of *Atzilut* belong to the section "*Taamim* of Torah," which are permitted to be disclosed, and these words are written in the books of Kabbalah.

28) You will find the source of these words in *Masechet Pesachim* (p 119), where it is said, it is written (Isaiah 23), "And her gain and her hire shall be holiness to the Lord; it shall not be treasured nor laid up; for her gain shall be for them that dwell before the Lord, to eat their fill, and for stately clothing [lit. covering *Atik*]." "What is 'stately clothing [covering *Atik*]'? This is what covers things that *Atik Yomin* covered. And what are those? The secrets of the Torah. Others say, this is what reveals things that *Atik Yomin* covered. What are those? The flavors of the Torah."

RASHBAM interprets, "*Atik Yomin* is the Creator," as it is written, "and *Atik Yomin* sits." The secrets of the Torah are *Maase Merkava* and *Maase Beresheet*. The meaning of "name" is as it is written, "This is My name forever." The "clothing" means that He does not give them to any person, but only to those whose heart is worried. As it is written in "one does not learn": "This is what reveals things that *Atik Yomin* covered." This means covering the secrets of the Torah, which were covered in the beginning, and *Atik Yomin* disclosed them and gave permission to disclose them. One who discloses them is granted what he said in this verse.

29) Now you evidently see the great difference between the secrets of Torah, where all who attain them receive this great reward (explained there in the Gemara, in the interpretation of the verse) for covering them and for not disclosing them. And it is to the contrary with the flavors of the Torah, where all who attain them receive this great reward for disclosing them to others.

Some say that there is no dispute regarding the first opinion, but only an examination of the different meanings between them. The first meaning explains the end, as it says, "covering *Atik*." Hence, they interpret the attainment of the great reward for covering the secrets of Torah.

Others say it explains the beginning, "eat their fill," meaning the *Taamim* [flavors] of the Torah, as it is written, "and the palate tastes food." This is because the lights of *Taamim* are called "eating"; hence, they interpret the attainment of the great reward, mentioned in the verse, regarding one who discloses the flavors of the Torah. However, both think that the secrets of the Torah must be covered, and the flavors of the Torah must be disclosed.

30) Thus you have a clear answer about the fourth and the fifth questions in the beginning of the introduction. What you find in the words of our sages, as well as in

the holy books, that it is only given to one whose heart is worried, meaning the part called "secrets of the Torah," which is the first three *Sefirot*, the *Rosh*, that it is given to only concealed ones and under certain conditions, you will not find even a trace of them in all the books of Kabbalah, in writing or in print, since those are the things that *Atik Yomin* covered, as it is written in the Gemara.

Moreover, do say if it is possible to even think or picture that all those holy and famous righteous, which are the greatest and best in the nation, such as *Sefer Yetzira* [Book of Creation], *The Book of Zohar*, and the Braita of Rabbi Ishmael, Rav Hai Gaon, and Rav Hamai Gaon, Rabbi Elazar of Garmiza, and the rest of the *Rishonim* [first ones] through Nachmanides, and Baal HaTurim and the Baal Shulchan Aruch through the Vilna Gaon [GRA], and the Ladi Gaon, and the rest of the righteous, from whom we received the whole of the revealed Torah, and by whose words we live, to know which act to do so as to be favored by the Creator. All of them wrote and published books in the wisdom of Kabbalah. And there is no greater disclosure than writing a book, whose author does not know who reads his book. It is possible that complete wicked will scrutinize it. Hence, there is no greater uncovering of secrets of Torah than this.

And we must not doubt these holy and pure, that they might infringe even an iota of what is written and explained in the Mishnah and the Gemara, that they are forbidden to disclose, as it is written in the prohibition to learn (in *Masechet Hagigah*).

Rather, all the written and printed books are necessarily considered the flavors of the Torah, which *Atik Yomin* first covered and then uncovered, as it is written, "the palate tastes food." Not only are these secrets not forbidden to disclose, but on the contrary, it is a great *Mitzva* [commandment] to disclose them (as it is written in *Pesachim* 119).

And one who knows how to disclose and discloses them, his reward is plentiful. This is because by disclosing these lights to many, particularly to the many, depends the coming of the Messiah, soon in our days, Amen.

31) There is a great need to explain once and for all why the coming of the Messiah depends on the study of Kabbalah in the masses, which is so prevalent in *The Zohar* and in all the books of Kabbalah. The public has discussed it pointlessly to the point that it has become intolerable.

The explanation of this matter is explained in *Tikkuney* [corrections of] *Zohar* [part of *The Zohar*] (*Tikkun* 30, "Second Path"). These are its words: Second path, "And the *Ruach* [spirit/wind] of God hovered over the face of the water. What is "and the *Ruach*"? Indeed, when the *Shechina* [Divinity] descends into exile, that *Ruach* [wind/spirit] blows upon those who engage in the Torah because the *Shechina* is among them.

All flesh is hay, they are all as beasts that eat hay, and all its mercy is as the flower of the field (Isaiah 40). Every mercy they do, they do for themselves. Even all those who exert in Torah, every mercy they do, they do for themselves.

At that time, and He remembered that they were flesh, a wind [spirit] that passes and will not return (Psalms 78) to the world. This is the spirit of the Messiah. Woe unto they who make it leave and not return to the world. They make the Torah dry and do not want to exert in the wisdom of Kabbalah. They cause the fountain of wisdom, which is the *Yod* in it, to depart. The spirit that leaves is the spirit of the Messiah, the spirit of holiness, the spirit of wisdom and understanding, the spirit of counsel and might, the spirit of knowledge and the fear of the Creator.

Second commandment: "And God said, 'Let there be light,' and there was light." This is love, which is the love of mercy, as it is written, "I have loved you with an everlasting love; therefore, I have drawn you with mercy." It is said about this, "If you awaken and if you stir up the love while it pleases," etc., love and fear are its core. Whether good or bad, for this reason, it is called fear and love in order to receive reward. And because of it, the Creator said, I adjure you, daughters of Jerusalem, by the gazelles and by the hinds of the field, if you awaken and if you stir up the love while it pleases, which is love without reward, and not in order to receive reward. This is because fear and love in order to receive reward are of a handmaid, and under three, the earth quakes, etc., under a slave when he becomes a king, and a handmaid that inherits her mistress.

32) We shall begin to explain the *Tikkunim* of *The Zohar* from toe to head. He says that the fear and the love one has in the practice of Torah and *Mitzvot* in order to receive reward, meaning while hoping for some benefit from the Torah and the work, this is considered the handmaid. It is written about her, "a handmaid that inherits her mistress."

This is seemingly perplexing, for it is accepted that "One should always engage in Torah and *Mitzvot*, even *Lo Lishma*," and why did the earth quake? In addition, we must understand the correlation of the engagement in *Lo Lishma* specifically to the handmaid, and also the allegory that she inherits her mistress. What inheritance is there here?

33) You will understand the matter with everything that has been explained above in this introduction, that they did not permit the study *Lo Lishma* but only since front *Lo Lishma* one comes to *Lishma*, since the light in it reforms him. Hence, engagement *Lo Lishma* is considered a helping handmaid who performs the ignoble works for her mistress, who is the *Shechina*.

This is because at last, one will achieve *Lishma* and will be rewarded with the installing of the *Shechina*. Then, the maid, which is the engagement *Lo Lishma*, will also be considered a handmaid of *Kedusha* [holiness], for she supports and prepares the *Kedusha*, though she will be considered the world of *Assiya* of the *Kedusha*.

However, if one's faith is incomplete, and he engages in the Torah and in the work only because the Creator commanded him to study, then we have seen above that in such Torah and work the light will not be revealed at all, since his eyes are flawed and turn the light into darkness like a bat.

Such engagement is no longer considered a maid of *Kedusha*, since he will not acquire *Lishma* through it. Hence, it comes to the domain of the handmaid of *Klipa* [shell/peel], which inherits these Torah and work and robs them for herself.

Hence, "the earth quaked," meaning the *Shechina*, called "earth," since those Torah and work that should have come to her, as possessions of the *Shechina*, that evil handmaid robs and lowers them into the possession of the *Klipot* [pl. of *Klipa*]. Thus, the handmaid inherits her mistress.

34) The *Tikkuney Zohar* interprets the meaning of the oath, "If you awaken and if you stir up the love while it pleases." The precision is that Israel will draw the light of the upper *Hesed* [mercy], called "love of mercy," since this is what is desired. This is drawn particularly by the engagement in Torah and *Mitzvot* not in order to receive reward. The reason is that the light of the upper wisdom is extended to Israel through this light of mercy, appearing and clothing in this light of mercy, which Israel extends.

And this light of wisdom is the meaning of the verse, "And the spirit of the Lord shall rest upon him, the spirit of wisdom and understanding, the spirit of counsel and might, the spirit of knowledge and of fear of the Lord" (Isaiah 11), said about the Messiah King. It is as is said there below, "And He will set up a standard for the nations, and will assemble the dispersed of Israel, and gather together the scattered of Judah from the four corners of the earth." This is because after Israel extends the light of wisdom through the light of mercy, as in "the spirit of wisdom and understanding," etc., the Messiah appears and assembles the dispersed of Israel.

Thus, everything depends on the practice of Torah and work *Lishma*, which can extend the great light of mercy where the light of wisdom clothes and extends. This is the meaning of the oath, "If you awaken and if you stir up." It is so because complete redemption and assembling the exiles are impossible without it, since so are the channels of *Kedusha* arranged.

35) They also interpreted "and the spirit of God hovered over the face of the waters." What is "the spirit of God"? When the *Shechina* is in exile, that wind [also "spirit"] blows on those who engage in Torah because the *Shechina* is with them. Interpretation: During the exile, when Israel were still occupied in Torah and *Mitzvot Lo Lishma*, if they are in this way because from *Lo Lishma* one comes to *Lishma*, then the *Shechina* is among them, though in a state of exile since he still did not achieve *Lishma*. As was said above, it is in the form of a handmaid of *Kedusha*.

This is the meaning of the *Shechina* being among them, meaning in concealment. However, they are bound to attain the revelation of *Shechina*, and then the spirit of the Messiah King hovers on the engaging and awakens them to come to *Lishma*, as in "the light in it reforms them," aiding and preparing the installation of the *Shechina*, which is her mistress.

Yet, if this learning *Lo Lishma* is not suitable to bring them to *Lishma*, for the above-mentioned reason, the *Shechina* regrets and says "All flesh is hay, they are all as beasts that eat hay." In other words, that spirit of man, which ascends upward, is not present among those who engage in Torah. Rather, they settle for the spirit of the beast, which descends downward.

They interpret the reason there: All its mercy is as the flower of the field. Even all those who exert in Torah, every mercy they do, they do for themselves. That is, their whole engagement in Torah and *Mitzvot* is only for their own benefit and pleasure, and the engagement in the Torah cannot bring them to *Lishma*.

He writes there, "At that time, and He remembered that they were flesh, a wind [spirit] that passes and will not return to the world, and this is the spirit of the Messiah. This means that the spirit of the Messiah does not hover on them but leaves them and will not return since the impure maid robs their Torah and inherits her mistress, since they are not on the way to come from *Lo Lishma* to *Lishma*.

For this reason, he deduces there that they are the ones who make the Torah dry and do not want to exert in the wisdom of Kabbalah. That is, even though they do not succeed through the practice in the revealed Torah, since there is no light in it and it is dry due to the smallness of their minds (see Item 16), they could still succeed by engaging in the study of Kabbalah, for the light in it is clothed in the clothing of the Creator—the Holy names and the *Sefirot*. Thus, they could easily come to that state of *Lo Lishma* that brings them to *Lishma*. Then the spirit of God would hover over them, as it is written, "the light in it reforms them."

Yet, they have no wish at all for the study of Kabbalah. And this is the meaning of "Woe unto them for they cause poverty, ruin, looting, killing, and destruction in the world. That spirit which departed is the spirit of the Messiah, as was said, the spirit of holiness, the spirit of wisdom and understanding," etc.

36) We learn from the *Tikkuney Zohar* that there is an oath that the light of mercy and love will not awaken in the world before Israel's works in Torah and *Mitzvot* will have the intention not to receive reward, but only to bestow contentment upon the Maker. This is the meaning of the oath, "I adjure you, daughters of Jerusalem."

Thus, the length of the exile and affliction that we suffer depends on us and waits for us to merit the practice of Torah and *Mitzvot Lishma*. And if we only merit this, this light of love and mercy, which has the power to extend as in the words, "And the spirit shall rest upon him, the spirit of wisdom and understanding," etc., will immediately awaken, and then we will be rewarded with complete redemption.

It has also been clarified that it is impossible for the whole of Israel to come to that great purity except through the study of Kabbalah, which is the easiest way, suitable even for commoners.

Conversely, while engaging only in the revealed Torah, it is impossible to be rewarded through it, except for a chosen few and after great efforts, but not for the majority of people for the reason explained in Item 22. This thoroughly explains the irrelevance of the fourth and fifth questions in the beginning of the introduction.

37) The third question, which is the fear that one will turn sour, well, there is no fear here at all. This is because the deviation from the path of the Creator that occurred before was for two reasons: 1) Either they broke the words of our sages with things they were forbidden to disclose, 2) or because they perceived the words of the Kabbalah in their superficial meaning, as corporeal instructions, breaching "You shall not make unto you a statue or any image."

Hence, until today there has indeed been a fortified wall around this wisdom. Many have tried to begin to study but could not continue for lack of understanding and because of the corporeal appellations. This is why I have labored with the interpretation, *Panim Meirot* and *Panim Masbirot*, to interpret the great book *Tree of Life*, by the ARI, to make the corporeal forms abstract and to establish them as spiritual laws, above time and place. Thus, any beginner can understand the matters, their reasons, and explanations with a clear mind and great simplicity, no less than one understands Gemara through the RASHI interpretation.

38) Let us continue to elaborate on the necessity to practice Torah and *Mitzvot Lishma* of which I began to speak. We must understand that name, "Torah *Lishma*," why the desirable and complete work is defined by the name *Lishma*, and the undesirable work named *Lo Lishma*.

The literal meaning implies that one who engages in Torah and *Mitzvot* to aim his heart to bring contentment to his Maker and not to himself should have been referred to as Torah *Lishmo* [for His sake] and Torah *Lo Lishmo* [not for His sake], meaning for the sake of the Creator. Why, then, is this defined by the name *Lishma* and *Lo Lishma*, meaning for the sake of the Torah?

There is certainly something more to understand here than the aforementioned, since the verse proves that Torah *Lishmo*, meaning to bring contentment to His Maker, is still not enough. Rather, the learning must be *Lishma*, meaning for sake of the Torah. This requires explanation.

39) The thing is that it is known that the name of the Torah is "Torah of life," as it is written, "For they are life unto they who find them" (Proverbs 4:22). It is also written, "For it is no vain thing for you, for it is your life" (Deuteronomy 32:47). Hence, the meaning of Torah *Lishma* is that the practice of Torah and *Mitzvot* brings one life and long days, and then the Torah is as its name. And one who does not aim his heart and mind to the aforesaid, the practice of Torah and *Mitzvot* brings him the opposite of life and longevity, meaning completely *Lo Lishma*, since its name is "Torah of life." These words are explained in the words of our sages (*Taanit* 7a): "Anyone who practices Torah *Lo Lishma*, his Torah becomes for him a potion of death, and anyone who practices Torah *Lishma*, his Torah becomes for him a potion of life."

However, their words require explanation, to understand how and by what does the holy Torah become a potion of death for him? Not only are his work and exertion in vain, and he receives no benefit from his labor and exertion, but the Torah and the work themselves become a potion of death for him. This is indeed perplexing.

40) First, we must understand the words of our sages (*Megillah* 6b), who said, "I labored and found—believe; I did not labor and found—do not believe."

We must ask about "I labored and found." They seem to contradict one another since labor refers to work and exertion that one gives in return for any desired possession. For an important possession, one makes great efforts, and for a lesser possession, one makes fewer efforts.

Its opposite is finding. Its conduct is to come to a person completely absentmindedly and without any preparation in labor, toil, and price. Hence, how can you say, "I labored and found"? And if there is effort here, it should have said, "I labored and purchased" or "I labored and was awarded," etc., and not "I labored and found."

41) *The Zohar* writes about the text "Those who seek Me shall find Me," and asks, "Where does one find the Creator?" They said that the Creator is found only in the Torah. Also, regarding the verse, "Indeed, You are a God who hides," that the Creator hides Himself in the holy Torah.

We must understand their words properly. It seems as though the Creator is hidden only in corporeal things and conducts, and in all the futilities of this world, which are outside the Torah. Thus, how can you say the opposite, that He hides Himself only in the Torah?

There is also the general meaning, that the Creator hides Himself in a way that He must be sought; why does He need this concealment? And also, "All who seek Him shall find Him," which we understand from the verse, "Those who seek Me shall find Me." We must thoroughly understand this seeking and this finding, what are they and why are they.

42) Indeed, you should know that the reason for our great distance from the Creator, and that we are so prone to transgress His will, is for but one reason which became the source of all the torment and suffering we suffer, and for all the sins and the mistakes that we fail in. Clearly, by removing that reason, we will instantly be rid of any sorrow or pain. We will immediately be granted adhesion with Him in heart, soul, and might. And I tell you that that preliminary reason is none other than "our lack of understanding of His guidance over His creations," that we do not understand Him properly.

43) If, for example, the Creator were to establish open Providence with His creations in that, for instance, anyone who eats something forbidden would choke on the spot, and anyone who performs a *Mitzva* would discover such wonderful pleasures in it, like the finest pleasures in this corporeal world, then 1) what fool

would even contemplate tasting something forbidden, knowing that he would immediately lose his life as a result, just as one does not contemplate jumping into a fire? 2) Also, what fool would leave any *Mitzva* without performing it as quickly as possible, just as one cannot retire from or linger with a great corporeal pleasure that comes into his hand, without receiving it as quickly as he can? Thus, if Providence were open to us, all the people in the world would be complete righteous.

44) Thus, you see that all we need in our world is open Providence. If we had open Providence, all the people in the world would be complete righteous and would also adhere to Him with absolute love, for it would certainly be a great honor for any one of us to befriend and love Him with our heart and soul, and always adhere to Him without losing even a minute.

However, since it is not so, and a *Mitzva* is not rewarded in this world, and those who defy His will are not punished before our eyes, but the Creator is patient with them, and moreover, sometimes the opposite seems to be the case, as it is written (Psalms 73), "Behold, those wicked and the tranquil in the world gained riches." Hence, not all who want to take the Lord may come and take. Instead, we stumble every step of the way, until, as our sages said (*VaYikra Rabba* 2) about the verse, "I have found one man out of a thousand, where a thousand enter a room, and one comes out to the light."

Thus, understanding His Providence is the reason for every good, and the lack of understanding is the reason for every bad. It turns out that this is the axis upon which all the people in the world circle, for better or for worse.

45) When we closely examine the attainment of Providence that people come to sense, we find four kinds there. Each and every kind receives specific Providence by the Creator, in a way that there are four discernments in the attainment of Providence here. In fact, they are only two: 1) concealment of the face, 2) and revelation of the face, but they are divided into four.

There are two discernments in Providence of concealment of the face, which are 1) "single concealment," 2) and "concealment within concealment," and two discernments in the Providence of revelation of the face, which are 3) Providence of "reward and punishment," 4) and "eternal Providence," as they will be explained below.

46) The verse says (Deuteronomy 31:17), "Then My anger shall be kindled against them in that day, and I will forsake them, and I will hide My face from them, and they shall be devoured, and many evils and troubles shall come upon them; so that they will say in that day: Are not these evils come upon us because our God is not among us? And I will surely hide My face in that day for all the evil which they have done, for they have turned to other gods."

When you examine these words you will find that in the beginning it states, "Then My anger shall be kindled... ...and I will hide My face," meaning one concealment. Afterward, it states, "and many evils and troubles shall come upon them... ...And I will surely hide My face [in Hebrew, "hide" appears twice]," meaning double concealment. We must understand what is this "double concealment."

47) We must first understand the meaning of the "face of the Creator," about which the writing says, "I will hide My face." It can be thought of as a person who sees his friend's face and knows him right away. However, when he sees him from behind he is not certain of his identity. He might doubt, "Perhaps he is another and not his friend?"

So is the matter before us: Everyone knows and feels that the Creator is good and that it is the conduct of the good to do good. Hence, when the Creator generously bestows upon His creations, it is considered that His face is revealed to His creations. This is because then everyone knows and senses Him, since He behaves according to His name, as we have seen above regarding open Providence.

48) Yet, when He behaves with His creations the opposite of the above-mentioned, meaning when they suffer afflictions and pains in His world, it is considered the posterior of the Creator. This is because His face, meaning His complete attribute of goodness, is entirely concealed from them, and this is not a conduct that suits His name. It is like a person who sees his friend from behind and might doubt and think, "Perhaps he is another?"

The writing says, "Then My anger shall be kindled... ...and I will hide My face from them." During the anger, when people suffer troubles and pains, it means that the Creator is hiding His face, which is His utter benevolence, and only His posterior is revealed. In that state, great strengthening in His faith is required, to beware of thoughts of transgression, since it is hard to know Him from behind. This is called "one concealment."

49) However, when troubles and torments accumulate to a great extent, it causes a double concealment, which the books name "concealment within concealment." It means that even His posterior is not seen, meaning they do not believe that the Creator is angry with them and punishes them, but attribute it to chance or to nature and come to deny His Providence in reward and punishment. This is the meaning of the verse, "And I will surely hide My face ... for they have turned to other gods." That is, they become heretic and turn to idol worshiping.

50) However, beforehand, when the writing speaks only from the perspective of one concealment, the text ends, "they will say in that day: Are not these evils come upon us because our God is not among us?" This means that they still believe in Providence of reward and punishment and say that the troubles and suffering come to them because they are not adhered to the Creator, as it is written, "these evils come upon us because our God is not among us." This is regarded as still seeing the Creator, but only from behind. For this reason, it is called "one concealment," only concealment of the face.

51) Now we have explained the two discernments of the perception of concealed Providence, which people sense: "one concealment" and "concealment within concealment." One concealment relates only to the concealment of the face, while the posterior is revealed to them. This means that they believe that the Creator gave them the affliction as a punishment. And although it is hard for them to always know the Creator through His posterior side, which brings them to transgress, even then they are considered "incomplete wicked." In other words, these transgressions are like mistakes because they come to them as a result of the accumulation of afflictions, since, in general, they believe in reward and punishment.

52) Concealment within concealment means that even the posterior of the Creator is hidden from them, since they do not believe in reward and punishment. These transgressions of theirs are considered sins. They are considered "complete wicked" because they become heretic and say that the Creator does not watch over His creations at all and turn to idolatry, as it is written, "for they have turned to other gods."

53) We must know that the whole matter of the work in keeping Torah and *Mitzvot* by way of choice applies primarily to the two aforementioned discernments of concealed Providence. Ben He He says about that time (*Avot*, Chapter 5): "The reward is according to the pain."

Since His Guidance is not revealed, it is impossible to see Him but only in concealment of the face, from behind, as one who sees one's friend from behind and might doubt and think he is another. In this manner, one is always left with the choice whether to keep His will or breach it. This is because the troubles and pains he suffers make him doubt the reality of His guidance over His creations, whether in the first manner, which are the mistakes, or in the second manner, which are the sins.

In any case, one is still in great pain and labor. The writing says about this time, "All that your hand finds to do by your strength, that do" (Ecclesiastes 9). This is so because he will not be granted the revelation of the face, the complete measure of His goodness, before he exerts and does whatever is in his power to do, and the reward is according to the pain.

54) When the Creator sees that one has completed one's measure of exertion and finished everything he had to do by the power of his choice and his strengthening of faith in the Creator, the Creator helps him. Then, one attains open Providence, meaning the revelation of the face. Then, he is rewarded with complete repentance, meaning he adheres to the Creator once more with his heart, soul, and might, as though naturally drawn by the attainment of the open Providence.

55) These above attainment and repentance come to a person in two degrees: The first is the attainment of absolute Providence of reward and punishment. Besides attaining the reward for every *Mitzva* in the next world in utter clarity, he is also rewarded with the attainment of the wondrous pleasure in immediate observation of the *Mitzva* in this world.

In addition, besides attaining the bitter punishment extending from every sin after one's death, one is also rewarded with feeling the bitter taste of every transgression while he is still alive.

Naturally, one who is rewarded with this open Providence is certain that he will not sin again, as one is certain that he will not cut his own flesh and cause himself terrible suffering. In addition, one is certain that he will not neglect a *Mitzva* without performing it the instant it comes to his hand, just as one is certain that he will not neglect any worldly pleasure or a great profit that comes into his hand.

56) Now you can understand the words of our sages, "What is repentance like? When He who knows the mysteries will testify that he will not return to folly." These are seemingly perplexing words, for who would rise to heaven to hear the testimony of the Creator? Also, before whom should the Creator testify? Is it not enough that the Creator Himself knows that the person repented with all his heart and will not sin again?

From the explanation, the matter becomes very simple: In truth, one is not absolutely certain that he will not sin again before he is rewarded with the above attainment of reward and punishment, meaning the revelation of the face. This revelation of the face, from the perspective of the Creator's salvation, is called "testimony," since His salvation in itself, to this attainment of reward and punishment, is what guarantees that he will not sin again.

It is therefore considered that the Creator testifies to him. It is written, "What is repentance like?" In other words, when will one be certain that he has been granted complete repentance? For this, one is given a clear sign: "When He Who knows the mysteries testifies that he will not return to folly." This means that he will attain the revelation of the face, at which time His salvation itself will testify that he will not return to folly.

57) This above-mentioned repentance is called "repentance from fear." This is because although one returns to the Creator with his heart and soul, until He who knows the mysteries testifies that he will not return to folly, that certainty that he will not sin again is due to one's attainment and sensation of the terrible punishment and wicked torment extending from the transgressions. Because of this, one is certain that he will not sin, just as he is sure that he will not afflict himself with horrible suffering.

However, in the end, these repentance and certainty are only because of the fear of punishment that extends from the transgressions. It turns out that one's repentance is only due to fear of punishment. Because of this, it is called "repentance from fear."

58) By this we understand the words of our sages, that one who repents from fear is rewarded with his sins becoming as mistakes. We must understand how this happens. According to the above (Item 52), you can thoroughly understand

that the sins one makes extend to him from the reception of a guidance of double concealment, namely concealment within concealment. This means that he does not believe in a guidance of reward and punishment.

One concealment means that he believes in a guidance of reward and punishment, but because of the accumulation of the suffering, he sometimes comes to thoughts of transgression. This is because although he believes that the suffering came to him as a punishment, he is still as one who sees his friend from behind, and might doubt and mistake him for another, as written there, that these sins are only mistakes, since in general, he believes in a guidance of reward and punishment.

59) Hence, when one is granted repentance from fear, meaning a clear attainment of reward and punishment until he is certain that he will not sin, the concealment within concealment is entirely corrected in him. This is because now he evidently sees that there is a guidance of reward and punishment. It is clear to him that all the suffering he ever felt was a punishment from His Providence for the sins he had committed. In retrospect, he made a grave mistake; hence, he uproots these sins.

However, this is not entirely so. Rather, they become mistakes, similar to the transgressions he committed in one concealment, when he failed due to the confusion that came to him through the multitude of torments that drive one out of one's mind. These are only regarded as mistakes.

60) Yet, in this repentance, he did not correct at all the first concealment of the face, which he had had before, but only from now on after he has been granted the revelation of the face. In the past, however, before he was rewarded with repentance, the concealment of the face and all the mistakes remained as they were, without any change or correction whatsoever, since then, too, he believed that the troubles and suffering came to him as a punishment, as it is written, "they will say in that day: Are not these evils come upon us because our God is not among us?"

61) Therefore, he is still considered an incomplete righteous because one who is awarded the revelation of the face, namely the complete measure of His goodness, as befits His name, is called "righteous" (Item 55). This is so because he justifies His guidance as it truly is, that He is utterly good and utterly perfect with His creations, that He is good to the good and to the bad.

Hence, since he has been awarded the revelation of the face, from here on he merits the name "righteous." However, since he has not completed the correction, but only the concealment within concealment, and has not corrected the first concealment, but only from here on, that time, before he was awarded repentance, still does not merit the name "righteous." This is because then he is left with the concealment of the face, as before. For this reason, he is called "incomplete righteous," meaning one who still needs to correct his past.

62) He is also called "medium," since after he is rewarded with repentance from fear he becomes qualified, through his completion in Torah and good deeds, to be

rewarded with repentance from love, as well. Then one attains being a "complete righteous." Hence, now one is the medium between fear and love, and is therefore named "medium." However, prior to that, he was not completely qualified to even prepare himself for repentance from love.

63) This thoroughly explains the first degree of attainment of the revelation of the face, the attainment and the sensation of a guidance of reward and punishment in a way that He who knows the mysteries will testify that he will not return to folly. This is called "repentance from fear," when his sins become for him as mistakes. This is also called "incomplete righteous" and "medium."

64) Now we will explain the second degree of the attainment of the revelation of the face—the attainment of the complete, true, and eternal guidance. It means that the Creator watches over His creations as The Good Who Does Good to the good and to the bad. Now one is considered "complete righteous" and "repentance from love," and is granted turning his sins to virtues.

This explains all four discernments of understanding of the guidance that apply in the creations. The first three discernments—double concealment, single concealment, and attainment of a guidance of reward and punishment—are but preparations by which one attains the fourth discernment: the attainment of the true, eternal Providence.

65) But we have yet to understand why the third discernment is not enough for a person, namely attainment of a guidance of reward and punishment. We said that he has already been rewarded with He who knows the mysteries testifying that he will not sin again. Hence, why is he still called "medium" or "incomplete righteous," whose name proves that his work is still not desirable in the eyes of the Creator, and there is still a flaw and blemish in his Torah and work?

66) First, let us scrutinize what the interpreters asked about the *Mitzva* of loving the Creator. How did the Torah oblige us to a *Mitzva* that we cannot keep at all? One can coerce and enslave oneself to anything, but no coercion or enslavement in the world will help with love.

They explained that by keeping all 612 *Mitzvot* appropriately, the love of the Creator extends to him by itself. Hence, it is considered possible to keep, since one can enslave and coerce oneself to keep the 612 *Mitzvot* properly, and then he will also be rewarded with the love of the Creator.

67) Indeed, their words require elaborate explanation. In the end, the love of the Creator should not have come to us as a *Mitzva*, since there is no act or enslavement on our part in it. Rather, it comes by itself after completing the 612 *Mitzvot*. Hence, we are quite sufficient with the commandments of the 612 *Mitzvot*, and why was the *Mitzva* of love written?

68) To understand this we must first acquire a genuine understanding of the nature of the love of the Creator itself. We must know that all the inclinations,

tendencies, and properties instilled in man, with which to serve one's friends, all these tendencies and natural properties are required for the work of the Creator.

To begin with, they were created and imprinted in man only because of their final role—the ultimate purpose of man, as it is written, "No outcast shall be cast out from Him." One needs them all so as to complement oneself in the ways of reception of the abundance and to complete the will of the Creator.

This is the meaning of "Everyone who is called by My name, I have created him for My glory" (Isaiah 43:7), and also "All that the Lord has worked was for His sake" (Proverbs 16:4). However, in the meantime, man has been given a whole world to develop and complete all these natural inclinations and qualities in him by engaging in them with people, thus yielding them suitable for their purpose.

It is as our sages said, "One must say, 'The world was created for me,'" for all the people in the world are required for a person, as they develop and qualify the attributes and inclinations of every individual to become a fit tool for His work.

69) Thus, we must understand the essence of the love of the Creator from the properties of love by which one person relates to another. The love of the Creator is necessarily given through these qualities, since they were only imprinted in man for His sake to begin with. When we observe the attributes of love between man and man, we find four measures of love, one atop the other, meaning two that are four.

70) The first is "conditional love." It means that because of the great goodness, pleasure, and benefit that one receives from one's friend, his soul clings to him with wondrous love.

There are two measures in this: The first measure is that before they met and began to love one another, they did harm to one another. However, now they do not want to remember it, for "Love will cover all crimes." The second measure is that they have always done good and helped one another, and there is no trace of harm or detriment between them.

[Editor's note: Item 71 is missing in the manuscript]

72) The second is "unconditional love." It means that one knows the virtue of one's friend to be sublime, beyond any imaginable measure. Because of this, his soul clings to him with immeasurable love.

Here, too, there are two measures: The first measure is before one knows every conduct and deed of one's friend with others. At that time, this love is considered "less than absolute love." This is because one's friend has dealings with others, and on the surface, he seems to be harming others out of negligence. In this manner, if the lover saw them, the merit of his friend would be entirely blemished and the love between them would be corrupted. Yet, since he has not seen these dealings, his love is still whole, great, and truly wonderful.

73) The second attribute of unconditional love is the fourth attribute of love in general, which also comes from knowing the merit of his friend. Yet, in addition, now he knows all his dealings and conducts with every person, none missing. He has checked and found that not only is there no trace of a flaw in them, but his goodness is greater than anything imaginable. Now it is "eternal and complete love."

74) Note that these four attributes of love between man and man also apply between man and the Creator. Moreover, here, in the love of the Creator, they become degrees through cause and consequence.

It is impossible to acquire any of them before one acquires the first attribute of conditional love. After it is completely acquired, that first attribute causes one to acquire the second attribute. After one has acquired the second attribute to the fullest, it causes him to acquire the third attribute. Finally, the third attribute to the fourth attribute, eternal love.

75) Accordingly, the question arises, "How can one acquire the first degree of love of the Creator, the first degree of conditional love, which is love that comes through the abundance of goodness that one receives from the loved one, when we accept that there is no reward for a *Mitzva* in this world?"

Moreover, according to the above, one must go through the first two forms of Providence by way of concealment of the face. In other words, His face, meaning His measure of goodness—the conduct of the good is to do good—is concealed at that time (Item 47). Therefore, at that time, one experiences pain and suffering.

Nevertheless, we learn that the whole practice of Torah and work out of choice is conducted primarily during that time of concealment of the face. If so, how can it be that one will be awarded the second attribute of conditional love, being that the loved one has always done only wondrous and plentiful good, and never caused him any harm at all, and it goes without saying that he will be granted the third degree or the fourth?

76) Indeed we dive into deep water here. At the very least, we must fish out a precious gem from this. For this reason, let us examine the words of our sages (*Berachot* 17), "When the sages would come out from the house of Rabbi Ami, and some say from the house of Rabbi Hanina, they told him the following, 'You will see your world in your life, and your end to the life of the next world, and your steps shall run to hear the words of *Atik Yomin*.'"

We must understand why they did not say, "You will receive your world in your life," but only "see." If they wanted to bless, they should have blessed wholly, meaning to acquire and receive his world in his life. We must also understand, why should one see his next world in his life? At least his end will be the life of the next world. Moreover, why did they place this blessing first?

77) First, we must understand how one sees the next world in one's life? Certainly, we cannot see anything spiritual with corporeal eyes. It is also not the Creator's

conduct to change the laws of nature. This is because the Creator originally arranged these conducts in this manner because they are the most successful for their purpose. Through them, one comes to adhere to Him, as it is written, "All that the Lord has worked was for His sake." Therefore, we must understand how one sees one's world in one's life.

78) I shall tell you that this seeing comes to a person through the opening of the eyes in the Torah, as it is written, "Open my eyes, that I may behold wondrous things from Your law." It is about this that the soul is sworn before it comes to the body (*Nida*, p 30b), where "Even if the whole world tells you that you are righteous, be wicked in your own eyes," specifically in your own eyes.

In other words, as long as you have not been rewarded with "opening of the eyes" in the Torah, regard yourself as wicked. Do not fool yourself with your reputation in the entire world as righteous.

Now you can also understand why they placed the blessing, "You shall see your world in your life," at the beginning of the blessings. It is because prior to that, one is not even awarded the property of "incomplete righteous."

79) We have yet to understand, if a person knows about himself that he has already kept the whole Torah, and the whole world agrees with him in that, why is that not enough for him at all? Instead, he is sworn to continue regarding himself as wicked. Is it because that wondrous degree of opening his eyes in the Torah is missing in him that you compare him to a wicked? Indeed, this is very perplexing.

80) Indeed, the four measures of people's attainment of His Providence over them have already been explained. Two of them are in concealment of the face, and two are in disclosure of the face.

Also, the reason for the concealment of the face from people has been explained: It is deliberately to give people room to labor and engage in His work in Torah and *Mitzvot* voluntarily, for then the contentment of the Creator from their work in His Torah and *Mitzvot* increases more than His contentment from the angels above, who have no choice and whose mission is compulsory. There are also other reasons, but this is not the place to elaborate on them.

81) Despite the above praise for concealment of face, it is still not considered wholeness, but only a "transition," as this is the place from which the longed-for wholeness is attained. This means that any reward for a *Mitzva* that is prepared for a person is acquired only through one's labor in Torah and good deeds during the concealment of the face, when he engages voluntarily. This is so because then one feels sorrow out of his strengthening in His faith in keeping His will. And one's whole reward is measured only according to the pain he suffers from keeping the Torah and the *Mitzva*, as in the words of Ben He He, "The reward is according to the pain."

82) Hence, every person must experience that transition period of concealment of the face. When he completes it, he is rewarded with open Providence, meaning the revelation of the face.

Before he is rewarded with revelation of the face, although he sees the posterior side, he cannot refrain from ever committing a transgression. Not only is he unable to keep all 613 *Mitzvot*, since love does not come by coercion and compulsion, but one is not complete even in the 612 *Mitzvot*, since even his fear is not fixed as it should be.

This is the meaning of the Torah being 611 in *Gematria*, for any *Gematria* is the posterior side, that one cannot properly observe even 612 *Mitzvot*. This is the meaning of "He will not contend forever." In the end, one will be awarded the revelation of the face.

83) The first degree of the revelation of the face is the attainment of a guidance of reward and punishment in utter clarity. This comes to a person only through His salvation, when one is awarded the opening of the eyes in the Torah in wondrous attainment and becomes "a flowing spring," as Rabbi Meir (*Avot* 6). In any *Mitzva* in the Torah that one has already kept of his own choice, one is granted seeing the reward of the *Mitzva* in it, intended for him in the next world, as well as the great loss in the transgression.

84) And although the reward is not yet in his hand, since the reward for a *Mitzva* is not in this world, the clear attainment is quite sufficient for him from now on, to feel the great pleasure while performing each *Mitzva*, since "All that is about to be collected is deemed collected."

For example, take a merchant who made a deal and gained a large sum. Even though the profit will come to him after a long time, if he is certain beyond any shadow of a doubt that the profit will come to him in time, he is as happy as if the money has come to him immediately.

85) Naturally, such open Providence testifies that from now on he will cling to Torah and *Mitzvot* with his heart and soul and might, and will retire from the transgressions as if escaping from a fire. And although he is not yet a complete righteous, since he has not been rewarded with repentance from love, his great *Dvekut* [adhesion] in the Torah and good deeds helps him be gradually granted repentance from love, meaning the second degree of the revelation of the face. Then one can keep all 613 *Mitzvot* in full, and he becomes a complete righteous.

86) Now we thoroughly understand what we asked concerning the oath, that the soul is sworn before it comes to this world: "Even if the whole world tells you that you are righteous, be wicked in your own eyes." We asked, "Since the whole world agrees that he is righteous, why must he still consider himself wicked? Does he not trust the entire world?"

We must also add, concerning the phrase, "Even if the whole world says." What is the connection between this and the testimony of the entire world, since one knows oneself better than the whole world? It should have sworn him, "Even if you know about yourself that you are righteous."

Yet, the most perplexing is that the Gemara explicitly states (*Berachot* 61), "Raba said, 'One must know in one's soul if he is righteous or not.'" Thus, there is an obligation and possibility to truly be completely righteous.

Moreover, one must delve and know this truth for himself. If this is so, how is the soul sworn to always be wicked in its own eyes, and to never know the actual truth, when our sages have obligated the opposite?

87) The words are very precise indeed. As long as one has not been awarded the opening of eyes in the Torah in wondrous attainment, sufficient for him for clear attainment of reward and punishment, he will certainly not be able to deceive himself and consider himself righteous. This is because he will necessarily feel that he lacks the two most comprehensive *Mitzvot* in the Torah, namely love and fear.

Even attaining complete fear, in a way that "He who knows the mysteries will testify that he will not return to folly," due to his great fear of punishment and the great loss from transgressing, is completely unimaginable before he is awarded complete, clear, and absolute attainment in Providence of reward and punishment.

This refers to the attainment of the first degree of revelation of the face, which comes to a person through the opening of the eyes in the Torah. It is all the more so with love, which is completely beyond one's ability, since it depends on the understanding of the heart, and no labor or coercion will help here.

88) Hence, the oath states, "Even if the whole world tells you that you are righteous." This is so because these two *Mitzvot*, love and fear, are given only to the individual, and no one else in the world can distinguish them and know them.

Thus, since they see that he is complete in 611 *Mitzvot*, they immediately say that he probably has the two *Mitzvot* of love and fear, too. And since human nature compels one to believe the world, one might fall into a grave mistake.

For this reason, the soul is sworn to this even before it comes into this world, and may it help us. Nonetheless, it is the individual himself who must certainly question and know in his heart if he is a complete righteous.

89) We can also understand what we asked concerning being rewarded with love. We asked, "How can we attain even the first degree of love when there is no reward for a *Mitzva* in this world?" Now it is clear that one does not need to actually receive the reward for the *Mitzva* in his life, hence their precision, "You will see your world in your life, and your end to the life of the next world," implying that the reward for a *Mitzva* is not in this world, but in the next world.

Yet, to know, see, and feel the future reward of the *Mitzva* in the next world, one must know it in complete certainty and clarity while in this life through his wondrous attainment in the Torah. This is because then one still attains conditional love, which is the first degree of the exit from concealment of the face and the entry to the revelation of the face, which one must have in order to keep Torah and *Mitzvot* correctly, in a way that "He who knows the mysteries will testify that he will not return to folly."

90) And by laboring to observe Torah and *Mitzvot* in the form of conditional love, which comes to him from knowing the future reward in the next world, as in "all that is about to be collected is deemed collected," one attains the second degree of revelation of the face—His guidance over the world from His eternity and truthfulness, meaning that He is good and does good to the good and to the bad.

In that state, one attains unconditional love and the sins become for him as merits. From then on, he is called "complete righteous," since he can keep the Torah and *Mitzvot* with love and fear. He is called "complete" because he has all 613 *Mitzvot* in completeness.

91) This answers what we asked above concerning one who attains the third measure of Providence, namely Providence of reward and punishment, when He who knows the mysteries already testifies that he will not return to folly. And yet, he is still considered incomplete righteous. Now we thoroughly understand that he still lacks one *Mitzva*, the *Mitzva* of love. Of course, he is incomplete, since he must necessarily complete the 613 *Mitzvot*, which is necessarily the first step on the threshold of wholeness.

92) With all that was said above, we understand what they asked, "How did the Torah obligate us to the *Mitzva* of love when this *Mitzva* is not even in our hands to engage in or even somewhat touch?" Now you see and understand that it is about this that our sages warned us, "I labored and did not find, do not believe," and also, "Let one always engage in Torah and *Mitzvot Lo Lishma* since from *Lo Lishma* one comes to *Lishma*" (*Pesachim* 50). Also, the verse, "Those that seek Me shall find Me" (Proverbs 8), testifies to that.

93) These are the words of our sages (*Megillah*, p 6b): "Rabbi Yitzhak said, 'If a person tells you, "I labored and did not find," do not believe; "I did not labor and found," do not believe; "I labored and found," believe.'" These matters concern words of Torah, but in negotiation, it is help from above. We asked above, in Item 40, about the words "I labored and found, believe." The words seem self-contradictory, since labor relates to possession, and finding pertains to what comes without any labor, absentmindedly. He should have said, "I labored and bought."

Yet, you should know that this term "finding," mentioned here, relates to the verse, "Those who seek Me shall find Me." It refers to finding the face of the Creator, as it is written in *The Zohar* that He is found only in the Torah, meaning that one is rewarded with finding the face of the Creator by laboring in the Torah. Hence, our sages were precise in their words, and said "I labored and found, believe," for the labor is in the Torah, and the finding is in the revelation of the face of His Providence (see Item 47).

They deliberately refrained from saying, "I labored and won, believe," or "I labored and bought." This is because then there would be room for error in the matters, since winning or possessing relate only to possession of the Torah. Hence, they made the precision of the word "found," indicating that it refers to something other than the acquisition of the Torah, namely the revelation of the face of His Providence.

94) That also settles the verse, "I did not labor and found, do not believe." It seems puzzling, for who would be so gullible as to think that it is possible to be rewarded with the Torah without having to labor for it? But since the words concern the verse, "They who seek Me shall find Me" (Proverbs 8:17), it means that anyone, small or great, who seeks Him, finds Him immediately. This is what the words "They who seek Me" imply.

One might think that this does not require such great labor, and even a lesser person, unwilling to make any effort for it, will find Him, too. In that regard, our sages warn us not to believe such an explanation. Rather, the labor is necessary here, and "I did not labor and found, do not believe."

95) Now you see why the Torah is called "life," as it is written, "See, I have set before you today life and good" (Deuteronomy 30:15), and also, "therefore choose life," and "For they are life unto those who find them" (Proverbs 4:22). This extends from the verse, "In the light of the King's face is life" (Proverbs 16), since the Creator is the source of all of life and every good.

Hence, life extends to those branches that adhere to their source. This refers to those who have labored and found the light of His face in the Torah, who have been imparted opening their eyes in the Torah in wondrous attainment until they were imparted the revelation of the face, meaning the attainment of the true Providence, which befits His name, The Good, and the conduct of the Good is to do good.

96) And those who were rewarded can no longer retire from observing the *Mitzva* correctly, as one cannot retire from a wonderful pleasure that comes to his hand. They also run away from transgression as one runs away from fire.

It is said about them: "But you who adhere to the Lord your God are alive every one of you this day," as His love is bestowed upon them in natural love through the natural channels prepared for one by the nature of creation. This is so because now the branch is properly adhered to its root, and life pours to him abundantly and incessantly from its origin. It is because of this that the Torah is called "life."

97) For this reason, our sages warned us in many places concerning the necessary condition in the practice of Torah, that it will be specifically *Lishma*, in a way that

through it, one will be awarded life, for it is a Torah of life and this is why it was given to us, as it is written, "Therefore, choose life."

Hence, during the practice of Torah, every person must labor in it, and set his mind and heart to find "the light of the King's face" in it, meaning attainment of open Providence, called "light of the face." Any person is capable of it, as it is written, "those who seek Me shall find Me," and as it is written, "I labored and did not find, do not believe."

Thus, one needs nothing in this matter except the labor alone. It is written, "Anyone who practices Torah *Lishma*, his Torah becomes for him a potion of life" (*Taanit* 7a). It means that one should only set one's mind and heart to attain life, which is the meaning of *Lishma*.

98) Now you can see that the question the interpreters asked about the *Mitzva* of love, saying that this *Mitzva* is out of our hands since love does not come by coercion and compulsion, is not at all a question since it is entirely in our hands. Every person can labor in the Torah until he finds the attainment of His open Providence, as it is written, "I labored and found, believe."

When one is rewarded with open Providence, the love extends to him by itself through the natural channels. One who does not believe he can attain it through his efforts, for whatever reason, is necessarily in disbelief of the words of our sages. Instead, he imagines that the labor is not enough for every person, which contradicts the verse, "I labored and did not find, do not believe." It also contradicts the words, "those who seek Me shall find Me," specifically, those who "seek," whomever they are, great or small. However, he certainly needs to labor.

99) From the above, you will understand the meaning of "Anyone who practices Torah *Lo Lishma*, his Torah becomes for him a potion of death" (*Taanit* 7a), and also what they said about the verse, "Indeed You are a God who hides," that the Creator hides Himself in the Torah.

We asked above, "It makes sense that the Creator is hidden specifically in worldly matters and in the vanities of this world, which are outside the Torah, and not in the Torah itself, as only there is the place of the disclosure. And we asked further: This concealment that the Creator hides Himself, to be sought and found, as it is written in *The Zohar*, "Why do I need all this?"

100) From the above explained you can thoroughly understand that this concealment that the Creator hides Himself so as to be sought is the concealment of the face, which He conducts with His creations in two manners: one concealment, and concealment within concealment.

The Zohar tells us that we should not even consider that the Creator wishes to remain in a guidance of concealed face from His creations. Rather, it is like a person who deliberately hides himself, so his friend will seek and find him.

Similarly, the Creator behaves in concealment of face with His creations only because He wants people to seek the disclosure of His face and find Him. In other words, there would be no way or inlet for people to attain the light of the King's face had He not first behaved with them in concealment of the face. Thus, the whole concealment is but a preparation for the disclosure of the face.

101) It is written that the Creator hides Himself in the Torah. Regarding the torments and pains one experiences during the concealment of the face, one who possesses transgressions and has done little in Torah and *Mitzvot* is unlike one who has engaged in Torah and good deeds extensively. The first is quite qualified to sentence his Maker to the side of merit, to think that the suffering came to him because of his sins and scarceness of Torah.

For the other, however, it is much harder to sentence his Maker to the side of merit since in his mind, he does not deserve such harsh punishments. Moreover, he sees that his friends, who are worse than him, do not suffer so, as it is written, "The wicked and the tranquil in the world gained riches," and also, "in vain have I cleansed my heart."

Thus, as long as one is not rewarded with a guidance of revelation of the face, the abundance of Torah and *Mitzvot* he has performed make his concealment of the face much heavier. This is the meaning of "The Creator hides Himself in the Torah."

Indeed, all that heaviness he feels through the Torah is but proclamations by which the Torah itself calls him, awakening him to hurry up and give the required measure of labor to promptly endow him with the revelation of the face, as God wills it.

102) This is why it is written that all who learn Torah *Lo Lishma*, their Torah becomes for them a potion of death. Not only do they not emerge from concealment of the face to disclosure of the face, since they did not set their minds to labor and attain it, the Torah that they accumulate greatly increases their concealment of the face. Finally, they fall into concealment within concealment, which is considered death, being completely detached from one's root. Thus, their Torah becomes for them a potion of death.

103) This clarifies the two names applied to the Torah: "revealed" and "concealed." We must understand why we need the concealed Torah, and why is not the whole Torah revealed?

Indeed, there is a profound intention here. The concealed Torah implies that the Creator hides in the Torah, hence the name, "the Torah of the hidden." Conversely, it is called "revealed" because the Creator is revealed by the Torah.

Therefore, the Kabbalists said, and we also find it in the prayer book of the Vilna Gaon [GRA], that the order of attainment of the Torah begins with the concealed and ends with the revealed. This means that through the appropriate labor, where one first delves in the Torah of the hidden, he is thus granted the revealed Torah, which is the literal. Thus, one begins with the concealed, called *Sod* [secret], and when he is rewarded, he ends in the literal.

104) It has been thoroughly clarified how it is possible to attain the first degree of love, which is conditional love. We learned that even though there is no reward for a *Mitzva* in this world, the attainment of the reward for the *Mitzva* exists also in this world. This comes to a person by opening the eyes in the Torah, and this clear attainment is completely similar to receiving instantaneous reward for the *Mitzva* (see Item 84).

For this reason, one feels the wonderful benefit contained in the thought of creation to delight His creatures with His full, good, and generous hand. Because of the abundance of benefit that one obtains, wondrous love appears between a person and the Creator. It pours to him incessantly, by the same ways and channels through which natural love appears.

105) However, all this comes to a person from the moment he attains onward. Yet, one does not want to remember all the torment caused by the Providence in concealment of the face he had suffered before he attained the above disclosure of the face, since "love will cover all crimes." Nevertheless, it is considered a great flaw, even with love among people, much less concerning the truthfulness of His Providence, since He is good and does good to the good and to the bad.

Therefore, we must understand how one can obtain His love in such a way that he will feel and know that the Creator has always done him wondrous good, since he was born onward, that He has never, nor will ever cause him an ounce of harm, which is the second manner of love.

106) To understand this, we need the words of our sages. They said, "One who repents from love, his sins become as merits." It means that not only does the Creator forgive his sins, He also turns each sin and transgression he had made into a *Mitzva*.

107) Hence, after one is rewarded with the illumination of the face to such an extent that each sin he had committed, even the deliberate ones, is turned and becomes a *Mitzva* for him, one rejoices with all the torment and affliction he had ever suffered since the time he was placed in the two states of concealment of the face. This is because it is they that brought him all those sins, which have now become *Mitzvot* by the illumination of His face, Who performs wonders.

And any sorrow and trouble that drove him out of mind and he failed with mistakes, as in the first concealment, or failed with sins, as in the double concealment, has now become a cause and preparation for keeping a *Mitzva* and the reception of eternal and wondrous reward for it. Therefore, any sorrow has turned for him into a great joy and any evil to wonderful good.

108) This is similar to a well-known tale about a Jew who was a house trustee for a certain landlord. The landlord loved him dearly. Once, the landlord went away and left his business in the hands of his substitute, who was an anti-Semite.

What did he do? He took the Jew and flogged him five times in front of everyone to thoroughly humiliate him.

Upon the landlord's return, the Jew went to him and told him all that had happened to him. His anger was kindled, he called the substitute and commanded him to promptly give the Jew a thousand coins for every lash he had struck him.

The Jew took them and went home. His wife found him crying. Fearful, she asked him, "What happened to you with the landlord?" He told her. She asked, "So why are you crying?" He answered, "I am crying because he only lashed me five times. I wish he had lashed me at least ten times, since now I would have had ten thousand coins."

109) Now you see that after one has been awarded repentance of the iniquities in a way that the sins became to him as merits, one is then awarded achieving the second degree of love of the Creator, where the loved one never caused his loved one any harm or even a shadow of a harm. Instead, He performs wondrous and plentiful good to him, always and forever (see Item 70), in a way that repentance from love and the turning of the sins into merits come as one, as in the words of our sages.

110) Thus far, we examined only the two degrees of conditional love. Yet, we must still understand how one is awarded coming in the two manners of unconditional love with one's Maker.

For this we must thoroughly understand the words of our sages who said (*Kidushin*, p 40b), "Our sages said, 'One must always regard oneself as half guilty and half innocent. If he performs one *Mitzva*, happy is he, for he has sentenced himself to the side of merit. If he commits one transgression, woe unto him for he has sentenced himself to the side of fault, as was said, 'And one sinner,' etc.'"

"Rabbi Elazar, son of Rabbi Shimon, says, 'Since the world is judged by its majority, and the individual is judged by the majority, if he performs one *Mitzva*, happy is he, for he has sentenced himself and the whole world to the side of merit. If he commits one transgression, woe unto him, for he has sentenced himself and the whole world to the side of fault, as was said, 'And one sinner,' etc.' For this one sin that he had committed, the world and he have lost much good."

111) These words seem puzzling from beginning to end. He says that one who performs one *Mitzva* immediately sentences to the side of merit for he is judged after the majority. Yet, this refers only to those who are half guilty and half innocent. And Rabbi Elazar, son of Rabbi Shimon, does not speak of those at all. Thus, the essence is absent from the book.

RASHI interpreted his words as referring to the words of the first Tanna, who says, "One must always consider oneself half guilty and half innocent." Rabbi Elazar adds that one should also regard the whole world as though they are half guilty and half innocent. Yet, the essence is absent from the book. Also, why did he change his words? Why is he not speaking like the first Tanna if the meaning is the same?

112) This is even more difficult on the object itself, meaning for one to see oneself as though he is only half guilty. This is a wonder: If one knows one's many iniquities, would he lie to himself saying that he is only half and half? But the Torah states, "Keep far from a false matter!"

Moreover, it is written, "One sinner destroys much good." This is because one transgression sentences the person and the entire world to the side of fault. Thus, it is about the actual reality, not some false imagination by which one should picture himself and the world.

113) There is another bewilderment: Can it be that there are not many people in each generation who perform one *Mitzva*? So how is the world sentenced to the side of merit? Does this mean that the situation does not change at all, and the world behaves as it always does? Indeed, great depth is required here, for the words cannot be understood superficially.

However, the Braita does not speak at all about a person who knows his transgressions are many, to teach him deception, that he is half this and half that, or to insinuate that he lacks only one *Mitzva*. This is not at all the way of the sages. Rather, the Braita speaks of one who feels and imagines that he is completely and utterly righteous, and finds himself utterly whole as he has already been awarded the first degree of love by opening his eyes in the Torah, and He Who knows the mysteries already testifies that he will not return to folly.

To him, the Tanna speaks, shows him his way, and proves to him that he is not yet righteous, but in between, meaning half guilty and half innocent. This is so because he still lacks one *Mitzva* of the 613 *Mitzvot* in the Torah, namely the *Mitzva* of love.

The whole testimony of He who knows the mysteries that he will not sin again is only because of the clarity in one's attainment of the great loss in transgressing. This is considered fear of punishment and is therefore called "repentance from fear."

114) We also learned above that this degree of repentance from fear still does not correct a person, but only from the time of repentance onward. Yet, all the sorrow and the anguish he had suffered prior to being awarded the revelation of the face remain as they were, without any correction. Also, the transgressions he had made are not entirely corrected but remain as mistakes.

115) This is why the first Tanna is said that such a person, who is still short of one *Mitzva*, will regard himself as half guilty and half innocent. This means that one should imagine that the time he was granted repentance was in the middle of his years. Thus, he is still half guilty, in that half of his years that had passed before he repented. At that time, one is certainly guilty since repentance from fear does not correct them.

It follows, also, that he is half innocent, in the half of his years since he has been awarded repentance onward. At that time, one is certainly innocent, for he is certain that he will not sin again. Thus, during the first half of his years he is guilty, and in the second half of his years, he is innocent.

116) The Tanna tells him to think that if he performs one *Mitzva*, that *Mitzva* which he lacks from the number 613, he will be happy, for he has sentenced himself to the side of merit. This is so because one who is granted the *Mitzva* of love by repentance from love, through it, he is rewarded with turning his sins to merits.

Then, every sorrow and grief that he had ever suffered, prior to being awarded repentance, is turned into wondrous, endless pleasures for him. Moreover, he regrets not having suffered several times more, as in the allegory about the landlord and the Jew who loved him.

This is called "sentencing to the side of merit," since all of his emotions, the mistakes and the sins, have become merits for him. Thus, sentencing to the side of merit means that the whole cup that was filled with sins has now been turned into a cup full of merits. In the words of the sages, this inversion is called "sentencing."

117) The Tanna further warns him and says that as long as he is in between and has not been granted the one *Mitzva* that is missing from the number 613, he should not believe in himself until his dying day. He should also not rely on the testimony of the One Who knows the mysteries, that he will not return to folly, but he might still transgress.

Hence, he should think for himself that if he commits one transgression, woe unto him, for he has sentenced himself to the side of fault. This is because then he will immediately lose all his wonderful attainment in the Torah, and all the disclosure of the face that he has been granted, and he will return to concealment of the face. Thus, he will sentence himself to the side of fault, for he will lose all the merits and the good, even from the latter half of his years. As evidence, the Tanna brings the verse, "One sinner destroys much good."

118) Now you will understand the addition that Rabbi Elazar, son of Rabbi Shimon, adds, and also why he does not bring the phrase, "half guilty and half innocent," like the first Tanna. This is so because the first Tanna speaks of the second and third discernments of love, as has been explained above (Items 70, 72), while Rabbi Elazar, son of Rabbi Shimon, speaks from the fourth discernment of love, the eternal love—the disclosure of face, as it truly is, as in The Good Who Does Good to the good and to the bad.

119) We learned there that it is impossible to be rewarded with the fourth discernment, except when one is proficient and knows all the dealings of the loved one, how he behaves with all the others, none missing. This is also why the great privilege, when one is awarded sentencing himself to the side of merit, is still not enough for one to be rewarded with complete love, meaning the fourth discernment. This is so because now he does not attain His merit as being good who does good to the good and to the bad, but only His Providence over himself, as said in Item 77.

Yet, he still does not know His Providence in this sublime and wonderful manner with the rest of the people in the world. Thus, we learned above that as long as one does not know all the dealings of the loved one with others, until none of them is missing, the love is still not eternal, as said in Item 73. Hence, one must also sentence the whole world to the side of merit, and only then is the eternal love revealed to him.

120) This is what Rabbi Elazar, son of Rabbi Shimon, says: "Since the world is judged by its majority and the individual is judged by its majority," and since he relates to the whole world, he cannot speak like the first Tanna, that he should regard them as half guilty half innocent, as this degree comes to a person only when he is granted the disclosure of the face and repentance from fear. Thus, how is this said about the whole world, when they have not been granted this repentance? For this reason, one must only say that the world is judged by its majority, and the individual is judged by its majority.

Explanation: One might think that one does not become a complete righteous, except when he has no transgressions and has never sinned. But those who failed with sins and transgressions no longer merit becoming complete righteous.

For this reason, Rabbi Elazar, son of Rabbi Shimon, teaches us that this is not so. Rather, the world is judged by its majority and so is the individual. This means that after one has emerged from being medium, after he has repented from fear, he is immediately rewarded with the 613 *Mitzvot* and is called "medium," meaning half his years guilty, and in half his years innocent. Afterward, if one adds but a single *Mitzva*, the *Mitzva* of love, it is considered that he is mostly innocent and sentences everything to the side of merit. Thus, the side of faults becomes merits, too, as in the words of the first Tanna.

It turns out that even if one has a cup full of iniquities and sins, they all become merits for him. Then, he is as one who never sinned and is considered "complete righteous." This is the meaning of the saying that the world and the individual are judged by the majority. Thus, the transgressions in his hand from before the repentance are not taken into consideration whatsoever for they have become merits. Accordingly, even "complete wicked" are considered "complete righteous" once they are granted repentance from love.

121) Therefore, he says that if an individual performs one *Mitzva*, meaning after the repentance from fear, then one is short of only one *Mitzva*, and "he is happy for he has sentenced himself and the whole world to the side of merit." Thus, not only is he rewarded, through his repentance from love, with sentencing himself to the side of merit, as the first Tanna says, but he is even awarded sentencing the whole world to the side of merit.

This means that he is awarded rising in wonderful attainments in the Torah until he discovers how all the people in the world will finally be awarded repentance from love. Then, they, too, will discover and see all that wonderful guidance as he has attained for himself. And they, too, will all be sentenced to the side of merit. At that time, "sins will cease from the earth and the wicked be no more."

And although the people in the world themselves have not yet been granted even repentance from fear, still, after an individual attains that sentencing to the side of merit destined to come to them in clear and absolute attainment, it is similar to "You will see your world in your life," said about one who repents from fear. We said that he is impressed and delighted by it as though he instantly had it, since "All that is about to be collected is deemed collected."

Also, here it is considered for that individual who attains the repentance of the whole world precisely as though they have been granted and came to repentance from love. Each of them sentenced their side of faults to merits sufficiently to know His dealings with every single person in the world.

This is why Rabbi Elazar, son of Rabbi Shimon, says, "Happy is he, for he has sentenced himself and the whole world to the side of merit." From now on, one thoroughly knows all the conducts of His guidance, with every single creation, by way of disclosure of His real face, meaning the Good who does good to the good and to the bad. And since he knows it, he has therefore been granted the fourth discernment of love, namely "eternal love."

Like the first Tanna, so Rabbi Elazar, son of Rabbi Shimon, warns that even after he has sentenced the whole world to the side of merit, he should still not believe in himself until his dying day. Should he fail with a single transgression, he will immediately lose all his wonderful attainments, as it is written, "One sinner destroys much good."

This explains the difference between the first Tanna and Rabbi Elazar, son of Rabbi Shimon: The first Tanna speaks only from the second discernment and the third discernment of love; hence, he does not mention sentencing the whole world. But Rabbi Elazar, son of Rabbi Shimon, speaks from the fourth discernment of love, which cannot be depicted except by attainment of sentencing the entire world to the side of merit. However, we must still understand how we attain this wonderful attainment of sentencing the whole world to the side of merit.

122) Here we must understand the words of our sages (*Taanit* 11a): "Another treatise, when the public is in grief, one should not say, 'I shall go to my house and eat and drink, and have my soul at peace.' If one does this, the writing says about him, 'And behold joy and gladness, slaying oxen and killing sheep, eating meat and drinking wine—Let us eat and drink, for tomorrow we shall die!' What does it say after this? 'And the Lord of hosts revealed Himself in my ears: Surely this iniquity shall not be atoned by you until you die.' Thus far regarding the attribute of medium. But what does it say about the attribute of wicked? 'Come you, I will fetch wine and we will fill ourselves with strong drink, and tomorrow shall be as this day.' What does it say after that? 'The righteous perishes and no one notices, for because of the evil,

the righteous perished.' Instead, when one grieves with the public, one is rewarded with seeing the comfort of the public."

123) These words seem completely irrelevant. He wishes to bring evidence from the text, that one must suffer with the public. Hence, why should we divide and separate the attribute of medium from attribute of wicked? Furthermore, what is the precision that it makes regarding the attribute of medium and the attribute of wicked? Why does it not say, "medium" and "wicked," why do I need the attributes?

Also, where does it imply that the writing speaks of an iniquity when one does not suffer with the public? Still more, we do not see any punishment in the attribute of wicked, but in what is written, "The righteous perishes and no one notices." If the wicked sins, what did the righteous do that he should be punished, and why would the wicked mind if the righteous is taken away?

124) Indeed, know that these attributes, "medium," "wicked," and "righteous," mentioned in this Braita, are not in separate people. Rather, all three are within every single person in the world. These three attributes are discernible in every person. During one's concealment of the face, before one attains repentance from fear, he is discerned as being in the attribute of wicked.

Afterward, if one is granted repentance from fear, he is discerned as being in the attribute of medium. Then, if one is granted repentance from love, too, in its fourth discernment, meaning eternal love, he is considered a "complete righteous." Hence, they did not say merely medium and righteous, but the attribute of medium and the attribute of wicked.

125) We should also remember that it is impossible to be rewarded with the above fourth discernment of love without first achieving the revelation of the face, which is destined to come to the entire world. This gives one strength to sentence the entire world to the side of merit, as Rabbi Elazar, son of Rabbi Shimon says. We have already learned that the matter of the disclosure of the face will inevitably turn every grief and sadness that came during the concealment of the face into wondrous pleasures, until one regrets having suffered so little, as was explained above.

Hence, we must ask, "When one sentences oneself to the side of merit, he certainly remembers all the grief and pains he had during the concealment of the face." This is why it is possible that they will all be turned into wondrous pleasures for him, as said above. But when he sentences the whole world to the side of merit, how does he know the measure of grief and pain that all the people in the world suffer, so as to understand how they are sentenced to the side of merit in the same manner we explained regarding one's own sentencing?

To avoid having the side of merit of the entire world lacking, when one is qualified to sentence them to the side of merit, one has no other tactic but to always suffer with the troubles of the public, just as he suffers with his own troubles. Then the side of fault of the entire world will be ready within him, like his own side of fault. Thus, if he is granted sentencing himself to the side of merit, he will be able to sentence the entire world to the side of merit, too, and will attain being "a complete righteous."

126) From what is explained, we properly understand the words of the Braita, that if one does not suffer with the public, then even when he is granted repentance from fear, which is the attribute of medium, the writing says about him and speaks in his favor, "And behold joy and gladness." This means that one who has been granted the blessing, "You will see your world in your life," and sees the whole reward for his *Mitzva*, which is prepared for the next world, is certainly "filled with joy and gladness." And he tells himself, "slaying oxen and killing sheep, eating meat and drinking wine—Let us eat and drink, for tomorrow we will die!"

In other words, he is filled with great joy because of his guaranteed reward in the next world. This is why he says so gladly, "for tomorrow we will die," and I will collect my complete next world's life after I die.

Yet, what does it write after this? "And the Lord of hosts revealed Himself in my ears: Surely this iniquity will not be atoned by you until you die." This means that the text rebukes him for the mistakes in his hand, for we learned that the sins of one who repents from fear become mere mistakes. Hence, since he did not suffer with the public and cannot attain repentance from love, at which time the sins become merits for him, it is necessary that his mistakes will never be atoned during his life. Thus, how can he rejoice in his life in the next world? This is why it is written, "Surely this iniquity will not be atoned by you," meaning the mistakes, "until you die," meaning before he dies. Thus, he is devoid of atonement.

127) The Braita also says that this is the "attribute of medium," meaning that this text speaks of a time when one has repented from fear onward. At that time, one is considered "medium."

Yet, what does it write about the "attribute of wicked"? That is, what shall become of the time when he was in concealment of the face, which was then called "attribute of wicked"? We learned that repentance from fear does not correct one's past before he has repented.

Hence, the Braita brings another verse: "Come you, I will fetch wine, and we will fill ourselves with strong drink, and tomorrow shall be as this day." This means that those days and years that have passed since the time of concealment of the face, which he has not corrected, called "attribute of wicked," they do not want him to die since they have no part in the next world after the death, as they are the attribute of the wicked.

Therefore, at a time when the attribute of medium in him is glad and rejoicing, "for tomorrow we shall die" and will be rewarded with the life of the next world, at the same time, the attribute of wicked in him does not say so. It rather says, "and tomorrow shall be as this day," meaning it wishes to live and be happy in this world forever, for it still has no part in the next world, since he has not corrected it, as it is corrected only by repentance from love.

128) The Braita ends, "What does it say after that? 'The righteous perishes.'" That is, the attribute of complete righteous, which that person should merit, is lost from him. "And no one notices ... for because of the evil, the righteous perished." This means that because that medium did not suffer with the public, he cannot attain repentance from love, which inverts sins to merits and evils to wondrous pleasures. Instead, all the mistakes and the evil he had suffered before he acquired repentance from fear still stand in the attribute of wicked, who feel harm from His Providence. And because of these harms that they still feel, he cannot be awarded being complete righteous.

The writing says, "and no one notices," meaning that that person does not notice "because of the evil." In other words, because of the harm that one still feels in His Providence from the past, "the righteous perishes," meaning he lost the attribute of righteous. And he will die and pass away from the world as mere medium.

All this concerns he who does not suffer with the public and is not awarded seeing the comfort of the public, for he will not be able to sentence them to the side of merit and see their consolation. Hence, he will never attain the attribute of righteous.

129) From all the aforementioned, we have come to know that there is no woman-born person who will not experience the three above attributes: the attribute of wicked, attribute of medium, and attribute of righteous.

They are called *Midot* [attributes] since they extend from the *Midah* [measure] of their attainment of His Providence. Our sages said, "One is allotted to the extent that he allots" (*Sutah* 8). Those who attain His Providence in concealment of the face are considered wicked or incomplete wicked, from the perspective of the single concealment, or complete wicked, from the perspective of the double concealment.

Because they feel and think that the world is conducted in bad guidance, it is as though they condemn themselves, since they receive torments and pains from His Providence and feel only bad all day long. And they condemn the most by thinking that all the people in the world are watched over like them, in bad guidance.

Hence, those who attain Providence from the perspective of concealment of the face are called "wicked," since that name appears in them out of the depth of their sensation. It depends on the understanding of the heart, and the words or the thought that justifies His Providence do not matter at all when it opposes the sensation of every organ and sense, which cannot force themselves to lie, as it does.

Hence, they who are in this measure of attainment of Providence are considered to have sentenced themselves and the whole world to the side of fault, as it is written in the words of Rabbi Elazar, son of Rabbi Shimon. This is because they imagine that all the people in the world are watched over in bad guidance, like them, as would befit His name, "The Good who does good to the good and to the bad."

130) Those who are granted the sensation of His Providence in the form of the first degree of disclosure of the face, called "repentance from fear," are

considered medium, since their feelings divide into two parts, called "two pans of the scales."

Now that they have achieved the disclosure of the face, by way of "You will see your world in your life," at the very least they have attained His good Providence as befits His name, The Good. Hence, they have the side of merit.

Yet, all the sorrow and the bitter torments that were thoroughly imprinted in their feelings by all the days and years they received Providence of concealed face, from the past, before they were awarded the above repentance, all those remain and are called "the side of fault."

And since they have these two pans standing one opposite the other, in a way that the side of fault is set from the moment of their repentance and before, and the side of merit is set and guaranteed to them from the moment of repentance onward, the time of repentance stands "between" the merit and the sin. This is why they are called "medium."

131) And the ones who merit the disclosure of the face in the second degree, called "repentance from love," when sins become as merits to them, are considered to have sentenced the above side of fault to the side of merit. This means that all the sorrow and affliction engraved in their bones while being under the Providence of concealment of the face have now been inverted and sentenced to the side of merit, since every sorrow and grief has now been turned into a wonderful, endless pleasure. Now they are called "righteous," for they justify His Providence.

132) We must know that the above attribute of medium applies even when one is under Providence of concealment of the face. By great exertion in faith in reward and punishment, a light of great confidence in the Creator appears to them. For a time, they are granted a degree of disclosure of His face in the attribute of medium. But the drawback is that they cannot remain in their degrees permanently, since standing permanently in a degree is possible only through repentance from fear.

133) We should also know that what we said, that there is choice only when there is concealment of the face, does not mean that after one has attained Providence of revealed face, one has no further labor or exertion in the practice of Torah and *Mitzvot*. On the contrary, the proper work in Torah and *Mitzvot* begins primarily after one has been awarded repentance from love. Only then is it possible to engage in Torah and *Mitzvot* with love and fear as we are commanded, and "The world was created only for the complete righteous" (*Berachot* 61).

It is like a king who wished to select for himself the most loyal of his subjects in the country and bring them to work inside his palace. What did he do? He issued a decree that anyone who wished, young or old, would come to his palace to engage in the works inside his palace.

However, he appointed many of his servants to guard the palace gate and all the roads leading to it, and ordered them to cunningly deflect all those nearing his palace and divert them from the way that leads to the palace.

Naturally, all the people in the country began to run to the king's palace. But the diligent guards cunningly rejected them. Many of them overpowered them and came near the palace gate, but the guards at the gate were the most diligent, and if someone approached the gate, they diverted him and turned him away with great craftiness until one despaired and returned as he had come.

And so they came and went, and regained strength, and came and went again, and so on and so forth for several days and years until they grew weary of trying. Only the mighty ones among them, whose patience endured, defeated the guards and opened the gate. And they were instantly awarded seeing the king's face, who appointed each of them in his right place.

Of course, from that moment on, they had no further dealings with those guards, who diverted and misled them and made their lives bitter for several days and years, running back and forth around the gate. This is because they have been rewarded with working and serving before the glory of the king's face inside his palace.

So it is with the work of the complete righteous. The choice applied during the concealment of the face certainly does not apply once they open the door to attain open Providence.

However, they begin their work primarily from the revelation of the face. At that time, they begin to climb up the many rungs in the ladder set up on the earth, and whose top reaches the heaven, as it is written, "The righteous shall go from strength to strength."

It is as our sages say, "Each and every righteous is burned by the canopy of his friend." These works qualify them for the will of the Creator, to realize His thought of creation in them, which is to "delight His creatures" according to His good and generous hand.

134) You should know this law, that there is disclosure only in a place where there was concealment. This is similar to matters of this world where the absence precedes the existence, since the growth of wheat appears only where it was sown and rotted.

It is the same with higher matters, where concealment and disclosure relate to each other as the wick to the light that catches it. This is because any concealment, once it is corrected, is a reason for disclosure of the light related to that kind of concealment, and the light that appears clings to it like light to a wick. Remember this on all your ways.

135) Now you can understand what our sages said, that the whole Torah is the names of the Creator. This seems puzzling, as there are many indecencies, such as names of wicked—Pharaoh, Balaam, etc., prohibition, *Tuma'a* [impurity], cruel curses

in the two admonitions, and so on. Thus, how can we understand that all these are names of the Creator?

136) To understand this, we must know that our ways are not His ways. Our way is to come from the imperfect to perfection. In His way, all the revelations come to us from perfection to the imperfect.

First, complete perfection emanates and emerges from Him. This perfection descends from His face and hangs down restriction by restriction, through several degrees, until it comes to the last, most restricted phase, suitable for our material world. And then the matter appears to us here in this world.

137) From the above-said you will learn that the Torah, whose height is endless, did not emanate or emerge from Him as it appears to us here in this world, since it is known that "The Torah and the Creator are one," and this is not at all apparent in the Torah of this world. Moreover, one who engages in it *Lo Lishma*, his Torah becomes a potion of death for him.

Rather, when it was first emanated from Him, it was emanated and emerged in utter perfection, meaning in the actual form of "The Torah and the Creator are one." This is called "The Torah of *Atzilut*," in the introduction to *Tikkuney Zohar*, p 3, that "He, His Life, and His Self are one." Afterward, it descended from His face and was gradually restricted through many restrictions, until it was given at Sinai, when it was written as it is before us here in this world, clothed in the crass dresses of the material world.

138) Yet, you should know that the distance between the dresses of the Torah in this world and the dresses of the Torah in the world of *Atzilut* is immeasurable. Nevertheless, the Torah itself, meaning the light within the dresses, is not changed at all between the Torah of *Atzilut* and the Torah of this world. This is the meaning of the verse, "I the Lord do not change" (Malachi 3:6).

Moreover, these crass dresses in our Torah of *Assiya* are not at all of inferior value compared to the light that is clothed in it. Rather, their importance is much greater, with respect to the end of their correction, than all its pure dresses in the upper worlds. This is so because the concealment is the reason for the disclosure. After its correction, during the disclosure, the concealment is to the disclosure as a wick is to the light that grips it. The greater the concealment, the greater light will cling to it when it is corrected. Thus, all these crass dresses in which the Torah is clothed in this world, their value is not at all inferior to the light that clothes it, but quite the contrary.

139) This is Moses' triumph over the angels with his argument, "Is there envy among you? Is there evil inclination among you?" (*Shabbat* 89). That is, the greater concealment discloses a greater light. He showed them that in the pure clothes that the Torah clothes in, in the world of the angels, the greater lights cannot appear through them the way it can in dresses of this world.

140) We thus learn that there is no change whatsoever from the Torah of *Atzilut*, where "The Torah and the Creator are one" through the Torah in this world. The only difference is in the dresses, since the dresses of this world conceal the Creator and hide Him.

Know that because of His clothing in the Torah, He is called "teacher." It tells you that even during the concealment of the face, and even during the double concealment, the Creator is present and clothed in the Torah, since He is *Moreh* [Teacher] and she is Torah, but the crass clothes of the Torah before our eyes are as wings that cover and hide the Teacher who is clothed and hides in them.

However, when one is granted the revelation of the face in repentance from love in its fourth discernment, it is said about him, "Your Teacher shall no longer hide Himself, and your eyes shall see your Teacher" (Isaiah 30:20). From then on, the clothes of the Torah no longer hide and conceal the Teacher, and one discovers for all time that "The Torah and the Creator are one."

141) Now you can understand the words of our sages about the words, "Leave Me and keep My law." They interpreted, "I wish that they left Me and kept My Torah—the light in it reforms them" (Jerusalem Talmud, *Hagigah*, Chapter 1, *Halacha* 7).

This is perplexing. They mean that they were fasting and tormenting to find the revelation of His face, as it is written, "They desire the nearness of God" (Isaiah 58:2). Yet, the text tells them in the name of the Creator, "I wish you would leave Me, for all your labor is in vain and futile, for I am nowhere but in the Torah. Hence, keep the Torah and look for Me there, the light in it will reform you, and you will find Me," as it is written, "Those who seek Me shall find Me."

142) Now we can somewhat clarify the essence of the wisdom of Kabbalah, enough for a reliable perception in the quality of that wisdom. Thus, one will not deceive oneself with false imaginations, as the masses imagine.

You should know that the Torah divides into four discernments, which encompass the whole of reality. Three discernments are discerned in the general reality of this world. They are called "world," "year," "soul." The fourth discernment is the conduct of existence of the above three parts of reality, their nourishment, conducts, and all their incidents.

143) That is, 1) the outer part of reality, like the sky and the firmaments, the earth and the seas, etc., that are written in the Torah, all these are called "world." 2) The inner part of reality—man and beast, animals and all kinds of fowl, etc., which are brought in the Torah and exists in the above places, called "outer part," are called "soul." 3) The evolution of reality through the generations is called "cause and consequence." For example, in the evolution of the heads of the generations from *Adam HaRishon* through Joshua and Caleb, who came to the land, which are brought in the Torah, the father is considered the "cause" of the son, who is "caused" by him. This evolution of the details of reality by way of the above cause and consequence is called "year." 4) All

the conducts of the existence of reality, external and internal, in their every incident and conduct brought in the Torah, are called "the existence of reality."

144) Know that when the four worlds called in the wisdom of Kabbalah, *Atzilut*, *Beria*, *Yetzira*, and *Assiya*, cascaded and emerged, they emerged from one another like a seal and imprint. This means that as anything that is written in the seal necessarily appears in what is imprinted from it, no more and no less, so it was in the cascading of the worlds. Thus, all four discernments—world, year, soul—and their modes of existence, which were in the world of *Atzilut*, emerged, were imprinted, and manifested in their image in the world of *Beria*, as well. It is the same from the world of *Beria* to the world of *Yetzira*, down to the world of *Assiya*.

Thus, all three discernments in the reality before us, called "world, year, soul," with all their modes of existence, which are set before our eyes here in this world, extended and appeared here from the world of *Yetzira*, and in *Yetzira* from the one above it.

In this manner, the source of the numerous details before us is in the world of *Atzilut*. Moreover, even the innovations that appear in this world today, each novelty must first appear above, in the world of *Atzilut*. From there, it cascades and appears to us in this world.

This is the meaning of what our sages said, "You have not a blade of grass below that does not have a fortune and a guard above, which strike it and tell it: 'Grow!'" (*Beresheet Rabba*, Chapter 10). This is the meaning of the words, "One does not move one's finger below, before one is declared above" (*Hulin*, p 7b).

145) Know that because of the clothing of the Torah in the three discernments of reality, "world," "year," "soul," and their existence in this material world, produce the prohibitions, *Tuma'a*, and blemish found in the revealed Torah. It has been explained above that the Creator is clothed in it by way of "The Torah and the Creator are one," but in great concealment because these material dresses are the wings that cover and hide Him.

However, the clothing of the Torah in the form of the pure "world," "year," "soul," and their existence in the three upper worlds, called *Atzilut, Beria, Yetzira*, are generally named "the wisdom of Kabbalah."

146) Thus, the wisdom of Kabbalah and the revealed Torah are one and the same. Yet, while a person receives from a Providence of concealment of the face, and the Creator hides in the Torah, it is considered that he is practicing the revealed Torah. In other words, he is incapable of receiving any illumination from the Torah of *Yetzira*, not to mention from above *Yetzira*.

And when one is granted the revelation of the face, he begins to engage in the wisdom of Kabbalah, since the dresses of the revealed Torah themselves were purified for him and his Torah became the Torah of *Yetzira*, called "the wisdom of Kabbalah."

Even for one who is granted the Torah of *Atzilut*, it does not mean that the letters of the Torah have changed for him. Rather, the very same dresses of the revealed Torah have purified for him and became very pure clothes. They have become like the verse, "Your Teacher shall no longer hide Himself, and your eyes shall see your Teacher." At that time, they become as "He, His life, and His self are one."

147) To make the matter somewhat clearer, I will give you an example. For example: While one was in concealment of the face, the letters and the dresses of the Torah necessarily hid the Creator. Hence, he failed, due to the sins and the mistakes he had committed. At that time, he was placed under the punishment of the crass dresses in the Torah, which are impurity, prohibition, and blemish.

However, when one is rewarded with open Providence and repentance from love, when his sins become as merits, all the sins and the mistakes he had failed in while being under the concealment of the face have now shed their crass and very bitter clothes, and have clothed in the garments of light, *Mitzva*, and merits.

This is so because the same crass clothes have turned to merits. Now they are as clothes that extend from the world of *Atzilut* or *Beria*, and they do not cover or hide the Teacher. On the contrary, "Your eyes shall see your Teacher."

Thus, there is no difference whatsoever between the Torah of *Atzilut* and the Torah in this world, between the wisdom of Kabbalah and the revealed Torah. Rather, the only difference is in the person who engages in the Torah. Two may study the Torah in the same portion and the same words, but to one, this Torah will be as the wisdom of Kabbalah and the Torah of *Atzilut*, while to the other, it will be the Torah of *Assiya*, the revealed.

148) Now you will understand the truth in the words of the Vilna Gaon in the prayer book, in the blessing for the Torah. He wrote that the Torah begins with *Sod* [secret], meaning the revealed Torah of *Assiya*, which is considered hidden, since the Creator is completely hidden there.

Afterward, in *Remez* [intimation], meaning that He is more revealed in the Torah of *Yetzira*. Finally, one attains the *Peshat* [literal], which is the Torah of *Atzilut*. It is called *Peshat* for it is *Mufshat* [stripped] of all the clothes that conceal the Creator.

149) Once we have reached thus far, we can provide some idea and insight into the four worlds, known in the wisdom of Kabbalah by the names *Atzilut, Beria, Yetzira, Assiya* of *Kedusha* [holiness], and the four worlds ABYA of *Klipot*, arranged one opposite the other, opposite the ABYA of *Kedusha*.

You will understand all this from the above explanation of the four discernments of attainment of His Providence, and the four degrees of love. First, we shall explain the four worlds ABYA of *Kedusha*, and we shall start from the bottom, from the world of *Assiya*.

150) We have already explained the first two discernments of Providence of concealment of the face. You should know that both are considered the world of *Assiya*. This is why it is written in the book *Tree of Life* (Gate 48, Chapter 3), that the world of *Assiya* is mostly bad, and even the little bit of good contained in it is mixed with bad and is unrecognizable.

Interpretation: From the perspective of the first concealment, it follows that it is mostly bad, meaning the torments and pains that those who receive this Providence feel. And from the perspective of the double concealment, the good is mixed with the bad, as well, and the good is completely indiscernible.

The first discernment of revelation of the face is the discernment of the world of *Yetzira*. This is why it is written in *Tree of Life* (Gate 48, Chapter 3) that the world of *Yetzira* is half good and half bad. This means that he who attains the first discernment of revelation of the face, which is the first form of conditional love, considered a mere "repentance from fear," is called "medium," and he is half guilty and half innocent.

The second discernment of love is also conditional, but there is no trace of any harm or detriment between them. Also, the third discernment of love is the first discernment of unconditional love. Both are regarded as the world of *Beria*.

Hence, it is written in *Tree of Life* (Gate 48, Chapter 3) that the world of *Beria* is mostly good and only its minority is bad, and that minority of bad is indiscernible. This means that since the medium is awarded one *Mitzva*, he sentences himself to the side of merit, and for this reason, he is considered "mostly good," meaning the second discernment of love.

The minute, indiscernible evil that exits in *Beria* extends from the third discernment of love, which is unconditional. Also, he has already sentenced himself to the side of merit, but he has not yet sentenced the whole world. Hence, a minority in him is bad since this love is not yet considered eternal. However, this minority is indiscernible because he still did not feel any harm or detriment, even toward others.

The fourth discernment of love, the unconditional love, which is also eternal, is considered the world of *Atzilut*. This is the meaning of what is written in *Tree of Life*, that in the world of *Atzilut* there is no evil whatsoever, and there, "evil will not dwell with You."

This is because after one has sentenced the entire world to the side of merit, too, love is eternal, complete, and no concealment or cover will ever be conceived, since there is the place of the absolute revelation of the face, as it is written, "Your Teacher shall no longer hide Himself, and your eyes shall see your Teacher." This is because now he knows all of the Creator's dealings with all the people, as true Providence that appears from His name, "The Good who does good to the good and to the bad."

151) Now you can also understand the discernment of the four worlds *ABYA* of *Klipa*, set up opposite the *ABYA* of *Kedusha*, as in "God has made one opposite

the other." This is because the *Merkava* [chariot/structure] of the *Klipot* of *Assiya* comes from the discernment of the concealed face in both its degrees. That *Merkava* dominates in order to make man sentence everything to the side of fault.

And the world of *Yetzira* of *Klipa* catches in its hands the side of fault, which is not corrected in the world of *Yetzira* of *Kedusha*. By this they dominate the medium, which receive from the world of *Yetzira*, by way of "God has made one opposite the other."

The world of *Beria* of *Klipa* has the same power to cancel the conditional love, meaning to cancel only the thing that love hangs on, meaning the imperfection in the love of the second discernment.

And the world of *Atzilut* of *Klipa* is what captures in its hand that minority of evil whose existence in *Beria* is not apparent, due to the third discernment of love. Even though it is true love, by the force of the Good who does good to the good and to the bad, regarded as *Atzilut* of *Kedusha*, still, because he has not been awarded sentencing the whole world to the side of merit, the *Klipa* has the strength to fail the love with regard to Providence over others.

152) This is the meaning of what is written in *Tree of Life*, that the world of *Atzilut* of the *Klipot* stands opposite the world of *Beria*, and not opposite from *Atzilut*. This is so because only the fourth discernment of love extends from the world of *Atzilut* of *Kedusha*. Hence, there is no dominion to the *Klipot* there at all, since he has already sentenced the whole world to the side of merit and knows all the dealings of the Creator in His Providence on people, too, from the Providence of His name, "The Good who does good to the good and to the bad."

However, in the world of *Beria*, from which extends the third discernment, there is still no sentencing of the whole world. Therefore, there is still a hold for the *Klipot*. Yet, these *Klipot* are considered the *Atzilut* of the *Klipa*, since they are opposite the third discernment, the unconditional love, and this love is considered *Atzilut*.

153) Now we have thoroughly explained the four worlds ABYA of *Kedusha* and the *Klipot*, which are the "vis-à-vis" of each and every world. They are considered the deficiency that exists in their corresponding world in *Kedusha*, and they are the ones named "the four worlds ABYA of *Klipot*."

154) These words suffice for any observer to feel the essence of the wisdom of Kabbalah to some degree. You should know that the majority of authors of books of Kabbalah intended their books only to such readers who have already attained a disclosure of the face and all the sublime attainments.

We should not ask, "If they have already been awarded attainments then they know everything through their own attainment, so why then would they still need to delve in books of Kabbalah by others?"

However, it is not wise to ask that question. It is like one who engages in the literal Torah but has no knowledge of the conducts of this world with respect to the "world, year, soul" of this world, and does not know people's behavior and their conducts with themselves and with others. And he also does not know the beasts and the animals and birds in this world. Would you even consider that such a person would be able to understand even a single issue in the Torah correctly? He would invert the issues in the Torah from good to bad and from bad to good, and he would not find his hands or legs in anything.

So is the matter before us: Even if one has been awarded attainment, and even at the level of the Torah of *Atzilut*, he will still not perceive more than relates to his own soul. Yet, one must know all three discernments, "world, year, soul," in their every incident and conduct in full consciousness, to be able to understand the issues in the Torah that relate to that world.

These issues are explained in *The Book of Zohar* and the genuine books of Kabbalah with all their details and intricacies. Thus, every sage and one who understands with his own mind must contemplate them day and night.

155) Therefore, we must ask, Why then did the Kabbalists obligate every person to study the wisdom of Kabbalah? Indeed, there is a great thing about it, which should be publicized: There is a wonderful, invaluable remedy to those who engage in the wisdom of Kabbalah. Although they do not understand what they are learning, through the yearning and the great desire to understand what they are learning, they awaken upon themselves the lights that surround their souls.

This means that every person from Israel is guaranteed to finally attain all the wonderful attainments with which the Creator contemplated in the thought of creation to delight every creature. And one who has not been awarded in this life will be granted in the next life, etc., until one is awarded completing His thought, which He had planned for him, as it is written in *The Zohar*.

And while one has not attained perfection, the lights that are destined to reach him are considered surrounding lights. This means that they stand ready for him but are waiting for him to purify his vessels of reception, and then these lights will clothe the able vessels.

Hence, even when he does not have the vessels, when he engages in this wisdom, mentioning the names of the lights and the vessels related to his soul, they immediately illuminate upon him to a certain extent. However, they illuminate for him without clothing the interior of his soul, for lack of vessels able to receive them. Yet, the illumination one receives time after time during the engagement draws upon him grace from above, and imparts him with abundance of sanctity and purity, which bring him much closer to achieving his wholeness.

156) Yet, there is a strict condition during the engagement in this wisdom not to materialize the matters with imaginary and corporeal issues. This is because thus they breach, "You shall not make unto you a statue or any image."

In that event, one is rather harmed instead of receiving benefit. Therefore, our sages cautioned to study the wisdom only after forty years, or from a rav, and other such warnings. All this is for the above reason.

For this reason, I prepared the commentaries *Panim Meirot* and *Panim Masbirot* on *Tree of Life* in order to rescue the readers from any materialization. However, after the first four parts of these commentaries were printed and circulated among the students, I saw that my explanation was not as clear as I had thought, and all the great effort I had made to explain and elaborate in order to make the matters understood with ease was almost completely futile.

This happened since the readers do not feel the grave necessity to delve into the meaning of each and every word before them and repeat it several times until they remember it well wherever that word appears throughout the book. And by forgetting a word, they become confused about the matters since the subtlety of the matter causes the lack of interpretation of one word to blur the whole matter for them.

In order to correct this, I began to write the "explanation of the words" according to the alphabet, relating to all the words appearing in the books of Kabbalah and that require explanation. On one hand, I collected the commentaries of the ARI and the rest of the first Kabbalists concerning all that they said about that word. On the other hand, I explained the essence from all those interpretations and compiled a solid definition to explain that word in a way that suffices for the reader to understand it in each and every place he meets that word in all the real books of Kabbalah, from the first to the last. This is what I did with all the words used in the wisdom of Kabbalah.

I have already printed the words beginning with the letter *Aleph* [A], and some from the letter *Bet* [B], but only on one side. This is already close to one thousand pages. Alas, for lack of money, I stopped the work in its beginning and for nearly a year now I have not continued this important work, and the Creator knows if I will ever come to it, for there are many expenses and at the moment, no support.

For this reason, I have taken on a different path, as in "Better to have little, but have," and this is the book *Talmud Eser Sefirot* [*The Study of the Ten Sefirot*] related to the ARI. There I collect from the books of the ARI—and especially from his book *Tree of Life*—all the principal essays concerning the explanation of the ten *Sefirot*. I positioned them at the top of each page and made a broad explanation about it called *Ohr Pnimi* [Inner Light], and another explanation called *Histaklut Pnimit* [Inward Observation]. These explain each word and issue presented in the words of the ARI at the top of the page as simply and as easily as I could.

I divided the book into sixteen parts so that each part will be a specific lesson about a specific topic in the ten *Sefirot*. The *Ohr Pnimi* mainly clarifies the words of the ARI presented in that lesson, and the *Histaklut Pnimit* mainly clarifies the matter in general. On top of them, I set up a Table of Questions and a Table of Answers for all the words and matters presented in that part.

Once the reader finishes that part, he should test himself to see if he can answer correctly every question presented in the Table of Questions. After he answers, he should look at the answer relating to that question in the Table of Answers, to see if he has answered correctly. Even if he can answer the questions well by memory, he should repeat the questions many times until it is as though they are placed in a box. At that time, he will remember every word when he needs it, or at least he will remember its place in order to look for it, "and the will of God will succeed through him."

The Order of Learning

Begin with learning the *Panim* [anterior/face], meaning the words of the ARI which are printed at the top of the pages, through the end of the book. Even though you will not understand, repeat them several times, as in "First learn, then understand." Afterward, learn the commentary *Ohr Pnimi*, and exert in it in a manner that you can learn and thoroughly understand the *Panim* even without the help of the commentary. Afterward, study the commentary *Histaklut Pnimit* until you understand and remember all of it.

After all this, test yourself with the Table of Questions. Once you answered a question, look in the answer that pertains to that question. Do so with each and every question; learn and memorize them and repeat them several times until you remember them well, as though they are placed in a box, since in each and every word in the third part, we must remember well the whole of the first two parts, without missing even a tiny meaning. The worst of all is that the reader will not feel what he has forgotten. Rather, either matters have become unclear to him or he adopts a wrong interpretation of the matter because he has forgotten. Naturally, one mistake leads to ten mistakes until he comes to complete misunderstanding and will have to stop learning altogether.

The Author

Introduction to "From the Mouth of a Sage"

It is known from books and from authors that the study of the wisdom of Kabbalah is an absolute must for any person from Israel. If one studies the entire Torah and knows the Mishnah and the Gemara by heart, if one is also filled with virtues and good deeds more than all his contemporaries, but has not learned the wisdom of Kabbalah, he must incarnate once more into this world to study the secrets of Torah and wisdom of truth. This is brought in several places in the writings of our sages.

This is what *The Zohar* writes in the interpretation of "Song of Songs," explaining the verse, "If you know not, O fairest among women," which our sages interpreted as the soul that comes before the Throne after a person's demise.

The Creator tells it, "If you know not, O fairest among women." Although you are the fairest among women and virtuous in good deeds more than all the souls, if you do not have knowledge in the secrets of Torah, "go forth by the footsteps of the flock," leave here and never return to this world. "And feed your kids [young goats] beside the shepherds' tents," go there to the seminaries and learn the secrets of Torah from the mouths of the disciples of our sages.

We must understand their words, conditioning the perfection of a person with the study of the wisdom of truth. Seemingly, how is it different from the other words of the revealed Torah? We found nowhere that one is obligated to understand all the subjects of the Torah and that he will not be completed if one subject in the Torah is missing. Moreover, our sages said that it is not the study that is the most important, but the act. Our sages also said, "One does much, and another does little, as long as they aim their hearts to Heaven," and there are many such sayings.

In order to attain the depth of their above words, we must first thoroughly understand what has been written many times in *The Zohar* and the *Tikkunim* [Corrections of *The Zohar*] with good taste and with reason: "The Torah, the Creator, and Israel are one." This seems very perplexing.

Before I elucidate their words, I will notify you that our sages have defined a great rule for us regarding all the holy names and appellations in the books. These are their golden words: "Anything that we do not attain, we do not define by a name."

Interpretation: It is known that there is no thought or perception in Him whatsoever, as it is written in the article "Elijah Started" in the beginning of the *Tikkunim* of *The Zohar*. For this reason, even the thought of the "self" of the Creator is forbidden, much less the speech.

All the names we call Him do not refer to His self, but only to His lights, expanding from Him to the lower ones. Even the holy name *Ein Sof* [Infinity], presented in the books of Kabbalah is also regarded as light that expands from His essence.

However, since He determined that His light, which expands from His self, will be attained by the lower ones as *Ein Sof*, we shall therefore define it by that name. Yet, this does not refer to His essence. Since there is absolutely no perception or thought in Him, how will we define Him by a name and a word? After all, all that we do not attain, we do not define by a name.

Any beginner in learning the wisdom of truth must contemplate the above great rule before any scrutiny in a book of Kabbalah, that even the thought is forbidden in His self since there is no thought or perception in Him at all, so how can we say a word or a name with regard to Him, which imply attainment?

However, it is a great *Mitzva* [commandment] to examine and research in His illuminations that expand from Him, which are all the holy names and appellations brought in the books. It is an utter must for any person from Israel to study and understand the secrets of Torah and all the ways of His bestowal upon the lower ones, which are the gist of the wisdom of truth and the future reward of the souls at the end of correction.

It is written in the words of our sages, in several places in *The Zohar* and the *Tikkunim*, that all the upper worlds and all the *Sefirot* of the five worlds AK and ABYA have been prepared in advance in quantity and quality to complement the children of Israel. This is so because the soul of one from Israel is a part of God above and "The end of an act is in the preliminary thought."

It arose in His simple will to delight the souls by way of reward for their labor, and for this reason the whole of reality expanded from before Him by way of a sequence of causes and their consequences in the descent of the degrees through the worlds AK and ABYA. Finally, they elicited two discernments clothed in one another, meaning the soul from the concealments of heaven that expands and robes the corporeal body.

The essence of reality expanded through the last degree, which is the corporeal body with a soul. Similarly, the cascading was made by way of cause and consequence relating to the essence of the existence of reality, which are the conducts of His giving that cascade by gradations.

Thus, the upper light, higher than high, will ultimately expand and come to the soul clothed in the corporeal body in this world, as it is written, "for the earth shall be full of the knowledge of the Lord, and they shall teach no more every man his neighbor to know the Lord, for they shall all know Me, from the greatest of them to the least of them."

It is written by our sages and in *The Book of Zohar* that "The whole Torah is the names of the Creator." All the stories and the laws and the sentences, all are His holy names.

According to the above explained, that "Anything that we do not attain, we do not define by a name," you will thoroughly understand that the holy names of the Creator are the attainments that expand from Him to His servants, the prophets and the righteous, each according to his merit, as it is written, "we are distinguished, I and Your people, from all the people that are on the face of the earth."

This distinguishing comes to us through the reception of the Torah and the keeping of Mitzvot [sing. of Mitzvot], first only in the revealed way, which has the merit of purifying our bodies and enhancing our souls to such an extent that we become worthy of attaining the whole Torah and its Mitzvot as His names. This is the entire reward intended for the souls at the end of correction. However, it is in this world, too, as it is written in the Gemara, "You will see your world in your life."

This explains to us why he calls the 613 Mitzvot in several places in *The Zohar* "613 Eitin [Aramaic: counsels] in the Torah." Also, in many places in *The Zohar*, he calls the 613 Mitzvot "613 Pekudin [Aramaic: deposits]." This is so because at first, one must keep the Torah and the Mitzvot in order to purify his body and enhance his soul. At that time, the 613 Mitzvot are as 613 Eitin for him, meaning "tips" by which to ultimately come before the King and be rewarded with the light of His face. Observing the Torah and keeping the Mitzvot gradually cleanse him until he is rewarded with the light of the King of life.

Also, it is written similarly in the Gemara: "Why should the Creator mind if one slaughters at the throat or at the back of the neck? Indeed, the Torah and Mitzvot were given only in order to purify Israel with them."

However, after one has been sufficiently purified and merits the light of His face, one's eyes and soul open and he is rewarded with attaining the 613 holy lights found in the 613 Mitzvot. These are his holy names, meaning the ones that come to our attainment.

By keeping each of the Mitzvot, one takes the part of the light deposited in that Mitzva since the Mitzva is a Kli [vessel] where the light is clothed, meaning a holy name that belongs explicitly to that Mitzva. This is the meaning of "The Mitzva is a candle and the Torah is light."

At that time, he calls the 613 Mitzvot "613 Pekudin." It is like one who deposits good stones and gems in a Kli and says to his loved one, "Take this Kli for yourself but guard it from the thieves and robbers." Thus, they only speak of the Kli, but their primary intention is the precious stones deposited there.

It is known in the books of Kabbalah that the meaning of the holy name "The Blessed Holy One" or *Kudsha Brich Hu* [the same in Aramaic] written by our sages and in *The Zohar* is named after the *HaVaYaH* [Yod-Hey-Vav-Hey]. This holy name contains all the holy names until one higher than high. Thus, we learn that "The Torah and the Creator are one," even though the masses do not see Him in the Torah, but only stories, sentences, and laws.

Indeed, I have already explained that "apples of gold in settings of silver" is how the 613 *Pekudin* are called. It is as our sages said, "The whole Torah is the names of the Creator." Hence, the Torah and the Creator are one.

Yet, there are general and particular, where the Creator is the assembly of all the names and the general light, and the Torah is divided into 613 lights. It follows, that all of them together are one, and are the Creator Himself.

Now there still remains for us to explain the discernment of Israel. First, you must understand the matter of the multiplicity of the separate forms in spirituality, meaning how they are divided and in what. (Author's proofreading) Corporeal things are separated by a knife and such, or time and place separate and distinguish them. Yet, this is unthinkable in spirituality, as it is known to be above time and space.

However, know that the whole difference in spirituality between the upper lights is only in the disparity of form. For example: The mental souls in people are certainly divided into separate souls. Each individual has a different soul.

Yet, the essential difference between them is nothing more than stemming from their disparity of form, meaning that the soul of one is good, the other's is bad, one has acquired wisdom, and the other folly, etc. Our sages say about this, "As their faces differ from each other, so their views differ from each other."

Yet, we can understand that if all the people were to come by the same concepts and the same inclinations without any difference whatsoever, all the souls of all the people would be regarded as a single soul. Its value would have been the same as the sunlight; the light clothes in all the inhabitants of the world, yet we do not discern that there are separate forms in the sunlight. Similarly, one mental soul would have robed in many bodies since places do not separate at all in spiritual matters if there are no separate forms in their attribute.

Now we shall come to the scrutiny, that it is known that the meaning of the souls of the children of Israel is that they are a part of God above. The soul cascaded by way of cause and consequence and descended degree by degree until it was suitable to come into this world and clothe the filthy corporeal body.

It ascends degree by degree until its stature is completed by keeping the Torah and observing its *Mitzvot*. Finally, it is worthy of receiving its complete reward, which has been prepared for it in advance, meaning attaining the holy Torah as the names of the Creator, which are the 613 *Pekudin*.

Now you can see with your mind's eye that "The Torah and Israel are one." The whole difference between the Torah and the soul is due to the disparity of form in the soul, which has been reduced to a very, very small light, and the Torah is simple light that expands from His essence, whose sublimity is endless, for "The Torah and the Creator are one."

However, when the soul is complete in its full stature and receives the Torah in the form of His names, namely attains all the light deposited in the Torah and *Mitzvot*, you find that the light of the soul is equal to the light of the Torah, since it has already attained all the light in the Torah.

It is considered incomplete as long as there is some deficit in attaining a small and subtle part of the general light of the Torah. This is because the entire light was prepared for the souls, as I have explained above, "Everything that we do not attain, we do not define by a name."

Since the light has been prepared for the attainment of the soul, and the soul did not attain all of it, it is therefore deemed incomplete. It is as it is written, "I shall keep the whole Torah except for one thing. Certainly, he is a complete evil."

However, such as that you can declare in the keeping of the Torah and *Mitzvot* in attaining the 613 commandments. It is incomplete when lacking even one thing, great or small.

Hence, in the end—for it will finally come to complete perfection, namely attain the entire light of the Torah—there will be no disparity of form between the light of the soul and the light of Torah. Thus, you tastefully find that the Torah and Israel are literally one.

They are one because there really is no difference and disparity of form between them. Since we have already proven that "The Creator and the Torah are one," and now we have proven that "The Torah and Israel are one," it is therefore evident that "The Torah and the Creator and Israel are one."

From all the above you find that there are two parts in the Torah and *Mitzvot*. The first is Torah and *Mitzvot* as they appear to all, being the keeping of *Mitzvot* and the learning of Torah in the form of 613 *Eitin*. These have the power to purify and cleanse the body, and enhance the merit of the soul to be worthy and fit to receive the light of the King of life as was the soul in its root before it diminished and came to this lowly body in the lowly world. The second part is observing the *Mitzvot* and learning the Torah in the form of 613 *Pekudin*, namely the matter of attaining His names and the full reward of the souls.

The merit of the latter part over the former is as the merit of Heaven over Earth. This is because the first part is merely the preparation, and the second part is the actual completeness and the purpose of creation.

This explains our above question about the words of our sages, that even if a person excels in the Torah and good deeds more than all his contemporaries, if he has not learned the secrets of Torah and the wisdom of truth, he must reincarnate in the world.

We asked: What is the difference between this subject in the wisdom of truth and other subjects in the Torah? We found nowhere that one is compelled to engage in all the topics in the Torah. On the contrary, we have found opposition to that in many places, such as, "One does much, and another does little, as long as they aim their hearts to Heaven," and also, "It is not the study that is of importance, but the act."

Now it becomes utterly clear: The entire part of the revealed Torah is but a preparation to become worthy and merit attaining the concealed part. It is the concealed part that is the very wholeness and the purpose for which man is created.

Hence, clearly, if a part of the concealed part is missing, although one may keep the Torah and observe its Mitzvot in the revealed part, he will still have to come to this world again to receive what he should receive, namely the concealed part in the form of the 613 Pekudin. Only in this is the soul completed, as the Creator had predetermined for it.

You can therefore see the utter necessity for anyone from Israel, whomever he may be, to engage in the internality of the Torah and its secrets. Without it, the intention of creation will not be completed in man.

This is the reason that we reincarnate, generation after generation, to our current generation, which is the residue of the souls upon which the intention of creation has not been completed, as they did not attain the secrets of the Torah in past generations.

This is why it was said in *The Zohar*: "The secrets of Torah are destined to be revealed at the time of the Messiah." It is clear to anyone who understands since they will be completing the intention of creation, and therefore merit the coming of the Messiah. Hence, inevitably, the secrets of the Torah will be revealed among them openly since if the correction is prevented, they will be compelled to reincarnate.

This will explain to you what we should ask about this interpretation in general, for who am I and who are my fathers that I have been awarded making the interpretation to expand the knowledge of the hidden secrets in *The Zohar* and the writings of the ARI? Moreover, why have we thus far found no other to interpret this wisdom as openly as I?

Now you can see that because our generation is really the time of the Messiah and we are all standing at the threshold of the complete correction, and the only prevention is the departure from the wisdom of truth that is present in this generation to the very end, because of the difficulty of the languages and the scattered matters, for one's view ... without knowledge.

In addition to all that, there is the smallness of the mind and the many troubles abundant in our generation. Hence, when the Creator wishes to hasten the redemption of our souls, He has passed a privilege through me to disclose the measure that is in this interpretation, and the will of God succeeded in my hand.

I did have another reason that brought me to interpret this disclosure, as it is written in *The Zohar*: "One must learn a little bit of folly," as it is written, "As the advantage of the light from within the darkness." After I completed my time in the city of Warsaw in the country of Poland, confined to my chamber and having nothing to do with the darkness of my surroundings, I have been blessed with settling in the holy City of Jerusalem.

When I walked among the people, I indeed saw the poverty of my people, the poverty of their mind. Their foolish laughter was in my ears as the crackling of thorns under a pot, mocking and trampling the heart and soul of our yearnings, slandering the Creator, His law, and His people in a loud voice, that there is no wisdom, understanding or knowledge in the wisdom of Kabbalah whatsoever. Rather, it is an assortment of words and names, no sense and no moral, only literal words.

It is a privilege to chatter idle words in the written text with complete faith that they are holy words, and that by this, the purpose of creation will be completed upon us. When the number of those who engage in the literal texts with complete faith increases, the Messiah King will come at once, for by that the whole correction will be completed, and nothing more is needed.

Finally, I met with the famous ones among them. These are people who have already worn out their years delving in the writings of the ARI and *The Zohar*. They have so succeeded, that they have memorized all the writings of the ARI.

They have a reputation as being the holiest people in the land. I asked them if they had studied with a teacher who attained the internality of the matters. They replied, "Heavens, no! There is no internality here at all, but a literally written text, and not more than that, God forbid."

I asked them if Rav Chaim Vital had attained the internality of the matters. They replied, "He certainly did not attain more than we attain." I then asked them about the ARI himself. They answered, "He certainly did not know about the internality more than we do, and all that he knew he'd passed on to his disciple Rav Chaim Vital and so they came to our hands."

I mocked them: "How then were the matters composed in the heart of the ARI without any understanding and knowledge?" They replied, "He received the composition of the matters from Elijah, and he knew the internality since he is an angel." Here I poured my wrath on them, for my patience to be with them had ended.

When I saw that their folly had been rooted in nearly everyone who engage in this wisdom at that time, woe to the ears that so hear, "Will he even force the queen with me in the house?"

The Zohar has already mourned bitterly the denial of the sins in their souls, saying that there are no internal secrets in the Torah, as it is written in the portion *VaYera*, "Has the Torah come to show us fables and historic tales? Such stories and fables are found among other nations, too." Our sages said that they uproot the plantings for they take only *Malchut*.

What would the authors of *The Zohar* say when seeing such a sinful culture of people, denying that there is any knowledge or wisdom in the words of *The Zohar* and the wisdom of truth themselves? They say about the very secrets of the Torah that there is no knowledge and perception revealed in this world, but merely empty words. Thus, they have come to force the *Shechina* [Divinity] inside the King's palace. Woe unto them, for they have caused their souls harm.

Our sages said that the Torah mourns before the Creator: "Your sons have made me a song in public-houses." But they do not even make of the Torah a semblance of a song, only frightening words to any listener that arise contempt and wrath.

Furthermore, they wish to be rewarded like Pinhas, saying that they do this in complete faith. The writing says about them: "Forasmuch as this people draws near, with its mouth and with its lips they honor Me, but have removed their heart far from Me," and this is the reason for the ruin of the First Temple.

The devil still dances among us precisely at the time of the Messiah, the time of the end of the secrets of the Torah. The zeal of the Lord of Hosts came as a fire that will not quench in my bones. Because of it, I have been awakened to disclose the robe to such an extent that they will know that there is wisdom in Israel.

This has been among the primary reasons that made me come to this explanation.

Author's Proofreading

You must see in every purpose and in every goal that it is utterly simple. All the wit, cleverness, and the many issues form during the preparation until they reach the goal. For example, when one wishes to sit in a house, he needs the wit and knowledge in the form of the design, the form of the inventions, the quality and quantity of the rooms and the possessions.

The final goal is but a simple thing: to dwell there. This is the meaning of the words, "according to the beauty of a man, to dwell in the house." It is a simple thought, without any philosophizing and without wit, only a simple will.

Know that all the sophistications in the knowledge are mostly mistakes that should fall before the truth. Yet, the truth itself is simple, without any wit.

There is a secret in this, that this is the iron wall that separates us from the Creator. There are things that are hidden because of their great height and depth, and there are things that are hidden because of their great subtlety, like flies in the air, which are too thin to be seen.

His light is so simple that the human mind, which feels only a tiny portion of an essence, simply does not perceive. It is like the smaller things from the measure needed for an actual tool to see.

This is so because although not all of the depth of the height and the depth of the width are perceived, you can nonetheless perceive the proximate. However, with subtle things, it seems as though they do not exist at all, since you do not attain even a slightest bit of them.

The Prophecy of Baal HaSulam

[from a manuscript]

And it came to pass in the days of the war, the days of the dreadful carnage, that I was praying, crying bitterly all through the night. And behold, at the break of dawn, it seemed as though all the people in the world have gathered in a group before my mind's eye. And a man was hovering among them with his sword over their heads, lashing at their heads. The heads soared upward, and their corpses fell to a great basin and became a sea of bones.

And a voice called out to me: "I am the Lord, God, who governs the whole world with great mercy. Reach out your hand and grip the sword, for now I have given you power and might." Then the spirit of God clothed me, I held the sword, and that man vanished instantly. As I looked unto his place, and he was gone, and the sword—in my possession, my own possession.

And the Lord said unto me: "Go out from your country to the pleasant land, the land of the holy fathers, where I will make you a great sage, and all the sages of the land will be blessed by you, for I have chosen you for a righteous sage in all this generation, to heal the human suffering with lasting salvation. Take this sword in your hand and guard it with your heart and soul, for it is a token between Me and you, that all those good things will happen through you, for until now, I had no such faithful man as you to give him this sword. For this reason, the evildoers did what they did, but from now on, every saboteur who sees My sword in your hand will promptly vanish and be uprooted from the land."

And I hid my face, for I was afraid to look upon He who was speaking to me. And the sword, which seemed to me like a simple iron sword that was a horrible destructor, has turned in my hands into glimmering letters of the holy name *Shadai* whose luster is filled with light, contentment, tranquility, and reassurance for the whole world. And I said to myself: "May I grant all the dwellers of the world a drop of the purity of this sword, for then they will know that there is pleasantness of the Lord in the land."

I raised my eyes, and behold, the Lord stood over me and said to me: "I am the Lord, God of your fathers. Raise your eyes from the place on which you stand before Me and see the whole of reality that I have created existence from absence, upper and lower together, from their very creation in the unfolding of reality through their continuous evolution to their completion, as befits the work of My hands by which to be glorified.

Then I saw and rejoiced over the glorious creation and all that is in it, and the delight and pleasure that all dwellers of the earth enjoy. And I was grateful to the Lord.

Then, I said unto the Lord: "We will serve You with tremor and fear and forever be grateful to Your name, because from You neither bad nor good emerge, but a long succession of pleasantness set before us from beginning to end. Happy are they who stride in Your world, which You have prepared for them, for pleasantness and gentleness and abundance. There is no deviousness or obstacles in all Your deeds, upper and lower together." And I was filled with wondrous wisdom, and atop them all, the wisdom of His absolute private Providence. And so I have gained wisdom day by day for many days—one hundred and eighty days.

In those days, I contemplated praying to the Lord saying, "Behold, I have been filled with wisdom more than all my predecessors, and there is nothing in the world that I do not know. Yet, I do not understand a word of the sayings of the prophets and the sages of the Lord. Also, I do not understand most of the holy names. And I thought—the Lord has promised me such wisdom and knowledge as to become a paragon among the sages and the created beings, yet I still do not understand their sayings."

And before I called, the Creator came over me and said, "But behold, your wisdom and attainment are far above all the sages who have lived on earth thus far. What have you asked of Me which I have not given you? Why torment yourself over understanding the words of prophecy, which you know for certain are uttered from a degree inferior to yours? Would you want Me to bring you down from your degree so you could understand their words as do they?"

I was silent, and I was jubilant, and I answered nothing. Afterward, I asked the Lord, "Thus far, I have not heard a thing about the persistence of my corpse; all the benefits and destinies that have come to me are solely from the spiritual, and there they all aim. What if some illness or bodily harm confuses my mind and I sin before You? Will You cast me from before You and lose all this abundance or punish me?"

And the Lord has sworn to me in His great and terrible Name and in His eternal throne that He will never let His mercy off me for eternity. Should I sin or should I not, His mercy and holiness will never part from me. And I heard and rejoiced. (For you have already achieved your goal, and I have pardoned all your sins, and this mercy.)

And after all these days, I listened attentively to all the promises and destinies I have been chosen for by the Lord, yet I found in them neither satisfaction nor the words by which to speak to the dwellers of this world and lead them to God's will, as He had told me. I could not stride among the people, who are vain and slandering the Lord and His creation, while I was satiated and praising, and walking merrily as though mocking those wretched ones.

Matters have touched me to the bottom of my heart, and I resolved that come what may, even if I descend from my sublime degree, I must make a heartfelt prayer to the Lord to grant me attainment and knowledge of the prophecy and wisdom, and the words by which to help the forlorn people of the world, to raise them to the same degree of wisdom and pleasantness as mine. Although I knew that I must not sadden my spirit, I could not hold back, and I poured my heart out in prayer.

In the morning, I raised my eyes and saw the Dweller of heaven laughing at me and at my words. He said unto me: "What do you see?" and I said, "I see two people struggling—one wise and perfect and strong, the other small and silly, like a newly born child. And the other, the weak, small and tasteless defeats the strong and the perfect." And the Creator said to me: "This little one is destined for greatness."

And the little one opened his mouth and told me some words I did not sufficiently understand, yet I felt in them all the treasures of wisdom and prophecy that abide among all the true prophets, until I knew that the Lord had answered me and gave me ways among all the prophets and sages of the Lord.

Then the Lord said to me, "Rise up, and look to the east." I raised my eyes and saw that that little one has at once rose and equaled himself and his level to the level of the big one, although he still lacked taste and reason as before. And I was bewildered.

Afterward, the Lord spoke to me with a vista, saying, "Lie down on your right-hand side." And I laid down on the ground. And He said to me, "What do you see?" And I said, "I see many peoples and nations, rising and falling, and their faces are deformed humans." Then the Lord said to me, "If you can give form to all these nations and blow into them the spirit of life, I will bring you to the land that I have sworn to your fathers, to give to you, and all my goals will have been fulfilled through you."

The Nation

Jerusalem, *Dalet Sivan, Tav-Shin* (June 5, 1940)

Title page of *The Nation*

Our Intention

This paper, *The Nation*, is a new entity on the Jewish street. It is an "inter-partisan" paper. And you may ask, "What does an 'inter-partisan' paper mean? How can there be a paper that can serve all parties together, despite all the opposition and contrasts among them?"

Indeed, it is a "being" that was born in dire straits, through hard and dreadful labor pains, from amidst the venom of hatred that had struck the nations of the world to obliterate us from the face of the Earth, the destruction of millions of our brothers, and they are prepared to do more. Their sadistic inclination is insatiable, and the calamity is twofold, for we cannot delude ourselves that all this is but a passing, transitory phenomenon, as with our past experiences in history, that if a nation erupts on us, we find a substitute in another.

However, now things are very different. Not only are we simultaneously attacked from all directions, but even the most developed nations have locked their doors before us without any sentiment of mercy or compassion, and in such a ruthless manner that is unprecedented in the whole of human history, even in the most barbaric times.

It is clear, save for relying on miracles, that our existence as individuals or as a nation is hanging between life and death. And the salvation is if we find the required ploy, that great scheme whose way is only to be found near danger, and which can tilt the scale to our favor—to give us a safe haven here for all our brothers in the Diaspora, as everyone says it is, at present, the only place of salvation.

Then the road of life will be open to us, to somehow continue our existence despite the difficulties. And if we miss the opportunity and do not rise as one, with the great efforts required at a time of danger, to guarantee our staying in the land, then the facts before us pose a great threat to us, since matters are developing favorably for our enemies, who seek to destroy us from the face of the Earth.

It is also clear that the enormous effort that the rugged road ahead requires of us mandates unity that is as solid and as hard as steel, from all parts of the nation, without exception. If we do not come out with united ranks toward the mighty forces that are standing on our way to harm us, we will find that our hope is doomed in advance.

And after all that, each person and party sits and meticulously guards its own possessions without any concessions. And under no circumstances can they, or more correctly *want* to reach national unity, as this perilous time for all of us requires. Thus, we are immersed in indifference as though nothing had happened.

Try to imagine that if some nation "showed us the door," as is so common these days, it is certain that then none of us would think about our factional belonging, for the trouble would mold all of us into a single mush, to defend ourselves or to pack up and flee by sea or by land. Had we felt the danger as real, we would undoubtedly be properly united, too, without any difficulty.

Under these circumstances, we have met here—a small group of us, from all sects, people who sense the dreadful whip on their backs as though it had already materialized. They had taken upon themselves to publish this paper, which they believe will be a faithful channel through which to convey their sensations to the whole nation, with all its sects and factions, none excluded. By doing so, the contrasts and the narrow-minded factionalism would be canceled. More correctly, they would be silenced and make way to what precedes them, and we will all be able to unite into a single, solid body, qualified to protect itself at this crucial time.

And although this danger is known to all, as it is known to us, perhaps it has not yet sufficiently evolved in all the public, as it truly is. If they had felt it, they would have long ago shaken off the dust of factionalism to the extent that it obstructs the unity of our ranks. If this is not so, it is only because this sentiment is still not shared by many.

Hence, we have taken upon ourselves the publication of this paper, to stand guard, warn of the trouble, and explain it to the public, until all the segregating elements are silenced and we are able to meet our enemy with united ranks, and give it its duly response in time.

Moreover, we are confident that among us there are still those who search the hearts, who can provide a successful scheme that will unite all the factions in the nation. From experience, we have learned that specifically those people go unnoticed and have no listeners. In this paper, we are willing to make room for anyone who carries a guaranteed solution for uniting the nation, to publicize it and to sound it in the public.

In addition to all the above, by publishing this paper, we aim to defend our ancient culture of two thousand years, since before the ruin of our country. We aim to reveal it and clean it from the piles that have accumulated over it during the years of our exile among the nations, so that their pure Jewish nature will be recognized, as they were at that time. This will bring us the greatest benefit, for we will be able to find a way to connect our Diaspora mode of thinking with that glorious time, and redeem ourselves from borrowing from others.

The Editors

The Individual and the Nation

We humans are social beings. Because we cannot satisfy our vital needs without assistance from others, partnership with many is necessary for our existence. This is not the place to explore the evolutions of the nations, and we can suffice for studying reality as it appears to our eyes.

It is a fact that we cannot fulfill our needs by ourselves, and we need a social life. Hence, individuals were compelled to unite into a union called "a nation" or "a state," in which each engages in one's own trade, some in agriculture, and some in artisanship. They connect through trading of their products. Thus the nations were made, each with its unique nature, both in material life and in cultural life.

Observing life, we see that the process of a nation is just as the process of an individual. The functioning of each person within the nation is like the functioning of the organs in a single body. There must be complete harmony among the organs of each person—the eyes see and the brain is assisted by them to think and to consult, and then the hands work or fight, and the legs walk. Thus, each stands on its guard and awaits its role. Similarly, the organs that comprise the body of the nation—counselors, employers, workers, deliverers, etc.—should function in complete harmony among them. This is necessary for the nation's normal life and for a secured existence.

As the natural death of the individual results from disharmony among one's organs, the nation's natural decline results from some obstruction that occurred among its organs, as our sages testified, "Jerusalem was ruined only because of unfounded hatred that existed in that generation." At that time, the nation was plagued and died, and its organs were scattered to every direction.

Therefore, it is a must for every nation to be strongly united within, so all the individuals within it are attached to one another by instinctive love. Moreover, each individual should feel that the happiness of the nation is one's own happiness, and the nation's decadence is one's own decadence. One should be willing to give one's all for the nation whenever needed. Otherwise, their right to exist as a nation in the world is doomed from the start.

This does not mean that all the people in the nation, without exception, must be so. It means that the people of that nation, who sense that harmony, are the ones who make the nation, and the measure of happiness of the nation and sustainability are measured by their quality. After a sufficient sum of individuals to the existence of the nation has been found, there can be a certain measure of loose limbs, which are not connected to the body of the nation in the above-mentioned measure, since the basis is already secured without them.

Hence, in ancient times, we did not find unions and societies without kinship among their members, since that primitive love, which is necessary for the existence of society, is found only in families that are offshoots of a single father.

However, as the generations evolved, there were already societies connected under the term "state," that is, without any familial or racial ties. The only connection of the individual to the state is no longer a natural, primitive connection, but stems from a common need where each individual bonds with the collective into a single body, which is the state. And the state protects the body and possessions of every individual with all the power of a state.

Indeed, that transition, where the generations moved from the natural nation to the artificial state, from ties that stem from primitive love to ties that stem from a common need, does not take anything from the conditions necessary in a natural, racial state. The rule is that as every healthy individual has complete control over one's organs, which is based solely on love, because the organs joyfully obey without any fear of punishment, the state should completely dominate all the individuals within it with respect to its general needs, based on love and instinctive devotion of the individuals to the collective. This is the most convenient force, sufficient to move the individuals toward the needs of the collective.

However, domination based on coercion and punishment is too weak a force to move every individual sufficiently to guard the needs of the public. The public, too, will weaken and will not be able to fulfill its commitment to guard and to secure each individual's body and possessions.

And we are not concerned with the form of governance of the state, whether autocratic, democratic, or cooperative. They do not change at all the essence of the establishment of the force of social unity. It cannot be established, much less persist, if not through ties of social love.

It is a shame to admit that one of the most precious merits we have lost during the exile, and the most important of them, is the loss of the awareness of the nationality, meaning that natural feeling that connects and sustains each and every nation. The threads of love that connect the nation, which are so natural and primitive in all the nations, have become degenerated and detached from our hearts, and they are gone.

And worst of all, even the little we have left of the national love is not instilled in us positively, as it is in all the nations. Rather, it exists within us on a negative basis: It is the common suffering that each of us suffers being a member of the nation. This has imprinted within us a national awareness and proximity, as with fellow-sufferers.

This is an external cause. As long as this external cause joined and blended with our natural national awareness, an odd kind of national love emerged and sparked off this jumble, unnatural and incomprehensible.

And most important, it is completely unfit for its task. Its measure of warmth suffices only to an ephemeral excitement, but without the power and strength with which we can be rebuilt as a nation that carries itself. This is because a union that exists due to an outside cause is not at all a national union.

In that sense, we are like a pile of nuts, united into a single body from the outside by a sack that envelops and unites them. Their measure of unity does not make them a united body, and each movement applied to the sack produces in them tumult and separation. Thus, they consistently arrive at new unions and partial aggregations. The fault is that they lack the inner unity, and their whole force of unity comes through outside incidents. To us, this is very painful to the heart.

Indeed, the spark of nationalism was kept within us to its fullest measure, but it has dimmed and has become inactive. It has also been greatly harmed by the mixture it had received from the outside, as we have said. However, this does not yet enrich us, and reality is very bitter.

The only hope is to thoroughly establish for ourselves a new national education, to reveal and ignite once more the natural national love that has been dimmed within us, to revive once more the national muscles, which have been inactive in us for two millennia, in every means suitable to this end. Then we will know that we have a natural, reliable foundation to be rebuilt and to continue our existence as a nation, qualified to carry itself as all the nations of the world.

This is a precondition for any work and act. In the beginning, the foundation must be built in a manner sufficiently healthy to carry the load it is meant to carry. Then the construction of the building begins. But it is a shame on those who build buildings without a solid enough basis. Not only are they not building anything, they are putting themselves and others next to them at risk, for the building will fall with the slightest movement and its parts will scatter to all directions.

Here I must stress concerning the above-mentioned national education: Although I aim to plant great love among the individuals in the nation in particular and for the entire nation in general, in the fullest possible measure, this is not at all similar to chauvinism or fascism. We loathe them, and my conscience is completely clear from them. Despite the apparent similarity of the words in their superficial sounds, since chauvinism is nothing but excessive national love, they are essentially far from one another as black from white.

To easily perceive the difference between them, we should compare them to the measures of egoism and altruism in the individual. As said above, the process of the nation is very similar to the process of the individual in all one's particular details. This is a general key by which to perceive all the national laws without deflecting right or left about them, even as a hair's breadth.

Clearly, the measure of egoism inherent in every creature is a necessary condition in the actual existence of the creature. Without it, it would not be a separate and distinct being in itself. Yet, this should not at all deny the measure of altruism in a person. The only thing required is to set distinct boundaries between them: The law of egoism must be kept in all its might, to the extent that it concerns the minimum existence. And with any surplus of that measure, permission is granted to relinquish it for the well-being of one's fellow person.

Naturally, anyone who acts in this manner is to be considered exceptionally altruistic. However, one who relinquishes one's minimal share, too, for the benefit of others, and thus risks one's life, this is completely unnatural and cannot be kept, but only once in life.

The excessive egoist, who has no regard at all for the well-being of others, is loathsome in our eyes, as this is the substance from which the looters, murderers, and all who are corrupt. It is similar with national egoism and altruism: The national love, too, must be imprinted in all the individuals in the nation, no less than the egoistic individual love in a person for one's own needs, sufficient to sustain the existence of the nation as such, so it can carry itself. And the surplus to that minimal measure can be dedicated to the well-being of humanism, to the whole of humanity, without any distinctions of nation or race.

Conversely, we are utterly hateful of the excessive national egoism, starting from nations that have no regard for the well-being of others, through ones that rob and murder other nations for their own pleasure, which is called "chauvinism." Thus, those who completely retire from nationalism and become cosmopolitan for humane, altruistic motives are making a fundamental error, since nationalism and humanism are not at all contradictory.

It is therefore evident that the national love is the basis of every nation, just as egoism is the basis of all individually existing beings. Without it, it would not be able to exist in the world. Similarly, the national love in the individuals of a nation is the basis of the independence of every nation. This is the only reason for which it continues or ceases to exist.

For this reason, this should be the first concern in the revival of the nation. This love is not presently within us, for we have lost it during our wandering among the nations for the past two millennia. Only individuals have gathered here, without any ties of pure national love among them. Rather, one is connected through a common language, another through a common homeland, a third through a common religion, and a fourth through common history. They all want to live here according to the measure by which they lived in the nation from which they came. They do not take into account that there it was a nation based on its own members before he or she had joined it, and which he or she took no active part in establishing it.

However, when a person comes to Israel, where there are no prearranged orders that suffice for a nation to function on its own, we have no other national substance on which structure we can rely, and we also have no wish for it. Rather, here we must rely entirely on our own structure; and how can we do this when there is no natural national connection that will unite us for this task?

These loose ties—language, religion, and history—are important values, and no one denies their national merit. However, they are still completely insufficient to rely on as a basis for the independent sustenance of a nation. In the end, all we have here is a gathering of strangers, descendants of cultures of seventy nations, each building a stage for oneself, one's spirit, and one's leanings. There is no elemental thing here that unites us all from within into a single mass.

I know that there is one thing that is common to all of us: the escape from the bitter exile. However, this is only a superficial union, like the sack that holds the nuts together, as was said above. This is why I said that we must establish for ourselves special education through widespread circulation, to instill in each of us a sense of national love, both from one person to another, and from the individuals to the whole, to rediscover the national love that was instilled within us since the time we were on our land as a nation among the nations.

This work precedes all others because besides being the basis, it gives the stature and successes to all the other actions that we wish to take in this field.

.A.G

The Name of the Nation, the Language, and the Land

We should examine the name of our nation. We have grown accustomed to calling ourselves "Hebrews," while our usual names, "Jew" or "Israel," have all but become obsolete. It is so much so that to distinguish the jargon from the language of the nation we call the language of the nation "Hebrew," and the jargon, "Yiddish."

In the Bible we find the name, Hebrew, pronounced only by the nations of the world, and especially by the Egyptians, such as, "See, he has brought in a Hebrew unto us to mock us" (Genesis 39:14), or "And there was with us there a young man, a Hebrew" (Genesis 41:13), or "This is one of the Hebrews' children" (Exodus 2:6). The Philistines also use this name: "Lest the Hebrews make a sword" (1 Samuel 13:19). We also find it in the relation between the nations and us, such as in the war of Saul with the Philistines, when he declared, "Let the Hebrews hear," and "the Hebrews crossed the Jordan" (1 Samuel 13:7).

Besides, we persistently find the name, "Hebrew," in proximity to slaves, such as a Hebrew slave or a Hebrew maidservant, etc. However, in truth, we will never meet in the Bible the name, "Hebrew," but only one of the two names, "Israel" or "Jew."

The origin of the name, "Hebrew," is that there was probably a famous ancient nation that went by that name, since the verse (Genesis 10:21) presents before us the name of Noah's son as the father of that nation: "And unto Shem, the father of all the children of Ever." Abraham the patriarch was from that nation, which is why the nations called him "Abraham the Hebrew," such as "and told Abram the Hebrew" (Genesis 14:13).

For this reason, before Israel became a nation among the nations, they were called "Hebrews," after the nation of Abraham the patriarch, the Hebrew. Although the children of Israel were distinguished in Egypt as a separate nation, such as "Behold, the people of the children of Israel are too many and too mighty for us; come, let us deal wisely with them, lest they multiply" (Exodus 1:10). However, that name is as a name of a tribe, and not of a nation, for they became a nation only after they had arrived at the land of Israel. From this we should conclude that this is why the nations did not wish to call us "the Israeli nation" even after we had arrived at the land, so as not to admit our existence as a nation. They emphasized it by calling us "Hebrews," as they had called us prior to arriving at the land.

It is not by chance that the name, "Hebrews," is absent in the Bible and in subsequent literature, except in relation to servants and maidservants, to whom the name, "Hebrew," persistently clings: "Hebrew slave," "Hebrew maidservant." But we will never encounter an "Israeli slave" or a "Jewish slave." This juxtaposition is probably a relic of the slavery in Egypt, which we are commanded to remember (Deuteronomy 5:15), "And you will remember that you were a slave in the land of Egypt."

Even today the majority of nations refer to us as "Jews" or "Israelis," and only the Russian nation still relates to us as "Hebrews." Supposedly, the haters of Israel among them have installed this label among them with the ill-will of denying its nationalism from it, just as the ancient peoples. It seems that they had delved into the meaning of this name far more than we, who have taken it absentmindedly due to being used in the Russian language, without much examination. It follows from all the above that if we wish to respect ourselves we should stop using the term, "Hebrew," in relation to any free person among us.

Indeed, regarding the name of the language, if we had a historic source, a language that the ancient Hebrew nation spoke, then perhaps we could call it "Hebrew." And yet, I have not found a single historic evidence that this ancient nation spoke this language.

For this reason, we should consider the Talmudic literature, which is closer to the source than we are by fifteen centuries. Among them, it was unequivocally accepted that the ancient Hebrews did not use this language at all. They said, "In the beginning the Torah was given to Israel in Hebrew letters and the holy language. It was given to them once more in the days of Ezra, in Assyrian letters and the Aramaic language. Israel had sorted out for themselves the Assyrian letters and the holy language, and left the uneducated with the Hebrew letters and Aramaic language" (*Sanhedrin*, 21b). Thus, we learn from their words that only the letters have come to us from the Hebrews, but not the language, because they said, "Assyrian letters and the holy language" and not "Hebrew letters and language."

We do find (*Megillah*, p 8), "Conversely, a Bible that is written in translation, and a translation that is written as the Bible, and Hebrew letters do not defile the hands." Thus, they emphasized, "a translation that is written as the Bible, and in Hebrew letters." They are not saying, "a translation that is written as Hebrew, and in Hebrew letters," like the Mishnah (*Yadaim*, 4:5). This "conversely" is taken from there in order to teach us that only the letters are attributed to the Hebrews, and not the language.

Also, there is no evidence from the words of the Mishnah because it seems that here there was Roman influence on the text. But when they were memorizing the Mishnah, they made the proper precisions.

Conversely, we find that several times the Tannaim referred to the language as "the holy language." One was (*Sifrey Beracha* [*Books of Blessing*], 13), "All who dwell in the land of Israel, read the *Shema* reading morning and evening, and speak the holy language, merit the next world." Also, (*Shekalim*, end of Chapter 3), "We learn from Rabbi Meir that all who are permanently in the land of Israel and speak the holy language..." etc.

Even if we assume that we can find some historic source that the ancient Hebrews spoke this language, it does not obligate us to name this language after them, since there is no trace of this nation among the living. As we have said, this name does not add to our national dignity, and only our enemies have attached it to us on purpose, to discard and slight the image of the nation's assets. Hence, we should also avoid following the English language, which calls the nation "Jews," and the language "Hebrew."

We should also determine which name suits us best: "Jews" or "Israelis." The name, "Israel," stems from our father, Jacob, who, as is written, is named as an expression of power and honor: "Your name will no longer be called Jacob, but Israel; for you have struggled with God and with men and you have prevailed" (Genesis 32:29). It is after him that we are called "Israel."

However, after King Solomon, the nation split in two: the ten tribes, which ordained Jeroboam son of Navat, and the two tribes, Judah and Benjamin, which remained under the kingship of Rehav'am, son of Solomon. The name, "Israel," remained with the ten tribes, and the two tribes, Judah and Benjamin, took for themselves the name, "Jews," as we have found in the story of Ester: "There was a certain Jew in Shushan the castle, whose name was Mordecai the son of Jair the son of Shimei the son of Kish, a Benjamite." Thus, the tribe of Benjamin also called themselves "Jews."

The ten tribes were exiled from the land long before the exile of Judah, and since then there has been no trace of them. The exile of Judah, who were exiled to Babylon, returned to the land after seventy years of exile and rebuilt the land. This is why throughout the period of the Second Temple, the name "Jews" is mentioned most often, and the name "Israel," is mentioned only rarely, under extraordinary circumstances.

We, the offspring of the exile of the Second Temple, are also called primarily by the name, "Jews," since we are from the exile of the Second Temple, the offspring of the two tribes, Judah and Benjamin, who have given themselves the name, "Jews." Accordingly, we should determine that the name of our nation is "Jews" and not "the Israeli nation" or "Israel," which is the name of the ten tribes.

And concerning the language, we should certainly choose the "Jewish language," and not the "Israeli language," for we do not find in the Bible this construct state of "Israeli language," as opposed to the mentioning of "Jewish": "they did not know how to speak Jewish" (Nehemiah 13:24), and also, "And God said ... 'speak now to your servants in Aramaic, for we understand it; and do not speak with us in Jewish in the ears of the people who are on the wall'" (2 Kings 18).

Rather, we should stress that this is why they called their language, "Jewish," since the people of King Hezekiah were called "Jews," as well as those who came from the exile in Babylon. But the ten tribes, which were called "Israelis," also called their language "Israeli language." And yet, even if we assume that it is so, it is still no reason for us, the offspring of Judah and Benjamin, to call our language "Israeli."

To summarize what we have said, both the nation and the language must be given only the name Judah. The nation should be named "Jews," and the language, "Jewish." This jargon language should be called "Yiddish." Only the land may be called "the land of Israel," as it is the inheritance of all the tribes.

Critique of Marxism in Light of the New Reality, and a Solution to the Question Regarding the Unification of All the Factions of the Nation

I have been asked to offer a solution, according to my view, regarding the painful problem of uniting all the parties and factions around a uniform background. At the outset, I must admit that I have no solution to this question in the way it was presented.

Nor will there ever be a solution to it, as wise men from all the nations and throughout the ages have probed it but have not found a natural solution that is accepted by all the factions among them. Many have suffered, and many will suffer still before they find the golden path that does not contradict the views among them.

The difficulty of the matter is that men cannot relinquish their ideals at all, since one can make concessions when it comes to one's material life, to the extent that it is necessary for one's physical existence, but it is not so with ideals. By nature, idealists will give all that they have for the triumph of their idea. And if they must relinquish their ideals even a little, it is not an honest concession. Rather, they stay alert and wait for a time when they can reclaim what is theirs. Therefore, such compromises cannot be trusted.

It is even more so with an ancient nation, with a civilization that is thousands of years old. Its ideals have already developed in it far more than in nations that have developed more recently, so there is no hope whatsoever that they will be able to compromise on this, not even a little. It is unwise to think that in the end, the more just idea will win over the other ideas, since over time they are all right, for "there is not a man without his place, nor a matter without an hour," as our sages have stated.

For this reason, ideals keep reappearing. Ideals that were ruled out in ancient times reappeared in the Middle Ages, and once they were ruled out in the Middle Ages, they have been revived in our generation. This indicates that they are all correct, and none of them is everlasting.

But although the nations of the world suffer terribly from this racket, they still have a strong backbone that allows them to tolerate this terrible burden. Somehow it does not immediately threaten their existence. But what can a poor nation do when its entire existence depends on the crumbs and leftover food that the nations throw to them by their mercy once they are fully satiated? Their back is too frail to carry the burden of this racket, especially in this fateful time when we are standing on the very edge of the abyss—it is not a time for vanity, disputes, and internal war among brothers.

In light of the gravity of the hour, I have a genuine solution to suggest, which I believe merits acceptance, and which will unite all the factions among us into a single unit. However, before I begin to present my suggestion, I would like to put the minds of the readers at rest concerning my political views.

I must admit that I see the socialistic idea of equal and just division as the truest. Our planet is rich enough to provide for all of us, so why should we fight this tragic war to the death, which has been dimming our lives for generations? Let us share among us the labor and its produce equally, and the end to all the troubles! After all, what pleasure do even the millionaires among us derive from their possessions if not the security of their sustenance for them and for their progeny several generations on? But in a regime of just division they will also have the same certainty and even more.

And should you say that they will not have the respect that they had while they were property owners, that, too, is nothing, for all those strong ones who have gained the power to earn respect as property owners will certainly find the same amount of honor elsewhere, for the gates of competition will never be locked.

Indeed, as truthful as this ideal might be, I do not promise its adherents even a shred of paradise. Quite the contrary, they are guaranteed to have troubles as in hell, as the living proof of Russia has already taught us. However, this does not negate the correctness of this ideal.

Its only fault is that to us it is unripe. In other words, our generation is not yet morally ready to accept this government of just and equal division. This is so because we have not had enough time to evolve sufficiently to accept the motto, "from each according to his skills, to each according to his needs."

This is like the sin of *Adam HaRishon* [the First Man]. Our ancient sages have explained that the sin was because he "ate fruit unripe," before it had ripened sufficiently. For that tiny misdeed the entire world was sentenced to death. This teaches us that this is the ancestor of every detriment in the world.

People do not know how to mind and watch everything to see if it has ripened sufficiently. Although the content of a matter may be advantageous, we must still delve more deeply to see if it is ripe, and if the receivers have grown sufficiently to digest it in their intestines. While they are still developing, the truthful and salutary will be turned to harmful and deceitful in their intestines. Thus, they are doomed to perish, for he who eats unripe fruit dies for his sin.

In light of this, the Russian entanglement has not proven that the socialist ideal is essentially unjust, as they still need time to accept this truth and justice. They are still unqualified to behave accordingly; they are only harmed by their own insufficient development and lack of aptitude for this ideal.

It is worthwhile to lend the ear to the words of M. Botkovsky (*Davar*, issue no. 4507). He asks, "Why would a politician, a member of the socialist movement, not do as that physicist, who—when faced with impairments in the interpretation he was accustomed to in the iron laws of his theory—did not deter from abandoning it? First, he gently tried to mend it, and finally, when he could no longer face reality, he was prepared to cast it off."

He explains: "In a time of ruin of the international Labor Movement, we must wash away prejudice. When facts speak the language of defeat, we must sit at the desk once more and vigorously examine the way and its principles. We must responsibly recognize the burden on the shoulders of those who carry on.

"This is the way of scientific thought when cornered by contradictions between the new reality and the theory that explained the old reality. Only an ideological breakthrough enables a new science, and a new life."

He concludes: "If we do not renounce our conscience, we will declare that the time has come for a fundamental debate, a time of labor pains. Now is the time for the leaders of the movement to stand up and answer the question: 'What does socialism mean today? What is the way by which the corps must go?'"

I doubt if anyone in the movement will answer his words, or perhaps be able to understand his words as they truly are. It is not easy for a hundred-year-old man who has been so successful in his studies thus far to get up and all at once strike a line through his past theory, sit at the desk, and resume his studies like that physicist, as comrade Botkovsky requires of the leaders of the socialist movement.

Yet, how do you ignore his words? While it is still possible to sit idly regarding the ruin of the international Labor Movement, since they are not facing immediate destruction, they are still secured a measure of life of submissive servants and slaves; it is not so concerning the danger that the Hebrew Labor Movement faces. They are truly facing annihilation under the slogan of the enemy "to destroy, to slay, and to cause to perish...little children and women," as during the time of Queen Ester.

We must not compare our state of ruin with the ruin of the movement among the nations of the world. If we were only sold to slavery and servitude, we would keep still, as they do. Yet we are denied even the security of the life of slaves.

Thus, we must not let the moment pass. We must attend school once more, reexamine the socialist ideal in light of the facts and contradictions that have surfaced in our days, and not fear of breaking ideological fences, for nothing stands in the way of saving lives.

For this purpose, we will briefly review the evolution of socialism from its earliest stages. In general, there are three eras: The first was humanistic socialism based on the development of morality. It was aimed solely at the exploiters.

The second was based on the recognition of the just and evil. It was aimed primarily at the exploited, to bring them to realize that the workers are the true owners of the work, and that the produce of society belongs to them. Since the workers are the majority in society, they were certain that once they realized that they are the just, they would rise as one, take what is theirs, and establish a government of just and equal division in society.

The third is Marxism, which succeeded more than all of them, and which is based on Historic Materialism. The great contradiction between the creative-forces, which are the workers, and the ones who exploit them, the employers, necessitates that society will ultimately come to peril and destruction. Then the revolution will come in production and distribution. The capitalistic government would be forced into ruin in favor of the government of the proletariat.

In his view, this government was to emerge by itself, by way of cause and consequence. But in order to bring the end sooner still, counsels must be sought, and obstacles must be placed before the bourgeois government, to bring the revolution sooner.

Before I come to criticize his method, I must admit his method is the most just of all its predecessors. After all, we are witnessing the great success it had in quantity and quality throughout the world before it came to practical experimentation among the many millions in Russia. Until then, almost all the leaders of humanity were drawn to it, and this is a true testimony to the justness of his method.

Besides, even theoretically, his words have merit, and no one has been able to contradict his historic stance that humanity is headed slowly and gradually upward, as if on a ladder. Each step is but the negation of its former, hence each movement and phase that humanity has taken in the political government is but a repudiation of its preceding state.

The duration of every political phase is just the time it takes to unveil its shortcomings and evil. While discovering its faults, it makes way for a new phase, liberated from these failings. Thus, these impairments that appear in a situation and destroy it are the very forces of human evolution, as they raise humanity to a more corrected state.

In addition, the faults in the next phase bring humanity to a third and better state. Thus, persisting successively, these negative forces that appear in the situations are the reasons for the progress of humanity. Through them, it climbs up the rungs of the ladder. They are reliable in performing their duty, which is to bring humankind to the last, most desirable state of evolution, purified of any ignominy and blemish.

In this historic process, he shows us how the feudal government manifested its shortcomings and was ruined, making way for the bourgeois government. Now it is time for the bourgeois government to show its faults and be ruined, making way for the better still governance, which according to him, is the government of the proletariat.

However, in this last point, where he promises us that after the ruin of the current bourgeois government, a proletariat government will immediately be instated, here is the flaw in his method: The new reality before us denies it. He thought that the proletariat governance would be the subsequent step to the bourgeois governance, and hence determined that by negating the bourgeois government, a proletariat one would be established instantly. Yet, reality proves that the step following the ruin of the present government is that of Nazis or Fascists.

Evidently, we are still in the middle stages of human development. Humanity has not yet reached the highest level of the ladder of evolution. Who can assume how many rivers of blood are yet to be shed before humankind reaches the desired level?

In order to find a way out of this complication, we must thoroughly perceive the above-mentioned gradual law of evolution upon which he based his entire method. We should know that this law is inclusive for the entire creation; all of nature's systems are based on it, organic and inorganic alike, up to the human species with all its idealistic properties, as well as the materials.

In all the above, there is none that does not obey the iron law of gradual evolution resulting from the collision of these two forces with one another: 1) a positive force, meaning constructive, and 2) a negative force, meaning negative and destructive.

They create and complement the entire reality, in general and particular, through their harsh and perpetual war with one another. As we have said above, the negative force appears at the end of every political phase, elevating it to a better state. Thus, the phases follow one another until they reach their ultimate perfection.

Let us take planet Earth as an example: First, it was but a ball of fog-like gas. Through the gravity inside it, over time, it concentrated the atoms in it into a closer circle. As a result, the ball of gas became a liquid ball of fire.

Over eons of terrible wars between the two forces in Earth, the positive and the negative, the chilling force in it was finally triumphant over the force of liquid fire. It cooled a thin crust around the Earth and hardened there.

However, the planet had not yet grown still from the war between the forces, and after some time the liquid force of fire overpowered and erupted in great tumult from the bowels of the Earth, rising and shattering the cold, hard crust to pieces, turning the planet back into a liquid ball of fire. Then an era of new wars began until the cool force overpowered the force of fire once more, and a second crust was chilled around the ball, harder, thicker, and more durable against the outbreak of the fluids from amidst the ball.

This time it lasted longer, but at last, the liquid forces overpowered once again and erupted from the bowels of the Earth, breaking the crust in pieces. Once more, everything was ruined and became a liquid ball.

Thus, the eons interchanged, and each time the cooling force prevailed, the crust it made grew thicker. Finally, the positive forces overpowered the negative ones and came into complete harmony: The liquids took their place in the bowels of the Earth, and the cold crust became thick enough around them to enable the creation of organic life atop it, as it is today.

All organic bodies develop by the same order. From the moment they are planted to the end of their ripening, they undergo several hundred periods of situations due to the two forces, the positive and the negative, and their war against each other, as described regarding the Earth. These wars yield the ripening of the fruit.

Also, every living thing begins with a tiny drop of fluid. Through gradual development over several hundred phases through the above-mentioned struggle of forces, it finally becomes "A big ox, fit for every work," or "A great man, fit for all his roles."

However, there should be yet another distinction between the ox and the human: Today, the ox has already reached its final phase of development. For us, however, the material force is yet insufficient to bring us to completion due to the contemplative power in us, which is thousands of times more valuable than the material force in us. Thus, for humans there is a new order of gradual development, unlike any other animal: the gradual development of human thought.

Also, being a social creature, the individual development is not enough. Rather, one's final perfection depends on the development of all the members of society. With respect to the development of one's intellectual capability, namely the ability to discern what is good and what is bad for him—though we must not think that man is still at the stage of a primitive man—it is clear that we have not reached perfection. Rather, we are still in the midst of our development, still given to the war between the positive and negative forces, as was said above regarding Earth—which are faithful messengers to their role of bringing humanity to its final completion.

As I have said, since the socialistic ideal is the most just of all the methods, it requires a highly developed generation that can process it and behave accordingly. Since today's humanity is in the middle rungs of the ladder of development, still in the midst of the conflict between the positive and negative forces, it is as yet unfit for this sublime idea. Rather, it is premature in it, like an unripe fruit. Hence, not only is it foul tasting, but the negative force in it is also harmful, sometimes deadly venom. This is the trouble of that nation, for which it suffers so, as they are premature and lack the elementary qualities suitable for assumption of this just governance.

The reader must not suspect that I have any spiritual concept on this matter, for Marx himself says the same thing: He admits that "on the first level of society, deficiencies are unavoidable." However, he promises that "on the highest level of the cooperative society, once the crass hierarchy of people in the division of the work has disappeared, along with the contradiction between physical work and spiritual work, when work itself becomes a necessity and not a means of provision, when along with the multifaceted development of the personality, production forces will grow and all of society's fountains will flow abundantly, then the narrow bourgeois perspective will vanish and society will write upon its banner: 'From each according to his ability, to each according to his needs.'" (Due to the pertinence of the words to our discussion, I have copied his excerpt in full.)

Thus, he, too, admits that it is hopeless to wait for completely just governance before humanity achieves the highest level, before work itself becomes a vital need, meaning life's principle, and not for the purpose of provision. However, he determines that while society is at a lower level, it should also be conducted by cooperative governance, for all its flaws.

But as was said above, this is the drawback in his method. Soviet Russia has already proven that an insufficiently developed society will invert the cooperative governance into the worst governance in the world. Moreover, he assumed that the subsequent phase to the ruin of today's governance is the governance of the workers, but reality has shown that the subsequent governance to today's governance is the Nazi or fascistic governance. This is a grave error. And worst of all, its completion, by and large, threatens specifically the Jewish nation, without any differentiation of class.

We should indeed learn from history. First arises the question: Such a supervisor who has shaken the world with his method, how did he make such a grave mistake? What is the obstacle that tripped him? Indeed, this mandates serious and meticulous consideration of his words.

As was said above, he based his method on historic materialism—that society develops through its conflicting forces by way of cause and consequence, from state to state. When the negative force prevails, it ruins the state, and a better state emerges in its stead through the positive force. They continue to fight until eventually the positive force appears in full.

However, this means that the perfection of society is guaranteed by default, since the negative force will not leave it before it brings it to completion. It follows that we can sit idly and wait for the anticipated self-development. So why all this trouble of this tactic he had placed upon us?

Indeed, it is a silly question, for this is the whole difference between man and beast: All animals rely entirely on nature. They are utterly unable to promote nature or help themselves without it. Not so with man. He is endowed with intellectual powers by which he becomes free of the shackles of nature and promotes it. His way is to emulate nature's work and do likewise. He does not wait for the fledglings to hatch naturally, for the hen to come and warm the eggs. Rather, he builds for himself a machine that warms the eggs and hatches the chicks, like the natural hen.

And if he does this in specific things, he will certainly do it with regard to the development of the whole of humanity. He will not rely on the conflicting forces, with him becoming an object in their collisions. Rather, he will advance nature and will thoroughly emulate its work in this development. He will arrange for himself a good and convenient tactic to bring about the happy end in less time and with less suffering.

This is what Marx wanted by his tactic: the organization, the Class Conflicts, and placing hurdles to undermine the capitalistic regime. His tactic would ease the pains of the suffering subjects, and the stomping on their backs. It would invigorate them to be their own subjects and rush the end of the backward regime to make room for the happy rule of the proletariat. In a word, the Marxist tactic turns the objects into subjects, establishing for them development as they wish.

Summary: The basis is the nature of human development through causal connection, which we see as a natural machine for development. The tactic is a kind of artificial machine for human development, similar to the natural machine. The benefit from the tactic is saving time and diminishing agony.

Now we can begin the critique of his method in a simple manner. It is clear that when we want to make a machine that replaces nature's work, we first need to closely observe nature's mechanism. Subsequently, we can set up an artificial mechanism similar to the natural machine.

For example, if we want to make a machine that replaces a hen's belly, which warms the eggs and hatches the chicks, we must first thoroughly understand nature's forces and manners of development, which operate in the hen's belly. We observe them and make a machine similar to a hen's belly, which can hatch chicks likewise.

It is likewise concerning our matter. When we want to make a machine that will replace the machine of natural human development, here, too, we must first examine those two forces—positive and negative—that operate in nature. It is a machine by which nature performs the procedure of development. Then we, too, will know how to establish a tactic that is similar to the mechanism of nature's natural machine of development, and which will be just as successful in developing humanity. Clearly, if we misunderstand the mechanism of the natural machine, our substitute will be useless, since the whole idea here is to mimic natural ways of creation and adapt artificial ones in their stead.

To be original, to define the matters in terms that will prevent any mistakes by any party, we should define the two forces—positive and negative—operating in the machine of human development by two names: "egoism" and "altruism."

I am not referring to the moral terms regarding them, which we ordinarily use. Rather, only to the material aspect of them, meaning the extent to which they are rooted in man's body to the point that one can no longer liberate oneself from them. That is, with respect to their being active forces in a person: 1) The egoistic force functions in a person similar to centripetal rays [a force that aims toward the center in a circular motion], drawing them from outside the person, and they gather within the body itself. 2) The altruistic serves as centrifugal rays [a force directing outward in a circular motion], which flow from within the body outward.

These forces exist in all parts of reality, in each according to its essence. They also exist in man, according to his essence. They are the key factors in all our actions. There are facts that are caused by a force that serves for one's own individual existence. This is like a force that draws from the external reality to the center of the body anything that is beneficial to itself. Were it not for this force, which serves one, the object itself would not exist. This is called "egoism."

Conversely, there are facts that are caused by a force that flows toward benefiting bodies outside of itself. This force works to benefit others, and it can be called "altruism."

By these distinctions, I name the two forces that struggle with one another on the path of human development. I will call the positive force, an "altruistic force," and I will call the negative force, an "egoistic force."

By the term, "egoism," I am not referring to the original egoism. Rather, I am referring to "narrow egoism." That is, the original egoism is nothing but self-love, which is all of one's positive, individualistic power of existence. In that respect, it is not at odds with the altruistic force, although it does not serve it.

However, it is the nature of egoism that the manner of using it makes it very narrow, since it is more or less compelled to acquire a nature of hatred and exploitation of others in order to make one's own existence easier. Also, it is not abstract hatred, but one that appears in acts of abusing one's friend for one's own benefit, growing murkier according to its degrees, such as deceiving, stealing, robbing, and murdering. This is called "narrow egoism," and in that respect it is at odds with—and the complete opposite from—love of others. It is a negative force that destroys the society.

Its opposite is the altruistic force. This is society's constructive force, since all that one does for another is done only by the altruistic force, as said above. Also, it ascends in its degrees: 1) The first facts of this constructive force are having children and family life. 2) The second ones are benefiting relatives. 3) The third is benefiting the state, 4) and the fourth is to benefit the entire world.

The whole cause of the social structuring is the altruistic force. As said above, these are the elements that operate in the natural machine of the development of humanity—the egoistic force, which is negative to society, and the altruistic, positive force, which is positive for society.

In his emulation of the natural machine of development, Marx regarded only the results of these negative and positive forces, which are the construction and destruction that take place in society. He established the plan of his tactic according to them and overlooked what causes these results.

This is similar to a physician not noticing the root cause of an illness but healing the patient only according to its superficial symptoms. This method always does more harm than good, since you must take both into account: the cause of the illness and the illness itself, and then you can prescribe a successful remedy. That same deficiency exists in the Marxist tactic: He did not take into account the subjective forces in society, but only the constructive and the flaws.

As a result, the direction of his tactic was opposite from the purposeful direction, for while the purposeful direction is altruistic, the direction of the tactic was to the contrary. It is clear that the cooperative governance must be conducted in an altruistic direction, since the very words, "just division," contain a pure altruistic perception, and is completely devoid of the framework of egoism.

Egoism strives to use the other entirely for oneself. For itself, there is no justice in reality whatsoever, as long as it is not working for its own good. The very word, "justice," means "mutual, fair relations," which is a concept in favor of the other. And to the same extent that it acknowledges the entitlement of the other, it necessarily loses its own egoistic entitlement.

It turns out that the very term, "just division," is an altruistic one. Factually speaking, it is impossible to mend the rifts that arise in society with just division, unless by exaggerated altruism. It is so because the reward for spiritual work is greater than that of physical work, and the work of the nimble is more rewarding than the work of the slow, and a bachelor should receive less than one who has a family. Also, the work hours should be equal to all, and the produce of the work should be equal to all. Indeed, how do we mend these rifts?

These are the main rifts, but they split into myriad other rifts, as it appears before us in the Soviet play. The only way to patch them is through a good altruistic will, where the spiritual workers relinquish some of their share in favor of the physical workers, and the bachelors in favor of the married ... or as Marx himself put it, "The work itself will become an imperative need and not merely a means of provision." This is nothing short of a complete altruistic direction.

And since the purposeful regime must be in the altruistic nature, it is necessary that the tactic that aims toward that goal should also be in the same direction as the goal, namely an altruistic direction.

However, in the Marxist tactic, we find the narrowest egoistic direction. This is the opposite direction from the goal: the nurturing of hatred of the opposite class, placing hurdles and ruining the old regime, and cultivating among the workers a feeling that the whole world is enjoying on the back of their work. All these overly intensify the narrow egoistic forces among the workers. It completely deprives them of the altruistic force inherent in them by nature. And if the tactic is in the opposite direction to the goal, how will one ever reach it?

This engendered the contradiction between his theory and the new reality: He thought that the subsequent stage to the bourgeois regime would be a cooperative workers' regime, but in the end, we are living witnesses that if the democratic bourgeois government were to be ruined now, a Nazi and fascist regime would promptly rise in its stead. Also, it will not necessarily be through the current war, but whenever the democratic government is ruined, a fascist, Nazi regime will inherit it.

There is no doubt that if this were to happen, the workers would be pushed back a thousand years. They will have to wait for several regimes to arise by cause and consequence before the world returns to today's democratic bourgeois regime. All this emerged out of the egoistic tactic that was given to those subjects that should be the workers' governance and led the movement in an opposite direction from the goal.

We should also take into account that all those who are ruining the natural process of the just governance actually came from the proletariat and emerged from their midst, and not necessarily the Soviets, but the majority of Nazis were also initially pure socialists, as well as the majority of fascists. Even Mussolini himself was initially an enthusiastic socialist leader. This completes the picture, how the Marxist tactic has led the workers in the complete opposite direction from the goal.

Indeed, it is difficult to determine that such a straightforward matter will be overlooked by the creator of the Marxist method, especially since he himself determined that "There is no remedy for the cooperative society before the crass hierarchy in division of work and conflicts between physical work and spiritual work disappears." Thus, it is clear that he was aware that a cooperative society without the members' complete relinquishment of their shares in favor of the fellow person is unsustainable.

And since he knew of that altruistic element that is mandatory in society, I say that he did not intend at all to offer us a purposeful procedure by his tactic. Rather, he intended primarily to hurry—through this tactic—the end of the present unjust governance, on the one hand, and on the other hand, to organize the international proletariat and prepare them to be a strong, decisive force when the bourgeois regime is ruined. These are two necessary fundamentals in the stages that facilitate the regime of a cooperative society.

In that respect, his tactic is a genius invention, the like of which we do not find in history. And concerning the establishing of the happy society, he relied on history itself to complete it, for it was clear to him that in dire times, when the bourgeois regime begins to die, the proletariat organization will find itself unprepared to assume governance. At that time, the workers will have to choose one of two options: 1) either to destroy themselves and let the true destructors, the Nazis and the fascists, take over the helm of governance, or 2) find a good tactic by which to qualify the workers to assume governance into their own hands.

In his mind, he was certain that when we come to a state where the international proletariat joins into a decisive power in the world, we will thank him for the validity of his method, which has brought us thus far, and we ourselves will seek the way to continue moving toward the goal. Indeed, there has never been an inventor who did not leave the completion of his work to his successors.

If we look deeper into his method we will see that, in fact, he could not invent for us the tactic to complete the qualification of the workers, as they are two procedures that contradict one another. To create the fastest movement and annihilate the governances of abusers, he had to use the procedure in the direction of the narrowest egoism, meaning to develop profound hatred to the class of abusers in order to increase the negative power into an instrument that can destroy the old regime in the quickest possible time, and to organize the workers in the strongest ties.

For this reason, he had to uproot and neutralize the altruistic force in the proletariat, whose nature is to tolerate and concede to its abusers. To qualify the workers in "practical socialism," so they could assume the governance *de facto*, he had to use the procedure in the altruistic direction, which contradicts the "organizational procedure." Thus, he must have left this work for us on purpose.

He did not doubt our understanding or ability since the matter was so straightforward that a cooperative government is feasible only on an altruistic basis, so we would have to adopt a new tactic in the altruistic direction and qualify the workers to take governance into their hands in a practical and sustainable manner. However, to comment on it, he found it necessary to depict for us the form of just governance of the proletariat in the abbreviated words, "Society will make its motto, 'From each according to his skills, to each according to his work.'" Thus, even a totally blind person would find these words to mean that just governance is inconceivable if not in an altruistic society in the full sense of the word.

From that perspective, Marxism did not encounter any confrontation due to the unsuccessful Russian experiment. And if Marxism has been stopped, it is only because its role in the first act has been completed, namely organizing the international proletariat into a force. Now we must find a practical way to qualify the movement to actually assume the government into its hands.

As said above, the current procedure must be in the completely opposite direction from the previous tactic. Where we had cultivated excessive egoism, which was very successful in the first act, we must now cultivate excessive altruism among the workers. This is utterly mandatory for the social nature of the cooperative regime. Thus, we will lead the movement with confidence to its practical role of assuming governance into its own hands in its final, happy form.

I know that it is not the easiest work to completely reverse the direction of the movement so that all who hear it will be burned by it as if by boiling water. Yet, it is not as bad as it is portrayed. We can bring the movement into recognition through proper explanation that the interest of the class depends on this, "whether it persists or perishes," whether to continue the Marxist movement or hand over the reigns of governance to the Nazis and the fascists—the most dangerous forces to the government of the workers, which pose the risk of regression by a thousand years.

When the masses understand this, it is certain that they will easily adopt the new, practical tactic leading them to actual assumption of the governance. Who does not remember how the whole world anxiously awaited the successful end of the Soviet regime? And were they not successful, the whole world would undoubtedly be under the reins of the cooperative government. Indeed, the Russians could not possibly succeed because the organizational direction to which the masses are accustomed is the egoistic one, which is necessary in the first act, and by nature, it is a power that destroys the cooperative governance.

Before the method is accepted, it is too soon to speak in detail about the practical program of this direction, especially since the essay has become too long already. Briefly, we can say that we must set up such dissemination, scientifically and practically, that will be certain to install in the public opinion that any member who does not excel in altruism is like a predator that is unfit to be among humans, until one feels oneself within the society as a murderer and a robber.

If we systematically engage in circulating this matter using the appropriate manners, it will not require such a long process. Hitlerism proves that within a short period of time, an entire country has been turned upside down through propaganda and accepted his bizarre notion.

Now that historic facts have clarified the right way in which the movement should go henceforth, I urgently appeal to our workers. As was said above, the nations of the world may wait, especially now that there is global upheaval and we must first be rid of the Hitlerian danger. But we have no time to waste. I ask that you will promptly pay attention to this new method that I have proposed, and which I call "practical socialism," for until now the role of socialism, in my view, was merely "organizational socialism," as said above.

If my method is accepted, we should also change the outward tactic, where instead of the old weapon of class hatred and hatred of religion, they will be given a new weapon of hatred of the excessive egoism in the proprietors. It is successful for its task from every angle because not only will the opposite class be unable to defend using the thick shields of moral and religious dogmas, it will also uproot along the way various noxious weeds of Nazism and fascism that have taken root quite strongly among the proletariat itself, risking its existence, as above said.

We should also take into account the beauty of this weapon, which is most enticing and can unite our youth around it. In fact, the change is not so much in the tactic, but only in the result. Until now, when they fought against the depriving of the class, the fighter always looks through the narrow possessive-egoistic perspective, as he is protecting his own possession. Thus, along with his war, the excessive egoistic force increases in him, and the warriors themselves are caught up in the same bourgeois perspective.

It is also very unlike the proprietors' approach, for they believe they have complete entitlement from all sides, by law, religion, and ethics, protecting themselves by all the means. However, when fighting against the egoism of the proprietors using the broad perspective of an altruistic perception, the result is that the power of altruism grows within them in proportion to the level of their struggle. Thus, the entitlement of the proprietors becomes very flawed and they cannot defend themselves, for this type of war relies heavily on the ethical and religious perception in the proprietors themselves.

Thus, my method holds the basis for national unity, for which we are so thirsty at this time. Presumably, history itself has already broken many of the political partitions among us, for now we can no longer distinguish between non-Zionists, spiritual Zionists, political Zionists, territorial ones, etc. Now that all the hopes of breathing free air outside our country have been shattered, even the most devout non-Zionists have become, by necessity, complete practical Zionists. Thus, in principle, the majority of rifts among us have been mended.

However, we are still suffering from two terrible partitions: 1) class partition; 2) religious partition. We must not slight these whatsoever, nor can we hope to ever be rid of them. However, if my new method of "practical socialism," which I have suggested, is accepted by the movement, we will be rid once and for all of the class wedge, too, which has been stuck in the nation's back.

As was said above, the new tactic takes much from religion, and does not aim at the abusing sinners, but only at their sins—only at the contemptible egoism within them. In truth, that same war will unfold in part within the movement, too, which will necessarily abolish class hatred and religious hatred. We will obtain the ability to understand one another and achieve complete unity of the nation with all its factions and parties, as this perilous time for all of us requires. This is the guarantee to our victory on all fronts.

Regarding the Question of the Day

We have grown weary of the contradicting pieces of information regarding Italy's joining the war that we receive each day. Once, we are promised that Mussolini would not dare to fight the Allies, and once, that he is promptly joining the war. Changes occur daily, and nerves are wrecked. All indications show that all these pieces of information are edited and presented to us by a Hitler-Mussolini factory, whose only aim is to weaken our nerves.

One way or the other, we must seek shelter from them. We must promptly turn away from all these odd pieces of news and try to follow the leading factors and all of these adventures by ourselves, so we might understand from them all those perplexing moves of Hitler-Mussolini.

But mainly, we should note the contract of their agreement. It is known that they have signed two contracts: The first was merely a political agreement, which they named the "Rome-Berlin Axis." Its content is mutual political aid and division of certain areas of influence between them. Following this agreement, Hitler provided political aid to Mussolini in his war in Ethiopia, and Mussolini did likewise for Hitler in his prewar adventures, and continues to do it still. 2) Near the outbreak of the war, they made a second, military pact, whose content we do not know. However, in general, we know that they have committed to actual mutual military aid.

There is sufficient proof to assume that they did not commit to wage the war together promptly, as with the England-France agreement. This agreement was built entirely on Hitler's initiative, for with it he wished to secure himself from any trouble that might come—should he be in military crisis and will need Italy's assistance. At such a time, the agreement commits Italy to come to his aid, following Hitler's invitation, and naturally, under certain conditions regarding the division of the spoil.

But essentially, Hitler did not think that he would need Italy's military assistance. There were two reasons for it: 1) He was confident of his strength and did not trust Italy's military skills. 2) The previous political agreement, too, the "Rome-Berlin Axis," already secured him substantial military aid, since by mere political maneuvers

Italy could occupy many of his enemies' forces on the borders of Italy. This is not far from taking an active role in the war. Thus, he had no desire at all to actually include Mussolini in his war. The military pact that he had made with him was only in case of a military crisis, which would commit Mussolini to come to his aid explicitly following Hitler's invitation, and the initiative would not be in Mussolini's hands at all.

Correspondingly, Mussolini was hoping to fulfill through this war all of his fascist plans to reinstate the ancient Roman Empire. He could not have hoped for a better opportunity than to fight his war alongside Hitler. Undoubtedly, he is anxious for the moment when Hitler asks him to join him in the war. Presumably, Hitler has not lost faith in his power and as yet has no desire whatsoever to include him in the war, or put differently, to share the spoil with him.

It therefore follows that as long as we do not feel that there is a real crisis among Hitler's armies, we have nothing to fear from Mussolini's threats and his preparations for the war. These are nothing but shrewd military maneuvers intended to stall the Allies on his borders and weaken the power of the Allies in the front as much as possible, in accord with the conditions of the "Rome-Berlin Axis" contract. (While writing, information has arrived that Italy has joined the war, so the essay was stopped midway. We will finish the article according to the present reality.)

Now that Italy's joining the war has become a fact, much has been clarified, if we discuss according to the line we have depicted. Now we know for certain that in the last battle, Hitler has come to a real crisis and his powers have been completely worn there. Otherwise, there is no doubt that he would not include Italy in the war. For this reason, Italy's joining the war is good news, of sorts, concerning Germany's downfall. We hope that Italy's assistance will not save it, too, and now the victory of the Allies is more certain than ever.

Public Stage

We hereby offer room in our paper for a "public stage" for anyone who discusses national matters, and especially the unification of the nation. Also, anyone with an important national matter, or a plan to unite the nation, as well as arguments that scrutinize these matters—we are willing to take them and publish them in our paper.

The Editors

The Study of the Ten Sefirot, Part One, Inner Observation

First, we must know that when dealing with spiritual matters, which have no concern with time, space, or motion, and moreover when dealing with Godliness, we do not have the words by which to contemplate and express. Our entire vocabulary is taken from sensations of imaginary senses. Thus, how can they assist us where sense and imagination do not reign?

For example, if you take the subtlest of words, namely "lights," it nonetheless resembles and borrows from the light of the sun or an emotional light of contentment. Thus, how can they be used to express Godly matters? They would certainly fail to provide the reader with anything true.

It is even truer in a place where these words should disclose the negotiations in the wisdom in print, as is done in any research of wisdom. If we fail with even a single inadequate word, the reader will be instantly disoriented and will not find his hands or legs in this whole matter.

For this reason, the sages of Kabbalah have chosen a special language that we can call "the language of the branches." There is not an essence or a conduct of an essence in this world that does not derive from its root in the upper world. Moreover, the beginning of every being in this world starts from the upper world and then cascades to this world.

Thus, the sages have found an adequate language without trouble by which they could convey their attainments to each other by word of mouth and in writing from generation to generation. They have taken the names of the branches in this world, where each name is self-explanatory, as though pointing to its upper root in the system of the upper worlds.

That should appease your mind regarding the perplexing expressions we often find in books of Kabbalah, and some that are even foreign to the human spirit. It is because once they have chosen this language to express themselves, namely the language of the branches, they could no longer leave a branch unused because of its inferior degree. They could not avoid using it to express the desired concept when our world suggests no other branch to be taken in its place.

Just as two hairs do not feed off the same foramen, so we do not have two branches that relate to the same root. It is also impossible to exterminate the object in the wisdom that is related to that inferior expression. Such a loss would inflict impairment and great confusion in the entire scope of the wisdom, since there is no other wisdom in the world where matters are so intermingled through cause and effect, reason and consequence as in the wisdom of Kabbalah, where matters are interconnected and tied to each other from top to bottom like one long chain.

Thus, there is no freedom of will here to switch or replace the bad names with better ones. We must always provide the exact branch that points to its upper root and elaborate on it until the accurate definition is provided for the scrutinizing readers.

Indeed, those whose eyes have not been opened to the sights of heaven, and have not acquired the proficiency in the connections of the branches of this world with their roots in the upper worlds are like the blind scraping the walls. They will not understand the true meaning of even a single word, for each word is a name of a branch that relates to its root.

Only if they receive an interpretation from a genuine sage who makes himself available to explain the matter in the spoken language, which is necessarily like translating from one language to another, meaning from the language of the branches to the spoken language, only then he will be able to explain the spiritual term as it is.

This is what I have troubled to do in this interpretation, to explain the ten Sefirot as the Godly sage the Ari had instructed us, in their spiritual purity, devoid of any tangible terms. Thus, any beginner may approach the wisdom without failing in any materialization or mistake. With the understanding of these ten Sefirot, one will also come to examine and know how to comprehend the rest of the issues in this wisdom.

Chapter One

"Know that before the emanated beings were emanated and the created beings created, an upper simple light had filled the whole of reality" (*Tree of Life*, 1:1). These words require explanation: How was there a reality that the simple light had filled before the worlds were emanated? Also, the matter of the ascent of the desire in order to be restricted so as to bring to light the perfection of His deeds. It is implied in the book that there was already some deficiency there.

Also, the issue of the middle point in Him, where the restriction occurred, is also quite perplexing, for he had already said that there is neither beginning nor end there, so how is there a middle? Indeed these words are deeper than the sea, and I must therefore elaborate on their interpretation.

> There is not one thing in the whole of reality that is not contained in Ein Sof. The contradicting terms in our world are contained in Him in the form of One, Unique, and Unified.

1) Know that there is not an essence of a single being in the world, both the ones perceived by our senses and the ones perceived by our mind's eye, that is not included in the Creator, for they all come to us from Him, and can one give that which is not in him?

This matter has already been thoroughly explained in the books, but we must understand the concepts that are separated or opposite for us, such as the term "wisdom" is regarded as different from the term "sweetness," as wisdom and sweetness are two separate terms. Similarly, the term "operator" certainly differs from the term "operation." The operator and its operation are necessarily two separate concepts. It is even more so with opposite terms such as "sweet" and "bitter"; these are certainly discerned as separate.

However, in Him, wisdom, pleasure, sweetness and acerbity, operation and operator, and other such different and opposite forms are all contained as one in His simple light. There are no differentiations among them whatsoever, as is the term "One, Unique, and Unified."

"One" indicates a single evenness. "Unique" implies that everything that extends from Him, all these multiplicities, are in Him as single as His self. "Unified" shows that although He performs the multiple operations, one force performs all these, and they all return and unite in the form of One. Indeed, this one form swallows all the forms that appear in His operations.

This is a very subtle matter and not every mind can tolerate it. Nachmanides explained to us the matter of His uniqueness, as "One, Unique, and Unified." These are his words in his commentary on *The Book of Creation*, Chapter 1, 47: There is a difference between One, Unique, and Unified: When He unites to act with one force, He is called "Unified." When He divides to act His act, each part of Him is called "Unique." When He is in a single evenness, He is called "One." Thus far his pure words.

Interpretation: "Unites to act with one force" means that His operations differ from each other and He seems to be doing good and bad. At that time, He is called "Unique" since all His different operations have a single outcome: doing good.

We find that He is unique in every single act and does not change by His different operations. "When He is in a single evenness," meaning "One," it points to His self, for in Him, all the opposites are in "single evenness," as written above. It is as Maimonides wrote, "In Him, the one who knows, the known and the knowledge are one, for His thoughts are far higher than our thoughts, and His ways than our ways."

Two discernments in bestowal: before it is received and after it is received.

2) We should learn from those who ate the manna. Manna is called "bread from heaven" because it did not materialize when clothing in this world. Our sages said that each one tasted in it everything he wanted.

This means that it had to have contained opposite forms: One person tasted it as sweet and another tasted it as acrid and bitter. Thus, the manna itself had to have contained both opposites together, for can one give what is not in him? Thus, how can there be two opposites in one subject?

It is therefore necessary that it is simple and devoid of both flavors, but is only included in them in a way that the corporeal receiver might discern the taste that one wants. Likewise, you can understand that anything spiritual is unique and simple in itself, but contains all the myriad forms in the world. When it comes to corporeal, limited receiver, the receiver makes in it a separate form from all the myriad forms united in that spiritual essence.

We should therefore always distinguish two discernments in His bestowal: The first is the form of the essence of that upper abundance before it is received, when it is still an inclusive, simple light. The second is that after the abundance has been received, for by this it acquired one separate form according to the properties of the receiver.

How can we perceive the soul as a part of Godliness?

3) Now we can come to understand what the Kabbalists wrote about the essence of the soul: "The soul is a part of God above and is not at all changed from the Whole, except in that the soul is a part and not the Whole." It is like a stone that is carved from a mountain. The essence of the mountain and the essence of the stone are the same and there is no distinction between the stone and the mountain, except that the stone is a part of the mountain, and the mountain is the Whole, thus far the essence of their words.

These words seem utterly perplexing, and the most difficult is to understand how it is possible to discern a difference and a part in Godliness to the point of resembling it to a stone that is carved from a mountain. The stone is carved from the mountain by an ax and a sledgehammer. But in Godliness, how and what would separate them from one another?

The spiritual is divided by disparity of form, as the corporeal is divided by an ax.

4) Before we come to clarify the matter, we shall explain the essence of the separation in spirituality: Know that spiritual entities become separated from one another only by disparity of form. In other words, if one spiritual entity acquires two forms, it is no longer one, but two.

Let me explain it in souls of people, which are also spiritual: It is known that the form of the spiritual law is simple. Certainly, there are as many souls as there are bodies, where the souls shine. However, they are separated from one another by the disparity of form in each of them, as our sages said, "As their faces are not the same, their opinions are not similar." The body can discern the form of the souls and tell if each specific soul is a good soul or a bad soul, and likewise with the various forms.

You now see that as a corporeal matter is divided, cut, and becomes separated by an ax and motion that increase the distance between each part, a spiritual matter is divided, cut, and separated by the disparity of form between each part. According to the measure of disparity, so is the distance between each two parts, and remember this well.

How can there be disparity of form in creation with respect to Ein Sof?

5) We are still not content. In this world, in souls of people, in relation to the soul, of which it was said to be a part of God above, it is still unclear how it is separated from Godliness to the point that we can call it "a Godly part." We should not say "by disparity of form," since we have already said that Godliness is simple light that contains the whole abundance of forms and opposite forms in the world in His simple uniqueness, as in "one, unique, and unified." Hence, how can we depict disparity of form in the soul, making it different from Godliness, rendering it distinct, to acquire a part of Him there?

Indeed, this question applies primarily to the light of Ein Sof [infinity/no end] prior to the restriction, for in the reality before us, all the worlds, upper ones and lower ones, are discerned by two discernments: The first discernment is the form of this entire reality as it is prior to the restriction. At that time, everything was without a boundary and without an end. This discernment is called "the light of Ein Sof." The second discernment is the form of this entire reality from the restriction downward. Then everything became limited and measured. This discernment is called the four worlds Atzilut, Beria, Yetzira, Assiya.

It is known that there is no thought or perception whatsoever in His self, and there is no name or appellation in Him, anything that we do not attain, how can we define it by a name? Any name implies attainment, indicating that we have attained it as that name. Thus, it is certain that there is no name or appellation whatsoever in His self, and all the names and appellations are but in His light which expands from Him. The expansion of His light prior to the restriction, which had filled the whole of reality, without a boundary or an end, is called Ein Sof. Thus, we should understand how the light of Ein Sof is defined in and of itself, and has departed from His self to the point that we may define it by a name, as we have said about the soul.

Explanation of the words of our sages: "Hence, work and labor have been prepared for the reward of the souls, for 'One who eats that which is not one's own is afraid to look upon one's face.'"

6) To somewhat understand this sublime place, we must go into further detail. We shall research the axis of the entire reality before us and its general purpose. Is there an operation without a purpose? And what is that purpose for which He has invented this entire reality before us in the upper worlds and in the lower worlds?

Indeed, our sages have already instructed us in many places that all the worlds were created only for Israel, who observe Torah and Mitzvot [commandments], etc., and this is well known. However, we should understand this question of our sages, who asked about it: "If the purpose of the creation of the worlds was to delight His creatures, why did He create this corporeal, turbid, and tormented world? Without it, He could certainly delight the souls as much as He wanted, so why did He bring the soul into such a murky and filthy body?"

They explained it with the verse, "One who eats that which is not one's own is afraid to look upon one's face." This means there is a flaw of shame in any free gift. To spare the souls this blemish, He has created this world where there is work, and they will enjoy their labor in the future, for they take their whole reward in return for their work, and are thus spared the blemish of shame.

What is the connection between working seventy years and eternal delight, as there is no greater free gift than this?

7) These words of theirs are perplexing through and through. First bewilderment: Our primary aim and prayer is "Spare us the treasure of a free gift." Our sages said that the treasure of a free gift is prepared only for the greatest souls in the world.

Their answer is even more perplexing: They said that there is a great flaw in free gifts, namely the shame that encounters every receiver of a free gift. To mend this, the Creator has prepared this world, where there is work and labor, so as to take the reward for their work and labor in the next world.

But their answer is very odd. What is this like? It is like a person who says to his friend, "Work with me for just one moment, and in return, I will give you every pleasure and treasure in the world for the rest of your life." There is indeed no greater free gift than this, since the reward is utterly incomparable with the work, for the work is in this world, a transient, worthless world compared to the reward and the pleasure in the eternal world, for what value is there to the passing world compared to the eternal world? It is even more so with regard to the quality of the labor, which is worthless compared to the quality of the reward.

Our sages said, "The Creator is destined to bequeath each and every righteous 310 worlds, etc." We cannot say that the Creator gives some of the reward in return for their work, and the rest as a free gift, for then what good would that do? The blemish of shame would remain in the rest of the gift! Indeed, their words are not to be taken literally, for there is a profound meaning here.

The whole of reality was emanated and created with a single thought. It is the operator; it is the very operation; it is the sought-after reward, and it is the essence of the labor.

8) Before we delve into the explanation of their words, we must understand His thought in creating the worlds and the reality before us. His operations did not come to be by many thoughts, as is our way, for He is one, unique, and unified. And as He

is simple, His lights, which extend from Him, are simple and unified, without any proliferation of forms, as it is written, "My thoughts are not your thoughts, neither are your ways My ways."

Therefore, understand and perceive that all the names and appellations, and all the worlds, upper and lower, are all one simple, unique, and unified light. In the Creator, the light that extends, the thought, the operation, the operator, and anything the heart can think and contemplate are in Him one and the same thing.

Thus, you can judge and perceive that this entire reality, upper ones and lower ones as one, in its final state of the end of correction, was emanated and created with a single thought. That single thought performs all the operations; it is the essence of all the operations, the purpose and the essence of the labor. It is by itself the very perfection and the sought-after reward, as Nachmanides wrote, "one, unique, and unified."

The matter of the restriction explains how an incomplete operation emerged from the perfect operator.

9) The ARI elaborated on the matter of the first restriction in the first chapters of this book. This is a very serious matter as it is necessary that all the corruptions and all the various shortcomings extend and come from Him.

It is written, "the maker of light and creator of darkness," but then the corruptions and the darkness are the complete opposite of Him, so how can they stem from one another? Also, how could they come together with the light and the pleasure in the thought of creation?

We cannot say that they are two separate thoughts; God forbid that we should even think that. Thus, how does all this extend from Him down to this world, which is so filled with scum, torment, and filth, and how do they exist together in the single thought?

Chapter Two

Explaining the thought of creation.

10) Now we shall come to clarify the thought of creation. Certainly, "The end of the work is in the preliminary thought." Even in corporeal humans, with their many thoughts, the end of the work is in the preliminary thought. For example, when one builds one's house, we understand that the first thought in this engagement is the shape of the house in which to dwell.

Therefore, it is preceded by many thoughts and many actions until this shape that he had predesigned is completed. This shape is what appears at the end of all his operations. Thus, you see that "The end of the work is in the preliminary thought."

The end of the work, which is the axis and the purpose for which all these were created, is to delight His creations, as it is written in *The Zohar*. It is known that His thought ends and acts immediately, for He is not a human, who is impelled to act. Rather, the thought itself completes the entire work at once.

Hence, we can see that as soon as He thought about creation, to delight His created beings, this light immediately extended and expanded from Him in the full measure and form of the pleasures He had contemplated. It is all included in that thought, which we call "the thought of creation," and understand this thoroughly since it is a place where they instructed to be concise. Know that we call this thought of creation "the light of Ein Sof [infinity/no end]" since we do not have a single word or utterance in His essence to define Him by any name at all, and remember this.

The will to bestow in the Emanator necessarily begets the will to receive in the emanated, and it is the vessel in which the emanated being receives His abundance.

11) The Ari said that in the beginning, an upper simple light had filled the whole of reality. This means that since the Creator contemplated delighting the created beings and the light expanded from Him and seemingly departed Him, the desire to receive His pleasure was immediately imprinted in this light.

You can also determine that this desire is the full measure of the expanding light, meaning that the measure of His light and abundance is as the measure of His desire to delight, no more and no less.

For this reason, we call the essence of that will to receive, imprinted in this light through the power of His thought, by the name, "place." For instance, when we say that a person has a stomach big enough to eat a pound of bread, while another person cannot eat more than half a pound of bread, which place are we talking about? It is not the size of the intestines, but the measure of the appetite. You see that the measure for the place of the reception of the bread depends on the measure and the desire to eat.

It is all the more so in spirituality, where the desire to receive the abundance is the place of the abundance, and the abundance is measured by the intensity of the desire.

The will to receive contained in the thought of creation brought it out of His self to acquire the name Ein Sof.

12) By this we can learn why the light of Ein Sof departed from His self, in which we cannot utter any word, and became defined by the name "light of Ein Sof." It is because of this above discernment that the will to receive from His self is included in this light. This is a new form that is not included whatsoever in His self, as from

whom would He receive? This form is also the full measure of this light. Examine this well for it is impossible to elaborate here.

Prior to the restriction, the disparity of form in the will to receive was indiscernible.

13) In His almightiness, this new form would not have been defined as a change from His light, as it is written in *Pirkey de Rabbi Eliezer*, "Before the world was created, there were He is one and His name One."

"He" indicates the light in Ein Sof, and "His name" implies the "place," which is the will to receive from His self, contained in the light of Ein Sof. He tells us that He and His name are one. "His name" is Malchut of Ein Sof, being the desire, namely the will to receive that has been imprinted in the entire reality contained in the thought of creation. Prior to the restriction, no disparity of form and difference from the light was discerned in it, and the light and the "place" are truly one. Had there been any difference and deficiency in the place compared to the light of Ein Sof, there would certainly have been two discernments there.

Restriction means that Malchut of Ein Sof diminished the will to receive in her. Then the light disappeared because there is no light without a vessel.

14) This is the meaning of the restriction, that the will to receive that is contained in the light of Ein Sof, called Malchut of Ein Sof, which is the thought of creation in Ein Sof, which contains the whole of reality, embellished herself to ascend and equalize her form with His self. Hence, she diminished her will to receive His abundance in phase four in the desire. Her intention was that by so doing, the worlds would be emanated and created down to this world.

In this manner, the form of the will to receive would be corrected and return to the form of bestowal, and that would bring her to equivalence of form with the Emanator. Then, after she had diminished the will to receive, consequently, the light departed from there, for it is already known that the light depends on the desire, and the desire is the place of the light, for there is no coercion in spirituality.

Chapter Three

Explanation of the origin of the soul.

15) Now we shall explain the matter of the origin of the soul. It has been said that it is a part of God above. We asked, "How and in what does the form of the soul differ from His simple light until it separates it from the Whole?" Now we can understand that there really is a great disparity of form in it. Although He contains all the

conceivable and imaginable forms, still, after the above said, you find one form that is not contained in Him, namely the form of the will to receive, as from whom would He receive?

However, the souls, whose creation came about only because He wanted to delight them, which is the thought of creation, were necessarily imprinted with this law of wanting and yearning to receive His abundance. This is where they differ from Him, since their form has changed from His. It has already been explained that a corporeal essence is separated and divided by the force of motion and remoteness of location, and a spiritual essence is separated and divided by disparity of form. According to the measure of disparity of form from one another, so is the measure of the distance between them. If the disparity of form comes to complete oppositeness, from one extreme to the other, they become completely severed and distinct, to the point where they can no longer suckle from one another, for they are regarded as alien to each other.

Chapter Four

After the restriction and the screen that were made on the will to receive, it became unfit to be a vessel of reception and departed from the system of Kedusha [holiness]. In its stead, the Reflected Light serves as a vessel of reception, and the vessel of the will to receive was given to the system of Tuma'a [impurity].

16) After the restriction and the screen that were placed on that vessel called "will to receive," it was canceled and departed from the system of Kedusha. In its stead, the reflected light became the vessel of reception, (as it is written in Part 3).

Know that this is the whole difference between ABYA of Kedusha and ABYA of Tuma'a. The vessels of reception of ABYA of Kedusha are from the reflected light that is established in equivalence of form with Ein Sof, while ABYA of Tuma'a use the will to receive that was restricted, being the opposite form from Ein Sof. That makes them separated and cut off from the "Life of Lives," namely Ein Sof.

Man feeds on the yeast of the Klipot [shells], and thus uses the will to receive as they do.

17) Now you can understand the root of the corruptions that were incorporated promptly in the thought of creation, which is to delight His created beings. After the cascading of the five general worlds, Adam Kadmon and ABYA, the Klipot appeared in the four worlds ABYA of Tuma'a, too, as in "God has made them one opposite the other." In that state, the turbid, corporeal body is set before us, of which it was said, "For the inclination of a man's heart is evil from his youth." This is so because its entire nursing from its youth is from the yeast of the Klipot. The whole matter of

Klipot and Tuma'a is the form of the desire only to receive that they have, and they have nothing of the will to bestow.

By this they are opposite from Him, for He has no will to receive whatsoever, and all He wants is to delight and bestow. This is why the Klipot are called "dead," since their oppositeness of form from the Life of Lives severs them from Him and they have nothing of His abundance.

Hence, the body, too, which feeds on the yeast of the Klipot, is also severed from life and is filled with filth. And all of this is because of the will to only receive and not to bestow that is imprinted in it. Its desire is always open to receive the whole world into its stomach. This is why "The wicked, in their lives, are called 'dead,'" since their fundamental disparity of form from their root, where they have nothing of the quality of bestowal, severs them from Him and they become truly dead.

Although it seems that the wicked, too, have the form of bestowal when they give charity, etc., it has been said about them in The Zohar, "Any grace that they do, they do for themselves, as their aim is primarily for themselves and for their own glory."

But the righteous, who engage in Torah and Mitzvot [commandments] not in order to receive reward but to bestow contentment upon their Maker, thus refine their bodies and invert their vessels of reception to the form of bestowal.

It is as our teacher said, "It is known and revealed," etc., "and I did not enjoy even with the little finger" (Ketubot 104). This makes them completely adhered to Him, for their form is identical to their Maker without any disparity of form. Our sages said about the verse, "Say unto Zion: 'You are My people.'" It was interpreted in the "Introduction of The Book of Zohar," Item 67, that you are with Me in partnership. This means that the righteous are partners with the Creator, since He started creation, and the righteous finish it by turning the vessels of reception into bestowal.

The whole of reality is contained in Ein Sof and extends existence from existence. Only the will to receive is new and extends existence from absence.

18) Know that the whole matter of innovation that the Creator had innovated with this creation, which our sages said He elicited existence from absence, applies only to the form of the desire to enjoy imprinted in every created being. Nothing more was innovated in creation, and this is the meaning of "maker of light and creator of darkness." Nachmanides interpreted the word "Creator" as indicating a novelty, meaning something that did not exist before.

You see that it does not say, "create light," since there is no innovation in it by way of existence from absence. This is because the light and everything contained in the light, all the pleasant sensations and conceptions in the world, extend existence from existence. This means that they are already included in Him; hence, there is no innovation in them. This is why it is written, "The maker of light," indicating that there is no innovation or creation in it.

However, it is said of the darkness, which contains every unpleasant sensation and conception, "and creator of darkness." This is because He invented them literally existence from absence. In other words, it does not exist in His reality whatsoever, but was rather innovated now. The root of all of them is the form of the "will to enjoy" included in His lights, which expand from Him.

Initially, it is only darker than the upper light, and is therefore called "darkness" compared to the light. But finally, the Klipot [shells/peels], Sitra Achra [other side], and the wicked cascade and emerge because of it, which cuts them off entirely from the root of life.

This is the meaning of the verse "Her legs descend to death." "Her legs" indicate the end of something. He says that in the end, death cascades from the legs of Malchut—the desire to enjoy that exists in the expansion of His light—to the Sitra Achra and to those that feed off her and follow her.

> Because we are branches that extend from Ein Sof,
> the things that are in our root are pleasurable to us,
> and those that are not in our root, are burdensome and painful.

19) We can ask, "Since this disparity of form of the will to receive must be in the created beings, for how else would they extend from Him and shift from being Creator to being created beings?" This is only possible by the above-mentioned disparity of form.

Furthermore, this form of the will to enjoy is the primary essence of creation, the axis of the thought of creation. It is also the measure of the delight and pleasure, as we have said above, for which it is called a "place."

Thus, how can we say about it that it is called "darkness" and extends to the discernment of death, since it creates separation and interruption from the Life of Lives in the receiving lower ones? We should also understand what is this great anxiety that comes to the receivers because of the disparity of form from His self and why the great wrath about it.

To explain this subtle matter sufficiently, we must first clarify the origin of all the pleasures and sufferings felt in our world. Know this: It is known that the nature of every branch is equal to its root. Therefore, the branch desires, loves, and covets every conduct in the root, and does not tolerate and hates any conduct that is not in the root.

This is an unbreakable law that applies to every branch and its root. Because He is the root of all His creations, everything in Him and that extends from Him directly is pleasurable and pleasant to us, for our nature is close to our root. Also, everything that is not in Him and does not extend to us directly from Him, but is rather opposite to creation itself, will be against our nature and will be hard for us to tolerate.

For example, we love rest, and vehemently hate movement, to the point that we do not make even a single movement if not to find rest. This is because our root is motionless and restful; there is no movement in Him whatsoever. For this reason, it is against our nature and hated by us.

Similarly, we love wisdom, power, wealth, and all the virtues because they are contained in Him, who is our root. We hate their opposites, such as folly, weakness, poverty, ignominy, and so on, since they are not at all in our root, making them despicable, loathsome, and intolerable to us.

We should still examine how there can be any extension that does not come directly from Him, but from the opposite of creation itself. It is like a wealthy man who called on a poor fellow, fed him and gave him drinks, and granted him silver and gold every single day, and each day more than the day before.

Note that this man simultaneously tastes two distinct flavors in the great gifts of the rich man: On the one hand, he tastes immeasurable pleasure due to the abundance of his gifts. On the other hand, it is hard for him to tolerate the abundant benefits and he is ashamed when receiving it. This matter causes him intolerance due to the abundant gifts showered on him every time.

It is certain that his pleasure from the gifts extends to him directly from the wealthy benefactor, but the impatience that he felt in the presents did not come from the wealthy benefactor, but from the very essence of the receiver—the shame awakened in him because of the reception and the free gift. The truth is that this, too, comes to him from the rich man, of course, but indirectly.

> Because the will to receive is not in our root, we feel shame and intolerance in it. Our sages wrote that in order to correct this, He has "prepared" for us labor in Torah and Mitzvot in this world, to invert the will to receive into a desire to bestow.

20) From all the above-said, we learn that all the forms that extend indirectly to us from Him present a difficulty for our patience and are against our nature. By this you will see that the new form that was made in the receiver, namely the desire to enjoy, is not in any way inferior or deficient compared to Him. Moreover, this is the primary axis of His creation. Were it not for this, there would be no creation here at all. However, the receiver, who is the carrier of this form, feels the intolerance due to his "self" since this form does not exist in his root.

By this we have succeeded in understanding the answer of our sages that this world was created because "One who eats that which is not one's own is afraid to look upon one's face." This seems very perplexing, but now their words feel very pleasant to us, for they refer to the matter of disparity of form of the desire to enjoy, which necessarily exists in the souls, since "One who eats that which is not one's own is afraid to look upon one's face." That is, any receiver of a present is ashamed when receiving it due to the disparity of form from the Root since the root does not have that form of reception. In order to correct this, He created this world where the soul comes and clothes a body. Through engagement in Torah and Mitzvot [commandments] in order to bring contentment to his Maker, the soul's vessels of reception are inverted into vessels of bestowal.

Thus, for herself, she did not want the distinguished abundance, yet she receives the abundance in order to bring contentment to her Maker, who wishes for the souls to enjoy His abundance. Because she is cleansed from the will to receive for herself, she is no longer afraid to look upon her face, and this reveals the complete perfection of the created being. The need and necessity for the long cascading to this world will be explained below, that this great labor of turning the form of reception into the form of bestowal can only be conceived in this world.

The wicked lose twofold, and the righteous will inherit twofold.

21) Come and see that the wicked lose twofold for they hold both ends of the rope. This world is created with absence and emptiness of all the good abundance, and in order to acquire possessions we need movement. It is known that profusion of movement pains man, for it is an indirect extension from His essence. However, it is also impossible to remain devoid of possessions and good, for this, too, is in contrast with the root, since the root is filled abundantly. Hence, we choose the torment of movement in order to acquire filling with possessions.

However, because all their possessions and property are for themselves alone, and "he who has a hundred wants two hundred," it follows that "One does not die with half one's wishes in one's hand." Thus, they suffer from both sides: from the pain of increased motion, and from the pain of deficiency of possessions, half of which they lack.

But "The righteous in their land will inherit twofold." In other words, once they turn their will to receive into a desire to bestow, and what they receive is in order to bestow, they inherit twofold. Not only do they attain the perfection of the pleasures and a variety of possessions, they also acquire the equivalence of form with their Maker. Thus, they come to true adhesion and are also at rest since the abundance comes to them by itself, without any movement or effort.

Chapter Five

The thought of creation compels every item in reality to stem from one another until the end of correction.

22) Now that we have been rewarded with all the above, we will have some understanding of His uniqueness, that His thoughts are not our thoughts, and all the abundance of matters and forms we perceive in this reality before us is united in

Him in a single thought, being the thought of creation to delight His creations. This singular thought encompasses the whole of reality in perfect unity through the end of correction, for this is the whole purpose of creation, and this is the operator, like the force that operates in the operated. This is because what is merely a thought in Him is a binding law in the created beings. Because He contemplated delighting us, it necessarily occurred in us that we receive His good abundance.

It is the operation. This means that after this law of the will to receive pleasure has been imprinted in us, we define ourselves by the name "operation." This is so because through this disparity of form, we stop being Creator and become a created being, and from being the Operator we become the operation.

This is the labor and the work. Due to the force that operates in the operated, the will to receive increases in us as the worlds cascade until we become a separated body in this world, opposite in form from The Life of Lives, who does not bestow outside of itself at all, which brings death to the bodies and every kind of torment and labor to the soul.

This is the meaning of the work of the Creator in Torah and Mitzvot. Through the illumination of the line in the restricted place, the holy names—Torah and Mitzvot—extend. By laboring in Torah and Mitzvot in order to bestow contentment upon the Maker, our vessels of reception gradually turn into vessels of bestowal, and this is the whole sought-after reward.

The more uncorrected our vessels of reception, the more we cannot open our mouths to receive His abundance, for fear of disparity of form, as in "One who eats that which is not one's own, is afraid to look upon one's face," as this was the reason for the first restriction. However, when we correct our vessels of reception to work in order to bestow, we thereby equalize our vessels with their Maker and become fit to receive His abundance unboundedly.

Thus, you see that all these opposite forms in the whole of creation before us, namely the form of operator and operated, the form of the corruptions and corrections, and the form of the labor and its reward are all included in His singular thought. In simple words, it is "to delight His created beings," precisely that, no less and no more.

The whole variety of concepts is also included in that thought, both the concepts in our holy Torah, and those of external teachings. All the many creations and worlds and various conducts in each and every one stem from this singular thought, as I will explain below in their proper place.

Malchut of Ein Sof means that Malchut does not place any Sof [end] there.

23) According to the above, we can understand what is presented in *Tikkuney Zohar* [part of *The Zohar*] regarding Malchut of Ein Sof, for which the doors trembled from the cries of the doubtful that it was possible to recognize a Malchut in Ein Sof? For if we can, it means that there are the first nine Sefirot there, too! From our words,

it becomes very clear that the will to receive that is necessarily included in the light of Ein Sof is called Malchut of Ein Sof. However, Malchut did not place a boundary and an end on the light of Ein Sof there because the disparity of form due to the will to receive had not yet become apparent in her. This is why it is called Ein Sof, meaning that Malchut does not put a stop there. Conversely, from the restriction downward, an end was made in each Sefira and Partzuf by the force of Malchut.

Chapter Six

It is impossible for the will to receive to appear in any essence, except in four phases, which are the four letters of HaVaYaH.

24) Let us elaborate a little on this matter, to fully understand the end that occurred in Malchut. First, we will explain what the Kabbalists have determined and is presented in *The Zohar* and the *Tikkunim*, that there is no light, great or small, in the upper worlds or in the lower worlds that is not arranged in the order of the four-letter name HaVaYaH.

This goes hand in hand with the law presented in *Tree of Life*, that there is no light in the worlds that is not clothed in a vessel. I have already explained the difference between His self and the light that expands from Him, that it is only due to the desire to enjoy that is contained in His expanding light, being a disparity of form from His self, for He does not have this desire.

This defines the expanding light by the name "emanated being" because due to this disparity of form, the light emerges from being the Emanator and becomes an emanated being. It is also explained that the desire to enjoy included in His light is also the measure of the greatness of the light. It is called the "place" of the light, meaning it receives its abundance according to its measure of will to receive and craving, not less and not more.

It also explains that this matter of the will to receive is the very innovation that was generated in the creation of the worlds by way of making existence from absence. This is so because this form alone is not included in His self whatsoever, and the Creator has only now created it for the purpose of creation. This is the meaning of "and creates darkness," since this form is the root of the darkness due to the disparity of form in it. For this reason, it is darker than the light that expands within her and because of her.

Now you see that any light that expands from Him instantly consists of two discernments: The first discernment is the expanding light itself, before the form of "desire to enjoy" appears in it. The second discernment is after the form of "desire to enjoy" appears in it, at which time it becomes coarser and somewhat darker due to the acquisition of disparity of form.

Thus, the first discernment is the light, and the second discernment is the vessel. For this reason, any expanding light consists of four phases in the impression on the vessel. This is because the form of the will to receive, called "a vessel to the expanding light," is not completed at once, but by way of operator and operated. There are two discernments in the operator and two discernments in the operated. They are called "potential" and "actual" in the operator, and "potential" and "actual" in the operated, which make up four discernments.

The will to receive is set in the emanated being only through its awakening to receive of its own accord.

25) Because the vessel is the root of the darkness, as it is opposite from the light, it must therefore be activated slowly, gradually, by way of cause and consequence. This is the meaning of the verse: "The water conceived and begot darkness" (*Midrash Rabbah, Shemot*, Chapter 22).

The darkness is a result of the light itself and is operated by it, as in conception and birth, meaning potential and actual. This means that the will to receive is necessarily included in any expanding light. However, it is not regarded as a disparity of form before this desire is clearly set in the light.

The will to receive that is included in the light by the Emanator is not enough for this. Rather, the emanated being itself must independently reveal the will to receive in him, in practice, meaning of his own choice. This means that he must extend abundance through his own will, more than the measure of the light of the expansion in him by the Emanator.

After the emanated being is operated by its own choice by increasing the measure of its desire, the yearning and the will to receive become fixed in it, and the light can clothe this vessel permanently.

It is true that the light of Ein Sof seemingly expands over all four phases, reaching the full measure of the desire by the emanated being itself, being phase four, since it would not emerge from His self anyhow and acquire a name for itself, meaning Ein Sof.

However, in His almightiness, the form did not change at all because of the will to receive, and no change is distinguished there between the light and the place of the light, which is the desire to enjoy; they are one and the same thing.

It is written in *Pirkey de Rabbi Eliezer*, "Before the world was created, there was He is one and His name One." It is indeed difficult to understand this double reference "He" and "His name." What has His name got to do there before the world was created? It should have said, "Before the world was created, He was one."

However, this refers to the light of Ein Sof, which precedes the restriction. Even though there is a place there and a will to receive the abundance from His self, it is still without change and distinction between the light and the "place."

"He is one" means the light of Ein Sof. "His name is One" means the desire to enjoy included there without any change whatsoever. Understand what our sages implied, that "His name" is desire in Gematria, meaning the "desire to enjoy."

All the worlds in the thought of creation, called "the light of Ein Sof," and what contains the receivers there is called Malchut of Ein Sof.

26) It has already been explained regarding "The end of the work is in the preliminary thought," that it is the thought of creation, which expanded from His self in order to delight His creations. We have learned that in Him, the thought and the light are one and the same thing. It therefore follows that the light of Ein Sof that expanded from His self contains the whole of reality before us through the end of the future correction, which is the end of the work. In Him, all the creations are already complete with all their perfection and joy that He wished to bestow upon them. This reality, which is complete sufficiently, is called "the light of Ein Sof," and that which contains them is called Malchut of Ein Sof.

Chapter Seven

Although only phase four was restricted, the light left the first three phases as well.

27) It has already been explained that the middle point, which is the comprehensive point of the thought of creation, namely the will to enjoy in it, embellished itself to enhance its equivalence of form with the Emanator. Although there is no disparity of form in His Almightiness from the perspective of the Emanator, the point of the desire felt it as a kind of indirect extension from His essence, as with the allegory about the rich man. For this reason, she diminished her desire from the last phase, which is the complete Gadlut [greatness/adulthood] of the will to receive, to increase the adhesion by way of direct extension from His essence.

Then the light was emptied from the entire place, meaning from all four degrees that exist in the place. Even though she diminished her desire only from phase four, it is the nature of the spiritual that it is indivisible.

Afterwards, he re-extended a line of light from the first three phases, and phase four remained a vacant space.

28) Afterwards, the light of Ein Sof extended once more to the place that was emptied. It did not fill the entire place in all four phases, but only three phases, as was the desire of the point of restriction. Hence, the middle point that has been restricted remained empty and hollow since the light illuminated only through phase four, but not all the way, and the light of Ein Sof stopped there.

We will henceforth explain the matter of the incorporation of the phases in one another applied in the upper worlds. Now you see that the four phases are incorporated in one another in such a way that within phase four itself there are all four phases, too. Thus, in phase four, too, the light of Ein Sof reached the first three phases in it, and only the last phase in phase four remained empty and without light.

Chapter Eight

Hochma is called "light," and Hassadim, "water." Bina is called "upper water," and Malchut, "lower water."

29) Now we will explain the meaning of the four phases of cause and consequence, necessary to complete the form of the will to receive, as in "The water conceived and begot darkness." There are two discernments in the light in Atzilut. The first discernment is called "light," which is Hochma, and the second discernment is called "water," which is Hassadim.

The first discernment extends from above downward without any assistance from the lower one. The second discernment extends with the help of the lower one, hence the name "water," for it is the nature of the light, whose foundation is above, and the nature of the water, whose foundation is below.

There are also two discernments in the water itself: upper water, by phase two in the four phases, and lower water, by phase four in the four phases.

Explanation of the expansion of the light of Ein Sof into the four phases in order to reveal the vessel, which is the will to receive.

30) For this reason, any expansion of the light of Ein Sof consists of ten Sefirot since the light of Ein Sof, which is the root and the Emanator, is called Keter. The light of the expansion itself is called Hochma, and this is the full measure of expansion of the light from above, from Ein Sof. It has already been said that the will to receive is incorporated in every expansion of light from above. However, the form of the will to receive does not actually become apparent before the desire awakens in the emanated being to extend more light than the measure of its expansion.

Thus, because the will to receive is included as potential immediately in the light of the expansion, the light is compelled to bring the potential to the actual. Consequently, the light awakens to extend additional abundance more than the measure of its expansion from Ein Sof. By this, the will to receive appears in practice in that light and acquires the form of the innovation through a slight disparity of form, for by this it becomes darker than the light, since it grew coarser by the new form.

Also, this part, which has become coarser, is called Bina. This is the meaning of "I am Bina [understanding], mine is the Gevura [strength]." In truth, Bina is a part of Hochma, meaning the actual light of expansion of Ein Sof. However, because she increased her desire and drew more abundance than the measure of the expansion in her from Ein Sof, she thus acquired disparity of form and grew slightly coarser than the light. Thus, she acquired her own name which is the Sefira Bina.

The essence of the additional abundance that she extended from Ein Sof by the power of the intensification of her desire is called "light of Hassadim," or "upper water." This is because this light does not extend directly from Ein Sof like the light of Hochma, but through the assistance of the emanated being who intensified the desire. Hence, it merits its own name, to be called "light of Hassadim" or "water."

Now you find that the Sefira Bina consists of three discernments of light: The first discernment is the light of Bina itself, which is a part of the light of Hochma. The second is her growing coarser and the disparity of form in her, acquired by the intensification of the desire. The third discernment is the light of Hassadim that came to her through her own extension from Ein Sof.

However, this still does not complete the entire vessel of reception, since the essence of Bina is the light of Hochma, which is very exalted, a direct expansion from the light of Ein Sof. Consequently, only the root for the vessels of reception and the operator for the operation of the vessel appeared in Bina.

Afterward, that same light of Hassadim that she extended through the power of her intensification extended from her once more, and some illumination of Hochma was added. This expansion of light of Hassadim is called Zeir Anpin, or HGT.

This light of expansion also increased its desire to extend a new abundance, more than the measure of illumination of Hochma in its expansion from Bina. This expansion is also regarded as two phases because the light of the expansion itself is called ZA or VAK, while the intensification in it is called Malchut.

This is how we come by the ten Sefirot: Keter is Ein Sof; Hochma is the light of the expansion from Ein Sof; Bina is the light of Hochma that intensified in order to increase abundance, by which it grew coarser. ZA, which consists of HGT NHY, is light of Hassadim with illumination of Hochma that expands from Bina, and Malchut is the second intensification to add illumination of Hochma more than there is in ZA.

The four phases in the desire are the four letters HaVaYaH, which are KHB TM.

31) This is the meaning of the four letters in the four-letter Name: The tip of the Yod is Ein Sof, meaning the operating force included the thought of creation, which is to delight His creations, namely the vessel of Keter. Yod is Hochma,

meaning phase one, which is the potential in the actual that is immediately contained in the light of the expansion of Ein Sof. The first Hey is Bina, meaning phase two, regarded as the actualization of the potential, meaning the light that has grown coarser than Hochma.

Vav is Zeir Anpin or HGT NHY, meaning the expansion of light of Hassadim that emerged through Bina. This is phase three, the potential for revealing the operation, the bottom Hey in HaVaYaH. It is Malchut, meaning phase four, the complete manifestation of the act in the vessel of reception that has intensified to extend more abundance than its measure of expansion from Bina. This completes the form of the will to receive and the light that clothes its vessel, being the will to receive that is completed only in this fourth phase and not before.

Now you can easily see that there is no light in the upper ones and lower worlds that is not arranged under the four-letter Name, being the four phases. Without it, the will to receive that should be in every light is incomplete, for this desire is the place and the measure of that light.

The letters Yod and Vav of HaVaYaH are thin because they are discerned as mere potential.

32) This might surprise us, since Yod implies Hochma and Hey implies Bina, and the entire light itself that exists in the ten Sefirot is in the Sefira of Hochma, while Bina, Zeir Anpin, and Malchut are merely garments with respect to Hochma. Thus, Hochma should have taken the greater letter in the four-letter Name.

The thing is that the letters of the four-letter Name do not imply or indicate the measure and amount of light in the ten Sefirot. Instead, they indicate measures of impression of the vessel. The white in the parchment of the scroll of Torah implies the light, and the black, being the letters in the scroll of Torah, indicates the quality of the vessels.

Thus, because Keter is only discerned as the root of the root of the vessel, it is implied only in the tip of the Yod. Hochma, which is the potential that has not appeared in practice, is implied by the smallest of the letters, namely the Yod.

Bina, in which the potential is carried out in practice, is indicated by the widest letter, the Hey. Since ZA is only the potential for revealing the act, it is implied by a long and thin letter, which is the Vav. Its thinness indicates that the essence of the vessel is still concealed in it in potential, in hiding. The length of the line indicates that at the end of its expansion, the complete vessel appears through it.

Hochma did not manage to reveal the complete vessel through her expansion, for Bina is still an incomplete vessel; rather, it is the operator of the vessel. This is why the leg of the Yod is short, implying that it is still short and did not reveal a complete vessel through the force concealed in it and through its expansion.

Malchut, too, is implied by the letter Hey, like Bina, which is a wide letter, appearing in its complete form. It should not surprise you that Bina and Malchut have the same letters because in the world of correction they are indeed similar and lend their vessels to one another, as in the verse, "And they two went."

Chapter Nine

Spiritual movement means a new change of form.

33) We should still explain the meaning of time and movement that we come across in almost every word in this wisdom. Indeed, you should know that spiritual movement is not like tangible movement from place to place. Rather, it refers to a new form. We denominate every new form by the title "movement." That innovation, meaning a new change of form that has occurred in the spiritual, unlike its general preceding form in that spiritual, is regarded as having been divided and distanced from that spiritual. It is considered to have emerged with its own name and authority, by which it is exactly like a corporeal being that some part departed from it and moves about from place to place. Hence, the new form is called "movement."

"Spiritual time" means a certain number of new changes of form that stem from one another. Former and latter mean cause and consequence.

34) Concerning the spiritual definition of time, understand that for us, the whole concept of time is only a sensation of movements. Our imagination pictures and devises a certain number of consecutive movements that it senses one by one and interprets them as a certain amount of "time." Thus, if one had been in a state of complete rest with one's environment, he would not even be aware of the concept of time. So it is in spirituality: A certain amount of new forms is regarded as "spiritual movements" which are intermingled in one another by way of cause and consequence, and they are called "time" in spirituality. Also, "before" and "after" always mean "cause and consequence."

Chapter Ten

The entire substance that is attributed to the emanated being is the will to receive. Any addition in it is attributed to the Emanator.

35) Know that the will to receive in the emanated being, it has been clarified that it is its vessel. Know also that it is all the general substance attributed to the emanated being. It follows that all that exists besides it is attributed to the Emanator.

> The will to receive is the first form of every essence. We define the first form as "substance" because we have no attainment in the essence.

36) Although we perceive the will to receive as an incident and a form in the essence, but how do we perceive it as the substance of the essence? Indeed, it is the same with essences that are near us. We call the first form in the essence by the name "the first substance in the essence" since we have no attainment or perception whatsoever in any substance, as all of our five senses are completely unfit for it. The sight, hearing, smell, taste, and touch offer the scrutinizing mind mere abstract forms of "incidents" of the essence, formulating through collaboration with our senses.

For example, if we take even the smallest, microscopic atoms in the smallest elements of any essence, which are separated through a chemical process, they, too, are merely abstract forms that appear that way to the eye. More precisely, we distinguish and discern them by the ways of the will to receive and to be received that we find in them.

Following these operations, we can distinguish and separate these various atoms to the very first matter of that essence. However, even then they would be no more than forces in the essence and not a substance.

Thus, you find that even in corporeality, we have no other way to understand the first matter, except by assuming that the first form is the first matter, which carries all other incidents and forms that follow it. It is much more so in the upper worlds, where tangible and imaginary do not apply.

Foreword to The Book of Zohar

1) The depth of wisdom in *The Book of Zohar* is enclosed and locked behind a thousand locks, and our human tongue is too poor to provide us with sufficient, reliable expressions to interpret one thing in this book to the fullest. Also, the interpretation I have made is but a ladder to help the examiner rise to the height of the matters and examine the words of the book itself. Hence, I have found it necessary to prepare the reader and give him a route and an inlet in reliable definitions concerning how one should contemplate and study the book.

2) First, you must know that all that is said in *The Book of Zohar*, and even in its legends, are denominations of the ten *Sefirot*, called KHB [*Keter, Hochma, Bina*], HGT [*Hesed, Gevura, Tifferet*], NHYM [*Netzah, Hod, Yesod, Malchut*], and the combinations of their denominations. Just as the twenty-two letters in the spoken [Hebrew] language, whose combinations suffice to uncover every object and every concept, the concepts and combinations of concepts in the ten *Sefirot* suffice to disclose all the wisdom in the book of heaven.

However, there are three boundaries we must be very prudent with and not exceed while studying the words of the book. First, I will offer them in brief, and then I shall elaborate on them.

3) First boundary: There are four manners in the ways of learning, called a) "matter," b) "form in matter," c) "abstract form," and d) "essence." It is the same in the ten *Sefirot*, as I will explain below. Know that *The Book of Zohar* does not engage at all in the essence and the abstract form in the ten *Sefirot*, but only in the matter in them, or in the form in them, while clothed in matter.

4) Second boundary: We distinguish three discernments in the comprehensive, Godly reality concerning the creation of the souls and the conduct of their existence. These are 1) *Ein Sof* [Infinity], 2) the world of *Atzilut*, 3) the three worlds called *Beria, Yetzira*, and *Assiya*.

You should know that *The Zohar* engages only in the worlds BYA [*Beria, Yetzira, Assiya*], and in *Ein Sof* and the world of *Atzilut*, to the extent that BYA receive from them. However, *The Book of Zohar* does not engage in *Ein Sof* and the world of *Atzilut* themselves at all.

5) Third boundary: There are three discernments in each of the worlds, BYA:

1. The ten *Sefirot*, which are the Godliness that shines in that world;
2. *Neshamot* [Souls], *Ruchot* [spirits], and *Nefashot* [life]* of people;
3. The rest of reality in it, called *Mala'achim* [angels], *Levushim* [clothes, dresses], and *Heichalot* [palaces], whose elements are innumerable.

---

* Translator's note: The usual translation for both *Neshama* and *Nefesh* is Souls, but here I had to choose a different word for *Nefesh* to distinguish it from *Neshama*.

Bear in mind that although *The Zohar* elucidates extensively on the details in each world, you should still know that the words of *The Zohar* always focus on the souls of people in that world. It explains other discernments only to know the measure that the souls receive from them. *The Zohar* does not mention even a single word of what does not relate to the reception of the souls. Hence, you should learn everything presented in *The Book of Zohar* only in relation to the reception of the soul.

Since these three boundaries are very strict, if the reader is not prudent with them and takes matters out of context, he will immediately miscomprehend the matter. For this reason, I have found it necessary to trouble myself and expand the understanding of these three boundaries as much as I can, in such a way that anyone can understand.

6) You already know that there are ten *Sefirot*, called *Hochma, Bina, Tifferet,* and *Malchut*, and their root, called *Keter*. (They are ten because the *Sefira* [singular for *Sefirot*] *Tifferet* contains six *Sefirot*, called *Hesed, Gevura, Tifferet, Netzah, Hod,* and *Yesod*. Remember this in all the places where we are used to saying ten *Sefirot*, which are HB TM.)

In general, they comprise all four worlds ABYA, since 1) the world of *Atzilut* is the *Sefira Hochma*, 2) the world of *Beria* is the *Sefira Bina*, 3) the world of *Yetzira* is the *Sefira Tifferet*, and 4) the world of *Assiya* is the *Sefira Malchut*. In greater detail, not only does each and every world have ten *Sefirot* HBTM, but even the smallest element in each world has these ten *Sefirot* HB TM, as well, as it is written in the introduction [to *The Book of Zohar*] in Items 44, 51, and 61.

7) *The Zohar* compared these ten *Sefirot*, HB TM, to four colors. These are 1) white for the *Sefira Hochma*, 2) red for the *Sefira Bina*, 3) green for the *Sefira Tifferet*, 4) black for the *Sefira Malchut* (as is written below, *Beresheet Bet*, Item 27).

It is similar to a mirror that has four panes painted in the four above colors. Although the light in it is one, it is colored when traversing the panes and turns into four kinds of light: 1) white, 2) red, 3) green, and 4) black.

Also, the light in all the *Sefirot* is simple Godliness and unity, from the top of *Atzilut* to the bottom of *Assiya*. The division into ten *Sefirot* HB TM is because of the *Kelim* [vessels] called HB TM. Each *Kli* [sing. for *Kelim*] is like a fine partition through which the Godly light traverses toward the receivers.

For this reason, it is considered that each *Kli* paints the light a different color. The *Kli* of *Hochma* in the world *Atzilut* transports white light, meaning colorless, as the *Kli* of *Atzilut* is like the light itself, and the light of the Creator does not undergo any change while traversing it. This is the meaning of what is written in *The Zohar* about the world of *Atzilut*: "He, His life, and His self are one." Hence, the light of *Atzilut* is considered white light.

But when it traverses the *Kelim* of the worlds *Beria, Yetzira,* and *Assiya*, the light changes and dims as it travels through them to the receivers. For example, the red light symbolizes *Bina*, which is *Beria*; the green light, like the sunlight, is for *Tifferet*, which is the world of *Yetzira*; and the black light is for the *Sefira Malchut*, which is the world of *Assiya*.

8) In addition to the above, there is a very important intimation in this allegory of the four colors. The upper lights are called *Sefer* [book], as it is written in *The Book of Creation*, Chapter One, Mishnah One, "He created His world in three books: A book, an author, and a story." It is also written, "The sky will be rolled up like a book" (Isaiah 34).

The disclosure of the wisdom in each book is not in the white in it, but only in the colors, meaning in the ink, from which the letters in the book, in the combinations of wisdom, come to the reader. On the whole, there are three kinds of ink in the book: red, green, and black.

Correspondingly, the world of *Atzilut*, which is *Hochma*, is all Godliness and is like the white in the book. This means that we have no perception in it whatsoever, but the whole disclosure in the book of heaven is in the *Sefirot Bina, Tifferet*, and *Malchut*, which are the three worlds *BYA*, as they are considered the ink in the book of heaven.

The letters and their combinations appear in the three above-mentioned kinds of ink, and it is only through them that the Godly light appears to the receivers. At the same time, we must note that the white in the book is the primary carrier of the book, and the letters are all "carried" on the white in the book, and had it not been for the white, the existence of the letters and all the manifestations of *Hochma* in them would not be possible whatsoever.

Similarly, the world of *Atzilut*, which is the *Sefira Hochma*, is the primary carrier of the manifestation of *Hochma*, which appears through the worlds *BYA*. This is the meaning of the verse, "In wisdom [Hochma] You have made them all."

9) We said above, in the third boundary, that *The Zohar* does not speak of the world *Atzilut* in and of itself since it is regarded as the white in the book, but according to its illumination in the three worlds *BYA*, since they are like the ink, the letters, and their combinations in the book. It is so in two manners:

1. Either the three worlds *BYA* receive the illumination of the world *Atzilut* in their own place, at which time the light is greatly reduced as it passes through the *Parsa* below the world *Atzilut* until it is discerned as mere illumination of the *Kelim* of *Atzilut*.

2. Or through the ascent of the worlds *BYA* above *Parsa*, to the place of *Sefirot Bina, Tifferet*, and *Malchut* of *Atzilut*, when they clothe the world of *Atzilut*, meaning receive the light in the place where it illuminates, as it is written in the Preface ["Preface to the Wisdom of Kabbalah"] from Item 155 onward.

10) Yet, the allegory and the lesson are not quite comparable because in the book of wisdom in this world, both the white and the ink in its letters are lifeless. The

disclosure of the wisdom induced by them is not in their essence itself but outside of them, in the mind of the scrutinizer.

However, in the four worlds ABYA, which are the book of heaven, all the *Mochin* in the spiritual and corporeal realities are present in them and extend from them. Thus, you should know that the white in it, which is the carrier in the book, is the learned subject matter itself, while the three colors of the ink elucidate this subject.

11) Here we should learn these four manners of perception, presented above in the first boundary. These are 1) matter, 2) form clothed in matter, 3) abstract form, 4) essence.

Yet, I shall first explain them using tangible examples from this world. For example, when you say that a person is strong, truthful, or deceitful, etc., you have the following before you:

1. His matter, meaning his body;

2. The form that clothes his matter, meaning strong, truthful, or deceitful;

3. The abstract form. That is, you can shed the form of strong, truthful, or deceitful from the matter of that person and study these three forms in and of themselves, unclothed in any matter or body, meaning examine the attributes of strength, truth, and deceitfulness, and discern merit or demerit in them, while they are devoid of any substance.

4. The person's essence.

12) Know that we have no perception whatsoever in the fourth manner, the essence of the person in itself, without the matter. This is because our five senses and our imagination offer us only manifestations of the actions of the essence, but none of the essence itself. For example, the sense of sight offers us only shadows of the visible essence as they are formed opposite the light. Similarly, the sense of hearing is but a force of striking of some essence in the air. The air that is rejected by it strikes the drum in our ear, and we hear that there is some essence in our proximity. The sense of smell is but air that emerges from the essence and strikes our nerves of scent, and we smell. Also, taste is but a result of the contact of some essence with our nerves of taste.

Thus, all that these four senses offer us are manifestations of the operations that stem from some essence and nothing of the essence itself.

Even the sense of touch, the strongest of the senses, separating hot from cold and solid from soft, all these are but manifestations of operations in the essence; they are but incidents of the essence. This is so because the hot can be chilled, the cold can be heated, the solid can be turned to liquid through chemical operations, and the liquid into air, meaning only gas where any discernment in our five senses has been expired. Yet, the essence still exists in it, since you can turn the air into liquid once again, and the liquid into solid.

Evidently, the five senses do not reveal to us any essence whatsoever, but only incidents and manifestations of operations from the essence. It is known that anything that we cannot grasp in our senses, we also cannot imagine. And what we cannot imagine will never appear in our thoughts and we have no way to perceive it.

Thus, the thought has no perception whatsoever in the essence. Moreover, we do not even know our own essence. I feel and know that I take up space in the world, that I am solid, warm, and that I think, and other such manifestations of the operations of my essence. But if you ask me what is my own essence, from which all these manifestations stem, I do not know what to reply to you.

You therefore see that Providence has prevented us from attaining any essence. We attain only manifestations and images of operations that stem from the essences.

13) We do have full perception in the first manner, which is matter, meaning the manifestations of operations that manifest from every essence. This is because they quite sufficiently explain to us the essence that dwells in the substance in such a way that we do not suffer at all from the lack of attainment in the essence itself.

We do not miss it, just as we do not miss a sixth finger in our hand. The attainment of the matter, meaning the manifestation of the operations of the essence, is quite sufficient for our every need and learning, both for attaining our own being and for attaining all that exists outside of us.

14) The second manner, form clothed in matter, is a satisfactory and clear attainment, too, since we acquire it through practical and real experiments we find in the behavior of any matter. All our higher, reliable knowledge stems from this discernment.

15) The third manner is abstract form. Once the form has been revealed to us while clothed in some matter, our imagination can abstract it from any matter altogether and perceive it regardless of any substance like the virtues and the good qualities that appear in ethics books, where we speak of properties of truth and falsehood, anger, and strength, etc., when they are devoid of any matter. We ascribe them merit or demerit even when they are abstract.

You should know that this third manner is unacceptable to the prudent erudite, since it is impossible to rely on it one hundred percent, since being examined while not clothed in matter, they might err in them.

Take, for example, one with idealistic morals, meaning one who is not religious. Because of his intensive engagement in the quality of truth while in its abstract form, that person might decide that even if he could save people from death by telling them a lie, he may decide that even if the whole world is doomed, he will not utter a deliberate lie. This is not the view of Torah since nothing is more important than saving lives (*Yoma* 82).

Indeed, had one learned the forms of truth and falsehood when they are clothed in matter, he would comprehend them only with respect to their benefit or harm to matter. In other words, after the many ordeals the world has been through, having seen the multitude of ruin and harm that deceitful people have caused with their lies, and the great benefit that truthful people have brought by restricting themselves to saying only words of truth, they have agreed that no merit is more important than the quality of truth, and nothing is more contemptible than the quality of falsehood.

And if the idealist had understood that, he would certainly agree to the view of Torah and would find that falsehood that saves even one person from death is far more important than the entire merit and praise of the abstract quality of truth. Thus, there is no certainty at all in those concepts of the third manner, which are abstract forms, much less with abstract forms that have never clothed in any substance. Such concepts are nothing but a waste of time.

16) Now you have thoroughly learned these four manners—matter, form in matter, abstract form, and essence—in tangible things. It has been clarified that we have no perception whatsoever in the fourth manner, which is the essence, and the third manner is a concept that might mislead. Only the first manner, which is matter, and the second manner, which is form clothed in matter, are given to us by the upper governance for clear and sufficient attainment.

Through them, you will also be able to perceive the existence of spiritual objects, meaning the upper worlds ABYA, since there is not a tiny element in them that is not divided by the four above manners. If, for example, you take a certain element in the world of *Beria*, there are *Kelim* there which are of red color, through which the light of *Beria* traverses to the dwellers of *Beria*. Thus, the *Kli* in *Beria*, which is the color red, is considered matter, or object, meaning the first manner.

Even though it is only a color, which is an occurrence and manifestation of an operation in the object, we have already said that we have no attainment in the essence itself, but only in the manifestation of an operation from the essence. We refer to that manifestation as essence, or matter, or body, or a *Kli*, as written in Item 13.

The Godly light, which travels and clothes through the red color, is the form clothed in the object, meaning the second manner. For this reason, the light itself seems red, indicating its clothing and illumination through the object, considered the body and the substance, meaning the red color.

And if you want to remove the Godly light from the object—the red color—and discuss it in and of itself, without clothing in the object, this already belongs to the third manner—form removed from matter—which might be subject to errors. For this reason, it is strictly forbidden in studying the upper worlds, and no real Kabbalist would engage in this, much less the authors of *The Zohar*.

It is even more so with regards to the essence of an element in *Beria*, since we have no perception whatsoever even in the essence of corporeal objects, all the more so in spiritual objects.

Thus you have before you four manners:

1. The *Kli* of *Beria*, which is the red color, considered the object, or the substance of *Beria*;
2. The clothing of the Godly light in the *Kli* of *Beria*, which is the form in the object;
3. The Godly light itself, removed from the object in *Beria*;
4. The essence of the item.

Thus, the first boundary has been thoroughly explained, which is that there is not even a single word of the third and fourth manners in the whole of *The Zohar*, but only from the first and second manners.

17) Along with it, the second manner has been clarified. Know that as we have clarified the four manners in a single item in the world of *Beria*, specifically, so are they in the general four worlds ABYA. The three colors—red, green, black—in the three worlds BYA, are considered the substance or the object. The white color, considered the world of *Atzilut*, is the form clothed in matter in the three colors called BYA.

Ein Sof in itself is the essence. This is what we said concerning the first manner, that we have no perception in the essence. This is the fourth manner, concealed in all the objects, even in the objects of this world (as written in Item 12). When the white color is not clothed in the three colors in BYA, meaning when the light of *Hochma* is not clothed in *Bina*, *Tifferet*, and *Malchut*, it is abstract form, in which we do not engage.

The Zohar does not speak in this manner whatsoever, but only in the first manner, being the three colors BYA, considered substance, namely the three *Sefirot Bina*, *Tifferet*, and *Malchut*, and in the second manner, which are the illumination of *Atzilut*, clothed in the three colors BYA, meaning light of *Hochma*, clothed in *Bina*, *Tifferet*, and *Malchut*, which are form clothed in matter. These are the two that *The Book of Zohar* is concerned with in all the places.

Hence, if the reader is not vigilant, restricting his thought and understanding to always learn the words of *The Zohar* strictly under the two above-mentioned manners, the matter will be immediately and entirely miscomprehended, for he will take the words out of context.

18) As the four manners in the general ABYA have been explained, so it is in each and every world, even in the smallest item of some world, both at the top of the world of *Atzilut* and at the bottom of the world of *Assiya*, because there are HB TM in it. You find that 1) the *Sefira Hochma* is considered "a form," and 2) *Bina* and TM are considered the "matter" in which the form clothes, meaning the first and second manners that *The Zohar* engages in. But *The Zohar* does not engage in the *Sefira Hochma* when stripped of *Bina* and TM, which is form without matter, and much less with the essence, considered the *Ein Sof* in that item.

Thus, we engage in *Bina*, *Tifferet*, and *Malchut* in every item, even in *Atzilut*, and we do not engage in *Keter* and *Hochma* of all the items, even in *Malchut* of the end of *Assiya*, when they are in and of themselves, unclothed, but only to the extent that they clothe *Bina* and *TM*. Now the first two boundaries have been thoroughly explained. All that the authors of *The Zohar* engage in is matter or form in matter, which is the first boundary, as well as in BYA, or the illumination of *Atzilut* in BYA, which is the second boundary.

19) Now we shall explain the third boundary. *The Zohar* engages in the *Sefirot* in each and every world, being the Godliness that shines in that world, as well as in every item of the still, vegetative, animate, and speaking, being the creatures in that world. However, *The Zohar* refers primarily to the speaking in that world.

Let me give you an example from the conducts of this world. It is explained (in the introduction [to *The Book of Zohar*], Item 42) that the four kinds, still, vegetative, animate, and speaking in each and every world, even in this world, are the four parts of the will to receive. Each of them contains these own four kinds of still, vegetative, animate, and speaking. Thus, you find that a person in this world should nurture and be nourished by the four qualities—still, vegetative, animate, and speaking—in this world.

This is so because man's food, too, contains these four qualities that extend from the four qualities, still, vegetative, animate, and speaking in man's body. These are a) wanting to receive according to the necessary measure for one's sustenance; b) wanting more than is necessary for sustenance, craving luxuries, but restricting oneself solely to physical desires; c) craving human lusts such as honor and power; d) craving knowledge.

These extend to the four parts of the will to receive in us:

1. Wanting the necessary provision is considered the still in the will to receive.

2. Wanting physical lusts is considered the vegetative in the will to receive since they come only to increase and delight one's *Kli* [vessel], which is the flesh of the body.

3. Wanting human lusts is considered the animate in the will to receive since they magnify one's spirit.

4. Wanting knowledge is regarded as the speaking in the will to receive.

20) Thus, in the first quality—the necessary measure for one's sustenance—and in the second quality—the physical desires that exceed one's measure for sustenance—one is nourished by things that are lower than the person—the still, the vegetative, and the animate. However, in the third quality, the human desires such as power and respect, one receives and is nurtured from his own species, his equals. And in the fourth quality, knowledge, one receives and is nurtured by a higher quality than one's own—from the actual wisdom and intellect, which are spiritual.

21) You will find it similar in the upper, spiritual worlds since the worlds are imprinted from one another from above downward. Thus, all the qualities of still, vegetative, animate, and speaking in the world of *Beria* leave their imprint in the world of *Yetzira*. And the still, vegetative, animate, and speaking of *Assiya* are imprinted from the still, vegetative, animate, and speaking of *Yetzira*. Lastly, the still, vegetative, animate, and speaking in this world is imprinted from the still, vegetative, animate, and speaking of the world of *Assiya*.

It has been explained in introduction [to *The Book of Zohar*], Item 42, that a) the still in the spiritual worlds are called *Heichalot* [palaces]; b) the vegetative is called *Levushim* [clothes or dresses]; c) the animate is named *Mala'achim* [angels]; and d) the speaking is considered the *Neshamot* [souls] of people in that world; e) and the ten *Sefirot* in each world are the Godliness.

The souls of people are the center in each world and are nourished by the spiritual reality in that world, as the corporeal speaking feeds on the entire corporeal reality in this world. Thus, the first quality, which is the will to receive one's necessary sustenance, is received from the illumination of *Heichalot* and *Levushim* there. The second quality, the animate surplus that increases one's body, is received from the quality of *Mala'achim* there (see *Tikkuney* [corrections of] *The Zohar*, *Tikkun* [correction] 69). These are spiritual illuminations beyond one's necessary measure for sustenance, to magnify the spiritual *Kelim* in which his soul clothes.

Thus, one receives the first quality and the second quality from lower qualities than one's own, which are the *Heichalot*, *Levushim*, and the *Mala'achim* there, which are lower than the souls of people. The third quality, which is human lusts that increase one's spirit, is received in this world from one's own species. It follows that one receives from one's own species, too, from all the souls in that world. Through them, one increases the illumination of *Ruach* of his soul.

The fourth quality of the desire—for knowledge—is received there from the *Sefirot* in that world. From them, one receives the *HBD* to one's soul.

It follows that man's soul, which is present in each and every world, should grow and be completed with all the qualities that exist in that world. This is the third boundary we have mentioned.

We must know that all the words of *The Zohar*, in every item of the upper worlds that are dealt with, the *Sefirot*, the souls, and the *Mala'achim*, the *Levushim*, and the *Heichalot*, although it engages in them as they are for themselves, the examiner must know that they are mentioned primarily with respect to the measure by which the human soul there receives from them and is nourished by them. Thus, all their words pertain to the needs of the soul. And if you learn everything according to this line, you will understand and your path will be successful.

22) After all that, we have yet to explain all these corporeal appellations explained in *The Book of Zohar* concerning the ten *Sefirot*, such as up and down, ascent and

descent, diminution and expansion, *Katnut* [smallness/infancy] and *Gadlut* [greatness/adulthood], separation and *Zivug* [mating], and numbers and so forth, which the lower ones induce through their good or bad deeds in the ten *Sefirot*.

These words seem perplexing. Can it be that Godliness would be affected and would change in such ways because of the lower ones? You might say that the words do not refer to Godliness itself, which clothes and shines in the *Sefirot*, but only to the *Kelim* of the *Sefirot*, which are not Godliness, but were rather generated with the creation of the souls to conceal or reveal degrees of attainment in the proper ration and measure for the souls to bring them to the desired end of correction. This resembles the mirror allegory with the four panes that are painted in four colors: white, red, green, and black. And there is also the white in the book and the substance of the letters in the book.

All this is possible in the three worlds BYA where the *Kelim* of the *Sefirot* are renewed and are not Godliness. However, it is not at all correct to attribute this to the world of *Atzilut* where the *Kelim* of the ten *Sefirot* are also complete Godliness, one with the Godly light within them.

It is written in the *Tikkunim* [corrections]: "He, His life, and His self are one." 1) He pertains to the essence of the *Sefirot*, which is *Ein Sof* [infinity]. 2) His Life pertains to the light that shines in the *Sefirot*, called "light of *Haya*," for the whole of the world of *Atzilut* is considered *Hochma*, and light of *Hochma* is called "light of *Haya*." This is why it is called "life." 3) His self pertains to the *Kelim* of the *Sefirot*. 4) Thus, everything is complete Godliness and unity. How then is it possible to perceive these changes that the lower ones induce there? At the same time, we must understand that if everything is Godliness in that world, and nothing of the generated creatures is to be found there, where do we discern there the three above discernments in the *Tikkunim* of *The Zohar*, He, His life, and His self, since it is utter unity?

23) To understand this, you must remember the explained above in Item 17. It explains that a necessary object is an essence that we have no perception of, even in the corporeal essences, and even in our own essence, all the more so in The Necessary One.

The world of *Atzilut* is a form and the three worlds *BYA* are matter. The illumination of *Atzilut* in *BYA* is form clothed in matter. Hence, you see that the name *Ein Sof* is not at all a name for the essence of The Necessary One, since how can we define by a name or a word what we do not attain?

Since the imagination and the five senses offer us nothing with respect to the essence, even in corporeality, how can there be a thought or a word in it, much less in The Necessary One Himself? Instead, we must understand the name *Ein Sof* as defined for us in the third boundary, that all that *The Book of Zohar* speaks of pertains precisely to the souls (as written in Item 21).

Thus, the name *Ein Sof* is not at all The Necessary One Himself, but pertains to all the worlds and all the souls being included in Him, in the thought of creation, by way of "The end of an act is in the preliminary thought." Thus, *Ein Sof* is the name of the connection in which the whole of creation is connected until the end of correction.

This is what we name above in the introduction [to *The Book of Zohar*], Item 13, "the first state of the souls," since all the souls exist in Him, filled with all the pleasure and the tenderness, at the final height they will actually receive at the end of correction.

24) Let me give you an example from the conducts of this world: A person wants to build a nice house. In the first thought, he sees before him an elegant house with all its rooms and details, as it will be when its building is finished.

Afterward, he designs all the details of the plan of execution. In due time, he will explain every detail to the workers: the wood, the bricks, the iron, and so on. Then he begins the actual building of the house to its completion, as it was arranged before him in the preliminary thought.

Know that *Ein Sof* pertains to that first thought in which the whole of creation was already pictured before Him in its utter completeness. However, the lesson is not quite like the example because in Him, the future and the present are the same. In Him, the thought completes, and He does not need tools of action as do we. Hence, in Him, it is actual reality.

The world of *Atzilut* is like the details of the thought-out plan that will later need to manifest when the building of the house actually begins. Know that in these two—the preliminary thought, which is *Ein Sof*, and the contemplated design of the details of execution in due time—there is still not even a trace of the creatures since this is still in potential, not in actual fact.

It is likewise in humans: Even though they calculate all the details—the wood, the bricks, and the metal—that will be required for carrying out the plan, it is essentially a mere conceptual matter. There is not even a trace of any actual wood or bricks in it. The only difference is that in a person, the contemplated design is not regarded as an actual reality. But in the Godly thought, it is a far more actual reality than the actual, real creatures.

Thus, we have explained the meaning of *Ein Sof* and the world of *Atzilut*, that all that is said about them is only with respect to the creation of the creatures. However, they are still in potential and their essence has not been revealed at all, as with our allegory about the person who designed the blueprint, which does not contain any wood, or bricks, or metal.

25) The three worlds *BYA*, and this world, are considered the execution from potential to actual, such as one who builds one's house in practice and brings the wood, bricks, and workers until the house is completed. Hence, the Godliness that shines in *BYA* clothes the ten *Kelim KHB HGT NHYM* to the extent that the souls should receive in order to reach their completion. These are real *Kelim* with respect to His Godliness, meaning they are not Godliness but are generated for the souls.

26) In the above allegory you find how the three discernments of one who contemplates building a house are interconnected by way of cause and consequence. The root of all of them is the first thought since no element appears in the planned blueprint except according to the end of the act, which emerged before him in the preliminary thought.

Also, one does not execute anything during the building but only according to the details arranged before him in the blueprint. Thus, concerning the worlds, you see that there is not a tiny innovation in the worlds that is not extended from *Ein Sof*, from the first state of the souls, which are there in their ultimate perfection of the end of correction, as in "The end of an act is in the preliminary thought." It follows that all that will manifest through the end of correction is included there.

In the beginning it extends from *Ein Sof* to the world of *Atzilut*, as in the allegory where the blueprint extends from the first thought. Each and every element extends from the world of *Atzilut* to the worlds *BYA*, as in the allegory, where all the details stem from the blueprint when they are actually executed during the building of the house.

Thus, there is not a single, tiny element that is generated in this world and is not extended from *Ein Sof*, from the first state of the souls. From *Ein Sof*, it extends to the world of *Atzilut*, meaning specifically associated to the thing actually being generated in this world. From the world of *Atzilut*, the innovation extends to the three worlds *BYA* where the innovation appears in actual fact, where it stops being Godliness and becomes a creature, and to *Yetzira* and *Assiya* until it extends to the lower one in this world. Understand this thoroughly and compare everything to what is done while building a house for a corporeal person, and then you will understand well.

It follows that there is no innovation in the world which is not extended from its general root in *Ein Sof*, and from its specific root in *Atzilut*. Afterward, it travels through *BYA* and adopts the form of a creature, and then it is made in this world.

27) Now you can understand that all these changes, described in the world of *Atzilut*, do not pertain to Godliness itself but only to the souls to the extent that they receive from *Atzilut* through the three worlds *BYA*. The meaning of the actuality of that world is in the relation of the blueprint to the preliminary thought, which is *Ein Sof*.

However, both in *Ein Sof* and in the world of *Atzilut*, there is still nothing in terms of the souls, just like there is nothing of the actual wood, bricks, or metal in the blueprint of the person who designs it. The existence of the souls begins to manifest in the world *Beria*. This is why the *Kelim* of the ten *Sefirot*, which allot a measure and a ration to the souls, are necessarily not Godliness but are innovated since there cannot be any changes or numbering in Godliness.

Hence, we attribute the three colors—red, green, and black—to the *Kelim* of the ten *Sefirot* in *BYA*. It is inconceivable that they will be discerned as Godliness since there is no innovation in Him whatsoever.

However, the light clothed in the ten *Kelim* in BYA is simple Godliness and unity, unchanged at all. Even the light clothed in the lowest *Kli* in *Assiya* is complete Godliness, without any change at all. This is because the light itself is one, and all the changes made in its illumination are made by the *Kelim* of the *Sefirot*, which are not Godliness. In general, they have the three above shades. In particular, numerous changes were made of these three shades.

28) Yet, the *Kelim* of the ten *Sefirot* of BYA certainly receive from *Atzilut* every little element and detail of the changes, since there is the blueprint of all the details that will unfold in the actual building of the house in BYA. Hence, it is considered that the *Kelim* of the ten *Sefirot* HB TM in BYA receive from their corresponding phase, from HB TM in Atzilut, meaning from the blueprint there.

This is so because every detail in the execution stems from every detail in the blueprint, as elaborated above. Hence, in this respect, we name the *Kelim* of *Atzilut* "white," although it is not at all a color.

Nevertheless, it is the source of all the colors. And like the white in the book of wisdom, where although there is no perception of the white in it, and the white in the book is meaningless to us, it is still the carrier of the entire book of wisdom for it shines around and inside each letter and gives each letter its unique shape and every combination its unique place.

And we might say the opposite: We have no perception of the substance of the red, green, or black letters. All that we perceive and know of the substance of the letters of the book is only through the white in it. It is so because through its illumination around and within each letter, it creates shapes in them, and these shapes reveal to us all the wisdom in the book.

We can compare it to the ten *Sefirot* of *Atzilut*: Even though they resemble the white color, it is impossible to discern anything in them, neither a number nor any change or other such appellations. Yet, all the changes necessarily come from the ten *Kelim* of the *Sefirot* of *Atzilut* in the illumination of the white to the worlds BYA, which are the three colors of the substance of the letters, although there are no *Kelim* there for itself, as it is all white. It is like the allegory of the white in the book with respect to the letters and their combinations, since its illumination to BYA makes the *Kelim* in them.

29) From what has been explained you will see that the *Tikkunim* of *The Zohar* divide the world of *Atzilut* into three discernments—He, His life, and His self—although it is simple unity there, and there is nothing of the creatures there. "He" pertains to Godliness as it is in itself, in which we have no perception, and it is imperceptible, as has been explained in all the essences, even the corporeal ones (as written in Item 12). His self pertains to the ten *Kelim* HB TM there, which we have likened to the white in the book of wisdom.

Even a number cannot be noted in the white for there is no one there to make a number as it is all white. Yet, we not only attribute a number to them, but all the changes that appear in *BYA*, which are the substance of the letters, are first found in the *Kelim HB TM* in *Atzilut* itself.

However, it is only in the manner of the white, which gives all the shapes of the letters in the book, while there is no form in it itself. Thus, you find that the white is divided into myriad forms, although in itself it has no form. Similarly, the ten *Kelim* in *Atzilut* are detailed with numerous changes, according to their illumination in *BYA*, as in the blueprint executed in the actual work of building the house.

Thus, all these changes, carried out in *BYA*, are only from the illumination of the *Kelim* of the ten *Sefirot HB TM* of *Atzilut*. And the multitude of changes we find in the white relate to the receivers in *BYA*. In relation to *Atzilut* itself, it is like the white in and of itself, unclothed in the ink in the letters; no number and nothing at all is found in it. Thus, we have thoroughly explained the self, which are the *Kelim*, which, in themselves, are simple unity, as is He.

30) His Life pertains to the light that is clothed in the white, which is the above-mentioned *Kelim*. We understand this light only with respect to the souls that receive from *Atzilut* and not in the Godliness itself. "He" means that when the three worlds *BYA* rise to *Atzilut* with the souls of people, the light they receive there is considered light of *Hochma*, called "light of *Haya*."

It is in that respect that we name the light there "His life." This is also the meaning of what is written in the *Tikkunim* of *The Zohar*, that "He, His life, and His self are one." All these three discernments relate to the receivers, where His self is the illumination of the *Kelim* in the place of *BYA* under the *Parsa* of *Atzilut*, since the light of *Atzilut* will never go below the *Parsa* of *Atzilut*, but only the illumination of the *Kelim*. The quality "His life" is the illumination of the light of *Atzilut* itself when *BYA* rise to *Atzilut*. And "He" pertains to the essence of Godliness, which is completely unattainable.

The *Tikkunim* of *The Zohar* say that although we, the receivers, should discern these three qualities in *Atzilut*, it nonetheless pertains only to the receivers. Yet, with respect to the world of *Atzilut* itself, even "His self" is considered "He," meaning the essence of Godliness. For this reason, there is no perception whatsoever in the world of *Atzilut* itself. This is the meaning of the white color in which there is no perception for itself, and it is all utterly simple unity there.

31) *The Zohar* describes the *Kelim HB TM* in *Atzilut* as growing or diminishing by people's actions. Also, we find in *The Zohar* (Bo, p 32b), "Israel... give anger and strength to the Creator," meaning it is not to be taken literally in Godliness itself, as there cannot be any changes in Godliness whatsoever, as it is written, "I the Lord do not change."

Yet, since the thought of creation was to do good to His creations, it teaches us that He has a desire to bestow. We find in this world that the Giver's contentment grows when the receivers from Him multiply, and He wishes to proliferate the receivers.

Hence, in this respect, we say that the *Mochin* in *Atzilut* grow when the lower ones are given the bestowal of *Atzilut*, or that they nurture it. Conversely, when there are no lower ones worthy of receiving His abundance, the *Mochin* diminish to that extent, meaning there is no one to receive from them.

32) You might compare it to a candle. If you light a thousand candles from it, or if you light none, you will not find that it caused any changes in the candle itself. It is also like *Adam HaRishon*: If he had progeny of thousands of offspring like us today, or if he had no progeny at all, it would not induce any change at all on *Adam HaRishon* himself.

Likewise, there is no change at all in the world *Atzilut* itself, whether the lower ones receive its great abundance lushly or receive nothing at all. The above-mentioned greatness lies solely on the lower ones.

33) Thus, why did the authors of *The Zohar* have to describe all those changes in the world of *Atzilut* itself? They should have spoken explicitly only with respect to the receivers in BYA, and not speak so elaborately of *Atzilut*, forcing us to provide answers.

Indeed, there is a very trenchant secret here: This is the meaning of "and by the hand of the prophets have I used similitudes" (Hosea 12). The truth is that there is a Godly will here, that these similitudes, which operate only in the souls of the receivers, will appear to the souls as He Himself participates in them to greatly increase the attainment of the souls.

It is like a father who constrains himself to show his little darling child a face of sadness and a face of contentment, although there is neither sadness nor contentment in him. He only does this to impress his darling child and expand his understanding so as to play with him.

Only when he grows will he learn and know that all that his father did was no more real than mere playing with him. So is the matter before us: All these images and changes begin and end only with the impression of the souls. Yet, by the will of God, they appear as though they are in Him Himself. He does that to enhance and expand the attainment of the souls to the utmost, in accordance with the thought of creation, to delight His creatures.

34) Let it not surprise you that you find such a conduct in our corporeal perception, too. Take our sense of sight, for example: We see a wide world before us, wondrously filled. But in fact, we see all that only in our own interior. In other words, there is a sort of a photographic machine in our hindbrain, which portrays everything that appears to us and nothing outside of us.

He has made for us there, in our brain, a kind of polished mirror that inverts everything seen there, so we will see it outside our brain, in front of our faces. Yet, what we see outside of us is not a real thing. Nevertheless, we should be so grateful to His Providence for having created that polished mirror in our brains, enabling us to see and perceive everything outside of us, for by this He has given us the power to perceive everything with clear knowledge and attainment, and measure everything from within and from without.

Without it, we would lose most of our perception. The same is true with the Godly will, concerning Godly perceptions. Even though all these changes unfold in the interior of the receiving souls, they nevertheless see it all in the Giver Himself since only in this manner are they awarded all the perceptions and all the pleasantness in the thought of creation.

You can also deduce this from the above parable. Even though we see everything as being in front of us, every reasonable person knows for certain that all that we see is only in our own brains.

So are the souls: Although they see all the images in the Giver, they have no doubt that all those are only in their own interior and not at all in the Giver.

35) Since these matters are at the core of the world, and I fear that the examiner will misperceive them, it is worth my while to trouble further and bring the golden words of *The Zohar* itself in these matters and interpret them to the best of my ability.

These are his words (in the portion *Bo*, Item 215) in his immaculate style: [Aramaic] "Should one ask, 'It is written, 'For you saw no image.''" [Hebrew] "Should one ask, 'But it is written in the Torah, 'For you saw no image,' so how do we depict names and *Sefirot* in Him?' [Aramaic] He will answer him, 'We saw this form.' [Hebrew] He will answer, 'I saw this form, as in the words, 'and the image of the Lord does he behold.'""

This means that the *Sefira Malchut*, where all the souls and the worlds are rooted, since she is the root of all the *Kelim*, by way of, "The ones that receive from her, and must acquire the *Kelim* from her," she is considered an image to them, as was said about her, "and the image of the Lord does he behold."

[Aramaic] Even that picture does not exist in its place but descends to *Malchut* on people and spreads over them, and will be seen by each one according to one's seeing and one's vision and imagination, and this is "and by the hand of the prophets have I used similitudes." [Hebrew] Even this image, which we name in the *Sefira Malchut*, is not in her place with respect to herself, but only when the light of *Malchut* descends and expands over the people. At that time, it appears to them, to each and every one, according to their own appearance, vision, and imagination, meaning only in the receivers and not at all in the *Sefira Malchut* herself. This is the meaning of "and by the hand of the prophets have I used similitudes."

[Aramaic] Because of this, He will say, "Although I manifest to you in your forms, to whom will you liken Me, that I should be equal?" [Hebrew] Because of this, the Creator tells them: "Although I manifest to you in your forms, in vision and imagination, yet, 'To whom will you liken Me, that I should be equal?'" [Aramaic] Before the Creator created a form in the world and depicted an image, He was unique, without a form or similitude. [Hebrew] After all, before the Creator created an image in the world, and before He formed a form, the Creator was unique, formless, and imageless.

[Aramaic] One who recognizes Him prior to creation, that He is outside the form, must not make for Him a shape or a form in the world, not in the letter *Hey* and not in the letter *Yod*, or even in the holy name, or in any letter and dot in the world. This is the meaning of "For you saw no image." [Hebrew] And one who attains Him there, prior to the degree of *Beria*, which is *Bina*, where He is beyond any similitude, it is forbidden to ascribe Him a form or an image in the world, neither in the letter *Hey* nor in the letter *Yod*, or even call Him by the holy name *HaVaYaH*, or by any letter or dot.

This is the meaning of the verse, "For you saw no image." In other words, the verse "For you saw no image" pertains to the ones rewarded with attaining Him above the degree of *Beria*, which is *Bina*. This is because there is no form or imagination whatsoever in the two *Sefirot Keter* and *Hochma*, meaning *Kelim* and boundaries, as written in Item 18. The *Kelim* begin from the *Sefira Bina* downward.

This is why all the implications in letters, in points, or in the holy names are only from *Bina* downward. They are also not in the place of the *Sefirot* themselves, but only with respect to the receivers, as with the *Sefira Malchut*.

36) (There seems to be a contradiction in their words: First they said that the forms extend to the receivers only from the *Sefira Malchut*, as he says "but only when the light of *Malchut* descends and expands over the people," which is the meaning of "and by the hand of the prophets have I used similitudes." But here he says that the forms extend to the receivers from *Beria* down, meaning from *Bina* downwards.

The thing is that in truth, the form and the image are extended only from phase four, which is *Malchut*. From her the *Kelim* extend to the place of the receivers and not at all from the first nine *Sefirot*, which are *Keter*, *Hochma*, *Bina*, and *Tifferet*, as it is written in the "Preface to the Wisdom of Kabbalah," Item 58.

Yet, the association of the quality of judgment with mercy was made in the world of *Tikkun*. This means that He raised the *Sefira Malchut*, considered the quality of judgment, and brought it into the *Sefira Bina*, regarded as the quality of mercy, as it is written in the "Preface to the Wisdom of Kabbalah," Item 58.

Hence, from that time on, the *Kelim* of *Malchut* have become rooted in the *Sefira Bina*, as he says here. For this reason, *The Zohar* begins to speak from the actual root of the images, which are the *Kelim*. It says that they are in *Malchut*, and then it says that they are in *Beria* because of the association that became the world of correction.

Our sages also said, "In the beginning the Creator created the world in the quality of judgment; He saw that the world cannot exist, He associated with it the quality of mercy." Know that the ten *Sefirot KHBTM* have many appellations in *The Book of Zohar*, according to their manifold functions.

When they are called *Keter*, *Atzilut*, *Beria*, *Yetzira*, and *Assiya*, their function is to distinguish between the anterior *Kelim*, called *Keter* and *Atzilut*, meaning *Keter* and *Hochma*, and the posterior *Kelim*, called *Beria*, *Yetzira*, and *Assiya*, meaning *Bina*, *Tifferet*, and *Malchut*. This discernment emerged in them by the association of the quality of judgment with the quality of mercy, as it is written in the "Preface to the Wisdom of Kabbalah," Item 183.

The Zohar wishes to insinuate the matter of the association of *Malchut* in *Bina*. Hence, *The Zohar* calls the *Sefira Bina* by the name *Beria*. This is so because prior to that association, there was no image or form in *Bina*, even with respect to the receivers, but only in *Malchut*.

37) It continues there: [Aramaic] But after it made that image of the *Merkava* [chariot/structure] of the upper Adam, it descended there and was called *HaVaYaH* since it recognized it in its qualities, in each and every quality. [Hebrew] After it made that form of the *Merkava* of the upper Adam, it descended and clothed there. It is named in it in the form of the four letters *HaVaYaH*, meaning the ten *Sefirot* KHBTM. This is because the tip of the *Yod* is *Keter*, *Yod* is *Hochma*, *Hey* is *Bina*, *Vav* is *Tifferet*, and the last *Hey* is *Malchut*, so they would attain Him through His attributes, meaning the *Sefirot*, in every single attribute in Him.

38) Explanation of the matters: From *Beria* on, meaning from *Bina*, after it had been associated with the quality of judgment, which is *Malchut*, the images and the forms extend to the receivers, which are the souls, though not in her own place but only in the place of the receivers.

He says that at that time he made the form of the *Merkava* of the upper Adam and descended and clothed in the form of this man. In other words, the whole form of man in his 613 *Kelim* extends from the *Kelim* of the soul, since the soul has 613 *Kelim*, called "248 organs and 365 spiritual tendons," divided into five divisions according to the four letters *HaVaYaH* and the tip of the *Yod*:

1. Her *Rosh* is considered *Keter*.

2. From *Peh* to *Chazeh* it is *Hochma*.

3. From *Chazeh* to *Tabur* it is *Bina*.

4. From *Tabur* to *Sium Raglin* it is the two *Sefirot Tifferet* and *Malchut*.

Additionally, the Torah, as a whole, is considered *Partzuf* Adam, pertaining to the 248 *Mitzvot* [commandments] to do, corresponding to the 248 organs, and the 365 *Mitzvot* not-to-do correspond to the 365 tendons. It contains five divisions, which are the five books of Moses, called "The image of the *Merkava* of the upper Adam," meaning Adam of *Beria*, which is *Bina*, from which the *Kelim* begin to extend in the place of the souls.

He is called "upper Adam" because there are three qualities of Adam in the *Sefirot*: Adam of *Beria*, Adam of *Yetzira*, and Adam of *Assiya*. However, in *Keter* and *Hochma* there is no similitude at all that could be named by some letter and dot or by the four letters *HaVaYaH*. Since here it speaks of the world of *Beria*, it makes the precision of saying upper Adam.

At the same time, you must always remember the words of *The Zohar*, that these images are not in the place of the *Sefirot Bina*, *Tifferet*, and *Malchut*, but only in the place of the receivers. Yet, because these *Sefirot* impart those *Kelim* and *Levushim* so they would know Him in His qualities, so the souls would attain Him through the light that extends to them by measure and boundary according to their 613 organs, we therefore call the givers by the name "Adam," as well, although there they are merely in the form of the white color (see Item 8).

39) It should not be puzzling for you since the four letters *HaVaYaH* and the tip of the *Yod* are five *Kelim*, since the *Kelim* are always called "letters," and they are the five *Sefirot KHBTM*. Thus, it is clear that there are *Kelim* in *Keter* and *Hochma*, as well, implied by the tip of the *Yod* and the *Yod* of *HaVaYaH*.

The thing is that the similitudes and the attributes it speaks of, which are the *Kelim*, begin from *Beria* downward, meaning only the three *Sefirot Bina*, *Tifferet*, and *Malchut*, and not in *Keter* and *Hochma*, meaning from the perspective of the essence of the *Sefirot*.

Yet, it is known that the *Sefirot* are integrated in one another. There are ten *Sefirot KHBTM* in *Keter*, *KHBTM* in *Hochma*, *KHBTM* in *Bina*, as well as in *Tifferet* and in *Malchut*.

Accordingly, you find that the three *Sefirot Bina*, *Tifferet*, and *Malchut*, that the *Kelim* come from, are found in each of the five *Sefirot KHBTM*. Now you see that the tip of the *Yod*, which is the *Kelim* of *Keter*, indicate *Bina* and *TM* that are included in *Keter*.

The *Yod* of *HaVaYaH*, which is a *Kli* of *Hochma*, indicates *Bina* and *TM* included in *Hochma*. Thus, the *Keter* and *Hochma* included even in *Bina* and *ZON* do not have *Kelim*, and in *Bina* and *TM* included even in *Keter* and *Hochma*, there are *Kelim*.

In this respect, there really are five qualities of Adam. The *Bina* and *TM* in all five *Sefirot* dispense in the form of the *Merkava* of Adam. For this reason, there is 1) Adam in the quality of *Keter*, called *Adam Kadmon*, and there is 2) Adam in the quality of *Hochma*, called "Adam of *Atzilut*." 3) There is Adam in the quality of *Bina*, called "Adam of *Beria*," 4) Adam in the quality of *Tifferet*, called "Adam of *Yetzira*," and 5) Adam in the quality of *Malchut*, called "Adam of *Assiya*."

40) [Aramaic] He is called *El*, *Elokim*, *Shadai*, *Tzvaot*, *EKYEH*, so they would know Him in each and every attribute, how He leads the world with power and grace according to people's work. [Hebrew] He named Himself *El*, *Elokim*, *Shadai*, *Tzvaot*, and *EKYEH*, so that every single attribute in Him would be known. The ten names in the Torah that are not to be erased pertain to the ten *Sefirot*, as it is written in *The Zohar*, *VaYikra*, Item 168:

1. The *Sefira Keter* is called *EKYEH*.

2. The *Sefira Hochma* is called *Yod-Hey*.

3. And the *Sefira Bina* is called *HaVaYaH* [punctuated *Elokim*].

4. The *Sefira Hesed* is called *Kel*.

5. The *Sefira Gevura* is called *Elokim*.

6. The *Sefira Tifferet* is called *HaVaYaH*.

7. The two *Sefirot Netzah* and *Hod* are called *Tzvaot*.

8. The *Sefira Yesod* is called *El Hay*.

9. The *Sefira Malchut* is called *Adni*.

41) [Aramaic] If His light does not spread over all the people, how will they know Him and how will there be "The whole earth is full of His glory"? [Hebrew] Had His light not expanded on all creations by seemingly clothing in these holy *Sefirot*, how would the creatures come to know Him, and how would they keep the verse, "The whole earth is full of His glory"? In other words, by this it explains the Godly desire to appear to the souls as if all these changes in the *Sefirot* are in Him. It is in order to give the souls room for sufficient knowledge and attainment in Him, for then the verse "The whole earth is full of His glory" shall come true, as was said above in Item 33.

42) [Aramaic] Woe unto he who ascribes to Him any attribute, even those attributes of His, much less those of people, whose foundation is in the dust, for they are fleeting and worthless. [Hebrew] Yet, woe unto one who ascribes any measure to Him, who would say that there is a measure in Him for Himself, even in these spiritual measures by which He appears to the souls. It is all the more so in the corporeal measures of the human nature, which are made of dust, and are transitory and worthless.

As we have said above, in Item 34, although it is a Godly wish for the souls to see that the changes in them are in the Giver, it should nonetheless be clear to the souls that there is no change or measure in Him whatsoever. It is only a Godly wish that they will imagine so, as it is written, "and by the hand of the prophets have I used similitudes."

And should they err in that, woe unto them, for they will instantly lose the Godly abundance. It is even more so with the fools who ascribe to Him some incident of the transitory, worthless flesh and blood incidents.

It would benefit the reader to learn all the rest of this *Zohar*, which explains the matter of the ten *Sefirot* and the three worlds *BYA*, as this is not the place to elaborate further.

Matter and Form
in the Wisdom of Kabbalah

As a whole, science is divided into two parts: one is called "material research," and the other, "formative research." This means that matter and form are perceived in every element of the entire reality before us.

For example, a table consists of matter, meaning the wood, and consists of form, the shape of a table. The matter, being the wood, is the carrier of the form, which is the table. Also, in the word "liar," there is matter, which is a person, and there is a form, which is the lie. The matter, which is the person, carries the form of a lie, meaning the custom of telling lies. So it is in everything.

Hence, science, too, which researches the elements of reality, is divided into two parts: material research and formative research. The part of science that studies the quality of the substances in reality, both materials without their form and materials along with their forms, is called "material research." This research is empirical, based on evidence and deductions derived from practical experimentation, and these practical experimentations are treated as a sound basis for valid conclusions.

The other part of science studies only forms abstracted from materials, without any contact with the substances themselves. In other words, they shed the forms of true and false from the materials, which are the people who carry them, and engage only in research to know such values of superiority and inferiority in these forms of truth and falsehood as they are for themselves, bare, as though they were never clothed in any matter. This is called "formative research."

This research is not based on practical experiments, for such abstract forms do not appear in practical experiments, as they do not exist in the actual reality since such an abstract form is imaginary, meaning only the imagination can picture it although it does not exist in the actual reality.

Hence, any scientific research of this kind is necessarily based solely on a theoretical basis. This means that it is not taken from practical experimentation but only from a research of theoretical negotiations.

All the high philosophy belongs to this kind; hence, many contemporary intellectuals have left it since they are displeased with any research built on a theoretical basis. They believe it is not a sound basis, for they consider only the experimental basis as sound.

The wisdom of Kabbalah, too, is divided into these two parts: "material research" and "formative research." But here there is a great advantage over secular sciences: Here, even the part of formative research is built entirely on the critique of practical reason, meaning on a practical, empirical basis.

General Preface

To the proficient in *The Tree of Life*, and to everyone,
as in "First, learn; then, comprehend."

1) Our sages said, "There is not a blade of grass below that does not have an angel above that strikes it and tells it, 'Grow!'" This seems very perplexing, for why would the Creator trouble an angel from above with striking and nursing a tiny, insignificant blade of grass?

Yet, this saying is one of creation's secrets that are too long to interpret. This is so because the heart of the infinitely wise wishes to reveal a portion and conceal two portions with their golden allegories, as they are wary of revealing the Torah to an unworthy disciple. It is for this reason that our sages said that one does not learn from legends, as legends are sealed and blocked before the masses, and are revealed only to a chosen few in a generation.

And we also find in *The Book of Zohar*, that Rashbi [Rabbi Shimon Bar-Yochai] instructed Rabbi Aba to write the secrets because he knew how to reveal with intimation. See in the *Idra*, where it is written that for each secret that Rashbi disclosed in the wisdom, he would cry and say, "Woe if I tell; woe if I do not tell. If I do not tell, my friends will lose that word; and if I tell, the wicked will know how to serve their Master."

This means that he was in distress from both angles: If he did not reveal the secrets of the Torah, the secrets would be lost from the true sages, who fear the Creator, and if he did reveal the secrets, people of no merit would fail in them, for they would not understand the root of the matters and would eat unripe fruit.

Hence, Rashbi chose Rabbi Aba to write because of his wisdom in allegories, to arrange things in such a way that it would be sufficiently revealed to those who are worthy of understanding them, and hidden and blocked from those unworthy of understanding them. This is why he said that Rabbi Aba knew how to reveal with intimation. In other words, although he revealed, it still remains a secret to the unworthy.

However, in *The Zohar* they promised us that this wisdom is destined to be completely revealed at the end of days, even for little ones. And they also said that with this composition, the children of Israel would be redeemed from exile, meaning that with the appearance of the wisdom of truth, Israel will be rewarded with complete redemption. And we also see that the words of *The Zohar* and the hidden secrets in the wisdom of truth are being gradually revealed, generation by generation, until we are rewarded with revealing all this wisdom, and at that time we will be rewarded with complete redemption.

To clarify the text with which we began, we shall first explain the verse in the famous *Book of Creation* where it is written of the ten Sefirot being ten and not nine, ten and not eleven. Most of the interpreters have already examined it, but we will explain it our own way, so matters will be revealed to all who seek the word of the Creator.

It is known that the ten Sefirot are called Keter, Hochma, Bina, Hesed, Gevura, Tifferet, Netzah, Hod, Yesod, Malchut. It is written in the ARI's *Gate to Introductions*, in the section *HaDaat*, that they are actually five phases: Keter, Hochma, Bina, Zeir Anpin, and Malchut; but Zeir Anpin comprises six Sefirot HGT NHY. I have written at length about the ten Sefirot within this composition [the commentary *Panim Meirot uMasbirot* on *The Tree of Life*], so here I would briefly say that in this general preface, I wish to give the student a true and general knowledge of the majority of this expansive wisdom, and true orientation in the style of study in the book *The Tree of Life*. Most students fail to understand the matters, since the spiritual concepts are above time and above place, but they are expressed in corporeal terms, pictured and set in times and places.

Additionally, no order for beginners is arranged in this wisdom in the writings of the ARI. The books were composed by the holy words that he would say before his students day by day, and the students themselves were proficient in the wisdom of truth. Hence, there is no text—long or short—in all the books that were composed, which does not require true proficiency in all the wisdom in general. Therefore, the students grow weary and cannot connect matters altogether.

Thus, I have come out with this preface, to connect the matters and the foundations of the wisdom in a concise manner, so it will be readily available to the student with every text he may wish to study in the writings of the ARI. And for this reason, I do not elaborate or interpret each matter to the fullest, for this will be clarified within my composition. Instead, I summarize sufficiently for my purpose. And our sages said, "First, learn; then, comprehend."

The ARI taught us that the ten Sefirot KHB, HGT, NHYM are actually five phases, KHB, ZA, and Malchut. This is the meaning of the four-letter-name, Yod-Hey-Vav-Hey. The tip of the Yod is Keter, Yod is Hochma, Hey is Bina, Vav is Zeir Anpin—containing six Sefirot HGT NHY—and the last Hey is Malchut.

You should know that the letters and the Sefirot are one thing. But following the rule that no light expands without a vessel, when we speak of both together, that is, when the light is clothed in the vessel, they are called Sefirot. And when we speak of the vessels alone, they are called letters.

It is written about the light that the white in the book of Torah implies the light, and the black in the book of Torah, meaning the letters, implies the vessels. This means, as the Nachmanides interprets concerning "I form the light, and create darkness," that the matter of eliciting existence from absence is called "Creator," since it is an innovation, something that did not exist prior to its creation. And in the light, and all the delight and pleasure included in the light, it is not an innovation and elicitation existence from absence, but rather existence from existence, for the light and all the abundance are already included in His essence.

For this reason, it is said, "form the light," for it is not a matter of creation, but of formation, that is, forming the light in a way that the dwellers below can receive it. But the darkness is an innovation that was generated with creation, in eliciting existence from absence, meaning it is not included in His essence. This is why it is said, "and create darkness." But the darkness is the real opposite from the light; hence, we should understand how darkness can be extended from the light.

In *Panim Masbirot* [*A Welcoming Face*], "Branch One," I elaborated on this point, and here I shall only stroll through it. It is known that it is written in *The Zohar* that the purpose of creation is to delight His creations, since it is the conduct of The Good to do good. Clearly, every wish in Him is a mandatory law for the created being. It follows that since the Creator contemplated delighting His creations, a mandatory nature of wanting to receive His pleasure was immediately imprinted in the created beings, that is, the great desire to receive His abundance. Know that this craving is called a vessel, with respect to its root.

For this reason, Kabbalists have said that there is no light without a vessel, since the will to receive included in each emanated created being is the vessel, and it is also the full measure of the light. In other words, it receives precisely the measure that it wants, no more and no less, since there is no coercion in spirituality, and even in corporeal beings, it is not from the side of Kedusha [holiness].

Clearly, the form of the vessel is different from that of the light. This is why it is called a vessel and not "light." But we need to understand the meaning of this disparity of form. Indeed, the will to receive for oneself is a great disparity of form, since this form does not apply to the Emanator whatsoever, as from whom would He receive? Rather, it has been initiated now in the first emanated being, by way of existence-from-absence, so that in it, there is a will to receive from The Cause of Causes, and see *Panim Masbirot*, "Branch One."

This clarifies what is written in *The Zohar* that the upper Keter is darkness compared to the Cause of Causes. They are referring to the will to receive included in the first emanated being, and they call this disparity of form "darkness" since it does not exist in the Emanator. For this reason, it is the root of darkness, which is the color black, compared to the light, and is opposite from it.

It has been explained in *Panim Masbirot* that as corporeal things are separated from one another by an axe and a hammer, the spirituals are separated from one another by the disparity of form between them. When the disparity of form increases to the point of oppositeness, from one extreme to the other, complete separation is created between them.

For this reason, it has been explained there that the form of the will to receive is immediately included in every light that expands from Him, but as a hidden, potential force. This hidden force is revealed to the emanated being only when the emanated being intensifies the desire to want additional abundance, more than the measure of its expansion from the perspective of the Emanator.

For example, when a food is tasty, one's desire for more food increases more than one's eating. Hence, after the emanated being increases the desire to draw additional abundance, more than the measure of its expansion, the actual vessel of reception appears. And the thing is that this disparity of form does not apply to Him, but to the emanated being. Hence, it is completed only by the awakening of the emanated being, and understand thoroughly.

2) Hence, the expansion of His light does not stop being an Emanator into being an emanated being until it goes through four phases, called Hochma, Bina, Zeir Anpin, and Malchut. This is so because the expansion of His light is called Hochma. This is the full measure of the essence of the light of that emanated being. When it intensifies and draws more abundance than the measure of its expansion, it is considered phase two, called Bina.

Also, three discernments should be made in the second phase: First discernment: The essence of the Sefira Bina is Hochma. Second discernment: The intensification of the desire that it manifested, for which the root of the vessel of reception was revealed in her, in that sense, there is disparity of form in her, meaning coarseness, compared to the light of Hochma. This is called upper Gevura.

Third discernment: This is the essence of the abundance that she has acquired through an awakening of her own desire. This light is given its own name—light of Hassadim, which is much lower than the light of Hochma, which expands solely from the Emanator. The light of Hassadim is associated also with the intensification of the emanated being, as it was mentioned, that the Gevura, which is a light that has grown coarser, became the root of the light of Hassadim. These three discernments together are called Bina, and the second phase from Hochma. Thus, the two Sefirot Hochma and Bina have been clarified, and the Keter is Ein Sof [Infinity], the root of the emanated being.

Although phase two manifested an intensified desire toward the Operator, she is still unfit to be a complete vessel of reception. The thing is that in spirituality, the vessel with the light in it are very close, virtually interdependent. When the light disappears, the vessel is canceled, and when the vessel disappears, the light is canceled. Thus, the importance of the vessel is as the importance of the light.

Hence, the form of the vessel of reception was not completed in Bina, since her essence is the light of Hochma. For this reason, the light of Hassadim, which she drew through her own intensification, was annulled before her essence as a candle before a torch. Thus, this light of Hassadim expanded further from Bina outward from herself and gained strength to draw additional abundance, more than the measure of its expansion through Bina. At that time, the vessel of reception was completed.

Hence, we discern two more phases, phase three and phase four, which are expansions that are extended from Bina, where the form of the vessel is still in potential, hidden, and as long as it did not intensify for addition, it is called Zeir Anpin. And its intensification for more abundance is called the "the vessel of Malchut," which is a vessel of reception that was completed in that emanated being, which now consists of light and vessel. By this it emerges from the state of Emanator and is discerned as an emanated being.

These are the four phases known as HB, ZA, and Malchut, which are the four-letter-name [Yod-Hey-Vav-Hey, HaVaYaH]. HB are Yod-Hey, and ZON are Vav-Hey. They are considered ten Sefirot because Zeir Anpin contains six Sefirot, which are Hesed, Gevura, Tifferet, Netzah, Hod, Yesod.

The thing is that the essence of ZA is the light of Hesed and Gevura, meaning the two phases light of Hassadim and upper Gevura, which expanded from Bina outward. We should note here that in Bina, Gevura is the first and the root of the light of Hassadim, but in Tifferet it is to the contrary: Hesed precedes the light of Gevura, since the main light that expands is Hesed, and the Gevura is ancillary within it, in Bina.

Now you can understand what was written in The Tree of Life and by Rashbi, that in the world of Nekudim, Gevura of [of] ZA preceded its Hesed, since ZON of Nekudim are considered ZON of Bina, and not the actual ZON, as in the two bottom phases of the four above-mentioned phases. This is why Gevura of ZA precedes its Hesed.

Also, the Sefira Tifferet of ZA is the unification of the above Hochma and Gevura to the act of the vessel of Malchut. It is called Tifferet since the light Mitpa'er [boasts] itself on phase one, which is Hochma, whose desire did not suffice to make a vessel. But phase three, which is Hassadim and Gevura that expand from Bina outward, sufficed to make the vessel of Malchut. This is the meaning of "according to the beauty [Tifferet] of a man, to dwell in the house." This explains the three Sefirot HGT of ZA, and they are called "the three patriarchs," as they are the essence of ZA. Also, Netzah, Hod, and Yesod are called "sons," since they expand from HGT.

The thing is that because of the first restriction, which is thoroughly explained inside the book, a hard screen was made in the vessel of Malchut. This means that phase four in the vessel of Malchut detains the upper light from expanding into phase four, due to the disparity of form there, as it is written there.

Yet, the light expands and wishes to come to phase four, too, as the nature of the upper light is to expand to the lower ones until it is almost separated from its place, as it is written in Panim Masbirot. Hence, a coupling by striking was made between the upper light that expands into the vessel of Malchut and the detaining screen in the vessel of Malchut.

This is like sunlight hitting a mirror, with sparks being reflected. Hence, ten new Sefirot emerged from this coupling by striking, called ten Sefirot of reflected light. It turns out that there are two sets of ten Sefirot in each emanated being: ten Sefirot of direct light over the four phases, and ten Sefirot of reflected light.

Know that this is the upper light that re-expanded from HGT of ZA for a coupling by striking in the screen in the vessel of Malchut. They are called Netzah, Hod, Yesod.

Now you can understand what is written in *Tikkuney Zohar* [*Corrections of The Zohar*], that Malchut is fourth to the fathers and seventh to the sons. This means that when she is first emanated, Malchut is discerned from the act of Tifferet of ZA and follows the HGT, which are called "fathers." And from the perspective of the illumination of the reflected light in her screen, she follows the NHY that expanded to her for coupling by striking. And the NHY are called "the sons of HGT"; hence, it is seventh to the sons.

Thus we have properly explained the essence of the ten Sefirot KHB, HGT, NHY, and Malchut at their root. This is the first concept in the wisdom of truth, and it must always be before the eyes of the student while delving into this wisdom.

Now we understand the sound warning in *The Book of Creation*, "ten and not nine." It means that since a detaining screen was made in phase four from the restriction downward, it is impossible to mistakenly say that phase four is excluded from the ten Sefirot, and only nine Sefirot remain in Kedusha [holiness]. For this reason, it warns, "ten and not nine."

And it warns further, "ten and not eleven." This means that you should not mistakenly say that phase four became a vessel of reception after the restriction. Thus, there are two Sefirot in one Malchut: One is the screen that always raises reflected light, and a vessel of reception to receive the direct light, as well. This is why it states, "ten and not eleven."

3) There are five prominent discernments in the ten above-mentioned Sefirot, which should not move from your eyes and will straighten your ways in studying the wisdom. The first discernment is the light of self, which is all the light from Ein Sof that exists in that emanated being. This is the essence, since the lower one does not participate here whatsoever, and it is called Hochma of direct light.

The second discernment is light of Hassadim that is extended from above downward. This light is conjoined with the awakening of the Gevura of the emanated being of phase two, which is the light of Bina that she drew. The third discernment is light of Hassadim that rises from below upward through a coupling by striking. It is called "reflected light" that rises and is extended only from the emanated being, due to the above-mentioned detainment.

The fourth discernment is the light of upper Gevura, meaning phase two, which is the coarseness of Bina that she acquired by her intensification.

The fifth discernment is the lower Gevura, meaning phase four, where the intensification of the desire is activated in the light of Hassadim that was added by the emanated being. This is called "the vessel of Malchut of direct light," and this Gevura is the vessel of ten Sefirot, and remember this.

Know that the screen in the vessel of Malchut is the root of the darkness because of the detaining force that exists in the screen, to stop the upper light from expanding in phase four. This is also the root of the labor in order to receive reward, since labor is an involuntary act, for the worker feels comfortable only when resting. But because the employer pays his salary, he cancels his will before the will of the employer.

Know that here, in this world, there is no being or conduct that is not rooted in the upper worlds, from which branches expand to the lower worlds until they are revealed to us in this world. And you see that in general, work and labor are rooted in the screen in the vessel of Malchut, which detains the upper light that she covets, due to the Emanator, Who wishes to bestow delight, and everything that is a thought in the Emanator is a mandatory law in the emanated being. Naturally, He needs no actions, but His thought completes. And yet, she chooses by herself to not receive the upper light, lest it will come to disparity of form, see in *Panim Masbirot*, "Branch One."

It follows that the detaining force in the screen is equal to the labor. And the reward that the employer gives to the worker is rooted in the reflected light emitted by the coupling by striking where by the screen, a root was made for the reflected light. It turns out that she returns to being Keter to these ten Sefirot of reflected light, as well as to direct light. As will be explained below, all this profit came to her because of this act of detaining.

From the above-mentioned, it follows that the ten Sefirot are really one vessel, called Malchut. But to complete its form, it is discerned with three roots—the three phases Hochma, Bina, and ZA that are extended from one another. Know that this Malchut is still included in the light of Ein Sof from before the restriction, and which is called Malchut of Ein Sof, in which was the first restriction.

As it is written in *Panim Masbirot*, "Branch One," because of the equivalence of form with the Emanator, her desire rose from wanting to receive in phase four, and the light of the line was extended to her from Ein Sof. The light of the line contains all the light that is extended through five worlds, called Adam Kadmon, Atzilut, Beria, Yetzira, and Assiya. This light is generally referred to as a line, from the words "measurement line", as it is extended into the worlds by measure and a rationed number in each world, according to the form of the vessel of Malchut in that world, as it is elaborated in *Panim* [*Panim Meirot uMasbirot*].

The matter of the five above-mentioned worlds are truly the matter of Keter and the four known phases in the ten Sefirot. Thus, the world of AK is the world of Keter, the world of Atzilut is the world of Hochma, the world of Beria is the world of Bina, the world of Yetzira is the world of Zeir Anpin, and the world of Assiya is the world of Malchut. However, in each world there are ten Sefirot, and each of the ten Sefirot of that world comprises ten Sefirot, as well, as it is written inside.

They are divided into the five above-mentioned worlds because the vessel of Malchut should first be included in each Sefira, through Keter. This occurs in 1) The first expansion of AHP of AK, where she was included in ZON. 2) In the second expansion of AHP, she was included in Bina. 3) In the world of Nekudim, she was included in Hochma, 4) and in the world of Atzilut she was included in Keter.

And since Malchut has been included in each Sefira, the world of Tikkun [correction] begins: Its Rosh [head] is the above-mentioned world of Atzilut, where the light of Ein Sof dresses in phase one. Then the light of Ein Sof dresses in phase two, creating the world of Beria. Following, it dresses in phase three, creating the world of Yetzira, and then it dresses in phase four, creating the world of Assiya. It will be elaborated in *Panim* [*Panim Meirot uMasbirot*] how they all stem from one another by a mandatory manner of cause and consequence, and how they are tied to one another.

4) First, we need to understand the quality of each of the worlds AK and ABYA, which I will explain one at a time. Let us begin with the world of Keter, which is the world of Adam Kadmon. Its first vessel is the world of Akudim [tied]. In *The Gate of Akudim*, Chapter Three, the ARI wrote that all ten Sefirot emerged, but not all of them emerged together. In the beginning, only Malchut came out in the world of Akudim, and this Malchut came out in the form of Nefesh. Following it, the rest of the parts emerged, through Keter.

When Keter came, Malchut was completed with all five inner lights—Nefesh, Ruach, Neshama, Haya, and Yechida. Yet, they were still missing all the above-mentioned Sefirot, which emerged incomplete. Hence, they had to rise back to the Emanator to be completed. But now, upon the return, Keter returns first.

When Keter rose, the light of Hochma rose to the place of Keter, Bina to the place of Hochma, ZA to the place of Bina, and Malchut to the place of ZA. Subsequently, Hochma rose to the Emanator, too. Then Bina rose to Keter, following Hochma, ZA to Hochma, and Malchut to Bina. Then Bina rose, too, and ZA rose to Keter, and Malchut to Hochma. Finally, ZA rose, as well, and Malchut rose to Keter until Malchut, too, rose to the Emanator.

After that, the light returned from the Emanator and expanded in them, though not in their initial order. Instead, the light of Keter did not return but departed and remained missing. Hence, the light of Hochma came out in the vessel of Keter, the light of Bina in the vessel of Hochma, the light of ZA in the vessel of Bina, and the light of Malchut in the vessel of ZA. The vessel of Malchut remained without light at all, thus far his words in brief. Additionally, the ten Sefirot of Akudim emerged from below upward. Malchut emerged first, then ZA, then Bina, then Hochma, and finally Keter, thus far his words.

We should thoroughly understand the matter of the elicitation of the Sefirot from above downward and from below upward, mentioned in the ARI's words. Certainly, this is not about measures of above, below, before, or after in time and place. Rather, it is in terms of reason and result, cause and consequence. Hence, how can Malchut emerge first, followed by ZA, followed by Bina, until Keter—the root of them all—emerges last? This seems perplexing. And who and what gave and inverted the upper to be lower and the lower to be above?

The thing is that the order of the ten Sefirot of direct light has already been explained above, being five degrees one below the other, by the measure of refinement of each of them from the coarse light whose form has changed, that is, phase four. Since phase one is considered a hidden potential, it is the most important in the degree. And phase two has already moved from potential to actual by intensifying with a worse desire than in phase one. Phase three is worse than phase two, and phase four, Malchut, is the worst, since the coarseness in her is greater than in the rest.

It is also known that once the vessel of Malchut emerged, it experienced the first restriction, not to receive in phase four. This detaining force is called screen, and when the direct light that descends from Ein Sof strikes the screen in Malchut, there is a coupling by striking, and thus ten Sefirot of reflected light emerge, as it is written in *Panim*, "Branch Three."

Within these ten Sefirot of reflected light, the degrees are inverted compared to the value of the ten Sefirot of direct light. In the ten Sefirot of direct light, the more refined is higher in merit and better. But in the ten Sefirot of reflected light, the coarser is higher and better because Malchut is the Keter and the root of these ten Sefirot of reflected light, since her coarse screen detains the light from descending into her phase four. Thus, Malchut returns to being Keter by way of "Its end is in its beginning," as it is written in *Panim Masbirot*, "Branch Three."

It turns out that ZA receives the light from Keter of reflected light; hence, ZA is considered a degree of Hochma, and Bina is considered a degree of Bina because she receives from ZA, who returns to being Hochma. Also, Hochma of direct light is considered ZA in the reflected light, since it receives the reflected light from Bina. And Keter of direct light is considered Malchut in the reflected light, since it receives from ZA. Thus, you find that the more refined in the degree will be lower in praise and merit, and understand that thoroughly.

Yet, the ten Sefirot of reflected light join and integrate together in the ten vessels. When they join as one, all the degrees are of equal merit, since Malchut's level is equal to that of Keter from the perspective of the reflected light, where Malchut returns to being Keter. Also, ZA is equal to Hochma, since ZA is considered Hochma of reflected light. And the level of Hochma is equal to that of Keter, since Keter receives the reflected light from her, as Hochma receives the direct light from Keter.

Since the level of ZA is equal to Hochma, and Hochma to Keter, it follows that the level of ZA is equal to that of Keter, too. It follows that by the elicitation of the ten Sefirot of reflected light from phase four, all the degrees in the ten Sefirot have been equalized, having the same level through Keter.

5) But the ten Sefirot of the world of Akudim disappeared once more. And we need to understand the reason for their departure. The ARI says that the reason is that when they emerged, they emerged incomplete and hence departed once more to receive their completion.

However, we need to understand the deficiency and the correction that came to them through this departure. Here the ARI wrote that the deficiency was because Keter emerged only in the quality of Nefesh. In another place, he wrote that the deficiency was because the inner light and the surrounding light came from the same foramen and were clashing with each other, as he writes in *Heichal AK, Shaar Vav, Shaar Akudim*, Chapter 1, Branch 4.

Afterwards, the lower Taamim [tastes, and also punctuation marks] came, below the letters, which are lights that emerge through the Peh of AK, and from there outward. And here the lights have completely joined, since they come out through a single channel. Since the surrounding lights and inner lights have conjoined, here begins the making of the vessels.

For this reason, the five inner lights and the surrounding lights emerged tied together. This is why they are called Akudim, from the verse, "and tied Isaac." Thus, when they emerge together outside of the Peh [mouth], tied together, they beat and strike each other, and their beatings beget the existence of the vessels.

This means that the lights of Ozen and Hotem where the inner light expands through the left foramens of the Ozen and the Hotem, and surrounding light expanded through the right foramens of Ozen and Hotem. Hence, they persisted and did not depart, since there is a special vessel for the inner light and a special vessel for the surrounding light.

But in the light of the Peh, where there is only one foramen, the inner light and the surrounding light were in the same vessel. Hence, they were beating on each other, as a result of which the light departed and the vessels fell down. In other words, they fell from their degree, and more coarseness was added to the previous coarseness, and by that the vessels were made, since the departure of the light completes the vessels.

To thoroughly understand the issue of the two foramens of Ozen and Hotem of AK, the issue of the single foramen in the Peh of AK, and the matter of the five internal and five surrounding, the clash and the vessels and the increasing coarseness, I must elaborate, since the ARI's words on these matters are quite succinct.

It is even more so concerning the surrounding, where he seemingly contradicts himself in each and every section. Once he says that they had inner lights KHB ZON and the five surrounding lights KHB ZON from the Hotem upward, but from the Peh down, the surroundings of Bina and ZON stopped and only two surrounding [lights], Keter and Hochma remained, and the five Partzufim KHB ZON. Another time, he said that from the world of Nekudim downward, the lower surroundings have stopped, but there are still five surrounding lights and five inner lights in the lights of the Peh. And another time, he says that there are five inner and five surrounding in the whole of ABYA, and other such contradictions.

6) I will elaborate inside the book [*Panim Meirot uMasbirot*], and here I will be brief so as to not stray from the issue. It is explained in Branch One and in Branch Four in the order of the ten Sefirot, concerning the four phases of ten Sefirot of direct light and reflected light, that in every ten Sefirot, there are two phases of expansion and two phases of increasing coarseness, which expand from the root, which is the Keter of these ten Sefirot.

Hochma, considered broad expansion, emerges first. This means that this expansion contains all the light that is extended from Ein Sof to that emanated being. And the vessel, called the coarse light, meaning the will to receive included in the expansion of the light, for which it acquires disparity of form from the Emanator, in whom there is no reception, and for which it becomes darker than the light, is still not revealed in this broad expansion, as long as its desire does not intensify, craving additional abundance more than the measure of its expansion. However, it is included in the above-mentioned coarse light from the perspective of the Emanator, who wishes to bestow upon it.

For this reason, it must reveal its vessel of reception and realize it from potential to actual. Hence, it grows coarser as it expands, meaning its desire to draw more abundance than its measure of expansion increases. And the increasing of coarseness that was made in this expansion is given its own name, due to its intensification. It is called Bina because it is darker than the light of Hochma, in which the will to receive was revealed in actuality.

This Bina is still unfit to be an actual vessel, since its essence is from Hochma, but she is the root of the vessel, for the vessel can only be completed from the increasing of coarseness that occurred in the second expansion. It is called "expansion through a window," meaning that the additional abundance that Bina drew through her intensification expands from her outwards. This is called light of Hassadim, the opposite of the broad first expansion, called the light of self.

The expansion through a window that expands from Bina is called ZA, and it becomes coarser as it expands, like the first expansion. This means that it, too, intensifies to draw additional abundance, more than the measure of its expansion from Bina. By this it actualizes the vessels of reception contained in it. This second increasing of coarseness is given its own name, since through this intensification, it grew darker than the light of expansion, and it is called Malchut.

Phase four, which is the increasing of coarseness created in the expansion through the window, called Malchut, is the complete vessel of reception, and not the three phases preceding it, which cascaded only in order to reveal this fourth phase. It is she who undergoes the first restriction, preventing herself from receiving abundance in this phase four, due to the disparity of form revealed in her. This detaining force is called a screen or a curtain, meaning that it detains the abundance from shining and expanding within it.

This is the whole difference between the first increasing of coarseness made in the broad expansion, and the increasing of coarseness that occurred in an expansion through a window. This is so because in the first increasing of coarseness, the restriction does not govern; hence, it is fit for reception of light. This is why she is called "a window," meaning receiving, as a house receives daylight through the window in it. But in the second increasing of coarseness, the force of restriction governs her and she prevents herself from receiving abundance in her coarseness. Hence, she is called a screen, meaning detaining the light.

After phase four appeared with her screen, the light expands to her again, and the screen detains it, as mentioned above. Consequently, a coupling by striking is made on it, and ten Sefirot of reflected light emerge, as it is written in Branch 3. The arrangement of these ten Sefirot is opposite from the ten Sefirot of direct light, which emerge from below upward, since the screen that elicited that great light, and which is its root, has become Keter.

This is the meaning of "Their end is embedded in their beginning." Just as Keter is the beginning and the Rosh [head] of the ten Sefirot of direct light, the end, which is Malchut, has become the beginning and the Rosh of the ten Sefirot of reflected light.

Thus, Malchut has returned to being a Keter to these ten Sefirot, and ZA of the ten Sefirot of direct light has now become Hochma, since the first receiver from the root is called Hochma. It is similarly with the rest, through Keter of direct light, which becomes Malchut in the ten Sefirot of reflected light, since it receives from ZA of reflected light, which is Hochma of direct light.

It turns out that in the ten Sefirot KHB ZON of direct light, the degrees are measured according to the refinement from the coarse light, where the more refined is higher and more important. But in the ten Sefirot KHB ZON of reflected light, the degrees are measured by the coarseness, where the greater the coarseness in the degree, the higher it is and more important. This makes the higher ones in the ten Sefirot of direct light lower in the ten Sefirot of reflected light, and the lower ones in the ten Sefirot of direct light higher in the ten Sefirot of reflected light.

The first ten Sefirot that expand from Ein Sof are called Adam Kadmon. These are the roots of the vessels of Rosh; hence, the ten Sefirot are named after the vessel of Rosh: Galgalta [skull], Einayim [eyes], Oznayim [ears] are the KHB of the ten Sefirot of AK, and Hotem [nose] and Peh [mouth] are ZA and Malchut of the ten Sefirot of AK. Also, it is known that the ten Sefirot are included in one another, as it is written in Panim. Hence, each of the above-mentioned Galgalta, Einayim, and AHP, expanded into ten Sefirot.

It is forbidden to speak of the ten Sefirot that expanded in Galgalta and Einayim, which are Keter and Hochma of the ten Sefirot of AK, and we do not deal with them. We begin to speak from the AHP down, from Bina and ZON of AK.

Also, it is known that the ten Sefirot are Keter and the four phases HB ZON, and there are inner light and surrounding light in them. This means that what has already been clothed in the vessel is called inner light, and what has not been clothed in the vessel is called surrounding light. Thus, in each of the ten Sefirot of AHP of AK there are five internal KHB ZON, and five surrounding KHB ZON.

7) Now we shall explain the inherent quality of the inner light and surrounding light of the ten Sefirot of AK. The matter of the ten Sefirot of direct light and ten Sefirot of reflected light that exist in each ten Sefirot has already been explained. In these ten Sefirot of AK, too, there are ten Sefirot of direct light from Keter to Malchut, and likewise, ten Sefirot of reflected light from Malchut to Keter, and the direct light is extended and comes in completeness to that emanated being. Yet, the ten Sefirot of reflected light are not fully and immediately extended to that emanated being. Instead, it is extended through all the Partzufim emanated after Adam Kadmon.

The thing is that everything that is extended from the Emanator is extended complete and with all the fillings. These are the ten Sefirot of direct light. But the ten Sefirot of reflected light that are extended from the emanated being, meaning from the detaining force in phase four, called screen, does not immediately emerge in full. Instead, each emanated being has a part in it, and is proliferated and multiplied according to the proliferation of the emanated beings, as it is written in Panim. Now you can see that the ten Sefirot of direct light and a part of the ten Sefirot of reflected light are the inner light, while the whole of the reflected light is the surrounding light.

Also, it has already been explained above that there are two Nukvaot [plural of Nukva] in the ten Sefirot: increasing of coarseness in the broad expansion, and increasing of coarseness in the expansion through a window, called Bina and Malchut. Know that Bina is discerned as an inner vessel, in which all the inner light is clothed, and Malchut is the outer vessel, in which all the surrounding light is clothed. This means that the surrounding light is tied to her, since she has a screen that is unfit for reception, due to the detaining force in it. Instead, it is the root of the ten Sefirot of reflected light.

Thus, the content of the inner light and surrounding light has been thoroughly explained, as well as the content of the inner vessel and the outer vessel. Now we can understand the ARI's words, brought above in Item 5 concerning the five internal and five surrounding that emerged tied to one another through the Peh of AK. This concerns what he had explained in *Shaar TANTA*, Chapter 1, that the inner light and surrounding light of the ten Sefirot of Oznayim [ears] and the inner light and surrounding light of the ten Sefirot of Hotem emerged in two vessels: an inner vessel for inner light and an outer vessel for surrounding light.

Also, they are remote from one another, since the five surrounding KHB ZON emerge from the foramen of the right Ozen, and the five internal KHB ZON emerge from the foramen of the left Ozen, and similarly in the Hotem. Hence, he tells us here, in the ten Sefirot of Peh of AK, that there are no two distinct vessels here, but both, the five internal and the five surrounding, emerged tied to a single vessel—the Peh, called Malchut of AK, meaning phase four. Yet, the inner vessel, which is phase two and the phase of Bina, is absent here.

We could ask about this: How is it possible for the inner light, which is the ten Sefirot of direct light, to clothe in the vessel of Peh, which is phase four that was erected with a screen, and is unfit for reception? The thing is that Malchut herself is discerned with four distinct phases, called Atzamot [bones], Gidin [tendons], Bassar [flesh], and Or [skin]. The Atzamot of Malchut indicate the Etzem ["essence" or "self"] of her structure. This is the actual phase of ZA, meaning the expansion through a window, except it has gained coarseness along its expansion due to the intensification of the desire to draw more abundance than in its expansion from Bina.

For this reason, it is defined by a name in and of itself. Thus, two phases are discerned in her: phase one is the Atzmut [self, spelled like Atzamot in Hebrew] in her, the part of ZA, and phase two is the coarseness added to her by her intensification. This is called Gidin [tendons]. And what she takes from the force of restriction—the detaining force so as to not receive abundance in this coarse light—called a screen, the one with the coupling of the ten Sefirot of reflected light, is phase four in Malchut, called Or [skin]. And the reflected light that rises from the screen by the force of the coupling is called Bassar [flesh], and this is the phase three of Malchut.

You find that Malchut consists of the expansion of Bina, too. Moreover, it is the core of its structure. Now you will understand that the self in Malchut becomes the inner vessel to the inner five in the lights of the Peh, and the skin in her becomes an outer vessel for the surrounding five in the lights of the Peh. Now it has been thoroughly clarified how the five internal KHB ZON and five surrounding KHB ZON emerged in a single vessel—Malchut—in which there are two vessels, as well, inner and outer, though connected to each other, since all four phases are but one vessel: Malchut.

8) Now we shall explain the issue of the striking and the clash that occurred between the surrounding light and the inner light due to their tying in one vessel. See in *The Tree of Life*, Heichal AK, Shaar 2, p 3, as well as in *Shaar Akudim*, Chapter 2, that the nature of the inner light is to refine the vessel in which it is clothed. Hence, since in the ten Sefirot of Peh of AK the inner light and surrounding light were tied in a single vessel in Malchut, the inner light was refining the vessel of Malchut degree by degree. This is the reason for the departure of the ten Sefirot of Peh, called "the world of Akudim."

The thing is that it has already been explained in Item 6 and Item 4 that the ten Sefirot of reflected light are of opposite value to the ten Sefirot of direct light. In the ten Sefirot of direct light, the degrees rise one above the other according to their refinement, up to their root, which is the most refined among them. But in the ten Sefirot of reflected light, the degrees rise one above the other according to their coarseness, up to the root, which is the coarsest among them. This is phase four, and Malchut that became Keter again, while phase three is Hochma, phase two is Bina, phase one is ZA, and Keter is considered Malchut.

In the beginning, the screen was refined by one degree. This means that the coarse form of light of phase four was refined and reacquired the form of coarseness of phase three. This is considered that the light of Malchut departed from its place and rose to vessel of ZA, since then, too, the direct light expanded from Ein Sof on the screen, and the detaining force controlled the screen until a coupling by striking was made and the ten Sefirot of reflected light emerged from the screen of phase three.

However, they are no longer at the level of Keter, as they were initially, but are at the level of Hochma. This is because the coarseness of the phase of ZA and phase three of direct light has the value of Hochma in the reflected light. It turns out that the screen did not return to being Keter due to the reflected light, but returned to being Hochma.

Afterward, it was refined further and received the refinement of phase two, which is Bina. There, too, the direct light expanded to it up to the coupling by striking and the raising of reflected light, though at the level of Bina. As the coarseness of phase three and phase four were lost, she lost the first two Sefirot of reflected light.

Subsequently, it was refined further, and received the refinement of phase one, the direct light from Ein Sof mated in it, and the reflected light rose, though at the level of ZA, lacking the phase of Bina, too. Then it was refined even more, up to the form of the root, which rose to the level of Keter.

At that time, there was no coarseness left in the screen; hence, there was no more coupling by striking on the direct light in it. For this reason, the reflected light completely disappeared from the ten Sefirot of Akudim, and see in *Panim* in Branch 3 and Branch 4, where all this is explained elaborately.

Thus, it has been clarified that since the inner light is clothed in the vessel of Malchut, it refines it degree by degree, and along with its refinement, the ten Sefirot KHB ZON of reflected light vanish, too. This is so because during her rise to the phase of Keter, the screen loses all its power to raise reflected light. Thus, the ten Sefirot of direct light also depart from it since the direct light and reflected light are interdependent and tied to [one another].

9) To explain this, I shall first explain the state of the Sefirot with a picture of the Taam [singular for Taamim—punctuation marks] Segolta, like this: ֠ , that is, the Keter is on top, below it on the right is Hochma, and at its left—Bina. We need to

understand this, for God forbid that we should understand it as a depiction of places that the tangible eye perceives. Also, the matter of face-to-face and back-to-back that apply in the ten Sefirot, God forbid that there should be back and front here.

The thing is that it has already been explained in the four phases of direct light that expand from Ein Sof, which is Keter, that the expansion of Keter is called Hochma. Also, it grows coarser as it expands, meaning the intensification of the desire to draw abundance more than the measure of its expansion. Hence, it is regarded as two phases: phase one is the whole of the light that expands from Ein Sof to that emanated being. This is called Hochma. Phase two is the increasing of coarseness, given to it by the intensification of the desire to draw new abundance, and this is called Bina.

For this reason, there are three discernments in the Sefira Bina: The first discernment is her own structure, which is a part of Hochma itself. The second discernment is the light that grew coarser in her through her intensification to draw new abundance from Keter. The third phase is the essence of the abundance that she draws from Keter, called light of Hassadim, which is much lower than the light of Hochma that is extended directly from the Emanator. But the light of Bina that she draws from the Keter is associated by her initial intensification, which became coarser for it.

And when Bina suckles the light of Hassadim from Keter, she does not suckle the light of Hochma from the Sefira of Hochma. Hence, she is considered to be back-to-back with Hochma. It turns out that the light of Hochma, which is the light of self of the general ten Sefirot in that emanated being, ceases from it, since Bina has turned her anterior to draw light of Hassadim from Keter.

Yet, when phase four appears, and the ten Sefirot of reflected light that emerge from her, which is also regarded as light of Hassadim, even more than the light of Hassadim in Bina, then Bina no longer needs to suckle light of Hassadim from Keter, since she receives abundantly from the reflected light of Malchut. Hence, she turns her anterior back to Hochma and suckles light of Hochma once more. At that time, the light of Hochma, too, is extended abundantly in the general ten Sefirot in that emanated being. This is called face-to-face of HB, which they gained through the reflected light that rises from the Malchut.

However, prior to the revealing of the vessel of Malchut, Bina turned her anterior to Keter, which is the state of the Taam Segolta, where Bina is below Keter, like Hochma, but Hochma draws the light of self from Keter, and Bina draws light of Hassadim from Keter. And since the light of self is the collective light in the emanated being, Hochma is considered "right," and the light of Hassadim is considered "left," as it is associated with Gevura.

Thus we have explained that the light of self cannot expand in the whole of the ten Sefirot of direct light, since Bina is back-to-back with it, except during a coupling by striking in the screen in the vessel of Malchut. At that time, Bina no longer needs the light of Hassadim and returns to being face-to-face with Hochma.

It turns out that when the ten Sefirot of reflected light depart from the world of Akudim, the light of self of the ten Sefirot of direct light depart along with it. This is because the light of Hochma and the reflected light are interdependent, and only the posterior of Bina remain there in the world of Akudim, meaning light of Hassadim and her Gevura.

Now you will understand the words of the ARI that we brought above, that the nature of the inner light is to refine the vessel it is clothed in, since it revolves around the light of Hochma that clothes in the internality of the emanated being through the Bina that returns to being face-to-face with it. Thus, the posterior of Bina are refined, and since the posterior of Bina, which is phase two, is the root of phase four, since the root is refined, the branch, phase four, is refined along with it.

10) Now we shall explain the issue of the clash of the inner lights with the surrounding lights, since they are tied to one another, which I introduced above in Item 5. I shall also bring the ARI's words in *Shaar Akudim*, Chapter 5, where he himself explains the issue of this clash at length. This is what he wrote, in brief: It follows that there are three kinds of light [in the expansion of light in the world of Akudim and its departure back to the Emanator]. The first light is the light of Akudim, called tastes. The second is the record of that light, which remains after its departure, and which is called tags. The third is the light that comes to it through the ascent of the Sefirot, at which time it is through the posterior, which is judgment and is called dots.

When the third light, called dots, comes and strikes the second light, called record, which is mercy, they beat and clash with each other. This is because they are opposites: One is direct light, which is mercy, and the other is reflected light, which is judgment. Then sparks fall from the descending reflected light, which is judgment, and these sparks are another, fourth light, called letters. These are the four phases—tastes, dots, tags, letters—all of which are included here in the Akudim. Also, these sparks that fell from the descending reflected light are like the 248 sparks of the breaking of the vessels in the world of Nekudim.

Interpreting his words: According to what has been explained above concerning the order of the expansion of the light in the world of Akudim, first the light expands from Ein Sof to the coupling by striking in the screen in the vessel of Malchut. Following, ten Sefirot of reflected light emerge from it, from below upward, as it is written in Item 6. They have an inverse relation, where the upper ones in direct light are below in the reflected light, since in the ten Sefirot of reflected light the degrees diminish according to the refinement.

Thus, ZA, which is more refined than Malchut, is of a lower degree than Malchut. But this is so only with respect to the Hochma in the ten Sefirot of reflected light.

Bina, which is more refined than ZA, was diminished in the degree and possesses only the value of Bina. Hochma, which is more refined than Bina, diminished in her degree and has only the value of ZA. And Keter has the value of Malchut, as it is written there in *Panim*, in Branch 3.

But once the direct light and reflected light unite and join together, it creates an equal value, where the level of each of the ten Sefirot reaches the level of Keter, as written in Item 4. And the whole of the world of Akudim, the expansion and return of the light of Ein Sof from Keter to Malchut and from Malchut to Keter, and the reflected light that conjoins with the direct light at an equal level through Keter is called the tastes or the first expansion of Akudim.

It has been explained above, Item 8, that because the inner light dresses in the vessel of Malchut, whose nature is to refine the vessel, it causes the refinement of the screen degree by degree. In the beginning, it receives the refinement as in phase three. This is considered that the screen rose to ZA. At that time, the light of Ein Sof expands once more from Keter to the screen in the vessel of ZA, and from ZA to Keter. This diminishes the value of the reflected light that rises from the screen to the degree of Hochma, similar to the value of ZA of reflected light. Similarly, the degrees descend in the refinement of the screen through the refinement of the phase of Keter of direct light, at which time the screen is canceled and the coupling by striking stops.

Thus, all this reflected light, which descends from degree to degree until it completely disappears, is called "light of dots" because the screen is extended from the point of restriction, and hence detains the direct light, too, from approaching and expanding in it. It is like the middle point of the first restriction that decorated itself and left the light in it, and assertively chose the refinement from its coarseness, in order to equalize her form with the Emanator, as has been explained in detail in *Panim Masbirot*, Branch 1. Hence, this force, the desire to be refined, is imprinted in the screen.

Now we shall explain the meaning of the record—the light of tags. It is known that even though the light departs, it still leaves a record behind it. Hence, the first expansion in the world of Akudim, which expanded and returned from Keter to Malchut and from Malchut to Keter, eliciting ten Sefirot whose level equals Keter in inner light, and similarly, ten Sefirot of surrounding light, as written in Item 7 [note that here there was no distinct vessel for inner light and a distinct vessel for surrounding light]. That vessel, as a whole, is called vessel of Keter, since all ten Sefirot were at the level of Keter. Hence, even though this expansion departed once more, a record of it nevertheless remained, keeping and sustaining the previous form there, so it would not be altogether revoked due to the departure of the light.

Accordingly, you can see how the light of record, which remained from the first expansion, and the descending reflected light, which is the light of dots, are two opposites, striking and beating one another. This is so because the light of record is strengthened by the first expansion, where the direct light expanded through the screen of phase four, and wished very much for the screen to remain specifically in coarseness of phase four, since only through the power in the excessive coarseness in phase four does it have the value of the level of Keter. However, the light of dots, the screen itself, intensifies with all its might only to be refined from its coarse light, discerned as judgment. It wishes to be utterly refined and equalize its form with the Emanator, since the first beginning of the point of restriction has been imprinted in it, and this is its root.

11) Now we can understand the fourth light, which fell through the clash of the light of record with the light of dots, called letters. They are like the 248 sparks in the breaking of the vessels in the world of Nekudim.

You should know that in every place in *The Zohar*, the *Tikkunim* [corrections of *The Zohar*], and in the writings of the ARI, the word sparks or sparkling indicates reflected light. This is because the illumination of direct light is defined by the names lights or Nehorin [Aramaic: lights], and the illumination of reflected light is defined by the name sparks or sparkling. Thus, you see that the issue of the sparks that fell through the clash of the record in the descending reflected light is also considered record, though it is a record of reflected light, and hence defined by the name sparks.

The order of the descent of the reflected light has been explained above, Item 8. In the beginning, it received for the refinement of ZA and was detached from phase four, which is the actual vessel of Malchut. And when the light of Ein Sof expands to the screen in vessel ZA once again, this light of Malchut will be at the level of Hochma, lacking the phase of Keter from the general light of Akudim, since the Malchut in ZA does not return to being Keter, but Hochma. [It has been explained that the essential giver of the level in the ten Sefirot of the emanated being is the light of Malchut, as above-mentioned, see *Panim Masbirot*, Branch 4.]

It follows that the real vessel of Malchut is without light, and two records should have remained in it. The first record is from the light of tastes, which keeps and sustains the coarseness of phase four as much as it can. The second record is from the light of dots, meaning the light ascribed to the screen and which craves the refinement.

However, both cannot remain together, since they are opposites. This is because the place of the record of tastes is called the vessel of Keter, since its ten Sefirot are at the level of Keter. And the place of the record of the descending reflected light is called the vessel of Hochma or "below Keter." Hence, her own record has departed Malchut, too, and rose to the vessel of ZA. And the record of the descending reflected light remained in its place. Thus, here the record for the sparks of reflected light were rejected. However, from here onward the sparks of reflected light are rejected for the light of the record.

Afterward, in the ascent of the screen to the place of Bina, when it received the refinement of phase two, and the light of Ein Sof expands once more from Keter to Bina and from Bina to Keter, the phase of Hochma is subtracted, too. Then the vessel of ZA remains without light, and two records remained there, too, from the light of tastes and from the reflected light, which are opposites. Here the record overpowers the sparks of reflected light, since the record of tastes remained in the vessel of ZA; hence, it remained in the form of the vessel of Keter.

Yet, the record of reflected light, which are the sparks of vessel Hochma, are rejected below Tabur, below the vessel of Keter, since the expansion of the world of Akudim is through Tabur, as Malchut of Akudim is called Tabur. Also, it is already known that sparks of Keter of the descending reflected light, whose value is considered Keter of Hochma, remain there since the record of Malchut of tastes, which are actual phase of Keter, rose to ZA. And the sparks that fell from vessel ZA, which are the sparks of Hochma in Hochma, fell below Tabur, where there is Keter of Hochma.

Similarly, in the ascent of the screen to Hochma, when it was refined into phase one, the light of Ein Sof was still expanding from Keter to Hochma and from Hochma to Keter, and this light is at the level of ZA. Hence, the level of Bina has been withdrawn, as well, and the vessel of Bina remained empty, without light. This left two records, as written above: a record of tastes that remained in their place, and a record of the descending reflected light that were rejected and fell below the sparks of Hochma below Tabur.

Subsequently, it was refined up to the phase of Keter, the root, and hence lost all the phases coarseness in it. Thus, the coupling by striking was naturally canceled, having no more reflected light. It turns out that no sparks fell from the phase of Keter at all, and only the record of tastes remained there.

Thus we have thoroughly explained the oppositeness between the record and the descending reflected light, for which the package was broken, and the record of the ten Sefirot of tastes that remain in their places. These are considered vessels KHB ZON of Keter, through Tabur of AK. And the sparks, which are record of the descending reflected light, fell outside the degree they were in. They are regarded as being below Tabur, meaning below Malchut of Akudim, which are considered vessels KHB ZON of Hochma, as we have said above, that they are called letters.

12) The reason for the refinement has already been explained above, at the end of Item 9: The inner light is connected to the vessel of Malchut, which is actually only an external vessel for the surrounding light, as it is written in Item 7. Hence, when the reflected light rises and brings HB back to face-to-face, as written in Item 9, coarseness of Bina leaves it, for it returns to being one with the Hochma, as they initially were. And when the coarseness in the root is canceled, the coarseness in the branch is canceled, too. Thus, when Bina becomes one object with Hochma, she

refined the screen along with her, and it, too, rises degree by degree, through her and because of her, until it disappears.

At the beginning of the entrance of the reflected light to Bina, she begins to turn her anterior back to Hochma. Thus, the screen rises from phase four and phase three. And when she draws the light of Hochma from the anterior of Hochma, the screen rises to phase two. And when she becomes one object with the Hochma, the screen rises to phase one, until it rises to the root phase. This is the meaning of what is mentioned in the *Idra Raba*, "the spark was sucked."

It follows that the light of Hochma, which is all the light of self in the first emanated being, meaning the world of Akudim, and the reflected light that rises from the vessel of Malchut are tied to one another and chase one another for without the reflected light, the light of Hochma would not able to expand in the emanated being, since Bina turns her face to suckle light of Hassadim from Keter, and her back to Hochma. This means she will not suckle the light of self from it.

However, when the reflected light comes out, Bina turns her face back to Hochma, and only then can the light of self expand in the emanated being. Thus, the light of self depends on the reflected light. But when HB return to being face-to-face, and her suckling from Keter stops, her coarseness is canceled, which naturally cancels the coarseness in the branch, which is the screen. Thus, the reflected light disappears, as well. Thus, the reflected light is repelled and chased due to the light of self.

This will thoroughly explain the ARI's words, which I presented above, Item 5, that the inner light and surrounding light beat on each other, and their beating begets the vessels. This is because the inner light is the light of Hochma that expands in the emanated being due to the reflected light. And the surrounding light is the screen, which is the outer vessel, which is tied to all the surrounding light that is destined to come out in the worlds by way of reflected light, as written in Item 7.

Although they are interdependent, nevertheless the inner light that expands through HB returning to face-to-face clashes with the surrounding light. This refines the screen and causes the departure of the light from the world of Akudim. Thus, the records of tastes and of reflected light were separated from one another, the record of reflected light was rejected outside her presence, meaning below the Tabur, called letters, and these are the vessels.

13) Thus, we have thoroughly clarified the reason for the departure, due to the gradual refinement of the screen until all the reflected light disappeared, and along with it, the light of self of Keter and Hochma of direct light. Yet, it did not remain so: Following the disappearance of the light of self, Bina turned its anterior back to Keter, for abundance of light of Hassadim, and hence, the previous posterior and coarseness returned to her. Therefore, her coarseness returned to the screen, as well, which is her branch.

It is known that the direct light from the Emanator does not stop from the emanated beings even for a moment. Hence, after the screen regained its coarseness, the direct light of Ein Sof was renewed on the four above-mentioned phases, up to the coupling of reflected light. And once again, the ten Sefirot of direct light and reflected light expanded in the world of Akudim. This is called the second expansion of the world of Akudim.

Yet, since HB in it returned to being face-to-face through the above-mentioned reflected light, the coarseness and posterior of Bina were refined once more, and with it, the coarseness of the screen, which is her branch. And once again, the coupling by striking and the reflected light were canceled, and Bina returns to drawing light of Hassadim from Keter. Thus, the light of self departs as before.

Similarly, once the posterior and coarseness returned to Bina, the coarseness was drawn on the screen, as well, and naturally, the direct light was renewed on the screen. Through it, the light of self expanded, too.

This is repeated similarly: When the reflected light comes, the light of self expands once more. And when the light of self comes, the reflected light leaves. When the reflected light leaves, the screen regains its coarseness, and the reflected light is renewed, and the light of self expands once more, and so on. It turns out that this second expansion is like a constant flame moving to and fro. This is why the ARI says that inner light and surrounding light that are tied in one vessel strike each other and clash with each other.

This clarifies the big difference between the first expansion of Akudim that was at the level of Keter, since the direct light made a coupling with the screen of phase four, and the current expansion, which is only on the level of Hochma. It is because the whole coarseness of the screen is only an expansion from the coarseness of Bina, as in the coarseness of ZA, hence it draws only the level of light of Hochma, as written in Item 8. But this light, too, is not permanent. Rather, it is like a flame that moves to and fro. This thoroughly explains that the matter of the second expansion of Akudim is extended from the departure of the first expansion itself.

14) Now we understand the ARI's words in *Shaar Akudim*, Chapters 1 and 2, that AK restricted itself and raised all the lights from below the Tabur to the Tabur and above, and they rose as MAN to AB of Galgalta. There, it placed a boundary in its internals, and the light that rose from NHY came out through the Einayim, extended below the Tabur, and expanded into the ten Sefirot of the world of Nekudim.

And from the light that was innovated by raising MAN, it expanded and breached the Parsa, and descended below the Tabur, expanding through the holes of Tabur and Yesod, into the ten Sefirot of the world of Nekudim. The ten Sefirot of Nekudim were built from these two lights. These two lights and this new restriction require great detail, which will be explained in its time. Here we shall explain them as needed in this place.

It has already been explained in Item 11 that the lights below Tabur of AK are the letters and sparks that fell through the clash of the record of Keter and tastes in the record of Hochma and dots. They came out below the whole record of Keter, and this exit place is called NHY and "below Tabur."

Now, after the second expansion—which is only light of Hochma in vessel of Keter—returned to the world of Akudim, the equivalence between the records of tastes and the records of dots was made once more. This is because they are both considered Hochma, and hence all the KHB ZON of the records of dots below the Tabur were drawn, rose, and reconnected with the records above Tabur. This is why the ARI says that AK raised the light from below its Tabur to above its Tabur.

However, we should understand why it is called restriction. The thing is that there are two discernments in these sparks that rose. The first is sparks of Keter of the descending reflected light that remained in the Tabur itself, which is Malchut of Akudim and phase four. The light of the second expansion does not reach it, since it is from phase three, and has coarseness from the expansion of the posterior of Bina. The second discernment is sparks of HB and ZON from phase three, as it is written in Items 11 and 12.

Hence, once HB ZON of the sparks rose, the lights increased there more than before, due to the coarseness that was added to them by their fall below the Tabur. Hence, the sparks of the Keter in the Tabur, which are phase four, were extended there, too. And naturally, the light of the direct light of Ein Sof, which never stops from the emanated beings, was renewed upon them. Thus, the coupling of reflected light was made in phase four, and as a result, ten new Sefirot emerged at the level of Keter, as in the first expansion.

Thus, you see how two phases of ten Sefirot were made of the sparks that rose: Ten Sefirot at the level of Hochma were made from the HB ZON of the sparks that were corrected only in their ascent, since they are from phase three, like the second expansion, and ten new Sefirot at the level of Keter were made of the sparks of Keter.

These two Partzufim are the roots of the Partzufim AVI and YESHSUT of Atzilut. The new Partzuf at the level of Keter is AVI, and it is called Hochma and Aba of Atzilut. And the Partzuf of the old light, at the level of Hochma, is YESHSUT, and is called Bina and Ima of Atzilut.

With these roots you will understand what is written in *Idra Zuta*, that Aba brought Ima out because of her son, and Aba himself was built as a kind of male and female. This is so because the upper Partzuf, which is at the level of Keter, called Aba, was built as a kind of male and female, since he raised phase four—Nukva and Malchut—to him. And Bina, the lower Partzuf, whose level is below Keter, went out from Aba because of the Nukva, which is phase four, which ends and detains the upper light from expanding below her. This is why this phase four is called Parsa [partition], without the Nekev [hole] that exists in phase two. And because of this Parsa, YESHSUT does not clothe the light of Keter.

It turns out that phase two, which is Bina, on which the first restriction did not apply at all, has now become deficient, since she was restricted, too, as she is below phase four. This is why the ARI said that AK restricted himself by raising light from below Tabur, concerning phase two that has now been restricted due to the ascent of MAN.

15) You should know the big difference between Rosh and Guf. The Rosh is called GAR, and the Guf is called VAK, ZAT, or ZON. The Guf itself is divided into GAR and ZON, too.

The root of this division is that up to the Peh—Malchut—the structure is made essentially of direct light. And the reflected light that rises and joins it is but clothing over it. The opposite of that is the Guf, which is a expansion of the screen itself, to the extent that it clothes the Sefirot of Rosh. Hence, it is made primarily of reflected light, and the ten Sefirot of direct light are like its branches.

Although it is called ZON, it is essentially only Malchut. This is so because there is no light of Malchut in reality at all, except with NHY of ZA that unite with it in a coupling by striking. Hence, they are regarded as one that expands through the reflected light. And it has already been explained above that the detaining screen and the reflected light that emerges as a result of it are not ascribed to the Emanator, but only to the emanated being. For this reason, the Rosh is regarded as the self of the light of the Emanator, and the Guf is regarded only as the act of the emanated being itself.

Now you understand the five general Partzufim of AK, called Galgalta, AB, SAG, MA, and BON, and the order of their emanation and clothing one another, how they are interconnected and emerge from one another by way of cause and consequence. This is so because of His one, unique, and unified thought—thoroughly explained in *Panim Masbirot*, Branch 1—which is to delight His creations. This thought is the root of the vessel, and of the first restriction that occurred in phase four, though indirectly, as it is written there in Item 7, as in the allegory about the rich man. See in Item 8, that this single thought encompasses the whole of reality, all the worlds, and all the many forms and conducts through the end of correction, when they all reunite with the light of Ein Sof from before the restriction, in simple unity, in the one form that stands above us—"to delight His creatures."

Immediately following the restriction in phase four, which is the Gadlut [greatness/adulthood] of the desire in Malchut of Ein Sof, four forms of gradations appeared in the record that has been emptied of the light—in the vessel. They are called HB, ZA, and Malchut, and they contain inner light and surrounding light, thus twelve forms.

Afterward, the light was extended on the above-mentioned record, up to the point of the restriction, since His light does not stop at all, and remember this. Then the thin line was extended into the record, and it is called "thin" because the light of self is extended to the emanated being only in the reflected light that rises in a coupling from the screen. And by the power of the reflected light, the image of AK was revealed in the form of Partzuf Galgalta, which is called, in the example, "the beginning of the line."

It expands over the twenty-five phases, since there are KHB ZON at the length and there are KHB ZON in thickness. As we have said, because Malchut returned to being Keter, each of the KHB ZON expands into ten Sefirot up to Keter, and it is called in the example, Galgalta, Einayim, AHP, or Galgalta, AB, SAG, MA, and BON. The level of each of them reaches Galgalta, and its lights emerge from the internality of this emanated being, as it has been explained in *Panim Masbirot*, Branch 3, Item 2, concerning the order of the emergence of the lights due to the refinement of the screen.

16) Therefore, initially, AB emerged. Emergence means subtracting. Due to the refinement of phase four of the inner AK, called Peh, she received coarseness of phase three. And after the light of Ein Sof was drawn over this screen, new ten Sefirot emerge at the level of Hochma, called AB. It turns out that the AB that comes out is subtracted from the AB that remains within AK, at the level of Keter.

Thus, Keter of the external AB clothes Hochma of Galgalta, and expands through the Tabur of the Inner AK. And it, too, contains twenty-five phases of its ten Sefirot of direct light, which are its Galgalta, Einayim, Ozen, Hotem, Peh, each of which expands by the power of the reflected light over the five phases, through Keter of AB.

Yet, the general Keter of the inner AK remains revealed, and it is regarded as having Rosh and Guf [head and body, respectively]. From the Peh down, it is called Guf, since it is only an expansion of the screen. Hence, the inner light and surrounding light are tied there only in phase four of AB. This is why they had to depart once more, and this is called "the world of Nekudim," which are ZON and Guf of the outer AB.

It has already been explained that the coarseness returned to the screen after the departure of its Guf, and a second expansion occurred there, as it is written in Items 13 and 14. It draws the lights from below the Tabur to above the Tabur, and by this ascent, the upper AVI are corrected. A Parsa is spread beneath them, and YESHSUT is from the Parsa to the Tabur. All this ascent is called "the outer Partzuf SAG," meaning it had departed its previous degree, which, in the outer AB was Bina at the level of Keter Hochma, which is the light of Ozen up to Shibolet haZakan.

However, at this Partzuf, which was made of the sparks that fell from the lights of Peh of the outer AB, Bina of this Partzuf is below all ten Sefirot of upper AVI, hence it is deficient of the Keter. Thus, its place is from Peh down, meaning from Shibolet haZakan, which is its Galgalta.

As the outer AB clothes only Malchut of the general Keter and the first nine remain revealed, the outer SAG, too, clothes only Malchut of Keter of AB, from Peh down, while its first nine—the whole of the Rosh—remain revealed. As the AB elicited its branches through the Se'arot [hair] of the Rosh, this SAG elicited its branches through the Se'arot AHP, which will be explained in their place. This is the meaning of the light that is withdrawn from them due to their exit, compared to the upper one that remains there in the Se'arot as surrounding, as in returning surrounding.

And this SAG clothes AK from Shibolet haZakan through its end. This means that its Rosh, which are GAR, is extended up to Tabur, which are equivalent to Galgalta, Einayim, Ozen, and Hotem. Its Peh expands into ten Sefirot of Guf in itself, as in the Peh of the outer AB. And the case of the lights of the Peh of the outer SAG, as in the case of the lights of Peh of the outer AB, due to their being tied in a single vessel, there was gradual refinement of the screen in them, as well, until it was refined into the phase of Keter, and the whole expansion disappeared.

This is the meaning of the breaking of the vessels and the fall of the 248 sparks. Yet, this happened only in their ZON, and not in their GAR, due to the correction of the Parsa, as will be explained in its place. Afterward, the sparks that fell from the Peh of the outer SAG were extended and rose in the form of MAN, the new MA came out, and the ten Sefirot of Atzilut were established in the form of twelve Partzufim.

Thus, all the previous phases are included in the world of Atzilut, as it is written in *The Tree of Life*, and the world of Beria was imprinted from the world of Atzilut, in a way that all that exists in Atzilut is imprinted in Beria. Yetzira is imprinted from Beria, Assiya is imprinted from Yetzira, and hence there is no existence or conduct in the lower ones that is not directly related to the upper ones, from which it stems and is extended down to its lower essence.

This is why our sages said, "There is not a blade of grass below that does not have an angel above that strikes it and tells it, 'Grow!'" This is so because all that is extended from a higher world to a lower one is extended through couplings. But the worlds are divided into internality and externality. The internality of the worlds, from Atzilut and below, is not extended through a coupling by striking in the screen, but through a coupling of Yesodot [plural for Yesod]. But the external phases that are extended from world to world, are extended through a coupling by striking.

This is the meaning of the striking, and this is why our sages accurately stated that the angel in the world of Yetzira, which is the root of the blade of grass in the world of Assiya, bestows upon it and nurtures it in the form of a coupling by striking. In other words, it strikes it and tells it, "Grow!" since saying means bestowing.

Thus, the matter of cause and consequence in Galgalta, AB, SAG of AK has been thoroughly explained, and the quality of their clothing over one another. Each lower one has the value of ZON of the upper one, which extends only from the sparks of the lights of the Peh of the upper one.

It has been clarified that in the emergence of AB, the screen was included in phase three. And in the emergence of SAG, the screen was included in phase two, to the Nukva of Aba. And in the emergence of MA from inside out, the screen was included in phase one. This will be explained in its place.

Also, Malchut of phase three is called Tabur, of phase two is called Parsa, and of phase one is called crust. There is nothing more to add here; I only tied the matters at their roots in an easy and brief manner. This was my intention in this place, but inside the book, the matters are explained elaborately.

Introduction to the Book Panim Meirot uMasbirot*

1) It is written at the end of the *Okatzin* [final treatise in the Mishnah], "The Creator did not find a vessel that holds a blessing for Israel, but peace, as it is written, 'The Lord will give strength unto His people; the Lord will bless his people with peace.'"

There is a lot to learn here: First, how did they prove that nothing is better for Israel than peace? Second, the text explicitly states that peace is the blessing itself, as it is written, "giving in strength and blessing in peace." According to them, it should have stated, "giving in peace." Third, why was this phrase written for the conclusion of the Mishnah? Also, we need to understand the meaning of the words "peace," "strength," and what they mean.

To interpret this article in its true meaning, we must go by a long way, for the heart of sayers is too deep to search. The author of *Afikey Yehuda* correctly interpreted the words of our sages about the verse "Support me with raisin cakes" is laws, "Cushion me with apples" is sayings. Our sages said that all the issues of the Torah and the *Mitzva* [commandment] bear revealed and concealed, as it is written, "Apples of gold in settings of silver. A word fitly spoken."

Indeed, the *Halachot* (laws) are like grails of wine. When one gives one's friend a gift, a silver grail with wine, both the insides and the outside are important because the grail has its own value, like the wine inside it.

The legends, however, are as apples whose interior is eaten and their exterior is thrown away, as the exterior is completely worthless. You find that all the worth and importance are only in the interior, the insides.

So is the matter with legends; the apparent superficiality seems meaningless and worthless. However, the inner content concealed in the words is built solely on the bedrock of the wisdom of truth, given to virtuous few, thus far his words, with slight changes.

Who would dare extract it from the heart of the masses and scrutinize their ways, when their attainment is incomplete in both parts of the Torah called *Peshat* [literal] and *Drush* [interpretation]? In their view, the order of the four parts of the Torah, PARDESS, begins with the *Peshat*, then the *Drush*, then *Remez* [insinuated], and in the end the *Sod* [secret] is understood.

However, it is written in the Vilna Gaon prayer book that the attainment begins with the *Sod*. After the *Sod* part of the Torah is attained, it is possible to attain the *Drush*, and then the *Remez*. When one is granted complete knowledge of these three parts of the Torah, one is awarded the attainment of the *Peshat* of the Torah.

---

* Shining and Welcoming Face

It is written in *Masechet Taanit*: "If one is rewarded, it becomes a potion of life to him. If he is not rewarded, it becomes a potion of death to him." Great merit is required in order to understand the *Peshat* of the texts, since first we must attain the three parts of the internality of the Torah, which the *Peshat* robes, and the *Peshat* will not be parsed. If one has not been rewarded with it, one needs great mercy, so it will not become a potion of death for him.

It is the opposite of the argument of the negligent in attaining the internality, who say to themselves, "We settle for attaining the *Peshat*. If we attain that, we will be content." Their words can be compared to one who wishes to step on the fourth step without first stepping on the first three steps.

2) However, accordingly, we need to understand the great concealing applied in the interior of the Torah, as it is said in *Masechet Hagiga*, one does not learn *Maase Beresheet* in pairs, and not the *Merkava* alone. Also, all the books at our disposal in this trade are sealed and blocked before the eyes of the masses. Only the few who are summoned by the Creator shall understand them, as they already understand the roots by themselves and in reception from mouth to mouth.

It is indeed surprising how the ways of wisdom and intelligence are denied of the people, for whom it is their life and the length of their days. It is seemingly a criminal offense, as about such our sages said in *Midrash Rabbah, Beresheet*, about Ahaz, that he was called Ahaz [lit. "held" or "seized"] for he seized synagogues and seminaries, and this was his great iniquity.

Also, it is a natural law that one is possessive concerning dispensing one's capital and property to others. However, is there anyone who is possessive concerning dispensing one's wisdom and intelligence to others? Quite the contrary, more than the calf wants to eat, the cow wants to feed, especially when it comes to the law of the Creator and His wish.

Indeed, we find such mysteries in the wisdom even in secular sages in previous generations. In Rav Butril's introduction to his commentary on *The Book of Creation*, there is a text ascribed to Plato who warns his disciples as follows: "Do not convey the wisdom unto one who knows not its merit."

Aristotle, too, warned, "Do not convey the wisdom to the unworthy, lest it shall be robbed." He (Rav Butril) interprets that if a sage teaches wisdom to the unworthy, he robs the wisdom and destroys it.

The secular sages of our time do not do so. On the contrary, they exert in expanding the gates of their sagacity to the entire crowd without any boundaries or conditions. Seemingly, they strongly disagree with the first sages, who opened the doors of their wisdom to only a handful of virtuous few, which they had found worthy, leaving the rest of the people fumbling the walls.

3) Let me explain the matter. We distinguish four divisions in the Speaking species, arranged in gradations one atop the other. Those are the masses, the strong,

the wealthy, and the sagacious. They are equal to the four degrees in the whole of reality, called 1) "still," 2) "vegetative," 3) "animate," and 4) "speaking."

The still can educe the three properties, vegetative, animate, and speaking, and we discern three values in the quantity of the force, from the beneficial and detrimental in them.

The smallest force among them is the vegetative. The flora operates by attracting what is beneficial to it and rejecting the harmful in much the same way as humans and animals do. However, there is no individual sensation in it, but a collective force, common to all types of plants in the world, which affects this operation in them.

Atop them is the animate. Each creature feels itself, concerning attracting what is beneficial to it and rejecting the harmful. It follows that one animal equalizes in value to all the plants in reality. It is so because the force that distinguishes the beneficial from the detrimental in the entire vegetative is found in one creature in the animate, separated to its own authority.

This sensing force in the animate is very limited in time and place, since the sensation does not operate at even the shortest distance outside its body. Also, it does not feel anything outside its own time, meaning in the past or in the future, but only at the present moment.

Atop them is the speaking, consisting of a feeling force and an intellectual force together. For this reason, its power is unlimited by time or place in attracting what is good for it and rejecting what is harmful to it like the animate.

This is so because of its science, which is a spiritual matter, unlimited by time or place. One can learn about others wherever they are in the whole of reality, and in the past and the future throughout the generations.

It follows that the value of one person from the speaking equalizes with the value of all the forces in the vegetative and the animate in the whole of reality at that time, and in all the past generations. This is so because its power encompasses them and contains them within its own self, along with all their forces.

This rule also applies to the four divisions in the human species, namely the masses, the strong, the wealthy, and the sagacious. Certainly, they all come from the masses, which are the first degree, as it is written, "all are of the dust."

It is certain that the whole merit of the dust and its very right to exist are according to the merit of the three virtues it educes—vegetative, animate, and speaking. Also, the merit of the masses corresponds to the properties they educe from them. Thus, they, too, connect in the shape of a human face.

For this purpose, the Creator installed three inclinations in the masses, called "envy," "lust," and "honor." Due to them, the masses develop degree by degree to educe a face of a whole man.

The inclination for lust educes the wealthy. The selected among them have a strong desire, and also lust. They excel in acquiring wealth, which is the first degree in the evolution of the masses. Like the vegetative degree in reality, they are governed by an alien force that deviates them to their inclination, as lust is an alien force in the human species borrowed from the animate.

The inclination for honor educes the famous heroes from among them, who govern the synagogues, the town, etc. The most strong-willed among them, which also have an inclination for honor, excel in obtaining dominion. These are the second degree in the evolution of the masses, similar to the animate degree in reality, whose operating force is present in their own essence, as we have said above. This is because the inclination for honor is unique to the human species, and along with it the craving for governance, as it is written, "You have put all things under his feet" (Psalms 8:7).

The inclination for envy elicits the sages from among them, as our sages said, "Author's envy increases wisdom." The strong-willed, with an inclination for envy, excel in acquiring wisdom and knowledge. It is like the speaking degree in reality, in which the operating force is not limited by time or place, but is collective and encompasses every item in the world, throughout all times.

Also, it is the nature of the fire of envy to be general, encompassing all times and the whole reality. This is because it is the conduct of envy: If one had not seen the object in one's friend's possession, the desire for it would not have awakened in one at all.

You find that the sensation of lack is not for what one does not have, but for what one's friends have, who are the entire progeny of Adam and Eve throughout the generations. Thus, this force is unlimited and therefore fit for its sublime and elated role.

Yet, those who remain without any merit, it is because they do not have a strong desire. Hence, all three above-mentioned inclinations operate in them together, in mixture. Sometimes they are lustful, sometimes envious, and sometimes they crave honor. Their desire breaks to pieces, and they are like children who crave everything they see and cannot attain anything. Hence, their value is like the straw and bran that remain after the flour.

It is known that the beneficial force and the detrimental force go hand in hand. In other words, as much as something can benefit, so it can harm. Hence, since the force of one person is greater than all the beasts and the animals of all times, one's harmful force supersedes them all, as well.

Thus, as long as one does not merit one's degree in a way that one uses one's force only to do good, one needs a careful watch so he does not acquire great amounts of the human level, which are wisdom and science.

For this reason, the first sages hid the wisdom from the masses for fear of taking indecent disciples who would use the power of the wisdom to harm and damage.

These would break and destroy the entire world with their lust and beastly savageness, using man's great powers.

When the generations have lessened and their sages themselves had started to crave both tables, meaning a good life for their corporeality, too, their views drew near to the masses. They traded with them and sold the wisdom as prostitutes for the price of a dog.

Since then, the fortified wall that the first had exerted on has been ruined and the masses have looted it. The savages have filled their hands with the force of men, seized the wisdom and tore it. Half was inherited by adulterers and half by murderers, and they have put it in eternal disgrace to this day.

4) From this you can deduce about the wisdom of truth, which contains all the external teachings within it, which are its seven little maids. This is the entirety of the human species and the purpose for which all the worlds were created, as it is written, "If My covenant be not day and night, if I have not appointed the ordinances of heaven and earth."

Hence, our sages have stated (*Avot* 4, *Mishnah* 5), "He who uses the crown passes." This is because they have prohibited us from using it for any sort of worldly pleasure.

This is what has sustained us thus far, to maintain the armies and the wall around the wisdom of truth, so no stranger or foreigner would break in or put it in their vessels to go and trade it in the market, as with the external sages. This was so because all who entered have already been tested by seven tests until it was certain beyond any concern and suspicion.

After these words and truth, we find what appears to be a great contradiction, from one extreme to the other, in the words of our sages. It is written in *The Zohar* that at the time of the Messiah, this wisdom will be revealed even to the young. However, according to the above, we learned that in the days of the Messiah, that whole generation will be at the highest level. We will need no guard at all, and the fountains of wisdom will open and water the whole nation.

Yet, in *Masechet Sutah*, 49, and *Sanhedrin* 97a, they said, "Impudence shall soar at the time of the Messiah, authors' wisdom shall go astray, and righteous shall be cast away." It interprets that there is none so evil as that generation. Thus, how do we reconcile the two statements, for both are certainly the words of the living God?

The thing is that this careful watch and door-locking on the hall of wisdom is for fear of people in whom the spirit of writers' envy is mixed with the force of lust and honor. Their envy is not limited to wanting only wisdom and knowledge.

Hence, both texts are correct, and one comes and teaches of the other. The face of the generation is as the face of the dog, meaning they bark as dogs *Hav, Hav* [give, give] righteous are cast away and authors' wisdom went astray in them.

It follows that it is permitted to open the gates of the wisdom and remove the careful guard, since it is naturally safe from theft and exploitation. There is no longer fear lest indecent disciples might take it and sell it in the market to the materialistic plebs, since they will find no buyers for this merchandise, as it is loathsome in their eyes.

Since they have no hope of acquiring lust or honor through it, it has become safe and guarded by itself. No stranger will approach except for lovers of wisdom and counsel. Hence, any examination shall be removed from those who enter, until even the very young will be able to attain it.

Now you can understand their words (*Sanhedrin* 98a): "The Son of David comes either in a generation that is all worthy, or all unworthy." This is very perplexing. Seemingly, as long as there are a few righteous in the generation, they detain the redemption. So when the righteous perish from the land, the Messiah will be able to come? I wonder.

Indeed, we should thoroughly understand that this matter of redemption and the coming of the Messiah that we hope will be soon in our days, Amen, is the uppermost wholeness of attainment and knowledge, as it is written, "and they shall teach no more every man his neighbor, saying: 'Know the Lord,' for they shall all know Me, from the greatest of them unto the least of them." And with the completeness of the mind, the bodies are completed, too, as it is written (Isaiah 65), "The youth, a hundred years old, shall die."

When the children of Israel are complemented with the complete knowledge, the fountains of intelligence and knowledge shall flow beyond the boundaries of Israel and water all the nations of the world, as it is written (Isaiah 11), "For the earth shall be full of the knowledge of the Lord," and as it is written, "and shall come unto the Lord and to His goodness."

The proliferation of this knowledge is the matter of the expansion of the Messiah King to all the nations. Yet, it is the opposite with the crude, materialistic plebs. Since their imagination is attached to the complete power of the fist, the matter of the expansion of the kingdom of Israel over the nations is engraved in their imagination only as a sort of dominion of bodies over bodies, to take their full fee with great pride, and boast over all the people in the world.

What can I do for them if our sages have already rejected them, and the likes of them, from among the congregation of the Creator, saying, "All who is proud, the Creator says, 'he and I cannot dwell in the same abode.'"

Conversely, some err and determine that as the body must exist prior to the existence of the soul and the complete perception, the perfection of the body and its needs precede in time the attainment of the soul and the complete perception. Hence, complete perception is denied of a weak body.

This is a grave mistake, harsher than death, since a perfect body is utterly inconceivable before the complete perception has been obtained, since in itself, it is a punctured bag, a broken cistern. It cannot contain anything beneficial, neither for itself nor for others, except with the obtainment of the complete knowledge.

At that time the body, too, rises to its completeness with it, literally hand in hand. This rule applies both in individuals and in the whole, and see all this in *The Zohar*, portion *Shlach*, concerning the spies, where it elaborates on this.

5) Now you will understand what is written in *The Zohar*: "With this composition, the children of Israel will be redeemed from exile." Also, in many other places, only through the expansion of the wisdom of Kabbalah in the masses will we obtain complete redemption.

Our sages also said, "The light in it reforms him." They were intentionally meticulous about it, to show us that only the light enclosed within it, "like apples of gold in settings of silver," in it lies the *Segula* [power/cure] that reforms a person. Both the individual and the nation will not complete the aim for which they were created, except by attaining the internality of the Torah and its secrets.

Although we hope for the complete attainment at the coming of the Messiah, it is written, "will give wisdom to the wise." It also says, "In the heart of every one who is wise-hearted, I have placed wisdom."

Hence, it is the great expansion of the wisdom of truth within the nation that we need first, so we may merit receiving the benefit from our Messiah. Consequently, the expansion of the wisdom and the coming of our Messiah are interdependent.

Therefore, we must establish seminaries and compose books to hasten the distribution of the wisdom throughout the nation. This was not the case before, for fear lest unworthy disciples would mingle, as we have elaborated above. This became the primary reason for the prolonging of the exile for our many sins, to this day.

Our sages said, "Messiah, Son of David comes only in a generation that is all worthy..." meaning when everyone retires from pursuit of honor and lust. At that time, it will be possible to establish seminaries among the masses to prepare them for the coming of the Messiah Son of David. "...or in a generation that is all unworthy," meaning in such a generation when "the face of the generation is as the face of the dog, and righteous shall be cast away, and authors' wisdom shall go astray in them." At such a time, it will be possible to remove the careful guard and all who remain in the house of Jacob with their hearts pounding to attain the wisdom and the purpose, "Holy" will be said to them and they shall come and learn.

This is so because there will no longer be fear lest one might not sustain one's merit and trade the wisdom in the market, as no one in the mob will buy it. The wisdom will be so loathsome in their eyes that neither glory nor lust will be obtainable in return for it.

Hence, all who wish to enter may come and enter. Many will roam, and the knowledge will increase among the worthy of it. And by this we will soon be rewarded with the coming of the Messiah, and the redemption of our souls.

With these words, I unbind myself from a considerable complaint, that I have dared more than all my predecessors in disclosing the usually covered rudiments of the wisdom in my book [*Panim Meirot uMasbirot*], which was thus far unexplored. This refers to the essence of the ten *Sefirot* and all that concerns them, *Yashar* [direct] and *Hozer* [reflected], *Pnimi* [inner] and *Makif* [surrounding], the meaning of *Hakaa* [beating/striking], and the meaning of *Hizdakchut* [purification/cleansing].

The authors that preceded me deliberately scattered the words here and there, and in subtle intimations so one's hand would fail to gather them. I—through His light, which appeared upon me, and with the help of my teachers—have gathered them and disclosed the matters clearly enough and in their spiritual form, above place and above time.

They could have come to me with a great complaint: If there are no additions to my teachers here, then the ARI and Rav Chaim Vital themselves, and the genuine authors, the commentators on their words, could have disclosed and explained the matters as openly as I. And if you wish to say that it was revealed to them, then who is this writer, for whom it is certainly a great privilege to be dust and ashes under their feet, who says that the lot given to him by the Creator is more than their lot?

However, as you will see in the references, I neither added to my teachers nor innovated in the composition. All my words are already written in the Eight Gates, in *The Tree of Life*, and in *Mavo Shearim* [*Entrance of the Gates*] by the ARI. I did not add a single word to them, but they aimed to conceal matters; hence, they scattered them one here and one there, since their generation was not yet completely unworthy and required great care. We, however, for our many sins, all the words of our sages are already true in us. They had been said for the time of the Messiah to begin with, for in such a generation there is no longer fear of disclosing the wisdom, as we have elaborated above. Hence, my words are open and orderly.

6) And now sons do hear me: The wisdom cries aloud outside; she calls you from the streets, "Whoso is on the Lord's side, let him come to me," "For it is no vain thing for you; because it is your life, and the length of your days."

"You were not created to follow the act of the grain and the potato, you and your asses in one trough." And as the purpose of the ass is not to serve all its contemporary asses, man's purpose is not to serve all the bodies of the people of his time, the contemporaries of his physical body. Rather, the purpose of the ass is to serve and be of use to man, who is superior to it, and the purpose of man is to serve the Creator and complete His aim.

As Ben Zuma said, "All those were created only to serve me, and I, to serve my Maker." He says, "All the works of the Lord are for His purpose," since the Creator yearns and craves our completion.

It is said in *Beresheet Rabbah*, Chapter 8, that the angels said to Him: "'What is man, that You are mindful of him, and the son of man, that You think of him?' Why do You need this trouble? The Creator told them: 'Therefore, why sheep and oxen?'" What is this like? It is like a king who had a tower filled abundantly but no guests. What pleasure has the king from his fill? They promptly said to Him: "O Lord, our Lord, how glorious is Your name in all the earth! Do that which seems good to You."

Seemingly, we should doubt that allegory, since where does that tower filled abundantly stand? In our time, we really would fill it with guests to the brim.

Indeed, the words are earnest, since you see that the angels made no complaint about any of the creatures created during the six days of creation, except about man. This is because he was created in God's image and consists of the upper and lower together.

When the angels saw it, they were startled and bewildered. How would the pure, spiritual soul descend from its sublime degree, and come and dwell in the same abode with this filthy, beastly body? In other words, they wondered, "Why do You need this trouble?"

The answer that came to them is that there is already a tower filled abundantly, and empty of guests. To fill it with guests, we need the existence of this man, made of upper and lower together. For this reason, this pure soul must clothe in the dress in this filthy body. They immediately understood it and said, "Do that which seems good to You."

Know that this tower filled abundantly implies all the pleasure and the goodness for which He has created the creatures, as our sages said, "The conduct of the Good is to do good." Hence, He created the worlds to delight His creatures.

(We have elaborated on our matter in *Panim Masbirot*, Branch 1, and learn it there.) And since there is no past or future in Him, we must realize that as soon as He thought to create creatures and delight them, they emerged and were instantly made before Him, they and all their fulfillments of delight and pleasure, as He had intended for them.

It is written in the book *Heftzi Bah* [*My Delight Is in Her*], by the ARI, that all the worlds, upper and lower together, are contained in the *Ein Sof* [Infinity], even before the *Tzimtzum* [restriction] by way of He is one and His name One, see there in Chapter 1.

The *Tzimtzum*, which is the root of the worlds ABYA, which reach up to this world, occurred because the roots of the souls themselves yearn to equalize their form with the Emanator. This is the meaning of *Dvekut* [adhesion], as separation and *Dvekut* in anything spiritual is possible only in values of equivalence of form or disparity of form.

Since He wanted to delight them, the will to receive pleasure was necessarily imprinted in the receivers. Thus, their form has been changed from His, since this form is not at all present in the Emanator, as from whom would He receive?

The *Tzimtzum* and the *Gevul* [boundary/limitation] were made for this correction, until the emergence of this world to a reality of a clothing of a soul in a corporeal body. When one engages in Torah and work in order to bestow contentment upon one's Maker, the form of reception will be reunited in order to bestow once more.

This is the meaning of the text, "and to cleave unto Him," since then one equalizes one's form to one's Maker, and as we have said, equivalence of form is *Dvekut* in spirituality. When the matter of *Dvekut* is completed in all the parts of the soul, the worlds will return to the state of *Ein Sof*, as prior to the *Tzimtzum*.

"In their land they will inherit doubly," since then they will be able to receive once more all the pleasure and delight, prepared for them in advance in the world of *Ein Sof*. Moreover, now they are prepared for the real *Dvekut* without any disparity of form, since their reception is no longer for themselves, but to bestow contentment upon their Maker. You find that they have equalized in the form of bestowal with the Maker, and I have already elaborated on these matters suitably in *Panim Masbirot*, Branch 1.

7) Now you will understand their words, that the *Shechina* [Divinity] in the lower ones is a high need. This is a most perplexing statement, though it does go hand in hand with the above *Midrash* that compared the matter to a king who has a tower filled abundantly, but no guests. It is certain that he sits and waits for guests, or his whole preparation will be in vain.

This is like a great king who had a son when he was already old, and he was very fond of him. Hence, from the day he was born he thought favorable thoughts about him, collected all the books and the finest scholars in the land, and built schools for him. He gathered the finest builders in the land and built palaces of pleasure for him, collected all the musicians and singers and built concert halls for him. He assembled the best chefs and bakers in the land and served him every delicacy in the world, and so forth.

Alas, the boy grew up to be a fool with no wish for knowledge. He was also blind and could not see or feel the beauty of the buildings, and he was deaf and could not hear the singers. Sadly, he was diabetic and was permitted to eat only coarse-flour bread, arising contempt and wrath.

Now you can understand their words about the verse, "I, the Lord, will hasten it in its time." The *Sanhedrin* (98) interpreted, "Not rewarded—in its time; rewarded—I will hasten it."

Thus, there are two ways to attain the above-mentioned goal: through their own attention, which is called a "path of repentance." If they are rewarded with it, "I will hasten it" will be applied to them. This means that there is no set time for it, but when they are rewarded, the correction ends, of course.

If they are not awarded the attention, there is another way, called "path of suffering," as our sages said, *Sanhedrin* 97, "I place upon them a king such as Haman, and they will repent against their will," meaning in its time, for in that there is a set time, and they will want it.

By this, they wanted to show us that His ways are not our ways. For this reason, the case of the flesh-and-blood king who had troubled so to prepare those great things for his beloved son and was finally tormented in every way, and all his trouble was in vain, bringing contempt and wrath, will not happen to Him.

Instead, all the works of the Creator are guaranteed and true, and there is no fraud in Him. This is as our sages said, "Not rewarded—in its time." What the will does not do, time will do, as it is written in *Panim Masbirot*, end of Branch 1, "Can you send forth lightning that they may go and say to you, 'Here we are'?"

There is a path of pain that can cleanse any defect and materialism until one realizes how to raise one's head out of the beastly trough in order to soar and climb the rungs of the ladder of happiness and human success, for one will cleave to one's root and complete the aim.

8) Therefore, come and see how grateful we should be to our teachers, who impart us their sacred lights and dedicate their souls to do good to our souls. They stand in the middle between the path of harsh torments and the path of repentance. They save us from the netherworld, which is harder than death, and accustom us to reach the heavenly pleasures, the sublime gentleness and the pleasantness that is our share, ready and waiting for us from the very beginning, as we have said above. Each of them operates in his generation, according to the power of the light of his teaching and sanctity.

Our sages have already said, "You have not a generation without such as Abraham, Isaac, and Jacob." Indeed, that Godly man, Rav [teacher/great one] Isaac Luria [the ARI], troubled and provided us the fullest measure. He did wondrously more than his predecessors, and if I had a tongue that praises, I would praise that day when his wisdom appeared almost as the day when the Torah was given to Israel.

There are not enough words to measure his holy work in our favor. The doors of attainment were locked and bolted, and he came and opened them for us. Thus, all who wish to enter the King's palace need only purity and sanctity, and to go and bathe and shave their hair and wear clean clothes, to properly stand before the upper Kingship.

You find a thirty-eight-year-old who subdued with his wisdom all his predecessors through the *Ge'onim* [pl. for genius] and through all times. All the elders of the land, the gallant shepherds, friends and disciples of the Godly sage, the RAMAK, stood before him as disciples before the Rav.

All the sages of the generations following them to this day, none missing, have abandoned all the books and compositions that precede him: the Kabbalah of the

RAMAK, the Kabbalah of the *Rishonim* [first], and the Kabbalah of the *Ge'onim*, blessed be the memory of them all. They have attached their spiritual life entirely and solely to his Holy Wisdom. Naturally, it is not without merit that a total victory is awarded, as this young in years father of wisdom has.

Alas, Satan's work succeeded, and obstacles were placed along the path of expansion of his wisdom into a holy nation, and only very few have begun to conquer them.

This was so primarily because the words were written by hearsay, as he had interpreted the wisdom day by day before his disciples, who were already elderly and with great proficiency in *The Zohar* and the *Tikkunim* [Corrections]. In most cases, his holy sayings were arranged according to the profound questions that they asked him, each according to his own interest.

For this reason, he did not convey the wisdom in a proper order, as with compositions that preceded him. We find in the texts that the ARI himself had wished to put order in the issues. In that regard, see the beginning of the words of Rashbi in the interpretation to the *Idra Zuta*, in a short introduction by Rav Chaim Vital.

There is also the short time of his teaching, since the entire time of his seminary was some seventeen months, as is said in *Gate to Reincarnations*, Gate 8, since he arrived in Safed from Egypt shortly before Passover in the year 1571, and at that time, Rav Chaim Vital was twenty-nine years old. And in July 1572, on the eve of Shabbat, *Parashat Matot-Masaey*,* the beginning of the month of *Av*, he fell ill, and on Tuesday, fifth of *Av* on the following week he passed away.

It is also written in *Gate to Reincarnations*, Gate 8, that upon his demise, he ordered Rav Chaim Vital not to teach the wisdom to others and permitted him to learn only by himself and in a whisper. The rest of the friends were forbidden to engage in it altogether because he said that they did not understand the wisdom properly.

This is why Rav Chaim Vital did not arrange the texts at all and left them unorganized. Naturally, he did not explain the connections between the matters so it would not be as teaching others. This is why we find such great caution on his part, as is known to those proficient in the writings of the ARI.

The arrangements found in the writings of the ARI were arranged and organized by a third generation, three times, and by three compilers. The first compiler was the sage MAHARI Tzemach. He lived at the same time of MAHARA Azulai, who passed away in the year 1644.

A large portion of the texts came by him, and he compiled many books from them. The most important among them is the book *Adam Yashar* [Upright Man], in which he collected the root and the essential teachings that were at his disposal. However, some of the books that this rav compiled were lost. In the introduction to his book, *Kol BeRama* [A Loud Voice], he presents all the books that he had compiled.

---

* Translator's note: name of the weekly Torah portion.

The second compiler is his disciple, MAHARAM Paprish. He did more than his rav, since some of the books that were held by the sage MAHARASH Vital came by his hands, and he compiled many books. The most important among them are the books, *Etz haChaim* [*The Tree of Life*] and *Pri Etz haChaim* [*Fruit of the Tree of Life*]. They contain the entire scope of the wisdom in its fullest sense.

The third compiler was the sage MAHARASH Vital, the son of Rav Chaim Vital. He was a great and renowned sage, who compiled the famous *Eight Gates* from the patrimony his father had left him.

Thus, we see that each of the compilers did not have the complete writings. This heavily burdened the arrangement of the issues, which are unsuitable for those without true proficiency in *The Zohar* and the *Tikkunim*. Hence, few are those who ascend.

9) In return for that, we are privileged by Him to have been rewarded with the spirit of The Baal Shem Tov, whose greatness and sanctity are beyond any word and any utterance. He was not gazed upon and will not be gazed upon, except by those worthy that had served under his light, and they, too, only intermittently, each according to what he received in his heart.

It is true that the light of his Torah and Holy Wisdom are built primarily on the holy foundations of the ARI. However, they are not at all similar. I shall explain this with an allegory of a person drowning in the river, rising and sinking as drowning people do. Sometimes, only the hair is visible, and then a counsel is sought to catch him by his head. Other times, his body appears as well, and then a counsel is sought to catch him from opposite his heart.

So is the matter before us. After Israel has drowned in the evil waters of the exile among the nations, since then until now they rise and fall, and not all times are the same. At the time of the ARI, only the head was visible. Hence, the ARI had troubled in our favor to save us through the mind. At the time of The Baal Shem Tov, there was relief. Hence, it was a blessing for us to save us from opposite the heart, and that was a great and true salvation for us.

And for our many sins, the wheel has been turned over again in our generation and we have declined tremendously, as though from the zenith to the nadir.

In addition, there is the collision of the nations, which has confused the entire world. The needs have increased and the mind grew short and corrupted in the filth of materialism which apprehends the lead. Servants ride horses and ministers walk on the earth, and everything that is said in our study in the above-mentioned *Masechet Sutah* has come true in us, for our many sins. Again, the iron wall has been erected, even on this great light the Baal Shem Tov, which we have said illuminated as far as the establishment of our complete redemption.

And the wise-at-heart did not believe in the possibility that a generation would come when they could not see by his light. Now, our eyes have darkened; we have been robbed of good, and when I saw this I said, "It is time to act!" Thus, I have come to open widely the gates of light of the ARI, for he is indeed capable and fit for our generation, too, and "Two are better than one."

We should not be blamed for the brevity in my composition, since it corresponds and is adapted to any wisdom lover, as too much wine wears off the flavor, and the attainment becomes harder on the disciple.

Also, we are not responsible for those fat-at-heart, since the language to assist them has yet to be created. Wherever they cast their eyes, they find folly, and there is a rule that from the same source from which the wise draws his wisdom, the fool draws his folly.

Thus, I stand at the outset of my book and warn that I have not troubled at all for all those who love to look through the windows. Rather, it is for those who care for the words of the Creator, who long for the Creator and His goodness, to complete the purpose for which they were created, for by the will of the Creator, the verse, "All who seek Me shall find Me" will come true in them.

10) Come and see the words of the sage Rabbi Even Ezra in his book *Yesod Mora*: "And now note and know that all the *Mitzvot* [commandments] that are written in the Torah or the conventions that the fathers have established, although they are mostly in action or in speech, they are all in order to correct the heart, 'for the Lord searches all hearts, and understands all the imaginations of the thoughts.'"

It is written, "to them who are upright in their hearts." Its opposite is "A heart that devises wicked thoughts." I have found one verse that contains all the *Mitzvot*, which is "You shall fear the Lord your God; and Him shall you serve."

The word "fear" contains all the *Mitzvot* not-to-do in speech, in heart, and in action. It is the first degree from which one ascends to the work of the Creator, which contains all the *Mitzvot* to-do.

These will accustom one's heart and guide one until one cleaves to the Creator, as for this was man created. He was not created for acquiring fortunes or for building buildings. Hence, one should seek everything that will bring one to love Him, to learn wisdom, and to seek faith.

And the Creator will open the eyes of his heart and will renew a different spirit within him. Then he will be loved by his Maker in his life.

Know that the Torah was given only to men of heart. Words are as corpses and the *Taamim* [flavors] as souls. If one does not understand the *Taamim*, one's entire effort is in vain, labor blown away.

It is as though one exerts oneself to count the letters and the words in a medicine book. No cure will come from this labor. It is also like a camel carrying silk; it does not benefit the silk, nor does the silk benefit it.

We draw only this from his words; hold on to the goal for which man was created. He says about it that this is the matter of the *Dvekut* with the Creator.

Hence, he says that one must search every means to bring one to love Him, to learn wisdom and to seek faith, until the Creator rewards one with opening the eyes of one's heart and renewing a different spirit within him. At that time, he shall be loved by his Maker.

He deliberately makes that precision, to be loved by his Maker in his life. It indicates that while he has not acquired this, his work is incomplete, and the work that was necessarily given to us to do today. It is as he ends it, that the Torah was only given to men of heart, meaning ones who have acquired the heart to love and covet Him. The sages call them "wise-at-heart," since there is no longer a descending, beastly spirit there, for the evil inclination is present only in a heart vacant from wisdom.

He interprets and says that the words are as corpses and the *Taamim*, as souls. If one does not understand the *Taamim*, it is similar to exerting oneself counting pages and words in a medicine book. This exertion will not yield a remedy.

He wishes to say that one is compelled to find the means to acquire the above-mentioned possession, since then one can taste the flavors of Torah, which is the interior wisdom and its mysteries, and the flavors of *Mitzva*, which are the love and the desire for Him.

Without it, one has only the words and the actions, which are dead bodies without souls. It is like one who labors counting pages and words in a medicine book, etc. Certainly, he will not perfect himself in medicine before he understands the meaning of the written medicine.

Even after one purchases it, for whatever price is asked, if the conduct of the study and the actions are not arranged to bring him to it, it is like a camel carrying silk; it does not benefit the silk and the silk does not benefit it, to bring it to complete the aim for which it was created.

11) According to these words, our eyes have been opened concerning the words of Rabbi Simon in *Midrash Rabbah*, Chapter 6, about the verse, "Let us make man." These are his words (When the Creator came to create man, He consulted the ministering angels), that they were divided into sects and groups. Some said, "Let him be created," and some said, "Let him not be created," as it is written, "Mercy and truth met; righteousness and peace kissed." Mercy said, "Let him be created, for he does acts of mercy." Truth said, "Let him not be created, for he is all lies." Righteousness said, "Let him be created, for he performs righteousness." Peace said, "Let him not be created, for he is all strife." What did the Creator do? He took Truth and threw it to the earth, as it is written, "and it cast down truth to the earth." The angels said to the Creator: "Why do You disgrace Your seal? Let truth come up from the earth, as it is written, 'Truth shall spring forth from the earth.'"

This text is perplexing all around:

1. It does not explain the seriousness of the verse, "Let us make man." Is it a counsel that He needs, as it is written, "Deliverance in the heart of a counsel"?

2. Regarding truth, how can it be said about the entire human species that it is all lies, when there is not a generation without such as Abraham, Isaac, and Jacob?

3. If the words of truth are earnest, how did the angels of mercy and righteousness agree to a world that is all lies?

4. Why is truth called "seal," which comes at the edge of a letter? Certainly, the reality exists primarily outside the seal. Is there no reality at all outside the borders of truth?

5. Can true angels think of the true Operator that His operation is untrue?

6. Why did truth deserve such a harsh punishment to be thrown to the earth and into the earth?

7. Why is the angels' reply not brought in the Torah, as their question is brought?

We must understand these two conducts set before our eyes, which are completely opposite. These are the conducts of the existence of the entire reality of this world and the conducts of the manners of existence for the sustenance of each and every one in the reality before us. From this end, we find a reliable conduct in utterly affirmed guidance, which controls the making of each and every creature in reality.

Let us take the making of a human being as an example. The love and pleasure are its first reason, certain and reliable for its task. As soon as it is uprooted from the father's brain, Providence provides it a safe and guarded place among the beddings in the mother's abdomen, so no stranger may touch it.

There, Providence provides it with its daily bread in the right measure. It tends to its every need without forgetting it for even a moment, until it gains strength to come out to the air of our world, which is full of obstacles.

At that time, Providence lends it power and strength, and like an armed, experienced hero, it opens gates and breaks walls until it comes to such people it can trust to help it through its days of weakness with love and great compassion to sustain its existence, as they are the most precious for it in the whole world.

Thus, Providence embraces it until it qualifies it to exist and to continue its existence onward. As is with man, so it is with the animate and the flora. All are wondrously watched, securing their existence, and every scientist of nature knows it.

On the other end, when we regard the order of existence and sustenance in the modes of existence of the whole of reality, large and small, we find confused orders, as if an army is fleeing the campaign sick, beaten, and afflicted by the Creator. Their whole life is as death, having no sustenance unless by tormenting first, risking their lives for their bread.

Even a tiny louse breaks its teeth when it sets off for a meal. How much frisking it frisks to attain enough food to sustain itself. As it is with it, so are all, great and small alike, and all the more so with humans, the elite of creation, who are involved in everything.

12) We discern two opposites in the ten *Sefirot* of *Kedusha* [Holiness]. The first nine *Sefirot* are in the form of bestowal, and *Malchut* is about reception. Also, the first nine are filled with light, and *Malchut* has nothing of her own.

This is the meaning of our discrimination of two discernments of light in each *Partzuf*: *Ohr Pnimi* [inner light] and *Ohr Makif* [surrounding light], and two discernments in the *Kelim* [vessels], which are the inner *Kli* [vessel] for *Ohr Pnimi* and an outer *Kli* for *Ohr Makif*.

This is so because of the two above-mentioned opposites, as it is impossible for two opposites to be in the same carrier. Thus, a specific carrier is required for the *Ohr Pnimi* and a specific carrier for the *Ohr Makif*, as I elaborated in *Panim Masbirot*, Branches 1 and 4.

However, they are not really opposite in *Kedusha*, since *Malchut* is in *Zivug* [copulation] with the first nine, and its quality is of bestowal, too, in the form of *Ohr Hozer* [reflected light], as written in *Panim Masbirot*, Branch 4, but the *Sitra Achra* [other side] have nothing of the first nine. They are built primarily from the vacant space, which is the complete form of reception, on which the *Tzimtzum Aleph* [first restriction] occurred. That root remained without light even after the illumination of the *Kav* [line] reached inside the *Reshimo* [recollection], as is written in *Panim Masbirot*, Branch 1.

For this reason, they are two complete opposites compared to life and *Kedusha*, as it is written, "God has made one opposite the other." This is why they are called "dead."

It has been explained above, Item 6, that the whole issue of the *Tzimtzum* was only for the adornment of the souls, concerning the equalizing of their form to their Maker, which is the inversion of the vessels of reception to the form of bestowal.

You find that this goal is still denied from the perspective of the *Partzufim* [pl. of *Partzuf*] of *Kedusha*, since there is nothing there of the vacant space, which is the form of *Gadlut* [greatness/adulthood] of reception, over which was the *Tzimtzum*. Hence, no correction will happen to it, as it does not exist in reality.

Also, there is certainly no correction here from the perspective of the *Sitra Achra*, although it does have a vacant space, since it is completely opposite, and everything it receives dies.

Hence, it is only a human in this world that we need. In infancy, he is sustained and supported by the *Sitra Achra*, inheriting the *Kelim* of the vacant space from it.

When he grows, he connects to the structure of *Kedusha* through the power of Torah and *Mitzvot* to bestow contentment upon his Maker.

Thus, one turns the complete measure of reception he has already acquired to be solely arranged for bestowal. In that, he equalizes his form with his Maker and the aim comes true in him.

This is the meaning of the existence of time in this world. You find that first, these two above opposites were divided into two separate carriers, namely *Kedusha* and *Sitra Achra*, by way of "one opposite the other." They are still devoid of the above correction, for they must be in the same subject, which is man.

Therefore, the existence of an order of time is necessary for us, since then the two opposites will come in a person one by one, meaning at a time of *Katnut* [smallness/infancy] and at a time of *Gadlut*.

13) Now you can understand the need for the breaking of the vessels and their properties, as it is written in *The Zohar* and in the writings of the ARI, that two kinds of light are present in each ten *Sefirot*, running back and forth. The first light is *Ohr Ein Sof* [light of infinity], which travels from above downward. It is called *Ohr Yashar* [direct light]. The second light is a result of the *Kli* of *Malchut*, returning from below upward, called *Ohr Hozer* [reflected light].

Both unite into one. Know that from the *Tzimtzum* downward, the point of *Tzimtzum* is devoid of any light and remains a vacant space. The upper light can no longer appear in the last *Behina* [discernment] before the end of correction, and this is said particularly about *Ohr Ein Sof*, called *Ohr Yashar*. However, the second light, called *Ohr Hozer*, can appear in the last *Behina*, since the case of the *Tzimtzum* did not apply to it at all.

Now we have learned that the system of the *Sitra Achra* and the *Klipot* [shells/peels] is a necessity for the purpose of the *Tzimtzum*, in order to instill in a person the great vessels of reception while in *Katnut*, when one is dependent on her.

Thus, the *Sitra Achra*, too, needs abundance. Where would she take it if she is made solely of the last *Behina*, which is a space that is vacant of any light, since from the *Tzimtzum* downward the upper light is completely separated from it?

Hence, the matter of the breaking of the vessels had been prepared. The breaking indicates that a part of the *Ohr Hozer* of ten *Sefirot* of the world of *Nekudim* descended from *Atzilut* out to the vacant space. And you already know that *Ohr Hozer* can appear in the vacant space, as well.

That part, the *Ohr Hozer* that descended from *Atzilut* outward, contains thirty-two special *Behinot* [discernments] of each and every *Sefira* of the ten *Sefirot* of *Nekudim*. Ten times thirty-two is 320, and these 320 *Behinot* that descended were prepared for the sustenance of the existence of the lower ones, which come to them in two systems, as it is written, "God has made one opposite the other," meaning the worlds *ABYA* of *Kedusha* and opposite them the worlds *ABYA* of the *Sitra Achra*.

In the interpretation of the verse (*Megillah* 6a), "And one people shall be stronger than the other people," our sages said that when one rises, the other falls, and Tzor is built only over the ruin of Jerusalem. This is so because all these 320 *Behinot* can appear for the *Sitra Achra*, at which time the structure of the system of *Kedusha*, with respect to the lower ones, is completely ruined.

Also, these 320 *Behinot* can connect solely to *Kedusha*. At that time, the system of the *Sitra Achra* is completely destroyed from the land, and they can divide more or less evenly between them, according to people's actions. And so they roll in the two systems until the correction is completed.

After the breaking of the vessels and the decline of the 320 *Behinot* of sparks of light from *Atzilut* outward, 288 of them were sorted and rose, meaning everything that descended from the first nine *Sefirot* in the ten *Sefirot* of *Nekudim*. Nine times thirty-two are 288 *Behinot*, and they are the ones that reconnected to building the system of *Kedusha*.

You find that only thirty-two *Behinot* remained for the *Sitra Achra* from what had descended from *Malchut* of the world of *Nekudim*. This was the beginning of the structure of the *Sitra Achra*, in its utter smallness, when she is as yet unfit for her task. The completion of her construction ended later by the sin of *Adam HaRishon* with the Tree of Knowledge.

Thus we find that there are two systems, one opposite the other, operating in the persistence and sustenance of reality. The ration of light needed for this existence is 320 sparks. Those were prepared and allotted by the breaking of the vessels. This ration is to be swaying between the two systems, and that is what the conducts of sustenance and existence of reality depend on.

You should know that the system of *Kedusha* must contain at least a ration of 288 sparks to complete her first nine *Sefirot*, and then it can sustain and provide for the existence of the lower ones. This is what it had prior to the sin of *Adam HaRishon*, and for this reason the whole of reality was then conducted by the system of *Kedusha*, since it had the full 288 sparks.

14) Now we have found the opening to the above Midrash [treatise] regarding the four sects, Mercy, Righteousness, Truth, and Peace, which negotiated with the Creator regarding man's creation. These angels are servants of man's soul (see *Tree of Life, Shaar Drushey ABYA*); hence, He negotiated with them, since the whole act of creation was created according to them, as each and every soul consists of ten *Sefirot* in *Ohr Pnimi* and *Ohr Makif*. Mercy is the *Ohr Pnimi* of the first nine of the soul. Righteousness is the *Ohr Pnimi* of *Malchut* of the soul. Truth is the *Ohr Makif* of the soul.

We have already said that *Ohr Pnimi* and *Ohr Makif* are opposites, since the *Ohr Pnimi* is drawn by the law of the illumination of the *Kav* [line], which is prevented from appearing at the point of the *Tzimtzum*, which is the *Gadlut* form of reception.

The *Ohr Makif* extends from *Ohr Ein Sof*, which surrounds all the worlds, since there, in *Ein Sof*, great and small are equal. For this reason, the *Ohr Makif* shines and bestows upon the point of *Tzimtzum*, too, much less for *Malchut*.

Since they are opposites, two *Kelim* are needed, since the *Ohr Pnimi* illuminates in the first nine. Even to *Malchut*, it shines only according to the law of the first nine, and not at all to her own quality. However, the *Ohr Makif* shines in the *Kelim* that extend specifically from the point of the *Tzimtzum*, which is called "external *Kli*."

Now you can understand why Truth is called "Seal." It is a borrowed name from a seal at the edge of a letter, at the end of the matters. However, it asserts them and gives them validity. Without the seal, they are worthless and the whole text is wasted.

It is the same with the *Ohr Makif*, which bestows upon the point of the *Tzimtzum*, which is the *Gadlut* measure of reception, until it equalizes its form with its Maker in bestowal. Indeed, this is the purpose of all the worlds, upper and lower, which are limited.

The protest of Truth regarding man's creation is its claim that he is all lies, since from the perspective of the creation of the Creator, man does not have an outer *Kli*, which must extend from the point of *Tzimtzum*, as she has already been separated from His light. Thus, the angels of Truth could not help man obtain the *Ohr Makif*.

All the limited worlds, upper and lower, which are limited, were created solely for this completion, and this man must be its only subject. But since this man is unfit for his role, they are all abyss and falsehood, and the labor in them—useless.

It is the opposite with the angels of Mercy and Righteousness, which belong specifically to the *Ohr Pnimi* of the soul. Because he has nothing of the vacant space, they could bestow upon him all the lights of *Neshama* abundantly, in the most sublime perfection.

Thus, they were happy to benefit him and wholeheartedly agreed to man's creation. (Because they are NHY that enter by *Zivug de Hakaa* [copulation by striking], they belong to the half of the *Ohr Makif* from the perspective of the *Ohr Hozer* in it.)

The angels of Peace claimed that he is all strife. In other words, how will he receive the *Ohr Makif*? In the end, they cannot come in the same subject with the *Ohr Pnimi*, as they are opposite from each other, as said above, "all strife."

(The *Ohr Makif* is discerned by two: the future *Ohr Hozer* and the future *Ohr Makif*. The outer *Kli* for the *Ohr Hozer* is the *Masach* [screen] and the outer *Kli* for the *Ohr Makif* is the *Aviut* of *Behina Dalet* [fourth discernment] itself, namely the stony heart. You find that *Adam HaRishon* lacked only the outer *Kli* that belongs to the angels of Truth. He did not lack the outer *Kli* that belongs to the angels of Peace. Hence, they agreed to the creation, but claimed that he is all strife, meaning that the *Ohr Yashar* cannot enter the inner *Kli* since they are opposites.)

15) Now we have been granted the understanding of the rest of the verses in the sin of the Tree of Knowledge of good and evil, which are most profound. Our sages, who disclosed a portion of them, concealed ten portions with their words.

As a foreword, it is written, "And they were both naked, the man and his wife, and were not ashamed." Know that clothing means an outer *Kli*, as written in *The Tree of Life, Shaar Drushey ABYA*. Hence, the text precedes to demonstrate the reason for the sin of the Tree of Knowledge, as our sages said in the verse, "Libel is terrible for the sons of man, for in libel you came upon him."

This means that his sin had been prepared in advance, and this is the meaning of the words that *Adam* and his wife did not have an outer *Kli* at the moment of creation, but only inner *Kelim*, which extend from the system of *Kedusha*. This is why they were not ashamed. They did not feel their deficiency, as shame is the matter of the sensation of a deficiency.

It is known that feeling the deficiency is the first reason for the fulfillment of the deficiency. It is similar to one who feels one's illness and is willing to receive the medication. However, when one does not feel that he is ill, he will certainly avoid all medications.

Indeed, this task is for the outer Kli to do. Since it is in the construction of the body and is empty of light, as it comes from the vacant space, it begets the sensation of emptiness and deficiency in it, by which one becomes ashamed.

Hence, one is compelled to fill the deficiency once again and draw the lacking *Ohr Makif*, which is about to fill that Kli. This is the meaning of the verse, "And the man and his wife were both naked," of the outer Kli. For this reason, they were not ashamed, since they did not feel their deficiency. In this manner, they are devoid of the purpose for which they were created.

Hence, one is compelled to fill the absence once again and draw the lacking *Ohr Makif*, which is about to fill that *Kli*. This is the meaning of the verse, "And the man and his wife were both naked," of the outer *Kli*. For this reason, they were not ashamed, since they did not feel their absence. In this manner, they are devoid of the purpose for which they were created.

Yet, we must thoroughly understand the sublimity of that man, the creation of the Creator, and also his wife, to whom the Creator administered greater intelligence than him, as they have written (*Nidah* 45) in the interpretation to the verse, "And the Lord made the rib."

Thus, how did they fail and became as fools, not knowing to beware of the serpent's cunningness? On the other hand, that serpent, of which the text testifies that it was more cunning than all the animals of the field, how did it utter such folly and emptiness that should they eat from the fruit of the Tree of Knowledge, they would be turned to God? Moreover, how did that folly settle in their hearts?

Also, it is said below that they did not eat because of their desire to become God, but simply because the tree is good to eat. This is seemingly a beastly desire!

16) We must know the nature of the two kinds of discernments customary for us: The first discernment is called "discernments of good and bad." The second discernment is called "discernments of true and false."

This means that the Creator has imprinted a discerning force in each creature that executes everything that is good for it and brings it to its desired completion. The first discernment is an active, physical force. It operates using the sensation of bitter and sweet, which loathes and repels the bitter form, since it is bad for it, and loves and attracts the sweet because it is good for it. This operating force is sufficient in the still, the vegetative, and the animate in reality, to bring them to their desired completion.

Atop them is the human species, in which the Creator instilled a rational operating force. It operates in sorting the above second discernment, rejecting falsehood and emptiness with loathing to the point of nausea, and attracts true matters and every benefit with great love.

This discernment is called "discernment of true and false." It is implemented solely in the human species, each according to his own measure. Know that this second acting force was created and came to man because of the serpent. At the time of creation, he had only the first active force, from the discernments of good and bad, which was sufficient for him at that time.

Let me explain it to you with an allegory: If the righteous were rewarded according to their good deeds, and the wicked punished according their bad deeds in this world, *Kedusha* would be determined for us in the reality of sweet and good, and the *Sitra Achra* would be defined in the reality of bad and bitter.

In this state, the commandment of choice would come to us in the form of "Behold, I have set before you the sweet and the bitter, and you shall choose the sweet." Thus, all the people would be guaranteed to achieve wholeness, for they would certainly run from the sin, as it is bad for them. They would be occupied in His *Mitzvot* day in and day out, ceaselessly, like today's fools regarding the bodily matters and its filth, since it is good and sweet to them. So was the matter of *Adam HaRishon* when He created him.

"And put him into the Garden of Eden to work in it and keep it." Our sages interpreted, "to work in it" are the *Mitzvot* to-do, "and to keep it" are the *Mitzvot* not-to-do. His *Mitzvot* to-do were to eat and delight in all the trees of the Garden, and his *Mitzvot* not-to-do were to not eat from the Tree of Knowledge of good and evil. The *Mitzvot* to-do were sweet and nice, and the *Mitzvot* not-to-do were retirement from the bitter fruit that is as hard as death.

Not surprisingly, these cannot be called *Mitzvot* and labor. We find the likes of this in our present work, where through the pleasures of Shabbat [Sabbath] and good days we are rewarded with the upper *Kedusha*. And we are also rewarded for retiring from reptiles and insects and everything that one finds loathsome.

You find that the choice in the work of *Adam HaRishon* was by way of "choose sweet." It follows that the physical palate alone was sufficient for all he needed, to know what the Creator commanded and what He did not command.

17) Now we can understand the serpent's cunningness, which our sages added, and notified us that SAM clothed in it, meaning because its words were very high. It started with, "Although God said: 'You shall not eat from any tree of the garden,'" meaning it began to speak with her since the woman was not commanded by the Creator. Hence, it asked her about the modes of scrutiny, meaning how do you know that the Tree of Knowledge was prohibited? Perhaps all the fruits of the garden were forbidden for you, too? "And the woman said... 'Of the fruit of the trees of the garden we may eat'; ...You shall not eat of it, neither shall you touch it, lest you die."

There are two great precisions here: 1) The touching was never forbidden; hence, why did she add to the prohibition? 2) Did she doubt the words of the Creator? The Creator said, "You will surely die," and the woman said, "lest you die." Could it be that she did not believe the words of the Creator even prior to the sin?

Yet, the woman answered it according to the serpent's question. She knew what the Creator had prohibited, that all the trees of the garden are sweet and nice and good to eat. However, she was already close to touching that tree inside the garden, and tasted in it a taste that is as hard as death.

She herself had proven that by her own observation, there is fear of death, even from mere touching. For this reason, she understood the prohibition further than what she heard from her husband, as there is none so wise as the experienced.

"Lest you die" concerns the touching. The answer must have been quite sufficient, for who would interfere and deny another's taste? However, the serpent contradicted her and said, "You shall not surely die; for God knows that in the day you eat thereof, your eyes shall be opened."

We must make the precision concerning the matter of the opening of the eyes to this place. Indeed, it informed her of a new and sublime matter. It proved to them that it is folly to think that the Creator created something harmful and detrimental in His world. Thus, with respect to the Creator, it is certainly not a bad or harmful thing.

Instead, that bitterness that you will taste in it, when even close to touching, is only on your part, since this eating is to notify you of the height of your merit. Thus, it is additional *Kedusha* that you need during the act, so your sole aim will be to bring contentment to Him, to keep the aim for which you were created. For this reason, it seems to you as bad and harmful so you will understand the additional *Kedusha* required of you.

"For in the day you eat thereof," meaning if the act is in *Kedusha* and purity as clear as day, "you shall be as God, knowing good and evil." This means that as it is certainly sweet to the Creator and completely equal, so the good and bad will be to you, in complete equivalence, sweet and gentle.

It is still possible to doubt the credibility of the serpent, since the Creator did not tell it this Himself. Therefore, the serpent first said, "for God knows that in the day you eat thereof, your eyes shall be opened."

This means that it is not necessary for the Creator to notify you of that, since He knows that if you pay attention to this, to eat on the side of *Kedusha*, your eyes shall be opened by themselves, to understand the measure of greatness in it. You will feel wondrous sweetness and gentleness in it; hence, He does not need to let you know, as for this He instilled in you the scrutinizing force, that you may know what is to your benefit by yourselves.

It is written right after that: "And the woman saw that the tree was good to eat and that it was a delight to the eyes." This means that she did not rely on His words, but went and examined with her own mind and understanding and sanctified herself with additional *Kedusha*, to bring contentment to the Creator in order to complete the aim desired of her, and not at all for herself. At that time, her eyes were opened, as the serpent had said, "And the woman saw that the tree was good to eat."

In other words, by seeing that "it was a delight to the eyes," before she even touched it, she felt great sweetness and lust, when her eyes saw by themselves that she had not seen such a desirable thing in all the trees of the garden.

She also learned that the tree is good for knowledge, meaning that there is far more to crave and covet in this tree than in all the trees of the garden. This refers to knowing that they were created for this act of eating, and that this is the whole purpose, as the serpent had revealed to her.

After all these absolute scrutinies, "she took of its fruit and ate, and gave also to her man with her, and he ate." The text accurately writes "with her," meaning with the pure intention only to bestow and not for her own sake. This is the meaning of the words "and gave to her man with her," with her in *Kedusha*.

18) Now we come to the heart of the matter and the mistake that concerned his leg. This Tree of Knowledge of good and evil was mixed with the vacant space, meaning with the *Gadlut* form of reception upon which the *Tzimtzum* was implemented, and from which the *Ohr Elyon* departed.

It has also been explained that *Adam HaRishon* did not have any of the *Gadlut* form of reception in his structure, which extends from the vacant space. Instead, he extended solely from the system of *Kedusha*, concerned only with bestowal.

It is written in *The Zohar*, *Kedoshim*, that *Adam HaRishon* had nothing of this world. For this reason, the Tree of Knowledge was forbidden to him, as his root and the whole system of *Kedusha* are separated from the *Sitra Achra* due to their disparity of form, which is the separation.

Thus, he, too, was commanded and warned about connecting to it, as thus he would be separated from his holy root and die like the *Sitra Achra* and the *Klipot*, which are dead due to their oppositeness and separation from the *Kedusha* and the Life of Lives.

However, Satan, which is SAM, the angel of death that clothed in the serpent, came down and enticed Eve with the lie in its mouth: "You shall not surely die." It is known that any lie does not stand if it is not preceded by words of truth. Hence, it started with a true word and revealed to her the purpose of creation, that came only to correct this tree, meaning to invert the great vessels of reception to the side of bestowal.

This is the meaning of what our sages said to her, telling her that God had eaten from this tree and created the world, meaning looked at that matter in the form of "The end of an act is in the preliminary thought," and for this reason He has created the world. As we have seen above, the whole matter of the first *Tzimtzum* was only for man, who is destined to equalize the form of reception to bestowal, and this was the truth.

For this reason, it succeeded and the woman believed it when she prepared herself to receive and enjoy solely in order to bestow. You find that at any rate, evil vanished from the Tree of Knowledge of good and evil, and the Tree of Knowledge of good remained. This is because the evil there is only the disparity of form of reception for oneself, which was imprinted in him but with reception in order to bestow. Thus, he is brought to his complete perfection, and you find that she made the great unification as it should be at the end of the act.

However, that sublime *Kedusha* was still untimely. She was only fit to endure it in the first eating but not in the second eating (as *The Zohar* writes, "It is all a lie"). I will explain to you that one who avoids a passion before one has tasted and grown accustomed is not like one who avoids a passion having tasted and becomes connected to it. The first can certainly avoid once and for all, but the other must exert to retire from one's craving bit by bit until he completes the matter.

So it is here. Since the woman had not yet tasted from the Tree of Knowledge and was completely in bestowal, it was easy for her to perform the first eating in order to bestow contentment upon the Creator in absolute *Kedusha*. But after she tasted it, a great desire and coveting for the Tree of Knowledge was made in her until she could not retire from her craving, since matters had gone out of her control.

This is why our sages said that she ate prematurely, meaning before it was ripe, before they acquired strength and power to rule over their desire. This is similar to what the sages said in *Masechet Yevamot*, according to Aba Shaul, who said that one who marries his dead brother's wife for beauty and for lust is as one who blemishes the pubes. They said, "The first intercourse is forbidden because of the second intercourse." This is the meaning of what our sages said, "I have eaten and I shall eat more." This means that even when he had explicitly heard that the Creator was in wrath with him, he still could not retire from it, since the lust had already been connected to him. You find that the first eating was on the side of the *Kedusha*, and the second eating was in great filth.

Now we can understand the severity of the punishment of the Tree of Knowledge, for which all people are put to death. This death extends from eating it, as the Creator had warned him, "in the day you eat from it you will surely die."

The thing is that the *Gadlut* form of reception extends into his limbs from the vacant space, and from the *Tzimtzum* onward it is no longer possible for it to be under the same roof with the upper light. Hence, that eternal breath of life, expressed in the verse, "and breathed into his nostrils the breath of life," had to leave there and depend on a slice of bread for its transient sustenance.

This life is not eternal life as before, when it was for himself. Rather, it is similar to sweat of life, a life that has been divided into tiny drops, where each drop is a fragment of his previous life. This is the meaning of the sparks of souls that were spread throughout his progeny. Thus, in all his progeny, all the people in the world in all the generations, through the last generation, which concludes the purpose of creation, are one long chain.

It follows that the acts of the Creator did not change at all by the sin of the Tree of Knowledge. Rather, this light of life that came at once in *Adam HaRishon* extended and stretched into a long chain, revolving on the wheel of transformation of forms until the end of correction. There is no cessation for a moment, since the actions of the Creator must be alive and enduring, and "Sanctity is raised, not lowered."

As is the case of man, so is the case with all the creatures in the world because they all descended from an eternal and general form, on the wheel of transformation of form, as did man.

Both man and the world have an inner value and an outer value. The external always ascends and descends according to the internal, and this is the meaning of "In the sweat of your brow shall you eat bread." Instead of the previous breath of life that the Creator had breathed in his nostrils, there is now a sweat of life in his nostrils.

19) Our sages said (*Babba Batra* 17), "He is the evil inclination; he is Satan; he is the angel of death. He descends and incites, ascends and slanders, he comes and he takes his soul." This is because two general corruptions occurred because of the sin of the Tree of Knowledge.

The first corruption is the matter of "ascends and slanders." He had been tempted to eat from the Tree of Knowledge and acquired a vessel of reception of the vacant space in the structure of his body. That, in turn, caused hatred and remoteness between the eternal light of life that the Creator had breathed in Adam's nostrils, and Adam's body.

It is similar to what our sages said, "All who is proud, the Creator says, 'he and I cannot dwell in the same abode.'" This is so because pride stems from the vessels of reception of the vacant space, from which the upper light had already departed from the time of the *Tzimtzum* onward.

It is written in *The Zohar* that the Creator hates the bodies that are built only for themselves. For this reason, the light of life fled from him, and this is the first corruption.

The second corruption is the descent of the 288 sparks that were already connected in the system of *Kedusha*. They were given and descended to the system of *Sitra Achra* and the *Klipot* so the world would not be destroyed.

This is so because the system of *Kedusha* cannot sustain and nourish people and the world, due to the hatred that had been made between the *Kedusha* and the *Kelim* of the vacant space. This follows the law of opposites, "he and I cannot dwell in the same abode." Hence, the 288 sparks were given to the system of the *Sitra Achra* so they would nurture and sustain man and the world all through the incarnations of the souls in the bodies, as it is written, "Ten thousand for a generation, and for a thousand generations," until the end of correction.

Now you can see why they are called *Klipot*. It is because they are like the peel on a fruit. The hard peel envelops and covers the fruit to keep it from any filth and harm until the fruit is eaten. Without it, the fruit would be corrupted and would not fulfill its purpose. Thus, you find that the 288 sparks were given to the *Klipot* to sustain and qualify reality until they connect and attain their desired goal.

The above-mentioned second corruption is the matter of "comes and takes his soul." I wish to say that even that tiny part of the soul that remains for a person, as "sweat of the previous life," is also robbed by the *Sitra Achra*, through that same bestowal that she gives him from the 288 sparks that have fallen into her.

To understand this, you need a clear picture of the *Sitra Achra* as she really is. Thus, you will be able to examine all her ways. I have already shown in *Panim Masbirot*, Branch 6, that all the parts of reality of the lower world are branches, extending from their roots like an imprint from a seal from the upper world, and the upper from the one above it, and that upper from its own upper.

Know that any discernment in branches about the roots is only in the basis of their substance. This means that the substances in this world are corporeal bases, and the substances in the world of *Yetzira* are spiritual bases, relating to the spirituality in *Yetzira*. So it is in each and every world.

However, the occurrences and the conducts in them have the same value from each branch to its root, like two drops of water, equal to each other, and like the imprint whose form is identical to the seal from which it was imprinted. Once you know this, we can seek that branch that the upper *Sitra Achra* has in this world, and through it we will also know its root, the upper *Sitra Achra*.

We find in *The Zohar*, Portion *Tazriya*, that the afflictions in people's bodies are branches of the upper *Sitra Achra*. Hence, let us take the animate level and learn from it. We find that the sprouting that occurs in its body through attainment of pleasure is what proliferates its life. For this reason, Providence has imprinted in the little ones, that every place they rest their eyes on gives them pleasure and contentment, even the most trifling things.

This is so because the level of the small must proliferate sufficiently to grow and sprout, and this is why their pleasure is copious. Thus, you find that the light of pleasure is the progenitor of life.

However, this law applies only in pleasures that come to the level as a whole. But in a pleasure of separation, when the pleasure is concentrated and received only by a separated part of the level of the animal, we find the opposite rule: If there is a defective place in its flesh, which demands scratching and rubbing, the act of scratching carries its reward with it, as one feels great pleasure pursuing it. However, this pleasure is sodden with a drop of the potion of death: If one does not govern one's desire and pays the haunting demand, the payment will increase the debt.

In other words, according to the pleasure from scratching, so will the affliction increase and the pleasure will turn to pain. When it begins to heal again, a new demand for scratching appears, and at a greater extent than before. And if one still cannot govern one's desire and pays to saturate the demand, the affliction will grow as well.

Finally, it brings it a bitter drop, poisoning all the blood in that animal. You find that it died by receiving pleasure, since it is a pleasure of separation, received only by a separate part of the level. Hence, death operates in the level in the opposite manner from the pleasure administered to the entire level.

Here we see before us the form of the upper *Sitra Achra* from head to toe. Her head is the will to receive only for herself, and not to bestow outside of herself, as is the property of the demand in the afflicted flesh with respect to the entire animal. The body of the *Sitra Achra* is a certain form of demand that is not going to be paid. The repayment one makes increases the debt and the affliction even more, as with the example of receiving pleasure by scratching.

The toe of the *Sitra Achra* is the drop of the potion of death, which robs it and separates it from the last spark of life it had left, like the drop of the potion of death that intoxicates all the blood in the animal.

This is the meaning of what our sages said, "In the end, it comes and takes his soul." In other words, they said that the angel of death comes with a drawn sword and a drop of poison at its tip; the person opens his mouth, he throws the drop inside, and he dies.

The sword of the angel of death is the influence of the *Sitra Achra*, called *Herev* [sword/ruin] because of the separation that grows according to the measure of reception, and the separation destroys him. One is compelled to open one's mouth, since one must receive the abundance for sustenance and persistence from her hands. In the end, the bitter drop at the tip of the sword reaches him, and this completes the separation to the last spark of his breath of life.

20) As a result of these two corruptions, man's body was corrupted, too, as it is precisely adapted by creation to receive the abundance of its sustenance from the system of *Kedusha*. This is so because in any viable act, its parts are guarded from any surplus or scarcity. An act that is not viable and sustainable is because its parts are unbalanced and there is some shortage or surplus in them.

As he says in the Poem of Unification: "Of all Your work, not a thing You have forgotten; You did not add, and You did not subtract." It is a mandatory law that perfect operations stem from the perfect Operator.

However, when a person passes from the system of *Kedusha* to the system of the *Sitra Achra*, due to the barnacle attached to his construction by the Tree of Knowledge, many parts of him are already in surplus, needless, since they do not receive anything from the abundance of sustenance dispensed from the authority of the *Sitra Achra*. It is as we find with the *Luz* bone, see in *The Zohar*, *Midrash HaNe'elam*, *Toladot*, and also in a certain portion of each and every organ.

Hence, one must receive sustenance into one's body more than is necessary, since the surplus joins every demand that rises from the body. Hence, the body receives for them. However, the surplus itself cannot receive its share; thus, its share remains in the body as surplus and litter that the body must later eject.

In consequence, the feeding and digesting tools exert in vain. They diminish and lessen to extinction because their sentence is predetermined, as that of any imbalanced act, destined to disintegrate. Thus you find that from the perspective of the construction of the body, too, its death depends on cause and effect from the Tree of Knowledge.

Now we have been awarded learning and knowing the two contradicting, opposite conducts (Item 11). The sustenance and keeping of the created beings has already passed from the system of *Kedusha* to the system of the *Sitra Achra* because of the barnacle of the great will to receive for oneself, connected to the created beings by the eating from the Tree of Knowledge. This induced separation, oppositeness, and hatred between the system of *Kedusha* and the structure of the bodies of the created beings in this world.

When the *Kedusha* can no longer sustain and nurture them from the high table, to not destroy reality and to induce an act of correction for them, it gives the collective abundance of the sustenance of reality–her 288 sparks–to the system of the *Sitra Achra*, so they will provide for all creations in the world during the correction period.

Hence, the conducts of existence are very confused, since evil sprouts from the wicked, and if the abundance is reduced to the created beings, it certainly brings ruin and destruction. And if abundance is increased, it brings excessive force of separation to the receivers, as our sages said, "He who has one hundred wants two hundred; he who has two hundred wants four hundred."

It is like the separated pleasure that the separated and defected flesh senses, where increased pleasure increases separation and affliction. Thus, self-love greatly increases in the receivers, and one swallows one's friend alive. Also, the life of the body shortens, since the accumulation of reception brings the bitter drop at the end sooner, and wherever they turn, they only condemn.

Now you can understand what is written in the *Tosfot, Ktubot* p 104: "Until one prays that Torah will enter one's body, one should pray that no delicacies will enter one's body." This is because the form of self-reception, which is the opposite of *Kedusha*, increases and multiplies by the measure of pleasure that one's body acquires.

Thus, how can one obtain the light of Torah within one's body when he is separated and in complete oppositeness of form from the *Kedusha*, and there is great hatred between them, as with all opposites: They hate each other and cannot be under the same roof.

Therefore, one must first pray that no delights or pleasures will enter one's body, and as the deeds in Torah and *Mitzvot* accumulate, one slowly purifies and inverts the form of reception to be in order to bestow. You find that one equalizes one's form with the system of *Kedusha*, and the equivalence and love between them returns, as prior to the sin of the Tree of Knowledge. Thus, one is awarded the light of the Torah, since he entered the presence of the Creator.

21) Now it is thoroughly understood why the answer of the angels regarding man's creation, which we learned in the *Midrash* in Item 11, is not presented. It is because even the angels of Mercy and Righteousness did not agree to the present man, since he has gone completely out of their influence and has become completely dependent on the *Sitra Achra*.

The *Midrash* ends: "He took Truth and threw it to the earth. They all said immediately, 'Let Truth rise from the earth.'" This means that even the angels of Mercy and Righteousness regretted their consent, as they never agreed that Truth would be disgraced.

This incident occurred at the time of the eating from the Tree of Knowledge, when Truth was absent from the management of the sustenance of reality, since the scrutinizing force imprinted in man by creation, which operates by the sensation of bitter and sweet, has weakened and failed, as it is written in Item 17.

This is so because the provision for sustenance, which are 288 different *Behinot*, were already as clear as day, connected in the system of *Kedusha*. And "the palate tastes its food" to attract in full all that is beloved and sweet, and reject all that is bitter and bad so no man will fail in them.

However, after the first tasting of the Tree of Knowledge, for which the *Gadlut* form of self-reception has stuck to them, their body and the *Kedusha* became two opposites. At that time, the abundance of sustenance, which is the 288 *Behinot*, went to the hands of the *Sitra Achra*.

You find that the 288 sparks that had already been sorted were remixed by the *Sitra Achra*. Thus, a new form was made in reality—the form whose beginning is sweet and whose end is bitter.

This was because the form of the 288 has been changed by the *Sitra Achra*, where the light of pleasure brings separation and a bitter drop. This is the form of falsehood, the first and foremost progenitor of every destruction and confusion.

It is written, "He took Truth and threw it to the earth." Thus, because of the serpent, a new discernment was added to man—the active cognitive force. It operates by discernments of true and false, and one must use it throughout the correction period, for without it the benefit is impossible, as written in Item 17.

Come and see all the confusion caused by the fall of the 288 sparks into the hands of the *Sitra Achra*. Before they tasted from the Tree of Knowledge, the woman could not even touch the forbidden thing, as written in Item 17. By mere nearness to the Tree of Knowledge, she tasted bitterness that tasted like death. For this reason, she understood and added the prohibition on touching. After the first eating, when the *Sitra Achra* and falsehood already controlled the sustenance of reality, the prohibition became so sweet in its beginning that they could no longer retire from it. This is why he said, "I have eaten and I shall eat more."

Now you understand why the reward in the Torah is intended only for the ripe bodies. It is because the whole purpose of the Torah is to correct the sin of the Tree of Knowledge, which induced the confusion of the conduct of the sustenance of reality.

It is for this correction that the Torah was given—to elevate the 288 sparks to *Kedusha* once more. At that time, the conduct of the sustenance will return to the *Kedusha* and confusions will cease from the modes of the sustenance of reality. Then, people will be brought to their desired wholeness by themselves, solely by the discernment of bitter and sweet, which was the first operator, prior to the sin of the Tree of Knowledge.

The prophets, too, speak only of this correction, as our sages said, "All the prophets prophesied only for the days of the Messiah." This is the meaning of the restoration of the modes of sustenance of the world under sorted Providence, as it was prior to the sin. "But for the next world" implies the end of the matter, which is the equivalence of form with the Maker, "neither has the eye seen a God besides You." It is also written that in the days of the Messiah, [if] Egypt does not rise, corporeality will not be on them, meaning through discernments of good and bad.

22) Now we understand the words of our sages that the Creator did not find a vessel that holds a blessing for Israel but peace. We asked, "Why was this statement chosen to end the Mishnah?"

According to the above, we understand that the eternal soul of life that the Creator had blown into his nostrils, only for the needs of *Adam HaRishon*, has departed because of the sin of the Tree of Knowledge. It acquired a new form, called "Sweat of Life," meaning the general has been divided into myriad parts, tiny drops, divided between *Adam HaRishon* and all his progeny through the end of time.

It follows, that there are no changes whatsoever in the acts of the Creator, but there is rather an additional form here. This common light of life, which was packed in the nose of *Adam HaRishon*, has expanded into a long chain, revolving on the wheel of transformation of form in many bodies, body after body, until the necessary end of correction.

It turns out that he died at the very day he ate from the Tree of Knowledge, and the eternal life departed him. Instead, he was tied to a long chain by the procreation organ (which is the meaning of the *Zivug*, called "Peace").

You find that one does not live for oneself, but for the whole chain. Thus, each and every part of the chain does not receive the light of life into itself, but only distributes the light of life to the whole chain. This is also what you find in one's days of life: At twenty, he is fit to marry a woman, and ten years he may wait to bear sons. Thus, he must certainly father by thirty.

Then he sits and waits for his son until he is forty years of age, the age of *Bina* [understanding], so he may pass onto him the fortune and knowledge he has acquired by himself, and everything he had learned and inherited from his forefathers, and he will trust him not to lose it for an ill matter. Then he promptly passes away and his son grips the continuation of the chain in his father's place.

It has been explained in Item 15 that the incident of the sin of the Tree of Knowledge had to happen to *Adam HaRishon*, as it is written, "Libel is terrible for the children of men." This is so because one must add to one's structure an external *Kli* to receive the surrounding light, so the two opposites will come in the same carrier in two consecutive times. During his *Katnut*, he will be dependent on the *Sitra Achra*. His vessels of reception of the vacant space will grow to their desired measure by the separated pleasures that one receives because of them.

Finally, when one reaches *Gadlut* and engages in Torah and *Mitzvot*, the ability to turn the great vessels of reception in order to bestow will be readily available. This is the primary goal, called "The light of truth," and "the seal," as it is written in Item 14.

However, it is known that before one connects to the *Kedusha*, one must retire once more from any form of reception that he had received from the table of the *Sitra Achra*, as the commandment of love came to us, "with all your soul and with all your might." Hence, what have the sages done by this correction if one loses everything he has acquired from the *Sitra Achra*?

For this reason, His Providence provided the proliferation of the bodies in each generation, as our sages said, "He saw that the righteous were few, He stood and planted them in each generation." This means that He saw that in the end, the righteous will repel the matter of self-reception altogether and thus their surrounding light would diminish, since the external *Kli* that is fit for it will be repelled from them.

For this reason, He planted them in each and every generation, because in all generations, a large number of the people are created primarily for the righteous, to be the carriers of the *Kelim* of the vacant space for them. Thus, the external *Kli* would necessarily operate in the righteous involuntarily.

This is so because all the people in the world are attached to one another. They affect one another both in bodily inclinations and in opinions. Therefore, they necessarily bring the inclination for self-reception to the righteous, and in this manner, they can receive the desired surrounding light.

However, accordingly, the righteous and the wicked should have been of equal weight in each generation. Yet, this is not so, and for each righteous, we find many thousands of vain ones. Yet, you must know that there are two kinds of governance in creation: 1) a qualitative force, 2) a quantitative force.

The force of those that hang about the feet of the *Sitra Achra* is meager, contemptible, and low, undesirable, and purposeless, and they are blown like chaff in the wind. Thus, how can such as those do anything to wise-hearted people whose way is clear with desire and aim, and a pillar of upper light shines before them day and night sufficiently to bring the tiny inclinations in their hearts?

Hence, He provided the quantitative force in creation, as this force does not need any quality. I will explain it to you by the way we find the qualitative force in strength, such as in lions and tigers, where because of the great quality of their strength no man will fight them.

Opposite them, we find strength and power without any quality but only quantity, as in the flies. But because of their numbers, no man will fight them. These wanderers roam man's house and set table freely and it is man who feels weak against them.

However, with wild flies, insects, and other such uninvited guests, although the quality of their strength is greater than domestic flies, man will not rest until he banishes them from his domain entirely. This is so because nature did not allot them the reproduction ability of flies.

Accordingly, you can see that there must necessarily be a great multitude for every single righteous. They instill their crude inclinations in him through the power of their numbers, as they have no quality whatsoever.

This is the meaning of the verse, "The Lord will give strength unto His people." It means that the eternal light of life, attained by the whole chain of creation, is called "strength." The text guarantees that the Creator will surely give us this strength.

Yet, we should ask, "How so? Since every person is not whole in and of himself, as our sages have written, 'It is better for one not to be born than to be born,' why then are we sure of His eternity?"

And the verse ends, "The Lord will bless his people with peace," meaning the blessing of the sons. It is as our sages said in *Masechet Shabbat*, "He who makes peace in the house is idle." It is so because through the sons, this chain is tied and linked through the end of correction. At that time, all the parts will be in eternity.

This is why our sages said, "The Creator did not find a *Kli* that holds a blessing for Israel, but peace," for as His blessing is eternal, the receivers should also be eternal.

Thus, you find that through the sons, the fathers hold and create among them the chain of eternity, fit to hold the eternal blessing. It follows that it is peace that holds and conducts the wholeness of the blessing.

Hence, our sages ended the Mishnah with this verse, since peace is the *Kli* that holds the blessing of the Torah and all the *Mitzvot* for us until the complete and eternal redemption soon in our days, Amen, and everything will come to its place in peace.

Introduction to the *Preface to the Wisdom of Kabbalah*

1) It is written in *The Zohar*, *Vayikra*, Portion *Tazria*, "Come and see: All that exists in the world exists for man, and everything exists for him, as it is written, 'Then the Lord God formed man,' with a full name, as we have established, that he is the whole of everything and contains everything, and all that is above and below, etc., is included in that image."

Thus, it explains that all the worlds, upper and lower, are included in man. And also, the whole of reality within those worlds is only for man. And we should understand these words: Is this world and everything in it, which serves him and benefits him, too little for man, that he needs the upper worlds and everything within them, too? After all, they were created solely for his needs.

2) To explain this matter to the fullest, I would have to introduce the whole of the wisdom of Kabbalah. But in general, matters will be sufficiently explained within the book, so as to understand them. The essence of it is that the Creator's intention in creation was to delight His creatures. Certainly, as soon as He contemplated creating the souls and delighting them abundantly, they immediately emerged from before Him, complete in form and with all the delights He had planned to bestow upon them. This is because in Him, the thought alone completes, and He does not need actions as we do. Accordingly, we should ask, "Why did He create the worlds restriction after restriction down to this murky world, and clothed the souls in the murky bodies of this world?

3) The answer to this is written in *The Tree of Life*—"to bring to light the perfection of His deeds" (*The Tree of Life*, Branch 1). Yet, we must understand how it is possible that incomplete operations would stem from a complete Operator, to the point that they would require completion through an act in this world.

The thing is that we should distinguish between light and *Kli* [vessel] in the souls. The essence of the souls that were created is the *Kli* in them, and all the bounty that He had planned to impart them with and delight them is the light in them. This is because since He had planned to delight them, He necessarily made them as a desire to receive His pleasure, since the pleasure and delight increase according to the measure of desire to receive the abundance.

Know that that will to receive is the very self of the soul with regard to the generation and elicitation existence from absence. This is considered the *Kli* of the soul, while the joy and the abundance are considered the light of the soul, extending existence from existence from His self.

4) Explanation: Creation refers to appearance of something that did not exist before. This is considered existence from absence. Yet, how do we picture something

that is not included in Him, since He is almighty and includes all of them together? Also, one does not give what is not in Him.

As we have said, the whole creation that He created is only the *Kelim* [plural for *Kli*] of the souls, which is the will to receive. This is clear, since He necessarily does not have a will to receive, as from whom would He receive? Hence, this is truly a new creation, not a trace of which existed previously, and is therefore considered existence from absence.

5) We should know that unification and separation applied in spirituality relate only to equivalence of form and disparity of form. This is because if two spiritual objects are of the same form, they are united, and they are one, and not two, as there is nothing to separate them from one another. They can only be discerned as two when there is some disparity of form between them.

Also, to the extent of their disparity of form, so is the measure of their distance from one another. Thus, if they are of opposite forms, they are considered as remote as the east from the west, meaning the greatest distance we can picture in reality.

6) But in the Creator, there is no thought or perception whatsoever, and we cannot utter or say anything with regard to Him. But since we know You by Your actions, we should discern that He is a desire to bestow, since He created everything in order to delight His creatures and bestow His abundance upon us.

Thus, the souls are in oppositeness of form from Him, since He is all bestowal and has no will to receive anything, while the souls were imprinted with a will to receive for themselves. And we have already said that there is no greater oppositeness of form than this.

It follows that had the souls remained with the will to receive, they would forever remain separated from Him.

7) Now you will understand what is written (*The Tree of Life*, Branch 1), that the reason for the creation of the worlds was that He must be complete in all His actions and powers, and if He did not carry out His actions and powers in practice, He would seemingly not be considered whole. This seems perplexing, for how can incomplete actions emerge from a complete operator, to the extent that they would need correction?

From what has been explained, you can see that the essence of creation is only the will to receive. On one hand, it is very deficient since it is opposite in form from the Emanator, which is separation from Him, but on the other hand, this is the entire innovation and the existence from absence that He created, by which to receive from Him what He planned to delight them and bestow upon them.

Yet, had they remained separated from the Emanator, He would seemingly be incomplete, for in the end, complete operations must stem from the complete Operator.

For this reason, He restricted His light and created the worlds restriction after restriction down to this world, and clothed the soul in a worldly body. And through the practice of Torah and *Mitzvot*, the soul obtains the perfection it lacked prior to creation—the equivalence of form with Him. Thus, it will be fit to receive all the abundance and pleasure included in the thought of creation, and will also be in complete *Dvekut* [adhesion] with Him, in equivalence of form.

8) The matter of the *Segula* [power/remedy] of Torah and *Mitzvot* to bring the soul to *Dvekut* with Him applies only when the engagement in it is not in order to receive any reward, and only to bestow contentment upon his Maker. This is so because then the soul gradually acquires equivalence of form with its Maker, as will be written below concerning Rabbi Hanina's words in the beginning of the book ["Preface to the Wisdom of Kabbalah"].

In all, there are five degrees—*Nefesh, Ruach, Neshama, Haya, Yechida* [NRNHY]—that come from the five worlds called *AK, Atzilut, Beria, Yetzira,* and *Assiya*. Also, there are five particular degrees NRNHY, which come from the five particular *Partzufim* [plural for *Partzuf*] in each of the five worlds. Then there are sub-particular NRNHY, which come from the ten *Sefirot* in each *Partzuf*, as is written inside the book.

And through Torah and *Mitzvot* to bestow contentment upon the Maker, one is gradually rewarded with the *Kelim* in the form of desire to bestow, which come in these degrees, degree by degree, until they achieve complete equivalence of form with Him. In that state, the thought of creation—to receive all the pleasure, tenderness, and abundance that He had planned for them—is carried out. Additionally, they receive the greatest reward, since they are awarded the true *Dvekut*, since they have obtained the desire to bestow, like their Maker.

9) Now it will not be difficult for you to understand the above words of *The Zohar*, that all the worlds, upper and lower and everything within them, were created only for man. This is so because all these degrees and worlds came only to complement the souls in the measure of *Dvekut* they lacked with respect to the thought of creation.

In the beginning, they were restricted and hung down degree by degree and world after world, down to our material world, to bring the soul into a body of this world, which is entirely to receive and not to bestow, like animals and beasts. It is written, "A wild ass' colt is born a man." This is considered the complete will to receive, which has nothing in terms of bestowal. In that state, one is regarded as the complete opposite of Him, and there is no greater remoteness than this.

Afterward, through the soul that clothes within one, he engages in Torah and *Mitzvot*. Gradually and slowly, from below upward, he obtains the same form of bestowal as his Maker, through all those qualities that hung down from above downward, which are but degrees and measures in the form of the desire to bestow.

Each higher degree means that it is farther from the will to receive and closer to being only to bestow. In the end, one is awarded being entirely to bestow and not to receive anything for himself. At that time, one is completed with true *Dvekut* with Him, for man was created only for this. Thus, all the worlds and everything in them were created only for man.

10) Now that you have come to know all this, you are permitted to learn this wisdom without any fear of materialization. This is because the students are very confused: On one hand, it is said that the ten *Sefirot* and the *Partzufim*, from the beginning of the ten *Sefirot* of *Atzilut* to the end of the ten *Sefirot* of *Assiya*, are complete Godliness and unity (*The Tree of Life*, Gate 44, Gate "Names," Chapter 1).

On the other hand, it is said that all these worlds are generated and appear after the *Tzimtzum* [restriction], but how can this even be conceived in Godliness? And there are also the numbers and above and below and other such changes and ascents and descents and *Zivugim* [couplings]. But it is written, "I the Lord do not change."

11) From what is clarified before us, it is clear that all these ascents, descents, restrictions, and the numbers are only regarded as *Kelim* [vessels] of the receivers, namely the souls. However, we should distinguish in them a potential and an actual fact in them, like a person who builds a house—the end of the act is in his preliminary thought.

But the quality of the house in his mind does not resemble the house that should actually be built, since the conceived house is spirituality, a conceptual substance, and is considered the substance of the thinking person. At that time, the house is only a potential. But when the building of the house begins in practice, it acquires an entirely different substance—that of wood and bricks.

Similarly, we should discern potential and actual in the souls. The beginning of their emergence from the Emanator into "actual" souls begins only in the world of *Beria*. And their *Hitkalelut* [inclusion] in *Ein Sof*, prior to the *Tzimtzum*, in relation to the thought of creation, as written in Item 2, concerns only the "potential," without any practical manifestation.

In that sense, it is said that all the souls were included in *Malchut de Ein Sof*, called "the middle point," since this point is included in potential in all the *Kelim* of the souls that are destined to emerge in practice from the world of *Beria* downward. And the first restriction occurred only in this middle point, meaning precisely in that discernment and measure considered the "potential" of the future souls, and not at all in itself.

Know that all the *Kelim* of the *Sefirot* and the worlds, through the world of *Beria*, which cascade and emerge from this point, or due to its *Zivug de Hakaa*, called *Ohr Hozer*, are also considered mere potential, without any essence of the souls. But these changes are destined to act on the souls later, when their essence begins to emerge from the world of *Beria* down, since there they have not yet departed from the essence of the Emanator.

12) Let me give you an allegory from the conducts of this world. For example, if a person who covers and hides himself behind clothes and garments so his friend

would not see him or notice him, can it even be conceived that he himself would be affected by the concealment made by all the garments with which he is covered?

Similarly, take the ten *Sefirot* we call *Keter, Hochma, Bina, Hesed, Gevura, Tifferet, Netzah, Hod, Yesod, Malchut* as an example. These are only ten covers by which *Ein Sof* is covered and concealed. The souls that are destined to receive from it will be compelled to receive by those measures that the ten *Sefirot* allot them. Thus, the receivers are affected by this number of ten *Sefirot*, and not at all by His light, which is one, unique, and unchanging.

Conversely, the receivers divide into ten degrees precisely according to the qualities of these names. Moreover, even these covers we spoke of pertain only to the world of *Beria* and below, since this is where the souls that receive from these ten *Sefirot* are found. But in the worlds *AK* and *Atzilut*, there is no existence even to the souls, since there they are only a potential.

Hence, the ten above covers in the ten *Sefirot* govern only in the three lower worlds, called *Beria, Yetzira*, and *Assiya*. But in the worlds *BYA*, the ten *Sefirot* are considered Godliness through the end of *Assiya*, just as in *AK* and *ABYA*, and as prior to the *Tzimtzum*.

The only difference is in the *Kelim* of the ten *Sefirot*: In *AK* and *Atzilut*, they do not even disclose their dominance, since they are only in "potential" there, and only in *BYA* do the *Kelim* of the ten *Sefirot* begin to manifest their concealing and covering power. But in the light in the ten *Sefirot*, there is no change whatsoever due to these covers, as was written in the allegory. This is the meaning of "I the Lord do not change."

13) We might ask, "Since there is no disclosure of the essence of the souls of the receivers in *AK* and *Atzilut*, what do those *Kelim*, called ten *Sefirot*, serve for, and whom do they conceal and cover in those measures?"

There are two answers to this: The first is the hanging down, as you will find inside the book. The second is that the souls, too, are destined to receive from those ten *Sefirot* in *AK* and *Atzilut*, through the ascent of the three worlds *BYA* to them, as will be written below in Item 163. Hence, we should discern these changes in the ten *Sefirot* in *AK* and *Atzilut*, as well, according to the light that they are destined to shine upon the souls once they rise there with the worlds *BYA*, for then they will receive according to the degree in those ten *Sefirot*.

14) Thus, we have thoroughly clarified that the worlds, the generation, the changes, and the number of degrees, etc., were said only with respect to the *Kelim* that give to the souls, and conceal and measure for them, so they can gradually receive from the light of *Ein Sof* in them. But they do not affect the light of *Ein Sof* itself in any way, since no covers affect the one who is covered, but only the other, who wishes to feel him and receive from him, as said in the allegory.

15) In general, we should discern these three discernments in the *Sefirot* and *Partzufim* wherever they are: *Atzmuto* [His Self], *Kelim*, and lights.

In *Atzmuto*—there is no thought or perception whatsoever. In the *Kelim*—there are always two opposite discernments: concealment and disclosure. This is so because in the beginning, the *Kli* covers *Atzmuto* in a way that these ten *Kelim* in the ten *Sefirot* are ten degrees of concealment.

But once the souls receive these *Kelim* under all the conditions in them, these concealments become disclosures for the attainments of the souls. Thus, the *Kelim* contain two opposite discernments, which are one, for the measure of disclosure in the *Kli* is precisely the measure of concealment in the *Kli*. The thicker the *Kli*, meaning the more it conceals *Atzmuto*, it reveals a higher degree. Thus, these two opposites are one.

And the lights in the *Sefirot* refer to that measure of degree suitable for appearing for the attainment of the souls. Since everything extends from *Atzmuto*, and yet, there is no attainment in Him, but only in the qualities of the *Kelim*, there are necessarily ten lights in these ten *Kelim*, meaning degrees of revelation to those receiving in the qualities of those *Kelim*.

Thus, His light and His essence are indistinguishable, except that in His essence, there is no attainment or perception whatsoever, except for what comes to us from Him through clothing in the *Kelim* of the ten *Sefirot*. And in that respect, we refer to anything that we attain by the name, "lights."

Preface to the Wisdom of Kabbalah

1) Rabbi Hanania Ben Akashia says, "The Creator wished to refine Israel; hence, He gave them plentiful Torah and *Mitzvot* [commandments], as was said, 'The Lord desires for the sake of His righteousness, to extol and glorify the Torah'" (*Makkot* 23b). It is known that *Zakkut* [refinement/cleansing] derives from the [Hebrew] word *Hizdakchut* [refining]. It is as our sages said, "The commandments were only given to refine Israel with them" (*Beresheet Rabbah*, beginning of Portion 44). We must understand this refinement that we achieve through Torah and commandments, and what is the coarseness within us, which we must refine using Torah and commandments.

Since we have already discussed it in my book *Panim uMasbirot*, and in *The Study of the Ten Sefirot*, I shall briefly reiterate that the thought of creation was to delight the created beings in accord with His abundant generosity. For this reason, a great desire and craving to receive His abundance was imprinted in the souls.

This is so because the will to receive is the vessel for the measure of pleasure in the abundance, since the measure and strength of the will to receive the abundance precisely corresponds to the measure of pleasure and delight in the abundance. And they are so connected that they are indivisible, except in what they relate to: The pleasure is related to the abundance, and the great desire to receive the abundance is related to the receiving created being.

These two necessarily extend from the Creator. However, they should be divided in the above-mentioned manner: The abundance comes from His self, extending existence from existence, and the will to receive included there is the root of the created beings. This means that it is the root of initiation, that is, emergence existence from absence, since there is certainly no form of will to receive in His self.

Hence, it is considered that the above-mentioned will to receive is the whole substance of creation from beginning to end. Thus, all the created beings, all their innumerable instances and conducts that have appeared and will appear, are but measures and various values of the will to receive. All that exists in those created beings, that is, all that is received in the will to receive imprinted in them, extends from His self, existence from existence. It is not at all a new creation, existence from absence, since it is not new at all. Rather, it extends from His Endlessness existence from existence.

2) As we have said, the will to receive is innately included in the thought of creation with all its values, along with the great abundance He had planned to delight them and impart upon them. And know that these are the light and vessel that we discern in the upper worlds. They necessarily come tied together and cascade together degree by degree. And the extent to which the degrees descend from the

light of His face and depart from Him is the extent of the materialization of the will to receive contained in the abundance.

We could also state the contrary: To the extent that the will to receive in the abundance materializes, it descends degree by degree, as written below, to the lowest of all places, where the will to receive is fully materialized. This place is called "the world of Assiya," the will to receive is considered "man's body," and the abundance one receives is considered the measure of "vitality in that body."

It is similar in other creatures in this world. Thus, the only difference between the upper worlds and this world is that as long as the will to receive incorporated in His abundance has not fully materialized, it is regarded as still being in the spiritual worlds, above this world. Once the will to receive has fully materialized, it is regarded as being in this world.

3) The above-mentioned order of cascading, which brings the will to receive to its final form in this world, follows a sequence of four phases that exist in the four-letter-name [HaVaYaH (Yod-Hey-Vav-Hey)]. This is because the four letters, HaVaYaH, in His name contain the whole of reality, without any exception.

In general, they are described in the ten Sefirot, Hochma, Bina, Tifferet, Malchut, and their root. They are ten Sefirot because the Sefira [sing. of Sefirot] Tifferet contains six internal Sefirot, called HGT NHY [Hesed-Gevura-Tifferet Netzah-Hod-Yesod], and the root is called Keter. Yet, in essence, they are called HB TM [Hochma-Bina Tifferet-Malchut].

These are four worlds called Atzilut, Beria, Yetzira, and Assiya. The world of Assiya contains this world within it. Thus, there is not a creature in this world that is not initiated in Ein Sof, in the thought of creation to delight His creations. Hence, it is innately comprised of light and vessel, meaning a certain measure of abundance with the will to receive that abundance.

The measure of abundance extends existence from existence from His self, and the will to receive the abundance is initiated existence from absence.

But for that will to receive to acquire its final quality, it must cascade along with the abundance within it through the four worlds—Atzilut, Beria, Yetzira, Assiya. This completes creation in light and vessel, called "body," and the "light of life" within it.

4) The reason why the will to receive must cascade by the four above-mentioned discernments in ABYA [Atzilut, Beria, Yetzira, Assiya] is that there is a great rule concerning the vessels: The expansion of the light and its departure make the vessel fit for its task. This means that as long as the vessel has not been separated from its light, it is included in the light and is annulled within it like a candle before a torch.

This annulment is because they are completely opposite from one another, on opposite ends. This is so because the light is abundance that is extended from His self, existence from existence. From the perspective of the thought of creation in Ein

Sof [infinity], it is all toward bestowal and there is no trace of a will to receive in it. Its opposite is the vessel, the great will to receive that abundance, and is the root of the innovated created being, in which there is no bestowal whatsoever.

Hence, when they are bound together, the will to receive is annulled in the light within it, and can determine its form only after the light has departed from it once. Following the departure of the light from it, it begins to crave it, and this craving properly determines and sets the shape of the will to receive. Subsequently, when the light dresses in it once more, it is henceforth regarded as two separate matters: vessel and light, or body and life. Observe closely, for this is most profound.

5) Hence, the four phases in the name HaVaYaH, called Hochma, Bina, Tifferet, Malchut, are required. Phase one, called Hochma, is indeed the whole of the emanated being, light and vessel. In it is the great will to receive with all the light included in it, called "light of Hochma" or "light of Haya," as it is all the light of *Hayim* [life] in the emanated being, dressed in its vessel. However, this phase one is regarded as all light, and the vessel in it is barely noticeable as it is mingled with the light and annulled in it as a candle in a torch.

Following it comes phase two, since at its end, the vessel of Hochma intensifies in equivalence of form with the upper light in it. This means that a desire to bestow upon the Emanator awakens in it, according to the nature of the light within it, which is entirely to bestow.

Then, using this desire that has awakened in it, a new light extends to it from the Emanator, called "light of Hassadim." As a result, it becomes almost entirely separated from the light of Hochma that the Emanator imprinted in it, since the light of Hochma can only be received in its own vessel—a desire to receive that has grown to its fullest measure.

Thus, the light and vessel in phase two are utterly different from those in phase one, since the vessel in it is the desire to bestow. The light within it is considered light of Hassadim, a light that stems from the adhesion of the emanated being in the Emanator, as the desire to bestow causes it equivalence of form with the Emanator, and in spirituality, equivalence of form is adhesion.

Next follows phase three, since once the light in the emanated being has diminished into light of Hassadim without any Hochma, and it is known that light of Hochma is the essence of the emanated being, hence, at the end of phase two, it awakened and drew into it a measure of light of Hochma to shine within its light of Hassadim. This awakening re-extended a certain measure of the will to receive, which forms a new vessel called phase three, or Tifferet. And the light in it is called "light of Hassadim in illumination of Hochma," since the majority of this light is light of Hassadim, and its lesser part is light of Hochma.

Following it came phase four, since the vessel of phase three, too, awakened at its end to draw the complete light of Hochma, as it was in phase one. Thus, this awakening is considered "craving" in the measure of the will to receive in phase one and exceeds it since now it has already been separated from that light, as the light of Hochma is no longer clothed in it but craves it. Thus, the form of the will to receive has been fully determined, since the vessel is determined following the expansion of the light and its departure from there. Later, when it returns, it will receive the light once more. It turns out that the vessel precedes the light, and this is why this phase four is considered the completion of the vessel, and it is called Malchut [kingship].

6) These four above discernments are the ten Sefirot discerned in each emanated being and each created being, both in the whole, which are the four worlds, and even in the smallest element in reality. Phase one is called Hochma or "the world of Atzilut." Phase two is called Bina or "the world of Beria." Phase three is called Tifferet or "the world of Yetzira," and phase four is called Malchut or "the world of Assiya."

Let us explain the four phases applied in each soul. When the soul extends from Ein Sof and comes into the world of Atzilut, it is phase one of the soul. There, it is still not discerned by that name since the name Neshama [soul] implies that there is some difference between it and the Emanator, and that through that difference, it departed Ein Sof and has been revealed as its own authority. But as long as it does not have a form of a vessel, there is nothing to distinguish it from His self, to merit its own name.

You already know that phase one of the vessel is not considered a vessel at all and is entirely annulled in the light. This is the meaning of what is said about the world of Atzilut that it is complete Godliness, as in "He, His life, and His self are one." Even the souls of all other living beings, while traversing the world of Atzilut, are regarded as still adhered to His self.

7) This above-mentioned phase two rules in the world of Beria—the vessel of the desire to bestow. Hence, when the soul cascades into the world of Beria and achieves the vessel that is there, it is regarded as Neshama. This means that it has already separated from His self and merits its own name—Neshama. Yet, this is a very refined and fine vessel, as it is in equivalence of form with the Emanator. For this reason, it is regarded as complete spirituality.

8) The above-mentioned phase three rules in the world of Yetzira, containing a little bit of the form of the will to receive. Hence, when the soul cascades into the world of Yetzira and achieves that vessel, it emerges from the spirituality of the Neshama and is then called Ruach. This is because here its vessel is already mixed with some coarseness, meaning the little bit of will to receive that is in it. Yet, it is still considered spiritual because this measure of coarseness is insufficient to completely separate it from His self and merit the name, "body," which stands in its own right.

9) Phase four rules in the world of Assiya, which is the complete vessel of the great will to receive. Hence, it obtains a completely separated and distinguished body from

His self, which stands in its own right. The light in it is called Nefesh, indicating that the light is motionless in and of itself. You should know that there is not a single element in reality that is not comprised of the whole ABYA.

10) Thus, you find that this Nefesh, the light of life that is dressed in the body, extends from His very self, existence from existence. As it traverses the four worlds ABYA, it becomes increasingly distant from the light of His face until it comes into its designated vessel, called Guf [body]. This is considered that the vessel has completed its desirable form.

And even if the light in it has so diminished that its origin becomes undetectable, through engagement in Torah and *Mitzvot* in order to bestow contentment upon the Maker, one refines one's vessel, called Guf, until it becomes worthy of receiving the great abundance in the full measure included in the thought of creation when He created it. This is why Rabbi Hanania Ben Akashia said, "The Creator wished to refine Israel; hence, He gave them plentiful Torah and *Mitzvot*."

11) Now you can understand the real difference between spirituality and corporeality: Anything that contains a complete desire to receive, in all its aspects, which is phase four, is considered "corporeal." This is what exists in all the elements of reality before us in this world. Conversely, anything above this great measure of desire to receive is considered "spirituality." These are the worlds ABYA, which are above this world, they and the whole reality within them.

Now you can see that the whole issue of ascents and descents described in the upper worlds does not relate to an imaginary place, but only to the four phases in the will to receive. The farther it is from phase four, the higher it is considered to be. And conversely, the closer it is to phase four, the lower it is considered to be.

12) We should understand that the essence of the created being, and of creation as a whole, is only the will to receive. Anything beyond it is not part of creation but extends from His self by way of existence from existence. Thus, why do we discern this will to receive as coarseness and turbidity, and we are commanded to refine it through Torah and *Mitzvot*, to the point that without it we will not achieve the sublime goal of the thought of creation?

13) The thing is that as corporeal objects are separated from one another by remoteness of location, spiritual matters are separated from each other by the disparity of form between them. This can be found in our world, too. For example, when two people share similar views, they like each other and the remoteness of location does not cause them to draw far from one another.

Conversely, when their views are far, they are hateful of each other and proximity of location will not bring them any closer. Thus, the disparity of form in their views removes them from each other, and the proximity of form in their views brings them closer to each other. If, for example, one's nature is the complete opposite of the other's, they are as far from one another as the east from the west.

Similarly, all matters of nearness and remoteness, coupling and unity that unfold in spirituality are but measures of disparity of form. They depart from one another according to their measure of disparity of form and attach to one another according to their measure of equivalence of form.

Yet, you should understand that although the will to receive is a mandatory law in the created being, as it is the essence of the created being and the proper vessel for reception of the goal of the thought of creation, it nonetheless completely separates it from the Emanator, as there is disparity of form to the point of oppositeness between itself and the Emanator. This is because the Emanator is complete bestowal without a shred of reception, and the created being is complete reception without a shred of bestowal. Thus, there is no greater oppositeness of form than this. It therefore follows that this oppositeness of form necessarily separates it from the Emanator.

14) To save the created beings from this titanic separation, the first restriction took place, separating phase four from the rest of the Partzufim [plural of Partzuf] of Kedusha [holiness] so that that great measure of reception remained an empty space devoid of any light, since all the Partzufim of Kedusha emerged with a screen erected in their vessel of Malchut so they would not receive light in this phase four. Then, when the upper light was extended and expanded to the emanated being, this screen rejected it. This is regarded as a striking between the upper light and the screen, which raises reflected light from below upward, clothing the ten Sefirot of the upper light.

That part of the light that was rejected and pushed back is called reflected light. As it dresses the upper light, it becomes a vessel for reception of the upper light instead of phase four, since afterward the vessel of Malchut expanded by the measure of reflected light—the rejected light—which rose and dressed the upper light from below upward, and expanded from above downward, too. Thus, the lights were clothed in the vessels within that reflected light.

This is the meaning of the Rosh [head] and Guf [body] in each degree. The coupling by striking from the upper light in the screen raises reflected light from below upward and dresses the ten Sefirot of the upper light in the form of the ten Sefirot of the Rosh, meaning the roots of the vessels, since there cannot be actual clothing there.

Subsequently, when Malchut expands with that reflected light from above downward, the reflected light ends and becomes vessels for the upper light. At that time, there is clothing of the lights in the vessels, and this is called the Guf of that degree, that is, complete vessels.

15) Thus, new vessels were made in the Partzufim of Kedusha instead of phase four after the first restriction. They were made of the reflected light of the coupling by striking in the screen.

Indeed, we should understand this reflected light and how it became a vessel of reception, since initially it was but a light that was rejected from reception. Thus, it now serves in an opposite role from its own essence.

I shall explain that with an allegory from life. Man's nature is to cherish and favor the quality of bestowal, and to despise and loathe reception from one's friend. Hence, when one comes to one's friend's house and he [the host] invites him for a meal, he [the guest] will decline even if he is very hungry, since in his eyes it is humiliating to receive a gift from his friend.

Yet, when his friend sufficiently implores him until it is clear that he would do his friend a big favor by eating, he agrees to eat as he no longer feels that he is receiving a gift and that his friend is the giver. On the contrary, he [the guest] is the giver, doing his friend a favor by receiving this good from him.

Thus, you find that although hunger and appetite are vessels of reception designated for eating, and that person had sufficient hunger and appetite to receive his friend's meal, he still could not taste a thing due to the shame. Yet, as his friend implored him and he rejected him, new vessels for eating began to form in him, since the power of his friend's pleading and the power of his own rejection, as they accumulated, finally added up to a sufficient amount that turned the measure of reception into a measure of bestowal.

In the end, he saw that by eating, he would do a big favor and bring great contentment to his friend. In that state, new vessels of reception to receive his friend's meal were born in him. Now it is considered that his power of rejection has become the essential vessel in which to receive the meal, and not the hunger and appetite, although they are actually the usual vessels of reception.

16) From the above allegory between two friends, we can understand the matter of coupling by striking and the reflected light that rises through it, which then becomes new vessels of reception for the upper light instead of phase four. We can compare the upper light, which strikes the screen and wants to expand into phase four, to the pleading to eat, because as he yearns for his friend to receive his meal, the upper light desires to expand to the receiver. And the screen, which strikes the light and repels it, can be likened to the friend's rejection and refusal to receive the meal, since he rejects his favor.

Just as you find here that precisely the refusal and rejection have been inverted and become appropriate vessels to receive his friend's meal, you can imagine that the reflected light that rises by the striking of the screen and its rejection of the upper light became new vessels of reception for the upper light instead of phase four, which served as a vessel of reception prior to the first restriction.

However, this was established only in the Partzufim of Kedusha of ABYA, not in the Partzufim of the shells, and in this world, where phase four itself is considered the vessel of reception. Hence, they are separated from the upper light, since the disparity of form in phase four separates them. For this reason, the shells are considered wicked and dead, as they are separated from the Life of Lives by the will to receive in them, as it is written in Item 13.

Five Phases in the Screen

17) Thus far we have clarified the three foundations in the wisdom. The first is the light and the vessel, where the light is a direct extension of His self, and the vessel is the will to receive, which is necessarily included in that light, where according to the measure of that desire, it emerged from the Emanator and became an emanated being. Also, this will to receive is considered the Malchut discerned in the upper light. This is why it is called Malchut, by way of "He and His name are One," as "His name" in *Gematria* is desire [in Hebrew].

The second matter is the clarification of the ten Sefirot and four worlds ABYA, which are four degrees one below the other. The will to receive must cascade through them until it is completed–vessel and content.

The third matter is the restriction and the screen placed on this vessel of reception, which is phase four, in return for which new vessels of reception were made in the ten Sefirot, called reflected light. Understand and memorize these three foundations and their reasons, as they had been clarified to you, since without them there is no understanding of even a single word in this wisdom.

18) Now we shall explain the five phases in the screen by which the levels change during the coupling by striking performed with the upper light. First, we must thoroughly understand that even though phase four was banned from being a vessel of reception for the ten Sefirot after the restriction, and the reflected light that rises from the screen through the coupling by striking became the vessel of reception in its stead, it must still accompany the reflected light with its power of reception. Had it not been for that, the reflected light would have been unfit to be a vessel of reception.

You should also understand this from the allegory in Item 15. We demonstrated there that the power to reject and decline the meal became the vessel of reception instead of the hunger and appetite. This is because hunger and appetite, the usual vessels of reception, were banned from being vessels of reception in this case due to the shame and disgrace of receiving a gift from one's friend. Only the powers of rejection and refusal have become vessels of reception in their stead, as through the rejection and refusal, reception has been inverted into bestowal, and through them he achieved vessels of reception suitable to receive one's friend's meal.

Yet, it cannot be said that he no longer needs the usual vessels of reception, namely the hunger and the appetite, as it is clear that without appetite for eating, he will not be able to satisfy his friend's wish and bring him contentment by eating at his place. But the thing is that the hunger and appetite, which were banned in their usual form, have now been transformed by the forces of rejection and refusal into a new form—reception in order to bestow. By this, the disgrace has been inverted into honor.

It turns out that the usual vessels of reception are still as active as ever but have acquired a new form. You will also conclude, concerning our matter, that it is true that phase four has been banned from being a vessel for reception of the ten Sefirot because of its coarseness, meaning the disparity of form from the Giver, which separates from the Giver. Yet, through establishing the screen in phase four, which strikes the upper light and repels it, her previous, faulty form, has been transformed and acquired a new form, called reflected light, like the transformation of the form of reception into a form of bestowal in the above allegory.

The content of its initial form was not changed there. Now, too, it does not eat without appetite. Likewise, here, all the coarseness, which is the force of reception that was in phase four, has come inside the reflected light, hence, the reflected light became suitable for being a vessel of reception.

Therefore, we must always discern two forces in the screen:

The first is hardness, which is the force within it that rejects the upper light.

The second is coarseness, which is the measure of will to receive from phase four included in the screen. By the coupling by striking through the force of the hardness in it, its coarseness has turned into refinement, meaning the inversion of reception into bestowal.

These two forces in the screen operate in five phases: the four phases HB TM and their root, called Keter.

19) We have already explained that the first three phases are still not considered a vessel, but only phase four is considered a vessel, as written in Item 5. Still, because the first three phases are its causes and induce the completion of phase four, once phase four is completed, four measures are recorded in its quality of reception.

Phase one in it is the slightest measure of the quality of reception. Phase two is somewhat coarser than phase one in terms of its quality of reception. Phase three is coarser than phase two in its quality of reception. Finally, phase four, its own quality, is the coarsest of them all, and its quality of reception is complete in every way. We should also discern that the root of the four phases, which is the most refined of them all, is included in it, too.

These are the five phases of reception contained in phase four, which are also called by the names of the ten Sefirot KHB [Keter-Hochma-Bina] TM [Tifferet-Malchut], incorporated in phase four, since the four phases are HB TM, as written in Item 5, and the root is called Keter.

20) The five qualities of reception in phase four are called by the names of the Sefirot KHB TM since prior to the restriction, while phase four was still the vessel of reception for the ten Sefirot incorporated in the upper light by way of "He is one

and His name One," since all the worlds are incorporated there, as it is written in The Study of the Ten Sefirot, Part 1. Its clothing of the ten Sefirot is discerned there according to the same five phases. Each phase of the five phases in her clothed its corresponding phase in the ten Sefirot in the upper light. The root phase in phase four clothed the light of Keter in the ten Sefirot, phase one in phase four clothed the light of Hochma in the ten Sefirot, phase two in her clothed the light of Bina, phase three in her clothed the light of Tifferet, and her own phase clothed the light of Malchut.

Hence, even now, after the first restriction, when phase four has been banned from being a vessel of reception, the five phases of coarseness in her are named after the five Sefirot KHB TM.

21) You already know that in general, the substance of the screen is called hardness, which means something very hard, which does not allow anything to push into its boundary. Similarly, the screen does not let any upper light pass through it into Malchut, which is phase four. Thus, it is considered that the screen detains and repels the entire measure of light that should clothe the vessel of Malchut.

It has also been made clear that those five phases of coarseness in phase four are incorporated and come in the screen, and join its measure of hardness. Hence, five kinds of coupling by striking are discerned in the screen, corresponding to the five measures of coarseness in it: A coupling by striking on a complete screen with all the levels of coarseness raises sufficient reflected light to clothe all ten Sefirot, up to the level of Keter. A coupling by striking on a screen that lacks the coarseness of phase four, and contains only the coarseness of phase three, raises sufficient reflected light to clothe the ten Sefirot only up to the level of Hochma, lacking Keter. And if it has only the coarseness of phase two, its reflected light diminishes and suffices only to clothe the ten Sefirot up to the level of Bina, lacking Keter and Hochma. If it contains only the coarseness of phase one, its reflected light diminishes even more and suffices only to clothe up to the level of Tifferet, lacking KHB. And if it lacks the coarseness of phase one, as well, and is left with only the coarseness of the root phase, its striking is very faint and suffices to clothe only up to the level of Malchut, lacking the first nine Sefirot, which are KHB and Tifferet.

22) Thus you see how the five levels of ten Sefirot emerge through five kinds of coupling by striking of the screen, applied to its five phases of coarseness. Now I shall tell you the reason, for it is known that light is not attained without a vessel.

Also, you know that these five phases of coarseness come from the five phases of coarseness in phase four. Prior to the restriction, there were five vessels in phase four, clothing the ten Sefirot KHB TM, as written in Item 18. After the first restriction, they were incorporated in the five phases of the screen, which, along with the reflected light it elevates, return to being five vessels with respect to the reflected light on the ten Sefirot KHB TM instead of the five vessels in phase four itself, prior to the restriction.

Accordingly, it is clear that if a screen contains all these five levels of coarseness, it contains the five vessels to clothe the ten Sefirot. But when it does not contain all five phases, since the coarseness of phase four is absent in it, it contains only four vessels. Hence, it can only clothe four lights, HB TM, and lacks one light—the light of Keter—just as it lacks one vessel—the coarseness of phase four.

Similarly, when it lacks phase three, too, and the screen contains only three phases of coarseness, meaning only up to phase two, it contains only three vessels. Thus, it can only clothe three lights: Bina, Tifferet, and Malchut. In that state, the level lacks the two lights Keter and Hochma, just as it lacks the two vessels, phase three and phase four.

And when the screen contains only two phases of coarseness, that is the root phase and phase one, it contains only two vessels. Hence, it clothes only two lights: the light of Tifferet and the light of Malchut. Thus, the level lacks the three lights KHB, just as it lacks the three vessels, phase two, phase three, and phase four.

When the screen has but one phase of coarseness, which is only the root phase of the coarseness, it has only one vessel; hence, it can clothe only one light: the light of Malchut. This level lacks the four lights KHB and Tifferet, as it lacks the four vessels, the coarseness of phase four, phase three, phase two, and phase one.

Thus, the level of each Partzuf depends precisely on the measure of coarseness in the screen. The screen of phase four elicits the level of Keter, phase three elicits the level of Hochma, phase two elicits the level of Bina, phase one elicits the level of Tifferet, and the root phase elicits the level of Malchut.

23) Yet, we must still find out why it is that when the vessel of Malchut—phase four—is absent from the screen, it lacks the light of Keter, and when the vessel of Tifferet is absent, it lacks the light of Hochma, etc. It seems as though it should have been the opposite, that when the vessel of Malchut, phase four, is absent from the screen, only the light of Malchut would be missing in the level, and it would have the four lights KHB and Tifferet. Also, in the absence of two vessels, phase three and phase four, it would lack the lights of Tifferet and Malchut, and the level would have the three lights KHB, etc. (see Item 20).

24) The answer is that there is always an inverse relation between lights and vessels. In the vessels, the higher ones grow first in the Partzuf: first Keter, then the vessel of Hochma, etc., and the vessel of Malchut grows last. This is why we name the vessels by the order KHB TM, from above downward, as this is the nature of their growth.

It is to the contrary with the lights. In the lights, the lower lights are the first to enter the Partzuf. First enters Nefesh, which is the light of Malchut, then Ruach, which is the light of ZA, etc., and the light of Yechida is the last to enter. This is why we name the lights by the order NRNHY [Nefesh-Ruach-Neshama-Haya-Yechida] from below upward, as this is the order by which they enter—from below upward.

Thus, when only one vessel has grown in the Partzuf, which is necessarily the highest vessel—Keter—the light of Yechida, related to that vessel, does not enter the Partzuf, but only the lowest light—the light of Nefesh. Thus, the light of Nefesh clothes the vessel of Keter.

When two vessels grow in the Partzuf, which are the highest two—Keter and Hochma—the light of Ruach enters it, as well. At that time, the light of Nefesh descends from the vessel of Keter to the vessel of Hochma, and the light of Ruach clothes the vessel of Keter.

Similarly, when a third vessel grows in the Partzuf—the vessel of Bina—the light of Neshama enters it. At that time, the light of Nefesh descends from the vessel of Hochma to the vessel of Bina, the light of Ruach to the vessel of Hochma, and the light of Neshama clothes the vessel of Keter.

When a fourth vessel grows in the Partzuf—the vessel of Tifferet—the light of Haya enters the Partzuf. Then the light of Nefesh descends from the vessel of Bina to the vessel of Tifferet, the light of Ruach to the vessel of Bina, the light of Neshama to the vessel of Hochma, and the light of Haya to the vessel of Keter.

And when a fifth vessel grows in the Partzuf, the vessel of Malchut, the light of Yechida enters it. At that time, all the lights enter their designated vessels. The light of Nefesh descends from the vessel of Tifferet to the vessel of Malchut, the light of Ruach to the vessel of Tifferet, the light of Neshama to the vessel of Bina, the light of Haya to the vessel of Hochma, and the light of Yechida to the vessel of Keter.

25) Thus, as long as not all five vessels KHB TM have grown in a Partzuf, the lights are not in their designated places. Moreover, they are in inverse relation: In the absence of the vessel of Malchut, the light of Yechida is absent, and when the two vessels, TM, are absent, Yechida and Haya are absent there, etc. This is so because in the vessels, the higher ones grow first, and in the lights, the last ones are the first to enter.

You will also find that each light that comes anew dresses only in the vessel of Keter. This is so because the receiver must receive in its most refined vessel, the vessel of Keter. For this reason, upon reception of each new light, the lights that are already dressed in the Partzuf must descend one degree from their place. For example, when the light of Ruach enters, the light of Nefesh must descend from the vessel of Keter to the vessel of Hochma to make room in the vessel of Keter to receive the new light, Ruach. Similarly, if the new light is Neshama, then Ruach, too, must descend from the vessel of Keter to the vessel of Hochma to vacate its place in Keter for the new light, Neshama. As a result, Nefesh, which was in the vessel of Hochma, must descend to the vessel of Bina, etc. All this is done to make room in the vessel of Keter for the new light.

Keep this rule in mind and you will always be able to discern in each issue if it is referring to the vessels or to the lights. Then you will not be confused, because there is always an inverse relation between them. Thus, we have thoroughly clarified the matter of the five phases in the screen, and how through them the levels change one below the other.

The Five Partzufim of AK

26) We have thoroughly clarified the issue of the screen that has been placed in the vessel of Malchut—phase four after having been restricted—and the issue of the five kinds of coupling by striking within it, which produce five levels of ten Sefirot one below the other. Now we shall explain the five Partzufim of AK that precede the four worlds ABYA.

You already know that this reflected light, which rises through the coupling by striking from below upward and dresses the ten Sefirot of the upper light, suffices only for the roots of the vessels, called "the ten Sefirot of the Rosh of the Partzuf." To complete the vessels, Malchut of the Rosh expands from those ten Sefirot of reflected light that clothed the ten Sefirot of the Rosh and expands from it and within it from above downward to the same extent as in the ten Sefirot of the Rosh. This expansion completes the vessels, called "the Guf of the Partzuf," as written in Item 14. Hence, we should always distinguish two phases of ten Sefirot in each Partzuf: Rosh and Guf.

27) In the beginning, the first Partzuf of AK emerged. This is because immediately following the first restriction, when phase four was banned from being a vessel of reception for the upper light, and was erected with a screen, the upper light was drawn to clothe in the vessel of Malchut, as before. Yet, the screen in the vessel of Malchut detained it and repelled the light. Through this striking in the screen of phase four, it raised reflected light up to the level of Keter in the upper light, and this reflected light became a clothing and the roots of the vessels for the ten Sefirot in the upper light, called "ten Sefirot of the Rosh" of "the first Partzuf of AK."

Subsequently, Malchut with the reflected light expanded and extended from her and within her by the force of the ten Sefirot of the Rosh into ten new Sefirot from above downward. This completed the vessels of the Guf. Then, the entire level that emerged in the ten Sefirot of the Rosh clothed in the ten Sefirot of the Guf, as well. This completed the first Partzuf of AK, Rosh and Guf.

28) Subsequently, that same coupling by striking repeated itself on the screen erected in the vessel of Malchut, which has only the coarseness of phase three. And then, only the level of Hochma, Rosh and Guf, emerged on it, since the absence of the screen in the coarseness of phase four caused it to have only four vessels, KHB Tifferet. Hence, the reflected light has room to clothe only four lights, *HNRN* [Haya, Neshama, Ruach, Nefesh], lacking the light of Yechida. This is called AB of AK.

Afterwards, that same coupling by striking repeated itself on the screen in the vessel of Malchut that contains only the coarseness of phase two. Then, ten Sefirot, Rosh and Guf, at the level of Bina emerged on it. This is called Partzuf SAG of AK. It lacks the two vessels, ZA and Malchut, and the two lights, Haya and Yechida.

Afterward, the coupling by striking emerged on a screen that has only the coarseness of phase one. Then ten Sefirot, Rosh and Guf, emerged at the level of Tifferet, lacking the three vessels, Bina, ZA, and Malchut, and the three lights, Neshama, Haya, and Yechida. It has only the lights Ruach and Nefesh, dressed in the vessels Keter and Hochma. This is called Partzuf MA and BON of AK. Remember the inverse relation between the vessels and the lights, as mentioned in Item 24.

29) Thus we have explained the emergence of the five Partzufim of AK, called Galgalta, AB, SAG, MA, and BON, one below the other. Each lower one lacks the higher phase of its upper one. Partzuf AB lacks the light of *Yechida*. Partzuf SAG lacks the light of *Haya*, as well, which its upper one, AB, has. Partzuf MA and BON lacks the light of *Neshama*, which its upper one, SAG, has.

This is so because it depends on the measure of coarseness in the screen on which the coupling by striking occurs, as explained in Item 18. Yet, we must understand who and what caused the screen to gradually diminish its coarseness, phase by phase, until it divided into the five levels that exist in these five kinds of coupling.

The Refinement of the Screen to the Emanation of the Partzuf

30) To understand the matter of the cascading of the degrees through five levels one below the other, explained above concerning the five Partzufim of AK, as well as in all the degrees appearing in the five Partzufim in each world of the four worlds ABYA, through Malchut of Assiya, we must thoroughly understand the matter of the refinement of the screen of the Guf that is implemented in each of the Partzufim of AK, the world of Nekudim, and the world of correction [Tikkun].

31) The thing is that there is no Partzuf, or any degree at all, that does not contain two lights, called "surrounding light" and "inner light," and we shall explain them in AK. The surrounding light of the first Partzuf of AK is the light of Ein Sof, which fills the whole of reality. Following the first restriction and the screen that was erected in Malchut, there was a coupling by striking from the light of Ein Sof on that screen. And through the reflected light that the screen raised, it drew the upper light to the restricted world once more, in the form of ten Sefirot of the Rosh and ten Sefirot of the Guf, as written in Item 25.

Yet, this extension from Ein Sof in Partzuf AK does not fill the whole of reality as prior to the restriction. Rather, it is discerned with a Rosh and a Sof [end]: From above downward, its light stops at the point of this world, which is the concluding Malchut, as in the verse, "His feet will stand on the Mount of Olives." And also from within outward, since as there are ten Sefirot KHB TM from above downward, and Malchut concludes the AK from below, so there are ten Sefirot KHB TM from within outward, called marrow, bones, tendons, flesh and skin [Mocha, Atzamot, Gidin, Bassar, and Or]. The skin is Malchut, which ends the Partzuf from the outside. In that respect, Partzuf AK is considered a mere thin line compared to Ein Sof, which fills the whole of reality. This is so because the Partzuf of skin ends it and limits it from all sides, from the outside, and it cannot expand and fill the entire restricted space. Thus, only a thin line remains standing in the middle of the space.

The measure of the light received in AK, the thin line, is called inner light. The difference between the inner light in AK and the light of Ein Sof prior to the restriction is called surrounding light, since it remains as surrounding light around Partzuf AK as it could not clothe within the Partzuf.

32) This thoroughly clarifies the meaning of the surrounding light of AK, whose immensity is immeasurable. Yet, this does not mean that Ein Sof, which fills the whole of reality, is in itself considered the surrounding light of AK. Rather, it means that a coupling by striking was made on Malchut of the Rosh of AK, where Ein Sof struck the screen that is placed there. In other words, it wished to dress in phase four of AK, as prior to the restriction, but the screen in Malchut of the Rosh of AK struck it. This means that it detained it from spreading into phase four and repelled it, as written in Item 14. Indeed, this reflected light that emerged from the pushing of the light back became vessels for clothing the upper light.

However, there is a very big difference between the reception in phase four prior to the restriction and the reception of the reflected light after the restriction, as now it clothed only a thin line in Rosh and Sof. This is what the screen did through its striking on the upper light. And the measure that was rejected from AK by the screen, the full measure of upper light from Ein Sof that wanted to clothe in phase four—had it not been for the screen that detained it—became the surrounding light surrounding AK.

The reason is that there is no change or absence in the spiritual. And since the light of Ein Sof is drawn to AK, to clothe in phase four, it must therefore be so. Hence, even though the screen has now detained it and repelled it, it does not contradict the extension of Ein Sof. On the contrary, it sustains it but in a different way: through proliferation of couplings in the five worlds AK and ABYA, until the end of correction, when phase four is completely corrected through them. At that time, Ein Sof will clothe in her as in the beginning.

Thus, no change or absence has occurred by the striking of the screen in the upper light. This is the meaning of what is written in *The Zohar*, "Ein Sof does not bring down His unification on her until He is given his mate." Meanwhile, that is, until that time, it is considered that this light of Ein Sof has become surrounding light, meaning it will clothe in it in the future. For now, it circles it and shines upon it from the outside with a certain illumination. This illumination accustoms it to expand by those laws that are fit to bring it to receive this surrounding light in the measure that Ein Sof was initially drawn to it.

33) Now we shall clarify the matter of the clashing of inner light and surrounding light on one another, which causes the refinement of the screen and the loss of the

last phase of coarseness. As these two lights are opposite yet connected through the screen in Malchut of the Rosh of AK, they beat and strike one another.

Interpretation: The coupling by striking in the Peh [mouth] of the Rosh of AK, in the screen in Malchut of the Rosh, called Peh, which was the reason for clothing the inner light of AK by the reflected light it raised (see Item 14), is also the reason for the exit of the surrounding light of AK. Because it detained the light of Ein Sof from clothing phase four, the light came out in the form of surrounding light.

In other words, that whole part of the light that the reflected light cannot clothe, like phase four herself, emerged and became surrounding light. Thus, the screen in the Peh is the reason for the surrounding light, as it is the reason for the inner light.

34) We have learned that both the inner light and surrounding light are connected to the screen, but in opposite actions. And to the extent that the screen draws a part of the upper light into the Partzuf through the reflected light that clothes it, so it drives the surrounding light away from clothing in the Partzuf.

And since the part of the light that remains outside as surrounding light is very large, due to the screen that detains it from clothing in AK, as written in Item 32, it is considered that it strikes the screen that removes it, since it wants to clothe within the Partzuf. In contrast, it is considered that the force of coarseness and hardness in the screen strikes the surrounding light, which wants to clothe within it, and detains it, as it strikes the upper light during the coupling. These beatings that the surrounding light and the coarseness in the screen beat on each other are called the clash of surrounding light and inner light.

Yet, this clash between them occurred only in the Guf of the Partzuf, since the clothing of the light in the vessels, which leaves the surrounding light outside the vessel, is apparent there. However, this clash does not apply to the ten Sefirot of the Rosh, since the reflected light is not considered vessels there whatsoever, but as mere thin roots. For this reason, the light in them is not regarded as limited inner light, to the point of discerning the light that remains outside as surrounding light. And since this distinction between them does not exist, there is no beating of inner light and surrounding light in the ten Sefirot of the Rosh.

Only once the lights extend from the Peh down to the ten Sefirot of the Guf—where the lights clothe in vessels, which are the ten Sefirot of reflected light from the Peh down—is there beating there between the inner light inside the vessels and the surrounding light that remained outside.

35) This clash continued until the surrounding light refined the screen from all its coarseness and elevated it to its upper root in the Peh of the Rosh. This means that it refined all the coarseness from above downward, called "screen and coarseness of the Guf," leaving it with only the root of the Guf, the screen of Malchut of the Rosh, called Peh. In other words, it had been refined of its entire coarseness from above downward, which divides between the inner light and the surrounding light,

leaving only the coarseness from below upward, where the distinction between the inner light and surrounding light has not occurred yet.

It is known that equivalence of form unites the spirituals into one. Hence, once the screen of the Guf has been refined of all the coarseness of the Guf, leaving in it only the coarseness that is equal to the screen of the Peh of the Rosh, its form was equalized with the screen of the Rosh. Thus, it was incorporated and became literally one with it, since there was nothing to divide them into two. This is considered that the screen of the Guf rose to the Peh of the Rosh.

Since the screen of the Guf was incorporated in the screen of the Rosh, it was incorporated once again in the coupling by striking in the screen of the Peh of the Rosh and a new coupling by striking was made on it. Consequently, ten new Sefirot emerged in it at a new level called AB of AK or Partzuf Hochma of AK. This is considered "a son" and a consequence of the first Partzuf of AK.

36) After Partzuf AB of AK emerged, complete with Rosh and Guf, the clash of surrounding light and inner light repeated itself there, too, as it was explained above concerning the first Partzuf of AK. Its screen of the Guf was refined from all its coarseness of the Guf, as well, until it equalized its form with its screen of the Rosh and was then incorporated in the coupling in its Peh of the Rosh.

Subsequently, a new coupling by striking was made on it, producing a new level of ten Sefirot at the level of Bina, called SAG of AK. This is considered a son and a consequence of Partzuf AB of AK, since it emerged from its coupling in the Peh of the Rosh. And the Partzufim from SAG of AK downward emerged in a similar manner.

37) Thus we have explained the emergence of the Partzufim one below the other by the clash of surrounding light and inner light, which refines the screen of the Guf until it brings it back to the state of the screen of the Peh of the Rosh. At that time, it is incorporated there in a coupling by striking, which takes place in the Peh of the Rosh, and through this coupling, it elicits a new level of ten Sefirot. This new level is considered the son of the previous Partzuf.

In this manner, AB emerged from Partzuf Keter, SAG from Partzuf AB, MA from Partzuf SAG, and so on with the remaining degrees in Nekudim and ABYA. Yet, we should still understand why the ten Sefirot of AB emerged only on phase three, and not on phase four, and why SAG was only on phase two, etc., meaning that each lower one is inferior to its upper one by one degree. Why did they not all emerge from one another on the same level?

38) First, we must understand why the ten Sefirot of AB are considered a consequence of the first Partzuf of AK, since it emerged from the coupling in the Peh of the Rosh of the first Partzuf, like the ten Sefirot of the Guf of the Partzuf itself. Thus, in what way did it emerge from the first Partzuf, to be considered a second Partzuf and its offshoot?

Here you must understand the big difference between the screen of the Rosh and the screen of the Guf. There are two kinds of Malchut in the Partzuf: The first is the mating Malchut—with the upper light—by the force of the screen erected in her. The second is the ending Malchut—the upper light in the ten Sefirot of the Guf—by the force of the screen erected in her.

The difference between them is as the distance between the Emanator and the emanated being. Malchut of the Rosh, which mates in a coupling by striking with the upper light, is considered "the Emanator of the Guf," since the screen erected in her did not reject the upper light as it struck it. On the contrary, through the reflected light that it raised, it clothed and drew the upper light in the form of ten Sefirot of the Rosh. Thus, it expands from above downward until the ten Sefirot of the upper light clothed in the vessel of reflected light, called Guf.

For this reason, the screen and the Malchut of the Rosh are considered the Emanator of the ten Sefirot of the Guf, and no limitation and rejection are apparent in that screen and Malchut. Yet, the screen and Malchut of the Guf, that is, after the ten Sefirot expanded from the Peh of the Rosh from above downward, they expand only down to the Malchut in those ten Sefirot. This is because the upper light cannot expand into Malchut of the Guf because of the screen erected there, which detains it from expanding into Malchut. Hence, the Partzuf stops there and a Sof [end] and Sium [conclusion] of the Partzuf are made.

Thus, the whole power of the restriction and limitation appears only in this screen and Malchut of the Guf. For this reason, the whole clash of surrounding light and inner light is only done in the screen of the Guf, as this is what limits and pushes the surrounding light away from shining in the internality of the Partzuf, and not in the screen of the Rosh, since the screen of the Rosh only extends and clothes the lights, and the power of the limitation is not yet revealed in it at all.

39) It follows that by the clash of surrounding light and inner light, the screen of the ending Malchut became the screen and Malchut of the mating Malchut once more (Item 35). This is because the clash of surrounding light refined the ending screen from all its coarseness of the Guf, leaving in it only fine records [Reshimot] of that coarseness, equal to the coarseness of the screen of the Rosh.

Also, it is known that equivalence of form attaches and unites the spirituals to one another. Hence, once the screen of the Guf equalized the form of its coarseness to the screen of the Rosh, it was immediately incorporated in it and they became seemingly one screen. In that state, it received the strength for coupling by striking like the screen of the Rosh, and ten Sefirot of the new level emerged on it.

Yet, along with this coupling, the records of the coarseness of the Guf, which were in it from the beginning, were renewed in its screen of the Guf. In that state, the disparity of form between it and the screen of the Rosh incorporated in it appeared in it once more to some extent. The recognition of this difference separates and removes it from the Peh of the Rosh of the upper one, since after its first origin from the Peh of the upper one downward has become apparent once more, it could not continue to stand above the Peh of the upper one, as the disparity of form separates the spirituals from one another. It follows that it was compelled to descend from there to the place from the Peh of the upper one downward.

Hence, it is necessarily considered a second Guf with respect to the upper one, as even the Rosh of the new level is considered as merely the Guf of the new level with respect to the upper one, since it extends from its screen of the Guf. Thus, this disparity of form distinguishes them into two separate Gufim [bodies]. And since the new level is entirely a consequence of the screen of the Guf of the previous Partzuf, it is considered its child, like a branch extending from it.

40) And there is another difference between the lower one and the upper one: Each lower one emerges with a different level in the five phases in the screen, as written in Items 22 and 24. Also, each lower one lacks the highest phase of the lights of the upper one and the lowest phase of the vessels of the upper one. The reason is that it is the nature of the clash of the surrounding light in the screen to eliminate from the screen its last phase of coarseness.

For example, in the first Partzuf of AK, whose screen contains all five levels of coarseness, down to phase four, the clash of surrounding light in the screen of the Guf completely refines the coarseness of phase four, not leaving even a record [Reshimo] of that coarseness. Only the records from the coarseness of phase three and above remain in the screen.

Hence, when that screen is incorporated in the Rosh and receives a coupling by striking on the coarseness that remained in its records from the Guf, the coupling emerges only on phase three of coarseness in the screen. This is because the record of coarseness of phase four is eliminated from there. Therefore, the level that emerges on that screen is only at the level of Hochma, called HaVaYaH of AB of AK, or Partzuf AB of AK.

We have already learned in Item 22 that the level Hochma that emerges on the screen of phase three lacks the Malchut of the vessels and the light of Yechida from the lights, which is the light of Keter. Thus, Partzuf AB lacks the last phase of the vessels of the upper one and the highest phase of the lights of the upper one. Because of this great disparity of form, the lower one is considered a separate Partzuf from the upper one.

41) Similarly, once Partzuf AB expanded in Rosh and Guf and there was the clash of surrounding light on the screen of the Guf of AB, which is a screen of phase three, this clash cancels and eliminates the record of coarseness of the last phase in the screen, which is phase three. It turns out that during the ascent of the screen to the Peh of the Rosh and its incorporation [Hitkalelut] in it in a coupling by striking, the striking was done only on the coarseness of phase two that remained in that screen,

since phase three has been eliminated from it. Hence, it elicits only ten Sefirot at the level of Bina, called HaVaYaH of SAG of AK, or Partzuf SAG, lacking ZA and Malchut in vessels, and Haya and Yechida in lights.

Similarly, when this Partzuf SAG expanded in Rosh and Guf, there was the clash of surrounding light in its screen of Guf, which is a screen of phase two. This clash cancels and eliminates the last phase of coarseness in the screen, which is phase two, leaving only the records of coarseness from phase one and above in the screen.

Hence, during the ascent of the screen to the Peh of the Rosh, and the incorporation in the coupling by striking there, the striking occurred only on the screen of phase one that remained in the screen, since phase two had already been eliminated from it. For this reason, it elicits only ten Sefirot at the level of Tifferet, called "the level of ZA," lacking Bina, ZA, and Malchut in the vessels, and Neshama, Haya, and Yechida in the lights, etc., similarly.

42) This thoroughly clarifies the reason for the decline of the levels one below the other during the cascading of the Partzufim from one another. It is because the clash of surrounding light and inner light, applied in each Partzuf, always eliminates the last phase of the record of coarseness that is there. Yet, we should know that there are two discernments in the records that remain in the screen after its refinement. The first is called the record of coarseness, and the second is called the record of clothing [Hitlabshut].

For instance, once the screen of the Guf of the first Partzuf in AK has been refined, we said that the last phase of the records of coarseness, the record of phase four, was lost, and all that remained in the screen was the record of coarseness of phase three. However the record of phase four contains two phases, as we have said—clothing and coarseness. Only the record of coarseness of phase four was eliminated from the screen by that refinement. But the record of clothing of phase four remained in that screen and was not eliminated from it.

A record of clothing refers to a very subtle phase from the record of phase four, which does not contain sufficient coarseness for a coupling by striking with the upper light. This record remains from the last phase in each Partzuf during its refinement. And our saying that the last phase is eliminated from each Partzuf during its refinement refers only to the record of coarseness in it.

43) The remainder of the records of clothing from the last phase that remained in each screen prompted the emergence of two levels—male and female—in the Roshim [heads] of all the Partzufim: beginning in AB of AK, SAG of AK, MA and BON of AK, and in all the Partzufim of Atzilut. This is so because in Partzuf AB of AK, where there is only a record of coarseness of phase three in the screen, which elicits ten Sefirot at the level of Hochma, the record of clothing from phase four, which remained there in the screen, is unfit for coupling with the upper light, due to its refinement. Yet, it is incorporated with the coarseness of phase three and becomes

one record. At that time, the record of clothing acquires the strength for coupling with the upper light. For this reason, the coupling by striking with the upper light emerged on her, eliciting ten Sefirot at nearly the level of Keter.

This is so because she had a clothing of phase four. This incorporation is called the incorporation of the female in the male, since the record of coarseness from phase three is called "female," as it carries the coarseness. And the record of clothing of phase four is called "male," as it comes from a higher place, and because it is refined from coarseness. Thus, although the record of the male is insufficient for a coupling by striking in itself, it becomes fit for a coupling by striking through the incorporation of the female in it.

44) Subsequently, there is incorporation of the male in the female, too. This means that the record of clothing is incorporated with the record of coarseness. This produces a coupling by striking only at the level of the female, the level of phase three, which is the level of Hochma, called HaVaYaH of AB. The upper coupling, when the female is incorporated in the male, is considered the level of the male, which is nearly the level of Keter. And the lower coupling, when the male is incorporated in the female, is considered the female level, which is only the level of Hochma.

Yet, the coarseness in the male level does not come from himself, but by means of incorporation with the female. And although it suffices to elicit the level of ten Sefirot from below upward, called Rosh, this level still cannot expand from above downward in the form of a Guf, which would mean clothing of lights in the vessels. This is so because a coupling by striking on coarseness that comes from the incorporation is insufficient to expand into vessels.

Hence, the male level contains only a phase of Rosh, without a Guf. The Guf of the Partzuf extends only from the female level, which has her own coarseness. For this reason, we name the Partzuf only after the female level, meaning Partzuf AB. This is so because the core of the Partzuf is its Guf—the clothing of the lights in the vessels. And it emerges only from the female level, as we have explained. This is why the Partzuf is named after her.

45) As we have explained concerning the two levels—male and female—in the Rosh of Partzuf AB, these two emerge in precisely the same manner in the Rosh of SAG. But there, the male level is nearly at the level of Hochma, as it is from the record of clothing of phase three incorporated with the coarseness of phase two. And the female level is at the level of Bina, from the coarseness of phase two. Here, too, the Partzuf is named solely after the female level, since the male is a Rosh without a Guf.

Similarly, in Partzuf MA of AK, the male level is nearly at the level of Bina, called "the level of YESHSUT," as it is from the record of phase two of clothing, incorporated with the coarseness from phase one, while the female level is only the level of ZA, as it is only phase one of coarseness. Here, too, the Partzuf is named solely after the female, meaning Partzuf MA or Partzuf VAK, since the male is a Rosh without a Guf. You will find it likewise in all the Partzufim.

Taamim, Nekudot, Tagin, Otiot
[Flavors, Dots, Tags, Letters (TNTO, pronounced Tanta)]

46) Now we have clarified the clash of surrounding light and inner light, occurring after the expansion of the Partzuf into a Guf. This causes the screen of the Guf to be refined, all the lights of the Guf depart, and the screen with the records that remain in it rise to the Peh of the Rosh, where they are renewed with a new coupling by striking, and produce a new level in the measure of coarseness in the records. Now we shall explain the four types of lights, Taamim, Nekudot, Tagin, Otiot, occurring with the clash of surrounding light and the ascents of the screen to the Peh of the Rosh.

47) It has been explained that through the clash of the surrounding light in the screen of the Guf, it refines the screen of all the coarseness of the Guf until it is refined and equalizes with the screen of the Peh of the Rosh. The equivalence of form with the Peh of the Rosh unites them as one, and it is incorporated in the coupling by striking in it.

However, the screen is not refined at once, but gradually: first from phase four to phase three, then from phase three to phase two, then from phase two to phase one, and then from phase one to the root phase. Finally, it is refined from all its coarseness and becomes as refined as the screen of the Peh of the Rosh.

The upper light does not stop shining for even a moment. It couples with the screen at each and every state of its refinement, since once it has been refined of phase four and the entire level of Keter has departed, and the screen has reached the coarseness of phase three, the upper light couples with the screen on the remaining coarseness of phase three and produces ten Sefirot at the level of Hochma.

Afterward, when the screen departs from phase three, too, and the level of Hochma departs, as well, leaving only phase two in the screen, the upper light couples with it on phase two and produces ten Sefirot at the level of Bina. Then, when it has been refined of phase two, too, and this level has departed, leaving only the coarseness of phase one in it, the upper light couples with the screen on the remaining coarseness of phase one and produces ten Sefirot at the level of ZA. And when it has been refined of the coarseness of phase one, too, and the level of ZA has departed, and it remains with only the root of the coarseness, the upper light makes a coupling on the coarseness of the root that remains in the screen and produces ten Sefirot at the level of Malchut.

And when the screen is refined of the coarseness of the root, as well, the level of Malchut departs thence, too, since no coarseness of the Guf remains there. In that state, it is considered that the screen and its records rose and united with the screen of the Rosh, became incorporated there in a coupling by striking and produced a new ten Sefirot over it, called a "son" and a "consequence" of the first Partzuf.

Thus we have explained that the clash of surrounding light and inner light that refines the screen of the Guf of the first Partzuf of AK and elevates it to its Peh of the Rosh, by which the second Partzuf, AB of AK, emerges, is not done at once. Rather, it occurs gradually, as the upper light couples with it at each state in the four degrees it traverses during its refinement, until it equalizes with the Peh of the Rosh.

As has been explained regarding the emergence of the four levels during the refinement of the Guf of the first Partzuf for the purpose of AB, three levels emerge during the time of the refinement of the screen of the Guf of Partzuf AB, as it emanates Partzuf SAG, and similarly in all the degrees. The rule is this: A screen does not become refined at once, but gradually. And the upper light, which does not stop expanding to the lower one, couples with it at each and every degree along its refinement.

48) Yet, these levels, which emerge on the screen during its gradual refinement, are not considered an expansion of real degrees, like the first level that emerged before the beginning of the refinement. Rather, they are considered Nekudot, and they are called reflected light and judgment [Din], since the power of judgment of the departure of the lights is already mingled in them. This is so because in the first Partzuf, as soon as the clash began to occur and it refined the screen of the Guf from phase four, it is considered as having been completely refined, since there is no "some (part)" in the spiritual.

Once it begins to be refined, it has to be refined completely. Yet, since the screen is refined gradually, there is time for the upper light to copulate with it at each degree of coarseness that the screen assumes during its refinement, until it is completely refined. Hence, the force of departure is mingled with the levels that emerge during its departure, and they are considered as only Nekudot and reflected light and judgment.

Therefore, we discern two types of levels in each Partzuf: Taamim and Nekudot. This is so because the first ten Sefirot of the Guf that emerge in each Partzuf are called Taamim, and the levels that emerge in the Partzuf as it refines, after the screen had already begun to be refined until it reaches the Peh of the Rosh, are called Nekudot.

49) The records that remain below, in the Guf, after the departure of the lights of Taamim, are called Tagin, and the records that remain from the levels of the Nekudot are called Otiot, which are vessels. Also, the Tagin, which are the records from the lights of Taamim, hover over the Otiot and the vessels and sustain them.

Thus we have clarified the four types of light, called Taamim, Nekudot, Tagin, Otiot. The first level to emerge in each Partzuf of the five Partzufim called Galgalta, AB, SAG, MA, and BON, is called Taamim. The levels that emerge in each Partzuf once it has started to be refined, until it is completely refined, are called Nekudot. The records that remain of the lights of Taamim in each level, after their departure, are called Tagin, and the records that remain from the lights of the levels of Nekudot after their departure are called Otiot or vessels. Remember this in all five Partzufim called Galgalta, AB, SAG, MA, and BON, for in all of them there is refinement and they all have these four types of lights.

The Rosh, Toch, Sof in Each Partzuf and the Order of Clothing of the Partzufim in One Another

50) You already know the difference between the two Malchuts in each Partzuf—the coupling Malchut and the ending Malchut. From the screen in the coupling Malchut, ten Sefirot of reflected light emerge from her and above, clothing the ten Sefirot of upper light, called "ten Sefirot of the Rosh," meaning only roots. From there down, the ten Sefirot of the Guf of the Partzuf expand in the form of clothing of lights in complete vessels.

These ten Sefirot of the Guf divide into two phases of ten Sefirot: ten Sefirot of Toch [inside], and ten Sefirot of Sof [end]. The ten Sefirot of Toch are positioned from the Peh [mouth] to the Tabur [navel], the place of the clothing of the lights in the vessels. The ten Sefirot of the Sium and Sof [both words mean "end"] of the Partzuf are positioned from the Tabur down to the Sium Raglin [end of the legs/feet].

This means that Malchut ends each Sefira until it reaches its own quality, which is unfit to receive any light, hence the Partzuf ends there. This cessation is called "the end of the Etzbaot Raglin [toes] of the Partzuf," and from there down it is a vacant and empty space without light.

Know that these two kinds of ten Sefirot extend from the root ten Sefirot, called Rosh, since both are incorporated in the coupling Malchut. This is so because there is the clothing power there—the reflected light that rises and clothes the upper light. There is also the screen's detaining force over Malchut so it would not receive the light. By this, the coupling by striking that raises reflected light occurs. At the Rosh, these two forces are only roots.

Yet, when they expand from above downward, the first force, which is a clothing force, is actualized in the ten Sefirot of Toch from the Peh down to the Tabur. The second force, which detains Malchut from receiving light, is actualized in the ten Sefirot of Sof and Sium, from Tabur down to the end of the Etzbaot Raglin.

These two kinds of ten Sefirot are always called HGT NHYM. All ten Sefirot of Toch, from Peh to Tabur, are called HGT, and all ten Sefirot of Sof from Tabur down are called NHYM.

51) We should also know that the restriction was only on the light of Hochma, whose vessel is the will to receive that ends at phase four, where the restriction and the screen occurred. Yet, there was no restriction at all on the light of Hassadim there, since its vessel is the will to bestow, in which there are no coarseness or disparity of form from the Emanator, and it does not need any corrections.

Hence, in the ten Sefirot of the upper light, these two lights, Hochma and Hassadim, are bound together without any difference between them, since they are one light that expands according to its quality. For this reason, when they come to clothe in the vessels after the restriction, the light of Hassadim stops at Malchut, too, even though it was not restricted. This is so because had the light of Hassadim expanded in a place where the light of Hochma could not expand even a bit, meaning the ending Malchut, there would be a shattering in the upper light, as the light of Hassadim would have to be completely separated from the light of Hochma. Hence, the ending Malchut became a completely vacant and empty space, devoid of even the light of Hassadim.

52) Now we can understand the content of the ten Sefirot of Sof of the Partzuf from Tabur down. It cannot be said that they are only considered light of Hassadim, without any Hochma, since the light of Hassadim is never completely separated from the light of Hochma. Rather, there is necessarily a small illumination of the light of Hochma in them, as well. You should know that we always call this small illumination "VAK without a Rosh." Thus, the three phases of ten Sefirot in the Partzuf, called Rosh, Toch, Sof, have been explained.

53) And now we shall explain the order of the clothing of the Partzufim Galgalta, AB, and SAG of AK on each other. Know that each lower one emerges from the screen of the Guf of the upper one, once it has been refined and has equalized its form with the Malchut and the screen at the Rosh. This is so because then it is incorporated in the screen at the Rosh, in the coupling by striking in it.

And once it undergoes the coupling by striking in the two records—coarseness and clothing—that remain in the screen of the Guf, its coarseness is recognized as coarseness of the Guf. Through this recognition, it is discerned that the level emerges from the Rosh of the first Partzuf of AK, descends, and clothes its Guf, meaning at her root, since she is from the screen of the Guf.

Indeed, the screen with the coupling Malchut of the new Partzuf had to descend to the place of Tabur of the first Partzuf, since the screen of the Guf with the ending Malchut of the first Partzuf begins there. Also, the root of the new Partzuf and its grip are there. Yet, the last phase of coarseness has been eliminated from the screen by the clash of inner light and surrounding light (see Item 40), and only the coarseness of phase three remained in the screen. This phase three of coarseness is called Chazeh [chest]. Hence, the screen and the coupling Malchut of the new Partzuf have no grip and root in the Tabur of the upper one, but only in its Chazeh, where it is attached like a branch to its root.

54) Hence, the screen of the new Partzuf descends to the place of the Chazeh of the first Partzuf, where it elicits ten Sefirot of the Rosh from it and above it through a coupling by striking with the upper light, up to the Peh of the upper one, which is the Malchut of the Rosh of the first Partzuf. But the lower one cannot clothe the ten Sefirot of the Rosh of the upper Partzuf at all, since it is considered merely the screen

of the Guf of the upper one. Subsequently, it elicits ten Sefirot from above downward, called "the ten Sefirot of the Guf" at the Toch and the Sof of the lower one.

Their place is only from the Chazeh of the upper Partzuf down to its Tabur, since from the Tabur down is the place of the ten Sefirot of the Sium of the upper one, which is phase four. The lower one has no grip of the last phase of the upper one since it loses it during its refinement (see Item 40). For this reason, that lower Partzuf, called Partzuf Hochma of AK, or Partzuf AB of AK, must end above the Tabur of the first Partzuf of AK.

Thus, it has been thoroughly clarified that any Rosh, Toch, Sof of Partzuf AB of AK, which is the lower one of the first Partzuf of AK, stand from the place below the Peh of the first Partzuf down to its Tabur. Thus, the Chazeh of the first Partzuf is the place of the Peh of the Rosh of Partzuf AB, meaning the coupling Malchut, and the Tabur of the first Partzuf is the place of the Sium Raglin of Partzuf AB, that is, the ending Malchut.

55) As has already been explained regarding the order of the emergence of Partzuf AB from the first Partzuf of AK, it is the same in all the Partzufim through the end of the world of Assiya. Each lower one emerges from the screen of the Guf of its upper one after it has been refined and incorporated in the screen of Malchut of the Rosh of the upper one in the coupling by striking there.

Afterward, it descends from there to its gripping point in the Guf of the upper one and elicits the ten Sefirot of the Rosh from below upward in its place through a coupling by striking with the upper light. Also, it expands from above downward into ten Sefirot of the Guf in Toch and Sof, as has been explained in Partzuf AB of AK. Yet, there are differences concerning the Sium of the Partzuf, as it is written elsewhere.

The Second Restriction [Tzimtzum Bet], Called the Restriction of NHY of AK

56) We have thoroughly explained the first restriction [Tzimtzum Aleph], carried out on the vessel of Malchut, which is phase four, so it would not receive the upper light within it. We have also explained the matter of the screen and its coupling by striking with the upper light, which raises reflected light. This reflected light became new vessels of reception instead of phase four.

Also explained was the refinement of the screen of the Guf, made in the Gufim [plural of Guf] of each Partzuf by the clash of surrounding light and inner light, which produces the four discernments Taamim, Nekudot, Tagin, Otiot of the Guf of each Partzuf and raises the screen of the Guf to be considered the screen of the Rosh. It qualifies it for a coupling by striking with the upper light, on which another Partzuf is born, one degree lower than the previous Partzuf. Finally, we have explained the emergence of the first three Partzufim of AK, called Galgalta, AB, SAG, and the order of their clothing on one another.

57) Know that in these three Partzufim, Galgalta, AB, and SAG of AK, there is not even a root for the four worlds ABYA, since there is not even a place for the three worlds BYA here. This is because the inner Partzuf of AK extended down to the point of this world, and the root of the desirable correction, which was the cause for the restriction, has not been revealed. This is so because the purpose of the restriction that occurred in phase four was to correct it, so there would be no disparity of form in it as it receives the upper light (see Item 10).

In other words, to create Adam's Guf from that phase four, and with his engagement in Torah and Mitzvot in order to bestow contentment upon his Maker, he will turn the force of reception in phase four to work in order to bestow. By this he will equalize the form of reception with complete bestowal, and that would be the end of correction, since this would bring phase four back to being a vessel of reception for the upper light, while also being in complete adhesion with the light, without any disparity of form.

Yet, thus far, the root of this correction has not been revealed, as this requires Adam to be incorporated also with the higher phases, above phase four, so as to be able to perform good deeds of bestowal. Had Adam emerged from the state of the Partzufim of AK, he would have been completely in the state of vacant space since then all of phase four, which should be the root of Adam's Guf, would have been below the Raglaim [feet] of AK, in the form of a vacant and empty space, devoid of light, as it would be of opposite form from the upper light. Thus, it would be considered separated and dead.

Had Adam been created from it, he would not have been able to correct his actions whatsoever, since there would be no sparks of bestowal in him at all. He would be deemed a beast that has none of the form of bestowal, and whose lives are only for themselves, like the wicked who are immersed in the lust of self-reception, and "even the grace that they do, they do for themselves." It is said about them, "The wicked in their lives are called 'dead,'" since they are in oppositeness of form from the Life of Lives.

58) This is the meaning of our sages' words (*Beresheet Rabbah*, end of Portion 12): "In the beginning, He contemplated creating the world with the quality of judgment [Din]. He saw that the world could not exist and brought forward the quality of mercy [Rachamim] and associated it with the quality of judgment."

Explanation: Every "first" and "next" in spirituality refers to cause and consequence. This is why it is written that the first cause for the worlds, meaning the Partzufim of AK that were emanated before all the worlds, were emanated in the quality of judgment, that is, in Malchut alone, called the quality of judgment. This refers to phase four, which has been restricted and departed as a vacant and empty space and the Sium of the Raglaim of AK. This is the point of this world, below the Sium Raglaim of AK's, in the form of a vacant and empty space, devoid of any light.

"He saw that the world does not exist" means that in this way, it was impossible for Adam, who should be created from this phase four, to acquire acts of bestowal, so that through him the world would exist in the desired measure of correction. This is why he "associated the quality of mercy with the quality of judgment."

Explanation: The Sefira of Bina is called the quality of mercy, and the Sefira Malchut is called the quality of judgment, since the restriction was made on her. The Emanator raised the quality of judgment, which is the force of Sium made in the Sefira of Malchut, and raised it to Bina— the quality of mercy. He associated them with one another, and through this association, phase four— the quality of judgment —was incorporated with the sparks of bestowal in the vessel of Bina (see Item 5).

This qualified Adam's Guf, which emerged from phase four, to be incorporated with the quality of bestowal, too. Thus, he will be able to perform good deeds in order to bestow contentment upon his Maker until he inverts the quality of reception in him to work entirely in order to bestow. Thus, the world will achieve the desired correction for which the world was created.

59) This association of Malchut in Bina occurred in Partzuf SAG of AK, and prompted a second restriction in the worlds from it downward. This is because a new Sium on the upper light was made on it in the place of Bina. It follows that the ending Malchut, which stood at the Sium Raglaim of SAG of AK, above the point of this world, ascended and ended the upper light at the place of half of Bina of the Guf of SAG of AK, called Tifferet, since KHB of the Guf is called HGT. Thus, Tifferet is Bina of the Guf.

Also, the coupling Malchut, which stood at the Peh of the Rosh of SAG of AK, ascended to the place of Nikvey Eynaim [pupils] of AK, which is half of Bina of the Rosh. Then, a coupling for the MA of AK, called "the world of Nekudim" was made there, at the Nikvey Eynaim

60) This is also called the restriction of NHY of AK, since SAG of AK, which ended equally with Partzuf Galgalta of AK, above the point of this world, ends above the Tabur of the inner AK through the association and the ascent of Malchut to the place of Bina, at half the Tifferet, which is half the Bina of the Guf of the inner AK. This is so because the ending Malchut ascended to that place and detained the upper light from expanding from it downward.

For this reason, a vacant and empty space was made there, devoid of light. Thus, the TNHY [Tifferet, Netzah, Hod, Yesod] of SAG became restricted and devoid of the upper light. This is why the second restriction is called "restriction of NHY of AK," since through the new Sium at the place of Tabur, NHY of SAG of AK were emptied of their lights.

It is also considered that the AHP of the Rosh of SAG departed from the degree of the Rosh of SAG and became its Guf, since the coupling Malchut ascended to Nikvey Eynaim and the ten Sefirot of the Rosh emerged from the screen at Nikvey

Eynaim and above. Also, from Nikvey Eynaim down it is considered the Guf of the Partzuf, since it can only receive illumination from Nikvey Eynaim and below, which is considered Guf.

The level of these ten Sefirot that emerged at the Nikvey Eynaim of SAG of AK are the ten Sefirot called "the world of Nekudim." They came down from the Nikvey Eynaim of SAG to their place below the Tabur of the inner AK, where they expanded with Rosh and Guf. Know that this new Sium, made at the place of Bina of the Guf, is called Parsa. Also, there is internality and externality here, and only the external ten Sefirot are called "the world of Nekudim," while the ten inner Sefirot are called MA and BON of AK itself.

61) Yet, we should understand that since the ten Sefirot of Nekudim and the MA of AK were emanated and emerged from the Nikvey Eynaim of the Rosh of SAG, they should have clothed the SAG from its Peh of the Rosh and below, as with the other Partzufim, where each lower one clothes its upper one from the Peh of the Rosh downward. Why was it not so? Why did they descend and clothe the place below Tabur of AK? To understand this, we must thoroughly understand how this association came about, when Bina and Malchut connected into one.

62) The thing is that during the emergence of Partzuf SAG, it ended entirely above the Tabur of the inner AK, as has been explained concerning Partzuf AB of AK. They could not expand from the Tabur down, since the governance of phase four of the inner AK begins there, in its ten Sefirot of Sium, and there is nothing of phase four whatsoever in the Partzufim AB and SAG (see Item 54).

Yet, when the Nekudot of SAG of AK began to emerge, after the screen of SAG, which is phase two of coarseness, has been refined through the clash of surrounding light in it, and came to phase two of clothing and phase one of coarseness, the Taamim of SAG departed. Then, the level of Nekudot emerged on the coarseness that remained in the screen, in VAK without a Rosh.

This is so because the ten Sefirot that emerge on phase one of coarseness are the level of ZA, lacking GAR. Also, there is no phase of Bina at the male level, which is phase two of clothing, but only nearly that, which is considered VAK of Bina.

Hence, this level of Nekudot of SAG has equalized its form with the ten Sefirot of Sium below the Tabur of AK, considered VAK without a Rosh, too (see Item 52). It is known that equivalence of form unites the spirituals into one. Hence, this level descended below the Tabur of AK and mingled there with ZON of AK, where they were as one, since they are of equal level.

63) We might wonder at the fact that there is still a great distance between them with respect to their coarseness, since Nekudot of SAG come from the coarseness of phase two and have nothing of phase four. And although they are the level of ZA, it is not like the level of ZA below the Tabur of AK, which is ZA of phase four. Thus, there is a big difference between them.

The answer is that the coarseness is not apparent in the Partzuf during the clothing of the light, but only after the departure of the light. Hence, when Partzuf Nekudot of SAG appeared at the level of ZA, descended, and clothed at the level of ZON from Tabur of AK downward, phase two and phase four were mingled together and caused the second restriction. This created a new Sium at the place of Bina of the Guf of that Partzuf, and also caused a change in the place of the coupling, making it the Peh of the Rosh instead of the Nikvey Eynaim.

64) Thus, you find that the origin of the association of Malchut in Bina, called the second restriction, occurred only below Tabur of AK, by the expansion of Partzuf Nekudot of SAG there. Hence, this level of ten Sefirot of Nekudim, which comes from the second restriction, could not expand above Tabur of AK, since no force or ruling can appear above its origin. And since the place of the forming of the second restriction began from Tabur and below, the level of Nekudim had to expand there, as well.

The Place for the Four Worlds ABYA, and the Parsa between Atzilut and BYA

65) Thus we have learned that the second restriction occurred only in Partzuf Nekudot of SAG, positioned from Tabur of AK downward through its Sium Raglin, that is, above the point of this world. Know that all the changes that followed that second restriction came only in that Partzuf Nekudot of SAG, and not above it.

When we said that above, through Malchut's ascent to half of Tifferet of AK she ended the Partzuf, and the lower half of Tifferet and NHYM of AK came out in the form of empty space, this did not occur in TNHY of AK itself, but only in TNHY of Partzuf Nekudot of SAG of AK. Yet, in AK itself, these changes are considered a mere raising of MAN. In other words, it clothed in these changes to emanate the ten Sefirot of Nekudim themselves, though no change took place in AK itself.

66) As soon as the restriction occurred, during the ascent of Malchut to Bina, even before the raising of MAN and the coupling that was made at the Nikvey Eynaim of AK, it caused Partzuf Nekudot of SAG of AK to divide into four divisions:

1. KHB HGT up to its Chazeh are considered the place of Atzilut.

2. The two lower thirds of Tifferet, from the Chazeh down to the Sium of Tifferet, became the place of the world of Beria.

3. Its three Sefirot NHY became the place of the world of Yetzira.

4. The Malchut in it became the place of the world of Assiya.

67) The reason for it is that the place of the world of Atzilut means the place worthy of the expansion of the upper light. And because of the ascent of the ending Malchut to the place of Bina of the Guf, called Tifferet, the Partzuf ends there and the light cannot pass from there down. Thus, the place of Atzilut ends there at half the Tifferet on the Chazeh.

You already know that this new Sium that was made here is called "the Parsa below the world of Atzilut." There are three divisions in the Sefirot below the Parsa, since indeed, only two Sefirot, ZON of the Guf, called NHYM, needed to emerge below the Atzilut. This is so because the Sium was made at the Bina of the Guf, which is Tifferet; hence, only the ZON below Tifferet are below the Sium, and not Tifferet, although the lower half of Tifferet emerged below the Sium, as well.

The reason is that Bina of the Guf is incorporated with the ten Sefirot KHB ZON, as well. Since these ZON of Bina are the roots of the general ZON of the Guf, which were incorporated in Bina, they are considered like them. Hence, ZON of Bina emerged below the Parsa of Atzilut, as well, along with the general ZON. For this reason, the Sefira Tifferet was fissured across at the place of the Chazeh, since Malchut that ascended to Bina stands there and brings out the ZON of Bina, that is, the two thirds of Tifferet from the Chazeh down to its Sium.

Yet, there is still a difference between the two thirds of Tifferet and the NHYM. The two thirds of Tifferet truly belong to the Bina of the Guf and did not emerge below the Sium of Atzilut of their own accord, but only because they are the roots of ZON. Hence, their flaw is not so great since their emergence is not because of themselves. Thus, they have become separated from the NHYM and became a world in and of themselves, called "the world of Beria."

68) ZON of the Guf, called NHYM, also divided into two phases: Since Malchut is considered Nukva [female], her flaw is greater, and she becomes the place of the world of Assiya. ZA, who is NHY, became the world of Yetzira, above the world of Assiya.

Thus we have explained how Partzuf Nekudot of SAG was divided by the second restriction and became the place of four worlds: Atzilut, Beria, Yetzira, Assiya. KHB HGT, down to its Chazeh, became the place of the world of Atzilut; the lower half of Tifferet, from the Chazeh to the Sium of Tifferet, became the place of the world of Beria; the NHY in it—the world of Yetzira; and its Malchut—the world of Assiya. Their place begins from the point of Tabur of AK and ends above the point of this world, that is, through the Sium Raglin of AK, which is the end of the clothing of Partzuf Nekudot of SAG over Partzuf Galgalta of AK.

The Katnut and Gadlut Initiated in the World of Nekudim

69) Now that you know about the second restriction that occurred in Partzuf Nekudot of SAG for the purpose of emanating the ten Sefirot of the world of Nekudim, the fourth Partzuf of AK, we shall go back and explain the emergence of the ten Sefirot of Nekudim in particular. The emergence of one Partzuf from another has already been explained. Each lower Partzuf is born and emerges from the screen of the Guf of the upper one, after its refinement and ascent for renewing the coupling in the Peh of the upper one. The cause of this refinement is the clash of surrounding light

with the screen of the upper Partzuf, which refines the screen from its coarseness of the Guf, and equalizes it with the coarseness of the Rosh (see Item 35).

In this manner, Partzuf AB of AK emerged from Partzuf Keter of AK, Partzuf SAG of AK from Partzuf AB of AK, and the fourth Partzuf of AK, called "the ten Sefirot of the world of Nekudim," was born and emerged from its upper one, being SAG of AK, in the same way.

70) Yet, there is another issue here. In the previous Partzufim, the screen was made only of the records of coarseness of the Guf of the upper one, during the refinement of the screen to the Peh of the Rosh of the upper one. But here, in the refinement of the screen of SAG of AK for Nekudim, this screen contained two kinds of records. Besides containing its own records of coarseness, with respect to the Sefirot of the Guf of SAG of AK, it also contains the records of coarseness of ZON of AK below the Tabur, due to their mixture together below Tabur of AK, as it is written in Item 61, that Nekudot of SAG descended below Tabur of AK and mixed with ZON of AK there.

71) Thus, the matter of Katnut [smallness/infancy] and Gadlut [greatness/adulthood] has been initiated here in Partzuf Nekudim. With respect to the records of coarseness in the screen, ten Sefirot of Katnut of Nekudim emerged over them. With respect to the records of ZON of AK below Tabur, which connected and mingled with the records of the screen, the ten Sefirot of Gadlut of Nekudim emerged over them.

72) You should also know that the ten Sefirot of Katnut of Nekudim that emerged on the screen are considered the core of Partzuf Nekudim, since they emerged by order of degrees, that is, from the actual screen of the Guf of the upper one, in the same way the three previous Partzufim of AK emerged. But the ten Sefirot of Gadlut of Nekudim are regarded as a mere addition to Partzuf Nekudim because they emerged only from the coupling on the records of ZON of AK below Tabur, which did not appear by order of degrees but were connected and added to the screen due to the decline of Partzuf Nekudot of SAG below the Tabur of AK, see Item 70.

73) First we shall clarify the ten Sefirot of Katnut of Nekudim. You already know that following the expansion of SAG of AK, it underwent the clash of surrounding light and inner light on its screen, which gradually refined it. The levels that emerged as it refined are called Nekudot of SAG, and they descended below Tabur of AK and mingled with phase four there (see Item 62). After it completed its refinement of all the coarseness of the Guf in the screen and remained with only coarseness of the Rosh, it is considered to have ascended to the Rosh of SAG, where it received a new coupling on the measure of coarseness that remained in the records in the screen, as has been explained above in Item 35.

74) Here, too, it is considered that the last phase of coarseness, the coarseness of phase two that was in the screen, was completely eliminated, leaving only the record of clothing. Thus, nothing was left of the coarseness but phase one. Hence, the screen

received two kinds of coupling in the Rosh of SAG (see Item 43). The incorporation of phase one of coarseness in phase two of clothing, called "the incorporation of the record of the female in the record of the male," elicited a level at nearly the degree of Bina, which is the degree of VAK of Bina. This level is called "the Sefira Keter of Nekudim." The incorporation of the male with the record of the female, the record of phase two of clothing in phase one of coarseness, elicited the level of ZA, considered VAK without a Rosh, called "Aba and Ima of Nekudim back to back."

These two levels are called GAR of Nekudim; that is, they are considered ten Sefirot of the Rosh of Nekudim, since each Rosh is called GAR or KHB. But there is a difference between them: Keter of Nekudim, which is at the male level, does not expand into the Guf and shines only at the Rosh. Only AVI [Aba (Father) ve (and) Ima (Mother)] of Nekudim, which are the female level, called "the lower seven Sefirot of Nekudim" or "HGT NHY of Nekudim" expand to the Guf.

75) Thus, there are three degrees here one below the other. The first is Keter of Nekudim, with the level of VAK of Bina. The second is the level of AVI of Nekudim, which has the level of ZA. These are both considered Rosh. The third is ZAT of Nekudim, HGT NHYM, considered Guf of Nekudim.

76) Know, that by Malchut's ascent to Bina, these two degrees of Nekudim split into two halves upon their emergence, called anterior [Panim] and posterior [Achoraim]. This is so because since the coupling was made at the Nikvey Eynaim, there are only two and a half Sefirot at the Rosh—Galgalta, Eynaim [eyes] and Nikvey Eynaim, that is, Keter, Hochma, and the upper half of Bina. These are called the anterior vessels.

The vessels of AHP, which are the lower half of Bina, ZA, and Nukva, emerged from the ten Sefirot of the Rosh and were considered the degree below the Rosh. Hence, the vessels of the Rosh, which departed from the Rosh, are considered posterior vessels. Each degree was split in this manner.

77) It follows that there is not a single degree that does not have anterior and posterior. This is because the AHP of the male level, the Keter of Nekudim, emerged from the degree of Keter and descended to the degree of AVI of Nekudim, the female level. And AHP of the female level—AVI of Nekudim—descended and fell to their degree of Guf, the degree of the seven Sefirot HGT NHY of Nekudim.

It turns out that AVI comprise two phases, anterior and posterior since within them is the posterior of the degree of Keter, that is, the AHP of Keter, and atop them clothe the anterior vessels of AVI themselves, that is, their own Galgalta, Eynaim, and Nikvey Eynaim. Also, ZAT of Nekudim comprise anterior and posterior: The posterior vessels of AVI, which are their AHP, are within the ZAT, and the anterior vessels of ZAT clothe them from the outside.

78) This issue of the division of degrees into two halves made the degrees of Nekudim unable to have more than Nefesh Ruach, meaning VAK without GAR.

This is so because each degree lacks the three vessels, Bina and ZON; hence, the lights of GAR, being Neshama, Haya, Yechida, are absent there (see Item 24). Thus we have thoroughly explained the ten Sefirot of Katnut of Nekudim, which are the three degrees called Keter, AVI, and ZAT. Each degree has only Keter Hochma in vessels, and Nefesh Ruach in lights, since the Bina and ZON in each degree fell to the degree below it.

Raising MAN and the Emergence of Gadlut of Nekudim

79) Now we shall explain the ten Sefirot of Gadlut of Nekudim, which emerged on the MAN of the records of ZON of AK below its Tabur (see Item 71). First, we must understand the matter of raising MAN. Thus far, we have only discussed the ascent of the screen of the Guf to the Peh of the Rosh of the upper one, once it has refined. There was a coupling by striking on the records incorporated in it, which elicits the level of ten Sefirot for the purpose of the lower one. Now, however, the issue of raising Mayin Nukvin [MAN/female water] has been initiated, for these lights, which rose from below Tabur of AK to the Rosh of SAG, which are the records of ZON of the Guf of AK, are called "raising MAN."

80) Know, that the origin of raising MAN is from ZA and Bina of the ten Sefirot of direct light [Ohr Yashar] that were explained above in Item 5. It is explained there that Bina, which is the phase of light of Hassadim, reunited with Hochma when she emanated the Sefira of Tifferet, called phase three, and extended from it illumination of Hochma for Tifferet, which is ZA. ZA emerged primarily from the light of Hassadim of Bina, and secondarily with the illumination of Hochma.

This is where the connection between ZA and Bina was made, as each time the records of ZA rise to Bina, Bina connects with Hochma and extends illumination of Hochma from it for ZA. This ascent of ZA to Bina, which connects it to Hochma, is always called "raising MAN." Without the ascent of ZA to Bina, Bina is not considered Nukva to Hochma, since she herself is only light of Hassadim and does not need light of Hochma.

She is always considered to be back-to-back with Hochma, which means that she does not want to receive from Hochma. Only when ZA ascends to her does she become Nukva for Hochma once more, in order to receive illumination of Hochma from it for ZA. Thus, the ascent of ZA makes her a Nukva, and this is why its ascent is called Mayin Nukvin, as the ascent of ZA brings her face-to-face with Hochma once more. This means that she receives from him as a female from a male. Thus we have thoroughly clarified the raising of MAN.

81) You already know that Partzuf AB of AK is Partzuf Hochma, and Partzuf SAG of AK is Partzuf Bina. This means that they are discerned according to the highest phase of their level. AB, whose highest phase is Hochma, is considered all Hochma. SAG, whose highest phase is Bina, is considered all Bina.

Thus, when the records of ZON of the Guf below Tabur of AK ascended to the Rosh of SAG, they became MAN to the SAG there, for which SAG, which is Bina, coupled with Partzuf AB, which is Hochma. Subsequently, AB imparted to SAG a new light for the purpose of the ZON below the Tabur that ascended there.

Once ZON of AK received this new light, they descended back to their place below the Tabur of AK where there are the ten Sefirot of Nekudim, and they shone the new light inside the ten Sefirot of Nekudim. This is the Mochin [light] of Gadlut of the ten Sefirot of Nekudim. Thus we have explained the ten Sefirot of Gadlut that emerged on the second type of records, which are the records of ZON below the Tabur of AK (see Item 71). Indeed, it is this Mochin of Gadlut that caused the breaking of the vessels, as will be written below.

82) It has been explained above, in Item 74, that there are two degrees in the Rosh of Nekudim, called Keter and AVI. Hence, when ZON of AK shone the new light of AB SAG to the ten Sefirot of Nekudim, it first shone to the Keter of Nekudim through Tabur of AK, where Keter clothes, and completed it with GAR in lights and Bina and ZON in vessels. Subsequently, it shone to AVI of Nekudim through the Yesod of AK, where AVI clothe, and completed them with GAR in lights and Bina and ZON in vessels.

83) First, let us explain the matter of the Gadlut which this new light caused in the ten Sefirot of Nekudim. The thing is that we may ask about what is written above (in Item 74), that the level of Keter and AVI of Nekudim were considered VAK because they emerged on coarseness of phase one. But we have said that through the descent of Nekudot of SAG below Tabur of AK, phase four connected to the screen of Nekudot of SAG, which is Bina. Thus, this screen has a record of phase four of coarseness, as well. In that case, during the incorporation of the screen in the Rosh of SAG, ten Sefirot should have emerged at the level of Keter and the light of Yechida, and not at the level of VAK of Bina in the Sefira of Keter, and the level of VAK without a Rosh in AVI.

The answer is that the place is the cause. Since phase four is incorporated in Bina, which is Nikvey Eynaim, the coarseness of phase four disappeared there inside Bina, as though it is not there at all. Hence, the coupling was made only on the records of phase two of clothing and phase one of coarseness, which are from the core of the screen of Bina alone, as written in Item 74, and only two levels emerged there: VAK of Bina and complete VAK.

84) Therefore, now ZON of AK below Tabur extended the new light through their MAN from AB SAG of AK and shone it to the Rosh of Nekudim (see Item 81). And since Partzuf AB of AK has no contact with this second restriction, which elevated phase four to the place of Nikvey Eynaim, when its light was drawn to the Rosh of Nekudim, it canceled the second restriction within it once again, which elevated the place of the coupling to Nikvey Eynaim and lowered phase four back to its place at the Peh, as it was at the time of the first restriction, that is, in the place of Peh of the Rosh.

Thus, the three vessels—Ozen [ear], Hotem [nose], and Peh [mouth]—that fell from the degree because of the second restriction (see Item 76), now returned to their place—their degree—as before. At that time, the place of the coupling descended once more from Nikvey Eynaim to phase four at the place of the Peh of the Rosh. Since phase four is already at her place, ten Sefirot emerged there at the degree of Keter.

Thus it has been explained that through the new light that ZON of AK extended to the Rosh of Nekudim, it gained the three lights Neshama, Haya, Yechida, and the three vessels AHP, which are Bina and ZON, that it lacked when it first emerged.

85) Now we have thoroughly clarified the Katnut and Gadlut of Nekudim. The second restriction, which raised the bottom Hey—phase four—to the place of Nikvey Eynaim, where it was concealed, caused the level of Katnut of Nekudim—the level of VAK or ZA in lights of Nefesh Ruach. There they were lacking Bina and ZON in vessels and Neshama, Haya, and Yechida in lights. And through the arrival of a new light of AB SAG of AK to the Nekudim, the first restriction returned to its place.

Bina and ZON of the vessels returned to the Rosh, since the bottom Hey descended from the Nikvey Eynaim and returned to her place—Malchut, called Peh. Then a coupling was made on phase four, which returned to her place, and ten Sefirot at the level of Keter and Yechida emerged. This completed the NRNHY of lights and the KHB ZON of vessels.

For short, we will henceforth refer to the second restriction and the Katnut by the name "ascent of the bottom Hey to Nikvey Eynaim and the descent of AHP below." Also, we will refer to the Gadlut by the name "the arrival of the light of AB SAG, which lowers the bottom Hey from the Nikvey Eynaim and brings the AHP back to their place." Remember this above explanation.

You should also remember that GE [Galgalta-Eynaim] and AHP [Ozen, Hotem, Peh, pronounced Achap] are names of the ten Sefirot KHB ZON of the Rosh, and the ten Sefirot of the Guf are called HGT NHYM. They, too, divide into GE and AHP, since Hesed and Gevura and the upper third of Tifferet through the Chazeh are Galgalta and Eynaim and Nikvey Eynaim, and the two thirds of Tifferet and NHYM are AHP, as has been written above.

Also, remember that Galgalta, Eynaim, and Nikvey Eynaim, or HGT through the Chazeh, are called anterior vessels, and AHP, or the two lower thirds of Tifferet and NHYM from the Chazeh down are called posterior vessels, as written in Item 76. You should also remember the matter of the fissuring of the degree that occurred with the second restriction, which left only anterior vessels in each degree, and each lower one has within it the posterior vessels of the upper one, as written in Item 77.

Explaining the Three Nekudot [dots] Holam, Shuruk, Hirik

86) Know that the Nekudot [dots] are divided into three phases—Rosh, Toch, and Sof. These are the upper Nekudot, above the Otiot [letters], incorporated in the name Holam, the middle Nekudot inside the Otiot, included in the name Shuruk or Melafom, meaning Vav and a dot within it, and the lower Nekudot below the Otiot that are incorporated in the name Hirik.

87) This is their explanation: Otiot [letters] are vessels, meaning the Sefirot of the Guf. This is because the ten Sefirot of the Rosh are but roots to the vessels, not actual vessels. Nekudot means lights, which sustain the vessels and move them, meaning light of Hochma, called light of Haya. This is considered a new light, which ZON of AK received from AB SAG and shone to the vessels of Nekudim, lowering the bottom Hey back to the Peh of each degree, and bringing the AHP of vessels and GAR of lights back to the degree.

Thus, this light moves the vessels of AHP and elevates them from the lower degree, connecting them to the upper one, as in the beginning. This is the meaning of the Nekudot that move the Otiot. Since this light extends from AB of AK, which is light of Haya, it revives those vessels of AHP by clothing within them.

88) You already know that ZON of AK shone this new light to the ten Sefirot of Nekudim through two places: It shone to the Keter of Nekudim through the Tabur and shone to AVI of Nekudim through the Yesod.

Know that this illumination through the Tabur is called Holam, which shines to the Otiot above them because the illumination of Tabur reaches only the Keter of Nekudim, the male level of the Rosh of Nekudim, as written in Item 74. And the male level does not expand into the ZAT of Nekudim, which are the vessels of the Guf, called Otiot; hence, it is considered to be shining on them only from its place above, without expanding in the Otiot themselves.

The illumination through the Yesod is called Shuruk, meaning a Vav with a dot that stands inside the line of the Otiot. The reason is that this illumination comes to AVI of Nekudim, which are the female level of the Rosh of Nekudim, whose lights expand to the Guf, as well, which are the ZAT of Nekudim, called Otiot. This is why you will find the dot of Shuruk inside the line of the Otiot.

89) Thus, the Holam and Shuruk have been thoroughly explained. The illumination of a new light through the Tabur, which lowers the bottom Hey from the Nikvey Eynaim of Keter to the Peh, and elevates the AHP of Keter once more, is the dot of Holam above the Otiot. The illumination of a new light through the Yesod, which lowers the bottom Hey from the Nikvey Eynaim of AVI to their Peh and returns their AHP to them, is the dot of Shuruk inside the Otiot. This is because these Mochin also come in the ZAT of Nekudim, called Otiot.

90) Hirik is considered the new light that the ZAT themselves receive from AVI, to lower the ending bottom Hey, which stands at their Chazeh, to the place of Sium Raglin

of AK. Thus, their AHP, namely the vessels from the Chazeh downward, which became the place of BYA, return to them. At that time, BYA once again became as Atzilut.

But ZAT of Nekudim could not lower the bottom Hey from the Chazeh and completely revoke the second restriction, the Parsa, and the place of BYA. Rather, when they extended the light into BYA, all the vessels of ZAT immediately broke, since the force of the ending bottom Hey, which stands at the Parsa, was mingled with these vessels.

Thus, the light had to instantaneously depart from there and the vessels broke, died, and fell into BYA. Their anterior vessels, which stand above the Parsa, meaning vessels above the Chazeh, also broke, since all the light departed from them, too. Thus, they broke, died, and fell into BYA, due to their joining with the posterior vessels into one Guf.

91) Thus, you see that the Nekuda [singular of Nekudot] of Hirik could not emerge and rule in the world of Nekudim. Moreover, it caused the breaking of the vessels. This was because it wanted to clothe inside the Otiot, in the TNHYM below Parsa of Atzilut, which became BYA.

However, later, in the world of correction, the dot of Hirik received its correction, since it was corrected into shining below the Otiot. This means that when ZAT of Atzilut receive the light of Gadlut from AVI, which should lower the ending bottom Hey from the place of the Chazeh to Sium Raglin of AK, and connect the vessels of TNHYM to Atzilut, and the lights will expand down to Sium Raglin of AK. Yet, they do not do so, but rather raise these TNHY from the place of BYA to the place of Atzilut, above the Parsa, and receive the lights while they are above the Parsa of Atzilut, so that no breaking of vessels would occur in them again, as in the world of Nekudim.

This is considered that the dot of Hirik, which raises the vessels of TNHY of ZAT of Atzilut, stands below these vessels of TNHYM that it raised; that is, it stands in the place of the Parsa of Atzilut. Thus, the dot of Hirik serves below the Otiot. This explains the three Nekudot, Holam, Shuruk, Hirik, in general.

The Matter of Raising MAN of ZAT of Nekudim to AVI and the Explanation of the Sefira Daat

92) It has already been explained that due to the ascent of the bottom Hey to Nikvey Eynaim, which occurred in the second restriction, when the Katnut of the ten Sefirot of Nekudim emerged, each degree divided into two halves: Galgalta and Eynaim remained in the degree, for which they are called anterior vessels, and Ozen, Hotem, Peh, which fell from the degree to the one below it, are therefore called posterior vessels, as it is written in Item 76.

Thus, each degree is now twofold, made of internality and externality, since the posterior vessels of the upper degree fell to the internality of its own anterior vessels. The fallen AHP of Keter of Nekudim are clothed inside Galgalta and Eynaim of AVI, and the fallen AHP of AVI are clothed inside Galgalta and Eynaim of ZAT of Nekudim.

93) In consequence, when the new light of AB SAG of AK comes to the degree and lowers the bottom Hey back to her place at the Peh, during the Gadlut of Nekudim, the degree returns her AHP to her, and its ten Sefirot of vessels and ten Sefirot of lights are completed. It is then considered that the lower degree, too, which was attached to the AHP of the upper one, rises along with them to the upper one.

This is so because the rule is that "there is no absence in the spiritual." As the lower one was attached to the AHP of the upper one during the Katnut, they are not separated from each other during the Gadlut, as well, when the AHP of the upper one return to their degree. It follows that the lower degree has now actually become a higher degree, since the lower one that rises to the upper one becomes like it.

94) It turns out that when AVI received the new light of AB SAG, lowered the bottom Hey from the Nikvey Eynaim back to their Peh, and raised their AHP to them, the ZAT, too, which clothe these AHP during the Katnut, now rose along with them to AVI. Thus, the ZAT became a single degree with AVI. This ascent of the ZAT to AVI is called "raising MAN." And when they are at the same degree as AVI, they receive the lights of AVI, as well.

95) It is called MAN since, as explained in Item 80, the ascent of ZA to Bina brings her back to being face-to-face with the Hochma. It is known that every ZAT are ZON; hence, when the ZAT ascended with the AHP of AVI to the degree of AVI, they became MAN to the Bina of the ten Sefirot of AVI. Then she returns to being face-to-face with the Hochma of AVI and imparts ZON, which are the ZAT of Nekudim that ascended to them, with illumination of Hochma.

96) Despite the above-mentioned ascent of ZAT to AVI, it does not mean that they became altogether absent from their place and ascended to AVI, since there is no absence in the spiritual. Also, any "change of place" in spirituality does not mean that it has left its former place and moved to a new place, as one relocates in corporeality. Rather, there is merely an addition here: They came to the new place while remaining in their previous place. Thus, although the ZAT ascended to AVI for MAN, they nevertheless remained in their place, at their lower degree, as before.

97) Similarly, you can understand that even though we say that once ZON ascended for MAN to AVI and received their lights there, they left there and returned to their place below, here, too, it does not mean that they left their place above and moved to the place below. Had ZON been absent from their place above in AVI, the coupling of AVI face-to-face would stop instantaneously, and they would return to being back-to-back as before. This would stop their abundance, and ZON, below, would lose their Mochin, too.

It has already been explained above that Bina naturally craves only light of Hassadim, as in "for he desires mercy." She has no interest whatsoever in receiving light of Hochma; hence, she is back-to-back with Hochma. Only when ZON ascend to them for MAN does Bina return in a coupling of face-to-face with Hochma, to bestow illumination of Hochma to ZA, as it is written in Item 80.

Hence, it is necessary that the ZON will always remain there to give subsistence and establishing to the coupling of AVI face-to-face. For this reason, it cannot be said that ZON left the place of AVI when they come to their place below. Rather, as we have said, any change of place is but an addition. Thus, although ZON descended to their place below, they nevertheless remained above, as well.

98) Now you can understand the Sefira of Daat, which was initiated in the world of Nekudim. In all the Partzufim of AK, through Nekudim, there are only ten Sefirot KHB ZON. But from the world of Nekudim onward, there is also the Sefira of Daat, which we regard as KHBD ZON.

The thing is that it has already been explained in Item 79 that there was no ascent of MAN in the Partzufim of AK, but only the ascent of the screen to the Peh of the Rosh. But you should know that the Sefira of Daat is drawn from the ascent of MAN of ZON to AVI, as it has been clarified that ZON, which ascended there for MAN to Hochma and Bina, remain there even after they depart from there to their place below, to provide subsistence and establishing to the coupling of AVI face-to-face. These ZON, which remain in AVI, are called "the Sefira of Daat." Hence, now HB have the Sefira of Daat, which sustains and positions them in a coupling of face-to-face. These are the ZON that ascended for MAN there and remained there even after the departure of ZON to their place.

Hence, from here on we call the ten Sefirot by the names KHBD ZON. But in the Partzufim of AK, prior to the world of Nekudim, before the raising of MAN, there was no Sefira of Daat there. You should also know that the Sefira of Daat is always called "five Hassadim and five Gevurot," since the ZA that remains there is considered five Hassadim, and the Nukva that remained there is considered five Gevurot.

Item 99 is absent in the original Hebrew.

100) We might ask about what is written in The Book of Creation, that the ten Sefirot are "ten and not nine, ten and not eleven." It was said that the Sefira of Daat was initiated in the world of Nekudim; thus, there are eleven Sefirot: KHBD ZON.

The answer is that this is not at all an addition to the ten Sefirot, since we have learned that the Sefira of Daat is ZON that ascended for MAN and remained there. Hence, there is no addition here, but rather two discernments in ZON. The first is the ZON in their place below, which are considered Guf. The second is the ZON that remained in the Rosh of AVI, since they were already there during the raising of the MAN, and there is no absence in the spiritual.

Thus, there is no addition to the ten Sefirot here, whatsoever, for ultimately there are only ten Sefirot KHB ZON here. And if ZON also remain in the Rosh in AVI, it does not add anything to the ten Sefirot.

The Breaking of the Vessels and Their Fall to BYA

101) Now we have thoroughly explained the raising of MAN and the Sefira of Daat, which are considered the anterior vessels of ZAT of Nekudim that were extended and rose to AVI. This is because AVI received the new light of AB SAG of AK from ZON of AK in the form of the dot of Shuruk. They lowered the bottom Hey from their Nikvey Eynaim to the Peh, and raised their posterior vessels, which were fallen in the ZAT of Nekudim. As a result, the anterior vessels of ZAT, which were attached to the posterior vessels of AVI (see Items 89 and 94), ascended, too, and the ZAT of Nekudim became MAN there and returned AVI to being face-to-face.

Since the bottom Hey, which is phase four, had already returned to her place at the Peh, the coupling by striking that was done on that screen of phase four elicited ten complete Sefirot at the level of Keter in the light of Yechida (see Item 84). Thus, ZAT, which are included there as MAN, received those great lights of AVI, too. Yet, all this is only regarded as being from below upward, since AVI are considered the Rosh of Nekudim, where the coupling that elicits ten Sefirot from below upward occurs.

Subsequently, they also expand into a Guf, meaning from above downward (see Item 50). At that time, the ZAT were extended with all the lights they had received in AVI to their place below, and the Rosh and Guf of Partzuf Gadlut of Nekudim is completed. This expansion is considered the Taamim of Partzuf Gadlut of Nekudim, see Item 26.

102) The four phases—Taamim, Nekudot, Tagin, Otiot—are discerned in Partzuf Nekudim, too (see Item 47), since all the forces that exist in the upper ones must exist in the lower ones, as well. But in the lower one, there are additional matters to the upper one. It has been explained that the primary expansion of each Partzuf is called Taamim. After it expands, the clash of surrounding light and inner light occurs in it, and through this clash, the screen is gradually refined until it equalizes with the Peh of the Rosh.

And since the upper light does not stop, the upper light couples with the screen in each state of coarseness along its refinement. This means that when it refines from phase four to phase three, the level of Hochma emerges on it. And when it reaches phase two, the level of Bina emerges on it. When it comes to phase one, the level of ZA emerges on it, and when it comes to the root phase, the level of Malchut emerges on it. All those levels that emerge on the screen through its refinement are called Nekudot.

The records that remain of the lights after they have departed are called Tagin. The vessels that remain after the departure of the lights from them are called Otiot. Once the screen has been completely refined of its coarseness of the Guf, it is incorporated in the screen of the Peh of the Rosh in the coupling there, and a second Partzuf emerges on it.

103) And here in Partzuf Nekudim, it was done in precisely the same manner. Here, too, two Partzufim emerge—AB and SAG—one below the other. And in each of them there are Taamim, Nekudot, Tagin, and Otiot.

The only difference is that the refinement of the screen was not done here because of the clash of surrounding light and inner light, but due to the force of judgment of the ending Malchut, incorporated in those vessels, as written in Item 90. For this reason, the empty vessels did not remain in the Partzuf after the departure of the lights, as in the three Partzufim Galgalta, AB, SAG of AK, but broke and died and fell to BYA.

104) Regarding the Partzuf of Taamim that emerged in the world of Nekudim, which is the first Partzuf in Nekudim, which emerged on the level of Keter, it has already been explained (Item 101) that it emerged with Rosh and Guf. The Rosh emerged in AVI, and the Guf is the expansion of ZAT from the Peh of AVI down. This expansion from the Peh of AVI downward is called Melech ha Daat [King of Daat].

And this is indeed the whole of the ZAT of Nekudim that expanded once again to their place after the raising of MAN. But since their root remained in AVI for subsistence and establishing to the face-to-face of AVI (see Item 98), called there Moach ha Daat, which makes AVI copulate, their expansion from above downward into a Guf is also called by that name—Melech ha Daat. This is the first Melech [king] of Nekudim.

105) It is known that all the quantity and quality in the ten Sefirot of the Rosh appear in the expansion from above downward to the Guf, as well. Hence, as in the lights of the Rosh, the coupling Malchut returned and descended from the place of Nikvey Eynaim to the Peh. Then, GE [Galgalta Eynaim] and Nikvey Eynaim, which are the anterior vessels, reunited with their posterior vessels, their AHP, and the lights expanded in them. Similarly, as they expanded from above downward to the Guf, the lights were drawn to their posterior vessels, too, which are the TNHYM in BYA, below the Parsa of Atzilut.

Malchut in the Parsa of Atzilut is mixed in those vessels; as soon as the lights of Melech ha Daat met this force, they all departed the vessels and ascended to their root. All the vessels of Melech ha Daat broke face and back, died, and fell to BYA, since the departure of the lights from the vessels is like the departure of vitality from the corporeal body, called "death." At that time, the screen was refined from the coarseness of phase four, since these vessels have already broken and died, and only coarseness of phase three remained in it.

106) And as the coarseness of phase four was revoked from the screen of the Guf by the breaking, that coarseness was revoked in the coupling Malchut of the Rosh in AVI, too. This is so because coarseness of the Rosh and coarseness of the Guf are the same thing, except one is in potential and the other is in practice (see Item 50).

Hence, the coupling at the level of Keter stopped at the Rosh in AVI, too, and the posterior vessels, the AHP that completed the level of Keter, fell once more to the degree below it, meaning to the ZAT. This is called "revoking the posterior of the level of Keter from AVI." It turns out that the whole level of Taamim of Nekudim, Rosh and Guf, has departed.

107) And since the upper light does not stop shining, it coupled once more on the coarseness of phase three that remained in the screen of the Rosh in AVI, and ten Sefirot emerged at the level of Hochma. The Guf from above downward expanded to the Sefira of Hesed and is the second Melech of Nekudim. It, too, extended to BYA, broke, and died, at which time the coarseness of phase three was revoked from the screen of the Guf and of the Rosh, as well. Also, the posterior vessels, the AHP that completed this level of Hochma of AVI, were revoked once more, and fell to the degree below it, to ZAT, as it happened at the level of Keter.

Afterwards, a coupling was made on coarseness of phase two that remained in the screen, and ten Sefirot emerged at the level of Bina. The Guf, from above downward, expanded in the Sefira of Gevura, and this is the third Melech of Nekudim.

It, too, extended into BYA, broke, and died, revoking the coarseness of phase two in Rosh and Guf, too, ending the coupling at the level of Bina in the Rosh, too. The posterior of the level of Bina of the Rosh fell to the degree below her in the ZAT, and then the coupling was made on the coarseness of phase one that remained in the screen, and ten Sefirot emerged on it at the level of ZA. Also, its Guf, from above downward, expanded in the upper third of Tifferet. Yet, it, too, did not last and its light departed it. Thus, the coarseness of phase one has also been refined with Guf and Rosh, and the posterior of the level of ZA fell to the degree below it, to ZAT.

108) This completed the descent of all the posteriors of AVI, which are the AHP, since with the breaking of the Melech of Daat, only the AHP that belong to the level of Keter were revoked in AVI. With the breaking of the Melech of Hesed, only the AHP that belong to the level of Hochma were revoked in AVI; with the breaking of the Melech of Gevura, the AHP that belong to the level of Bina were revoked; and with the departure of the upper third of Tifferet, the AHP of the level of ZA were revoked.

It follows that all the Gadlut of AVI was revoked and only GE of Katnut remained in them, and only the coarseness of the root remained in the screen. Afterward, the screen of the Guf was refined from all its coarseness and equalized with the screen of the Rosh. At that time, it was included in the coupling by striking of the Rosh, and the records in it were renewed, except for the last phase (see Item 41). By this renewal, a new level emerged on it, called YESHSUT.

109) Since the last phase was lost, only phase three was left in it, on which ten Sefirot at the level of Hochma emerged. And when its coarseness of the Guf was recognized, it departed from the Rosh of AVI, descended, and clothed the place of Chazeh of the Guf of Nekudim (see Item 55), and elicited the ten Sefirot of the Rosh

from the Chazeh upward. This Rosh is called YESHSUT, and it produced its Guf from the Chazeh down in the two thirds of Tifferet through the end of Tifferet. This is the fourth Melech of Nekudim, and it, too, extended to BYA, broke, and died. Thus, the coarseness of phase three has been refined in Rosh and Guf. Its posterior vessels of the Rosh fell to the degree below it, in the place of their Guf.

Subsequently, the coupling was made on the coarseness of phase two, which remained in it, and the level of Bina emerged on it. Its Guf, from above downward, expanded in the two vessels Netzah and Hod, which are both one Melech—the fifth Melech of Nekudim. And they, too, extended to BYA, broke, and died. Thus, the coarseness of phase two has been refined in Rosh and Guf, and the posterior vessels of the level fell to the degree below it: the Guf.

Then the coupling was made on the coarseness of phase one that remained in it and the level of ZA emerged on it. Its Guf, from above downward, expanded in the vessel of Yesod, and this is the sixth Melech of Nekudim. It, too, extended into BYA, broke, and died. Thus, the coarseness of phase one has been refined in Rosh and Guf, as well, and the posterior vessels in the Rosh fell to the degree below them, to the Guf.

Then there was the coupling on the coarseness of the root phase that remained in the screen, and the level of Malchut emerged on it. Its from above downward extended into the vessel of Malchut, and this is the seventh Melech of Nekudim. It, too, extended into BYA, broke, and died. Thus, the coarseness of the root was refined in Rosh and Guf, as well, and the posterior of the Rosh fell to the degree below it, in the Guf. Now all the posterior vessels of YESHSUT have been canceled, as well as the breaking of the vessels of all the ZAT of Nekudim, called "the seven Melachim [kings]."

110) Thus we have explained the Taamim and Nekudot that emerged in the two Partzufim AVI and YESHSUT of Nekudim, called AB SAG. In AVI, four levels emerged one below the other. These are the level of Keter, called "looking of the Eynaim of AVI," the level of Hochma, called the Guf of Aba, and the level of Bina, called the Guf of Ima, and the level of ZA is called Yesodot [plural of Yesod] of AVI. Four bodies expanded from it: Melech [king] of Daat; Melech of Hesed; Melech of Gevura; and the Melech of the upper third of Tifferet, through the Chazeh.

These four Gufim [plural of Guf] broke in both anterior and posterior. But with respect to their Roshim [plural of Rosh], that is, the four levels in AVI, all their anterior vessels remained in the levels, that is, the GE and Nikvey Eynaim of each level, which were in them since the Katnut of Nekudim. Only the posterior vessels in each degree, which joined them during the Gadlut, were revoked once more by the breaking, fell to the degree below them, and remained as they were prior to the emergence of Gadlut of Nekudim, as written in Items 76-77.

111) The emergence of the four levels, one below the other, in Partzuf YESHSUT was in precisely the same manner. The first level is the level of Hochma, called

"looking of the Eynaim of YESHSUT at one another," as well as the level of Bina, the level of ZA, and the level of Malchut, from which four Gufim expanded, which are the Melech of the two lower thirds of Tifferet, the Melech of Netzah and Hod, the Melech of Yesod, and Malchut.

Their four Gufim broke in both anterior and posterior. But in the Roshim, that is, in the four levels of YESHSUT, the anterior vessels in them remained, and only their posterior was revoked by the breaking, and fell to the degree below them. After the revoking of the two Partzufim AVI and YESHSUT, the level of MA of Nekudim emerged. And since only corrections of vessels expanded from her to the Guf, I will not elaborate on it, and it has already been explained in *The Study of the Ten Sefirot*, Part 7, Item 70.

The World of Correction and the New MA that Emerged from the Metzach of AK

112) From the beginning of the preface ["Preface to the Wisdom of Kabbalah"] to this point, we have thoroughly explained the first four Partzufim of AK.

The first Partzuf of AK is called Partzuf Galgalta, whose coupling by striking is performed on phase four and its ten Sefirot are at the level of Keter.

The second Partzuf of AK is called AB of AK. The coupling by striking in it is done on coarseness of phase three, and its ten Sefirot are at the level of Hochma. It clothes from the Peh of Partzuf Galgalta downward.

The third Partzuf of AK is called SAG of AK. The coupling by striking in it is done on coarseness of phase two, and its ten Sefirot are at the level of Bina. It clothes from the Peh of Partzuf AB of AK downward.

The fourth Partzuf of AK is called MA of AK. The coupling by striking in it is done on coarseness of phase one, and its ten Sefirot are on the level of ZA. This Partzuf clothes from the Tabur of SAG of AK downward and is divided into internality and externality. The internality is called MA and BON of AK, and the externality is called "the world of Nekudim." This is where the association of Malchut in Bina, called the second restriction, takes place, as well as the Katnut, Gadlut, the raising of MAN, and the Daat, which determines and copulates the HB face to face, and the issue of the breaking of the vessels, since all these were initiated in the fourth Partzuf of AK, called MA or "the world of Nekudim."

113) These five phases of coarseness in the screen are named after the Sefirot in the Rosh, that is, Galgalta Eynaim and AHP. The coarseness of phase four is called Peh, on which the first Partzuf of AK emerges. The coarseness of phase three is called Hotem, on which Partzuf AB of AK emerges. The coarseness of phase two is called Ozen, on which Partzuf SAG of AK emerges. The coarseness of phase one is called Nikvey Eynaim, on which Partzuf MA of AK and the world of Nekudim emerge.

The coarseness of the root phase is called Galgalta or Metzach, on which the world of correction emerges. It is called "the new MA" since the fourth Partzuf of AK is the core of Partzuf MA of AK, as it emerged from the Nikvey Eynaim at the level of ZA, called HaVaYaH of MA.

But the fifth Partzuf of AK, which emerged from the Metzach, that is, the phase of Galgalta, considered as the coarseness of the root, actually has only the level of Malchut, called BON. Yet, because the first phase of clothing remained there, too, namely the phase of ZA, it is called MA, as well, though by the name of MA that emerged from the Metzach of AK, meaning from the incorporation of the coarseness of the root, called Metzach. It is also called "the new MA," to distinguish it from the MA that emerged from Nikvey Eynaim of AK. This new Partzuf of MA is called "the world of correction" or "the world of Atzilut."

114) We should still understand why the first three levels of AK, called Galgalta, AB, SAG, are not considered three worlds but three Partzufim, and why the fourth Partzuf of AK changed into being called "world." It is likewise with the fifth Partzuf of AK, since the fourth Partzuf is called "the world of Nekudim," and the fifth Partzuf is called "the world of Atzilut" or "the world of correction."

115) We should know the difference between a Partzuf and a world. Any level of ten Sefirot that emerges on a screen of the Guf of an upper one after it has been refined and incorporated in the Peh of the Rosh of the upper one (see Item 50) is called Partzuf. After its departure from the Rosh of the upper one, it expands into its own Rosh, Toch, Sof, and it contains five levels one below the other, called Taamim and Nekudot (see Item 47). Yet, it is named only after the level of Taamim in it. The first three Partzufim of AK—Galgalta, AB, SAG (see Item 47)—emerged in that manner. However, a world means that it contains everything that exists in the world above it, like a seal and an imprint, where everything that exists in the seal is transferred to its imprint.

116) Thus you see that the first three Partzufim, Galgalta, AB, and SAG of AK are considered as only one world, the world of AK, which emerged in the first restriction. But the fourth Partzuf of AK, where the second restriction occurred, became a world in and of itself, due to the doubling that occurred in the screen of Nekudot of SAG in its descent from the Tabur of AK. This is because it was doubled by the coarseness of phase four in the form of the bottom Hey in the Eynaim (see Item 63).

During the Gadlut, phase four returned to its place at the Peh and elicited the level of Keter (see Item 84), and this level was equal to the first Partzuf of AK. After it expanded into Rosh, Toch, Sof in Taamim and Nekudot, a second Partzuf emerged on it, at the level of Hochma, called YESHSUT, which is similar to the second Partzuf of AK, called AB of AK. Following its expansion into Taamim and Nekudot, a third Partzuf emerged, called MA of Nekudim (see Item 111), which is similar to the third Partzuf of AK.

Thus, everything that existed in the world of AK emerged here in the world of Nekudim, that is, three Partzufim one below the other. Each of which contains Taamim and Nekudot and all their instances, like the three Partzufim Galgalta, AB, SAG of AK in the world of AK. For this reason, the world of Nekudim is regarded as an imprint of the world of AK, and because of it, it is considered a complete world in and of itself. (The reason why the three Partzufim of Nekudim are not called Galgalta, AB, SAG, but rather AB, SAG, MA, is that the coarseness of phase four that connected to the screen of SAG is incomplete due to the refinement that occurred in the first Partzuf of AK. This is why they descended into being AB, SAG, and MA.)

117) Thus we have learned how the world of Nekudim was imprinted from the world of AK. Similarly, the fifth Partzuf of AK, that is, the new MA, was entirely imprinted from the world of Nekudim. Thus, although all the discernments that served in Nekudim were broken and canceled there, they were renewed in the new MA. This is why it is considered a separate world.

Also, it is called "the world of Atzilut" because it ends completely above the Parsa that was erected in the second restriction. It is also called "the world of correction" because the world of Nekudim could not persist because of the revoking and breaking that occurred in it. Only afterward, in the new MA, when all those phases that were in the world of Nekudim returned and came in the new MA, they were established and persisted there.

This is why it is called "the world of correction," for indeed, it is actually the world of Nekudim, but here, in the new MA, it receives its full correction. This is because through the new MA, all the posterior that fell from AVI and YESHSUT to the Guf, as well as the anterior and posterior of all the ZAT that fell to BYA and died, reunite with the GAR and rise through it to Atzilut.

118) The reason for it is that each lower Partzuf returns and fills the vessels of the upper one after the departure of their lights during the refinement of the screen. This is because after the departure of the lights of the Guf of the first Partzuf of AK, because of the refinement of the screen, the screen received a new coupling at the level of AB, which refilled the empty vessels of the Guf of the upper one, that is, the first Partzuf.

Also, following the departure of the lights of the Guf of AB because of the refinement of the screen, the screen received a new coupling at the level of SAG, which refilled the empty vessels of the upper one, which is AB. Also, after the departure of the lights of SAG, due to the refinement of the screen, the screen received a new coupling at the level of MA, which emerged from Nikvey Eynaim, being the Nekudim, which refilled the empty vessels of the upper one, which is Nekudot of SAG.

And exactly in the same way, following the departure of the lights of Nekudim because of the revoking of the posteriors and the breaking of the vessels, the screen received a new coupling at the level of MA, which emerged from the Metzach of

Partzuf SAG of AK. This fills the empty vessels of the Guf of the upper one, which are the vessels of Nekudim that were revoked and broken.

119) Yet, there is an essential difference here in the new MA: It became a male, and an upper one to the vessels of Nekudim which it corrects. Conversely, in the previous Partzufim, the lower one does not become a male and an upper one to the vessels of the Guf of the upper one, even though it fills them through its level.

That change is because in the previous Partzufim there was no flaw in the departure of the lights, because only the refinement of the screen caused their departure. But here, in the world of Nekudim, there was a flaw in the vessels, since the force of the ending Malchut was mixed with the posterior vessels of ZAT, making them unfit to receive the lights. This is why they broke and died and fell into BYA.

Hence, they are completely dependent on the new MA to revive them, sort them, and raise them to Atzilut. As a result, the new MA is regarded as male and giver. And these vessels of Nekudim, which were sorted by it, became Nukva [female] to the MA. Thus, their name has been changed to BON, meaning they have become a lower one to the MA. Even though they are the upper one to the new MA, since they are vessels from the world of Nekudim and are considered MA and Nikvey Eynaim, whose highest phase is VAK of SAG of AK (see Item 74), they now became a lower one to the new MA, for which reason they are called BON.

The Five Partzufim of Atzilut and the MA and BON in Each Partzuf

120) It has been explained that the level of the new MA expanded into a whole world in and of itself, as well, like the world of Nekudim. The reason is, as it has been explained regarding the level of Nekudim, the doubling of the screen from phase four, too (see Item 116). This is because the illumination of the ZON of AK that shone through the Tabur and Yesod to GAR of Nekudim brought the first restriction back to its place, and the bottom Hey descended from Nikvey Eynaim to the Peh, which caused all these levels of Gadlut of Nekudim to emerge (see Item 101). Yet, all these levels were revoked and broken once more, and all the lights departed them. Consequently, the second restriction returned to its place and phase four was reunited with the screen.

121) Hence, in the new MA that emerged from the Metzach, there are two phases of Katnut and Gadlut, too, as in the world of Nekudim. The Katnut emerges first, according to the coarseness disclosed in the screen, which is the level of ZA of clothing, called HGT, and the level of Malchut of coarseness, called NHY, due to the three lines made on the level of Malchut. The right line is called Netzah, the left line is called Hod, and the middle line is called Yesod.

Yet, since there is only clothing in phase one, without coarseness, it has no vessels. Thus, the level of HGT is devoid of vessels, and it clothes the vessels of NHY. This level is called embryo [Ubar], which means that there is only coarseness of the root there, which remained in the screen after its refinement, during its ascent for coupling at the Metzach of the upper one. The level that emerges there is only the level of Malchut.

Yet, within there is a concealed bottom Hey, regarded as "the bottom Hey at the Metzach." Once the embryo receives the coupling in the upper one, it descends from there to its place (see Item 54), and receives the Mochin of suckling [Yenika] from the upper one, which are coarseness of phase one, considered "the bottom Hey in Nikvey Eynaim." Thus, it acquires vessels for HGT, too, HGT expand from NHY and it has the level of ZA.

122) Afterwards, it rises for MAN to the upper one once again. This is called the second impregnation [Ibur Bet]. It receives there Mochin from AB SAG of AK, and phase four descends from Nikvey Eynaim to her place at the Peh (see Item 101). At that time, a coupling is made on phase four at her place, ten Sefirot emerge at the level of Keter, the vessels of AHP ascend back to their place at the Rosh, and the Partzuf is completed with ten Sefirot of lights and vessels. These Mochin are called "Mochin of Gadlut of the Partzuf," and this is the level of the first Partzuf of Atzilut, called Partzuf Keter or Partzuf Atik of Atzilut.

123) You already know that after the breaking of the vessels, all the AHP fell from their degrees, each to the degree below it (see Items 77, 106). Thus, the AHP of the level of Keter of Nekudim are in GE of the level of Hochma, and the AHP of the level of Hochma are in the GE of the level of Bina, etc. Therefore, during the second impregnation of Gadlut of the first Partzuf of Atzilut, called Atik, which elevated its AHP once more, GE of the level of Hochma ascended along with them. They were corrected along with the AHP of the level of Atik and received the first impregnation there.

124) Once GE of Hochma received their level of impregnation and suckling (see Item 121), they ascended once again to the Rosh of Atik, where they received their second impregnation for Mochin of Gadlut. Phase three descended to her place at the Peh, and ten Sefirot emerged on her, at the level of Hochma, and their vessels of AHP ascended back to their place at the Rosh. Thus, Partzuf Hochma was completed with ten Sefirot of lights and vessels. This Partzuf is called Arich Anpin of Atzilut.

125) The GE of the level of Bina ascended along with these AHP of AA, and received there their first impregnation and suckling. Afterward, they ascended to the Rosh of AA for a second impregnation, raised their AHP, and received the Mochin of Gadlut. Thus, Partzuf Bina was completed with ten Sefirot of lights and vessels. This Partzuf is called AVI and YESHSUT, since the GAR are called AVI, and the ZAT are called YESHSUT.

126) And GE of ZON ascended along with these AHP of AVI, and received there their first impregnation and suckling. This completes the ZON in the state of VAK to ZA and Nekuda [dot] to the Nukva. Thus we have explained the five Partzufim of the new MA that emerged in the world of Atzilut in permanence, called Atik, AA, AVI,

and ZON. Atik emerged at the level of Keter, AA at the level of Hochma, AVI at the level of Bina, and ZON in VAK and Nekuda, which is the level of ZA.

Also, there can never be any diminution in these five levels, since the actions of the lower ones never reach the GAR in a way that they can blemish them. The actions of the lower ones do reach ZA and Nukva, that is, their posterior vessels, which they obtain during the Gadlut. But the actions of the lower ones cannot reach the anterior vessels, which are GE in lights of VAK and Nekuda. Hence, these five levels are considered permanent Mochin in Atzilut.

127) The order of their clothing of each other and on Partzuf AK is that Partzuf Atik of Atzilut, although it emerged from the Rosh of SAG of AK (see Item 118), it still cannot clothe from the Peh of SAG of AK downward, but only below the Tabur since above the Tabur of AK it is considered the first restriction and it is called Akudim.

Since Partzuf Atik is the first Rosh of Atzilut, the second restriction does not control it, so it should have been worthy of clothing above the Tabur of AK. But since the second restriction had already been established in its Peh of Rosh, for the rest of the Partzufim of Atzilut, from it downward, it can only clothe from the Tabur of AK downward.

Thus, the level of Atik begins at the Tabur of AK and ends equally with the Raglaim of AK, that is, above the point of this world. This is so because of its own Partzuf. Yet, because of its connection to the rest of the Partzufim of Atzilut, from whose perspective it is regarded as consisting of the second restriction, too, in that respect, it is considered that its Raglaim end above the Parsa of Atzilut, since the Parsa is the new Sium of the second restriction, as written in Item 68.

128) The second Partzuf in the new MA, called AA, which was emanated and emerged from the Peh of Rosh of Atik, its level begins from the place of its emergence, meaning from the Peh of Rosh of Atik, and clothes the ZAT of Atik, which end above the Parsa of Atzilut. The third Partzuf, called AVI, which were emanated from the Peh of Rosh of AA, they begin from the Peh of Rosh of AA and end above the Tabur of AA. The ZON begin at the Tabur of AA and end equally with the Sium of AA, meaning above Parsa of Atzilut.

129) You should know that when each level of these five Partzufim of the new MA emerged, it sorted and connected to itself a part of the vessels of Nekudim, which became its Nukva. Thus, when Partzuf Atik emerged, it took and connected to itself all the GAR of Nekudim that remained complete during the breaking of the vessels. This refers to the GE in them, which emerged during their Katnut, called the anterior vessels (see Item 76). In the Katnut of Nekudim, only the upper half of each degree came with them, that is, GE and Nikvey Eynaim. The bottom half of each one, which is called AHP, descended to the lower degree.

Hence, it is considered that Partzuf Atik of the new MA took the upper half of Keter from the vessels of Nekudim, as well as the upper half of HB, and the seven roots of ZAT, incorporated in the GAR of Nekudim. These became a Partzuf Nukva to Atik of the new MA, and joined with one another. They are called MA and BON of Atik of Atzilut, since the male of Atik is called MA, and the vessels of Nekudim that joined it are called BON (for the reason explained in Item 119, see there). They are positioned face and back: Atik of MA at the anterior, and Atik of BON in its posterior.

130) Partzuf AA of the new MA, which emerged at the level of Hochma, sorted and connected to itself the lower half of Keter of Nekudim—AHP of Keter—which, during the Katnut, were at the degree below Keter, that is, in Hochma and Bina of Nekudim (see Item 77). It became a Nukva to the AA of the new MA, and they joined with one another. They are positioned right and left: AA of MA, which is the male, stands on the right, and AA of BON, which is the Nukva, stands on the left.

The reason why Partzuf Atik of MA did not take the lower half of Keter of Nekudim is that since Atik is the first Rosh of Atzilut, whose merit is very high, it connected to itself only the anterior vessels of the GAR of Nekudim, in whom no flaw occurred during the breaking. This is not so at the bottom half of Keter, the AHP that were fallen in HB during the Katnut. Afterward, during the Gadlut, they rose from HB and joined the Keter of Nekudim (see Item 84). Afterwards, at the time of the breaking of the vessels, they fell from the Keter of Nekudim once more and were revoked. Thus, they were flawed by their fall and revocation, and are therefore unworthy of Atik. This is why AA of MA took them.

131) The new Partzuf of AVI, which are at the level of Bina, sorted and connected to themselves the lower half of HB of Nekudim, which are the AHP of HB that fell in the ZAT of Nekudim during the Katnut. But afterward, during the Gadlut of Nekudim, they ascended and joined HB of Nekudim (see Item 94). During the breaking of the vessels, they fell once more to the ZAT of Nekudim and were revoked (see Item 107), and AVI of MA sorted them into being their Nukva.

They are called the ZAT [Zayin Tachtonot (bottom seven)] of Hochma and the VAT [Vav Tachtonot (bottom six)] of Bina of BON, since Hesed of Bina remained with the GAR of HB of BON in Partzuf Atik, and only the VAT from Gevura downward remained at the bottom half of Bina. It follows that the male of AVI is the level of Bina of MA, and the Nukva of AVI is the ZAT of HB of BON. They are positioned on the right and on the left: AVI of MA on the right, and AVI of BON on the left. And YESHSUT of MA, which are the ZAT of AVI, took the Malchuts of HB of BON.

132) Partzuf ZON of the new MA, at the level of VAK and Nekuda, sorted and connected to themselves the anterior vessels of ZAT of Nekudim, out of their shattering in BYA, that is, the GE of ZAT of Nekudim (see Item 78). They became the Nukva to the ZON of MA and stand on the right and on the left: ZON of MA on the right, and ZON of BON on the left.

133) Thus we have explained the MA and BON in the five Partzufim of Atzilut. The five levels of the new MA that emerged in the world of Atzilut sorted the old

vessels that worked at the time of Nekudim, and made them into a Nukva, called BON. BON of Atik were made and established from the upper half of the GAR of Nekudim. BON of AA and AVI were sorted and established from the bottom half of the GAR of Nekudim, which served them during the Gadlut of Nekudim and were revoked once again. BON of ZON were sorted and established from the anterior vessels that emerged during the Katnut of Nekudim, which, during the Gadlut, broke and fell along with their posterior vessels.

A Great Rule Concerning the Permanent Mochin and the Ascents of the Partzufim and the Worlds during the Six Thousand Years

134) It has already been explained (from Item 86 and below) that the emergence of the Gadlut of the GAR and ZAT of Nekudim came in three sequences, by way of the three dots Holam, Shuruk, Hirik. From this you can understand that there are two kinds of completion of ten Sefirot for reception of Mochin of Gadlut.

The first is through its ascent and incorporation in the upper one, that is, when ZON of AK shone the new light through the Tabur to Keter of Nekudim and lowered the bottom Hey from Nikvey Eynaim of Keter to its Peh. Thus, the fallen AHP of Keter that were in AVI ascended and returned to their degree in Keter, completing its ten Sefirot.

It is discerned that in that state, GE of AVI, which were attached to the AHP of Keter, ascended along with them. Hence, AVI, too, are incorporated in the complete ten Sefirot of Keter (see Item 93), since the lower one that ascends to the upper one becomes like it. It is therefore considered that AVI, too, obtained the AHP they lacked to complete their ten Sefirot, by their incorporation in the Keter. This is the first kind of Mochin of Gadlut.

135) The second kind is a degree that was completed into ten Sefirot by itself when ZON of AK shone the new light through Yesod of AK, called "the dot of Shuruk," to AVI, and lowered the bottom Hey from Nikvey Eynaim of AVI themselves to their Peh. By this, they elevated the vessels of AHP of AVI from the place to which they fell in the ZAT to the Rosh of AVI and completed their ten Sefirot. Thus, now AVI are completed by themselves since now they have obtained the actual vessels of AHP that they lacked.

Conversely, in the first kind, when they received their completion from the Keter through adhesion with its AHP, they were actually still deficient of the AHP. But due to their incorporation in the Keter, they received through it an illumination from their AHP, which sufficed only to complete them in ten Sefirot while they were still in the place of the Keter, and not at all when they departed from there to their own place.

136) Similarly, these two kinds of completion are found in the ZAT as well. The first is during the illumination of Shuruk and the ascent of the AHP of AVI. At that time, the GE of ZAT that are attached to them ascended along with them to

AVI, too, where they received the discernment of AHP to complete their ten Sefirot. These AHP are not yet their actual AHP, but only an illumination of AHP, sufficient to complete the ten Sefirot while they are in AVI, but not at all when they descend to their own place.

The ZAT obtained the second kind of completion of the ten Sefirot during the expansion of Mochin from AVI to the ZAT. By this they, too, lowered their ending bottom Hey from their Chazeh to the Sium Raglin of AK, elevated their TNHY from BYA, and connected them to their degree, to Atzilut. Then, had they not been broken and died, they would have been completed with ten complete Sefirot by themselves, since now they have obtained the actual AHP that they lacked.

137) In the four Partzufim that emerged from AVI into vessels of HGT, as well as in the four Partzufim that emerged from YESHSUT to the vessels of TNHYM (Items 107, 109), there are these two kinds of completion of ten Sefirot, too. This is because first, each of them was completed by their adhesion with the AHP of AVI and YESHSUT while they were still at the Rosh. This is the first kind of completion of the ten Sefirot. Afterward, when they expanded to BYA, they wanted to be completed by completing the second kind of ten Sefirot. This applies to the Sefirot within Sefirot, as well.

138) You should know that these five Partzufim of Atzilut, Atik, AA, AVI, and ZON were established in permanence, and no diminution applies to them (see Item 126). Atik emerged at the level of Keter, AA at the level of Hochma, AVI at the level of Bina, and ZON at the level of ZA, VAK without a Rosh.

Thus, the vessels of AHP that were sorted for them at the time of Gadlut, were considered the completion of the first kind of ten Sefirot, by way of the dot of Holam that shone in Keter of Nekudim. At that time, AVI, too, were completed by the Keter and obtained illumination of the vessels of AHP (see Item 134). Hence, although Atik, AA, and AVI all had ten complete Sefirot at the Rosh, no GAR from it reached their Gufim. Even Partzuf Atik had only VAK, without a Rosh, at the Guf, and so did AA and AVI.

The reason for this is that the more refined is sorted first. Hence, only the completion of the first kind of ten Sefirot was sorted in them, from the perspective of its ascent to the upper one, that is, the illumination of the vessels of AHP, which suffices to complete the ten Sefirot in the Rosh. But there is still no expansion from the Rosh to the Guf, since when AVI were incorporated in Keter of Nekudim, the illumination of AHP through the Keter sufficed for them, and not at all upon their expansion to their own place, from the Peh of Keter of Nekudim downward (see Item 135). And since the Gufim of Atik and AA and AVI were in VAK without a Rosh, it is all the more so with the ZON themselves, considered the general Guf of Atzilut— they emerged in VAK without a Rosh.

139) Yet, this was not so in AK. Rather, the entire quantity that emerged in the Roshim of the Partzufim of AK expanded to their Gufim, as well. Hence, all five

Partzufim of Atzilut are regarded as merely VAK of the Partzufim of AK. This is why they are called "the new MA" or "MA of the five Partzufim of AK," meaning the level of ZA, which is MA without GAR. GAR are Galgalta, AB, SAG, since the core of the degree is discerned according to its expansion to the Guf, from the Peh down. Since the first three Partzufim do not expand into the Guf, but only VAK without a Rosh, they are considered MA, which is the level of VAK without a Rosh, with respect to the five Partzufim of AK.

140) Thus, Atik of Atzilut, who has the level of Keter at the Rosh, is considered VAK to the Partzuf of Keter of AK, and lacks Neshama, Haya, Yechida of Keter of AK. AA of Atzilut, having the level of Hochma at the Rosh, is considered VAK to Partzuf AB of AK, which is Hochma, lacking Neshama, Haya, Yechida of AB of AK.

AVI of Atzilut, with the level of Bina at the Rosh, are considered VAK of Partzuf SAG of AK, and lack Neshama, Haya, Yechida of SAG of AK. ZON of Atzilut are considered VAK of Partzuf MA and BON of AK, and lack Neshama, Haya, Yechida of MA and BON of AK. And YESHSUT and ZON are always on the same degree—one being the Rosh and the other being the Guf.

141) The completion of the AHP of the ten Sefirot of the second kind are sorted through raising MAN from good deeds of the lower ones. This means that they complete AVI, with respect to themselves, as in the dot of Shuruk. At that time, AVI themselves lower the bottom Hey from their Nikvey Eynaim and raise their AHP to them. Then they have the strength to bestow to the ZAT, as well, which are ZON, that is, to the Gufim from above downward. This is because the GE of ZON, attached to the AHP of AVI, are drawn along with them to AVI, and receive the completion of their ten Sefirot from them (see Item 94).

At that time, the full amount of Mochin in AVI are imparted also to the ZON that ascended along with them to their AHP. Hence, when the five Partzufim of Atzilut receive this completion of the second kind, there is GAR to the Gufim of the first three Partzufim—Atik, AA, and AVI of Atzilut—as well as to the ZON of Atzilut, which are the general Guf of Atzilut.

At that time, the five Partzufim of Atzilut ascend and clothe the five Partzufim of AK, since during the expansion of GAR to the Gufim of the five Partzufim of Atzilut, as well, they equalize with the five Partzufim of AK. Atik of Atzilut ascends and clothes Partzuf Keter of AK, AA clothes AB of AK, AVI–SAG of AK, and ZON clothes MA and BON of AK. Then each of them receives Neshama, Haya, and Yechida from its corresponding phase in AK.

142) Yet, with respect to ZON of Atzilut, these Mochin are regarded as merely the first kind of completion of ten Sefirot, since these AHP are not complete AHP, but merely illumination of AHP, which they receive through AVI while they are at the place of AVI. But in their expansion to their own place, they still lack their own AHP (see Item 136).

For this reason, all the Mochin that the ZON obtains during the 6,000 years are considered "Mochin of ascent," since they can obtain Mochin of GAR only when they rise to the place of GAR, as then they are completed by them. But if they do not rise to the place of GAR, they cannot have Mochin, since the ZON still have to sort the second kind of Mochin, and this will happen only at the end of correction.

143) Thus we have explained that the Mochin of the five permanent Partzufim in Atzilut are from the first kind of sorting of vessels of AVI. In the world of Nekudim, this illumination is called "illumination of Tabur" or "the dot of Holam." Even AVI have only the first kind of completion; hence, no illumination of GAR reaches from the Roshim of Atik, AA, and AVI to their own Gufim and to ZON, since ZAT of Nekudim, too, received none of that illumination of the Holam (see Item 88).

The Mochin of the 6,000 years, through the end of correction, which come through the raising of MAN of the lower ones, are considered sorting of vessels to complete the second kind of ten Sefirot of AVI. In the world of Nekudim, this illumination is called "illumination of Yesod" or "the dot of Shuruk," since then AVI raise their own AHP, to which the GE of ZAT are attached, as well. Hence, ZAT, too, receive Mochin of GAR in the place of AVI. Thus, these Mochin reach the Gufim of the five Partzufim of Atzilut and the general ZON, as well. However, they must be above, in the place of GAR, and clothe them.

In the future, at the end of correction, ZON will receive the completion of the second kind of ten Sefirot, and will lower the ending bottom Hey from their Chazeh, which is the Parsa of Atzilut, to the place of Sium Raglin of AK (see Item 136). At that time, TNHY of ZON in BYA will connect to the degree of ZON of Atzilut, and Sium Raglin of Atzilut will equalize with Sium Raglin of AK. Then the Messiah King will appear, as it is written, "His feet will stand on the Mount of Olives." Thus, it has been thoroughly clarified that there is no correction to the worlds during the 6,000 years, except through ascent.

Explaining the Three Worlds Beria, Yetzira, and Assiya

144) There are seven basic principles to discern in the three worlds BYA:

1. From where was the place for these three worlds made?

2. The levels of the Partzufim BYA and the initial position of the worlds when they were emanated and emerged from the Nukva of Atzilut.

3. All the levels from the added Mochin and their position, which they had obtained prior to the sin of Adam ha Rishon.

4. The Mochin that remained in the Partzufim BYA and the place to which the worlds fell after they were blemished by the sin of Adam ha Rishon.

5. The Mochin of Ima that the Partzufim BYA received after their fall below Parsa of Atzilut.

6. The posterior Partzufim of the five Partzufim of Atzilut, which descended and clothed the Partzufim BYA and became the phase of Neshama to Neshama for them.

7. The phase of Malchut of Atzilut that descended and became Atik to the Partzufim of BYA.

145) The first discernment has already been explained (above, from Item 66 onward): Because of the ascent of the ending Malchut, which was below the Sium Raglin of AK, to the place of the Chazeh of ZAT of Nekudot of SAG, which occurred during the second restriction, the two lower thirds of Tifferet and NHYM fell below the new point of Sium at the Chazeh of Nekudot. Thus, they are no longer worthy of receiving the upper light, and the place of the three worlds BYA was made of them. The place of the world of Beria was made of the two lower thirds of Tifferet, the place of the world of Yetzira was made of the three Sefirot NHY, and the place of the world of Assiya was made of Malchut.

146) The second discernment is the levels of the Partzufim BYA and their position upon their exit and birth from the Nukva of Atzilut. Know that at that time, ZA had already obtained the phase of Haya from Aba, and the Nukva had already obtained the phase of Neshama from Ima.

You already know that the ZON receive the Mochin from AVI only by ascent and clothing (see Item 142). Hence, ZA clothes Aba of Atzilut, called upper AVI, and the Nukva clothes Ima of Atzilut, called YESHSUT. Then the Nukva of Atzilut sorted and emanated the world of Beria with its five Partzufim.

147) Since the Nukva stands at the place of Ima, she is regarded as the degree of Ima, since the lower one that ascends to the upper one becomes like it. Hence, the world of Beria, which was sorted by her, is regarded as the degree of ZA, since it is a lower degree than the Nukva, regarded as Ima, and the one below Ima is ZA. Thus, the world of Beria stands at the place of ZA of Atzilut below the Nukva of Atzilut, which was then regarded as Ima of Atzilut.

148) Thus, it is considered that the world of Yetzira, which was sorted and emanated by the world of Beria, is then at the degree of Nukva of Atzilut. This is because it is the degree below the world of Beria, which was then the phase of ZA of Atzilut. And the one below ZA is the phase of Nukva.

However, not all ten Sefirot of the world of Yetzira are considered Nukva of Atzilut, but only the first four of Yetzira. The reason is that there are two states to the Nukva: face-to-face and back-to-back. When she is face-to-face with ZA, her level is equal to that of ZA. When she is back-to-back, she occupies only the four Sefirot TNHY of ZA.

And since at that time the state of all the worlds was only back-to-back, there were only four Sefirot in the Nukva. Hence, the world of Yetzira, too, has only its first four

Sefirot at the place of Nukva of Atzilut, and the remaining bottom six of Yetzira were at the first six Sefirot of the current world of Beria, according to the qualities of the place of BYA in the first discernment (Item 145), where the worlds BYA fell after the sin of Adam ha Rishon, which is now their permanent place.

149) The world of Assiya, which was sorted by the world of Yetzira, is considered the current degree of Beria. Since the world of Yetzira was previously at the degree of Nukva of Atzilut, the degree below it—the world of Assiya—is regarded as the current world of Beria. But since only the first four of Yetzira were in the phase of Nukva of Atzilut, and its lower six were in the world of Beria, therefore, only the first four of the world of Assiya below it are regarded as the bottom four Sefirot of the world of Beria. And the bottom six of the world of Assiya were in the place of the first six of the current world of Yetzira.

At that time, the fourteen Sefirot—NHYM of the current Yetzira and all ten Sefirot of the current world of Assiya—were devoid of any Kedusha [holiness] and became the shell section [Mador ha Klipot]. This is so because there were only shells [Klipot] in the place of these fourteen Sefirot, since the worlds of Kedusha ended at the place of the Chazeh of the current world of Yetzira. Thus we have clarified the levels of the Partzufim BYA and their position when they were initially emanated.

150) Now we shall explain the third discernment—the levels of the Partzufim BYA and the position they had from the added Mochin prior to the sin of Adam ha Rishon. This is because through the illumination of the addition of Shabbat [Sabbath], they had two ascents.

The first was on the fifth hour on the eve of Shabbat when Adam ha Rishon was born. At that time, the illumination of the addition of Shabbat begins to shine in the form of the Hey of the sixth day. At that time, ZA obtained the phase of Yechida and rose and clothed AA of Atzilut, Nukva the phase of Haya, and it rose and clothed AVI of Atzilut. Beria rose to YESHSUT, the whole of Yetzira rose to ZA, the first four Sefirot of Assiya rose to the place of Nukva of Atzilut, and the bottom six of Assiya rose to the place of the first six of Beria.

The second ascent was on the eve of Shabbat at dusk. Through the addition of Shabbat, the bottom six of Assiya rose to the place of Nukva of Atzilut, as well, and the worlds of Yetzira and Assiya stood in the world of Atzilut, in the place of ZON of Atzilut, in a manner of face-to-face.

151) Now we shall explain the fourth discernment—the level of Mochin that remained in BYA, and the place to which they fell after the sin. Because of the flaw of the sin of the Tree of Knowledge, all the added Mochin they had obtained through the two ascents departed from the worlds, and ZON returned to being VAK and Nekuda. And the three worlds BYA were left with only the Mochin with which they initially emerged. The world of Beria was at the degree of ZA, which means VAK, and Yetzira and Assiya in the above-mentioned measure, too (Item 148).

Additionally, the phase of Atzilut had completely left them and they fell below Parsa of Atzilut, to the quality of the place of BYA, prepared by the second restriction (see Item 145). Thus, the bottom four of Yetzira and the ten Sefirot of the world of Assiya fell and stood at the place of the fourteen Sefirot of the shells (see Item 149), called the "shell section."

152) The fifth discernment is the Mochin of Ima that BYA received at the place to which they fell. After BYA departed from Atzilut and fell below Parsa of Atzilut, they had only VAK (see Item 151). Then YESHSUT clothed ZON of Atzilut, and YESHSUT coupled from the clothing in ZON, and imparted Mochin of Neshama to the Partzufim BYA in their place: The world of Beria received from them ten complete Sefirot at the level of Bina, the world of Yetzira received from them VAK, and the world of Assiya, only the state of back-to-back.

153) The sixth discernment is the Neshama to Neshama, which the Partzufim BYA obtained from the posterior Partzufim of the five Partzufim of Atzilut. This is because during the diminution of the moon, the posterior Partzuf of Nukva of Atzilut fell and clothed in the Partzufim BYA. It contains three Partzufim, called impregnation, suckling, Mochin: The state of Mochin fell into Beria, the state of suckling fell into Yetzira, and the state of impregnation fell into Assiya. They became the state of Neshama to Neshama to all the Partzufim BYA, which is the state of Haya with respect to them.

154) The seventh discernment is Nukva of Atzilut, which became the RADLA [Reisha de Lo Etyada - The Rosh that is unknown] and the illumination of Yechida in BYA. This is because it has been explained that during the diminution of the moon, the three states—impregnation, suckling, Mochin—of the posterior Partzuf Nukva of Atzilut fell and clothed in BYA. They are at the state of the posterior of the bottom nine of Nukva, which are impregnation, suckling, and Mochin: NHY is called impregnation, HGT is called suckling, and HBD is called Mochin.

However, the posterior of the phase of Keter of Nukva became Atik to the Partzufim BYA in a way that the lights of the current Partzufim BYA are primarily from the remnants left in them after the sin of Adam ha Rishon, which is the VAK of each of them (see Item 151).

They received the phase of Neshama from Mochin of Ima (see Item 152), and they received the phase of Neshama to Neshama, which is the phase of Haya, from the bottom nine of the posterior Partzuf of Nukva, and they received the phase of Yechida from the phase of posterior of Keter of Nukva of Atzilut.

Explaining the Ascents of the Worlds

155) The main difference between the Partzufim of AK and the Partzufim of the world of Atzilut is that the Partzufim of AK are from the first restriction where each degree contains ten complete Sefirot. Also, there is only one vessel in the ten Sefirot—the vessel of Malchut, but the first nine Sefirot are only considered lights.

Conversely, the Partzufim of Atzilut are from the second restriction, as it is written, "In the day that the Lord God made earth and heaven," when He associated mercy with judgment (see Item 59). The quality of judgment, which is Malchut, ascended and connected to Bina, which is the quality of mercy, and they were conjoined. Thus, a new Sium was placed over the upper light in the place of Bina. The Malchut that ends the Guf ascended to Bina of the Guf, which is Tifferet, at the place of the Chazeh, and the coupling Malchut at the Peh of the Rosh ascended to Bina of the Rosh, called Nikvey Eynaim (see Item 61).

Thus, the level of the Partzufim diminished into GE, which are Keter Hochma in vessels, at the level of VAK without a Rosh, which is Nefesh Ruach in lights (see Item 74). Hence, they are deficient of AHP of the vessels, which are Bina and ZON, and the lights Neshama, Haya, Yechida.

156) It has been explained above, in Item 124, that by raising MAN for the second impregnation, the Partzufim of Atzilut obtained the illumination of Mochin from AB SAG of AK, which lowers the bottom Hey from Nikvey Eynaim back to her place at the Peh, as in the first restriction. Thus, they regain the AHP of the vessels and Neshama, Haya, Yechida of lights. Yet, this helped only to the ten Sefirot of the Rosh of the Partzufim, but not to their Gufim [bodies], since these Mochin did not spread from the Peh down to their Gufim (see Item 138).

Therefore, even after the Mochin of Gadlut, the Gufim remained in the second restriction, as during the Katnut. Hence, all five Partzufim of Atzilut are considered to have only the level of the ten Sefirot that emerge on the coarseness of phase one, the level of ZA, VAK without a Rosh, called "the level of MA." They clothe the level of MA of the five Partzufim of AK, meaning from Tabur of the five Partzufim of AK downward.

157) Thus, Partzuf Atik of Atzilut clothes Partzuf Keter of AK from its Tabur down and receives its abundance from the level of MA of Partzuf Keter of AK there. Partzuf AA of Atzilut clothes Partzuf AB of AK from Tabur down and receives its abundance from the level of MA of AB of AK there. AVI of Atzilut clothe Partzuf SAG of AK from the Tabur down and receive their abundance from the level of MA of SAG there. ZON of Atzilut clothe Partzuf MA and BON of AK from Tabur down and receive their abundance from the level of MA of Partzuf MA and BON of AK.

Thus, each of the five Partzufim of Atzilut receives from its corresponding Partzuf in AK, only VAK without a Rosh, called "the level of MA." And even though there is GAR in the Roshim of the five Partzufim of Atzilut, only the Mochin that expand from the Peh down into their Gufim, which are merely VAK without a Rosh, are taken into consideration (see Item 139).

158) This does not mean that each of the five Partzufim of Atzilut clothes its corresponding phase in AK. This is impossible, since the five Partzufim of AK clothe one atop the other, and so do the five Partzufim of Atzilut. Rather, this means that the level of each Partzuf of the Partzufim of Atzilut aims to its corresponding phase

in the five Partzufim of AK, from which it receives its abundance (see the book *Ha'Ilan*, Diagram no. 3).

159) For the Mochin to flow from the Peh down to the Gufim of the five Partzufim of Atzilut, it has been explained in Item 141 that raising MAN from the lower ones is required, when the completion of the ten Sefirot of the second kind are given to them, which suffices for the Gufim, as well.

There are three discernments in these MAN that the lower ones raise. When they raise MAN from the coarseness of phase two, ten Sefirot at the level of Bina emerge, called "the level of SAG." These are Mochin of light of Neshama. When they raise MAN from the coarseness of phase three, ten Sefirot at the level of Hochma emerge, called "the level of AB." These are Mochin of the light of Haya. When they raise MAN from the coarseness of phase four, ten Sefirot at the level of Keter emerge, called "the level of Galgalta." These are Mochin of the light of Yechida (see Item 29).

160) Know that the lower ones that are suitable for raising MAN are only considered NRN [Nefesh, Ruach, Neshama] of the righteous, which are already incorporated in BYA and can raise MAN to ZON of Atzilut, considered their upper one. At that time, the ZON raise MAN to their upper one, which are AVI, and AVI higher still, until they reach the Partzufim of AK. Then the upper light descends from Ein Sof to the Partzufim of AK on the MAN that ascended there, and the level of ten Sefirot emerges, according to the measure of coarseness of the MAN that they raised. If it is from phase two, it is at the level of Neshama; if it is from phase three, it is the level of Haya.

From there the Mochin descend degree by degree through the Partzufim of AK until they arrive at the Partzufim of Atzilut. And they also travel degree by degree through all the Partzufim of Atzilut until they arrive at the Partzufim ZON of Atzilut, which impart these Mochin upon the NRN of the righteous that raised these MAN from BYA. The rule is that any initiation of Mochin comes only from Ein Sof, and no degree can raise MAN or receive abundance except from its adjacent upper one.

161) This tells you that it is impossible for the lower ones to receive anything from ZON of Atzilut before all the higher Partzufim in the world of Atzilut and the world of AK are brought into Gadlut by them. This is because it has been explained that there is no initiation of Mochin except from Ein Sof.

Yet, the NRN of the righteous can only receive them from their adjacent upper one, which are ZON of Atzilut. Hence, the Mochin must cascade through the upper worlds and Partzufim until they reach the ZON, which then give to the NRN of the righteous.

You already know that there is no absence in the spiritual, and that transference from place to place does not mean becoming absent from the first place and arriving at the next place, as in corporeality. Rather, they remain in the first place even after they have moved and arrived at the next place, as though lighting one candle from another, without the first being deficient.

Moreover, the rule is that the essence and the root of the light remains in the first place, and only a branch of it extends to the next place. Now you can see that the abundance that traverses the upper ones until it reaches the NRN of the righteous remains in each degree it had traversed. Thus, all the degrees grow because of the abundance that they pass onto the NRN of the righteous.

162) Now you can understand how the actions of the lower ones cause ascents and descents in the upper Partzufim and worlds. This is because when they improve their actions and raise MAN and extend abundance, all the worlds and degrees through which the abundance passed grow and ascend because of the abundance that they pass. When they corrupt their actions once more, the MAN is spoiled and the Mochin depart the higher degrees, too, since the transference of abundance from them to the lower ones stops and they descend once more to their permanent state as in the beginning.

163) Now we shall explain the order of the ascents of the five Partzufim of Atzilut to the five Partzufim of AK, and the three worlds BYA to YESHSUT and ZON of Atzilut, beginning with their constant state up to the level that can be reached during the 6,000 years before the end of correction.

Overall, they are only three ascents, but they divide into many details. The constant state of the worlds AK and ABYA has already been explained above: The first Partzuf that was emanated after the first restriction is Partzuf Galgalta of AK, clothed by the four Partzufim of AK—AB, SAG, MA, and BON. And the Sium Raglin of AK is above the point of this world (see Items 27, 31). It is circled by the surroundings of AK from Ein Sof, whose magnitude is infinite and immeasurable (see Item 32). Just as Ein Sof surrounds it, it clothes within it, and it is called "the line of Ein Sof."

164) Within MA and BON of AK lies Partzuf TNHYM of AK, called Nekudot of SAG of AK (Item 63, 66). During the second restriction, the ending Malchut, which stood above the point of this world, ascended and determined its place at the Chazeh of this Partzuf, below its upper third of Tifferet, where it created a new Sium on the upper light, so it would not spread from there down. This new Sium is called "Parsa below Atzilut" (see Item 68).

These Sefirot from the Chazeh down of Partzuf Nekudot of SAG of AK that remained below the Parsa became a place for the three worlds BYA: The two thirds of Tifferet through the Chazeh became the place of the world of Beria; NHY became the place of the world of Yetzira; and Malchut, the place of the world of Assiya (see Item 67). It turns out that the place of the three worlds BYA begins below the Parsa and ends above the point of this world.

165) Thus, the four worlds, Atzilut, Beria, Yetzira, and Assiya begin from the place below Tabur of AK and end above the point of this world. This is because the five Partzufim of the world of Atzilut begin from the place below Tabur of AK and end above the Parsa. And from the Parsa down to this world stand the three worlds BYA.

This is the permanent state of the worlds AK and ABYA, and there will never be any diminution in them.

It has already been explained (Item 138) that in that state there is only state VAK without a Rosh in all the Partzufim and the worlds. This is so because even in the first three Partzufim of Atzilut, in whose Roshim there is GAR, they are still not imparted from their Peh down, and all the Gufim are VAK without a Rosh, all the more so in the Partzufim BYA. Even the Partzufim of AK, with respect to their surroundings, are regarded as lacking GAR (see Item 32).

166) Hence, overall, there are three ascents to complete the worlds in the three levels, Neshama, Haya, Yechida, which they lack. These ascents depend on the lower ones' raising of MAN. The first ascent is when the lower ones raise MAN from coarseness of phase two. At that time, the AHP of the level of Bina and Neshama, with respect to the ten Sefirot of the second kind, are sorted, from the illumination of the dot of Shuruk (see Item 135). These Mochin shine to the ZAT and the Gufim, as well, like in the Partzufim of AK, when the full quantity that exists in the ten Sefirot in the Roshim of the Partzufim of AK traverses and spreads to the Gufim, as well.

167) It turns out that when these Mochin traverse the Partzufim of Atzilut, each of the five Partzufim of Atzilut receives Mochin of Bina and Neshama, called Mochin of SAG, which illuminate GAR to their Partzufim, as well, as in AK. Hence, it is then considered that they grow and rise and clothe the Partzufim of AK, to the extent of the Mochin that they achieved.

168) Thus, when Partzuf Atik of Atzilut obtained these Mochin of Bina, it rises and clothes Partzuf Bina of AK, opposite the level of SAG of Partzuf Galgalta of AK, from which it receives its state of Neshama of Yechida of AK, which shines for his ZAT, too.

When the Mochin come to Partzuf AA of Atzilut, it ascends and clothes the Rosh of Atik of the constant state, opposite the level of SAG of Partzuf AB of AK, from which it receives the state of Neshama of Haya of AK, which shines for its ZAT. When the Mochin come to Partzuf AVI of Atzilut, it ascends and clothes the constant GAR of AA, opposite the level of Bina of SAG of AK, from which it receives the state of Neshama of Neshama of AK, which shines to their ZAT, too. And when these Mochin come to YESHSUT and ZON of Atzilut, they ascend and clothe the constant AVI, opposite the level of Bina of Partzuf MA and BON of AK, from which they receive the state of Neshama of Nefesh Ruach of AK. Then the NRN of the righteous receive the Mochin of Neshama of Atzilut.

When the Mochin come to the Partzufim of the world of Beria, the world of Beria ascends and clothes Nukva of Atzilut, from which it receives the state of Nefesh of Atzilut. And when the Mochin come to the world of Yetzira, it ascends and clothes the constant world of Beria, from which it receives the state of Neshama and GAR of Beria. When the Mochin come to the world of Assiya, it ascends and clothes the world of Yetzira, from which it receives the state of Mochin of VAK in Yetzira. Thus we have explained the first ascent that each Partzuf in ABYA obtained by the MAN of phase two, which the lower ones raised (see the book *Ha'Ilan*, Diagram no. 7).

169) The second ascent occurs when the lower ones raise MAN from coarseness of phase three. At that time, the AHP of the level of Hochma and Haya are sorted with respect to the completion of the second kind of ten Sefirot. These Mochin shine for the ZAT and the Gufim, too, as in the Partzufim of AK. And when the Mochin pass through the Partzufim ABYA, each Partzuf rises and grows through them, according to the Mochin it had attained.

170) Thus, when the Mochin came to Partzuf Atik of Atzilut, it ascended and clothed the GAR of Partzuf Hochma of AK, called AB of AK, opposite the level of AB of Galgalta of AK, from which it receives the light of Haya of Yechida. When the Mochin reach Partzuf AA of Atzilut, it rises and clothes GAR of SAG of AK, opposite the level of AB of Partzuf AB of AK, from which it receives the light of Haya of Haya of AK. When the Mochin reach the Partzufim AVI of Atzilut, they rise and clothe the constant GAR of Atik, opposite the level of AB of Partzuf SAG of AK, from which they receive the light of Haya of Neshama of AK, which shines for the ZAT and the Gufim, as well. When the Mochin reach YESHSUT of Atzilut, they rise and clothe the constant GAR of AA, opposite the level of AB of MA of AK, from which they receive the light of Haya of MA of AK. When the Mochin reach ZON of Atzilut, they rise to GAR of AVI, opposite the level of AB of BON of AK, from which they receive the light of Haya of BON of AK. Also, they receive the souls of the righteous from ZON.

When the Mochin reach the world of Beria, it rises and clothes ZA of Atzilut, from which it receives the state of Ruach of Atzilut. When the Mochin reach the world of Yetzira, Yetzira ascends and clothes Nukva of Atzilut and receives from it the light of Nefesh of Atzilut. When the Mochin reach the world of Assiya, it rises and clothes the world of Beria and receives from it the state of GAR and Neshama of Beria. At that time, the world of Assiya is completed with the full NRN of BYA. Thus we have explained the second ascent of each Partzuf of the Partzufim ABYA that ascended and grew by the MAN of phase three, which the NRN of the righteous raised (see the book *Ha'Ilan*, Diagram no. 8).

171) The third ascent is when the lower ones raise MAN from coarseness of phase four. At that time the AHP of the level of Keter of Yechida are sorted with respect to the completion of the second kind of ten Sefirot. These Mochin shine to the ZAT and their Gufim, too, as in the Partzufim of AK. When these Mochin traverse the Partzufim ABYA, each Partzuf rises, grows, and clothes its upper one according to the measure of that Mochin.

172) Thus, when the Mochin reach Partzuf Atik of Atzilut, it rises and clothes the GAR of Partzuf Galgalta of AK and receives its light of Yechida of Yechida from there. When the Mochin reach Partzuf AA of Atzilut, it rises and clothes GAR of

Partzuf AB of AK and receives the light of Yechida of Haya of AK from there. When the Mochin reach Partzuf AVI of Atzilut, they rise and clothe GAR of SAG of AK and receive the light of Yechida of Neshama of AK from there. When the Mochin reach Partzuf YESHSUT, they rise and clothe the GAR of MA of AK and receive the light of Yechida of MA of AK from there. When the Mochin reach ZON of Atzilut, they rise and clothe GAR of BON of AK and receive the light of Yechida of BON of AK from there. Then the NRN of the righteous receive the light of Yechida from ZON of Atzilut.

When the Mochin reach the world of Beria, it rises and clothes Partzuf YESHSUT of Atzilut and receives from there Neshama of Atzilut. When the Mochin reach the world of Yetzira, it rises and clothes Partzuf ZA of Atzilut and receives from it the state of Ruach of Atzilut. When the Mochin reach the world of Assiya, it rises and clothes Nukva of Atzilut and receives the state of light of Nefesh of Atzilut from her (see the book *Ha'Ilan*, Diagram no. 9).

173) It turns out that now, during the third ascent, the five Partzufim of Atzilut have each been completed with three levels, Neshama, Haya, Yechida from AK, which they lacked in the constant state. It is therefore considered that the five Partzufim of Atzilut ascended and clothed the five Partzufim of AK, each in its corresponding phase in the Partzufim of AK.

Also, the NRN of the righteous received the GAR they lacked, and the three worlds BYA that were under Parsa of Atzilut had only NRN of light of Hassadim in the constant state, departed from Hochma by the force of the Parsa atop them. Now, however, they have risen above the Parsa and clothed YESHSUT and ZON of Atzilut, and have NRN of Atzilut, where the light of Hochma shines in their Hassadim.

174) We should know that the NRN of the righteous permanently clothe only the Partzufim BYA below the Parsa: Nefesh clothes the ten Sefirot of Assiya; Ruach—the ten Sefirot of Yetzira; and Neshama—the ten Sefirot of Beria.

It turns out that although they receive from ZON of Atzilut, it still reaches them only through the Partzufim BYA, which clothe over them. Thus, the NRN of the righteous, too, rise along with the ascents of the three worlds BYA. It turns out that the worlds BYA, too, grow only according to the measure of reception of abundance by the NRN of the righteous according to the MAN sorted by them.

175) Thus, it has been made clear that in the constant state, there is only VAK without a Rosh in all the worlds and Partzufim, each according to its phase. Even the NRN of the righteous are only considered VAK. Although they have GAR of Neshama from the world of Beria, these GAR are regarded as VAK compared to the world of Atzilut, since they are considered light of Hassadim, separated from Hochma.

Also, although there is GAR in the Roshim of the Partzufim of Atzilut, they are merely regarded as VAK, since they do not shine to the Gufim. And all the Mochin that reach the worlds, which are more than the VAK, come only through the MAN that the righteous raise.

Yet, these Mochin can only be received in the Partzufim through the ascent of the lower one to the place of the upper one. This is so because although they are considered completion of the second kind of ten Sefirot, with respect to the Gufim and the ZAT themselves, they are still regarded as sorting of AHP of the first kind, which are not completed in their own place, but only when they are at the place of the upper one (see Item 142). Hence, the five Partzufim of Atzilut cannot receive Neshama, Haya, and Yechida of AK, except when they rise and clothe them.

Likewise, NRN and the three worlds BYA cannot receive NRN of Atzilut except when they ascend and clothe YESHSUT and ZON of Atzilut, since these AHP of the second kind, which belong to ZAT, and expand from above downward to the place of ZAT, will only be sorted at the end of correction. Hence, when the three worlds BYA rise and clothe YESHSUT and ZON of Atzilut, their constant place, from Parsa downward, remains utterly vacant of any light of Kedusha.

And there is a difference there between from the Chazeh and above of the world of Yetzira, and from its Chazeh and below. This is because it has been explained above that from the Chazeh of the world of Yetzira and below it is the permanent place of the shells (see Item 149). But because of the flaw of the sin of Adam HaRishon, the bottom four of Yetzira of Kedusha and the ten Sefirot of Assiya of Kedusha descended and clothed there (see Item 156). Hence, during the ascents of BYA to Atzilut, there is neither Kedusha nor shells from the Chazeh of Yetzira upward. But from the Chazeh of Yetzira downward, there are shells, as this is their section.

176) Since the additional Mochin from the levels of VAK come only through MAN of the lower ones, they are not constantly present in the Partzufim, as they are dependent on the actions of the lower ones. When they corrupt their actions, the Mochin leave (see Item 162). However, the constant Mochin in the Partzufim, which were established by the force of the Emanator Himself, will never suffer any change, since they do not grow by the lower ones and are hence not flawed by them.

177) Do not wonder about AA of BON being considered Keter of Atzilut, and AVI as AB (see Item 130). This is because AA is the bottom half of Keter of BON, and AVI are the bottom half of HB of Nekudim. Hence, its corresponding phase of AA in AK should have been Partzuf Keter of AK, and the phase corresponding AVI in AK should have been AB of AK.

The answer is that the Partzufim of BON are females, having no reception of their own, except what the males—the Partzufim of MA—impart upon them. Hence, all these discernments in the ascents, which mean obtaining Mochin from the upper one, are discerned only in the males, which are the Partzufim of MA. Since AA of MA has nothing of the state of Keter, but only the level of Hochma, and AVI of MA have nothing of the state of Hochma, but only the level of Bina (see Item 126), it is considered that their corresponding phase in AK is AB of AK to AA, and SAG of AK to AVI, and Partzuf Keter of AK relates only to Atik, which took the whole of the level of Keter of MA.

178) You should also discern in the above said, that the ladder of degrees as they are in the permanent Mochin never changes because of all these ascents. After all, it has been explained (Item 161) that the reason for all these ascents was that the NRN of the righteous, which stand at BYA, cannot receive anything before all the higher Partzufim transfer it to them from Ein Sof. To that extent, the upper ones themselves, through Ein Sof, grow and ascend, as well, each to their own upper one.

It turns out that to the extent that one degree rises, all the degrees through Ein Sof must rise, as well. For example, when ZON rise from their constant state, below Tabur of AA, clothing Chazeh of AA downward, then AA, too, ascended one degree above his constant state from Peh of Atik downward, clothing GAR of Atik. Following him, all his internal degrees rose, too: His HGT ascended to the place of the constant GAR, and his from the Chazeh to Tabur ascended to the place of the constant HGT, and his from Tabur down ascended to the place from the Chazeh through Tabur.

Accordingly, ZON, which ascended to the place from the Chazeh through Tabur of the constant AA, is still below Tabur of AA. This is because at that time, the below Tabur of AA had already ascended to the place from the Chazeh to Tabur (see the book *Ha'Ilan*, Diagram no. 4, where you will see the ascents of ZON in the constant state of the five Partzufim of Atzilut, which rise and clothe during the obtainment of Neshama to GAR of YESHSUT that stand from Peh of AVI downward, which stand from Chazeh of AA downward).

However, all the Partzufim of Atzilut rise at that time (see the book *Ha'Ilan*, Diagram no. 7). For this reason, you will find that there the ZON still clothes YESHSUT from the Peh down, atop from Chazeh of AVI downward, atop from Tabur of AA downward. Thus, the ladder of degrees has not changed at all by the ascent. And it is likewise in all the ascents (see the book *Ha'Ilan*, Diagram no. 3 through the end of the book).

179) We should also know that even after the ascent of the Partzufim, they leave their entire degree in the constant place or in the place where they were in the beginning, since there is no absence in the spiritual (see Item 96). Thus, when GAR of AVI rise to GAR of AA, GAR of AVI still remain in the permanent place from Peh of AA down. And YESHSUT rise atop the HGT of the raised AVI and receive from the actual GAR of AVI, which were there prior to the ascent.

Moreover, it is considered that there are three degrees together there. The raised GAR of AVI stand at the place of the constant GAR of AA, and bestow upon their constant place from Peh of AA downward, where YESHSUT are now present. Thus, GAR of AA and AVI and YESHSUT illuminate at the same time in the same place.

This is also the manner with all the Partzufim of AK and ABYA during the ascents. For this reason, when a Partzuf ascends, we should always note the meaning of the ascent with respect to the upper ones in their constant state, and its value toward the upper ones, who also ascended by one degree. (Examine all that in the book *Ha'Ilan*. In Diagram no. 3, you will find the state of the Partzufim in their constant state. And in Diagrams 4-6 you will find the three ascents of ZA by the value of the five constant Partzufim of Atzilut. In Diagrams 7-9 you will find the three ascents of all five Partzufim of Atzilut by the value of the five permanent Partzufim of AK. And in Diagrams 10-12 you will find the three ascents of all five Partzufim of AK in relation to the line of the permanent Ein Sof.)

The Division of each Partzuf to Keter and ABYA

180) We should know that the general and the particular are equal, and all that is discerned in the general is also present in its details, and even in the smallest detail that can be. Also, reality as a whole is discerned as the five worlds AK and ABYA, where the world of AK is considered the Keter of the worlds, and the four worlds ABYA are regarded as HB and ZON (see Item 3). Similarly, there is not a single element in all four worlds ABYA that does not comprise these five: The Rosh of each Partzuf is considered its Keter, corresponding to the world of AK; and the Guf, from the Peh to the Chazeh is considered its Atzilut. From the place of the Chazeh through the Tabur, it is considered its Beria, and from the Tabur down to its Sium Raglin, it is considered its Yetzira and Assiya.

181) You should know that there are many appellations to the ten Sefirot KHB, HGT, NHYM. Sometimes they are called GE and AHP, or KHB and ZON, or NRNHY, or the tip of the Yod and the four letters Yod-Hey-Vav-Hey, or simple HaVaYaH and AB, SAG, MA, and BON, being the four kinds of fillings in HaVaYaH. The filling of AB is Yod, Hey, Viv, Hey [Yod replaces the Aleph in the Vav]; the filling of SAG is Yod, Hey, Vav, Hey; the filling of MA is Yod, He, Vav, He [Aleph replaces the Yod in the Heys]; the filling of BON is Yod, Heh, Vv, Heh [Hey replaces the Yod in the Heys, and the Aleph is removed in the Vav].

They are also called AA, AVI, and ZON. AA is Keter, Aba is Hochma, Ima is Bina, ZA is HGT NHY, and the Nukva of ZA is Malchut.

They are also called AK and ABYA, or Keter and ABYA. Malchut of Keter is called Peh, Malchut of Atzilut is called Chazeh, Malchut of Beria is called Tabur, Malchut of Yetzira is called Ateret Yesod, and the general Malchut is called Sium Raglin.

182) Know that you should always distinguish two instructions in these different names of the ten Sefirot: The first is its equality to the Sefira to which it relates. The second is how it differs from that Sefira to which it relates, and for which its name changed in the specific appellation.

For example, Keter of the ten Sefirot of direct light is Ein Sof, and each Rosh of a Partzuf is also called Keter. Similarly, all five Partzufim of AK are called Keter, too. Partzuf Atik is also called Keter, and AA is also called Keter. Hence, we should consider this: If they are all Keter, why do their names change to be called by these appellations? Also, if they all relate to Keter, should they not be equal to Keter?

In one sense, they are all equal to Keter, as they are considered Ein Sof, for the rule is that as long as the upper light has not clothed in a vessel, it is considered Ein Sof. Hence, all five Partzufim of AK are regarded as light without a vessel with respect to the world of correction, since we have no perception in the vessels of the first restriction. Thus, for us, its lights are considered Ein Sof.

Also, Atik and AA de Atzilut are both considered Keter of Nekudim. Yet in a different sense they are far from one another, since Keter of direct light is one Sefira, but in AK it contains five complete Partzufim, each of which with Rosh, Toch, Sof (see Item 142). Also, Partzuf Atik is only from the upper half of Keter of Nekudim, and Partzuf AA is from the bottom half of Keter of Nekudim (see Item 129). Similarly, these two instructions should be discerned in all the appellations of the Sefirot.

183) Know that the specific instruction concerning these appellations of the ten Sefirot named Keter and ABYA is to show that it refers to the division of the ten Sefirot into anterior vessels and posterior vessels, made because of the second restriction. It has been explained above (Item 60), that at that time, the ending Malchut ascended to the place of Bina of Guf, called "Tifferet at the place of the Chazeh," ended the degree there, and created a new Sium called "the Parsa below the Atzilut" (see Item 68).

And the vessels from the Chazeh down went outside of Atzilut, and they are called BYA. The two thirds of Tifferet from Chazeh to Sium are called Beria, NHY are called Yetzira, and Malchut is called Assiya. It has also been explained that for this reason, each degree divided into anterior vessels and posterior vessels: From the Chazeh up it is called anterior vessels, and from the Chazeh down it is called posterior vessels.

184) Hence, this discernment of the Parsa at the place of the Chazeh splits the degree into four special phases, called ABYA: Atzilut—through the Chazeh, and BYA—from the Chazeh down. The beginning of the distinction is in AK itself. But there, the Parsa descended to its Tabur (see Item 68); hence its phase of Atzilut is the AB SAG that end above its Tabur.

From its Tabur down is its BYA, where there are the two Partzufim MA and BON in it. This is how the five Partzufim of AK divide into ABYA by the force of the Sium of the second restriction, called Parsa: Galgalta is the Rosh, AB SAG through its Tabur are Atzilut, and the MA and BON from its Tabur down is BYA.

185) Similarly, all five Partzufim of the world of Atzilut divide into their own Keter and ABYA: AA is the Rosh of the whole of Atzilut. Upper AVI, which are AB, clothing from the Peh of AA down to the Chazeh, are Atzilut. There, at the point of Chazeh, stands the Parsa, which ends the phase of Atzilut of the world of Atzilut. YESHSUT, which are SAG, clothing from the Chazeh of AA to its Tabur, are Beria

of Atzilut. ZON, which are MA and BON that clothe from the Tabur of AA to the Sium of Atzilut, are Yetzira and Assiya of Atzilut.

Thus, the world of Atzilut, too, in its five Partzufim, divided into Rosh and ABYA, as do the five Partzufim of AK. But here the Parsa stands at its place in the Chazeh of AA, which is its true place (see Item 127).

186) However, in the worlds in general, all three Partzufim Galgalta, AB, SAG of AK are regarded as the general Rosh. And the five Partzufim of the world of Atzilut, clothing from the Tabur of AK down to the general Parsa, being the Parsa that was made at the Chazeh of Nekudot of SAG (see Item 66), are the general Atzilut. And from the Parsa down stand the three general worlds BYA (Items 67-68).

187) In this very way, each particular degree in each of the worlds ABYA is divided into Rosh and ABYA, even the phase of Malchut of Malchut of Assiya, because Rosh and Guf are discerned in it. The Guf is divided into Chazeh, Tabur, and Sium Raglin; the Parsa below the Atzilut of that degree stands at its Chazeh and ends the Atzilut. From the Chazeh to the Tabur, it is considered the Beria of the degree, which the point of the Tabur concludes. From the Tabur down to its Sium Raglin it is considered Yetzira and Assiya of the degree. With respect to the Sefirot, HGT through the Chazeh are considered Atzilut, the two bottom thirds of Tifferet from the Chazeh to the Tabur are considered Beria, NHY is Yetzira, and Malchut is Assiya.

188) For this reason, the Rosh of each degree is attributed to the phase of Keter or Yechida or Partzuf Galgalta. The Atzilut in it, from the Peh to the Chazeh, is attributed to Hochma, to the light of Haya, or to Partzuf AB. The Beria in it, from the Chazeh to the Tabur, is attributed to Bina, to the light of Neshama, or to Partzuf SAG. The Yetzira and Assiya in it, from the Tabur down, are attributed to ZON, to the lights Ruach Nefesh, or to Partzuf MA and BON. Examine the book Ha'Ilan, from Diagram no. 3 onward, and you will see how each Partzuf is divided by these phases.

Preface to the Sulam Commentary

Ten Sefirot

1) First, we must know the names of the ten *Sefirot*: KHB, HGT, NHYM. These are acronyms for *Keter, Hochma, Bina, Hesed, Gevura, Tifferet, Netzah, Hod, Yesod, Malchut*. These are also the ten coverings of His light, established so the lower ones can receive His light.

This is like the light of the sun, which is impossible to look at unless through a darkened glass that diminishes its light and makes it suitable for the eyes' ability to see. Similarly, had His light not been covered by these ten coverings, called "ten *Sefirot*," in which each lower one further covers His light, the lower ones would have been unable to obtain it.

2) These ten *Sefirot* are the ten holy names in the Torah: The name *Ehyeh* [pronounced *Ekyeh*] is the *Sefira Keter*, the name *Yah* [pronounced *Koh*] is the *Sefira Hochma*, and the name *HaVaYaH* with punctuation of *Elokim* is *Bina*. The name *El* [pronounced *Kel*] is *Hesed*; the name *Elohim* [pronounced *Elokim*] is *Gevura*; and the name *HaVaYaH* with punctuation of *Shwah, Holam, Kamatz* is *Tifferet*. The name *Tzvaot* [pronounced *Tzakot*] is *Netzah* and *Hod*; the name *Shadai* [pronounced *Shadi*] is *Yesod*; and the name *Adonai* [pronounced *Adni*] is *Malchut* (The Zohar, VaYikra, Items 157-163, 166-177).

3) Although we count ten *Sefirot*, there are no more than five *Behinot* [discernments] in them. These are called *Keter, Hochma, Bina, Tifferet, Malchut*, and their content is clearly explained in the "Preface to the Wisdom of Kabbalah" from its beginning to Item 7. Read it there because there is no need to repeat it here, but these are the foundations of the wisdom. The reason we count ten *Sefirot* is because the *Sefira Tifferet* contains six *Sefirot*, called *Hesed, Gevura, Tifferet, Netzah, Hod, Yesod*, which makes them ten. To understand this, see "Introduction of The Book of Zohar," "Mirrors of the Sulam" (p 5).

These five *Behinot* KHB TM are discerned in every emanated and in every creature in all the worlds—the five worlds called *Adam Kadmon, Atzilut, Beria, Yetzira, Assiya*, which correspond to the five *Behinot* KHB TM—and in the smallest item in reality. We discern that the *Rosh* [head] in it is *Keter*, from its *Rosh* to *Chazeh* [chest] it is *Hochma*, from *Chazeh* to *Tabur* [navel] it is *Bina*, and from *Tabur* down it is *Tifferet* and *Malchut*. The meaning of the five worlds is explicated in the "Preface to the Wisdom of Kabbalah" (Items 6-10).

Why *Tifferet* Includes HGT NHY

4) When the five *Behinot* KHB TM emerged, they were incorporated in one another in such a way that each of them contained KHB TM. However, in the *Sefira Tifferet*, the level of the *Sefirot* descended from being GAR; hence, the names of the KHB

TM included in it changed to *HGT NH* and *Yesod*, which contains them. Therefore, when we say that *Tifferet* contains six *Sefirot*, it is not because of its merit over the first three *Sefirot*. On the contrary, it is the lack of light of GAR in it that caused the five *Behinot* KHB TM in it to receive different names: *HGT NH*.

Thus, *Hesed* is *Keter*, *Gevura* is *Hochma*, and *Tifferet* is *Bina*, *Netzah* is *Tifferet*, and *Hod* is *Malchut*. The *Sefira Yesod* is added to them, but it is not an additional *Behina* [sing. of *Behinot*] to the five *Behinot*. Rather, it is only a container that contains all five *Sefirot HGT NH* within it. Also, they are always called *VAK*, which is an acronym for *Vav* [six] *Ktzavot* [ends], which are these six *Sefirot HGT NHY*. Since this descent of the five *Behinot* to *HGT NHY* occurred only in *ZA*, we attribute the five changed *Behinot* only to *ZA*.

Light and *Kli*

5) It is impossible to have light in all the worlds without a *Kli*. The matter of the spiritual *Kli* is explained in the "Preface to the Wisdom of Kabbalah," Items 3-4. Initially, there was only one *Kli* in the ten *Sefirot*—*Malchut*. The reason why we say that there are five *Behinot KHB TM* is that they are all parts of *Malchut*, called *Behina Dalet*. This means that they are arranged by their proximity to the completion of the *Kli*, which is *Malchut*, called *Behina Dalet* (as written in the "Preface to the Wisdom of Kabbalah," Item 5).

But after *Tzimtzum Aleph* [first restriction], a *Masach* [screen] was erected in the *Kli* of *Malchut*, which stops the upper light from dressing in it. Hence, when the upper light reaches the *Masach*, the *Masach* strikes it and repels it. This striking is called "*Zivug de Hakaa* [coupling by striking] of the upper light with the *Masach* in the *Kli* of *Malchut*," and the repelled light is called "ten *Sefirot* of *Ohr Hozer* [reflected light]."

This is so because the repelled light rises from below upward and clothes the ten *Sefirot* in the upper light, called "ten *Sefirot* of *Ohr Yashar* [direct light]." New *Kelim* [pl. of *Kli*] were made of this *Ohr Hozer*, to clothe the upper light instead of *Malchut*, which had been restricted so as not to receive light. The content of those new *Kelim*, called "ten *Sefirot* of *Ohr Hozer*," is explained in the "Preface to the Wisdom of Kabbalah," Items 14-26.

Rosh-Toch-Sof, Peh-Tabur-Sium Raglin

6) Because of the new *Kelim* of *Ohr Hozer*, each *Partzuf* has three parts called *Rosh, Toch, Sof* [Head, Interior, End]. It has been explained that by the force of the *Masach* that stops the light from reaching *Malchut*, there was a *Zivug de Hakaa* with the light, which produced the ten *Sefirot de* [of] *Ohr Hozer* and clothed the ten *Sefirot de Ohr Yashar* in the upper light.

These ten *Sefirot de Ohr Yashar* and *Ohr Hozer* are called "ten *Sefirot de Rosh*." However, these ten *Sefirot de Ohr Hozer*, which emerged from the *Masach* upward and clothe the ten *Sefirot de Ohr Yashar*, are still not actual *Kelim*. This is because the name *Kli* indicates the *Aviut* in it, that is, the force of *Din* [judgment] in the *Masach*, which prevents the clothing of the light in *Malchut*.

There is a rule that the force of *Din* operates only from the place of the emergence of the *Din* downward, and not from the place of the emergence of the *Din* upward. Since the ten *Sefirot de Ohr Hozer* emerged from the *Masach* upward, the force of *Din* is not apparent in the *Ohr Hozer* and is unfit to be a *Kli*. For this reason, these ten *Sefirot de Ohr Hozer* are called *Rosh*, meaning a root for the *Kelim*, and not actual *Kelim*.

And *Malchut*, in which the *Masach* for the *Zivug de Hakaa* had been established, is therefore called *Peh* [mouth]. This implies that as in a corporeal mouth, *Otiot* [letters] are made through a *Zivug de Hakaa* of the five outlets of the mouth. The spiritual *Peh* contains a *Zivug de Hakaa* to produce ten *Sefirot de Ohr Hozer*, being the five *Behinot KHB TM*, which are the *Kelim* for the ten *Sefirot de Ohr Yashar*, and *Kelim* are called *Otiot*. Thus, the ten *Sefirot de Rosh* have been explained.

7) Thus, the ten *Sefirot de Ohr Yashar* and ten *Sefirot de Ohr Hozer* had to expand from the *Masach* downward, at which time the ten *Sefirot de Ohr Hozer* became *Kelim* that receive and clothe the ten *Sefirot de Ohr Yashar*. This is because now there is a *Masach* over the ten *Sefirot de Ohr Hozer*. For this reason, its thickness controls the ten *Sefirot de Ohr Hozer*, and by that the *Kelim* were made.

Also, these ten *Sefirot*, which are actual *Kelim*, are called *Toch* and *Guf* [body]; they are the very insides and the *Guf* of the *Partzuf*. And *Malchut* of the *Toch* is called *Tabur*, as in the phrase, "the *Tabur* [navel/center] of the land," referring to the center and the middle. This indicates that *Malchut de Toch* is the central *Malchut*, and it is from her *Ohr Hozer* that the actual *Kelim* of the *Guf* were made.

It can also be said that *Tabur* comes from the words *Tov Ohr* [good light], indicating that thus far the light is good, as it is dressed in *Kelim* that are suitable to receive it. Thus we have explained the ten *Sefirot de Toch* through the *Tabur*.

8) We find two discernments in *Malchut de Rosh*: 1. The ending *Malchut*: the *Masach*'s detaining of the upper light from clothing in the *Kli* of *Malchut*. 2. The mating *Malchut*: Had it not been for the *Zivug* of the upper light with the *Masach* through a *Zivug de Hakaa*, which raises *Ohr Hozer* to clothe the upper light, there would have been no vessels of reception in the upper light, and there would be no light in reality, since there is no light without a *Kli*.

But in *Malchut* of the *Rosh*, these two discernments are only two roots. The ending *Malchut* is the root of the *Malchut* that ends the degree, and the mating *Malchut* is the root of the clothing of light in the *Kelim*.

These two actions appeared and occurred in the *Guf* of the *Partzuf*: From *Peh* to *Tabur*, the mating *Malchut* shows its strength there, where the upper light is clothed in *Kelim*. From *Tabur* down, the ending *Malchut* shows its strength and produces ten

Sefirot de Sium [ending]. Each *Sefira* [sing. of *Sefirot*] emerges with illumination of only *Ohr Hozer*, without the upper light. When it reaches the *Malchut* of these ten *Sefirot de Sium*, the entire *Partzuf* ends, since this *Malchut* is the ending *Malchut*, which does not receive anything. Hence, the expansion of the *Partzuf* ends in it.

And we call this *Malchut*, *Malchut de Sium Raglin*, which cuts the light and ends the *Partzuf*. And these ten *Sefirot de Sium* that expand from the *Tabur* down to its *Sium Raglin* are called "ten *Sefirot de Sof*" [end], and they are all parts of the *Malchut* of *Sof* and *Sium*. Also, when we say that there is only *Ohr Hozer* in them, it does not mean that they have no *Ohr Yashar* at all. Rather, it means that they do have some illumination of *Ohr Yashar*, but it is considered VAK without a *Rosh*, and see the "Preface to the Wisdom of Kabbalah," Items 50-53.

Chazeh

9) Thus far we have discussed the *Partzufim* [pl. of *Partzuf*] of *Adam Kadmon*. But in the *Partzufim* of the world of *Atzilut*, another *Sium* was added in the ten *Sefirot de Toch*: *Malchut de Toch*, called *Tabur*, rose to *Bina* of the ten *Sefirot de Toch* and ended the ten *Sefirot* of the degree of *Toch* there. This *Sium* is called *Chazeh*, and the *Parsa* has been set there.

This means that the new *Sium* that was made by the ascent of *Malchut* to *Bina* at the place of the *Chazeh* is called *Parsa*, as in the firmament that separates the higher water—*Keter* and *Hochma* that remained in the *Toch* degree—from *Bina* and TM, which departed from the degree of ten *Sefirot de Toch* and became the degree of ten *Sefirot de Sof*.

For this reason, the ten *Sefirot de Toch* divided into two degrees: From *Peh* to *Chazeh* it is considered ten *Sefirot de Toch*, *Atzilut*, GAR of the *Guf*. From the *Chazeh* down to *Tabur*, it is considered ten *Sefirot de Sof*, *Beria*, VAK without a *Rosh*, like the ten *Sefirot de Sof*. On the matter of the ascent of *Malchut* to *Bina* and the new *Sium* that was made in the middle of each degree (see below letters 15-16).

Inverse Relation between *Kelim* and Lights

10) There is always an inverse relation between lights and *Kelim*. In the *Kelim*, the order is that upper ones are the first to grow in a *Partzuf*. First, *Keter* comes to the *Partzuf*, then *Hochma*, then *Bina*, then *Tifferet*, and then *Malchut*. For this reason, we name the *Kelim* KHB TM, that is, from above downward, because so is their order of appearance in the *Partzuf*.

But the lights are opposite. The order of the lights is that the lower ones enter the *Partzuf* first. The first to enter is the light of *Nefesh*, then the light of *Ruach*, then the light of *Neshama*, then the light of *Haya*, and then the light of *Yechida*.

Thus, in the beginning comes the light of *Nefesh*, which is the light of *Malchut*, the smallest of all the lights. And the last to come is the light of *Yechida*, the biggest of all the lights. This is why we always name the lights NRNHY, that is, from below upward, as this is their order of entering the *Partzuf*.

11) It therefore follows that while there is only one *Kli* in the *Partzuf*, which is necessarily the highest *Kli—Keter—*which is the first to emerge, the great light related to *Keter*, the light of *Yechida*, does not enter the *Partzuf*. Rather, the light that enters and clothes in *Kli de Keter* is the smallest light, the light of *Nefesh*.

When two *Kelim* grow in the *Partzuf*, which are the bigger *Kelim—Keter* and *Hochma—*the light of *Ruach* enters, too. In that state, the light of *Nefesh* descends from *Kli de Keter* to *Kli de Hochma*, and the light of *Ruach* clothes in *Kli de Keter*. Similarly, when the third *Kli* grows in the *Partzuf—*the *Kli* of *Bina—*the light of *Neshama* enters the *Partzuf*. In that state, the light of *Nefesh* descends from the *Kli* of *Hochma* to the *Kli* of *Bina*, the light of *Ruach* leaves the *Kli* of *Keter* and enters the *Kli* of *Hochma*, and the light of *Neshama* dresses in the *Kli* of *Keter*.

When a fourth *Kli* grows in the *Partzuf*, being the *Kli* of *Tifferet*, the light of *Haya* enters the *Partzuf*. In that state, the light of *Nefesh* descends from the *Kli* of *Bina* to the *Kli* of *Tifferet*, the light of *Ruach* to the *Kli* of *Bina*, the light of *Neshama* to the *Kli* of *Hochma*, and the light of *Haya* to the *Kli* of *Keter*.

When a fifth *Kli* grows in the *Partzuf*, the *Kli* of *Malchut*, all the lights enter their respective *Kelim*. This is because then the light of *Yechida* is drawn into the *Partzuf*: The light of *Nefesh* descends from *Kli de Tifferet* to the *Kli* of *Malchut*, the light of *Ruach* descends from *Kli de Bina* and enters the *Kli* of *Tifferet*, the light of *Neshama* descends from *Kli de Hochma* and enters the *Kli* of *Bina*, and the light of *Haya* descends from *Kli de Keter* and comes into the *Kli* of *Hochma*, and the light of *Yechida* comes and clothes in the *Kli* of *Keter*.

12) You find that as long as not all five *Kelim* KHB TM have grown in the *Partzuf*, the lights are not in their designated places. Moreover, they are in an inverted ratio, since if the *Kli* of *Malchut—*the smallest *Kli—*is lacking in the *Partzuf*, the light of *Yechida—*the biggest light—will be missing. If the two bottom *Kelim—Tifferet* and *Malchut—*are missing, the two biggest lights—*Haya* and *Yechida—*will be missing. If the three bottom *Kelim—Bina, Tifferet*, and *Malchut—*are missing, the three biggest lights—*Neshama, Haya*, and *Yechida—*will be missing, etc.

Thus, as long as not all five *Kelim* KHB TM have grown in a *Partzuf*, there is an inverse relation between the *Kelim* and the lights. If one light and one *Kli* are missing, the biggest light, the light of *Yechida*, will be missing. And it is the opposite in the *Kelim*: The smallest *Kli* will be missing—the *Kli* of *Malchut*.

13) Now you can see why we say that through *Malchut*'s ascent to *Bina*, the degree ends under the *Hochma*. And for this reason, only two *Sefirot* remained in the degree—*Keter* and *Hochma—*while *Bina* and TM of the degree were canceled and descended

from the degree (as written below, Item 17). Yet, this relates only to the *Kelim*. It is the opposite in the lights: The lights *Nefesh-Ruach* remained in the degree, and the lights *Neshama*, *Haya*, and *Yechida* were canceled from the degree.

14) Now you can understand why *The Zohar* sometimes says that with the ascent of *Malchut* to *Bina*, the five *Otiot* [letters] of the name *Elokim* were divided in a way that the two *Otiot MI* [*Mem*, *Yod*] remained in the degree and the three *Otiot ELEH* [*Aleph*, *Lamed*, *Hey*] departed and were canceled in the degree (as written in the "Introduction of The Book of Zohar," p 20 [in Hebrew]).

Sometimes *The Zohar* says the opposite, that when *Malchut* rose to *Bina*, the two letters *EL* [*Aleph*, *Lamed*] remained in the degree, and the three letters *HYM* [*Hey*, *Yod*, *Mem*] were canceled and descended from the degree (as written in *The Zohar*, *Beresheet* 1, Item 59). The thing is that the five letters *Elokim* are the five *Sefirot KHB TM* or five lights *NRNHY*. When *Malchut* rises to *Bina*, only the *Kelim Keter* and *Hochma*, which are the two letters *EL*, remain in the degree, and the three letters *HYM* descend from the degree.

In the lights, it is the opposite: The two bottom letters *MI*, which imply the two lowest lights, *Nefesh-Ruach*, remained in the degree, and the three higher letters, *ELEH*, which imply *Yechida*, *Haya*, *Neshama*, departed and were canceled from the degree.

Hence, in the "Introduction of The Book of Zohar," *The Zohar* speaks of five lights *NRNHY*, implied in the five letters *Elokim*. This is why it says that *MI* remained and *ELEH* departed the degree. Also, in *The Zohar*, *Beresheet* 1, it speaks of five *Kelim KHB TM*, implied in the five letters *Elokim*.

For this reason, it states the opposite: *EL* remained in the degree and the three *Otiot HYM* departed the degree. We should remember these words and examine every place to see if it speaks of lights or of *Kelim*, and this will resolve many apparent contradictions.

Malchut's Ascent to Bina

15) We should thoroughly understand the issue of the sweetening of *Malchut* in *Bina*, as it is the root of the whole wisdom. *Malchut* is *Midat ha Din* [quality of judgment], in which the world cannot exist. For this reason, the Emanator elevated it to the *Sefira* of *Bina*, which is *Midat ha Rachamim* [quality of mercy]. Our sages hinted about this: "In the beginning, He contemplated creating the world with *Midat ha Din*," meaning only in *Malchut*, which is *Midat ha Din*. "He saw that the world does not exist, and He preceded *Midat ha Rachamim* and associated it with *Midat ha Din*" (*Beresheet Rabbah*, end of Portion 12).

Through *Malchut's* ascent to *Bina*, *Malchut* acquires the form of *Bina*, which is *Midat ha Rachamim*, and then *Malchut* leads the world with *Midat ha Rachamim*. This issue of *Malchut's* ascent to *Bina* occurs in each and every degree, from the top of the world of *Atzilut* to the bottom of the world of *Assiya*, since there is no degree without ten *Sefirot* KHB, HGT, NHYM. And the *Malchut* in each degree rose to *Bina* in that degree and was sweetened there.

The Division of Each Degree into Two Halves

16) It is known that *Malchut* ends each *Sefira* and each degree. This means that by the *Tzimtzum* [restriction] that was made on her, of not receiving the upper light, *Malchut* stops the light in the degree from spreading into it. Hence, the light of the degree extends only through *Malchut* and stops when it reaches the *Masach* in *Malchut*, and a *Zivug de Hakaa* with the light is performed on the *Masach* in *Malchut* (as written in the "Preface to the Wisdom of Kabbalah," Item 14).

Therefore, since *Malchut* of the degree has risen to *Bina* in that degree, *Malchut* ends the light in the place to which it climbed, that is, in the middle of *Bina*. Thus, half of *Bina*, *Tifferet*, and *Malchut*, which are under the ending *Malchut*, exit their degree and become another degree, below *Malchut*.

Thus, by *Malchut*'s ascent to *Bina*, each degree is cut in two: *Keter*, *Hochma*, and half of *Bina* above the *Malchut* remained in the degree, and half of *Bina*, *Tifferet* (including HGT NHY), and *Malchut* departed the degree and became a degree below it. This ending that *Malchut* created in the middle of *Bina* is called *Parsa*.

17) Each degree must have five lights, called *Yechida*, *Haya*, *Neshama*, *Ruach*, and *Nefesh* clothed in five *Kelim* called *Keter*, *Hochma*, *Bina*, *Tifferet* (including HGT NHY), and *Malchut*. Since due to *Malchut*'s ascent to *Bina*, only two complete *Kelim* remained in the degree—*Keter* and *Hochma*—and three *Kelim*, *Bina*, *Tifferet*, and *Malchut* are missing in it, only two lights remain in it—*Nefesh*, *Ruach*—clothing the two *Kelim Keter* and *Hochma*. The three lights *Neshama*, *Haya*, and *Yechida* are missing in it since they have no *Kelim* in which to clothe.

It turns out that the degree is deficient of the first three *Sefirot*, since due to *Malchut*'s ascent to *Bina*, the degree was cut into two halves: Half of it remained in the degree—*Keter-Hochma* in the *Kelim* and *Nefesh-Ruach* in the lights—and half of it departed the degree—*Bina* and TM in *Kelim*, and *Neshama*, *Haya*, *Yechida* in lights. This is why this ascent of *Malchut* to *Bina* is implied by the *Yod* that entered the light of the degree, and the *Ohr* [light] became *Avir* [air]. As a result of *Malchut*'s ascent to *Bina*, the degree lost the light of its first three *Sefirot* and remained at the level of *Ruach Nefesh* called *Avir* (as written in *Beresheet* 1, Item 32 in the *Sulam* [Ladder commentary on *The Zohar*]).

This matter is also implied in the five letters of the name *Elokim*, which divided into two halves: MI-ELEH. The two letters MI imply the two lights *Ruach Nefesh*, clothed in the two *Kelim Keter Hochma* that remained in the degree, and the three letters ELEH imply the three *Kelim Bina*, *Tifferet*, and *Malchut* that departed the degree (as written above, Item 14).

Malchut's Descent from Bina to Its Place

18) However, through raising Mayin Nukvin from Torah and prayer of the lower ones, higher illumination is drawn from Hochma and Bina de AK, which brings Malchut out of Bina in all the degrees and lowers it to its place (The Zohar, VaYikahel, p 41). The three Kelim, Bina, Tifferet, and Malchut previously departed the degree because of the entrance of the Yod, which is Malchut, into the light of the degree, thus ending the degree under Hochma and turning the Ohr into Avir.

But now, after Malchut has descended from there and departed the Avir, the Kelim return to their degree. Thus, once again there are five Kelim KHB TM in the degree. And since there are five Kelim, all five lights Yechida, Haya, Neshama, Ruach, Nefesh return and clothe in them, and the Avir becomes Ohr once more, since the level of the first three, called Ohr, has returned to the degree.

A Time of Katnut and a Time of Gadlut

19) Thus, it has been explained that because of Malchut's ascent to Bina, two times were made in each degree: a time of Katnut [smallness/infancy] and a time of Gadlut [greatness/adulthood]. With Malchut's ascent to Bina, it ends the degree under the Hochma, and Bina, Tifferet, and Malchut of the degree depart the degree and come to the degree below it. Hence, only Keter Hochma in Kelim and Ruach Nefesh in lights remain in the degree, lacking the GAR [first three]. This is the time of Katnut (see above Item 17).

But after the lower ones raise Mayin Nukvin and extend illumination from Hochma Bina de [of] AK, which brings Malchut out of Bina, the three Kelim Bina and TM that fell to the degree below it return and rise from there to their initial degree. Since there are now five Kelim KHB TM in the degree, five lights return and clothe in them: Nefesh, Ruach, Neshama, Haya, Yechida (see above Item 18). This is the time of Gadlut of the degree (and we have already elaborated on these matters in the "Introduction of The Book of Zohar," p 20 [in Hebrew]). Thus we have explained that due to the fall of Bina and TM of the degree to the degree below it, the degree is in Katnut, lacking GAR. And through the return of Bina and TM to the degree, the degree is in Gadlut, that is, with filling of GAR.

How the Lower One Rises to Its Upper One

20) By this ascent of Malchut to Bina, the connection and the possibility of raising each lower one to its upper one has been prepared. This is because the rule is that when the upper one descends to the lower one, it becomes like it. And also, when the lower one rises to the upper one, it becomes like it.

Hence, in the state of Katnut of the degree, when the ending Malchut rises to Bina, it drives Bina and TM outside the degree into the degree below it. Then, these

Bina and *TM* become one degree with the degree below it, since the upper one that descends to the lower one becomes like it. For this reason, in the state of *Gadlut* of the degree, when *Malchut* returns and exits *Bina* and comes to its place, *Bina* and *TM* that fell from *Bina* return to their degree and take the lower degree in which they were while they were fallen, along with them.

Because they have now become one degree with the lower one, when they were fallen, and became as one with it, they take it with them on their return to the degree and elevate the lower degree to the upper degree. According to the rule that the lower one that rises to the place of the upper one becomes like it, now the lower degree receives all the lights and *Mochin* that exist in the upper degree.

Thus it has been clarified how the ascent of *Malchut* to *Bina* induced a connection between the degrees, so each degree can rise to the degree above it. Thus, even the lowest degree can rise to the highest level through this connection made by the fall of *Bina* and *TM* from each degree to the degree below it (as it is written in the *Sulam* [Ladder commentary on *The Zohar*], *VaYikahel*, p 41 [in Hebrew]).

Katnut and Gadlut of YESHSUT and ZON

21) Once the issue of *Malchut's* ascent to *Bina*, applied in each and every degree in the four worlds ABYA, has been explained in general, I will now explain them in detail. Let us take two degrees, called YESHSUT and ZON in the world of *Atzilut* as an example. Through the ascent of *Malchut de* YESHSUT to *Bina de* YESHSUT in the state of *Katnut*, the three *Sefirot*, *Bina* and *TM de* YESHSUT departed and fell to the degree below YESHSUT, being ZON. These *Bina* and *TM* clung to the degree of ZON during their fall.

Hence, upon the arrival of the time of *Gadlut*, *Malchut* departed *Bina de* YESHSUT back to her own place. Thus, *Bina* and *TM de* YESHSUT rose from their fall and came to the degree of YESHSUT. Along with them, they brought ZON, since they were attached to them during the *Katnut*, when they were fallen. It turns out that ZON, too, rose and became the degree of YESHSUT, receiving the same illuminations and *Mochin* fit for the degree of YESHSUT.

Had It Not Been for Malchut's Ascent to Bina, ZON Would Not Have Been Worthy of Mochin

22) Here we should know that for themselves, ZON are completely unfit to receive *Mochin*, since the origin of ZON is below *Tabur de* AK (see Item 17 above), where *Malchut* of *Midat ha Din* rules, which is governed by the force of *Tzimtzum* and is unfit to receive the upper light. Yet, now that *Bina* and *TM de* YESHSUT elevated ZON to the degree of YESHSUT, ZON became as the degree of YESHSUT and can receive the upper light as they do.

23) Now you can thoroughly understand why our sages said (*Beresheet Rabbah*, end of Portion 12): "In the beginning, He contemplated creating the world with *Midat ha Din*," that is, with *Malchut* of the first restriction, which is *Midat ha Din*. And "world" should be understood as ZON *de Atzilut*, called "world." And it should also be understood as "this world," which receives from ZON *de Atzilut*. This is because all that is received in ZON *de Atzilut* can be received by people in this world, and all that is not received in ZON is not received by people in this world, as we cannot receive above the degree of ZON.

Hence, since the root of ZON is below *Tabur de AK*, where *Malchut* of *Midat ha Din* rules, they cannot receive the upper light and exist, since they are under the *Tzimtzum* in *Malchut*. All the more so, this world cannot exist.

This is the meaning of "He saw that the world does not exist, he preceded *Midat ha Rachamim* and associated it with *Midat ha Din*." This means that He elevated *Malchut* of each degree, which is *Midat ha Din*, to the *Bina* of the degree, which is *Midat ha Rachamim*. It follows that *Malchut de YESHSUT* rose to *Bina de YESHSUT*, by which *Bina* and TM *de YESHSUT* fell to the degree below it, which is ZON, and clung to them.

For this reason, during the *Gadlut* of YESHSUT, when *Malchut* descended from *Bina de YESHSUT* and returned to her place, and the three *Kelim Bina* and TM *de YESHSUT* returned to their place, YESHSUT, as in the beginning, they took the ZON that were attached to them along with them and raised them to the degree of YESHSUT. Thus, ZON became like the degree of YESHSUT, worthy of receiving the upper light like YESHSUT (see above Item 21). For this reason, they receive the upper light of YESHSUT and give to this world, and now the world can exist.

But had it not been for the association of *Midat ha Din* with *Midat ha Rachamim*, meaning if *Malchut de YESHSUT* had not risen to *Bina de YESHSUT*, *Bina* and TM *de YESHSUT* would not have fallen to ZON, and there would be no possibility for ZON to rise to YESHSUT. In that state, they would not be able to receive the upper light for the world, and the world would not be able to exist. Thus we have explained the issue of *Malchut's* ascent to *Bina*.

Tikkun Kavim

24) In the first three *Partzufim de AK*, called *Galgalta*, AB, SAG *de AK*, the *Sefirot* were in a single line, one below the other. But in the world of *Nekudim*, clothing from *Tabur de AK* downward, there was a *Tikkun Kavim* [correction of lines] in their GAR, but not in the seven lower *Sefirot*. In the world of *Atzilut*, there was a *Tikkun Kavim* in the seven lower *Sefirot*, as well.

Two Discernments in Tikkun Kavim

25) The reason for it is that the *Tikkun Kavim* performed in the ten *Sefirot* extends from *Malchut's* ascent to *Bina*, which became *Nukva* [female] to *Hochma*. As a result, two sides were made in the ten *Sefirot*, since the *Malchut* that was mingled into each

Sefira became the left side of the *Sefira*, and the actual *Sefira* is considered the right line in the *Sefira*. Also, the left line blemished the right line.

In that state, the upper light mated on the *Masach* of the *Dinim* [pl. of *Din*] in this *Malchut*, and the level of *Hassadim* that emerged in the *Zivug de Hakaa* of the upper light on the *Masach* of that *Malchut* became the middle line, uniting and equalizing the two lines with one another. Were it not for the *Dinim* in *Malchut*, there would be no *Zivug de Hakaa*, nor would there be the many *Hassadim*. Hence, *Malchut*, which is "left," became as important as the actual *Sefira*, which is "right."

It is known that the beginning of the *Tikkun* of *Malchut*'s ascent to *Bina* was in the world of *Nekudim*, which emerged after *Partzuf SAG de AK*. Hence, the *Tikkun* of the three *Kavim* begins in the world of *Nekudim*, too, for one is dependent on the other. But in the first three *Partzufim*, *Galgalta*, *AB*, *SAG* that preceded the world of *Nekudim*, where there was no such issue as *Malchut*'s ascent to *Bina*, hence, there weren't three lines in them, but only one line.

26) All this is possible only in GAR of the world of *Nekudim*, considered GAR *de Bina*, whose *Hassadim* are GAR, since they are *Ohr Hassadim* by their very essence, since they never receive *Ohr Hochma* (as written in the "Introduction of The Book of Zohar," p 6 [in Hebrew]). For this reason, the level of *Hassadim* that emerged on the *Masach* of *Malchut* is sufficient to unite the two lines, right and left, with one another, and return the GAR to the *Sefirot*.

This is not so in the seven lower *Sefirot* in the world of *Nekudim*, which are considered ZA, whose essence is illumination of *Hochma* in *Hassadim* (as written in *The Study of the Ten Sefirot*, Part 1, Chapter 1, Item 50), since they need *Hochma*. Since *Malchut* is involved in all the *Sefirot*, they cannot receive *Hochma*; they are deficient and flawed as long as *Hochma* does not shine in them.

Thus, the level of *Hassadim* that emerged on the *Masach de Malchut* does not help them at all to equalize the two lines, right and left, with one another. This is because the *Dinim* in the left, which are the *Dinim* of *Malchut* that rose to *Bina*, blemish the right line and remove the light of GAR from it. Thus, the *Tikkun Kavim de* GAR does not help at all in correcting the two lines, right and left in VAK, since the VAK in all the *Sefirot* is from the *Hitkalelut* [mixture, integration] of ZA there. And as long as it does not have illumination of *Hochma*, it is deficient and flawed.

Tikkun Kavim in ZAT and in YESHSUT

27) Hence, the first *Tikkun* the lower seven *Sefirot* need is to remove the *Dinim* in *Malchut* that have been mingled in the *Sefirot*, that is, to simply extend illumination from *Hochma Bina de AK*, which lowers the *Malchut* from *Bina* and returns it to its place (as written in Item 18). At that time, the three *Kelim Bina* and TM return to the *Sefira* and become the left line, and *Keter* and *Hochma* that remained become the right line. Since the degree is completed with five *Kelim*, KHB TM, all five

lights *NRNHY* return to it and the light of *Hochma* returns to the degree. Then the middle line can unite the two lines with one another and complete the degree with all its corrections.

28) The second *Tikkun* is to strengthen the *Parsa* (mentioned above in Item 17), which is the ending force of *Malchut* that rose to *Bina*, so it will never be canceled. And even when *Malchut* descends from *Bina*, her ending force remains in *Bina's* place. Then *Bina* and *TM*, which unite with the degree, should rise above the *Parsa* and unite there with the degree. Yet, when they are below the *Parsa*, they cannot connect to the degree, even though *Malchut* has already descended from there, since her ending force remains after her descent from there, as well.

29) When *Bina* and *TM* rise above the *Parsa* and connect to the degree, they do not actually become one degree with the two *Kelim Keter* and *Hochma*. This is because there remains a difference between the two *Kelim Keter* and *Hochma*, which were never blemished because they never left their degree, and the three *Kelim Bina* and *TM* that departed their degree were blemished during the *Katnut* and have now returned. That difference turns them into two lines, right and left, where *Keter* and *Hochma* of the degree become the right line, and *Bina* and *TM* of the degree become the left line (as it is written in *VaYakhel*, Item 130).

30) This difference and these right and left do not refer to a location because the spiritual is above place and above time. Instead, a difference means that they do not want to connect with one another. Also, right refers to *Ohr Hassadim* and left refers to *Ohr Hochma*.

The thing is that *Keter* and *Hochma* of the degree, which remain in it during the *Katnut*—with *Ohr Hassadim*—settle for this *Ohr Hassadim* during the *Gadlut*, as well, after *Malchut* has descended from *Bina*. This is because this light was not flawed. They do not want to receive the *Ohr Hochma* and *GAR* that have now returned to the degree, with the return of *Bina* and *TM* to the degree (written above in Item 18).

For this reason, *Keter* and *Hochma* are considered the right line, meaning *Ohr Hassadim*, and these *Bina* and *TM*, which, upon their return to the degree, introduce *Ohr Hochma* and *GAR* to the degree, do not want to unite with *Keter* and *Hochma*, since they keep to the *Ohr Hassadim* that they had during the *Katnut*. *Bina* and *TM* have higher regard for the *Ohr Hochma* that has now come to the degree; hence, they are considered the left line since they keep to the *Ohr Hochma*.

31) This difference between the right line and the left line is also considered the division of the right from the left (see *Beresheet 1*, p 57, and the *Idra Raba*, Item 214). The right line holds the *Hassadim* and wishes to cancel the *Ohr Hochma* in the left line and ordain the *Ohr Hassadim* alone. Conversely, the left line, which keeps to *Ohr Hochma*, wishes to cancel the *Ohr Hassadim* in the right line and ordain the *Ohr Hochma*. Because of this dispute, neither shines, since the *Ohr Hassadim* in the right line is deficient of *Ohr Hochma*, like a *Guf* without a *Rosh*, and the *Ohr Hochma* in the

left line is complete darkness because *Ohr Hochma* cannot shine without *Hassadim* (as it is written in *Beresheet* 1, p 47).

32) There is no correction to this dispute except through the middle line, created by the lower one that ascends there for MAN in the form of the middle line. A *Zivug* from the upper light is made on the *Masach* of the lower one, called *Masach de Hirik*, and the level of *Hassadim* emerges on it, and this is the middle line. On one hand, this *Masach* diminishes the GAR of the left line, and on the other hand, it increases the *Ohr Hassadim*. By these two, it compels the left line to unite with the right line.

Thus, the light of VAK *de Hochma* of the left line clothes the *Hassadim* in the right line, and now it can shine, completing the left line. Also, the *Ohr Hassadim* in the right line unites with the *Hochma* in the left line, thus obtaining the light of GAR, which completes the right line. Thus, you see how the middle line completes the two lines, right and left. This explains in general terms the *Tikkun* of the three lines that was established in the seven lower *Sefirot*.

The Emergence of the Three Lines in YESHSUT

33) Now we shall explain the order of emergence of three lines in one particular degree. And from it, you will be able to deduce about all the degrees.

Take the degree of YESHSUT, for example, that is, the seven bottom *Sefirot* of *Bina*. GAR *de Bina de* AA were established in the upper AVI, and ZAT *de Bina de* AA were established in YESHSUT. The first to emerge was the right line of YESHSUT—*Keter* and *Hochma de* YESHSUT. It was established during the ascent of *Malchut de* YESHSUT to *Bina de* YESHSUT, which ended the degree of YESHSUT under the *Hochma*, and *Bina* and TM *de* YESHSUT fell below to the degree of ZA (see Item 21).

Then, these two *Kelim*, *Keter* and *Hochma*, remained in the degree of YESHSUT and became the right line. Since there are only two *Kelim* there, *Keter* and *Hochma*, they have only two lights, *Nefesh Ruach*, lacking GAR (see Item 26).

34) Then the left line emerged—the three *Kelim* of *Bina* and TM of YESHSUT—after they returned and rose from their fall. It was established by the illumination of *Hochma* and *Bina de* AK, which brought the ending *Malchut* from *Bina de* YESHSUT and returned it to her place. At that time, *Bina* and TM *de* YESHSUT rise back to their degree (see Item 21).

And since the five *Kelim* in the *Partzuf* are now completed, the full NRNHY clothe in them. At that time, they become the left line of YESHSUT (see Item 29). Also, with the emergence of the left line, there is a division between the right and the left: The right wishes to cancel the left and rule by itself, and the left, too, wishes to cancel the right and rule by itself (see Item 31). For this reason, neither can shine as long as the middle line, which unites them, has not been erected.

35) Afterward emerged the middle line. It emerged by the *Masach* of the lowest degree in YESHSUT, ZA, which rose as MAN to YESHSUT (see Item 32). It rose to YESHSUT along with the three *Kelim Bina* and TM when they rose back to their degree (see Item 21).

The level of light that emerges on this *Masach* unites the right and left in YESHSUT into one. However, the right shines from above downward and the left shines from below upward. In that state, the *Hochma* is dressed with *Hassadim* and can shine, while the *Hassadim* are included in the illumination of *Hochma* and are completed with GAR.

Thus, you find that before the establishment of the middle line, the right line and the left line were disputed and wanted to revoke one another: The right line, being unflawed and the root of the degree, wished to revoke the dominion of the left and subdue it, as is the root's relation to its branch. And since the left line holds the *Ohr Hochma*, which is greater than the *Ohr Hassadim* in the right line (see Item 30), its power is therefore great to revoke the *Ohr Hassadim* in the right line. This is why neither could shine, since *Hochma* cannot shine without a clothing of *Hassadim*, and *Hassadim* without illumination of *Hochma* are VAK without a *Rosh*.

36) The reason *Hochma* cannot shine without *Ohr Hassadim* is that it is YESHSUT—the seven lower *Sefirot* of *Bina*—HGT NHYM *de Bina*. These HGT NHYM *de Bina* are not the actual *Bina*, but from the *Hitkalelut* of ZA in *Bina*. This is because all ten *Sefirot* are included in one another and each *Sefira* contains ten *Sefirot*.

For example, the *Sefira Bina* is comprised of all ten *Sefirot* KHB TM, and its *Bina* is discerned as its self. *Keter* and *Hochma* in it are from *Keter* and *Hochma* that were included in it, and *Tifferet* and *Malchut*, which are its HGT NHYM, are from the *Hitkalelut* of ZON in it. It is known that the *Sefira* ZA from its source in the ten *Sefirot de Ohr Yashar* is primarily *Ohr Hassadim*, but the *Ohr Hochma* shines in its *Hassadim* (see *The Study of the Ten Sefirot*, Part 1, Chapter 1, Item 50). Hence, it is impossible for *Hochma* to shine without *Hassadim* in all seven lower *Sefirot*, since they lack the core and the carrier of the illumination of *Hochma*—the *Hassadim*—the essence of ZA of the ten *Sefirot de Ohr Yashar*, which is the root of every seven lower *Sefirot* included in all the degrees.

Hence, the rule is that *Hochma* can shine without *Hassadim* only in the light of the first three *Sefirot*. But in the seven lower *Sefirot*, wherever they are, they are considered ZA, and *Hochma* cannot shine without *Hassadim*, since *Hassadim* are its main essence. For this reason, if *Hochma* is deficient of *Hassadim*, it is darkness and not light.

37) Because of the height of the *Hochma* that the left is holding, the left line does not surrender whatsoever to unite with the *Hassadim* in the right line. Moreover, it fights it and wishes to revoke it. It does not surrender to the right unless by the two forces that rise from the middle line, which act on it and subdue it:

1. The *Masach* of *Behina Aleph* in the middle line, which is ZA. This *Masach* diminishes the level of *Hochma* in the left line from the level of GAR *de Hochma* to the level of VAK

de Hochma. This is so that Hochma would not expand and shine from above downward but from below upward. This illumination is regarded as only VAK de Hochma.

2. The Zivug of the upper light on this Masach de Behina Aleph, which extends the level of Ohr Hassadim. Then, on one hand, the level of Hochma in the left descended into VAK de Hochma by the force of the Masach. On the other hand, the Hassadim on the left line increased from two sides: from the side of the right line and from the side of the Zivug of the upper light on the Masach in the middle line. At that time, the left line surrenders and unites with the Hassadim in the right line and in the middle line (see The Zohar, Emor, Item 197 in the Sulam [Ladder commentary on The Zohar]). However, as long as the Masach in the middle line does not diminish the level of GAR de Hochma, there is no power in the world that can unite it with the right line (see Beresheet 1, p 60 [in Hebrew]).

38) We should know that two forces operate in this Masach of the middle line to diminish the level of GAR de Hochma in the left line. This is because it has been explained above (Item 22) that in themselves, ZON are unfit to receive Mochin, as they are controlled by Malchut of Midat ha Din, who is ridden by the force of Tzimtzum so as to not receive illumination of Hochma. We call this Malchut of Midat ha Din, Man'ula [lock] (as written in the "Introduction of The Book of Zohar," p 59 [in Hebrew]). But afterward, Malchut was associated with Midat ha Rachamim, meaning Bina, and in Behinat Malchut that is associated with Bina, they are worthy of receiving Mochin—light of Hochma. We call this Malchut, which is associated with Bina, Miftacha [key] (see "Introduction of The Book of Zohar," p 57 [in Hebrew]).

Hence, in Masach de ZA, too, which is their middle line, there are these two forces of Man'ula and Miftacha. In the beginning, when it needs to diminish the GAR of the left line, it works in this Masach of Man'ula, that is, in Malchut of Midat ha Din. Wherever it appears, the upper light flees (see in the Sulam [Ladder commentary on The Zohar], YaYetze, Item 13). However, since it wishes VAK de Hochma to remain, it subsequently removes this Masach de Man'ula and operates with the Masach de Miftacha, which is Malchut that is associated with Bina. And through its force, an illumination of VAK de Hochma remains, nevertheless (see all this in the Sulam, Lech Lecha, p 13 [in Hebrew]).

Thus, we have thoroughly explained how ZA rises along with Bina and TM de YESHSUT to the degree of YESHSUT, and through its Masach, it unites and completes the two lines, right and left in YESHSUT, where it becomes a middle line. And these three lines in YESHSUT are called Hochma, Bina, Daat de YESHSUT. The two lines, right and left, are called HB, and ZA, the middle line that decides between them, is called Daat.

Holam, Shuruk, Hirik

39) These three lines are also called "the three dots, Holam, Shuruk, Hirik." The right line is the dot of Holam, the left line is the dot of Shuruk, the Melafom, which is a Vav with a dot within it, and the middle line is the dot of Hirik. The reason for it is that

dots imply illumination of *Hochma*, which revive and move the *Otiot* [letters], which are the *Kelim*.

Hence, the right line, erected during *Malchut*'s ascent to *Bina*, which lacks *Hochma* (see Item 30) is implied by the dot of *Holam*, which stands above the *Otiot*. This indicates that the dot, which is *Hochma*, is not clothed in the *Kelim*, which are the *Otiot*, but is above the *Kelim*.

And the left line is made of *Bina* and *TM*, which have *Ohr Hochma* after they have returned to their degree (see Item 30). For this reason, it is implied by the dot of *Shuruk*, which is a *Vav* with a dot within it. This indicates that the dot, which is *Hochma*, is clothed inside the *Kelim*, called *Otiot*. And the middle line is made of the degree below it, which rose to the higher degree, deciding and completing its two lines (see Items 32, 35).

Had it not been for the middle line, *Hochma* would never have been able to shine (see there). And since this *Tikkun* comes from the degree below it, it is implied by the dot of *Hirik*, which stands below the *Otiot*—the *Kelim*—as it is its inferior degree. Because of it, we always refer to the *Masach* of the middle line as *Masach de Hirik* (see all this in the *Sulam* [Ladder commentary on *The Zohar*], *Beresheet* 1, Item 9).

The Middle Line Above the Two Lines

40) Indeed, there is a middle line above the two lines, in the first *Roshim* [heads] of *Atik*, where the *Reisha de lo Etyada* decides and unites the two lines, right and left, which are the two *Roshim*, *Keter* and *Hochma Stimaa de AA*, which are below it (as written in *Idra Zuta*, p 15, 27 [in Hebrew]). But although they were erected as the root for the three lines, in all three lines, the middle line comes from below, except in these.

And you find that there are three *Behinot* [discernments] of *Tikkun Kavim*:

1. *Tikkun Kavim* in the three *Roshim de Atik*, where the middle line is above the two lines;
2. *Tikkun Kavim* in GAR, where there is no appearance of *Hochma* even in the left line (see Item 26);
3. *Tikkun Kavim* in the seven lower *Sefirot*, where there is appearance of *Hochma* in the left line (see Items 27-39).

Three Kinds of Hochma in Atzilut

41) There are three *Hochmas* in *Atzilut*:

1. *Hochma* in the ten *Sefirot de Ohr Yashar*, which, in the *Partzufim*, is *Hochma Stimaa de AA*;
2. GAR *de Bina*, which, in the *Partzufim*, is AVI, and is called "*Hochma* of the right";

3. ZAT *de Bina*, which, in the *Partzufim*, is YESHSUT, and is called "*Hochma* of the left."

The first two *Hochmas* are blocked and do not shine to the lower ones. Only the third *Hochma*, the *Hochma* of the left, is apparent at the place of *Malchut* and shines to ZON and to the lower ones.

42) You already know that AA is *Hochma de Atzilut*, and AVI are GAR *de Bina de Atzilut*, and YESHSUT are the seven lower *Sefirot de Bina de Atzilut*. It is known that there are only two *Sefirot*, *Keter* and *Hochma*, in *Rosh de* AA, called *Kitra* and *Hochma Stimaa*. Its *Bina* departed its *Rosh* and became a *Guf* without a *Rosh* because of the ending *Malchut* that rose and ended the *Rosh* under its *Hochma*.

For this reason, *Bina* and TM are below the ending *Malchut* in the *Rosh* (see Item 33), and hence was discerned as a *Guf*. Also, these *Bina* and TM are all named after the highest *Behina* in them, which is *Bina*. Since it departed the *Rosh* to form a *Guf* without a *Rosh*, it is no longer worthy of receiving *Hochma* until it returns to *Rosh de* AA.

43) This *Bina* divided into two *Behinot*, GAR and ZAT, since the flaw of the absence of *Hochma* that was made in it by its exit from *Rosh* of AA does not affect the GAR *de Bina* whatsoever, since they are always in the state of "for he desires mercy." Thus, *Bina* craves only *Ohr Hassadim*, and not *Ohr Hochma*. Even when it was in the *Rosh de* AA, its GAR did not receive *Hochma*, but only *Hassadim*.

This extended to it from *Bina de Ohr Yashar*, whose essence is *Hassadim* without *Hochma* (as written in the "Preface to the Wisdom of Kabbalah," Item 5). For this reason, GAR *de Bina* are not flawed in any way by their exit from the *Rosh*, and they are considered completely perfect while still at the *Rosh de* AA. Hence, GAR *de Bina* were separated into a degree in and of themselves. Also, upper AVI, clothing from *Peh de* AA downward, which are always considered GAR, are made of them, although they are below the *Rosh* of AA.

But the seven lower *Sefirot de Bina* are not *Bina's* essence, but are from the *Hitkalelut* of ZON in *Bina* (see Item 26). And the essence of ZA is the illumination of *Hochma* in *Hassadim* (as written in the "Preface to the Wisdom of Kabbalah," Item 5). Hence, they need illumination of *Hochma* in order to give to ZON. Since they are not worthy of receiving *Hochma* for ZON upon their exit from *Rosh de* AA, they are considered flawed.

For this reason, they were separated from the complete GAR *de Bina* and became a separate degree in itself, from which *Partzuf* YESHSUT *de Atzilut* that clothes from *Chazeh de* AA downward was made. Also, they are considered VAK without a *Rosh*, until *Bina* returns to *Rosh de* AA, at which time they obtain GAR.

44) Thus, you see that *Hochma* is primarily at the *Rosh de* AA, called *Hochma Stimaa*, since this initial *Hochma* was blocked at the *Rosh* of AA and does not shine to the lower ones, below *Rosh de* AA. AVI and YESHSUT are the original *Bina de Atzilut*, called "the level of SAG *de* MA," whose essence is *Hassadim* and not *Hochma*.

And upon the exit of *Bina* from *Rosh de AA*, only ZAT *de Bina*—YESHSUT—were flawed, and hence remained without GAR. They are completed only upon the return of *Bina* to *Rosh de AA*, at which time *Hochma* receives for ZON.

At that time, they are regarded as *Hochma* of the left line. This means that this *Hochma* appears only through the three lines that emerge in YESHSUT, where the *Hochma* appears in the left line of these three lines (see Item 34).

Even though GAR and ZAT *de Bina*, which are AVI and YESHSUT, returned to *Rosh de AA*, YESHSUT do not receive the *Hochma* directly from *Hochma Stimaa* in *Rosh de AA*, since each degree receives only from its adjacent upper one. Thus, AVI receive the *Hochma* from *Hochma Stimaa* at the *Rosh de AA* and give to YESHSUT.

45) AVI are regarded as *Hochma* of the right. This is because even when they are below the *Rosh*, they are as complete as they were at the *Rosh*. They are always united with the *Hochma Stimaa* at the *Rosh de AA*, but do not receive from it, since they are always in the state of "for he desires mercy" (see the *Sulam* ["Ladder" commentary on *The Zohar*], *Tzav*, Item 151, and Pinhas, Item 206).

This thoroughly explains that the essence of *Hochma* is at the *Rosh de AA*, but it is blocked and does not shine at all below its *Rosh*. Also, the illumination of *Hochma Stimaa*, included in AVI, is considered *Hochma* of the right, although they do not actually receive it. Upon their return to the *Rosh*, they are called *Hochma Ilaa* [upper *Hochma*].

And the reason they are considered *Hochma*, although they do not receive it, is that their unification with the *Hochma* turns the *Hassadim* in AVI into complete GAR. Also, the *Hochma* that shines in YESHSUT is *Hochma* of the left, since it shines only in the left line. This *Hochma* of the left is called "Thirty-two paths of *Hochma* [wisdom]" (as written in the *Idra Zuta*, Item 73), and this is the *Hochma* that appears to ZON and to the lower ones.

But *Hochma* of the right does not shine any *Hochma*, but only *Hassadim*, since AVI do not receive the *Hochma*, much less the *Hochma de Ohr Yashar* in the *Rosh de AA*, which does not shine below its *Rosh*. This is why it is called *Hochma Stimaa*. Thus, illumination of *Hochma* does not appear, but only *Hochma* of the left, even though this is not the actual *Hochma*, but *Bina* that receives *Hochma* for ZON.

Three Letters in *Tzelem*: Mem, Lamed, Tzadik

46) The *Mochin de Gadlut*, after *Malchut* came back down from *Bina*'s place to her own, and *Bina* and TM returned to their degree and the degree was completed with five *Kelim* KHB TM and five lights NRNHY (see above Item 18). This is considered that *Malchut*, which is the *Yod* that entered the *Ohr* and turned it into *Avir*, returned and departed the *Avir*, and the *Avir* went back to being *Ohr* (see there). There are three degrees to discern in these *Mochin*, implied by the three letters—Mem, Lamed, Tzadik—which is *Tzelem*.

First Degree: This is the GAR *de Bina* that were established in upper *AVI*. They are in a state of "for he desires mercy," and never receive *Hochma*. For this reason, it is discerned in them that the *Yod* does not leave their *Avir*. This is because *Avir* implies the level of *Ruach*, *Hassadim*, and in *AVI* these *Hassadim* are regarded as actual GAR, and they have no interest in removing the *Yod* from their *Avir*.

Also, they are called *Mem de Tzelem*, since this letter implies that they contain four *Mochin*: *Hochma*, *Bina*, the right of *Daat*, and the left of *Daat*. Each *Moach* [sing. of *Mochin*] comprises ten *Sefirot*, hence they are forty *Sefirot*. It also implies that the *Mochin* are closed as though by a ring, which is the form of the *Mem*, so as to not receive *Hochma*.

47) Second Degree: This is the seven lower *Sefirot* of *Bina* that were erected in YESHSUT, which require *Hochma* in order to give to ZON (see Item 43). Hence, during the *Gadlut*, the *Yod* leaves their *Avir* and the *Ohr Hochma* returns to them in order to give to ZON. Yet, they, too, do not receive *Hochma* for themselves, since they are from *Bina*, and every *Bina*, whether GAR or ZAT, is from *Ohr Hassadim*. The only difference is in the ZAT, which receive *Hochma* in order to give to ZON.

This degree is called *Lamed de Tzelem*. This letter implies that there are three *Mochin* in them: *Hochma*, *Bina*, *Daat*. Each *Moach* contains ten *Sefirot*, hence they are thirty *Sefirot*. This is because the right in *Daat* and the left in *Daat* are regarded as one here, since they are considered the middle line, uniting *Hochma* and *Bina*.

48) The third degree is ZON, in which the *Hochma* appears from the *Chazeh* down, since the place where *Hochma* appears is in them. It is called *Tzadik de Tzelem* after the nine *Sefirot* in ZON. Each comprises ten, hence they are ninety [in *Gematria*, the numeric value of *Tzadik* is 90]. Thus we have explained the three *Otiot Mem*, *Lamed*, *Tzadik* [MLTz] in the three *Partzufim* AVI, YESHSUT, and ZON in the world of *Atzilut* in general. Yet, this is so in every detail, too, since there is no degree in which these three *Behinot* MLTz are not discerned, since each of them contains MLTz.

49) Yet, the place where *Hochma* appears is not in ZA but in *Malchut*. When we say that *Hochma* appears from the *Chazeh de ZA* downward, it is because from *Chazeh de ZA* downward it is considered *Malchut*. Thus, *Hochma* does not appear in the first nine *Sefirot*, but only in *Malchut*. This is why *Malchut* is called *Hochma Tataa* [lower *Hochma*] (as written in the *Sulam* ["Ladder" commentary on *The Zohar*], *Beresheet* 1, p 276 [in Hebrew]).

Two Discernments in Raising MAN

50) There are two *Behinot* [discernments] in raising MAN *de ZA*: 1) GAR *de Bina*, which are the upper AVI, are always in *Achoraim* to *Hochma*, meaning they do not want to receive *Hochma*, but *Hassadim*, as it is written, "for he desires mercy," and YESHSUT cannot receive *Hochma* from AA, but only through AVI (see Item 44). Hence, YESHSUT cannot receive *Hochma* through AVI, unless ZA rises to YESHSUT

for MAN. At that time, *AVI* remove their *Achoraim* from *Hochma*, and *Hochma* passes through *AVI* to *YESHSUT*.

This awakening extends from *Bina de Ohr Yashar*, which extends illumination of *Hochma* in *Hassadim* for ZA *de Ohr Yashar* (see the "Preface to the Wisdom of Kabbalah," Item 5). Therefore, whenever ZA rises for MAN, *AVI* awaken to extend *Hochma* for it (see below Item 83).

51) The second discernment in the raising of MAN by ZA is to unite the two lines, right and left, in *YESHSUT* (see Item 35). This is because when the left line of *YESHSUT* emerges, a division is made between the right and the left. For this reason, neither shines until ZA unites them with one another through the middle line, and then both shine (as written there).

Three Emerge from One, One Exists in Three

52) Thus, it has been explained that the second discernment in raising MAN *de* ZA to *YESHSUT* is to unite the two lines right and left of *YESHSUT*. They can only shine through the *Masach de Hirik* in ZA (see end of Item 39), which completes the middle line in them and determines the two lines of *Bina*. This is considered that three lines emerge in *Bina* through the *Masach de* ZA, called *Hochma*, *Bina*, and *Daat*.

The rule is that the lower one is rewarded with the full illumination that it causes in the upper one. Hence, since ZA, with its *Masach*, caused the emergence of the three lines *Hochma*, *Bina*, and *Daat* in *YESHSUT*, ZA, too, is rewarded with the three lines, *Hochma*, *Bina*, and *Daat*. This is the meaning of what is written in *The Zohar* (*Beresheet* 1, Item 363): "Three emerge from one, one exists in three" (see there).

The Root of *Nukva de* ZA, Meaning the *Malchut*

53) During the *Katnut* of the world of *Nekudim*, ZA, which is HGT NHY *de Nekudim*, had six *Kelim*, HBD HGT (because from the perspective of the lights, where the small ones grow first, they are called HGT NHY and they lack GAR. From the perspective of the *Kelim*, where the higher ones grow first, they are called HBD HGT and lack NHY *de Kelim* (as written in the "Preface to the Wisdom of Kabbalah," Item 24)).

Thus, it lacked NHY *de Kelim* because of *Malchut*'s ascent to the place of *Bina de* ZA, namely the *Sefira Tifferet*, since HGT *de* ZA are KHB (see Item 9), on the upper third of *Tifferet* in the place of the *Chazeh*. And the two thirds, *Bina* and TM, which, in ZA, are called the two thirds *Tifferet* and NHY (see there), fell from its degree to the degree below it, to the worlds *Beria*, *Yetzira*, and *Assiya*, below ZA *de Atzilut*.

For this reason, only HBD HGT *de Kelim* through the point of *Chazeh* remained in it. The point of *Chazeh* is the *Malchut* that ends the degree in the place of *Bina*, and lowers *Bina* and TM, called TNHY, to the degree below it (see Item 16). This is why ZON in *Katnut* are always called *Vav* and *Nekuda*, since the six *Kelim* HBD HGT in it are called VAK, meaning *Vav Ktzavot* [six ends], and the point of *Chazeh*, which is the *Malchut* that ends its degree is called *Nekuda* [point/dot]. (From the perspective of the lights, where the smaller ones grow first, they are called HGT NHY, and the ending *Malchut* is called "*Nekuda* under the *Yesod*.")

54) For this reason, *Malchut* took all the *Kelim* in BYA into her own domain, which is the point of the *Chazeh*. This is because this point took the *Kelim de* TNHY *de* ZA out to BYA. Also, she returned those *Kelim* to the degree of *Atzilut* when the *Gadlut de Nekudim* emerged, before they broke. This is because during the *Gadlut*, the ending *Malchut* declined from the place of the *Chazeh* back to her own place, under NHY *de Kelim de* ZA. Then the *Kelim de Bina* and TM that fell to BYA, which are TNHY, rose back to *Atzilut*. And since ZA acquired the complete TNHY *de Kelim*, it had lights of GAR (see Item 19).

Since there is no absence in the spiritual, it is considered that even now *Malchut* remains in the place of *Chazeh de* ZA as before, and that only the force of *Din* and *Sium* [ending] in her descended to the point of this world. Hence, those *Kelim* TNHY *de* ZA that were under its authority during the *Katnut*, and now returned and united with ZA, unite with her during the *Gadlut*, as well, after they have been united and completed the TNHY *de* ZA.

Also, they become her lower nine *Sefirot*, since the point of *Chazeh*, which is the root of *Malchut* that she has had since the time of *Katnut*, has become *Keter*. And in the three *Kelim* NHY *de* ZA, each *Kli* divided into three thirds. The three thirds of *Netzah de* ZA became for *Malchut*, *Hochma*, *Hesed*, *Netzah*. And the three thirds of *Hod de* ZA became for *Malchut*, *Bina*, *Gevura*, *Hod*, and the three thirds of *Yesod de* ZA became for *Malchut*, *Daat*, *Tifferet*, *Yesod*. Thus, these TNHY *de* ZA that rose from BYA during the *Gadlut* and united with its degree, causing its GAR of lights, unite with *Malchut*, too, and become her nine lower *Sefirot* in *Kelim* and the first nine in lights.

55) And you find that the root of *Nukva de* ZA is the point of the *Chazeh*, which is not absent in it even during the *Katnut*. And it is called by the name *Keter* of *Malchut*. These *Kelim* TNHY *de* ZA that fell to BYA during the *Katnut* and return to *Atzilut* during the *Gadlut* divide into two *Partzufim*: ZA and *Malchut*. This is because they serve as TNHY *de Kelim* for ZA and HBD HGT NHY *de Kelim* for *Malchut*.

From *Chazeh de* ZA Down, It Belongs to *Nukva*

56) This yields the rule that from *Chazeh de* ZA downward, that is, the *Kelim* TNHY *de* ZA, are considered *Malchut*, called "the separated *Nukva de* ZA." This is because all bottom nine *Sefirot* of *Malchut* are made of these TNHY *de* ZA after they unite with it during the *Gadlut*. Also, we thoroughly understand what we say, that in *Katnut*, ZA and *Malchut* are in the form of VAK and *Nekuda*, meaning HBD HGT *de Kelim* and *Nekuda* of *Chazeh*. ZA lacks GAR of lights because of the absence of NHY *de Kelim*, and *Malchut* lacks the first nine *Sefirot* of lights due to the absence of the lower nine in the *Kelim*.

Thus, it has been thoroughly clarified that the root of the *Nukva de ZA* in *Katnut* and *Gadlut* is from the *Katnut* and *Gadlut* of the world of *Nekudim*. Although the *Kelim de Nekudim* broke, they still returned and were erected in the world of *Atzilut* in both these times of *Katnut* and *Gadlut*. Thus, both ZA and *Malchut de Atzilut* are VAK and *Nekuda* in *Katnut*, as in the *Katnut* of the seven *Sefirot de Nekudim*.

At that time, TNHY *de ZA de Atzilut* are fallen in BYA, and this point is the root of the *Nukva*. During the *Gadlut*, they return to their degree in ZA *de Atzilut* and complete NHY *de Kelim* to ZA and the lower nine of *Kelim* to its *Nukva*, which is *Malchut*, as in *Katnut* and *Gadlut* of the world of *Nekudim*. Thus, these TNHY *de ZA* from its *Chazeh* down are the roots of *Gadlut de Nukva*.

Twelve *Partzufim* in *Atzilut*

57) Each degree that contains three times ten *Sefirot*—ten *Sefirot de Rosh*, ten *Sefirot de Toch*, and ten *Sefirot de Sof* (see above Items 5-6)—is called a *Partzuf*. It is discerned by its highest *Behina*. If the highest *Behina* is *Keter*, all thirty *Sefirot* in it are named *Keter*; and if the highest *Behina* is *Hochma*, they are all called *Hochma*, etc.

Also, there are five *Partzufim* whose level is measured by the *Zivug de Hakaa* on the five *Behinot* in the *Masach*. A *Zivug de Hakaa* on *Masach de Behina Dalet* extends the level of *Keter*, *Masach de Behina Gimel* extends the level of *Hochma*, *Masach de Behina Bet* extends the level of *Bina*, *Masach de Behina Aleph* extends the level of ZA, and *Masach de Behinat* [*Behina* of] *Shoresh* extends the level of *Malchut* (see the "Preface to the Wisdom of Kabbalah," Item 21).

58) Yet, there are twelve *Partzufim* in *Atzilut*: the four *Partzufim* of *Keter*, called *Atik* and *Nukva*, and *Arich* and *Nukva*; the four *Partzufim* of *Bina*, called upper AVI and YESHSUT; and the four *Partzufim* of ZON, called "the big ZON" and "the little ZON." The reason they are divided in this manner is that each *Partzuf* in *Atzilut* comprises two kinds of *Kelim*: 1) *Kelim* that emerged in the world of *Atzilut* in the *Zivugim de Hakaa* [plural of *Zivug de Hakaa*]. Those are called *Kelim de MA*. 2) *Kelim* that broke in the world of *Nekudim*, called *Kelim de BON*. These are corrected, rise from BYA, and connect to the levels that emerged through a *Zivug de Hakaa* in the world of *Atzilut*, called MA. Also, the *Kelim de MA* are considered "male" and the *Kelim de BON* are considered "female." Hence, each *Partzuf* contains male and female.

59) In addition, each *Partzuf* is divided into GAR and ZAT. It turns out that there is male and female in the GAR of the *Partzuf*, and there is male and female in the ZAT of the *Partzuf*. For this reason, four *Partzufim* emerged in each *Partzuf*.

The two *Partzufim* of GAR of *Keter* are called *Atik* and *Nukva*, where *Atik* is MA and *Nukva* is BON. The two *Partzufim* of ZAT *de Keter* are called *Arich Anpin* and *Nukva*, where *Arich Anpin* is MA and *Nukva* is BON. The two *Partzufim* of GAR *de Bina* are called upper AVI, the two *Partzufim* of ZAT *de Bina* are called YESHSUT, the two *Partzufim* of GAR *de* ZON are called "the big ZON," and the two *Partzufim* of ZAT in ZON are called "the little ZON."

60) The reason we do not count four *Partzufim* in *Hochma* is that AA is the level of *Hochma de* MA, but the *Hochma* in it has been blocked inside its *Keter*, by way of "one inside the other" (as written in *Idra Zuta*, Item 37). Also, *Hochma* never shines in *Atzilut* at all. Instead, all the *Hochma* that shines in *Atzilut* is from *Bina* that returned to *Rosh de* AA and became *Hochma* (see above Item 44). This *Bina* clothed in AVI and YESHSUT. And AVI are regarded as *Hochma* of the right, and YESHSUT are regarded as *Hochma* of the left (see Item 41). Hence, we do not count four *Partzufim* in *Hochma*, but in *Bina*, which is also considered *Hochma*, which shines in ZA and *Malchut* in all the worlds.

A Great Rule in Time and Place

61) Know that all the expressions in the wisdom of Kabbalah that are with time and place do not refer to the imaginary time and place in corporeality, since here everything is above time and above place. Rather, "before" and "after" refer to cause and consequence. We refer to the cause as "before," and to the consequence as "after," since every cause precedes its consequence.

Also, "above," "below," "ascent," and "descent" are measures of *Aviut* and *Zakkut* [purity].* This is because an "ascent" means *Hizdakchut* [purification] and "descent" means *Hit'abbut* [increasing the *Aviut*]. When we say that a lower degree rose, it means that the lower one has been purified and became as pure as the higher degree. Hence, it is considered to have clung to it because equivalence of form attaches the spirituals to one another.

Also, when we say that the lower one clothes the upper one, it means that equivalence of form with the externality of the upper one has been made in it. This is because we call the *Dvekut* to the externality of the upper one "clothing the upper one." And it is the same in all other things perceived in time or in space. Study them in this manner, that is, in spiritual meanings, according to the issue.

Two Differences between the *Partzufim* of GAR and the *Partzufim* of VAK

62) Each *Partzuf* is emanated and born from the *Masach de Guf* of the higher *Partzuf* by way of cause and consequence. This applies to all the *Partzufim*, from *Partzuf Keter de* AK, which emerged after the first restriction, to the end of the *Partzufim* of *Assiya*. They clothe each other; that is, each lower one clothes the *Guf* of its upper one. Concerning the meaning of *Partzuf*, see above (Item 57).

63) The *Partzufim* divide into *Partzufim* of GAR, which are *Partzuf Keter*, *Partzuf Hochma*, and *Partzuf Bina*, and to *Partzufim* of VAK: *Partzuf* ZAT *de Bina*, called

---

* Translator's note: In Kabbalah, *Zakkut* refers to the power of the *Masach*, rather than to the traditional meaning of the word: purity.

YESHSUT, *Partzuf ZA*, and *Partzuf Malchut*. These three *Partzufim* are always considered *Partzufim* of VAK. Even when they receive GAR, they do not stop being VAK, since they lack KHB from their very root, as it is written in *The Zohar*, *Mishpatim*, Item 520. There is a difference between the *Partzufim* of GAR and the *Partzufim* of VAK, both in their emergence and birth and in how they clothe the *Guf* of the upper one.

The *Partzufim* of GAR exit from *Peh de Rosh* of their adjacent upper one. This begins in *Partzuf Keter de AK*, since once *Partzuf Keter de AK* emerged in *Rosh* and *Guf* (see above Items 5-6), there was the *Bitush* of *Ohr Makif* [surrounding light] and *Ohr Pnimi* [inner light] in the ten *Sefirot* of the *Guf*.

This means that that light, which the *Aviut* of the *Masach* detained from entering the *Guf* of the *Partzuf*, is called *Ohr Makif*. It struck the *Aviut* of the *Masach*, whose *Ohr Pnimi* is dressed in its *Ohr Hozer* [reflected light], and through this striking of the *Ohr Makif* in the *Aviut* on the *Masach*, the *Masach* in the *Guf* was purified and its form equalized with the mating *Masach* at the *Rosh* of the *Partzuf*. This is considered that the *Masach de Guf* rose and was included in the *Masach* at the *Peh de Rosh*, inside the *Zivug* there, since equivalence of form is considered *Dvekut* [adhesion].

Hence, through its *Hitkalelut* [inclusion/mixture] in the *Zivug* of the *Rosh*, all the *Behinot* of *Aviut* in the *Masach* were renewed, apart for the last *Behina*. Then, a *Zivug de Hakaa* on the measure of *Aviut* that remained in the *Masach*—*Aviut de Behina Gimel*—emerged on it from the upper light in the *Rosh*, and the level of *Partzuf Hochma* emerged on it.

At that time, it was recognized that the *Masach* was from another *Behina*, since the upper one is *Partzuf Keter*, and this level that was renewed on the *Masach* is the level of *Hochma*, since the last *Behina* had been lost. This recognition is considered "birth," meaning it departed the level of *Keter* and became a distinct *Partzuf* that has only the level of *Hochma*. Thus, the source of the newly born *Partzuf Hochma* is the *Masach de Guf* of the level of *Keter*, which purified and rose to the *Peh de Rosh*, and the exit, birthplace, is *Peh de Rosh* of *Partzuf Keter* (see all this in the "Preface to the Wisdom of Kabbalah," Item 35).

After *Partzuf Hochma* was born and emerged from *Peh de Rosh* of *Partzuf Keter*, it is considered clothing only the *Guf* of *Partzuf Keter*, that is, GAR *de Guf*, which is HGT. This is because the *Masach de Guf* is the root from which it was born. Also, it clothes only the externality of the *Guf* of *Partzuf Keter*, since the level of *Behina Gimel* is external to *Partzuf Keter*, whose level is from the *Ohr Hozer* of *Behina Dalet*. Hence, this is regarded as clothing, indicating *Dvekut* in the externality.

64) As has been explained concerning the birth of *Partzuf Hochma de AK* from *Peh de Rosh* of *Partzuf Keter de AK*, *Partzuf Bina* emerged from *Peh de Rosh* of *Partzuf Hochma* in precisely this manner. After *Partzuf Hochma* had been completed with *Rosh* and *Guf*, there was another *Bitush* of *Ohr Makif* and *Ohr Pnimi*, which purifies the *Aviut* of the *Masach* and equalizes its form with the *Masach de Malchut* of the *Rosh*.

Since it is included in the *Zivug* of the *Rosh*, the *Behinat Aviut* in it has been renewed, except for the last *Behina*, which was lost.

Then, ten *Sefirot* emerged on the remaining *Aviut* in it, *Aviut de Behina Bet*, at the level of *Bina*. And since it has been recognized that it is a lower level than *Partzuf Hochma*, it was discerned as separated from it and was born into its own domain. Yet, it clothes the *Guf* of the upper one, which is its root. And it also clothes the GAR de *Guf* at the place of HGT.

65) The three *Partzufim* of VAK—YESHSUT, ZA, and Malchut—emerged in this very way, except there are two differences in them:

1. Their lower one does not emerge from the *Peh de Rosh* of its adjacent upper one, but from the *Peh de Rosh* of the one above its upper one. For example, ZA does not emerge from *Peh de Rosh de* YESHSUT, but only after YESHSUT has become one *Partzuf* with AVI, which are one above its upper one. Similarly, *Nukva* does not emerge from *Peh de Rosh* of ZA, but only after ZA has risen to AVI. Likewise, *Partzuf Atik de Atzilut* did not emerge from the first *Rosh* of *Nekudim*, but from the *Rosh* of SAG de AK. The reason is that these *Roshim* [pl. of *Rosh*], considered VAK from their very root, are unfit for *Zivug* with the upper light in a way that they can emanate a lower *Partzuf*.

2. This concerns the clothing: The *Partzufim* of VAK do not clothe GAR de *Guf* of their upper one, HGT, but VAK of the *Guf* of the upper one, which is NHY from the *Chazeh* downward. Since they are VAK at their root, they cannot cling to GAR de *Guf* of the upper one. Thus, the two differences between the *Partzufim* of GAR and the *Partzufim* of VAK have been thoroughly clarified: One concerns the emergence, where only *Partzufim* of GAR emerge from the *Peh* of their adjacent upper one. This is not so in the *Partzufim* of VAK, which emerge from the one above their upper one. And the other concerns the clothing, that only *Partzufim* of GAR can cling to the HGT of the upper one, which are GAR de *Guf*, but not the *Partzufim* of VAK, which cling only from the *Chazeh* downward in the VAK de *Guf*.

Three Conditions for the Emergence of a Lower *Partzuf*

66) There are three conditions for a *Zivug* to beget a lower *Partzuf*:

The first condition is the *Masach* that mates with the upper light in *Zivug de Hakaa* and raises *Ohr Hozer*, which clothes the upper light. The level of the lower one is according to the measure of clothing of *Ohr Hozer* (as written in the "Preface to the Wisdom of Kabbalah," Item 21). Similarly, after the *Masach* elicited all the *Partzufim* and degrees in the world of *Nekudim*, they did not persist but broke and canceled, and the *Masach* was purified of all five *Behinot Aviut* in it, returned to *Rosh de SAG* (as written in *The Study of Ten Sefirot*, Part 8, Items 2,4), and all the degrees that emerged in *Nekudim* left their *Reshimot* in the *Masach*.

Hence, when the Masach was included in the Zivug in Rosh de SAG, its previous Reshimot were renewed in it. Initially, the Masach elicited its highest Behina, the Reshimo of Partzuf Keter, called Atik de Atzilut, at Aviut of Behina Dalet. The rest of the Reshimot, which remained in the Masach, emerged along with the birth of Atik to the place of Atik.

And once Atik had been completed, there was a Zivug de Hakaa in it, on the highest Behina in the remainder of the Masach within it, which is Behina Gimel, and elicited the level of AA on it. The rest of the Reshimot in the Masach, on which the Zivug de Hakaa had not yet been made, descended along with the birth of AA to the place of AA.

And when AA was completed, a Zivug was made in it on the highest Behina in the remainder of the Masach, which is Behina Bet, and elicited the level of AVI, etc., similarly. Thus, all the Partzufim emerge through a Zivug de Hakaa of the upper light with the Masach.

67) The second condition is that Keter and Hochma of each lower one are attached to the Bina and TM of their upper one. Hence, when the upper one is completed and raises its Bina and TM, Keter and Hochma of the lower one rise along with them to the place of the upper one (see above Item 20) and are included in the Zivug of the upper one. Thus, each lower one receives its level from the Zivug of the Rosh of the upper one.

68) The third condition is that ZA rises to YESHSUT and completes and unites the lights of the right and left of YESHSUT. Had it not been for the ascent of ZA for MAN, the right and left of YESHSUT would have been unable to shine. It follows that the ascent of ZA to YESHSUT caused the elicitation of the three lines—right, left, and middle—which are HBD de YESHSUT.

There is a rule: The lower one is rewarded with the full measure of light that it causes its illumination in the upper one. Hence, ZA receives the same Mochin de HBD from YESHSUT. This is the meaning of "Three emerge from one; one exists in three" (as it is written in *The Zohar*, Bo, and above in Item 52). Thus, we have explained the three conditions for the Zivug to elicit the lower one.

69) In essence, the Zivug to elicit the lower one emerges from the Zivug de Hakaa of upper light on the Masach, since this measures the level of the lower one. Yet, it requires an awakening of MAN of the lower one, and this awakening is done by Keter and Hochma of the lower one, which are attached to Bina and TM of the upper one. Therefore, both are required for eliciting a lower Partzuf.

Yet, in ZA there is another matter: Its Masach does not extend Kelim de GAR, since it is a Masach of Behina Aleph. Thus, the upper one cannot give it Mochin from a Zivug of the Masach in the upper light. Hence, the third condition is required—to receive the Mochin by inducing Mochin in its upper one, as in "Three emerge from one; one exists in three."

Three Stages in the Elicitation of the Ten *Sefirot*

70) The first stage is in the first *Partzufim* of AK where all ten *Sefirot* emerged at once. In the *Zivug de Hakaa* on the *Masach* of *Behina Dalet*, the ten *Sefirot* of the level of *Keter* emerged. In the *Zivug de Hakaa* on the *Masach* of *Behina Gimel*, ten *Sefirot* at the level of *Hochma* emerged. In the *Zivug de Hakaa* on the *Masach* of *Behina Bet*, ten *Sefirot* at the level of *Bina* emerged.

71) The second stage is the world of *Nekudim*, which emerged on a *Masach de Behina Aleph*, connected with the *Malchut*, and in which ten *Sefirot* emerged in two times. First, *Malchut* rose to *Bina de SAG de AK*. Then, when the *Masach* of *SAG* purified into *Behina Aleph*, called *Nikvey Eynaim*, *Malchut* rose and conjoined with *Behina Aleph*, ending the degree under the *Hochma*, called *Eynaim*. It follows that only two *Kelim* remained in the degree, *Keter* and *Hochma*, with two lights, *Ruach* and *Nefesh*. And the three *Kelim Bina* and *TM* fell from the degree. This is called *Katnut* [smallness/infancy] *de Nekudim*.

At the time of *Gadlut* [greatness/adulthood], the three *Kelim Bina* and *TM* returned to the degree and the five *Kelim KHB TM* in the degree were completed with the five lights *NRNHY* (see above Item 19). Thus, it has been clarified that in the world of *Nekudim*, the ten *Sefirot* did not emerge at once, as in the first three *Partzufim* of AK, but rather emerged at two times—a time of *Katnut* and a time of *Gadlut*. During the *Katnut*, only two *Sefirot* emerged, and during the *Gadlut*, the remaining three *Sefirot* emerged.

72) The third stage is the world of *Atzilut*, in which the ten *Sefirot* emerged in three times, called *Ibur* [conception], *Yenika* [nursing], and *Mochin*. It is so because here the *Hizdakchut* of the *Masach* at the last degree was added to the world of *Atzilut*. This is because the *Masach* was purified from *Behina Aleph*, called *Nikvey Eynaim*, into a *Masach* with *Aviut* of *Behinat Shoresh* (see the "Preface to the Wisdom of Kabbalah," Item 21), whose *Ohr Hozer* clothes only the level of the light of *Malchut* in the *Kli* of *Keter*, called *Metzach*. Hence, this light is called "MA that emerges from the *Metzach* [forehead]." This is because *KHB TM de Rosh* are called *Galgalta*, *Eynaim*, *AHP*, and *Metzach* is *Galgalta*.

Hence, two descents of *Malchut* are required here:

1. A decline from the *Metzach* to *Nikvey Eynaim*, which is called *Yenika*.

2. A decline from the *Nikvey Eynaim* to her place at the *Peh*, which is called *Mochin*.

Thus, the first level that emerges on the *Masach* of *Aviut Shoresh* is called *Ibur*. The second level, emerging on the *Masach* after *Malchut*'s descent to *Behina Aleph*, is called *Yenika*. The third level, emerging on the *Masach* after *Malchut*'s decline to her place, is called *Mochin*. Thus, it has been clarified that in the world of *Atzilut*, the ten *Sefirot* emerge in three times, called *Ibur*, *Yenika*, and *Mochin*, as will be explained below.

Ibur, Yenika, Mochin de Achor, and Ibur, Yenika, Mochin de Panim

73) It has already been explained that the level that emerges on a *Masach* with merely *Aviut Shoresh* is called "the level of *Ibur*." This is the level of the light of *Nefesh* in the *Kli* of *Keter*. With respect to its three lines, it is called "the level of *NHY*." Yet, there is the level of *Ruach* in it, too, called "the level of *HGT*," except it is without *Kelim*. Hence, *HGT* must clothe in *Kelim de NHY*, which is why the level of *Ibur* is called "three inside three," meaning *HGT* inside *NHY*.

74) The meaning of it is that although the *Hizdakchut* of the *Masach* causes the loss of the last *Behina*, for which the five levels are one below the other (as it is written in the "Preface to the Wisdom of Kabbalah," Items 40, 41), the last *Behina* is not entirely lost, but a *Reshimo de Hitlabshut* of it remains in the *Masach* (as written there in Item 42). For example, when the *Masach* of *Partzuf Keter de AK* was purified and rose to *Peh de Rosh*, it was included in the *Zivug* there and its *Reshimot* were renewed. With respect to the *Aviut* in the *Masach*, on which the *Zivug de Hakaa* was made, only the *Reshimo* of *Aviut de Behina Gimel* remained in the *Masach*, since the last *Behina*, *Behina Dalet*, had been lost. But the part of the *Hitlabshut of Behina Dalet* still remained in the *Masach*.

It follows that there are two upper *Behinot* in the *Masach* that are fit for *Zivug*:

1. The *Aviut* of *Behina Gimel*, which detains the upper light and receives the *Zivug de Hakaa*, on which the level of *Hochma* emerges.

2. The *Hitlabshut* of *Behina Dalet*. Even though it is unfit for a *Zivug de Hakaa*, since it has no *Aviut* that detains the expansion of the light, when it is included and associated with *Aviut de Behina Gimel*, a *Zivug de Hakaa* is done on it, too, producing nearly the level of *Keter*.

These two levels are called "male" and "female." The level that emerged on *Behina Dalet de Hitlabshut*, associated with *Behina Gimel de Aviut* is called "male," and the level that emerged only on *Behina Gimel de Aviut* is called "female" (see there in Item 42).

Similarly, when the *Masach de Guf* of *Partzuf Hochma de AK* purified and rose to its *Peh de Rosh*, two *Reshimot* remained in it—male and female—as in *Partzuf Keter*. This is because the *Reshimo de Behina Gimel de Hitlabshut*, associated with *Behina Bet de Aviut*, produces nearly the level of *Hochma*. This is considered the male. And the *Reshimo de Behina Bet de Aviut*, which is the primary one that receives the *Zivug de Hakaa*, produces the level of *Bina*. This is considered a female.

In the same way, there are male and female in the *Hizdakchut* of the *Masach de Guf de Partzuf Bina*. The male is nearly on the level of *Bina*, and the female is on the level of *ZA*, which is the *Zivug* for *Partzuf Nekudim*. In this manner, there are male and female in the *Hizdakchut* of the *Masach de Guf de Partzuf Nekudim* where the male, meaning the *Reshimo de Behina Aleph de Hitlabshut* that remained in the *Masach*, is associated with *Behinat Aviut de Shoresh* at nearly the level of *Behina Aleph*, meaning the level of ZA, which is the level of *Ruach*, meaning the level of *HGT*. The female, which is the *Aviut* of *Behinat Shoresh*, receiving the *Zivug de Hakaa*, is on the level of the light of *Nefesh*, *Malchut*, which, from the perspective of the three lines, is called *NHY*.

75) Therefore, we discern two levels on the level of *Ibur*: the level of *HGT* and the level of *NHY*. The level of *HGT*, which is male, emerges on the *Reshimot de Behina Aleph de Hitlabshut*, which is joined with *Aviut de Shoresh*. And the level of *NHY*, which is female, emerges only on the *Reshimo de Aviut Shoresh*.

Since the *Reshimo de Hitlabshut* is unfit to receive a *Zivug de Hakaa*, except through association with *Aviut Shoresh*, the level of *HGT* does not stand on its own but must clothe inside the *NHY*. For this reason, the level of *Ibur*, which is *HGT* and *NHY* together, is regarded as "three within three," that is, *HGT* inside *NHY*.

76) After the two levels *HGT* within *NHY* emerged in the *Hitkalelut* of the *Zivug de Rosh* of the upper one, and it was recognized that they are new levels, different from the upper one, this recognition is considered "birth." This means it has been recognized that a new *Partzuf* has been born here, different from the upper one, and they decline and clothe the *Guf* of the upper one. If they are *Partzufim* of GAR, they clothe the GAR *de Guf*, which are *HGT*, and if they are *Partzufim* of VAK, they clothe the VAK *de Guf*, which are *TNHYM* from the *Chazeh* downward.

Also, they suck the light from the upper *Partzuf*, a suction that makes for *Malchut's* descent from the *Metzach* to the *Nikvey Eynaim*. At that time, it receives *Aviut de Behina Aleph* once more, which is connected to *Malchut*, as it was in the *Partzufim* of *Nekudim*. Then the level of *HGT* acquires *Behinot Kelim*, as well, and they no longer need the *Kelim de NHY*. It is therefore considered that through the nursing, *HGT* expand and exit the *NHY*. And then it has the complete level of *Ruach*.

For example, in *Partzuf Atik de Atzilut*, the *Masach de Nekudim* rose first—through its *Hizdakchut*—to *Rosh de SAG de AK*. After the last *Behinat* [*Behina* of] *Aviut* in it had been lost, the *Masach* remained with *Aviut de Behinat Shoresh*, called *Metzach*, and *Reshimo de Hitlabshut de Behina Aleph*. And then two levels, *HGT NHY*, emerged on it, three within three, since *HGT* has no *Kelim*.

When they were recognized as a new level, it is considered that they had departed and were born and came to their place to clothe from *Tabur de AK* downward. Because it is *Partzuf VAK*, it clothes only VAK *de Guf*, and this is called *Partzuf Atik*.

Afterward, through *Yenika*, when it sucks from *SAG de AK*, it lowers the *Masach* from *Metzach* to *Nikvey Eynaim*. Following, the *Kelim* come out to its *HGT*, as well, expanding from within the *NHY*. Thus, the two *Behinot*, called *Ibur* and *Yenika*, have been clarified.

77) Now we shall explain *Partzuf Mochin*. After the *Partzuf* received the two *Behinot Ibur* and *Yenika*, it rises for MAN to the upper one and brings HB of the upper one

back to being face to face. Then they give the lower one the illumination that lowers *Malchut* from *Nikvey Eynaim* to her own place—the *Peh*.

At that time, these three *Kelim*, *Bina* and *TM*, which fell because of *Malchut's* ascent to *Bina*, rise back to their degree, and the *Partzuf* is completed with five *Kelim* KHB TM and five lights NRNHY. This is called *Partzuf Mochin*, since the first three lights *Neshama*, *Haya*, *Yechida* are called *Mochin*.

For example, after *Atik* received the complete two *Behinot Ibur* and *Yenika*, which are the levels of *Nefesh* and *Ruach*, it rises back to *Rosh de SAG* for MAN and returns the *Hochma* and *Bina* there to being face to face. And since the *Bina* in *Partzuf Hochma de AK* is not mixed with *Malchut*, when *Atik* receives its illumination it lowers its *Malchut* from its *Bina*, too. At that time, it raises the three *Kelim Bina* and *TM*, which fell by the mixture of *Malchut* in *Bina*, to its own degree, and now it has KHB TM de *Kelim*, in which the lights NRNHY can clothe.

78) When these *Mochin* emerge for the first time, it causes a dispute between the right and the left (as written above Items 29-30). This is because the left line, which carries the illumination of *Hochma*, wishes to cancel the right line, which carries the light of *Hassadim*. Because of this dispute and *Bitush* [beating] of right and left that occur in these *Mochin*, they are called *Mochin de Achor*. Thus, the three *Behinot Ibur*, *Yenika*, and *Mochin de Achor* have been clarified.

79) This *Bitush* of left and right causes the *Partzuf* to return to raising MAN to the upper one. This is because the illumination of the left, which is illumination of *Hochma*, strikes and purifies all the *Aviut* in the *Partzuf* until the *Masach* becomes as pure as it was when it first rose to the *Rosh* of the upper one. This means that only *Aviut Shoresh* and *Reshimo de Hitlabshut de Behina Aleph* remained in it. Through this equivalence, it adheres to the *Rosh* of the upper one.

Once it is incorporated in the *Zivug de Rosh* of the upper one, it receives a *Zivug de Hakaa* from the upper light once more, on the *Aviut* of *Behinat Shoresh* and *Behina Aleph de Hitlabshut* that were renewed in the *Masach*. This elicits the level of three within three on it once more, meaning the level of HGT, clothed in the level of NHY, called "the level of *Ibur*" (see above Item 75). Thus we have explained that the *Bitush* of the left and the right that occurred in *Mochin de Achor* caused the *Partzuf* to return to the upper one and receive a new *Ibur* from the upper one.

80) Once it received the new *Ibur*, it departed the *Rosh* of the upper one once more and clothed the *Guf* of the upper one. Through this clothing, it sucked the lights from the upper one once more, and these lights of *Yenika* lowered the *Aviut de Shoresh* into *Aviut* of *Behina Aleph*. They lowered *Malchut* from the *Metzach* to the place of *Nikvey Eynaim*, at which time a complete level of *Behina Aleph* emerged on the *Masach*. This is regarded as the *Hitpashtut* [expansion] of HGT from within the NHY (see Item 76). It follows that it has obtained a new *Yenika*, which is the level of *Ruach*.

81) After it obtained new *Ibur* and *Yenika*, it rises for MAN to the upper one once more, and this ascent is by itself, since by leaving its root attached to *Bina* and *TM* of the upper one (see Item 67), it can now return there whenever it needs. It unites the *HB* that are there face to face (see below Item 83), and they bestow upon it the illumination that lowers *Malchut* from *Nikvey Eynaim* to its place. At that time, *Bina* and *TM* rise and unite in it as before, and it obtains *KHB TM de Kelim* and *NRNHY* of lights.

To prevent the rift of right and left from reawakening, the middle line rises from below and unites the right and the left so they shine together: The *Hochma* on the left will clothe in the *Hassadim* on the right, and the *Hassadim* on the right will be integrated in the *Hochma* on the left (see Item 37). Then the *Mochin* shine in their fullest perfection, and at that time they are called *Mochin de Panim*. Thus we have explained how due to the *Bitush* of left and right in the *Mochin de Achor*, the three *Behinot Ibur*, *Yenika*, and *Mochin de Panim* reemerged.

82) Hence, a *Partzuf* is complete only after it receives *Ibur*, *Yenika*, and *Mochin de Achor* and *Ibur*, *Yenika*, and *Mochin de Panim*. Because of the *Hizdakchut* of the *Masach* that was added in *Atzilut* to the degree of *Aviut* of *Behinat Shoresh*, the *Partzufim* of *Atzilut* will not be able to receive their ten *Sefirot*, except after three consecutive times, called *Ibur*, *Yenika*, *Mochin* (see above Item 72). Since on the first elicitation of *Mochin* there was the *Bitush* of right and left until the left purified all the *Aviut* in the *Masach*, all the lights, *Ibur*, *Yenika*, and *Mochin* it had received departed.

This is so because when the *Aviut* in the *Masach* is canceled, the *Zivug* is canceled and the lights depart. The *Partzuf* returns to the *Rosh* of the upper one for an *Ibur*, receiving new three within three. Then it is born and receives a new *Yenika*, which lowers the *Malchut* from *Metzach* to *Eynaim*, the *HGT* exit the *NHY*, and it receives the level of *Ruach* once more. Subsequently, it rises for MAN and receives *Neshama*, *Haya*, *Yechida* once more, in which there is already the middle line, which unites the right and the left with each other. These are called *Mochin de Panim*, and then they shine and persist. Thus, before the *Mochin* is obtained for the second time, they cannot persist.

Panim and *Achor* [face-to-back], and *Panim be Panim* [face to face]

83) Even while the *Partzuf* has already received the *Mochin de Panim*, the *Hochma* and *Bina* there are still in a state of *Panim* and *Achor*. This means that only *Hochma* receives the *Mochin de Panim*. But *Bina* is always in a state of delighting in mercy and wants *Hassadim* and not *Hochma*; hence, it is considered that its *Achoraim* are toward the *Hochma*, and it does not want to receive the *Mochin de Panim* from it.

Hochma and *Bina* are at that state of *Panim* and *Achor* until ZA rises to them for MAN. Also, there is a connection between *Bina de Ohr Yashar*, imparting illumination of *Hochma* to ZA *de Ohr Yashar* (see the "Preface to the Wisdom of Kabbalah," Item 5). Hence, when ZA rises for MAN to *Bina*, *Bina* immediately turns her *Panim* back to *Hochma* to receive *Mochin de Panim* from it—which are *Mochin* of illumination of

Hochma—for ZA, as it does in the five *Behinot* of *Ohr Yashar*. Then it is considered that *Hochma* is already *Panim be Panim* with *Bina*.

Who Measures the Level in *Atzilut*?

84) We should ask this: "The *Masach de Atzilut* has only *Behinat Shoresh de Aviut*, called *Metzach*, having only the level of *Ohr Nefesh*. Thus, who caused the emergence of the five *Partzufim* in *Atzilut*, *Atik*, AA, AVI, and ZON, where *Atik* is the level of *Yechida*, AA—the level of *Haya*, AVI—the level of *Neshama*, and ZON—the level of *Ruach*?" This question applies also to the world of *Nekudim*, since only *Aviut de Behina Aleph* remained in the *Masach*, called *Nikvey Eynaim*. Thus, how could five *Partzufim* emerge in *Nekudim*?

85) The thing is that *Behina Dalet*, too, was connected in the *Masach de Nekudim* and in the *Masach de Atzilut* through the *Malchut* that rose to *Nekudot de SAG de AK*. Had *Behina Dalet* not associated in the *Masach* in them, no *Partzuf* would have been able to emerge on that *Masach*, since even the *Aviut de Behina Aleph* in *Nekudim* is regarded as "thin *Histaklut*" [looking], from which the *Zivug de Hakaa* does not produce any *Partzuf*. It is all the more so in the *Aviut de Metzach* in *Atzilut*: It is unfit for a *Zivug de Hakaa* for the elicitation of a *Partzuf*.

But since *Behina Dalet* conjoined with those screens, they became fit for *Zivug de Hakaa*. Now we may ask, "In that case, the level of *Keter* should have emerged on the *Masach*, since *Behina Dalet* is attached to the *Masach*!"

86) The answer is that *Behina Dalet* does not produce the level of *Keter*, except when it is at the place of *Malchut*. At that time, the *Ohr Hozer* that rises from the *Zivug de Hakaa* on it clothes the five *Kelim* KHB TM over the five lights NRNHY. But if *Behina Dalet* stands at the place of ZA, where there are only four *Kelim* KHB *Tifferet*, the *Ohr Hozer* draws only four lights NRNH in four *Kelim* KHB and *Tifferet*.

If *Behina Dalet* stands at the place of *Bina* where there are only three *Kelim* KHB, the *Ohr Hozer* draws only three lights NRN. If *Behina Dalet* stands at the place of the *Kli de Hochma* where there are only two *Kelim*—*Keter* and *Hochma*—its *Ohr Hozer* draws only two lights, *Nefesh Ruach*. This is what happened in *Nekudim* where the *Zivug* was made at the *Nikvey Eynaim*, which is the *Kli de Hochma*. Hence, only the level of *Nefesh Ruach* emerged in *Katnut*.

And if *Behina Dalet* stands at the place of *Keter*, where there is but one *Kli*, its *Ohr Hozer* draws only one light: *Nefesh*. This is what happened in *Atzilut*—only the level of *Nefesh* emerged in the *Ibur*, since the *Zivug* was in the place of the *Metzach*, which is the *Kli de Keter*.

Yet, after the illumination of *Yenika*, which *Behina Dalet* rejected to the place of *Behina Aleph*, called *Nikvey Eynaim*, the level of *Ruach* emerged. But then, through illumination of HB *Panim be Panim* of the upper one, which lowered *Behina Dalet* to her place in *Malchut*, which raises the fallen *Bina* and *TM* to their degree, there are five *Kelim KHB TM* there once again. At that time, *Behina Dalet* elicits the level of *Keter* in the light of *Yechida*, and this is the level of *Atik de Atzilut*.

87) Now we need to explain how the rest of the *Partzufim* below *Atik* came out. In the beginning, after the breaking of the vessels, *Masach de Nekudim* rose to *Rosh de SAG*. It was purified of all five *Behinot Aviut* that emerged in it in five *Partzufim*, until it equalized with the *Masach of Rosh de SAG*. Yet, the *Reshimot* from the *Aviut* of the five *Partzufim* that emerged in it remained in it, except for the last *Behina*, which was lost, as it is written about all the *Partzufim*. Thus, when it was included in the *Zivug* of the *Masach of Rosh de SAG*, the *Aviut* of all five *Partzufim* was renewed in the *Masach de Nekudim*, and a *Zivug de Hakaa* emerged on the *Aviut* in the *Masach*.

However, not all the *Behinot* in the *Aviut* participated in the *Zivug de Hakaa*, but only its highest *Behina*, which is *Aviut de Metzach*, connected to *Behina Dalet*. Through the three *Behinot Ibur, Yenika*, and *Mochin*, its ten *Sefirot* were completed at the level of *Keter*.

The other *Reshimot*, from the rest of the *Partzufim de Nekudim* that were in the *Masach*, did not receive anything from this *Zivug* at *Rosh de SAG*, since they are below the level of *Keter* and are waste compared to its value. For this reason, upon the emergence of *Atik* from *Rosh de SAG*, all the *Reshimot* from the rest of the *Partzufim* that were not included in its *Zivug* came down with it.

After *Atik* was completed in *Ibur, Yenika, Mochin de Panim*, the upper light shone on the highest *Behina* from the *Reshimot* that remained in it, which is *Aviut de Behina Gimel*. Through the three *Behinot, Ibur, Yenika*, and *Mochin*, ten *Sefirot* at the level of *Hochma* emerged, and this is *Partzuf AA*.

It is the same here: All the *Reshimot de Aviut* that are less than *Aviut de Behina Gimel* are waste compared to the value of the *Zivug* at the level of *Behina Gimel* that emerged in *Rosh de Atik*. Hence, when AA was born and departed *Rosh de Atik* to its place, all those *Reshimot* were drawn to its place along with it.

After AA obtained all three *Behinot Ibur, Yenika, Mochin* in completeness, the upper light shone on the highest *Behina* that remained in those *Reshimot*, which is *Aviut de Behina Bet*. Then, through the three *Behinot Ibur, Yenika, Mochin*, ten *Sefirot* at the level of *Bina* emerged on it. This is *Partzuf AVI*, and the rest of the *Partzufim* emerged similarly. Thus we have explained how the *Partzufim* of *Atzilut* emerged from one another.

Two States in *Malchut*

88) *Malchut* is the *Nukva de ZA*. Her root begins in *Malchut de Tzimtzum Bet*, which ended the seven *Sefirot de Katnut de ZA de Nekudim*. It is a separate degree from *ZA*, since *ZA* includes *HGT NHY de Nekudim*, and the degree below it is *Malchut*, which ends the *Nekudim*. Hence, this *Malchut* is considered a separate *Nukva* from *ZA* and a lower degree than *ZA*.

And there is also *Behinat Nukva* in the *Guf* of ZA, since the left side of ZA is considered its *Nukva*. Yet, this *Nukva* is considered ZA's own *Guf* [body], since ZA is the middle line, which receives from the two lines, right and left, of *Bina*. The right in it receives from *Bina's* right line, which is *Ohr Hassadim*, considered the male side in it, and the left side in it receives from the left line of *Bina*, which is *Ohr Hochma*, considered the *Nukva* side in it. Yet, both are one degree, included in one another.

It is known that in the beginning, the sun and the moon, which are the separate *Nukva* and ZA, were considered the two great lights. The level *Nukva* was equal to that of ZA, and she was as big as him. But then the moon—the *Nukva* that is separated from ZA—complained and said, "Two kings cannot use the same *Keter* [crown]." Then she was told, "Go, diminish yourself." Thus she became the small light.

Thus, you find two states here in *Nukva*: In the first state, she was with ZA, in the state of the two great lights, equal to ZA. The second state is after the *Nukva* was diminished and became the small light.

Explanation: In the beginning of the correction of the separate *Nukva de ZA*, the Emanator connected her with the *Nukva* in the *Guf* of ZA, which is the left side in it, and the two became one *Nukva* for ZA. When *Mochin* of right and left were drawn for them from *Bina*, ZA, which is the right in it, took the lights of the right of *Bina*, and the separate *Nukva* took the lights of the left line of *Bina*, like the *Nukva* in the *Guf* of ZA, since she was joined into a single *Nukva* with her.

And you already know that the lights of the right line *de Bina* are *Hassadim*, and the lights of the left line *de Bina* are *Hochma*. It follows that now ZA received the *Hassadim* of the right of *Bina* without *Hochma*, and the separate *Nukva* received the *Hochma* of the left of *Bina* without *Hassadim*, and it is known that *Hochma* cannot shine without *Hassadim*. For this reason, the *Hochma* froze in it and became darkness and not light.

This is the meaning of the moon's complaint, saying that two kings cannot use the same *Keter*. This is because when they both use the same *Keter*, which is *Bina*, considered their *Keter*, ZA becomes *Hassadim* without *Hochma*, and the *Nukva* becomes *Hochma* without *Hassadim*, which is darkness, and she could not tolerate that state.

We could ask, "But before the separate *Nukva* joined with the *Nukva* in his *Guf*, the right in it, which is the male, did receive *Hassadim*, and the left in it, which is the *Nukva* in his *Guf* received *Hochma*; yet, the *Nukva* in his *Guf* could tolerate it and was not darkness!" The thing is that the *Nukva* in his *Guf* is ZA's own self. Hence, the *Hochma* in her is not separated from the *Hassadim* in ZA. But this is not so with the separate *Nukva*, which is truly a different degree from ZA. But because it joined with the *Nukva* in his *Guf*, she received the *Hochma* of the left of *Bina* like her. Hence, after she received the *Hochma* within her, the *Hochma* separated from the *Hassadim* since she had no connection with the *Hassadim de ZA*.

Thus, we thoroughly explained the first state of the separated *Nukva*. To be able to shine for the lower ones, she was told, "Go, diminish yourself," meaning diminish yourself from that great degree of being equal with the degree of ZA and receiving from *Bina*. Rather, she is to descend below *Yesod de ZA*, as she was at her root: below the whole degree of ZA, and receive all of her lights from ZA.

Since she receives her lights from ZA, which is the middle line, the *Hochma* that he gives her is integrated with *Hassadim* and she can shine. This is the second state of the separate *Nukva*. What she received in the first state is regarded as *Nefesh, Ruach, Neshama de Achor*, meaning they do not shine. And what she receives in the second state is regarded as *Nefesh, Ruach, Neshama de Panim*, meaning they shine in completeness. To understand the matters to the fullest, you must delve in *The Zohar, Beresheet* 1, Items 111-116, and the *Idra Raba*, Item 323-325.

There are merits to her first state, since then her highest level was *Bina* and she could receive *Hochma* from her and did not need to receive from ZA. Yet, she could not shine to the lower ones due to the absence of *Hassadim*. For this reason, she is regarded as being in *Achoraim*.

But in the second state, after she was diminished under the *Masach* of *Yesod de ZA*, she was no longer fit to receive *Hochma*, since the *Masach de Yesod ZA* detained her. Hence, she had to receive *Hochma* in *Kelim de Achoraim* that remained in her from the first state. But there are more merits to the second state than to the first state since then she could shine to the lower ones both *Hochma* and *Hassadim*, whereas in the first state, she could not shine to the lower ones.

HaIlan (The Tree)

Illustrations and References

Diagram 1

Item 1 depicts the *Rosh, Toch, Sof* of *Partzuf Keter de* (of) AK. Item 2 depicts *Partzuf AB de AK* in *Rosh-Toch-Sof* and how it clothes *Partzuf Keter de AK* from its *Peh* down. Item 3 depicts *Partzuf SAG de AK* in *Rosh-Toch-Sof* and how it clothes *Partzuf AB de AK* from its *Peh* down.

Diagram 1, Item 1

This is *Partzuf Keter de AK*, the first ten *Sefirot* that expanded from *Ein Sof* into the space after the *Tzimtzum*. Its *Rosh* touches *Ein Sof* above, and its *Sium Raglin* is in the middle, central point, which is this world. It contains three *Behinot* of ten *Sefirot*: ten *Sefirot de Rosh*, ten *Sefirot de Toch*, and ten *Sefirot de Sof*.

The ten *Sefirot de Rosh* are called "the roots of the ten *Sefirot*," since there is the beginning of their creation, through the meeting of the ten *Sefirot de Ohr Yashar* in the *Zivug de Hakaa* in the *Masach* in *Malchut de Rosh* that raises ten *Sefirot de Ohr Hozer* that clothe the ten *Sefirot de Ohr Yashar*, which extend from *Ein Sof* (as it is written in *Tree of Life*, Gate 47, Chapter 1). The ten *Sefirot de Ohr Yashar* are arranged from above downward, and their opposite is the *Ohr Hozer*, which are arranged from below upward. *Malchut* of the ten *Sefirot de Rosh* is called *Peh*.

The ten *Sefirot de Toch* in the *Partzufim* of AK is called *Akudim*, in *Partzuf Keter*, in AB, as well as in SAG. Yet, in *Partzuf Keter*, the upper light was not yet distinguished in ten *Sefirot*, and the difference between them was only in impressions (as the ARI wrote in *Tree of Life*, Section Mati ve Lo Mati, Chapter 1). Also, *Malchut* of the ten *Sefirot de Toch* is called *Tabur*.

The ten *Sefirot de Sof* are considered the *Sium* of each *Sefira* of the ten *Sefirot* through *Malchut*. The *Partzuf* ends at the *Sefira* of *Malchut*, which is why she is called *Sium Raglin*.

Diagram 1, Item 2

This is *Partzuf AB de AK*, the second *Hitpashtut* of ten *Sefirot* from *Ein Sof* into the space, after the *Tzimtzum*. It begins from *Hochma*, and lacks the light of *Keter*. It was emanated and came out of *Malchut de Rosh* of *Partzuf Keter*, which is called *Peh*. Hence, it clothes *Partzuf Keter* from its *Peh* down to *Tabur* of *Partzuf Keter*.

Its ten *Sefirot de Rosh* are like the ten *Sefirot de Rosh* of *Partzuf Keter de AK*, except that it lacks *Keter*. The elicitation of these ten *Sefirot* is elaborated on in *Tree of Life*,

Section *Mati ve Lo Mati*, Chapters 1 and 2, as well as in *Talmud Eser Sefirot*, Part 5, where these words of the ARI are thoroughly explained.

Here, the ten *Sefirot de Toch* become more conspicuous than the ten *Sefirot de Toch* in *Partzuf Keter*, since here there were ten entrances and ten exits in the order of *Mati ve Lo Mati* (as it is written in *Tree of Life*, Section *Mati ve Lo Mati*, and in *Talmud Eser Sefirot*, Part 5). In the *Sefira Keter* of the ten *Sefirot de Toch*, there are two *Kelim*, called *Yod-Hey*. This is so in their *Sefira Hochma*, too, but in the *Sefira Bina*, the *Yod-Hey* are only in one *Kli*, and the *Vav* is in the *Kli* of *Yesod*, and the bottom *Hey* is in *Malchut*.

The ten *Sefirot de Sof* are the same as in *Partzuf Keter de AK*, except its *Sium Raglin* is above the *Tabur* of *Partzuf Keter*.

Diagram 1, Item 3

This is *Partzuf SAG de AK*, the third expansion of ten *Sefirot* from *Ein Sof* into the space after the *Tzimtzum* in *Rosh, Toch, Sof*. It was emanated and came out of the *Peh* of *Partzuf AB de AK*. It begins from *Bina* and lacks the lights *Keter* and *Hochma*, and clothes from the *Peh* of *Partzuf AB de AK* downward, although below it is longer than it, since it expanded downward, to the same level as the *Sium Raglin* of *Partzuf Keter de AK*.

Diagram 2, Item 1

This is the state of *Partzuf SAG de AK* during *Tzimtzum Aleph*. It is presented above, in Diagram 1, Item 3, but here there is the additional distinction of its own two *Partzufim* that emerged in it: *Partzuf Taamim* from *Peh* to *Tabur*, and *Partzuf Nekudim* from *Tabur* down. You will find their explanation in *Talmud Eser Sefirot*, Part 6, p 390 [in Hebrew].

Thus far, the three lower worlds *Beria, Yetzira,* and *Assiya* did not come to any existence, since *SAG de AK*, too, extended through the point of this world. It follows that it was considered *Atzilut* down to the point of this world.

Diagram 2, Item 2

This is the state of *SAG de AK* during *Tzimtzum Bet*, prior to the *Zivug* in *Nikvey Eynaim*, which was done in order to emanate the ten *Sefirot de Nekudim*. Because of the descent of *SAG* into the inner *MA* and *BON de AK*, *Bina* received the *Behinat Malchut*. Thus, the ending *Malchut*, which stood at the point of this world, rose to the place of *Tabur*, and the mating *Malchut*, which stood at *Peh de Rosh de SAG*, rose to the place of *Nikvey Eynaim de Rosh de SAG*, and the *AHP de Rosh* descended to *Behinat Guf de SAG*. Also, the light was emptied from *Tabur* down, and this, in general, is *Partzuf SAG*.

And there is *Rosh, Toch, Sof*, called *HBD, HGT, NHYM* in its own *Partzuf Nekudot de SAG*, standing entirely below the *Tabur* (Diagram 2, Item 1). In it, too, as in general, it is considered that the ending *Malchut* rose to *Bina de Guf*, called *Tifferet*, in the place of its *Chazeh*, where the line of *Ein Sof* ended, and below it the *Parsa* was established, since this is where *Behinat Atzilut* ended.

From there down it became the place of the three worlds BYA. The world of *Beria* was made of the two bottom thirds of *Tifferet*, down to its *Sium*. The world of *Yetzira* was made from NHY, and the world of *Assiya* was made of *Malchut*. This is thoroughly explained in the words of the ARI, p 8, and in *Ohr Pashut* there.

Diagram 2, Item 3

This is the state in SAG de AK during the *Zivug* that was made in *Nikvey Eynaim*: The *Ozen, Hotem, Peh* came out of *Behinat Rosh* and into the *Guf*, below the place of the *Zivug de Rosh*. Yet, since there is no absence in the spiritual, two kinds of *Ozen, Hotem*, and *Peh* are discerned here: The first are the *Ozen, Hotem, Peh* at their exit spot, their place at the *Rosh*, as in the beginning. The second are the *Ozen, Hotem, Peh* that descended into actual *Behinat Guf* below *Peh de Rosh de SAG*. They are called AHP not in the place of their exit. And all those are called "inner AHP."

Here, the ten *Sefirot de Toch* through *Tabur* are called *Akudim*, as prior to *Tzimtzum Bet*, since the ten *Sefirot* that emerged from the *Zivug de Nikvey Eynaim* could only manifest below *Tabur*. These are called "ten *Sefirot de Nekudim*," and they emerged primarily outside of *Partzuf* SAG, although their internality emerged in AK itself. They are called MA and BON de AK, since the internality of GAR de Nekudim is called MA de AK and the internality of ZAT de Nekudim is called BON de AK. They end at the point of *Sium* of *Tzimtzum Bet*, called "the *Parsa* between *Atzilut* and *Beria*." Below it are the three lower worlds BYA.

Diagram 2, Item 4

This is an external *Partzuf* AHP de SAG de AK, through *Tabur*. From *Tabur* down, it is *Partzuf* of ten *Sefirot de Nekudim* which end at the *Parsa*. Below *Parsa* stand the three lower worlds BYA.

The external AHP are divided into two *Behinot* AHP: external AHP at the place of their emergence, standing above the *Peh*, and external AHP not at the place of their emergence, standing from below the *Peh* through *Tabur*. Their GAR are attached to the bottom lip. It is called *Shibolet HaZakan* (the bit of hair under the bottom lip), and the GAR are primarily the light of *Ozen*, but their *Behinot Hotem, Peh* are included in them, too. These are the roots of GAR de Nekudim.

Their ZAT, which are the actual *Hotem* and *Peh*, stand below *Shibolet HaZakan* and spread through the *Tabur*. These external AHP are also called *Dikna* (beard) de SAG de AK, and you will find a detailed explanation of them in *Talmud Eser Sefirot*, Part 6, p 409, Item 20, and in *Ohr Pnimi* there.

The ten *Sefirot de Nekudim* stand from *Tabur* downward. Their GAR are in *Tikkun Kavim* and clothe MA de AK, and their ZAT are one below the other, as in *Tzimtzum*

Aleph, clothing BON *de* AK. Below them are the *Parsa* and the three worlds BYA below the *Parsa*.

Diagram 3, Item 1

This is the constant state of the five *Partzufim* of AK, from which the five *Partzufim* of the new MA emerged, called "the five constant *Partzufim* of *Atzilut*." Once they were established, no diminution will ever occur in them.

It also explains the division of each *Partzuf* into *Keter* and ABYA, which are also called *Keter*, AB, SAG, MA, and BON, or *Yechida*, *Haya*, *Neshama*, *Ruach*, *Nefesh*. Each *Rosh*, through the *Peh*, is called *Keter* or *Yechida*. From *Peh* through *Chazeh* in each of them, it is called *Atzilut* or AB or *Haya*. And from *Chazeh* to *Tabur* in each of them, it is called *Beria* or *Neshama* or SAG. And from *Tabur* down of each of them, it is called *Yetzira* and *Assiya*, or MA and BON, or *Ruach-Nefesh*.

Additionally, it explains their clothing within one another. Each clothes its superior from the *Peh* of its superior downward in such a way that the *Rosh* of each lower one clothes the AB and *Atzilut* of the upper one, and AB and *Atzilut* of the lower one clothe the SAG and *Beria* of its upper one.

Also, SAG and *Beria* of each lower one clothe MA and BON, which is *Yetzira* and *Assiya* of the upper one. Thus, the *Peh* of the upper one is considered the *Galgalta* of the lower one, and the *Chazeh* of the upper one is considered the *Peh* of the lower one, and *Tabur* of the upper one is considered the *Chazeh* of the lower one.

Also, it explains the emergence of the new MA in each of the five *Partzufim* of *Atzilut*, the MA in its corresponding *Partzuf* in AK.

Diagram 4

The state of ZA during its ascension to obtain *Neshama* pertaining to the constant five *Partzufim* of AK and *Atzilut*, and how it takes and nourishes from *Beria de* BON *de* AK—its corresponding *Partzuf* in AK.

Diagram 5

The state of ZA during its ascension to obtain *Haya* pertaining to the constant five *Partzufim* of AK and *Atzilut*, and how it takes and nourishes from *Atzilut de* BON *de* AK—its corresponding *Partzuf* in AK.

Diagram 6

The state of ZA during its ascent to obtain *Yechida* pertaining to the constant five *Partzufim* of AK and *Atzilut*, and how it takes and nourishes from *Rosh de* BON *de* AK—its corresponding *Partzuf* in AK.

Diagram 7

The states of the five *Partzufim* of *Atzilut* upon their ascent to obtain *Neshama* pertaining to the five constant *Partzufim* of AK, and how each takes and nourishes from its corresponding *Partzuf* in AK.

Diagram 8

The states of the five *Partzufim* of *Atzilut* upon their ascent to obtain *Haya* pertaining to the five constant *Partzufim* of AK, and how each takes and nourishes from its corresponding *Partzuf* in AK.

Diagram 9

The states of the five *Partzufim* of *Atzilut* upon their ascent to obtain *Yechida* pertaining to the five constant *Partzufim* of AK, and how each takes and nourishes from its corresponding *Partzuf* in AK.

Diagrams 10, 11, 12

These depict how the ladder of degrees never changes, and the degrees, as a whole, always remain as they were in their beginning, at the time of the emergence of the new MA, as in the constant state. This is so because when ZA ascends and obtains *Neshama*, all the degrees rise along with it—the five *Partzufim* of AK and *Atzilut*—and each obtains the *Behinat Neshama* related to it. It is similar in obtaining *Haya de ZA* and obtaining *Yechida de ZA*.

Diagram 10 is the state of the five *Partzufim* of AK as they ascend to obtain *Neshama*. Diagram 11 depicts their state when they obtain *Haya*, and Diagram 12 is their state when they obtain *Yechida*.

Diagram No. 1

The first three Partzufim of AK, called Keter, AB, SAG

1

Expansion of the first Ten Sefirot from Ein Sof into the space after the Tzimtzum. It is called Partzuf Keter de AK or Inner AK

Ten Sefirot de Rosh	
Ohr Yashar	Ohr Hozer
Keter	Malchut
Hochma	Tifferet
Bina	Bina
Tifferet	Hochma
Malchut	Keter

Masach in the Kli of Malchut

Peh

Reshimo of Kli of Keter
Reshimo of Kli of Hochma
Reshimo of Kli of Bina
Reshimo of Kli of Hesed
Reshimo of Kli of Gevura
Reshimo of Kli of Upper third of Tifferet

Chazeh

Reshimo of Kli of two bottom thirds of Netzah
Reshimo of Kli of Hod
Reshimo of Kli of Yesod
Reshimo of Kli of Malchut

These Ten Sefirot are regarded as Reshimot of Sefirot and not as actual Ten Sefirot

Tabur

Ten Sefirot de Sof

KHB
HGT
NHYM

Sium Raglin
Point of This world

Line of Ein Sof

2

The Second expansion of AK called Partzuf AB de AK

Ten Sefirot de Rosh	
Ohr Yashar	Ohr Hozer
Keter	Malchut
Hochma	Tifferet
Bina	Bina
Tifferet	Hochma
Malchut	Keter

Masach in Kli of Malchut

Peh

Ten Sefirot de Toch
Two Kelim Yod-Hey in Keter
Two Kelim Yod-Hey in Hochma
One Kli Yod-Hey in Bina
Hesed
Gevura
Upper Third of Tifferet

Chazeh

Two bottom thirds of Tifferet
NHY
Malchut

Tabur

Sium Raglin

3

The expansion of Partzuf SAG de AK called Behina Bet of the constant Present and Not Present

Ten Sefirot de Rosh	
Ohr Yashar	Ohr Hozer
Keter	Malchut
Hochma	Tifferet
Bina	Bina
Tifferet	Hochma
Malchut	Keter

Masach in the Kli of Malchut

Peh

Ten Sefirot de Toch
KHB HG
Upper third of Tifferet

Chazeh

Two bottom thirds of Tifferet
NHY
Malchut

Tabur

Ten Sefirot de Sof
KHB
HGT
NHYM

Sium Raglin
Point of This world

Diagram No. 2

1	2	3	4
Partzuf SAG de AK during Tzimtzum Aleph	Partzuf SAG de AK during the ascent to Tzimtzum Bet	Partzuf SAG de AK during the elicitation of the Melachim and the breaking of the vessels	The external Partzuf AHP called Dikna de SAG de AK
Ten Sefirot de Rosh Galgalta Keter Eynaim Hochma Ozen Bina Hotem Tifferet Peh Malchut	Ten Sefirot de Rosh Galgalta Eynaim Keter Hochma Bottom Hey in Nikvey Eynaim The Ozen Hotem Peh Fell from Rosh to Behinat Guf	Ten Sefirot de Rosh Galgalta Eynaim Bottom Hey in Nikvey Eynaim The Masach for Zivug de Hakaa Inner AHP Yod Ozen Hey Hotem Vav Peh Peh	Outer AHP in the place of their exit Ozen Hotem
Partzuf Taamim from Peh to Tabur Keter Hochma Bina Hesed Gevura Upper third of Tifferet Chazeh Two bottom thirds of Tifferet Netzah Hod Malchut Thus far Akudim	Ten Sefirot de Toch called Akudim Keter Hochma Bina Hesed Gevura Upper third of Tifferet Chazeh Two bottom thirds of Tifferet Netzah Hod Malchut This is where the ten Sefirot that departed from Tabur arose	Ten Sefirot de Toch called Akudim Keter Hochma Bina Hesed Gevura Upper third of Tifferet Chazeh Two bottom thirds of Tifferet Netzah Hod Malchut The ten Sefirot that Arose here from below Tabur did not ascend again	Peh Shibolet HaZakan This is the light of Ozen and the general Hotem Peh that descended here. They are the roots of KHB de Nekudim
Tabur	Tabur	Tabur	Hotem Peh Of externality that descended here. They are the roots of ZAT de Nekudim
Partzuf Nekudot de SAG with Tagin and Otiot included with them Keter Hochma Bina	All ten Sefirot departed from here and rose above Tabur. This is called Tzimtzum NHY de AK	Partzuf MA de AK is the internality of GAR de Nekudim Keter Hochma Bina	World of Nekudim Keter Hochma Bina
Thus far Behinat Rosh		Partzuf BON de AK This is the internality of ZAT de Nekudim, which are Daat, HGT, NHY, Malchut one inside the other	Daat Hesed Gevura tifferet Netzah Hod Yesod Malchut
Hesed Gevura Upper third of Tifferet			
Behinat Chazeh	Here is the new point of Tzimtzum Bet called Parsa	Parsa below Atzilut	Parsa below Atzilut
Two bottom thirds of Tifferet through the Sium of all of Tifferet	Place of Beria	The world of Beria Which is made of the two bottom thirds of Tifferet	World of Beria
Netzah Hod Yesod	Place of the world of Yetzira	The world of Yetzira Which is made from NHY	World of Yetzira
Malchut	Place of the world of Assiya	The world of Beria Which is made from Malchut	World of Assiya
The point of This World	The point of This World	The point of This World	The point of This World

Diagram No. 3

The constant state of the five Partzufim of AK and the five Partzufim of Atzilut that are never diminished from that measure.

The lines of Nekudot extending from each Rosh of the five Partzufim of Atzilut to its corresponding Partzuf in AK indicate the measure that they took and from which they nurse.

The Five Partzufim of AK

The Five Partzufim of Atzilut

1 — Partzuf Keter de AK
- Rosh: Keter Yechida — Peh
- AB: Atzilut Haya — Chazeh
- SAG: Beria Neshama — Tabur
- MA: Yetzira Ruach
- BON: Assiya Nefesh — Sium
- Raglin of the five Partzufim of AK — Point of This World

2 — Partzuf AB de AK
- Rosh: Keter Yechida — Peh
- AB: Atzilut Haya — Chazeh
- SAG: Beria Neshama — Tabur
- MA: Yetzira Ruach
- BON: Assiya Nefesh

3 — Partzuf SAG de AK
- Rosh: Keter Yechida — Peh
- AB: Atzilut Haya — Chazeh
- SAG: Beria Neshama — Tabur
- MA: Yetzira Ruach
- BON: Assiya Nefesh

4 — Partzuf MA de AK
- Rosh: Keter Yechida — Peh
- AB: Atzilut Haya — Chazeh
- SAG: Beria Neshama — Tabur
- MA: Yetzira Ruach
- BON: Assiya Nefesh

5 — Partzuf BON de AK
- Rosh: Keter Yechida — Peh
- AB: Atzilut Haya — Chazeh
- SAG: Beria Neshama — Tabur
- MA: Yetzira Ruach
- BON: Assiya Nefesh

6 — Partzuf Atik de Atzilut
- Rosh: Keter Yechida — Peh
- AB: Atzilut Haya — Chazeh
- SAG: Beria Neshama — Tabur
- MA: Yetzira Ruach
- BON: Assiya Nefesh

7 — Partzuf AA de Atzilut
- Rosh: Keter Yechida — Peh
- AB: Atzilut Haya — Chazeh
- SAG: Beria Neshama — Tabur
- MA: Yetzira Ruach
- BON: Assiya Nefesh

8 — Partzuf AVI de Atzilut
- Rosh: Keter Yechida — Peh
- AB: Atzilut Haya — Chazeh
- SAG: Beria Neshama — Tabur
- MA: Yetzira Ruach
- BON: Assiya Nefesh

9 — Partzuf YESHSUT de Atzilut
- Rosh: Keter Yechida — Peh
- AB: Atzilut Haya — Chazeh
- SAG: Beria Neshama — Tabur
- MA: Yetzira Ruach
- BON: Assiya Nefesh

10 — Partzuf ZON de Atzilut
- Rosh: Keter Yechida — Peh
- AB: Atzilut Haya — Chazeh
- SAG: Beria Neshama — Tabur
- MA: Yetzira Ruach
- BON: Assiya Nefesh

Sium Raglin of the five Partzufim of Atzilut — Point of This World

Parsa | Parsa | Parsa | Parsa | Parsa

World of Beria
World of Yetzira
World of Assiya

Line of Ein Sof

HaIlan (The Tree)

Diagram No. 4

The position of ZA after attainment of Neshama in the constant state of the five Partzufim of AK and Atzilut.

1 Partzuf Keter de AK	2 Partzuf AB de AK	3 Partzuf SAG de AK	4 Partzuf MA de AK	5 Partzuf BON de AK	6 Partzuf Atik de Atzilut	7 Partzuf AA de Atzilut	8 Partzuf AVI de Atzilut	9 YESHSUT de Atzilut	10 Partzuf ZON de Atzilut
Rosh Keter Yechida Peh									
AB Atzilut Haya Chazeh	**Rosh** Keter Yechida Peh								
SAG Beria Neshama Tabur	**AB** Atzilut Haya Chazeh	**Rosh** Keter Yechida Peh							
MA Yetzira Ruach	**SAG** Beria Neshama Tabur	**AB** Atzilut Haya Chazeh	**Rosh** Keter Yechida Peh		**Rosh** Keter Yechida Peh				
BON Assiya Nefesh	**MA** Yetzira Ruach	**SAG** Beria Neshama Tabur	**AB** Atzilut Haya Chazeh	**Rosh** Keter Yechida Peh	**AB** Atzilut Haya Chazeh	**Rosh** Keter Yechida Peh			
	BON Assiya Nefesh	**MA** Yetzira Ruach	**SAG** Beria Neshama Tabur	**AB** Atzilut Haya Chazeh	**SAG** Beria Neshama Tabur	**AB** Atzilut Haya Chazeh	**Rosh** Keter Yechida Peh		
		BON Assiya Nefesh	**MA** Yetzira Ruach	**SAG** Beria Neshama Tabur	**MA** Yetzira Ruach	**SAG** Beria Neshama Tabur	**AB** Atzilut Haya Chazeh	**Rosh** Keter Yechida Peh	**Rosh** Keter Yechida Peh
			BON Assiya Nefesh	**MA** Yetzira Ruach	**BON** Assiya Nefesh	**MA** Yetzira Ruach	**SAG** Beria Neshama Tabur	**AB** Atzilut Haya Chazeh	**AB** Atzilut Haya Chazeh
				BON Assiya Nefesh		**BON** Assiya Nefesh	**MA** Yetzira Ruach	**SAG** Beria Neshama Tabur	**SAG** Beria Neshama Tabur
							BON Assiya Nefesh	**MA** Yetzira Ruach	**MA** Yetzira Ruach
								BON Assiya Nefesh	**BON** Assiya Nefesh
									World of Beria
				Sium	Raglin	of the five	Partzufim of Atzilut		
				Parsa	Parsa	Parsa	Parsa		Parsa
									World of Yetzira
									World of Assiya
Sium Point of	Raglin This World	of the five	Partzufim	of AK			Place of the	world of Point of	Assiya This World

Diagram No. 5

The position of ZA after attainment of Haya in the constant state of the five Partzufim of AK and Atzilut.

1 Partzuf Keter de AK	2 Partzuf AB de AK	3 Partzuf SAG de AK	4 Partzuf MA de AK	5 Partzuf BON de AK	6 Partzuf Atik de Atzilut	7 Partzuf AA de Atzilut	8 Partzuf AVI de Atzilut	9 YESHSUT de Atzilut	10 Partzuf ZON de Atzilut
Rosh Keter Yechida **Peh**									
AB Atzilut Haya **Chazeh**	**Rosh** Keter Yechida **Peh**								
SAG Beria Neshama **Tabur**	**AB** Atzilut Haya **Chazeh**	**Rosh** Keter Yechida **Peh**							
MA Yetzira Ruach	**SAG** Beria Neshama **Tabur**	**AB** Atzilut Haya **Chazeh**	**Rosh** Keter Yechida **Peh**		**Rosh** Keter Yechida **Peh**				
BON Assiya Nefesh	**MA** Yetzira Ruach	**SAG** Beria Neshama **Tabur**	**AB** Atzilut Haya **Chazeh**	**Rosh** Keter Yechida **Peh**	**AB** Atzilut Haya **Chazeh**	**Rosh** Keter Yechida **Peh**			
	BON Assiya Nefesh	**MA** Yetzira Ruach	**SAG** Beria Neshama **Tabur**	**AB** Atzilut Haya **Chazeh**	**SAG** Beria Neshama **Tabur**	**AB** Atzilut Haya **Chazeh**	**Rosh** Keter Yechida **Peh**		**Rosh** Keter Yechida **Peh**
		BON Assiya Nefesh	**MA** Yetzira Ruach	**SAG** Beria Neshama **Tabur**	**MA** Yetzira Ruach	**SAG** Beria Neshama **Tabur**	**AB** Atzilut Haya **Chazeh**	**Rosh** Keter Yechida **Peh**	**AB** Atzilut Haya **Chazeh**
			BON Assiya Nefesh	**MA** Yetzira Ruach	**BON** Assiya Nefesh	**MA** Yetzira Ruach	**SAG** Beria Neshama **Tabur**	**AB** Atzilut Haya **Chazeh**	**SAG** Beria Neshama **Tabur**
				BON Assiya Nefesh		**BON** Assiya Nefesh	**MA** Yetzira Ruach	**SAG** Beria Neshama **Tabur**	**MA** Yetzira Ruach
							BON Assiya Nefesh	**MA** Yetzira Ruach	**BON** Assiya Nefesh
								BON Assiya Nefesh	World of Beria
									World of Yetzira
			Sium	Raglin	of the five	Partzufim	of Atzilut		
			Parsa	Parsa	Parsa	Parsa	Parsa		
						Place of the	world of		World of Assiya Yetzira
Sium	Raglin	of the five	Partzufim	of AK		Place of the	world of	Point of	Assiya
Point of	This World							Point of	This World

Diagram No. 6

The position of ZA after attainment of Yechida in the constant state of the five Partzufim of AK and Atzilut.

1. Partzuf Keter de AK	2. Partzuf AB de AK	3. Partzuf SAG de AK	4. Partzuf MA de AK	5. Partzuf BON de AK	6. Partzuf Atik de Atzilut	7. Partzuf AA de Atzilut	8. Partzuf AVI de Atzilut	9. YESHSUT de Atzilut	10. Partzuf ZON de Atzilut
Rosh — Keter Yechida — Peh									
AB — Atzilut Haya — Chazeh	**Rosh** — Keter Yechida — Peh								
SAG — Beria Neshama — Tabur	**AB** — Atzilut Haya — Chazeh	**Rosh** — Keter Yechida — Peh							
MA — Yetzira Ruach	**SAG** — Beria Neshama — Tabur	**AB** — Atzilut Haya — Chazeh	**Rosh** — Keter Yechida — Peh		**Rosh** — Keter Yechida — Peh				
BON — Assiya Nefesh	**MA** — Yetzira Ruach	**SAG** — Beria Neshama — Tabur	**AB** — Atzilut Haya — Chazeh	**Rosh** — Keter Yechida — Peh	**AB** — Atzilut Haya — Chazeh	**Rosh** — Keter Yechida — Peh			**Rosh** — Keter Yechida — Peh
	BON — Assiya Nefesh	**MA** — Yetzira Ruach	**SAG** — Beria Neshama — Tabur	**AB** — Atzilut Haya — Chazeh	**SAG** — Beria Neshama — Tabur	**AB** — Atzilut Haya — Chazeh	**Rosh** — Keter Yechida — Peh		**AB** — Atzilut Haya — Chazeh
		BON — Assiya Nefesh	**MA** — Yetzira Ruach	**SAG** — Beria Neshama — Tabur	**MA** — Yetzira Ruach	**SAG** — Beria Neshama — Tabur	**AB** — Atzilut Haya — Chazeh	**YESHSUT** — Rosh — Keter Yechida — Peh	**SAG** — Beria Neshama — Tabur
			BON — Assiya Nefesh	**MA** — Yetzira Ruach	**BON** — Assiya Nefesh	**MA** — Yetzira Ruach	**SAG** — Beria Neshama — Tabur	**AB** — Atzilut Haya — Chazeh	**MA** — Yetzira Ruach
				BON — Assiya Nefesh		**BON** — Assiya Nefesh	**MA** — Yetzira Ruach	**SAG** — Beria Neshama — Tabur	**BON** — Assiya Nefesh
							BON — Assiya Nefesh	**MA** — Yetzira Ruach	World of Beria
								BON — Assiya Nefesh	World of Yetzira
									World of Assiya
Sium	Raglin	of the five	Partzufim	of AK		Sium Parsa	Raglin Parsa	of the five Parsa — Place of the world of — Place of the world of — Place of the world of	Partzufim of Atzilut Parsa — Beria — Yetzira — Assiya

Point of This World below the Raglin of all five Partzufim of AK

Point of This World below the Raglin of all five Partzufim of the world of Assiya

Diagram No. 7

The position of all five Partzufim and three worlds BYA after Attainment of their **Neshama** in the constant state of the five Partzufim of AK.

1 Partzuf Keter de AK	2 Partzuf AB de AK	3 Partzuf SAG de AK	4 Partzuf MA de AK	5 Partzuf BON de AK	6 Partzuf Atik de Atzilut	7 Partzuf AA de Atzilut	8 Partzuf AVI de Atzilut	9 YESHSUT de Atzilut	10 Partzuf ZON de Atzilut
Rosh — Keter Yechida — Peh									
AB — Atzilut Haya — Chazeh	**Rosh** — Keter Yechida — Peh								
SAG — Beria Neshama — Tabur	**AB** — Atzilut Haya — Chazeh	**Rosh** — Keter Yechida — Peh			**Rosh** — Keter Yechida — Peh				
MA — Yetzira Ruach	**SAG** — Beria Neshama — Tabur	**AB** — Atzilut Haya — Chazeh	**Rosh** — Keter Yechida — Peh		**AB** — Atzilut Haya — Chazeh	**Rosh** — Keter Yechida — Peh			
BON — Assiya Nefesh	**MA** — Yetzira Ruach	**SAG** — Beria Neshama — Tabur	**AB** — Atzilut Haya — Chazeh	**Rosh** — Keter Yechida — Peh	**SAG** — Beria Neshama — Tabur	**AB** — Atzilut Haya — Chazeh	**Rosh** — Keter Yechida — Peh		
	BON — Assiya Nefesh	**MA** — Yetzira Ruach	**SAG** — Beria Neshama — Tabur	**AB** — Atzilut Haya — Chazeh	**MA** — Yetzira Ruach	**SAG** — Beria Neshama — Tabur	**AB** — Atzilut Haya — Chazeh	**Rosh** — Keter Yechida — Peh	
		BON — Assiya Nefesh	**MA** — Yetzira Ruach	**SAG** — Beria Neshama — Tabur	**BON** — Assiya Nefesh	**MA** — Yetzira Ruach	**SAG** — Beria Neshama — Tabur	**AB** — Atzilut Haya — Chazeh	**Rosh** — Keter Yechida — Peh
			BON — Assiya Nefesh	**MA** — Yetzira Ruach		**BON** — Assiya Nefesh	**MA** — Yetzira Ruach	**SAG** — Beria Neshama — Tabur	**AB** — Atzilut Haya — Chazeh
				BON — Assiya Nefesh			**BON** — Assiya Nefesh	**MA** — Yetzira Ruach	**SAG** — Beria Neshama — Tabur
								BON — Assiya Nefesh	**MA** — Yetzira Ruach
									BON — Assiya Nefesh
									World of Beria

Sium Raglin of the five Partzufim of Atzilut — Parsa

World of Yetzira

World of Assiya

Sium Raglin of the five Partzufim of AK

Point of This World

Diagram No. 8

The position of all five Partzufim and three worlds BYA after Attainment of their **Haya** in the constant state of the five Partzufim of AK.

1 Partzuf Keter de AK	2 Partzuf AB de AK	3 Partzuf SAG de AK	4 Partzuf MA de AK	5 Partzuf BON de AK	6 Partzuf Atik de Atzilut	7 Partzuf AA de Atzilut	8 Partzuf AVI de Atzilut	9 YESHSUT de Atzilut	10 Partzuf ZON de Atzilut
Rosh Keter Yechida **Peh**									
AB Atzilut Haya **Chazeh**	**Rosh** Keter Yechida **Peh**				**Rosh** Keter Yechida **Peh**				
SAG Beria Neshama **Tabur**	**AB** Atzilut Haya **Chazeh**	**Rosh** Keter Yechida **Peh**			**AB** Atzilut Haya **Chazeh**	**Rosh** Keter Yechida **Peh**			
MA Yetzira Ruach	**SAG** Beria Neshama **Tabur**	**AB** Atzilut Haya **Chazeh**	**Rosh** Keter Yechida **Peh**		**SAG** Beria Neshama **Tabur**	**AB** Atzilut Haya **Chazeh**	**Rosh** Keter Yechida **Peh**		
BON Assiya Nefesh	**MA** Yetzira Ruach	**SAG** Beria Neshama **Tabur**	**AB** Atzilut Haya **Chazeh**	**Rosh** Keter Yechida **Peh**	**MA** Yetzira Ruach	**SAG** Beria Neshama **Tabur**	**AB** Atzilut Haya **Chazeh**	**Rosh** Keter Yechida **Peh**	
	BON Assiya Nefesh	**MA** Yetzira Ruach	**SAG** Beria Neshama **Tabur**	**AB** Atzilut Haya **Chazeh**	**BON** Assiya Nefesh	**MA** Yetzira Ruach	**SAG** Beria Neshama **Tabur**	**AB** Atzilut Haya **Chazeh**	**Rosh** Keter Yechida **Peh**
		BON Assiya Nefesh	**MA** Yetzira Ruach	**SAG** Beria Neshama **Tabur**		**BON** Assiya Nefesh	**MA** Yetzira Ruach	**SAG** Beria Neshama **Tabur**	**AB** Atzilut Haya **Chazeh**
			BON Assiya Nefesh	**MA** Yetzira Ruach			**BON** Assiya Nefesh	**MA** Yetzira Ruach	**SAG** Beria Neshama **Tabur**
				BON Assiya Nefesh				**BON** Assiya Nefesh	**MA** Yetzira Ruach
									BON Assiya Nefesh
									World of Beria
				Sium	Raglin	of the five	Partzufim of Atzilut		**World of Yetzira**
				Parsa	Parsa	Parsa	Parsa	Parsa	Parsa
						Place of the	world of		**World of Assiya** Yetzira
Sium	Raglin	of the five	Partzufim	of AK	Point of	This World	Place of the	world of	Assiya
Point of	This World								

Diagram No. 9

*The position of all five Partzufim and three worlds BYA after Attainment of their **Yechida** in the constant state of the five Partzufim of AK.*

1 Partzuf Keter de AK
- Rosh — Keter Yechida — Peh
- AB — Atzilut Haya — Chazeh
- SAG — Beria Neshama — Tabur
- MA — Yetzira Ruach — Tabur
- BON — Assiya Nefesh

2 Partzuf AB de AK
- Rosh — Keter Yechida — Peh
- AB — Atzilut Haya — Chazeh
- SAG — Beria Neshama — Tabur
- MA — Yetzira Ruach
- BON — Assiya Nefesh

3 Partzuf SAG de AK
- Rosh — Keter Yechida — Peh
- AB — Atzilut Haya — Chazeh
- SAG — Beria Neshama — Tabur
- MA — Yetzira Ruach
- BON — Assiya Nefesh

4 Partzuf MA de AK
- Rosh — Keter Yechida — Peh
- AB — Atzilut Haya — Chazeh
- SAG — Beria Neshama — Tabur
- MA — Yetzira Ruach
- BON — Assiya Nefesh

5 Partzuf BON de AK
- Rosh — Keter Yechida — Peh

Sium Raglin of the five Partzufim of AK
Point of This World

6 Partzuf Atik de Atzilut
- Rosh — Keter Yechida — Peh
- AB — Atzilut Haya — Chazeh
- SAG — Beria Neshama — Tabur
- MA — Yetzira Ruach — Tabur
- BON — Assiya Nefesh

7 Partzuf AA de Atzilut
- Rosh — Keter Yechida — Peh
- AB — Atzilut Haya — Chazeh
- SAG — Beria Neshama — Tabur
- MA — Yetzira Ruach
- BON — Assiya Nefesh

8 Partzuf AVI de Atzilut
- Rosh — Keter Yechida — Peh
- AB — Atzilut Haya — Chazeh
- SAG — Beria Neshama — Tabur
- MA — Yetzira Ruach
- BON — Assiya Nefesh

9 YESHSUT de Atzilut
- Rosh — Keter Yechida — Peh
- AB — Atzilut Haya — Chazeh
- SAG — Beria Neshama — Tabur
- MA — Yetzira Ruach
- BON — Assiya Nefesh

10 Partzuf ZON de Atzilut
- Rosh — Keter Yechida — Peh
- AB — Atzilut Haya — Chazeh
- SAG — Beria Neshama — Tabur
- MA — Yetzira Ruach
- BON — Assiya Nefesh

World of Beria

World of Yetzira

World of Assiya

Sium Raglin of the five Partzufim of Atzilut
Parsa — Parsa — Parsa — Parsa — Parsa
Place of the world of Beria
Place of the world of Yetzira
Place of the world of Assiya
Point of This World

HaIlan (The Tree)

Diagram No. 10

The position of all the worlds and Partzufim, namely the five Partzufim of AK, five Partzufim of Atzilut, and three worlds BYA after attainment of their **Neshama** in the constant state of the line of Ein Sof.

	1 Partzuf Keter de AK	2 Partzuf AB de AK	3 Partzuf SAG de AK	4 Partzuf MA de AK	5 Partzuf BON de AK	6 Partzuf Atik de Atzilut	7 Partzuf AA de Atzilut	8 Partzuf AVI de Atzilut	9 YESHSUT de Atzilut	10 Partzuf ZON de Atzilut
Rosh of the line of Ein Sof	AB / Atzilut Haya / Chazeh	Rosh / Keter Yechida / Peh								
	SAG / Beria Neshama / Tabur	AB / Atzilut Haya / Chazeh	Rosh / Keter Yechida / Peh							
	MA / Yetzira Ruach	SAG / Beria Neshama / Tabur	AB / Atzilut Haya / Chazeh	Rosh / Keter Yechida / Peh		Rosh / Keter Yechida / Peh				
	BON / Assiya Nefesh	MA / Yetzira Ruach	SAG / Beria Neshama / Tabur	AB / Atzilut Haya / Chazeh	Rosh / Keter Yechida / Peh	AB / Atzilut Haya / Chazeh	Rosh / Keter Yechida / Peh			
		BON / Assiya Nefesh	MA / Yetzira Ruach	SAG / Beria Neshama / Tabur	AB / Atzilut Haya / Chazeh	SAG / Beria Neshama / Tabur	AB / Atzilut Haya / Chazeh	Rosh / Keter Yechida / Peh		
			BON / Assiya Nefesh	MA / Yetzira Ruach	SAG / Beria Neshama / Tabur	MA / Yetzira Ruach	SAG / Beria Neshama / Tabur	AB / Atzilut Haya / Chazeh	Rosh / Keter Yechida / Peh	
				BON / Assiya Nefesh	MA / Yetzira Ruach	BON / Assiya Nefesh	MA / Yetzira Ruach	SAG / Beria Neshama / Tabur	AB / Atzilut Haya / Chazeh	Rosh / Keter Yechida / Peh
					BON / Assiya Nefesh		BON / Assiya Nefesh	MA / Yetzira Ruach	SAG / Beria Neshama / Tabur	AB / Atzilut Haya / Chazeh
								BON / Assiya Nefesh	MA / Yetzira Ruach	SAG / Beria Neshama / Tabur
									BON / Assiya Nefesh	MA / Yetzira Ruach
										BON / Assiya Nefesh
					Sium	Raglin	of the five	Partzufim of Atzilut		World of Beria
					Parsa	Parsa	Parsa	Parsa		Parsa
										World of Yetzira
										World of Assiya
	Sium	Raglin	of the five	Partzufim	of AK	Point of	This World	Place of the	world of	Assiya
	Point of	This World								

Diagram No. 11

The position of all the worlds and Partzufim, namely the five Partzufim of AK, five Partzufim of Atzilut, and three worlds BYA after attainment of their **Haya** in the constant state of the line of Ein Sof.

	1 Partzuf Keter de AK	2 Partzuf AB de AK	3 Partzuf SAG de AK	4 Partzuf MA de AK	5 Partzuf BON de AK	6 Partzuf Atik de Atzilut	7 Partzuf AA de Atzilut	8 Partzuf AVI de Atzilut	9 YESHSUT de Atzilut	10 Partzuf ZON de Atzilut
Rosh of the line of Ein Sof	SAG — Beria Neshama — Tabur	AB — Atzilut Haya — Chazeh	Rosh — Keter Yechida — Peh							
	MA — Yetzira Ruach	SAG — Beria Neshama — Tabur	AB — Atzilut Haya — Chazeh	Rosh — Keter Yechida — Peh		Rosh — Keter Yechida — Peh				
	BON — Assiya Nefesh	MA — Yetzira Ruach	SAG — Beria Neshama — Tabur	AB — Atzilut Haya — Chazeh	Rosh — Keter Yechida — Peh	AB — Atzilut Haya — Chazeh	Rosh — Keter Yechida — Peh			
		BON — Assiya Nefesh	MA — Yetzira Ruach	SAG — Beria Neshama — Tabur	AB — Atzilut Haya — Chazeh	SAG — Beria Neshama — Tabur	AB — Atzilut Haya — Chazeh	Rosh — Keter Yechida — Peh		
			BON — Assiya Nefesh	MA — Yetzira Ruach — Tabur	SAG — Beria Neshama	MA — Yetzira Ruach — Tabur	SAG — Beria Neshama	AB — Atzilut Haya — Chazeh	Rosh — Keter Yechida — Peh	
				BON — Assiya Nefesh	MA — Yetzira Ruach	BON — Assiya Nefesh	MA — Yetzira Ruach	SAG — Beria Neshama — Tabur	AB — Atzilut Haya — Chazeh	Rosh — Keter Yechida — Peh
					BON — Assiya Nefesh		BON — Assiya Nefesh	MA — Yetzira Ruach	SAG — Beria Neshama — Tabur	AB — Atzilut Haya — Chazeh
								BON — Assiya Nefesh	MA — Yetzira Ruach	SAG — Beria Neshama — Tabur
									BON — Assiya Nefesh	MA — Yetzira Ruach
										BON — Assiya Nefesh
										World of Beria
	Sium	Raglin	of the five	Partzufim	of AK	Sium	Raglin	of the five	Partzufim of Atzilut	World of Yetzira
						Parsa	Parsa	Parsa	Parsa	Parsa
										World of Assiya
						Place of the	world of	Yetzira		
	Point of	This World				Place of the	world of	Assiya		Point of This World

Diagram No. 12

The position of all the worlds and Partzufim, namely the five Partzufim of AK, five Partzufim of Atzilut, and three worlds BYA after attainment of their **Yechida** in the constant state of the line of Ein Sof.

1 Partzuf Keter de AK	2 Partzuf AB de AK	3 Partzuf SAG de AK	4 Partzuf MA de AK	5 Partzuf BON de AK	6 Partzuf Atik de Atzilut	7 Partzuf AA de Atzilut	8 Partzuf AVI de Atzilut	9 YESHSUT de Atzilut	10 Partzuf ZON de Atzilut
Rosh of the line of Ein Sof	MA — Yetzira Ruach	SAG — Beria Neshama / Tabur	AB — Atzilut Haya / Chazeh	Rosh — Keter Yechida / Peh		Rosh — Keter Yechida / Peh			
	BON — Assiya Nefesh	MA — Yetzira Ruach	SAG — Beria Neshama / Tabur	AB — Atzilut Haya / Chazeh	Rosh — Keter Yechida / Peh	AB — Atzilut Haya / Chazeh	Rosh — Keter Yechida / Peh		
		BON — Assiya Nefesh	MA — Yetzira Ruach	SAG — Beria Neshama / Tabur	AB — Atzilut Haya / Chazeh	SAG — Beria Neshama / Tabur	AB — Atzilut Haya / Chazeh	Rosh — Keter Yechida / Peh	
			BON — Assiya Nefesh	MA — Yetzira Ruach	SAG — Beria Neshama / Tabur	MA — Yetzira Ruach	SAG — Beria Neshama / Tabur	AB — Atzilut Haya / Chazeh	Rosh — Keter Yechida / Peh
				BON — Assiya Nefesh	MA — Yetzira Ruach	BON — Assiya Nefesh	MA — Yetzira Ruach	SAG — Beria Neshama / Tabur	AB — Atzilut Haya / Chazeh
					BON — Assiya Nefesh		BON — Assiya Nefesh	MA — Yetzira Ruach	SAG — Beria Neshama / Tabur
								BON — Assiya Nefesh	MA — Yetzira Ruach
									BON — Assiya Nefesh
									World of Beria
									World of Yetzira
					Sium	Raglin	of the five	Partzufim of Atzilut	World of Assiya
					Parsa	Parsa	Parsa	Parsa	Parsa
						Place of the	world of	Beria
						Place of the	world of	Yetzira
Sium	Raglin	of the five	Partzufim	of AK		Place of the	world of	Assiya
Point of	This World				Point of	This World			

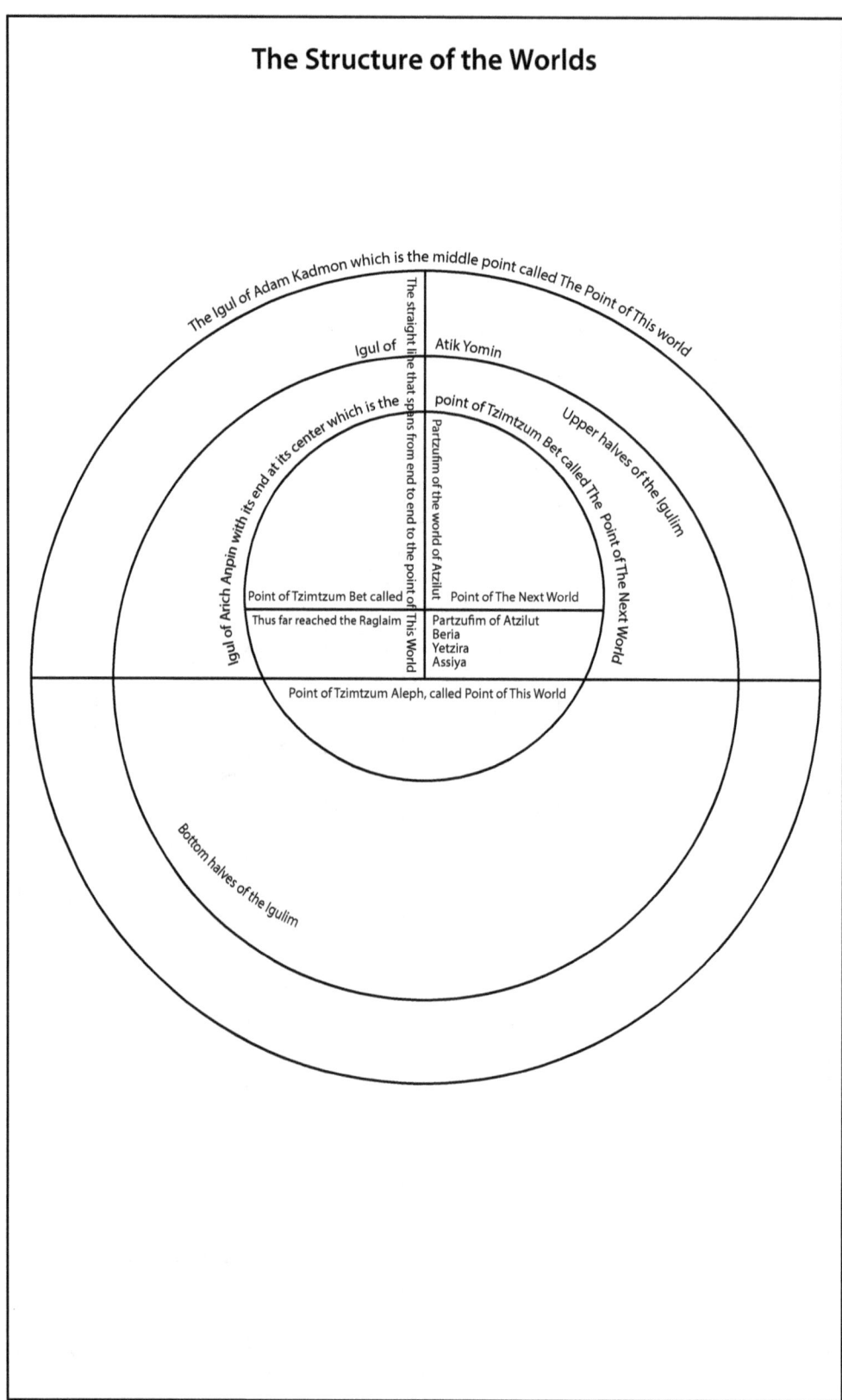

Poems of Baal HaSulam

A Poem of Sanctity

My God, the soul You have placed in me is pure.
You blew in my nostrils and I became a living soul.
How wonderful is Your love, for beauty and for light.
My lips are too villainous to speak fairly of it,
And my Creator has fashioned me, I am still budding.
My soul is desperate, a wound within my heart,
I delight to serve Him, for He is my Father
And I so desire Him, and He desires me.
He is generous, and there is much work,
And I am a learned man, destined for redemption,
As befits the queen, with faith and duty.
Indeed, He pushed me and my heart is torn.
My soul is as a wheel, turning on its hinge.
From its end and onward, it will not move at all.
Its sunlight shone beyond her face,
And since then, of all her wishes, she is worse.
A hidden hand shattered my bones,
And I became ignoble and became two camps.
One obeyed the orders of my corpse,
And the rest follow my soul.
Indeed, my body knows no lust from them,
For they did not honor its God with delight.
Like a bewildered eunuch, it is deprived of love,
Its labor leaves it and it does not know.
One who eats with it from the cakes of my lust,
From the wonders of love, the revealing of the concealed,
Or lustful words from my nectar and potion,

Will hush me with mockery, "What will the people say?"

It is he who will never taste of my pleasantness,

And I, where will I turn? To His delights,

And he, too, was added to my troubles,

To anger me with his rage and with his blows.

On the day of relief, he will still not give me a blessing,

Rather, his mockery of me will be as plentiful as locusts.

Why walk in the clouds and be so troubled,

For you will surely burn as a flame.

If time has been kind and has turned to you,

Together, they did not know you or your dreams.

For in degradation they encounter you at every corner,

One will spit in your face, and one will pull out your hair.

I Am Content

Happy is the man whose strength is in You, and the Lord is the highway in his heart.

Happy is the man who hears Your commandments and on whose heart You place Your law and Your word.

You fashion light and create darkness, make peace and create everything,

And if You made me an ear with which to hear You with the soul's love forever,

And did not show me how Your eyes observe from the end of the world to its end, I am content.

If You promised me that I would attain all Your secrets and be among those who approach You,

And did not clothe them in me in the actual present, I am content.

And if You clothed them in me in the actual present,

And I did not attain that Your glory is not forgiven and that even spirits will not limit You, I am content.

If I attained that spirits will not limit You,

And You did not establish for me a house of prayer to receive from You all my deficiencies, I am content.

If I were awarded Your calling and to accept as one demands of one's friends for all my contemplations,

And You did not bewilder me with the inheritance of a land in one day and the birth of the nation in one time, I am content.

If You showed so as to know the secret that can be seen on the earth from His throne,

And You did not place me at the start, to feel Your clothing there within my heart, I am content.

If I merited to feel all Your lights in inner light, to shine the light of the face,

And You did not alert me that this is the purpose You want from all Your creation and all that gives You pleasure, I am content.

If You alerted me Your unique pleasure, that You wish from all the work of heaven and earth,

And did not teach me to know how You blessed it from all the days and sanctified it from all the times, I am content.

If I merited the blessing of all the days, and the sanctity of all the times, past and future put together,

And You did not trouble Yourself to appease me with much wisdom and friendship to remove from me the shame, I am content.

If I merited being purified as the object of the heaven and their host, and the secret of addressing my prayer to You, etc.,

And You did not ask me about the meaning of the words, "Should your sons praise My covenant," etc., I am content.

If I heard from You the oath by Your holiness, if it is for David, it is not a lie,

And You did not instruct me that besides Your pleasure, it pertains to my own pleasures, I am content.

If my palate uttered every wisdom and every lust, and all my pleas would be to You,

And You did not make clear to me that I have nothing to add and I may go from the world, I am content.

If I understood with all my mind that I must leave the world at once,

And You did not awaken me to search for some gift in the vessels, and did not find a thing, I am content.

If You alerted me that it is labor that You want and more mere pleasure,

And You did not alert me with a kind expression where is the place of understanding in the books, I am content.

If You alerted me to yearn for understanding in the books,

And did not teach me that what matters most is the certainty and purity of heart, and that the light has no value, I am content.

If I attained that there is no importance to the light but only to the certainty and purity of heart,

And You did not grant me yearning for the Lord, and I were unable to receive without blemishing You, I am content.

If I perished from the world after fulfilling my complete purpose,

And I did not merit what is written, "Let the wise not boast of his wisdom," and the ability to accept the renewal of a faithful craftsman, I am content.

If I merited the renewal of a faithful craftsman and who sustains the question,

And I were not rewarded with all the wondrous lights and the whole Torah in one moment, and the pen of a quick writer, I am content.

If I merited there all the glory and the faithful mercies in a never-ending coupling,

And I did not merit the blessing of a man to rule over the fish of the sea, etc., until a complete withdrawal from within, I am content.

If I departed from the world after this privilege of dwelling in heaven and in earth at once,

And You did not illuminate for me the solution of a righteous who is saved, I am content.

If You illuminated for me the solution of a righteous who is saved,

And did not stop me in Ahiman and the closing of the gates of righteousness up to those who say to God, "Move away," etc., I am content.

If I departed from the world after filling out this wholeness,

And You did not teach me the meaning of the verse, "We have a little sister who has no breasts," etc., I am content.

If You renewed my vitality with "What shall with do to our sister on the day when she is spoken for,"

And You did not illuminate me with the wondrous lights and "Indeed, the matter has become known," and the silver mansion and a cedar tablet, I am content.

If at that time, You showed me all Your wondrous mercies by the installing of the crown,

And You did not teach me the meaning of the flood and the breaking of the vessels and the cherubim, and present and not present, etc., I am content.

If You established Your faith in my heart through the cherubim and present and not present through the Parsa of the two that I had heard,

And did not teach me the meaning of the verse, Korah, Nafag, and Zichri, I am content.

If You taught me the great unification of Korah, Nafag, and Zichri,

And did not draw me into the purifying bath with my head held high through "God, do bring near the redemption of they who await You," I am content.

If I merited revealing all the blessing and sacristy from Rosh and Toch of MIKVEH in multiplication through "God, do bring near the redemption of they who await You,"

And I did not merit seeing the great abundance in KLA to the point of carrying more on the Rosh of MIKVEH, I am content.

If I merited attainments in the whole Torah instead of the KLA and the meaning of rest and light...

And I did not merit seeing Jerusalem decisively built so it will never be ruined again, I am content.

If I departed from the world after the eternal attainment of the built Jerusalem,

And You did not instruct me with great faith the meaning of the verse, "Hear O Israel, the Lord is our God, the Lord is one," I am content.

If You showed me the absolute certainty in ATA before the eyes of all the nations in utter clarity,

And did not alert me to return into the purifying bath since the connection has not stopped, and You will be glorified in me, I am content.

If You alerted me to interfere with Your work inside,

And did not bewilder me with the sight of how the Yod takes and ascends from me until I depart, I am content.

If You bewildered me with the rising of the Yod that I drew until it departed above,

And did not establish in me the desire to interfere because of "How will God know," etc.,

For behold, these are the wicked who obtained riches, and as "Who is like You in might

And who is similar to You," and since the might is not eternal, You therefore drew me inside, etc., etc., I am content (for how sweet is the light of certainty, etc.).

If You established me by interfering with Your work,

And did not offer me the meaning of the words, "Should a man give all his fortune," etc., I am content.

If I endured the trial not to think of all Your future in return for Your love,

And You did not give me sweetness in the ascents and the disclosure of the secrets of Your law abundantly, I am content.

If I were rewarded, through the ascents and through the revealing of the secrets, to continue two years,

And I was not rewarded with being combed in iron combs to death in the one, I am content.

If I were rewarded with devotion of NRN in the one until my whole being is annulled,

And I were not rewarded with the dew of revival that will slowly be shaken on my head, I am content.

And moreover, I have been rewarded with a benefit that is many greater by meriting all the above, and even the revival of the dead with great compassion to bring me closer in complete repentance with fear and love and true work.

You have brought me back to the whole of Israel and to Your law with great and faithful love. How can I repay You for all that You have imparted me?

Your benefit to me is several times greater for You have lent an ear to listen. You, with the love of the soul and abundant peace for absolute eternity, have shown me Your eyes watching from the end of the world to its end, to attain with certainty all Your secrets as all those near You, who sit first in Your kingdom. You have clothed them in me in complete and absolute present and I attained that Your glory is never forgiven. Even lights and spirits do not limit You, and You determine the place for a house of prayer, as one demands and receives from one's friend all my contemplations, none excluded.

You have bewildered me with the inheritance of a land and the birth of a nation unto Your great secret that watches over the land from His dwelling place. You also alerted me that this is all that You desire from all the creation of heaven and earth. You taught me that You have blessed it from all the days and times, and You appeased me with abundant wisdom until You completely removed from me the shame, as an object of the heaven, as in "My face to Your prayer when you run to see the favor," etc. You also swore to me by Your holiness that You will never remove Your mercy and the light of Your face from me, and You alerted me that anything but Your delight belongs to myself, and my palate expelled any wisdom and lust; I wish only to see Your brightness.

You notified me that I must depart from the world at once since I have nothing more to add. You awoke me to seek some gift, and did not find one, and You awoke me to yearn for the return to the beginning but I could not without blemishing Your sublime glory. You alerted me that there is no importance to the lights and wisdoms, only to the certainty and purity of heart.

You also showed me the renewal of a faithful craftsman and who sustains the question, the green line that surrounds all the worlds, and You renewed my vitality, extolled Your name on everything, Your robe like a throne embracing heaven and earth as one, and You bewilder with Your lights, You are more beautiful than the sons of men; grace is poured, etc., and from the work of creation and the whole of the Torah, as in "My tongue is as the pen of a quick writer," and the blessing of the man to rule over the fish of the sea and every creature crawling on the earth, etc. I also added Your wonders to explain the meaning of righteous who is saved, and the Ahiman and the closing until it was. ...

You have also given me the little sister and renewed my vitality. You also crowned it with the wondrous lights from "Indeed, the matter has become known," and the silver mansion and the cedar tablet. You also brought me into the breaking of the vessels, the flood, the present and not present, until I heard with two. You bewildered me with seeing Korah and Nafag and Zichri, and the great and holy unification of "God, do bring near the redemption of they who await You," to extend me into the purifying bath and to the revelation of all the lights of the 613 commandments, and the abundance of KLA over ... a purifying bath.

I also set before my eyes the meaning of the built Jerusalem and the meaning of the verse, "The Lord is our God, the Lord is one," until the decisiveness in the 613 commandments before the eyes of all the nations. You also taught me that the connection from within the purifying bath has not stopped, and You still take pride in me as in the beginning, to see how You crave the work of Your hands, and the great vision without the ability to extend the Yod into the Hey, and in the middle of the way, it rises up like a rising start until it disappears there. And I sorted out for me the permission to interfere with Your work, as in the words, "Behold, these wicked and those who are tranquil obtained riches," etc., etc. You tested me as in the verse, "Should one give all the fortune of his household, he shall be ridiculed and mocked." You also granted me with Your humility, a pleasant sweetness in the ascents, and commanded me to reveal the secrets of Your law through compositions more wondrous than my predecessors. Also, I was rewarded with being combed with iron combs for the love of Your unification. Also, I merited extracting my whole soul in one. You returned and revived me with a dew of revival.

The Bright One

The bright One, from the Heavens He shines.
There—within the curtain of the screen.

The secret of the righteous is there made clear,
And light and darkness shine together.

How good it is to explore His deeds,
But beware not to reach out your hand to Him.

Then shall you hear Him, and so will you meet Him,
In the tower of might, the All-Inclusive Name.

You shall relish in words of truth,
To speak untainted words.

And all you will see,
Your own eyes will see, and not that of a stranger!

A Psalm - His Foundation Is in the Mountains of Holiness

The light of *Atzilut* is sublime and pure
It oversees the *Hod* of *Beria*,
Nourished by His brightness, firmly made
His vineyard He has given to the guards.
He sits me and raises me with His *Hod*
As do all who grasp the meaning of Him.
So I heard Him and saw Him glorified,
Taste and see for my future I hasten.
Hurray! Who gives me a friend?
Who knows the meaning of all things,
They are His witnesses, and happy are they.
Of all that their eyes sought,

The concealed and above any mystery.

Indeed, I saw the fountain of every wisdom,

Please, He who teaches man understanding.

The wisdom and knowledge are given to You!

My faults are many, but more than they is my affront.

Will they pardon my iniquity, comfort me from my grief?

The one who found gumption found faith

That delights him in his labor, and who like Him answers?

In His hand is all of my futures

He pities me and rushes me in order to redeem me

And my generation remembers what is in the hearts

And between Him and me are words of love.

He will consider by my years and my spirit did not blemish,

He rejuvenates me like an eagle and the wisdom is revealed.

His own mercies, from within, from without, and from all around me,

And the clouds of my darkness, the time of concealment of my sins.

The heaven will not sustain Him and in my stomach He desires,

His delight is wedged in my heart like lava.

I have tasted the life of truth, from the hall that is built inside,

I uttered His might, and my belly fills with secrets,

He is glorified with *Hassadim* and *Gevurot*,

And guards the *Yesod* of *Yetzira*,

Like a crown upon him He hovers

By breakings, he is cleansed from the excess.

He will show me wonders from His law

And my eyes shall behold from all His the majesty of His kingdom

Here am I, and all that is good in me shall stand together.

Indeed, test me, choose for Yourself one

From the favored ones, desirable men

Who have touched His secret and have yielded results,

That His Almightiness fills their palms,

And all that comes into their hearts.

Where there is wisdom, there is He,

And before I understood, I found Him and studied Him.

To You is the glory, pardon me and say a word,

That You are the operator of every operation,

I lent to both men and angels,

And so understood that there is none else besides Him.

With his finger, he shows God that which he wants,

Under the iniquity of love and under the affront of pride,

From Him are all my joy and all my grief.

Since then, I have been love sick,

To the light, my desire awaits in the corner,

My Redeemer lives, He counts the drops of my sweetness.

He hid me, and do not know how and with what,

My dust is more lush than is milk, and my sheaf has risen.

Let my falls be my time to attain my precious things.

I will always enlighten them, were they the passion of my hills?

And from all His sides and angles, enjoyment and affection

It ignites by itself and its flame will not quench.

I did not labor in Him, and all was built so as to establish it.

As a shadow, I was pulled into the room, and the kingdom is established.

I established Him in my poverty on the 8th of *Heshvan*, *Tav-Reish-Peh-Tet* [October 22, 1928], Jerusalem.

Yehuda HaLevi Ashlag

www.ingramcontent.com/pod-product-compliance
Lightning Source LLC
Chambersburg PA
CBHW080606170426
43209CB00007B/1349